CW01018812

The Official History of
Hartlepool United Football Club
1908 – 2008

Designed by Charles Bradshaw.

Printed in Great Britain by Printability2000 Ltd.

British Library Catalogue in Publication Data:
A catalogue record for this book is available from the British Library.

ISBN No: 9780955767104

© Hartlepool United Football Club.
Book first published 2009.

H'Angus is a registered trademark – registration number 2219911.

Acknowledgements
Hartlepool United acknowledge the contributions of the following in the production of this book:
Colin Foster, Nick Loughlin, Becky McNamee, John Phillips (www.inthemadcrowd.co.uk), Mark Simpson and Jeff Stelling.

The Club would also like to thank the many supporters who provided us with memorabilia, photographs and information to help with the production of this history book.

Photographic Acknowledgements
Photographs courtesy of The Northern Echo www.thenorthernecho.co.uk and Frank Reid/ Hartlepool Mail www.hartlepoolmail.co.uk

History of Club strips courtesy of www.historicalkits.co.uk

Increased Oil Recovery Ltd

An IOR Ltd Company

The Official History of
Hartlepool United
Football Club
1908 – 2008

Contents

Foreword

by Jeff Stelling

MY life changed in November 1962. It was the day I persuaded my sister Susan to take me to see Pools play Stockport. My first game. We won 3-0! The icy wind off the North Sea and snow flurries didn't matter. I was hooked.

We didn't win for the next 18 matches but it didn't matter. The Club was part of my life. In those days I would often have to wait for the gates on the Mill House side to open 10 minutes before the end to get in free. Now I'm lucky enough to be able to sit with the hoi-polloi! My circumstances have changed – my passion hasn't.

Fans of serial title winners like Manchester United or Chelsea must find it hard to understand the pleasure – and pain of course – this Club has given us.

The relief of re-election to the Football League, the despair of being beaten at Rochdale or Grimsby, the goalscoring exploits of Phythian and Mulvaney, the Cup wins over Crystal Palace and West Brom, the extra time agony of losing in the Play-Off Final at the Millennium Stadium, the joy of winning at Darlington. These are things that will live forever in our memories – especially winning at Darlo!

But the Club is about more than just results on the field. It's the heartbeat of the community.

It's a Club where the players are still part of that community. Fans can still approach them and speak to them. They are not spirited away after matches without so much as an autograph.

At Hartlepool United, the supporters are as much a part of this Club as the directors and players and as the Club progresses and improves that must continue to be the case.

Just as my father supported this Club and I have done, so my two sons Robbie and Matthew are Junior Poolies. I'm hoping that a hundred years from now, their children and grandchildren will still be able to say "Hartlepool United – that's my Club!"

Jeff Stelling

The Official History of Hartlepool United Football Club 1908 – 2008

Introduction

by Nick Loughlin
Sports Editor, Northern Echo Newspaper

WHEN some parties take control of football clubs with it comes the big, brash and bold opening statement.

Increased Oil Recovery's buyout of Hartlepool United in September 1997 wasn't quite like that.

And while the eye-catching opening gambits more often than not come back to haunt, it's fair to say that Ken Hodcroft's initial declaration has rung true.

There was no promise of reaching the Premiership in five years, no talk of a lavish budget to be dished out to the manager and no tacky PR stunts to grab the headlines.

Understated and not overstated it may have been. True to life it was proved to be.

"We aren't coming in here with pots of money to invest, but I want to build up a squad with good, local players, some niche players, and see the Club do well," said the newly-installed chairman in September 1997.

"There will be no rash promises immediately. But we have some good ideas we want to put into practice and, working together, we can take the Club forward."

In over eleven years of control at Victoria Park after Hodcroft took over as Chairman when Harold Hornsey's controlling stake was bought out, Hartlepool United have never had it so good.

For 100 years – most of it on the side of failure than success on the grand sliding scale – it was mainly about survival. Progression was a thought for dreamers. Two promotions in 89 years in the Football League was the sum total of success pre-IOR.

Since then and there's been five play-off campaigns, two promotions and the biggest day

Ken Hodcroft, Chairman of Hartlepool United

of them all when Pools reached the League One play-off final in May 2005 and, in front of almost 70,000 people and a live Sky Sports audience, Hartlepool United were eight minutes away from playing their football in the second tier of English football only to be denied by a referee's dubious decision.

Hartlepool United have been hauled out of the doldrums and become a respected Club throughout the leagues.

Perhaps, after years of achieving little and being run by local, self-made chairmen, there was one big question being asked when Hornsey, who saved the Club from the trauma of the Garry Gibson era (1989-1994) and put it back on an even footing, decided IOR were right for his Club: Why Hartlepool United?

After all, IOR were unheard of in Hartlepool, bar perhaps a few oil industry workers.

Until recent times outsiders didn't buy football clubs. Football clubs weren't even sold in normal times, it was only in the midst of a financial crisis that they changed hands.

"I was first approached in June 1997 by IOR's solicitors, Baker Botts from London, and it took a lot of soul-searching," admitted the late Harold Hornsey. "But I am certain that Hartlepool United will prosper under IOR.

"Ken, who is from Newcastle, wants football at youth and first team level to develop and prosper and I am certain it will happen."

Hodcroft revealed how Hartlepool United proved an attractive proposition for a company in the oil industry based 300 miles away in Aberdeen.

"Harold was interested in taking the Club forward, but had gone as far as he could financially and he was looking for help to do it," said Ken Hodcroft.

"I think he was a bit cautious about anyone coming in, but that was his nature. He agreed to chat with us about helping. IOR's interest in the Club came about because there was an article in the Sunday Sun with Harold saying he was looking for some help – my ears pricked up on reading it.

"At the time IOR was quite aggressive in the North Sea in the oil business. We wanted to raise our profile.

"Able Offshore in Hartlepool were approved to dismantle old oil platforms and we were hoping to be involved in that side of the business. A large North Sea platform was to be decommissioned and one area being looked at was Hartlepool.

"We were looking for some good public relations at the time.

"IOR are an international business and football is an international language – perhaps getting involved with the Club would be a good business move.

"Reading between the lines of the article in the Sunday Sun about Harold, he was asking for some help and assistance – that's one reason why we focused on Hartlepool.

"The Club wanted help, we wanted to raise

the profile of IOR, it worked out for everyone."

Hodcroft added: "If we had arrived and promised this and promised that, people might have thought 'who do this company think they are?'. The more good PR you can build up the better – looking back over eleven plus years we can say that it's worked for all parties.

"We have business dealings all over the world and a lot of times we go into meetings without knowing people well. But you get talking about football and people come to life – then we mention about owning a football club and, yes, it's not the Premier League, but it's a team and a Club we are very proud of."

The benefits of football and Pools has rubbed off for others as well. IOR deal with a welter of companies across the globe, which has ensured the good name of Hartlepool United spreads far and wide.

"Other businesses who we work with have come on board and raised their own profile," said Hodcroft. "Dove Energy and DNO have benefited from it – especially DNO who were our shirt sponsors when H'Angus the Monkey, our Club mascot, aka Stuart Drummond, was standing for election – this gave DNO worldwide publicity.

"The concept we started when we first expressed an interest in the Club has come to fruition.

"Our philosophy has remained the same since day one and we keep a low profile. We don't go public and we keep it within ourselves. Yes, of course. we have to deal with supporters and with the media, but we have our own ways."

Part of that philosophy was keeping former Chairman Hornsey on board as a consultant.

Dove Energy were Pools' sponsors when H'Angus ran for Mayor of Hartlepool

Revered by the fans for his work and financial wizardry in keeping the Club alive after entering into financial strife in the early 1990s, plenty of supporters knew Harold well.

A town businessman, Hornsey often preferred to stand and watch from the terraces rather than sit in the director's box.

The short, unassuming figure of Hornsey proved a big assistance as the IOR revolution begun.

"Apart from paying Harold back the money he had personally put into the Club, keeping Harold on was part of the deal – we didn't want to come in and remove Harold from the Club, that would have earned us zero brownie points and he played a valuable part when we took over," said Hodcroft.

"We have never promised things we couldn't deliver because that would be no good for our image. But we won the fans over and kept the fans with us over the years which has been a very pleasing thing.

"There was some scepticism from Harold when we spoke to him at the time of wanting to purchase the Club, there was some scepticism from supporters as well – maybe that's the nature of football fans. But even if you take over a Club and promise to plough £100m in they will be the same.

"At the time there was an issue over the greyhound stadium next to the ground. People were saying it would be a supermarket or housing – we came in at the same time and had to be careful because people were wondering about us.

"But we also learned a quick lesson –

Harold Hornsey, Owner and Chairman (1994-1997)

innocent Ken Hodcroft gave an interview in the first few days and was asked how far the Club could go. I said "look at what Wimbledon have done" and they had come from the bottom division to top, it was a fair comparison.

"Next day and the interview appeared – it was about how 'Ken can do a Wimbledon' and make the top!"

At the time "the top" was a million miles away. Even the top of division four was viewed from afar. "After the first game IOR were in charge, I recall being in the Vic Lounge at the Club watching the results and tables on teletext. In those days the table for Division Four was split into two pages. Frankie Baggs (Commercial Manager) at the time quipped, "We are on page one and 12th. That is going up in the world!"

Making An Early Mark At Victoria Park

A little over two years into their tenure and Pools were in something of a precarious position. Things weren't going well under Mick Tait and the team was struggling. As Pools said goodbye to 1998 and rang in 1999, a new signing was announced.

Former England international Peter Beardsley had been playing in the Premier League months before.

His Victoria Park signing raised a few eyebrows.

Even Mick Tait asked 'do I have to play him?!'

"Peter Beardsley signed and bringing him in helped raise the profile," admitted the chairman. "At the time the Club wasn't doing well – we wondered how we could help.

"We had no experience in hiring and firing managers and we were still learning from Harold. We wanted to bring in a high profile player who could help and we introduced Peter. It raised the profile of the Club in the national media and it showed to everyone that IOR were trying to help.

"His arrival helped set the standards off the field and on it as well. Without making promises it was the sort of signing we wanted to make and we hoped he would be the first of many.

"He scored on his debut and I thought straight away that the idea had paid off – if he didn't do anything else in his time with us then he had made an impact."

And while Beardsley's long-term impact may have been somewhat limited, there's little doubt that IOR's first stellar recruit made a stunning impact and IOR appreciated Peter's contribution at a very important time for the Club.

Jan Ove Pedersen made only 18 appearances in a blue and white shirt in 1998. It was enough for many to label him the best Hartlepool United player seen by many.

"It was the same with signing Peter as it was Jan Ove Pedersen – we needed experience and we had few contacts within football in this country," said Hodcroft.

"We could talk to potential players but we had nothing to offer them. So we used our Norwegian links and our contacts. Getting him on a short term deal put the Club on the map.

"He was a great player and imagine what he would be like in the current side?

"He only played 18 games for us but made a big impact – we tried to get him back again and very nearly did it. He got an offer from Austria and went there – it was down to his wife in the end and she'd been to England with Hartlepool but wanted to try somewhere else!"

Both Beardsley and Pedersen played under Mick Tait.

But, with a team low on confidence and struggling at the foot of the table, a change in the dugout was afoot.

Hodcroft recalled: "We had Mick in charge – we lost on the Saturday and he resigned the following day. I was in Brazil and Harold rang me to tell me. I said to Harold 'so what do we do now?' Then Mick came in on the Monday and said to Harold that he hadn't resigned.

"So we were in limbo a bit – would he carry on after that? He told Harold he would only leave by mutual consent and it was all part of the steep learning curve for us. Our first manager was gone."

Assistant Manager Brian Honour and Paul Baker took temporary charge of first team affairs while IOR began the search for the next manager.

Interviews started and the appointment of a new manager was something of a key one. Pools were in a precarious position. The right choice had to be made. It was IOR's first major football decision and one which still has strong implications today.

"Chris Turner came to the interview with a very good track record, from his time with the youth team at Wolves. He was the only candidate who we saw who had actually prepared and presented a dossier on the Club and told us what he could do," said the Chairman. "And he was talking during the interview about 'us' and 'we' so I knew he had a feeling for the Club and the job ahead. And even though he was based in the Midlands, he was prepared to move to Hartlepool.

"He went to Exeter to watch the team play in the week before he took over – we were confident we were bringing the right man in.

"We were new to league football and putting Chris in place was adding another block – we were learning and building something up all the time.

"We could have gone for an old head, an experienced manager who had been there and done that in the game and had his ways and means of doing things. Or we could go for a

Chris Turner was chosen by IOR to take the helm at Pools in 1999

young, up and coming manager, someone who was new to that side of things but was determined to be successful.

"That's why we took Chris. Harold wanted an older manager, but we felt if we did that we would have lost the plot. An older type would come in and have his methods – we were trying to get people to work to our ways."

And that philosophy has been part of IOR's recruitment process each time a managerial vacancy has become available.

The Three Rules Of Hartlepool United

FROM Chris Turner – number one in 1999 – to Danny Wilson – number five in 2006, IOR have stood by their own way of doing things.

"We have a criteria to stick to when we make an appointment – we look for someone fresh and new," revealed Hodcroft. "Mike Newell replaced Chris in 2002 and Mike had helped with reserve team football and in other positions at other clubs and wanted the next step up. He needed us so he could break into management and we needed his keenness to do well.

"Neale Cooper didn't know the English managerial game when he came to us in 2003, we could show him how to adapt to our ways. However, he had to return to Scotland for family reasons. Martin Scott had been trained up from Youth Team Coach over the years. He was the ideal candidate to move up in 2005 – he had learned the IOR way and it was our first attempt at a home-grown manager.

"He had potential, however he broke the IOR rule and just tried to do it his way and it didn't work out.

"Prior to the appointment of Danny Wilson we had the same problem as in 1999 – do we go for an old head or a younger manager? However, the Club had changed – we also had experience of running a football club.

"We considered Danny. We already had Chris in place as Director of Sport and he was a friend of Danny, who had lots of experience.

"Chris met him and explained how the Club and IOR work – it was an important move. We had just been relegated. Danny did an excellent job to get us promoted but departed in December 2008.

"Maybe we left Martin in charge a bit too long, but he deserved the chance and in the end we had to change. He will benefit from it.

"We brought Chris back in with one eye on the future. After relegation we had one aim – to get out of League Two, we had to do it in one season and couldn't afford to hang around.

"Relegation wasn't part of the plan. We had enjoyed some good times and season 2005/6 wasn't one of them.

"At Hartlepool United we have three rules – enjoy the work you are doing, don't embarrass yourself or the Club and don't get relegated. Everyone of those was broken in the relegation season!

"That's the philosophy of IOR running the Club. Maybe if you break one of them you can get away with it – but not all three!

"The gut reaction was to bring someone in straight away after Martin left. But then what happens? If the new manager takes the team down he will say it's not his team, if he doesn't then it's job done and we have him for the next season. We wondered if we should take the risk or learn from our decisions.

"We decided to give Paul Stephenson the caretaker job with no pressure to stay in League One and it was a great experience for him. He has done a very good job for the Club over the years – but there was going to be a pressure from the media and fans after relegation because we needed to be promoted the next season.

"If he failed to get promotion immediately, his career, when it was just getting off the ground, could have been ruined and we didn't want that.

"However, despite trying to do the best for him long-term, he later walked out on the Club."

Hodcroft and IOR have never been afraid to make a change when necessary. While Turner left of his own accord to take over at Sheffield Wednesday with the blessing of all at Victoria Park, although Hodcroft didn't want him to leave, in other cases it hasn't been as simple.

Neale Cooper replaced Mike Newell as Manager in June 2003

"As a company we don't put pressure on individuals, we work with them and give them the chance to progress and succeed," said Hodcroft of the IOR business mantra. "Maybe we did leave it too long with Martin (Scott) and could have made a change in November or December. But he had worked hard to be the manager and he was the right man for the job at the time.

"The problem was that he tried to do everything his way. Maybe, and we will never know, he might have got us out of the situation but because of the dressing room incident we had to make a decision.

"One of our three rules had been broken and the other two were in the balance.

"But even then, maybe that wasn't the real Martin Scott. He was feeling the pressure and could see all his hard work over the years slipping away. His career was in jeopardy and you cannot blame him for trying to make it work.

"We are always as supportive as we can be and Martin left the Club with my best wishes for the future."

There's little doubt that such a supportive nature towards players, managers and staff at the Club has brought its rewards.

Cardiff – The Biggest Game

POOLS never have – and more than likely never will – reach an FA Cup or League Cup final.

Making the 2004/05 play-off final in the grand splendour of Cardiff's Millennium Stadium was the Club's highest juncture.

"Cardiff was a memorable day and a memorable occasion, but 12 months later we were relegated," said Hodcroft. "It brought everyone back down to earth with a bang.

"We have been so close to being promoted to the Championship and we had a great crack at it, but we were robbed eight minutes from time by a very dubious referee decision.

"Getting to the Championship would be nice – then again, it would have been nice to get to Wembley!

"Cardiff was a proud occasion for everyone connected with the Club and the town. It was a fantastic atmosphere and it gives us great pride when you think that something like 18,000 – that's almost a quarter of the town's population – travelled to support us.

"One of the abiding memories for me from getting to Cardiff came when we were travelling back to the hotel and stopped at a service

The Millennium Stadium, Cardiff, 2005

Hartlepool Mail

It was Pools v Sheffield Wednesday at the Millennium Stadium

station for petrol and there were some Pools supporters there.

"We were expecting them to be upset and moaning about the outcome – everyone knows we were robbed on the day – because people felt hard done by by questionable refereeing decisions.

"Instead they couldn't stop talking about how proud they were of the team and the day itself. After what had just happened, it was music to my ears."

To play on the biggest stage of all meant a thorough preparation and build-up. Instead of playing in front of around 5,000 fans, there would be near-70,000 in the arena.

"We had the team prepared so well for Cardiff," recalled Hodcroft. "On the Friday we arranged a visit to the Millennium Stadium so they could have a look at it – they went in the dressing rooms, the tunnel and everywhere they would be on the Sunday.

"Then they went to the League Two play-off game on the Saturday so they could see the ground with a crowd in it. Everything was done correctly and professionally so that when they arrived for the game there was no sense of being overawed by it all – they had a feeling for the place.

"It's just a shame how the day ended, but I'm sure everyone has their own fond memories of the day and the occasion."

The story doesn't end there though, and an interesting account can be found later in the book.

He added: "I think the only other thing that comes close for me personally is taking the team to play at Elland Road in September 2007 – and that's because although I was born in Newcastle (and a Newcastle supporter), I was brought up in Leeds from the age of five and used to go and occasionally watch them during the Don Revie years – albeit not as a supporter. I never dreamed I would go back there in a Chairman's role and see my team play so well."

Special occasions were rare before 1997. Occasions since 1997 have been many. From reaching the play-offs for the first time in 2000 to finally earning promotion in 2003 and playing at the likes of the City Ground, Hillsborough, the Stadium of Light and Elland Road.

Victoria Park

VICTORIA Park has been improved by IOR no end, just as the town has. Hartlepool is a flourishing town. The old image of cloth caps and whippets has gone.

The image of Victoria Park hosting football as ramshackle as the old surroundings has been consigned to the past.

"As for the future we will continue to look for steady progress and aim to do the best we can," insisted Hodcroft. "We won't be making brash statements that we will be doing this or doing that.

"But the most important thing is for us to own the ground. The Government allow you to buy a council house after you have rented it for so long and we've been here nearly twelve years now!

"That is our key objective. Progress to buy the land from the council is being made and hopefully things will happen but the length of time to achieve the purchase is very frustrating for the owners and something needs to be resolved soon.

"To be honest it was us who did not follow up the initial negotiations several years ago after the council's initial rejection because all our focus was on getting out of the bottom division and getting back into League One.

"However, I still can't understand the council's logic or the reasons they say for rejecting our very substantial offer at the time. After all, they bought it from the previous owners very cheap at a time when the Club was in financial distress.

"But now we are making it top of the agenda again. If we had come in from day one and tried to start talking with the council over it, then we could understand if things didn't happen or go well.

"Hopefully we have proved we are here for the right reasons and we are very active in all parts of the community. I would like to think we have helped raise the profile of both the town and the town's Football Club over the years – that's with the oil business, with Jeff Stelling on Sky Sports every Saturday and with H'Angus. Put the whole package together and crowds are up, the supporters have watched some excellent football. We look forward to the council returning the ground to the owners. Without IOR where would it all be now?"

And Hodcroft proudly concluded: "Hartlepool as a town is looking fantastic now, the football Club is no longer a laughing stock and we have rid ourselves of the image which we used to have.

"Within football the Club now has a good name and reputation. Opponents know they are in for a good game and a good test when they come up against us – be it home or away in a league or cup game.

"Players and staff know that their wages will be paid on a set day every month without fail and wages and salaries have steadily increased for everyone across the board at the Club. The VAT man is happy with the fact that we pay him on time too!"

Despite the current world economic crisis and after the excellent progress in the first 11 years under IOR, Hodcroft remains very positive and added: "Although we will still have the highs and lows because that's football, perhaps the best years are still to come although there have been some very interesting times in the last 100 years which I hope everyone will enjoy reading about in this book."

IOR are working hard to purchase the ground from the local council

Chapter 1

East and West

AT the time of the formation of Hartlepools United in 1908, what is known now as the town of Hartlepool was then two individual boroughs.

Hartlepool, to the east, was an established working class community with roots going back to prehistoric times.

The area was an important part of the coastline, with panoramic views north and south. It had a long and varied history and had finds from the 5th Century Roman era, both Roman and Celtic in origin.

In the 7th Century Anglo-Saxons settled there and a monastery was founded which was later run by a nun called Hilda, and this became known as St Hilda. After the Norman Conquest and the destruction of land between the Ouse and the Tees, a Norman nobleman called

Hartlepool Rovers team in 1895

CHARITY CRICKET CARNIVAL, WEST HARTLEPOOL, 1897

IN COSTUME OF PERIOD OF QUEEN'S ACCESSION.

GARRY'S TEAM v. YOUNG'S TEAM.

W. Swain.	A. Young.	Rev. W. Heath.	J. Clarke. J. W. Humphreys. C. Gallen.	J. H. Bell.	M. Cox. T. Noblings, J.
Capt. C. Brockett. (Umpire).	J. Garry.	J. Hartas. Rev. A. Curwood.	H. Botham. F. J. Theaker T. Marshall. (Hon. Sec.)	B. C. Waddington.	(Umpire).
	C. R. Theaker (Scorer).	T. Wood.	W. Armstrong.	W. H. Hopper.	W. Martin.

Charity Cricket Carnival, 1897

Robert de Brus was given land and the title of the Lord of the Manor of Hartlepool. His descendants developed the docks extensively throughout the 12th Century and the Headland area was protected by a town wall, the building of which commenced in 1315. A large section still stands today.

West Hartlepool was a more modern town established around the 1830s from the expansion of various villages such as Stranton, California and Seaton Carew. Following the industrial revolution at the end of the previous century and the ever-expanding Victorian British Empire, many towns and ports flourished. West Hartlepool was no exception.

The construction of a new railway line from the coal fields of County Durham commenced in 1832. It was to lead direct to the dock area resulting in a further increase in trade. Additional rail links were established and the docks were expanded as the combined population of the two areas rocketed from around 1,300 in 1831 to around 90,000 in 1901, the town of West Hartlepool becoming twice the size of the older town.

Even now the population of Hartlepool, at the 2001 census, stands less than this at around 89,000. Both towns benefited from the trade in and out of the harbour resulting in the port becoming the fourth busiest in Britain for many a year.

Pre 1908 – Hartlepool People Prove To Be Good Sports

SPORT in the Hartlepools before 1908 had plenty of variety and was beginning to become organised as the area improved and developed.

There were regular open air boxing bouts, cycling and athletic events intended for both track and field – including regular prestigious 'foot races'. Prior to this, West Hartlepool even had it's own racecourse in the Stranton area, where horse racing was a regular event. Other sports such as quoits, fives and tennis had local circles. However, the main sports in the towns were cricket, rugby football and association football.

Cricket had been played in the area for almost 90 years and the main club in the town was West Hartlepool Cricket Club.

The Club was formed in 1855 and played in the Stranton area before merging with another club, West Hartlepool Temperance, and moving to play at Clarence Road in the 1880s to become one of the most successful teams of that era, winning the North Yorkshire and South Durham League (a league in which they still play today) on consecutive occasions between 1899 and 1902.

However, rugby football was by far and away the most popular sport. There were several clubs in the towns, many of which are still in existence today. Those no longer around are West Hartlepool Nomads, Hartlepool Wanderers, New Stranton Celtic, Empress Rovers and West Hartlepool East End. The clubs competed in the Pyman League and local cup tournaments as well as Durham County tourneys such as the Durham Senior Cup.

Clubs from the era still alive and kicking include Hartlepool Old Boys, West Hartlepool (albeit known for three or four years as Greatham from 1908 onwards) and Hartlepool Rovers. The latter two were more prominent and encountered local success and county success with several Rovers players selected to play at international level.

The Emergence of Football in the Town

ASSOCIATION football was establishing itself slowly but surely with the foundation of the FA in 1862. With several attempted forays into forming leagues and teams in the 1870s, the first major town Club was established in 1881, the West Hartlepool Amateur Football Club.

They started playing in the Northumberland & Durham Association and a couple of years later found themselves in the Durham Association (South) playing the likes of Darlington and Stockton.

However, the Club struggled for support and folded. It was taken over by the local railway concern (NER), until in 1898 when they regrouped and renamed as West Hartlepool.

In 1898 the Club were allowed into the Northern League second division, playing at their Park Road base against such opposition as Stockton Vulcan, Scarborough and Thornaby Utopians.

By now association football in the Hartlepools was gaining a foothold with a competitive Church League and other competitions formed such as the Lightfoot League, the Waller League and the Lormor League. Various local cups – The Westland Cup and the Hartlepool Challenge Cup among them – were competed for.

Countless clubs were formed, closed and re-formed, West Hartlepool Temperance Institute, Arncliffe, Hartlepool Olympic, Middleton St. John's, Nursery Villa and Belle Vue Congretionalists to name but a few.

Two of the better teams were West Hartlepool Expansion and West Hartlepool St. Joseph's. What is noticeable from the naming of the sides, despite the two towns being so close, is that they fervently sought to retain their individual identity.

West Hartlepool struggled in their first two seasons in the Northern League, but surprised

West Hartlepool Cricket Team, 1902

Rugby was played at The Vic in 1905

all when they achieved a cup success on April 28, 1900, winning the Durham Amateur Cup. They secured a 1-0 victory over Sunderland's reserve team in front of 2,000 spectators at Feethams, Darlington.

West lined up as follows: A Lindsay, G Hutchinson, T Watson, J Parker, A Middlemiss, R Stringer, G Shinton, J McGuire, T Blumer, W Bowman and W Dillon, with outside left Dillon grabbing the winner in the first half. Keeper Lindsay left West in the summer of 1902 and played league football for Sunderland and Glossop North End.

In 1900 the Northern League reformatted and the Club was in the single division competition.

At the time West played at a ground in Park Road and struggled, finishing second bottom in 1901, third bottom 1902, and bottom in both 1902/3 and the following season.

The following campaign West performed a little better, but surprised all when they qualified for the Northern Final of the Amateur Cup after beating Saltburn, Skinningrove, Grangetown, Nottingham Jardine's and Darlington St Augustine's.

In the final at Stockton, they beat Bishop Auckland 2-1 to qualify for the FA English Amateur Cup final.

The final, on April 8, 1905, was a pulsating affair at the ground of Shepherd's Bush FC in Loftus Road, London.

West Hartlepool players and dignitaries in 1905

STEWARTS CLOTHIERS Ltd., 22, Lynn Street, WEST HARTLEPOOL.

HARTLEPOOL ROVERS RUGBY.

1907.
Sept. 7—Gosforth Nomads L... h
14—Leicester .... a
21—Tynedale L .... a
28—West Hartlepool L .. h
Oct. 5—Westoe L .... a
12—North Durham L ... h
19—Durham City L .... a
26—Westoe L .... a
Nov. 2—Old Novocastrians L. h
9—Winlaton Vulcans L. a
16—Northern L .... h
23—Sunderland L ..... a
30—Gosforth Nomads L.. h
Dec. 7—Rockcliff L .... a
14—Headingley .... h
21—Winlaton Vulcans L. a
26—West Hartlepool L .. h
28—Northern L .... a
1908.
Jan. 1—Kersal .... h
2—Leicester .... h
4—Sunderland L ..... h
11—Old Novocastrians L. a
25—Durham University .. h
Feb. 1—Headingley .... h
8—Percy Park L ...... h
15—West Hartlepool L .. h
22—North Durham L ... h
29—Durham University .. a
Mar. 7—Cup Tie ..
14—Cup Tie ....
21—Cup Tie ....
28—Cup Tie ....
April 4—Percy Park L ...... a
11—Tynedale L .... h
18—Rockcliff L .... a
20—(Easter Monday)....

WEST HARTLEPOOL RUGBY.

1907.
Sept. 7—Castleford .... h
14—Tynedale .... h
21—Leicester .... a
28—Rovers .... h
Oct. 5—North Durham .... h
12—Winlaton .... a
19—Westoe .... h
26—Sunderland .... a
Nov. 2—Hamsteels .... h
9—Durham City ...... h
16—Percy Park .... a
23—Northern .... h
30—Hamsteels .... h
Dec. 7—North Durham .... a
14—Old Novocastrians .. h
21—Rockcliff .... a
26—Rovers .... h
28—Skipton .... h
1908.
Jan. 1—Leicester .... h
2—Percy Park .... a
4—Percy Park .... h
11—Northern .... a
18—Westoe .... h
25—Ilkley .... h
Feb. 1—Sunderland .... a
8—Durham City ...... h
15—Rovers .... a
22—Castleford .... h
29—Ilkley .... a
Mar. 7—Cup Tie (1st round) .. h
14—Cup Tie (2nd round). h
21—Tynedale .... a
28—Gosforth Nomads .. h
Apl. 4—Rockcliff .... h
11—Winlaton .... a
18—Gosforth Nomads .. a

WEST HARTLEPOOL ASSOCIATION.

1907.
Sept. 7—Scarborough (L) .... h
9—Expansion .... h
11—Middlesbrough .... h
14—Grangetown L .... a
21—W.Auckland (E.C.P. rd.)a
28—Bishop Auckland L .. a
Oct. 12—Darlington L ...... h
26—Spennymoor L ..... h
Nov. 2—Leadgate Park ......
(E.C. 3rd rd.) L a
9—South Bank L ..... h
16—Crook L .... a
23—St. Augustines L ....
(E.C 4th rd.) h
Dec. 7—Scarbro'(E.C. 5th rd.) h
21—Stockton L .... h
25—Caledonians ...... h
26—West Norwood ....
27—Shepherd's Bush ...
28—Saltburn L .... a
1908.
Jan. 1—Rutherglen Glencairn h
Feb. 1—Grangetown L .... h
8—Stockton ....
(D.S. 3rd rd.) L a
15—South Bank ....
(A.C. 3rd rd.) L a
22—Spennymoor L .... a
29—Saltburn L .... h
Mar. 7—Crook (A.C. 4th rd.) L h
14—Bishop Auckland ...
(D.C. Final) L h
21—Darlington ....
(A.C.S. Final) h
28—Leadgate Park L .... a
Apl. 18—St. Augustines L .... a
L—Northern League. EC—English Cup.
DS—Durham Senior Cup.

Sports Fixtures 1908-1909

Ted Magner

West lined up with keeper Jim Bainbridge in goal. In front of him were two full backs, the Hegarty brothers Dick and Tom. The three half backs were composed of Fred Black, captain Jim Hyslop and Sammy Stokes. The forward line featured Davie Larkin, Wilf Fairweather, Alf Robinson, Otto Trechmann and Bob Hodgson.

Opponents Clapton took to the field encouraged by the predominantly southern crowd, with West backed by a distinctly smaller, but equally loud, support.

West were the underdogs and, as was the norm, skipper Hyslop lost the toss, so they were forced to kick-off with the sun blazing into their faces. Clapton took the advantage, playing in high balls, which the Hegartys found difficult to clear.

Clapton were a physically bigger and stronger team and used their advantage, as well as their greater skills, to dominate the first 20 minutes or so, but were unable to breach the West back line.

West eventually began to break into Clapton territory, but found themselves up against some rough treatment from the Clapton backs and the referee, with Stokes and Robinson both receiving treatment for unpunished challenges.

However, West took a shock lead when, from a Larkin corner, Trechmann gave the keeper no chance with a powerful strike.

The West half backs began to turn the screw and frustrated the Londoners, so much so that the Clapton keeper was penalised for handling outside the box. Dick Hegarty took the resultant free-kick and left the keeper floundering as it rolled into the net and put West two goals up just before half time.

Upon the restart, West carried on where they left off and ex-public school-boy Trechmann scored a third with a high curling shot.

Three-down

Bob Pailor

and with just 20 minutes left, Clapton came to life. With 15 minutes to go, Clyde Purnell grabbed one back. Again, they pushed, Black had to clear a shot off the line and shortly after Purnell netted a second to make it 3-2.

However, West held solid. They had done the unthinkable and returned home with the cup, to a marvellous reception.

Local Talent Snapped Up

SEVERAL local players went on to have decent careers after small beginnings. Alf Robinson, who played in the amateur cup final for West, had started out playing Church League football for Stranton Parish Church before joining the amateur concern. He later had a spell on trial at Sunderland, before playing league football at Stockport County in seasons 1905/6 and 06/7. He later had spells at Carlisle, Sheffield United and Spennymoor.

Others who played their first football in the Hartlepools and went onto league football were Cup-winning brothers Dick and Tom Hegarty, who played for Stockport after starting out with Belle Vue Athletic and West Hartlepool Perseverance respectively. The latter's promising career in Scotland with Hearts was cruelly terminated by injury.

Arthur Swift, who started with Seaton Carew Ironworks and later West Hartlepool Expansion and Perseverance, played for West Bromwich Albion and Crystal Palace.

Expansion became a breeding ground for talent and previously on their books were players such as Bill Hastings, Ted Magner, while West produced the likes of Ernie Pinkney and Bob Pailor.

Hastings had a successful career in the south and Magner played league football for Gainsborough Trinity and Everton. He later became a successful coach and had spells as a manager at Huddersfield and Derby County. Pinkney played top flight football for Everton and Bob Pailor had a successful career curtailed only by injury shortly after he joined Newcastle United from West Brom.

With the success of West Expansion, the growing popularity of association football and the increasing financial problems that the West Rugby Club were having, the board of the latter deliberated over a period of months before deciding to dip their paws in the water and consider changing sports and the business of the Club to a professional association football Club.

It was the beginning of the Hartlepool United Football Club we know today.

Chapter 2

1908 – WW1

The Beginning

A behind-closed-door meeting was held at the Grand Hotel on April 30, 1908, attended by various existing football organisations in West Hartlepool – among them West Hartlepool Association Football Club and West Hartlepool Expansion Association FC.

The Victoria Ground, on which rugby was to be played, was named after Queen Victoria, and built the year before her Golden Jubilee. The land was owned by the North Eastern Railway Company, with the rugby club paying rent to the NER.

One of the main ideas was that West Hartlepool AFC and the new Club try to work together, but remain separate concerns. Despite initial objections from West, it was suggested that West cease playing at their Park Road home and groundshare with the new

Club at the Victoria Ground, in Clarence Road, West Hartlepool.

With no decision made the attendees reported back to their committees. The overall feeling was positive. The two towns were to have their own professional team, following the winding up of the rugby club just days earlier.

Association Football Comes To Hartlepool

ON May 2 it was announced that the newly-formed association football Club would proceed on professional terms and had applied to join the North Eastern League. The league was formed in season 1906-7 and included the reserve sides of Middlesbrough, Sunderland and Newcastle, as well as Huddersfield Town, South Shields Athletic and Workington. Teams from Darlington, Seaham White Star and Spennymoor United had applied to join at the same time as the proposed new Hartlepools side.

Three days later and a further meeting took place at the Grand Hotel attended by those interested in the adoption of professional association football in the Hartlepools. Councillor Coates (who became Mayor of West Hartlepool in 1913) was the chair person. Also present, among others, were Councillors Martin (who became Mayor of West Hartlepool in 1911 & 1912) and Paterson. All three were board members of the now defunct rugby club. The meeting was a

Grand Hotel, Hartlepool – the birthplace of Hartlepool United

defining one, as several key matters were promoted, discussed and settled upon.

The Club was to be called the Hartlepools United Football and Athletic Club Company Limited, with their headquarters confirmed as the Victoria Ground, and offices in Scarborough Street, West Hartlepool.

The Club could not be called West Hartlepool for obvious reasons due to the amateur team, nor could they be called Hartlepool United for, at the time, a team using the same name had operated in both the Lightfoot League in 1906-7 and the Hewitt League in 1907-8.

The term Hartlepools was intended to show that the new team was to represent both towns in the district.

Although the ground was in West Hartlepool it was quite close to the boundary of the sister towns and it was hoped the joint title would be attractive to followers of association football in both boroughs.

However, it later became apparent that despite serving the two areas, the board believed themselves to be a West Hartlepool team. The majority of the directors, and therefore most of the money, came from West.

The sponsors were optimistic that a good team would stop the flow of people leaving the towns on weekends to follow professional football elsewhere.

Shares Sold For New Football Club

THE Club was to be formed with a capital of shares and they decided on shares at ten shillings each and not £1 as widely anticipated.

In order to make it within reach of the ordinary working man, these could be purchased in instalments – 2s 6d on application, 2s and 6d on allotment, a third instalment two months after allotment and a final tranche two months after that.

All attending the meeting were asked to become shareholders. It was hoped that if they were successful in joining the NEL, of which they were confident, lovers of the association code would support the team.

Although the rugby code seemed to be on the wane in West Hartlepool, the rugby teams in the town of Hartlepool retained their hardcore supporters, in particular Hartlepool Old Boys and Hartlepool Rovers.

However, there were possibly now as many followers of association football in the Hartlepools as in other towns in the region. They were to be the target audience and it was hoped they would now follow the team of their home town, rather than Middlesbrough, Newcastle and Sunderland.

When it was decided to disband the rugby club it was also resolved that the assets, such as stands and other property, be handed over to the trustees of the ground on the understanding that they discharged the liabilities of the Club.

This allowed the rugby club to die a natural death, with every penny owed being paid, making their demise an honourable one.

The company was formally registered with a capital of £2,000 in ten shilling shares. All shareholders still had to pay admission for entrance to the ground.

In To The Unknown

THE gentlemen of the day who were establishing the Club had no estimate, accurate or otherwise, of the cost of maintaining the Club. The first outlay was the rugby club debts.

In return for redemption of these liabilities the Club would get use of the Victoria Ground and the fixtures and fittings.

Objections were raised over the condition of the stands on the ground. Some of the board were concerned that they were not built of the best wood and that the timber, in contact with the earth for over 20 years (the ground was built in 1886), would deteriorate and have only scrap value.

However, reassurance was given that although these fittings were to be purchased out of the Club capital for approximately £180, they were still in order and the fee was still considered nominal when compared to the cost of new fittings. Leading figures who had visited the ground appeared satisfied with the condition.

The old rugby club committee appointed three Councillors to interview various clubs connected with the North Eastern League. All but two had been interviewed and they found clubs all differed in the way they operated.

In the case of Hartlepools United the entrance to the NEL was not to be the end of the ambitions of the Club, but a means to an end. It was viewed as a start.

As a professional team they desired to play in the professional Football League. They were to run just one team due to the expense and uncertainty of running a reserve side.

Two To Become One?

THE matter of a possible merging of the talents of West Hartlepool Expansion and

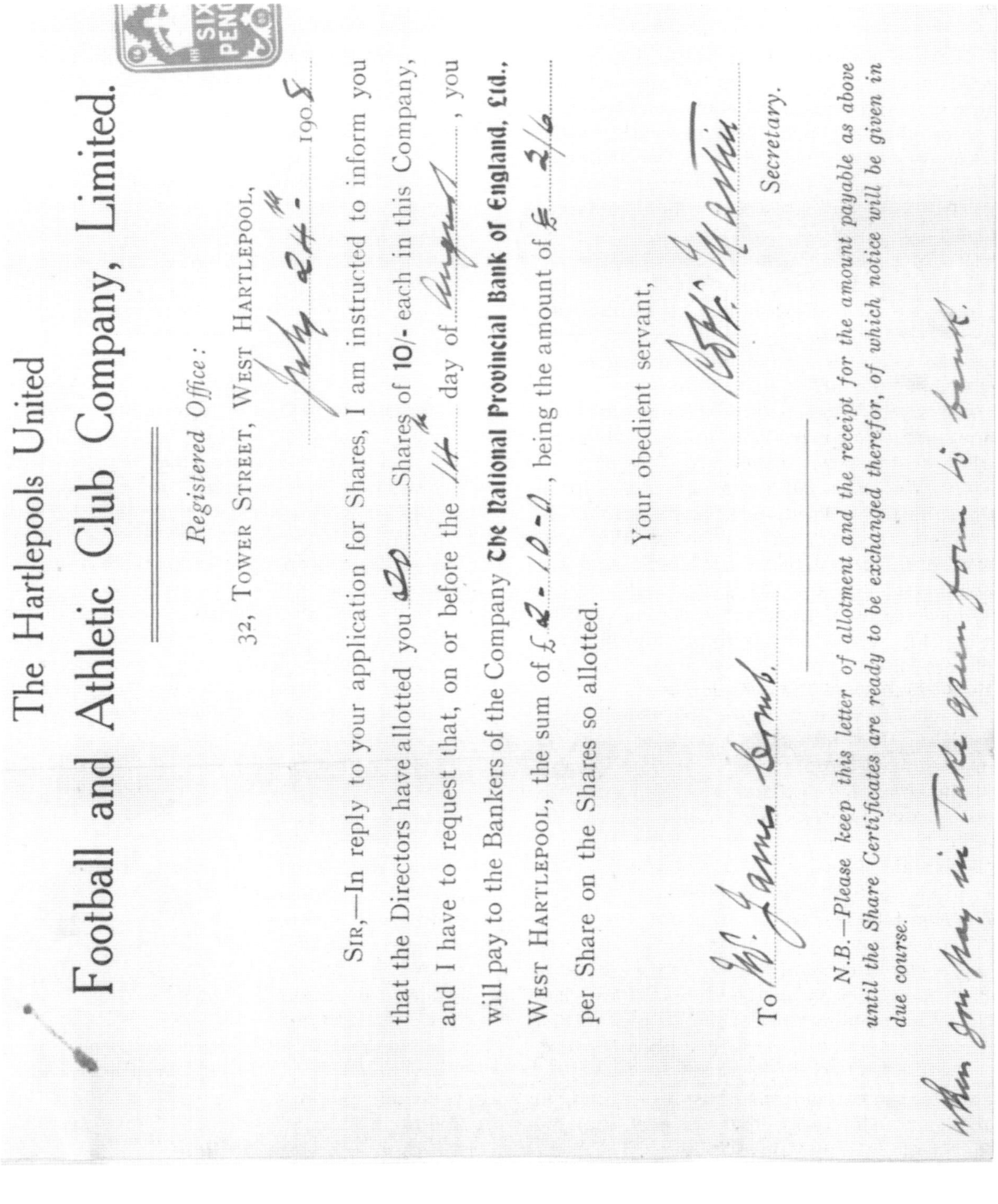

The Hartlepools United

Football and Athletic Club Company, Limited.

Registered Office :

32, Tower Street, West Hartlepool,

July 24 - 1908

Sir,—In reply to your application for Shares, I am instructed to inform you that the Directors have allotted you *20* Shares of **10/-** each in this Company, and I have to request that, on or before the *14th* day of *August*, you will pay to the Bankers of the Company **The National Provincial Bank of England, Ltd.,** West Hartlepool, the sum of £ *2 - 10 - 0*, being the amount of £ *2/6* per Share on the Shares so allotted.

Your obedient servant,

C.E. Martin

Secretary.

To *Mr James Boyd.*

N.B.—Please keep this letter of allotment and the receipt for the amount payable as above until the Share Certificates are ready to be exchanged therefor, of which notice will be given in due course.

when you pay in take green form to Bank.

Share Application Return Form, 1908

Hartlepools United was still being debated.

Pools had discussed merging with the Expansion Club, but in effect they were a works side and not keen on losing amateur status. It was revealed that if negotiations with West fell through, the new Club would still proceed despite the fact that the two clubs would be competing for spectators.

However if the new Club was to get into the NEL, there was nothing to prevent an arrangement between the clubs at a later date.

Although the clubs were in negotiation it seemed clear they wished to continue on their own, permitting people to see association football at the Vic each week, with two different teams to support.

It was finally announced by Mr John Proud, a member of the West Hartlepool Expansion Club since their establishment, that both clubs would continue to be separate and he hoped that good and trusted working arrangements with the new Club could be adopted.

Mr Proud was a former centre forward, honourable secretary and was at the helm when West won the Amateur Cup in 1905.

His West team had a much-coveted place in the competitive Northern League. Adamant on maintaining their amateur status, they had offered to assist the new Club in any way possible.

An agreement was reached stating that the new Club would not approach any of West's players directly, but if they applied to play applications would be considered.

Townsfolk were surprised that it had taken so long for the Hartlepools to form a professional Club.

The combined population of the towns was greater than that of several league clubs at the time.

The First Manager Is Appointed

ON the first day of June 1908 the Club was officially established and only a few days later the Club announced the details of its first manager.

Former England international full back, Fred Priest was chosen from a list of around 30 applicants who applied for the post after the Club's advert in the Athletic News.

Darlington-born, he played for South Bank, Sheffield United and Middlesbrough.

Priest was vastly experienced and while with Sheffield he was on both a winning and losing FA Cup final side, scoring in both ties. He also won a league championship medal and was the league's top scorer in 1902. His pedigree for the job was enhanced further by a spell as

assistant trainer at Middlesbrough.

Fred Priest

He had the experience needed and, at the age of 33, it was hoped that he would be able to help out on the pitch too.

Goalkeeper Fred Mearns joined from Bury in July 1908. Born in Sunderland, he was returning to the area (where he had played with his hometown team in 1901) after spells with Tottenham Hotspur, Bradford City and Bury amongst others. The former joiner was a proven keeper with experience and a great reputation.

Newcastle Form Opposition For First Game

AS a curtain raiser to the first season, a friendly was arranged to face a team representing Newcastle United at the Victoria Ground on September 2 1908. The opponents declared they were to send down a competitive side.

The game was just three days before the Club's first league fixture at Hebburn Argyle.

Another prominent signing was made in the form of pub landlord Joshie Fletcher from Wearside League side Wingate Albion.

Of the 70 goals Albion netted in season 1907/8, Fletcher scored 38 of them. He spent the three seasons previous with Queens Park Rangers of the Southern League, where he had also figured for Reading and West Ham United.

More signings followed – Hewston (ex-West Hartlepool), Ridsdale (Wingate), Wilson (Middlesbrough), Higgins (Lincoln) and Tweddle (Darlington St. Augustine's).

Fred Mearns

An Agreement

An Agreement made this _Eighth_ day of _April_ One Thousand Nine Hundred and _Nine_ between _Robert Martin_ as Secretary and on behalf of the Hartlepools United Football and Athletic Club Company, Limited (hereinafter called the Club), of the one part and _Alfred Ernest Priest_ of the other part.

1.—The said _Alfred Ernest Priest_ shall from the _First_ day of _May_, One Thousand Nine Hundred and _Nine_ until the 30th day of April, One Thousand Nine Hundred and _Twelve_ (both inclusive), serve the said Club as a Professional Football Player.

2.—The said _Alfred Ernest Priest_ shall and will obey all the lawful commands of the Committee for the time being of the said Club.

3.—The said _Robert Martin_ for such services as aforesaid shall and will pay to the said _Alfred Ernest Priest_ weekly and every week during the said employment, the sum of _Three Pounds_ (£3.)

4.—The said _Alfred Ernest Priest_ hereby expressly agrees with the said _Robert Martin_ that he will play to the best of his ability, and in accordance with the laws of the game and the Rules of the Football Association in force for the time being, and will devote his whole time and services exclusively for the benefit of the said Club, and will implicitly obey the directions of the Committee, and not at any time during the said employment play for any other Football Club, nor with any other Football Team than the Hartlepools United Football Team; and further if he is guilty of any misconduct the Committee shall have power to cancel this Agreement, and dismiss him from their service.

As witness the hands of the said parties the day and year first above written.

Robt. Martin

A. E. Priest

Fred Priest's contract signed in 1909

Joshie Fletcher

On August 13 the Club held their first open practice which attracted a decent crowd. No game took place but the players on show were made up of those who had signed and hopefuls on trial.

Those present included Mearns, Priest, Smith, Hand, Prosser, S Tweddle, Edgley, Seal, Lenaghan, Hewson and Higgins. Freddie Seal (from West Stanley) and Jacky Hand (Shildon Athletic) were signed for £5 each.

A week later a trial match took place at the Victoria Ground between the Whites and the Blues and Whites. The latter won 2-1 with Hodgson and Lenaghan scoring for the victors and Edgley replying.

On September 2, the friendly fixture with Newcastle United failed to live up to its promise as the visitors brought a team including a mere two players with first team experience.

The first Pools team to take to the pitch was Fred Mearns, Richard Hegarty, Fred Priest, Steve Tweddle, Jacky Hand, Chris Smith, Fred Tweddle, Joshie Fletcher, Frank Edgley, John Lenaghan and Freddie Seal.

Newcastle were subsequently hammered 6-0 by the new Hartlepools United, with goals from Smith, Fletcher, Edgley, Seal and two from trialist Lenaghan.

Whether or not this fixture was arranged to encourage the townsfolk of Hartlepool and West Hartlepool to follow the new Club is open to conjecture.

1908/09

First Season

THE first league fixture in the NEL on September 5 resulted in a 2-2 draw at Hebburn Argyle with the Club's first goals scored by Joshie Fletcher.

The only changes in the line-up were the swapping over of Priest and Hegarty from left to right full back and the replacement of Fred Tweddle with former West Hartlepool player Fred Hewston.

The following Saturday saw the first professional North Eastern League fixture at the Vic, when 5,000 expectant fans were in attendance. However, the game was little more than a drab affair as Seaham White Star kept United at bay and the game ended goalless.

On September 26, United registered their first victory, a 2-0 triumph over fellow NEL debutants North Shields Athletic.

After four unbeaten NEL games the Club played their first FA Cup match, the opposition none other than West Hartlepool.

Pools were drawn away, but the tie was played at home due to the groundshare and, in front of 7,000 spectators, United ran out 2-1 winners with Chris Smith and Tommy Brown doing the damage. Pools were knocked out in the next round by Middlesbrough amateur side South Bank, after a replay.

First Meeting Called For Shareholders

ON October 23 the Club held the first statutory shareholders meeting at the Grand Hotel.

Members were exceedingly satisfied with how both the financial and playing situations stood.

A scheme was to be drawn up where

Pools in action in the FA Cup for the first time in October 1908

shareholders could benefit from the success of the Club, possibly in form of dividend payments at the end of the season, considering the expenses that had already been encountered to date.

Former Fulham and Reading forward Frank Edgley became the Club's first scorer of a hat-trick in a 4-1 home victory over Carlisle United on November 7 and, by Christmas, matters were progressing nicely.

Pools had lost only two of their first 11 league fixtures. Despite the FA Cup setback the Club were progressing in the Durham Senior Cup after beating Tow Law, Spennymoor United and West Stanley to place them in the second round proper.

Soon to be bitter neighbours, Darlington came to the Vic three days after Christmas 1908.

The result was the Club's biggest victory to date – 8-1. Edgley again bagged three.

Two more home games followed and on New Year's Day, Huddersfield were sent packing 4-1. The following day, in front of the record crowd to that date for association football at the Vic of 10,000, last season's second-placed team and NEL champions in 1906, Sunderland A were resoundingly beaten by the same scoreline.

Trouble Brews For Match Official

DISGRACEFUL scenes followed the 2-2 draw at Shildon Athletic on March 13, 1909. Tommy Brown scored an equaliser in the last minute for Pools which resulted in bedlam.

The referee had experienced difficulty throughout the game with keeping control. Most of the 750 or so Shildon spectators did not see eye to eye with his decisions and a section of the crowd reacted badly to the result, verbally abusing the referee as he crossed the ropes to go to the dressing room.

He was surrounded by around 50 people who threw stones and mud at him. One stone hit him on the right side of the face causing a large cut, while a half brick narrowly missed his head.

Club officials unsuccessfully attempted to stop the trouble. Fortunately for the referee, two police constables arrived to quell the disturbance and one of them was also hit by a stone.

Police escorted the referee to a nearby hotel and then on to the railway station for a hasty departure.

The referee had to miss four days of work because of the assault, later submitting a claim to the Durham FA for lost earnings.

The Shildon club later admitted the assault, but claimed it was only of a trivial nature on the basis that they had put the matter in the hands of the local constabulary, with no arrests being made.

At a hearing 18 days later, Shildon were found guilty and had to pay the official's lost earnings along with his doctor's bill.

They were further reprimanded as evidence proved that two members of the Club's committee had sworn at the referee after the game in his dressing room. The guilty parties were suspended until the end of the season.

The use of their ground was suspended for two weeks and they couldn't play home games within six miles of Shildon. They were also fined the sum of £3.

Illustrations of Hebburn Match, Pools first NEL outing

THE HARTLEPOOLS UNITED

Football and Athletic Club Co.,

LIMITED.

Notice is hereby given that the STATUTORY MEETING of the above Company will be held in the GRAND HOTEL, West Hartlepool, on FRIDAY, the 23rd day of October, 1908, at 8 p.m., to receive the Directors' and Auditor's Report, to Elect Directors and Auditor, and to transact any other ordinary business of the Company.

By Order of the Board,

ROBT. MARTIN,

Secretary.

Registered Office :
32, Tower Street,
West Hartlepool,
16th October, 1908.

R. MARTIN, CROWN PRINTING WORKS WEST HARTLEPOOL

Notice of a Statutory Meeting to be held in October 1908

Silverware In The First Season

A week after the game, Pools faced Seaham White Star in the Durham Senior Cup final.

They had qualified for the final after beating Bishop Auckland and Stockton in the quarter and semi-finals. Since the victory over Sunderland's A team in early January, United were in poor form, winning only two of their eight league games, with the defence leaking four goals on three occasions.

To make sure the players were fit and at their best, they endured a week of strict training and were declared in 'fine fettle'.

The squad line up was as follows – Mearns, T Hegarty, R Hegarty, Hand, Smith, F Tweddle, W Ledger, Fletcher, Edgley, Tommy Brown and W P Roberts.

Nine minutes into the game and United went in front through Tommy Brown before a header from skipper Jacky Hand put Pools two goals up at the interval.

Shortly after the restart, Frank Edgley netted his 16th goal of the season and gave United a seemingly unassailable three-goal lead.

However, in an oft-repeated fashion over the next hundred years, Pools let things slip and left their supporters on tenterhooks as Seaham rallied and scored two goals.

The backs stood firm, however, and, in their inaugural season, United had won a trophy.

Although a regional tournament, the Durham Senior Cup was of great importance.

The team enjoyed a small celebration in Stockton while waiting for their train to West Hartlepool. They were greeted by a crowd of around 5,000 who cheered loudly as Jacky Hand, the skipper, held the cup aloft for all to see.

The team made the short journey to the Grand Hotel where Councillor Martin addressed the crowd thanking them for their support throughout the first season.

He also hoped that they would continue to support Pools in the future. After several more celebratory speeches and back slapping, the cup was filled with alcohol and passed around. Finally each player received a medal.

But the season petered out with Pools winning just five of the remaining 12 NEL games. There were some good performances in there, with Pools scoring 15 goals in the space of six days in one purple patch.

They beat Workington (5-0), Hebburn Argyle (5-1) and Seaham White Star (5-2) with leading scorer Fletcher grabbing his first hat-trick of the season in the Seaham game. He went on to become top scorer, grabbing 31 goals in total, 27 in the league.

A Strong Start For The Team

THE Club's first season was a decent one by any standards.

Winning the much-coveted Durham Senior Cup at the first attempt and finishing fourth in the North Eastern League ahead of the A teams of Sunderland and Middlesbrough and Darlington was no mean feat for an infant Club.

Newcastle United's second string won the title, their seventh title in their last eight seasons.

Team Heads For Europe

POOLS success brought recognition from outside of the area and at the end of April 1909 it was announced that an offer had been made to Pools to show their prowess abroad. The offer originated from the Hamburg Club in Germany to play there in the Whitsun holidays.

All the club needed was a suitable guarantee to cover expenses.

Arrangements were agreed and the tour went ahead as Pools joined the latest fashion of clubs touring Europe to display their footballing talents.

The party left West Hartlepool on Thursday, May 27 heading for Grimsby, where they caught a ship bound for Hamburg.

They reached their destination at dinnertime on Saturday, May 29. The weather was fine and the crossing good. The players aboard were Kelly, the Hegarty brothers, the Tweddles, Hand, Ledger, Fletcher, Edgley, Brown and new signing Thompson, previously of Fulham and Clapton Orient.

United played two matches, the first on May 31 against Hamburg.

The game was a one-sided affair with Pools winning 4-1 and the following day Pools beat a good Bremen side 4-2, playing some fine football, reported as 'the game of their lives'.

The German teams praised the manager, Mr Priest, for the performances. After each match the team were elaborately entertained.

The squad returned to West Hartlepool looking bronzed and fit, after enjoying delightful weather throughout the tour.

Reasons To Be Cheerful

THE Club was now awash with optimism. They had enjoyed a great season which exceeded all expectations, but at the same time not surprising anybody as they believed that they had the potential to do well. The tour, cup win and the good league showing

No. 45

The Hartlepools United Football and Athletic Club Company, Limited.

Incorporated under the Companies Acts, 1862 to 1900.

This is to Certify, that Mr. James Cook

of Queen Hotel Mainsforth Terrace West Hartlepool

is the Registered Proprietor of 20 Shares of Ten Shillings each,

Numbered 534 to 553 both inclusive, in

The Hartlepools United Football and Athletic Club Company, Limited,

subject to the Memorandum of Association, and the Rules and Regulations
thereof, and that up to this date there has been paid in respect of each of such
Shares, the sum of Seven Shillings and Sixpence.

Given under the Common Seal of the said Company,

this 28th day of June 1909

Robt. Martin
Secretary.

Wm. R. Paterson
Wm. I. Forbes
Directors.

No Transfer of any of the above-mentioned Shares can be Registered without the production of this Certificate.

The Hartlepools United Football & Athletic Club Company, Limited.

An original share certificate from 1909

Auditor's Report.

To the Shareholders of The Hartlepools United
Football and Athletic Club Company, Ltd.,
per Mr. R. Martin, Secretary.

I beg to report that I have examined the Balance Sheet and Accounts for the year ending April 30th, 1909, with the Books and Vouchers relating thereto, and that I have obtained all the information and explanations I have required, and that, in my opinion, the Balance Sheet referred to in this Report is properly drawn up so as to exhibit a true and correct view of the state of the Company's affairs, according to the best of my information and the explanations given to me, and as shown by the Books of the Company.

JAS. MARCHBANK,

Auditor.

33, Lynn Street,
West Hartlepool,
May 18th, 1909.

The Hartlepools United

Football and Athletic Club Company,

Limited.

NOTICE is hereby given, that the First Annual General Meeting of the above-named Company will be held at the Grand Hotel, West Hartlepool, on Wednesday, May 26th, 1909, at 8 p.m., to receive the Directors' and Auditor's Reports, to declare a Dividend, to elect Directors and Auditor, and to transact the ordinary business of the Company.

By Order of the Board,

ROBT. MARTIN,

Secretary.

Registered Office :
32, Tower Street, West Hartlepool,
May 18th, 1909.

Notice of the Club's First AGM and an Auditor's Report from 1909

THE HARTLEPOOLS UNITED FOOTBALL AND ATHLETIC CLUB COMPANY, LIMITED.

Balance Sheet, 1st Year ending, April 30th, 1909.

LIABILITIES.

	£ s. d.	£ s. d.
Share Capital—		
Authorised, 4,000 Shares, 10/- each...		2,000 0 0
Issued, 747 Shares at 10/- (7/6 called) ...	274 12 6	
Sundry Creditors ...	143 6 5	
Profit and Loss A/c—Profit ...	177 17 9	
		£595 16 8

ASSETS.

	£ s. d.	£ s. d.
By Stands, Turnstiles, Ground Fittings, etc. ...	524 19 8	
Less Depreciation, 10% ...	52 10 0	472 9 8
" R. Martin, Petty Cash ...		3 0 0
" North Eastern League, Deposit ...		10 0 0
" National Provincial Bank ...		110 7 0
		£595 16 8

Profit and Loss Account, 1st Year ending April 30th, 1909.

	£ s. d.	£ s. d.	£ s. d.
To Promotion Expenses ...			26 4 2
" Players' Wages ...	717 10 0		
" Money Takers' do. ...	32 1 6		
" Trainers' do. ...	60 0 0		809 11 6
" Train Fares, &c. ...			132 11 4
" Refreshments and Hotel Expenses ...			96 13 0
" Referees ...			19 11 10
" Police ...			15 6 0
" Ground Rent ...			22 10 0
" Rates, Taxes, &c. ...			20 3 8
" Insurances ...			19 7 6
" Transfer Fees, &c. ...			17 10 0
" Entry Fees and Subscriptions ...			8 2 6
" Forms and Stationery ...			1 19 6
" Advertising ...			5 1 9
" Gas and Water, Fuel, &c. ...			12 19 0
" Printing ...			36 5 9
" Billposting ...			21 5 0
" Medical Stores ...			6 12 0
" Outfitting ...			44 17 4
" Sundries ...			25 17 9
" Bank Charges, Cheque Books, &c. ...			2 4 11
" Legal Fees and Charges ...			6 18 6
" Registration and Stamping Fees ...			1 11 0
" Postages and Telegrams ...			8 7 4
" Carriage ...			0 1 10
" Audit Fee ...			5 5 0
" Depreciation on Stands, Turnstiles, Ground Fittings, &c.—10% on £524 19s. 8d. ...			52 10 0
			1689 14 3
By Takings at Gate and Stands ...		1517 7 5	
Less Visiting Teams ...	159 14 1		
" Charities ...	12 12 9	172 6 10	
" Season Tickets ...		29 2 0	
" Rent of Field, &c. ...		50 16 6	
To Balance, Profit ...		177 17 9	
	£1,597 5 11		£1,597 5 11
By Balance, Profit ...			£177 17 9

WM. PATERSON, (CHAIRMAN.)

THOMAS RELTON, } DIRECTORS.

May 18th, 1909.

Club's Balance Sheet from 1909

		P	W	D	L	F	A	POINTS
1	Newcastle United A	34	26	4	4	106	48	56
2	South Shields Adelaide	34	22	4	8	80	41	48
3	Bradford Park Avenue A	34	19	5	10	84	49	43
4	**HARTLEPOOLS UNITED**	**34**	**16**	**9**	**9**	**79**	**51**	**41**
5	Middlesbrough A	34	17	6	11	82	45	40
6	Sunderland A	34	18	3	13	81	54	39
7	West Stanley	34	18	3	13	73	56	39
8	Darlington	34	15	8	11	76	73	38
9	North Shields Athletic	34	14	6	14	63	48	34
10	Spennymoor United	34	13	7	14	55	63	33
11	Wallsend Park Villa	34	13	6	15	55	66	32
12	Workington	34	12	5	17	50	80	29
13	Seaham White Star	34	10	7	17	55	64	27
14	Hebburn Argyle	34	10	6	18	55	91	26
15	Carlisle United	34	10	4	20	61	84	24
16	Huddersfield Town	34	10	4	20	47	74	24
17	Shildon Athletic	34	7	6	21	51	101	20
18	Sunderland Royal Rovers	34	7	5	22	39	100	19

North Eastern League
1908-1909

promised much.

The details of the first financial report for the year ending 30/4/1909 were issued on May 19 showing a profit of £177 17s 9d (£177.89) with the shareholders taking a five per cent dividend.

The directors were very proud of the success achieved on and off the pitch. There was a lot of initial expense involved with the Club's set up, which could now be capitalised.

Gate receipts totalled £1689 14s 3d, of which £12 12s 9d from the practice games was donated to charity.

The total annual wage bill for players was £717 10s. The trainer, Mr Spoors, received an annual income of £60. Also highlighted in the accounts were train fares and travel expenses of £132 11s 4d with £96 13s spent on refreshments and hotels.

A week later at the first AGM, the board mentioned they intended to 'lick the ground into shape'. They had already spent the £274 of share money, along with an additional £110 from gate monies on improvements and repairs to the ground. At the start of the first season £400 had been pledged in share monies but far more was received.

Despite assurances made at the start of the season that the grandstand was in good order, it was reported as being dilapidated.

Repair work was carried out over the summer by local carpenters and joiners. The rest of the ground was taking shape though. Banking of the terrace at the end of the ground (now the Town End) adjacent to where West Hartlepool Cricket Club once played had already taken place.

This action was also carried out at the allotment end (now the Rink End). A scoreboard was also in place where a selection of half-time and full-time scores would be displayed.

1909/10

THERE were changes to the NEL for the start of the second season. The Bradford Park Avenue reserve side resigned along with Huddersfield. Wingate Albion were admitted and Seaham White Star changed their name to Seaham Harbour.

Hartlepools had a poor start with only one win in their first four NEL games and were knocked out of the Durham Benevolent Bowl in their debut match in the competition, losing 2-0 to Darlington.

Their single win was away to the strong reserve side of Sunderland, proving the potential performance was there when they played better opposition.

Goals Galore

KNOCKED out of the FA Cup on October 16, again to Darlington, the Club gained revenge by registering their first league home win of the season over the Quakers two weeks later. This victory set the ball rolling and the Club went on a fantastic run of results, remaining unbeaten at Christmas, with revenge in the form of a 4-0 drubbing of Darlington in the first round of the DSC in mid-December.

Two days after Christmas, Pools entertained Hebburn Argyle and treated 4,600 fans, scoring ten goals without reply with Frank Edgley bagging four and Josh Fletcher netting a hat-trick. Brown, Ledger and Tom Hegarty were also on the scoresheet.

The Club had hit form and to follow was a 2-0 victory over the reserve side of Newcastle United, a 6-2 victory at Seaham Harbour and another great home display, scoring eight without reply against Wallsend Park Villa with Tommy Brown scoring four.

However, sour news was received when it was reported that a gateman had been physically assaulted by a spectator at a home game over the festive period. The board had agreed to back him and pay all fees should he pursue legal action against his assailant. The gateman opted not to pursue the case after the individual involved apologised in person both to him and Fred Priest.

Good Form And Merger Talks

MEANWHILE, in contrast to Pools' good run, the West Hartlepool amateur side were encountering financial difficulties and dropping support due to some rather mediocre performances. Another factor was the attraction to follow the better Club of the two, Pools. A meeting was to be held between the two boards to consider the question of amalgamation.

Towards the end of the month Joshie Fletcher scored another hat-trick in the 5-1 victory over a struggling Sunderland Rovers.

Tragedy Hits The Football Club

MEANWHILE, Frank Edgley, who had been complaining of weakness in his legs, was admitted to Cameron's Hospital on February 1, 1910. A week later he was operated on for appendicitis.

Pools were drawn against Spennymoor United in the semi-final of the DSC. The tie ended 2-2 at Spennymoor, the replay a week later on February 12. Bizarrely the referee called a halt to proceedings only one minute into the second half of extra time due to the worsening conditions with Spennymoor 3-2 up. A replay was scheduled for a fortnight later.

On February 16, came the devastating news that Edgley, possibly Pools' best player, had died in hospital failing to recover after his operation.

He had first complained of being ill during the tour of Germany in May 1909. Testament to his commitment was that despite being ill, he played on and never missed a game. He suffered a relapse on Valentine's Day 1910 and died as a result of gangrenous appendicitis. He was to be buried in his home town of Crewe and when his body was moved from the hospital to the train station a couple of days later, many people watched the procession.

Despite the sad loss, the business of the Club had to continue and meetings with the amateur club went ahead. West had seemingly conceded

The 1909 Durham Senior Cup winners

A selection of pages from the Frank Edgley
Memorial Programme, 1910

defeat and agreed to the surrender of their lease on the ground, while drawing up a list of their liabilities.

The next home game was postponed and a week later Pools tried again against Spennymoor in the semi-final replay of the DSC. Both teams wore black armbands as a mark of respect. With a sleet and hail storm crashing down, United thrilled the 7,000 fans with a 5-0 victory, a fitting tribute to their departed team-mate.

A letter was presented before the board from the West Hartlepool Expansion stating their liabilities stood at £195 and that they had assets of only £66, leaving net liabilities of £129, with five home and two away fixtures to play.

Pools' great run of form finally ended at Middlesbrough on March 25 when Boro's reserve team won 3-1. The Club had gone 18 league games unbeaten, 23 in all competitions.

To The Final Again

THE day after defeat the same side, bar one change with Smith replacing Steve Tweddle, represented United in the Durham Senior Cup Final for the second year running.

Played in Bishop Auckland, an estimated 3,600 people travelled on the train from the towns of Hartlepools. Taking to the field for Pools were W McIver, T Hegarty, G Billam, J Hand, C Smith, W Ledger, F Tweddle,

J Fletcher, F Thompson, J Bennett, J Hogg.

South Shields took the lead after only five minutes, but after 17 minutes, Pools drew level through Fletcher when he deflected a shot from Hogg into the net. Early in the second half Fletcher netted a Tweddle cross, only for the referee to blow for offside. There were only ten minutes remaining when Fletcher got his second, to give Pools a 2-1 lead. The game was soon over as a contest as, with a couple of minutes to go, Jack Bennett made it 3-1 to Pools. As in the previous final the score ended 3-2 to Pools as King scored for Shields straight from the restart.

Once again the team received a fantastic reception from townsfolk upon their return and held speeches before an enthusiastic crowd on the balcony of the Grand Hotel, where only two years earlier the Club had been founded.

West Struggle To Cope Financially

ON April 9, the board of Pools unanimously agreed to take over the liabilities of the amateur club with the main condition that West surrender their lease of the ground, as agreed. The necessary steps were then taken to wind up the Club.

Irrespectively, two days later, Pools again played the amateur side in the Cricket Club Medal Competition winning 2-0, with goals from George Billam and the unstoppable Fletcher.

Pools remained unbeaten throughout the rest of the season with the highlights the DSC victory and an amazing game against Workington on April 24, 1910.

The replacement striker for the late Edgley was Jack Hogg, who joined before Christmas from West Stanley for £10, originally playing in defensive roles, but moving up front after Edgley's death. Pools romped to a 12-0 triumph. Fletcher netted another hat-trick and Hogg stunned Workington with a brilliant nine goals, a record that still stands and is unlikely to be bettered.

United could even afford a missed penalty taken by goalkeeper McIver.

Less than two weeks after playing Pools it was revealed that West were set to go out of business. They finished their Northern League campaign with a defeat to the hands of Stockton in front of just a few hundred supporters. West finished eighth and honoured an agreement to play a friendly at Wingate on April 30, which they won 3-2 and never played again, just five years after making their name by winning the English Amateur Cup.

It was not the first time that West had gone bust – in the 1880s they encountered financial difficulties and were taken over by the NER club, changing their name back to West in 1898.

Since Pools were formed, West had continuously struggled to make ends meet, receiving decreasing support and the directors had incurred heavy expenses leaving the Park Road ground.

Although there was only one Pools home game postponed due to the weather, it was unfortunate for West that they suffered postponements on a more regular basis. With some of their better players leaving to play either professionally or for local amateur clubs on a better financial footing, West were left with no alternative but to cease trading.

Pools won another trophy on April 25 by defeating Wingate Albion 4-2 in the final of the Cricket Club competition, with goals from Fletcher, a Tom Hegarty penalty and a brace from Thompson.

Pools had lost just one league game since the reverse at South Shields Adelaide on October 23, 1909 – a run of one defeat in 28 games. Despite the slow start and the loss of Edgley, it was another fantastic season for Pools, although they finished fourth behind the reserve teams of Newcastle and Middlesbrough.

Spennymoor United, who joined the NEL at the same time as Pools, won their maiden championship.

Fletcher again topped the scoring charts with an astounding 36 goals, 25 of them in the league.

Looking Upwards At United

AFTER such a great campaign, United believed they were clearly capable of playing in a higher league and decided to apply for election to the second division of the Football League.

The board visited over two dozen clubs and petitioned others by post. Possibly too early to gain admittance, Pools were rejected rather bluntly receiving only one vote from the 40 member clubs of the first and second divisions.

Huddersfield Town, who finished 16th in the NEL in 1908-9 and fifth in the Midland League in 1909/10 were surprisingly elected. It was, however, a determined effort by Pools to get into the league – but possibly too bold an attempt by such a young Club and, with no doubt, politics playing a big part. The same politics that will later help Pools gain re-election in the decades still to come.

1910/11

WANTING to build on their success of the previous season, Pools made some promising signings. George Featherstone, a forward, from Brighton joined. Jack Bainbridge, another forward who had served three seasons with Southampton, signed along with highly-rated former Liverpool players Michael Griffin and James Gorman. With George Hedley from Hull brought in to replace the Watford-bound Smith and Jack Hogg converting to defence to accommodate the extra forwards, the rearguard was also strengthened.

The squad had been bolstered to such a depth that the board registered to run a reserve team in the Wearside League.

Pools disappointed in their first game of the season at the Vic, losing 3-0 to new boys Jarrow. The reserves, meanwhile, drew 1-1 at Seaham Albion, Jack Bainbridge registering their first goal.

Once again the Club started the season slowly and won three of their first six matches. The sixth match was a 2-2 draw at Sunderland, with Bainbridge and Hedley, a penalty, getting their first goals in the NEL for the Club.

Pools had been knocked out of the FA Cup at home to Darlington. There then followed a good run of results in the league with Fletcher, Featherstone and Bainbridge all amongst the goals.

Jack Hogg

The wing play of Griffin was attracting attention from Middlesbrough who wrote to the Club regarding his availability, so a £250 transfer fee was placed on his head.

Victoria Ground Stages Charity Match

ON November 23 1910, a match took place at The Vic for the benefit of local boilermakers who were locked out during a national shipyard dispute which had been running for around two months and, as it turned out would still have another two months to run.

The unrest greatly affected attendances as a lot of support came from men working in the shipyards and associated businesses. The Club was to be plagued by support levels affected by slides in trade in the area for decades to come.

A side made up of workers from Hartlepool played against a team representing those from West Hartlepool, who took a 2-0 lead through Wood and Mahoney, Elwine got one back and future Pools reserve player Joseph Lobb netted twice, to give the spoils to the Hartlepool XI.

On the same day Pools lost 2-1 to Seaham Harbour in a replay of the Durham Benevolent Bowl semi-final. The only remaining cup interest was the Durham Senior Cup, and Pools were scheduled to play Darlington a week

before Christmas Eve.

On December 12, Pools had a hard-fought 3-1 victory over Spennymoor United at the Vic. The visiting centre half Harrison, whose methods towards the end of the game left something to be desired, was followed to the dressing tent after the game by a large amount of Hartlepools fans who jeered and verbally abused him. Nothing untoward happened and the crowd gradually and peacefully dispersed.

The following week United gained revenge for their FA Cup exit at the hands of Darlington, beating them 1-0 at the Vic. Into the New Year and Pools played host to perennial strugglers Sunderland Royal Rovers, scoring their customary five goals, this time without reply.

On January 7, 1911 a new centre forward was signed. Robert Blanthorne had experienced league football with Grimsby and Liverpool before signing for Newcastle United where he was injured on his debut. After failing to return to the Newcastle first team he joined Pools.

Battling For Honours Once Again

ON January 21 in the reserve game against Seaham Villa, defender Gorman badly displaced the cartilage in his knee and was put on the sick list along with teammate Brown. He was a player with good pedigree who had already suffered niggling injuries during the season. He returned later in the season and played a bit part the next, but failed to live up to his billing.

Once again United were progressing well in the Durham Senior Cup. In February they qualified for their third consecutive final with a 3-1 win at Bishop Auckland. Pools were cheered on by a large away support that had travelled on specially provided trains. In the NEL Pools were neck and neck with the Newcastle United A team for the title.

With Steve Tweddle suffering from an injury sustained at a blast furnace where he worked and Gorman injured, Pools were in need of another half back.

Teddy McIntyre, who had been playing for West Stanley, had approached Pools and, although a centre forward, he could play in a half back position. He signed but ended up playing only two of his 12 NEL games in that position.

Another long unbeaten league spell of 17 games ended at the hands of champions Spennymoor, who were 2-1 victors on March 11, in what was Robert Blanthorne's final game for the Club. He was again injured, bringing an end to his playing days.

United bounced back the next weekend with a 7-4 victory over Middlesbrough A, where Fletcher helped himself to four goals. The following week Seaham Harbour were the visitors to the Vic and Pools put them to the sword, winning 5-0. Pools now seemed favourites for the title but form suddenly nosedived and the Club won only one of their last ten games.

Three thousand Pools fans saw United lose the DSC Final to South Shields, ending their hopes of a third straight win.

The losing XI were W McIver, G Hedley, G Billam, J Hand, J Hogg, W Ledger, J Bainbridge, J Fletcher, G Featherstone, J Stokoe, and M Griffin. George Featherstone netted Pools only goal as they lost by the odd goal in three.

This poor run of form was compounded by the defeat at Sunderland Rovers who were stranded at the foot of the table. The game was held in benefit of Rovers' former West Hartlepool keeper Albert Lindsay in recognition of his long career.

Pools slipped to third place behind the reserve teams of Sunderland and champions Newcastle. Once again the outstanding Fletcher topped the scoring charts, this time bagging 15 NEL goals, 21 in all.

The reserve team performed well and were in contention for the title but finished third, behind champions Haswell Swifts.

Further Attempts Made To Join Football League

IT was declared on April 21 that the Club would make another bid for election to the second division of the Football League.

Despite only receiving one vote last year, the application was lodged in May along with applications from Rochdale (Lancashire Combination champions), Darlington (who finished fourth in the NEL and reached the third round proper in the FA Cup), Grimsby Town (Midland League champions) and Chesterfield (fifth in the Midland League but who reached the second round of the FA Cup). The bottom two, Barnsley and Lincoln City, applied for re-election.

A letter sent to support the application offered a background on the Club and the two towns. It also advised that the Club had a large fan base despite people leaving the towns each weekend to watch league football, despite the performance of the team in the NEL and DSC.

The Club further advised that the capacity of the ground was 14,000 with scope for increase. Attention was also brought to the fact that the ground was close to West Hartlepool railway station which, at the time, had excellent links.

On May 26 1911, the third AGM took place at the Grand Hotel.

Chairman Coates stated that the accounts for the last year end would not be ready until the end of the following month. He added that fortunes were not so good due to the protracted shipyard dispute which had affected attendances. Councillor Brown and Mr Lees Whitehead were to accompany the chairman to attend the Football League meeting later in the month.

Four days later, United were again unsuccessful in gaining election, getting just one vote. Grimsby were elected after failing the season before and Barnsley were re-elected. Lincoln City were confined to the Midland League.

Idea For A New Division

THE representatives who failed in their attempt to be elected met afterwards and proposed the formation of a third division.

They quickly drafted a scheme and the majority of the proposals were approved by the league's management committee. The proposed new venture would comprise 20 clubs – including Pools. The Football League advertised the possibility of the division in the Athletic News in order to obtain applicants from across the country.

The three representatives from Pools reported back from the meeting and it became apparent that teams from the Durham County area were practically barred from the second division due to their geographical position and the difficulties and costs with reaching the area.

It seemed odd, however, as besides Chelsea and Clapton Orient the majority of the teams in the second division were predominantly northern or midlands teams. The sporting prowess of North-East clubs was never in doubt at the election meetings, but the clubs simply never got sufficient votes due to the mentality of the members.

The other team from County Durham, Darlington, boasted that they had 24 votes before the election.

Full of confidence that they would achieve election, they were astonished and left with egg on their face when they received a mere seven votes. Nevertheless, it was almost certain that the five who failed at the election stage would be members of the new division.

A period of meetings across the north of England followed, with the likes of Cardiff, Walsall, Crewe Alexandra and St Helen's Town all wanting to be part of the new venture.

Clubs needed to be on a solid financial footing and Pools once again appealed for aid. The Football League had agreed to the idea of a third division in principal, but delayed their decision following a complaint from the Southern League, regarding the possible loss of some of their members.

They delayed a decision until the winter of 1911, which would hopefully give Pools ample time to sort their finances out.

Meanwhile, Pools' management were preparing for the future and secured the services of Micky Griffin for another season. Jack Martin, a forward of some repute, joined from Millwall where he had finished leading scorer the previous season.

Four days later, on June 16, the FL management committee met at Blackpool and dealt a huge blow to the idea of a third division. The committee of the Southern League wrote to the FL advising that they thought that the formation of the third division would be 'an unfriendly act'.

The management committee of the Football League took the view that too many problems had arisen and had ultimately decided that the proposed formation of the third division would not proceed now.

Although the proposal for the new venture came on rather suddenly, the idea was adopted with great enthusiasm by many.

Despite this setback, the board of Hartlepool diplomatically stated they believed the enforced delay was beneficial for the majority of the parties involved giving them more time to get their houses in order.

It seemed that the NEL would be the only campaign that the Club would be vying for the following season, as on June 21 the Club announced the reserve team had tendered their resignation from the Wearside League.

Club Concerned Over Small Following

THE annual report was released days later showing a loss of £363 17s 11d. It was stated that the deficit was mainly down to four reasons.

First was the dispute at the shipyards. During the protracted lock out period, the revenue on the gate fell by £262. The second reason was that the A team had generated a working loss of £100. The third was that there was an unusually high number of injuries to players resulting in the need to bring in new blood and finally the Club had been receiving rental income of around £77 from the amateur Club who now were no more.

Some features of the accounts were players wages of £1238 10s, with train fares being £129 13s 9d. Gate money totalled £1750 4s 2d with payments to visitors of £154 3s 11d and local charities benefiting to the tune of £24 7s 10d.

The only main topic on the agenda was the reserve side. The Club had never envisaged that this team was going to make a profit and the idea behind it was to keep good men in employment and to groom players.

However, they were surprised at the lack of interest and support in the area for a competitive team. Pools were not alone in this respect and several other teams in the Wearside League were struggling to attract decent crowds. Despite wanting to pull out of competition, it served a purpose and the board voted to reverse their previous resignation and re-enter.

In July 1911, Robert Grierson arrived from Rochdale, a prolific scorer the previous season. Pools were desperately trying to sign a new Frank Edgley and they hoped Grierson would fit the bill. The signature of Woolwich Arsenal right back Duncan McDonald was also completed.

Improvements were carried out to the Victoria Ground. The main grandstand had been totally repaired and the middle section, traditionally reserved for the well-off Club patrons, had been refurbished providing more comfortable seating for around 100 spectators.

Two clubs joined the NEL for the forthcoming season, Newcastle City, from the Northern Alliance and newly-formed Gateshead Town. Workington had disbanded.

1911/12

THE season started with a loss, a draw and a victory. Pools then went on a run of seven league games without a win, before victory over Sunderland Rovers, by four goals to one, started a decent run of form.

In September, George Hedley requested the board advance him some monies from his wages. The board, however, were not overly keen on amending the details of his contract but would have been prepared to make an exception as he had a good season previously. However they refused on the grounds that his behaviour away from the Club was less than desired and they warned him about his future conduct. He demanded to be released from his contract, but it was left in the hands of the manager to calculate a transfer fee that would cover the amount paid to him as salary since he joined the Club.

Winger Micky Griffin made his first start of the season on September 13 in the game at

No. of
Certificate } 98191.

COMPANIES ACTS, 1862 TO 1907.

REPORT

pursuant to s. 12 of the Companies Act, 1900 (63 and 64 Vict. c. 48) of

The Hartlepools United

Football and Athletic Club Company, Limited.

The total number of shares allotted is 705, wholly for cash.

The total amount of cash received by the Company in respect of the shares issued wholly for cash is £156 12s. 6d.

The Receipts and Payments of the Company on Capital Account to the 13th day of October, 1908, are as follows :—

Particulars of Receipts.				Particulars of Payments.			
	£	s.	d.		£	s.	d.
On Share Capital—Application	88	2	6	On account of Stands, Turn-stiles, Ground Fittings, &c. .	10	0	0
Do. Allotment .	68	10	0	Labour on Ground, Turnstiles, Indicator, Flag, &c.... ...	38	5	2

First Annual Report to the Shareholders

Hebburn Argyle – and with it came an infamous place in history. He was ordered from the field of play by the referee for kicking an opposition player, becoming the first player to be sent off while playing for Hartlepools United.

During October and November several meetings took place nationwide about the set up of the new division. Despite the protests from the Southern League, it seemed the Football League were at last keen for the expansion to proceed.

Pools were again dumped out of the FA Cup at the first hurdle, losing 2-1 at North Shields Athletic.

Fussy Official Causes Chaos At The Vic

ON 11/11/11 Pools beat Gateshead Town 2-1 at the Vic. But after the game finished and the players had made their way to the dressing rooms, they were called back out by the referee. On leaving the field the pedantic official noticed he had blown for full time almost two minutes early. The players managed to squeeze the additional time in as the light faded, with no change to the result.

Financial Issue Begin To Bite

THE Club was still encountering problems off the pitch. Player wages were late in being paid during November and a meeting of the board and the players resolved that they be settled directly in cash from gate money. Players and directors thrashed out a deal to make improvements to the way that the Club was run. Members of the board loaned the Club £33 but with little effect on the situation.

On the last day of the month a shareholders meeting was held in the Alma Hotel. Debt had risen to around £500. The directors decided it was wise, before undertaking any further liability, to openly lay the state of the finances on the table for the shareholders to review.

Initially, in order to ease the situation, the management team and players agreed to a wage deferral of one third, to be paid when the Club were in a position to do so. While it was a big cut from their wages, it was better than the limit the board originally wanted of no more than 30 shillings per week.

Shareholders believed the condition of the accounts was not altogether due to indifferent play on the part of the team, more a long running series of unfortunate events, spanning to the season before and culminating with the early FA Cup exit at North Shields.

They predicted that cash would flow through the turnstiles with more home games due, particularly over Christmas, with three home games over four days. It was also hoped that Pools could maintain their good record in the DSC, gaining income from that tournament.

At the end of the meeting several shareholders agreed on the spot to subscribe to more shares, giving immediate extra revenue. Over 60 extra shares were subscribed to.

Replies and votes from the member clubs were needed at the Football League by December 14 for further consideration regarding the new venture of a third division.

The result of the vote by the 40 members was once again not in favour of a new division three.

The majority of the members who were asked to vote decided that the scheme was 'at the present time inappropriate'. Six months previously at least three-quarters of the clubs were full of support for the scheme – and now they were totally against it.

One theory is that they had been swayed by the voices of both the Southern League clubs and ex-members of the Southern League who persuaded them to vote against the new format.

Eleven clubs voted in favour, 26 against and three either abstained or the votes were spoiled.

Pools, as usual, retained a diplomatic silence. All the clubs who dedicated so much time and effort in order to attempt to get division three off the ground would have to abide by the questionable decision.

Disciplinary Issues Dealt With As Form Improves

AS if the Club didn't have enough problems of their own owing to the financial situation, one of the players, Harvey Carmichael, turned up for the game on December 9 against South Shields in a 'condition which made him unable to play'. Carmichael had been dropped the previous week and had played for the reserves. The manager was authorised to investigate the matter fully and suspend him from the Club if necessary. Fred Priest never felt justified enough to suspend him, but confined him to the reserves for the rest of the season and released him on a free transfer when the season had ended.

Results started to improve and an impressive Christmas Day display at the Vic saw Pools beat Wallsend Park Villa, scoring five without reply. One of the goals was scored by Harry Carr, who hailed from a well-known footballing family in South Bank. The former England amateur international had previously played for Middlesbrough and Sunderland. On January 1, another home game saw United beat Seaham Harbour by the same scoreline.

Knocked out of the DSC by Darlington in January, Pools failed to reach the final for the first time. However, the bumper gate entitled them to over £150 in takings, enabling them to clear £27 of back wages to players and a further £18 the following week.

In mid-February, Jack Martin scored his first hat-trick in a 5-2 home win over Shildon Athletic.

Despite the brief financial respite given by the Darlington game things were still dire and following the 4-2 home victory over Jarrow Croft on March 2, the board could only afford to pay the staff half their weekly salary. It clearly didn't go down too well with trainer Spoors as he was dismissed two days later, having to return the keys for the Vic when he collected the monies due to him.

Duncan McDonald, George Hedley and Jack Martin seemed to be the least pleased with the arrangement and they demanded an agreement be made regarding the amount of monies due. Hedley didn't stop there and again was abusive to members of the board, which led to him being suspended on the spot. He never played for the Club again.

Players Defer Payments To Help Club

CAPTAIN Josh Fletcher offered to help out by playing for nothing for the rest of the season. The rest of the squad agreed to wait for payment. To raise money a medal competition took place at the Vic amongst local teams with entrance fees and a share of the gate going to Pools. They also agreed to allow the cricket club to have summer dances on the field, for a small retainer.

Results remained inconsistent, culminating in their biggest defeat to date, a 5-0 reverse at the hands of Middlesbrough's reserve side. Pools ended the season in a disappointing ninth place. For the fourth season in a row Joshie Fletcher finished top scorer, with 23 goals.

At the end of the season, the board offered a lump sum to the players to settle the outstanding monies. It represented all funds due to them under the arrangement of full wages to the end of November 1911 and half salary from then on.

All players, except McDonald and Martin, accepted. The only drawback to the arrangement from the players' point of view was that the Club had a year to pay.

Harry Carr

Away from football the area was in a state of political unrest again. Railway strikes were random and had been ongoing for several months. There was also a great deal of unrest in heavy industry. Once more, when the workers who followed Pools had no cash, the first thing to suffer were the attendances at the Club.

Rumours Of Downfall Denied By Club

FOLLOWED by the financial problems earlier in the season, the cost of the failed division three venture was another unwanted setback. Rumours were rife that the Club might not even be around next season.

The board was forced to declare in the Press that this was simply not the case. They advised the Club was to have a thorough examination of how the Club was run and how it conducted business both on and off the pitch.

Pools were in no position, on or off the pitch, to apply for election to the Football League as it had done so before. Darlington, after another good FA Cup run where they reached round two, and Newcastle City applied but both without success.

Club Seeks New Player Manager

AT a board meeting in the Alma Hotel, West Hartlepool in May 1912, confirmation was made that Fred Priest's agreement was to be terminated and that the board had decided that they should seek a player/manager.

In order to keep costs low only a limited number of young professionals were to be employed, hopefully forming the spine of the team. The board was to encourage the coaching staff to make full use of local amateur talent.

Applications were invited for the post of manager and for players of all positions, following the placing on the transfer list of all players, except Ledger whose registration was held by Sunderland and Grierson who was granted a free transfer.

Two weeks after the request, there was an abundance of local players offering their services for free to the A team.

Several signings had been made following the release of most of the playing staff. James Stokoe, a forward, and John Gatenby, a defender, had re-signed and amateur back Harry Little signed professional forms.

When Pools were formed in 1908, the players of the former West Rugby Club moved to play for the Greatham side and in the summer of 1912 had regrouped sufficiently to reform as West Hartlepool Rugby Football Club.

They approached Pools in May to discuss the possibility of a ground share, but it was rejected by the board due to difficulties of playing different codes on a pitch and that was also used by the reserve XI. They also rejected a plea from the local West Hartlepool St Joseph's side to use the pitch.

Towards the end of June came the fourth annual report, and losses for the year amounted to £807 9s 4d.

Before the start of the 1911/12 season the formation of a Football League third division seemed assured and the directors brought in good players, with good credentials and experience, but at a price.

The formation of the new division fell through, results in the money-spinning FA Cup were poor, and the league performance was unsatisfactory. Gate receipts were down in excess of £450.

New Manager And New Gate Prices

FOUR days after the May meeting came the appointment of Percy Humphreys as player/manager.

The ex-England international and league representative had played for Notts County, Chelsea and Spurs, and joined from Leicester Fosse. He could play in most forward positions and also in the half back line. The board and the manager were to continue the selection arrangements established under Fred Priest – teams were selected by the board and the manager.

Further signings followed – Hibbert from West Brom, Wood from Eston United – and the prolific Joshie Fletcher re-signed.

The Directors seemed happy with the appointment. It transpired that Fred Priest had appointed several players following the receipt of postal reports. The Club also decided to reduce admission from 6d to 4d in an attempt to gain more spectators and it was deemed necessary as adjacent to the Victoria Ground was the Clarence Road Stadium where the West Hartlepool Rugby Club were to play. Entrance to games at the Rugby Club was only 3d.

The previous occupiers of that ground, West Hartlepool Cricket Club, had moved to new headquarters at Park Drive, West Hartlepool. The rugby club and Pools were at loggerheads for many months in relation to work carried out on their side of the boundary that was damaging the fencing built by Pools.

Percy Humphreys was busy in the transfer market, Barnsley full back Ellis joined, along with Mayo of Reading, and a mass of players on amateur terms – Miller from Deaf Hill United, Calder from local side Arncliffe and Frankland from Shotton Albion to name but a few. H Measor, well known in local rugby circles, was appointed groundsman and the trainer, H McNeill, was put in charge of the reserves.

Practice games, with proceeds going to charity, were arranged allowing the Club to assess players on trial. A young squad had been amassed, and results were expected to justify the patient policy of the board.

1912/13

THE season was to begin on September 2 at Gateshead Town, who numbered in their ranks former player William Ledger.

The campaign settled into an inconsistent format after a good start. There was a 5-0 victory at Gateshead on October 18, but summer signing Hibbert was laid up in the same month after contracting blood poisoning following a foot injury, and player/manager Humphreys was also sidelined.

By the end of October the board had to make a decision to increase gate prices back to 6d, as they could not afford to run the Club on the 4d fee with the volume of support that they were receiving.

FA Cup games against Wingate and Houghton Rovers were due to be played away, but an agreement was reached, which meant the games would be played in Hartlepool, with the potential of a bigger crowd and therefore greater revenue.

Further signings were made in November. Albert Butler, a half back, joined from Reading. His transfer was held at £350. Norman Mason, a young forward, joined from Heworth Colliery. Forwards Bennett and Rumney were selected to represent the Wearside League against the Sunderland & District League and Bennett captained the team to a 3-2 victory.

However, it wasn't all good news as Hibbert was hospitalised after contracting typhoid.

During November Pools were sniffing around Middlesbrough to see what the possibility was of signing former England forward Fred Pentland. Aged only 29 Pentland was deemed surplus to requirements at Ayresome Park and would have moved, but Pools could neither afford a fee or his services.

Train Strike Forces Postponement Of Game

FEW matches were missed in this era, but on December 7, the home game against West Stanley had to be postponed because of a train strike and West Stanley claimed to have no other method of transport.

They wired Pools stating that they could not make the game, when it was subsequently found that some trains were running from nearby Birtley. A charabanc was also available at South Hetton if the train could not have reached West Hartlepool.

It seemed that West Stanley were being petulant as the scheduled NEL game at their ground was postponed due to Pools' FA Cup run. By coincidence, the A team fixture on the same day at Shotton Albion had to be cancelled too, as the reserve team had lost their kit upon arrival at Shotton. They were later fined seven shillings and ten pence for this offence.

Joshie Fletcher bagged another hat-trick in the 6-0 win on December 28 at home to Hebburn Argyle. At the end of the year the Club had been knocked out of the FA Cup, after a fair run (but failing to make the first round proper again), but were still in the North Riding Challenge Cup, the Durham Senior and Amateur Cups. Out of 14 league games, six had been won, with three drawn and five lost.

Inconsistent Form In League And Cup

IN the New Year the team struggled, winning only one of their next seven league games.

Forwards were inconsistent and the manager struggled to find a settled half back line. The team was chopped and changed with the manager dropping back into the half back role where he played at the start of his career.

A new half back, G Stevenson, joined from the Belfast Distillery Club and Robert Brewis was signed from Burnley – it was hoped he would solve the forward line problems. However, Mayo, Stokoe and amateur F Henderson (broken leg) were all injured and Humphreys was starting to suffer more problems, ruled out in both January and February due to separate complaints.

The team were knocked out of the DSC at Birtley in January and out of the DAC the following month to Expansion, losing to two goals by former player Arthur Taylor. They made it to the semi finals of the North Riding Challenge Cup, losing at Darlington in a March replay, an extremely physical and poorly refereed encounter. Mayo was carried off injured, and then John Gatenby was sent from the field of play by the referee, making him the second player from the Club to be dismissed.

Not surprisingly, the nine men were hammered 6-2.

Another keeper, Alfred Cockerill, joined from Middlesbrough on a free transfer and results stabilised. The sporting side of the team showed through when in March during a friendly against a Leeds League XI, Percy Humphreys and Jim Baker both missed penalties on purpose, as not to over embarrass the already well-beaten opponents.

On March 24 the long-awaited return of Hibbert came in a 1-1 draw against Seaham Harbour. Hibbert was out of sorts and it was apparent he was rushed back too early and he never appeared again that season.

On April 11 an appeal was heard at the Crown Hotel in Newcastle, Pools claiming £106 from West Stanley for lost revenue for the cancelled home game in December when a large gate was expected. However, the Club was allocated only £10 and West Stanley were fined two guineas.

Difficult Campaign Leads To Change Of Direction

THE board had struggled throughout the season to make ends meet and only prudence, determination and low player wages helped keep their heads above water.

The majority of players had terms in their contract whereby if the board could not find them employment during the week then they would be paid more money, which meant board members found as much work for them as possible.

In the second week of April, player/manager Percy Humphreys announced his decision to sever ties with the Club at the end of his contract. The season was not as successful as expected and while Humphreys gave his best on and off the pitch he suffered from injuries, played himself out of position and was hindered by under performing players.

When he joined he was on a salary of £2 per week and was demanding a 75 per cent increase to stay. He later went on to become one of the first English coaches on the continent, working both in Switzerland, with FC Basle, and Italy.

In April, the first team played seven games in three weeks and, including reserve games, the pitch was used twice on the same day.

At the end of the season the Club finished in their lowest position to date, 12th, for the first time since its foundation in 1908 losing more games than they won. Fletcher was again top scorer with 22.

The close season saw the use of the Victoria Ground for some different sporting events in order to increase revenue.

There was a horse tournament on May 12, which featured an exhibition of 'leaping over hurdles' – showjumping – and pony scampering. On June 14 a school sports day took place, featuring sprinting, sack race, obstacle race, and the high jump. Music was provided by the Boys Brigade band.

On June 12, the annual report was issued, which showed a loss of £177 2s 11d, until year end 30/4/1913. The loss needed no difficult explanation.

There was the lost Saturday home gate for the West Stanley game. The Club were only awarded costs of £10 by the DFA, when £100 was more appropriate. The £10 was still outstanding when the report was issued. Also, due to the high volume of cup games, league games were rearranged, and the revenue was drastically reduced, taking only £6 14s 2d for the Carlisle game, and £3 8s 4d, for the Wingate game. The reduction of gate price to 4d at the start of the season did not attract more fans and the re-introduction of the 6d charge didn't help.

The team had performed fairly well in the cups but large sums were paid to visitors and the monies received from the tie at Birtley fell way short of what would have been received if the tie had been played at the Vic.

The cost of travel and hotels at Gainsborough far exceeded the share of the gate monies.

Financial Problems Come To The Fore

THE following day the board held their annual meeting. The Club toyed with the idea of entering the locally prestigious Sunderland Shipowner's Cup, but as they felt they were in enough cups for now, it would review the decision the following season.

The board were reminded that they owed £418 to sundry creditors and tradesmen, etc, and that some of these monies had been outstanding for two to three seasons. Among those owed were players from the previous season, who had been promised payment by the end of April. Many had got the Player's Union and solicitors involved in their plea for what was owed. Grierson, Priest, Martin, McDonald, Hogg, Tweddle and others were all advised that they would be paid at the start of the season.

The A team loss of £100 was discussed, and it was revealed that as several players lived out of town, and despite being amateurs, expenses

Ernest Ellis

were paid. Teas and refreshments were also provided for the players both home and away.

This is all some players got, and some "took good care they got it". Yet again the A team had not been the breeding ground for success that the Club had hoped, and the A team was to be disbanded, with a squad of around 15 to be maintained. The reserves didn't get the support they deserved with takings for some games not even reaching a pound and the players had to be released even though several were of a good quality.

The board were trying to keep the Club afloat but the lack of support and the general public apathy at a few bad results forced gates to reduce even further. It was going to be a long struggle to keep the Club alive.

New Appointment To Club Hotseat

POOLS went to West Bromwich for their next player/manager. On July 7, 1913, Jack Manners was given the task of turning fortunes around. Manners had played for two different clubs in his home town of Morpeth before spending eight seasons at West Brom where he played in nearly 200 league games, mainly as a half-back. Although in his mid-30s, it was still assumed that he could play important roles both on and off the pitch.

Following the appointment, his first task was to re-sign John Gatenby. Jack Bennett also agreed to play as an amateur. New signings followed and James Varty, a former England junior international arrived from West Brom, while forward John Lowe and Newcastle City keeper George Gill signed. The recruits encouraged Jim Baker, Jimmy Hibbert and Ernest Ellis to re-sign.

It was hoped the change of management and the new squad would show improvement on the previous season.

1913/14

BLYTH Spartans replaced wooden spooners Wingate Albion in the league and Pools' season began with a home match against a strong South Shields side, who included former England player Arthur Bridgett.

With Gill in goal and new signing Graham, preferred to Gatenby, to partner Ellis, the back line promised to be solid. The half backs, Hibbert (recovered from typhoid), Manners and Baker oozed quality. Expectations were high and a 1-1 draw was a good result against a resolute Shields team with J W Smith bagging his first goal for the Club.

This good start continued and after five games the team stood in fifth place, losing only to Middlesbrough reserves. The team were also through to the first qualifying round of the FA Cup, drawn to play at Annfield Plain. An arrangement was

Jim Baker

reached between the clubs, assumed to be £20, and the game was played at the Vic. It was the first in a run of six consecutive wins, finishing in another FA Cup game played at home, despite being drawn away to Horden.

In September, Councillor Coates announced his intention to resign his position as Chairman due to ill health but would stay in place until he had finished off his business with the council. His desire, drive and financial backing were so important with not only the establishment of the Club, but also the financial battle.

Cup Fever Followed By Disappointment

AFTER being knocked out of the North Riding Challenge Cup by Spennymoor, the Club faced the most anticipated home game in their history, against NEL league leaders South Shields in the FA Cup fourth qualifying round.

Pools had won at a strong Newcastle United reserves the week before and had Smith in form, netting nine goals in the past five games. A record crowd of 12,000 saw Shields progress (their reward a tie at Luton Town), by the only goal.

During October and November, the Club finally settled some of the debts due to ex-players with sums ranging from just over £3 to John Gatenby and a little in excess of £13 for Jack Martin.

With Middlesbrough among several clubs, including Brighton, Bury, Stoke and Huddersfield, watching in-form JW Smith, his departure looked imminent and manager Manners had no option but to recruit more players. Following the signing of the excellent forward Bryden in October, he signed two further attacking players in December, Mitchell and Flanagan.

On Christmas Eve it was announced that the installation of 250 seats in the main grandstand was completed.

The Club had also arranged to house out of

town players in West Hartlepool over the Christmas period, with the players staying at the Birk's Café, immediately adjacent to West Hartlepool railway station. Players had Christmas dinner at the Boot and Shoe Inn in Darlington centre, after a 1-1 draw there on Christmas Day.

Pools had dropped to seventh, but due to the protracted cup runs they had games in hand on teams above them and had still only leaked five goals.

Success in the DSC continued and they were drawn at Sunderland Reserves, following a win over Stockton. The game was a big test, as both sides were having a good season. Having held them to a draw, United were beaten in the replay 1-0, ending their interest in all cups.

Striker's Form Leads To Exit From The Vic

AT the end of February 1914, striker Smith was selected to represent the NEL against the Central League and two more forwards arrived, 20-year-old John Culif and 17-year-old McGill. However, Culif injured his leg in training and his debut was delayed.

Pools ran into their best run of form in February, starting a four-game winning run with a 2-0 victory over Sunderland Rovers. Pools bagged 16 goals without conceding and the highlight was scoring eight without reply against Wallsend, with Smith nabbing four.

The departure of Smith took place in mid-March when he moved, somewhat surprisingly, to Scottish side Third Lanark for a sizeable, but undisclosed fee, after scoring 32 goals.

It was something of a shock as the player had been seriously courted by Huddersfield, with contact and a meeting taking place during February. The Club had a new forward line compared to the start of the season.

The last few weeks of the season proved a struggle.

Manners suffered a cut to his eye and Ellis, Graham and Baker all missed games. Things were so desperate that for the match at Sunderland on April 13, McGill and Young were absent and trainer Harry Measor had to don a shirt and adopt the centre forward position – Pools lost 2-1. They never recovered from the sale of Smith and won only one in 13, finishing the season in seventh spot.

Although this was their best finish in the previous three seasons it was still way short of expectations following such an excellent start.

Manners' good judgement and controlling presence in the half-back line was a major factor in the performances. Smith was missed, but the replacement forwards didn't fare badly,

they just were nowhere near as prolific or consistent. Smith finished top scorer, despite departing with 13 games remaining.

J W Smith

Manners Begins His End Of Season Wheeling And Dealing

ON the way back from the last game of the season at Carlisle, there were hurried talks at Newcastle station regarding the future of the outstanding Jim Baker and he was soon on his way to Huddersfield. Coupled with the possibility of losing some of their excellent defence, together with Lowe and Bryden, Pools would need to be shrewd in the transfer market in the close season or try to retain the best of their existing players.

Again the Club released several players and put some on the NEL transfer list, which meant that if a player moved to another NEL Club then a fee would need to be paid, or Pools' consent sought. A club could hold a player's registration in this way for many years.

It was apparent that Manners wasn't intending to wait until the end of the close season and made signings aplenty in May and June.

Former Villa inside right H H Strugnell joined from Queens Park Rangers. Jack Bennett had again offered to play on amateur terms. Reuben Butler, a prolific scorer for Middlesbrough reserves, defender William Taylor, along with J Ridley, once of Newcastle United, agreed to join. The Club also appointed a new trainer, Mr A Cooper, who had been at Portsmouth.

The Annual Report was issued on June 6, 1914. After a fairly successful season on the pitch, particularly in the first half, the Club made a healthy profit of £793 11s 3d. It enabled the bank overdraft to be cleared and part of their loans

Jack Manners

Fourth in from right (back row) J W Smith played for Pools in 1913-14 and then played for the Football Battalion XI during the Great War

were repaid, while leaving a balance for team building.

There had been a good attendance, again especially in the first half of season. Good crowds and sound financial management would have to be maintained, as the class of football in the NEL was improving. A profit of £176 4d on transfers was recorded.

It was all down to Smith's move to Third Lanark, as he was the only player to leave for any funds, although the fee had never been disclosed at the time.

In July 1914, the Club were still carrying on negotiations with the appointed liquidators for the West Amateur club and offered to pay a lump sum of £35 to settle all debts owed by this organisation.

Later that month three further players signed on amateur terms. William Cunningham, a right half signed along with J Brown, an inside right and George Vivian who was a forward who apparently hailed from Newbiggin. He held a South African amateur international cap and became the first overseas international to pull on a Hartlepools shirt.

Great Hopes For Season 1914-15 Cut Down By The Great War

OPTIMISM was high for the new season. The Club had made a good profit and had been active in the transfer market.

However, no-one could have predicted the impending darkness during the sunshine of the early close season. Although there had been trouble in the Balkans and nearby areas with a war raging for some time, there was no indication that war would soon be upon Britain.

The assassination of Archduke Ferdinand, the heir to the Austro-Hungarian Empire, on June 28, by a Serb-sponsored terrorist was to be the catalyst for the onset of the Great War.

Just weeks later men in their hundreds of thousands would be at war and on August 4, 1914, Britain declared war on Germany who were already engaged in hostilities with Russia and France.

Chapter 3

WW1 – 1920

DESPITE the declaration of War, it was, somewhat naively, the belief that the national winter game should not be stopped on any account.

Interest and support would decrease, but all players who were meant to be playing would be kept as fit as possible to maintain standards and it was promised that "much good football would be enjoyed over the coming months".

Trials And Tribulations

ERNEST Ellis left for Heart of Midlothian, along with outside left George Bryden. JE Smith was signed from Shildon Athletic, and with the team almost settled on, trial games were arranged.

The first took place on August 19, and the gate proceeds were designated to the Prince of Wales war fund.

South African International G Vivian bagged a brace on his debut. A week later, the second pre-season game, a friendly against Middlesbrough, took place with the proceeds heading the same way as previous. The match was advertised in the local press, under the slogan "Don't miss this glorious opportunity to help those who rely on the Men at the Guns".

Smith, the signing from Shildon, was an absentee. He was employed in the mining industry by Pease & Partners of Crook and was holidaying in Switzerland when war was declared and was due to arrive home on August 31.

However, to return he had to endure a journey through war-torn Europe. On the morning of Friday, August 28, he travelled by mountain railway from Finhaut to Martigny and then to Geneva. From there he went by train to Reims and onto Paris.

On the Saturday he passed four troop trains near Paris, full of wounded British soldiers, returning from Mons. At Paris, he encountered hundreds of French people cheering, chanting 'Vive L'Angleterre' and bands playing the British National Anthem.

By the Saturday evening, he arrived in Dieppe at about the same time as his team-mates were leaving the pitch after beating Middlesbrough 2-0.

Again a grand reception was encountered in Dieppe with people on roof tops cheering "victory to the two armies". He boarded the cross channel steamer ferry bound for Folkestone – it was overcrowded and no bunks were available, despite the extortionate prices charged.

While on the main deck, he noticed 'a new motor car' which was all covered up for the journey. Cannily, he crept under the covering of the car and had a comfortable sleep during the crossing. He arrived in Folkestone the next morning, London in the afternoon and the following day he finally reached West Hartlepool – able to recant his tale and bring home, in a small way, the reality of what was happening in Europe, to his new team-mates.

1914-15

THE season began with a NEL fixture at West Stanley, ending in a 2-1 reverse with new forward Butler opening his account.

It continued in a broken fashion with no real

WE, THE UNDERSIGNED, PLAYERS OF THE HARTLEPOOLS UNITED FOOTBALL CLUB AGREE TO ACCEPT 25% REDUCTION FROM THE WAGES AGREED UPON WHEN SIGNING ON FOR SEASON 1914 & 1915. IF ANY FURTHER REDUCTION IS MADE WE AGREE TO TREAT SUCH REDUCTION AS ARREARS, BUT SAME TO BE REFUNDED TO US ON OR BEFORE THE 30th. APRIL 1915, OTHERWISE WE WILL APPEAL TO THE FOOTBALL ASSOCIATION FOR SAME. *Signed Jan 4th 1915*

George McGill
David Young
J B Jameson
J W Hibbert
R. Butler
J W Graham
H. Strugnell
A. McDougall
Wm Rushe

Pay Reduction Letter

pattern of results. In order to attempt to engineer more interest the Club allowed all military personnel in uniform into the ground for half price – 3d. The Club also announced that no obstacles were to be placed in the way of any of their players who wanted to leave to join the colours.

Hall was injured in his NEL debut in September against Hebburn and never played again.

At Spennymoor on September 12, Jack Manners was forced to go off after taking a knock and the Spennymoor fans booed and jeered him while being helped from the pitch. The referee also came under verbal attack for aiding the injured player.

The once-stranded Smith finally made his debut against Blyth on September 19, but he was soon called up for active service and appeared for Pools only twice.

Nine days later and Jack Bennett was presented with a case of pipes and a pouch by the Club directors. He left for Durham on Tuesday, September 29, as he was called up for service along with E Smith.

In the first round of the SSC, United were originally due to play North Shields, but their opponents were compelled to withdraw and were replaced by Sunderland St. Joseph's who Pools beat 2-0.

War Starts To Affect The Game

A meeting was held in Darlington on November 23, 1914 to consider wartime football. Eleven of the 20 NEL sides wanted to end the season, but Pools weren't one of them.

At a further meeting in Newcastle three days later it was disclosed that Hartlepools were one of nine teams in the NEL that had already lost players who had volunteered for military service. The main reason for clubs wanting to pull out, hostilities aside, was income reduction due to the drop in gates.

The poorer clubs wanted help from the league with travel costs, etc. The committee advised that players from most clubs had taken pay cuts of up to 50 per cent to help finances. It was decided that the fixtures should continue, at least until the end of the current season.

In early December, Pools were knocked out of the FA Cup by Rochdale, an arduous battle in which Pools ended up with nine men, while Taylor and Manners both missed the next fixture, due to injuries. On December 12, Pools trounced Spennymoor 11-0 in the first round of the NRCC with Reuben Butler scoring four to take him to 18 for the season. In an attempt to further reduce costs the Club sought to get the

players agreements to accept a reduction in their salaries. Several drawn out meetings took place, this time ensuring that a signed document was obtained. Pools had built up a run of six unbeaten league games, and prospects on the field seemed to be improving, but events were due to take a dramatic turn.

Hartlepool Hit By German Attack

ON December 16, 1914 Hartlepool suffered a naval bombardment at the hands of the Imperial German Navy. In excess of 100 people died, including the first civilian and soldier to be killed on British soil during the Great War.

The next fixture, at Jarrow three days later, was cancelled due to funerals taking place that day, of townsfolk who perished in the attack.

On the pitch, the inconsistent results resumed with a 6-2 hammering at South Shields on Christmas Day. In the Boxing Day game against Darlington, Gill, Young and Hibbert were all late for the start so Taylor had to play in goal for the eight men.

When the other players turned up Pools were a goal to the good. Jameson was also absent despite being selected to play, so when Gill arrived and went in goal, Taylor played at half back.

No half time break was allowed as the referee thought the light was poor and at the finish Pools won 3-0.

Two more wins followed – 5-1 v Newcastle City and 9-0 against Gateshead, with Butler scoring his seventh goal in three games. The good results were then followed by a 5-0 reverse against Darlington in the New Year.

Pools Reach Double Figures

THE Club joined an elite group on February 13, 1915 by hammering Carlisle United 10-0.

Three different players each scored individual hat tricks – Butler, McGill and Strugnell, with McDougall getting the tenth. Nottingham Forest had achieved the feat in April 1909, and St. Alban's City later the same year, the only previous recorded instances.

In the spring, in form striker Reuben Butler announced he was joining the services as a despatch rider, only playing when military duties would permit. His pace and goals would be a loss.

In April the Club qualified for the finals of both the Sunderland Shipowners Cup and the North Riding Charity Cup. They lost the NRCC to Middlesbrough by the odd goal in five, with

The Hartlepools United Football and Athletic Club Company, Limited.

———

Notice is hereby given, that the SEVENTH ANNUAL GENERAL MEETING of the above-named Company will be held at the Commercial Hotel, West Hartlepool, on Friday, June 25th, 1915, at 8 p.m., to receive the Directors' and Auditor's Reports, to elect Directors and Auditor, and to transact the ordinary business of the Company.

By order of the Board,

THOMAS P. ROBERTSON,

Secretary.

Registered Office :—
11, Byron Street,
West Hartlepool.
15th June, 1915.

Robt. Martin, Ltd., Printers, West Hartlepool.

Notice of the AGM from 1915

makeshift centre forward Angus McDougall netting two.

The team on display was G Gill, W Taylor, J Graham, J Jamieson, J Hibbert, J Manners, N Luke, T McGill, A McDougall, H Strugnell and J Bennett.

Two weeks later in the SSC final against South Shields the match was tied at 0-0 when Mahon went off injured after 65 minutes. He was unable to retake the field of play and Pools ended up losing by one goal.

At the end of the season the Club finished in the same position as the season before, seventh. Despite short FA Cup and DSC runs, Pools performed well in the SSC and the NRCC and now the close season approached with a not too difficult decision to be made about the future of the sport.

Top scorer was Reuben Butler, with 34 in total.

Squad Depleted By Enlistments And Club Has Financial Problems Again

MANY Pools players had already enlisted during the previous season and it was believed that Luke, Mahon, Taylor, Hibbert, Graham and McDougall would follow suit and commit themselves to the war effort.

At the end of April rumours were rife at how much the Club had lost during the season.

Money was lost by the week, the total assumed to be around £500. If the Club had not been so surprisingly successful with their finances the season before it was in doubt whether or not they would have been able to bear the strain.

Bills hadn't been paid, the overdraft was at its limit and players had endured reductions in their salaries. As it was likely that no football was to take place in the coming season, many would have to enlist to find a source of income.

The Military had occupied the ground on a sub-let basis from the Club and had decided to establish a Military Sports Committee.

This organisation had immediately appreciated the efforts of the men stationed in the town. By May a small number of matches had taken place at various grounds around the town which the Military had also secured the use of.

It was decided that an inter-billet competition league would be established.

Over £20 had been raised from a whist drive and these funds had been placed at the disposal of the committee for providing medals and kit for the players etc, although an appeal for boots was made in the local press.

A medal competition was also planned with

some games taking place at the Vic. There were many capable players in the regiments stationed in Hartlepool and in addition to keeping soldiers fit, which was the main objective, the matches would prove entertainment for football fans of the two towns and help boost morale.

At the end of May a Seaman's Mission XI and a Royal Navy XI met. The Mission won 1-0 with the goal scored by a 'jolly member of the team' known only as 'Tubby'!

The Inter Regimental Gold Medal Tournament started on June 5, 1915 with a game between Durham Royal Garrison Artillery (RGA) and the 3rd Yorks Regiment (The Green Howards). The game was drawn, but after a replay four days later the 3rd Yorks qualified for the final winning by the odd goal in seven.

The Royal Engineers beat the 7th Welsh Regiment scoring seven goals without reply and went on to beat the 3rd Yorks Regiment in the final.

Finances Affected Badly By War

THE annual report for year end April 30, 1915 was issued on June 22. A loss of £650 7s 5d was recorded. Taking into account the amount of supporters enlisted in the army, or called to industrial work, attendances were as good as could be expected.

At the AGM at the Commercial Hotel, it was mentioned that Pools thought that the FA should have cancelled all football at the start of the season and, under the circumstances, the directors had done their best.

The finance committee director, Mr Stonehouse, said that due to the war he didn't think the Club's business should have continued and it was suggested that before any further liabilities it was necessary to be sure that an end to the war was in sight.

The board agreed that business should have ceased but they had not been given authority by either the NEL or Durham FA to stop playing. The only increase in costs incurred was travel, which had escalated dramatically since war started. The decision was made to suspend the business of the Club until a ruling was made further by the FA and NEL.

A week after the regimental final, the Vic was the venue for a Grand Military and Sports Display with the band of the A.P.W. 6th Yorkshire Regiment playing 'well known airs'. There were stalls aplenty selling goods made and donated by locals and raising monies for countries across Europe, such as flag days for Belgium who were under occupation. Sporting events included sprint races, relay races, boot

The Hartlepools United Football & Athletic Club Company, Limited.

Balance Sheet as at 30th April, 1915.

LIABILITIES.

	£ s. d.	£ s. d.	£ s. d.
Capital—			
Authorised:—			
4,000 Shares at 10/- each	2,000 0 0		
Issued and Fully Paid:—			
1,446 Shares at 10/- each		723 0 0	
Sundry Creditors—			
Hartlepools United	292 19 9		
West Hartlepool Association Football and Athletic Club Company, Limited	71 19 9		364 19 6
Loans		392 7 6	
Bank Overdraft		223 3 8	
			980 10 8
			£1,703 10 8

WM. J. COATES, } Directors.
WM. BAKER, }

ASSETS.

	£ s. d.	£ s. d.	£ s. d.
Stands, Turnstiles, Ground Fittings, etc.:—			
As at 30th April, 1914	324 15 0		
Additions	9 5 8	334 0 8	
Less Depreciation 10% £33 8 0			
" Loss by Bombardment	50 0 0	83 8 0	250 12 8
Sundry Debtors			4 19 0
North-Eastern League Deposit			10 0 0
Cash in hand			2 10 0
Profit and Loss Account:—			
As at 30th April, 1914	785 1 7		
Loss during year, as per Account	650 7 5		1,435 9 0
			£1,703 10 8

Profit and Loss Account for year ended 30th April, 1915.

	£ s. d.	£ s. d.
To Players' Wages		813 10 1
" Money Takers' Wages		36 10 5
" Trainer's Wages	75 2 4	
" Travelling		925 2 10
" Refreshment and Hotel Expenses		72 8 8
" Referees		17 12 4
" Ground Rent		45 0 0
" Rates and Taxes		19 2 4
" Insurance		13 3 2
" Entry Fees and Subscriptions		2 11 0
" Advertising		8 17 9
" Gas, Water and Fuel		8 13 5
" Printing		16 7 0
" Bill Posting		12 6 0
" Medical Stores		4 12 1
" Outfitting		15 11 9
" Sundries (including Washing)		19 7 9
" Bank Charges and Interest		12 6 9
" Registration Fees		0 5 0
" Postages and Telegrams		11 9 10
" Audit Fee		6 6 0
" Ground Expenses		20 6 3
" Secretary's Salary		15 0 0
" Office Expenses		1 3 3
" North-Eastern League		4 5 4
" Transfer Fees		16 0 0
" Depreciation on Stands, Turnstiles and Ground Fittings, 10% on £334/0/8	33 8 0	
" Loss by Bombardment	50 0 0	
" Liquidation Expenses, re West Hartlepool Association Football and Association Club Company, Limited		3 10 4
		£1,488 6 11

	£ s. d.	£ s. d.	£ s. d.
By Takings—Gates and Stands			962 2 9
Less Visiting Teams, £102 14 9			
Charities 92 19 3		195 14 0	
			766 8 9
" Season Tickets			30 5 0
" Sports			13 12 7
" Rents Received			21 1 4
" Sports Training Permits			0 12 0
" Discounts and Allowances			0 6 0
" Aid from North-Eastern League			5 13 10
" Loss on Year's Working			650 7 5
			£1,488 6 11

Auditor's Report.

In accordance with Sub-section 2 of Section 113 of the Companies (Consolidation) Act, 1908, I report as follows:—

I have audited the above Balance Sheet of the Hartlepools United Football and Athletic Club Company, Limited, for the year ended 30th April, 1915, and have obtained all the information and explanations I have required. In my opinion such Balance Sheet is properly drawn up so as to exhibit a true and correct view of the state of the Company's affairs at 30th April, 1915, according to the best of my information and the explanations given to me, and as shown by the books of the Company.

H. H. KILVINGTON,
Chartered Accountant.

West Hartlepool,
4th June, 1915.

Club's Balance Sheet from 1915

races and a three-legged race.

The cold reality of the war hit home when the death was announced of former player Thomas Penman who was killed in action back in May.

The NEL was contemplating running two small local leagues throughout the war, but Pools decided not to partake and had intended to close down for the duration of the war.

Their decision seemed vilified when on July 19, 1915 the FA finally announced that no official league competitions were to take place. Some teams decided to continue, but it was all unofficial and not endorsed by the FA.

At a further meeting the directors stated they were inclined to abandon the games whilst hostilities were ongoing saying 'Football of any kind would be useless under the circumstances'.

The Club did not want to surface until the end of the war although they agreed that friendlies would take place for soldiers and players not enlisted whenever possible.

A few local teams continued, particularly Hartlepool YMCA (captained by former trialist R Redshaw) and Central Marine Engineering Works.

On October 16, by permission of the military, a game took place at the Vic between a side representing the Steelworks, (which consisted of former Pools players such as Jack Manners and former West players including Charlie Hewitt and Bill Hastings) and a team of The Royal Engineers. Entrance was 3d for the public and free to soldiers, sailors and boys. Funds were donated to the Grange Road Red Cross Hospital.

The half-time 1-1 score was changed into an emphatic 4-1 victory for a very fit and athletic army side. Ex-Pools player Tiplady scored for the Steelworks side with Thompson, Spencelayh and Lloyd, with a brace, scoring for the Engineers.

Of the Royal Engineers team, Corporal Thomas Gale, the goalkeeper, played football after the war with Harrogate Town, Barnsley and Stockport. Lance Corporal Hobson played for several clubs including Sunderland, Rochdale, Jarrow, Darlington and Spennymoor. Sapper Thompson was on the books of Sheffield Wednesday and Sapper Spencelayh was with Redcar of the Northern League.

Despite the recommencement of football, albeit in a friendly, more sad news came from France with the death of John Gatenby. He died from wounds incurred on the battlefield. Gatenby was a near regular just a couple of seasons ago, well-respected and a reliable player.

Come And See The Stars

THE Vic was used for a spell for games between various military sides, mainly the local artillery garrison.

'Come and see the stars' was the headline in the advertisement for a match at the Vic on January 3, 1916, between a Jack Manners XI and a Bob Pailor XI with all funds going to the VAD Normanhurst hospital in Hartlepool.

Injured soldiers were admitted free of charge. A crowd of 3,000 saw the Hartlepools team, managed by Manners, playing in blue and white losing easily to the white shirted opposition by four goals to one.

Bob Pailor's XI – A Hogg (Leeds City), Hedley (ex-Hartlepools Utd), Hudspeth (Newcastle Utd), Spink (Newcastle Utd), Low (Newcastle Utd), Harrison (Horden), Thompson (QPR), C Stephenson (Aston Villa), Walker (Bishop Auckland), Mason (Grimsby), Griffin (Barnsley, and ex-Pools).

Pailor, formerly of the West Hartlepool club, selected a side that constituted either military personnel based in the area, or workers who had not yet enlisted.

His team included many players with top flight experience, such as Wilf Low and Frank Hudspeth of Newcastle and Clem Stephenson of Aston Villa.

Walker, of Bishop Auckland, scored twice and Griffin, once of Pools but now with Barnsley, and Thompson (QPR) scored one each for Pailor's XI, with an unidentified player scoring an own goal in reply.

A month later a Hartlepools side selected by Manners faced the 21st DLI based in Richmond, with the proceeds to benefit members of the DLI who were prisoners of war, and their families.

The Pools side won 2-1, with Billy Hogg (Sunderland) and Arthur Swift (West Brom) getting the goals.

The next entertainment at the Vic, was on April 8, 1916 when a representative United XI took on a Teesside Engineers team, selected by George Elliott, the England international and prolific scorer for Middlesbrough.

A great crowd attended as the Engineers had a strong side of some repute. Once more the proceeds went to the VAD Normanhurst hospital.

The team mainly consisted of many former Pools players, including keeper Kelly and Jackie Hand, who were on the Club's books when they first formed.

Lieutenant Hollis and Bob Pailor scored for United with Elliott getting a penalty for the visitors and an equaliser after the interval in a 2-2 draw.

The final game to take part in the traditional season timescale was on April 24, the 631st day of the war, between a Pools side and a team representing the 3rd Yorks Regiment with Pools scoring a resounding 6-1 victory. Goals came from Thornton (3), Hastings with two and Hewitt. Binns replied for the army side.

Before the end of the month a military rugby match took place on the Victoria Ground with a team of North of England Soldiers well beaten by the Tees & Hartlepool Garrison.

War Efforts Greaten As Enlistment Rises

WITH the demand for troops increasing, the criteria for conditions were altered with the age limit reduced. Not only were more men needed at the front, but the demand for skilled persons to work on the industrial side of things increased and women were called into the factories to aid the war effort.

It meant less, if that was possible, was to be seen of Hartlepools United.

On June 3, 1916 the 19th Alexandra, Princess of Wales Own (Yorkshire Regiment) held their regimental sports day at the ground. The band played and there were various sporting events including long jump, sprints and tug of war.

Dilapidated Victoria Ground Vandalised

ON June 14, two youths appeared in the Hartlepool Juvenile Court for causing wilful damage to a fence at the ground.

Evidence was that the youths were pulling the fence down but they claimed to be putting it up. William Green and Jonathon Normanton were fined 3d each. The total estimated cost of repairs to the exterior fencing was approximately £50. Five other boys – James Killen, Alex Nossiter, John Godley, Michael Lahaney and Joseph Cosgrave – were each fined 1s and 6d for wilful damage to the grandstand.

The ground obviously seemed in quite a state of disrepair due to the lack of maintenance and unaided by the bizarre range of uses during the tenancy of the military.

On June 17, 1916, the Club's 8th Annual Report for the year ending 30, April 1916 revealed a loss of £19 15s 8d.

The board unanimously agreed, in the best interests of national welfare, that to run a team during wartime would have been unusual.

The Military had the full use of the property of the football Club and the income contributed towards rent, wages and other costs still incurred despite no sport taking place.

On August 5, the NEL held their annual meeting and decreed that no football should take place in the forthcoming 'season'.

The Wearside League would operate but with only eight teams. There was also a Tyneside Alliance and local and district teams from across the region were playing some form of football. However, the NEL decided they could not advocate a full competition with so many enlisted in the war effort.

Bombers Attack Victoria Ground

ON the night of November 27 further damage was inflicted on the ground.

This time it was not by half a dozen or so tearaways fooling around, but by a German Zeppelin raid, just before midnight.

The stand on the Clarence Road side of the ground was hit and badly damaged. It had to be replaced after the war. However the two Zeppelins involved did not return home.

One was attacked by a plane of the Royal Flying Corps based at Seaton Carew, brought down off the coast at 11.45pm, by Lieutenant IV Pyott.

The other was tracked down the coast, attacked and crashed at 6.45 am the following morning off the Norfolk coast. The bodies were later recovered and buried at Seaton Carew.

This incident resulted in the Bombardment Anniversary Friendly match taking place at Expansion's ground, and not the Vic, on December 8, 1916, the RNAS beating the RFC by three goals (Stapleton 2, Parish) to two (Keen, Verrill).

It should also be noted that 90 years later Ken Hodcroft would make a claim for damages to the German Embassy in London. The Club received a small donation to Youth Development.

With conscription increasing and only the specialised skilled workforce remaining at home to aid the war effort the possibility of more matches taking place was minimal.

Consequently, and despite the state of the ground, a game took place at the Vic on Easter Monday 1917 to raise funds for Yorkshire POW's. A crowd of 5,000 saw Central Marine Engineering Works take on The Expanded Metal Company's (Expansion) side. Unusually, the game was an all-female affair and it was followed by a Military XI v Munitions Workers XI, which was in effect a Hartlepools side.

The games were arranged by the Pools manager Jack Manners. The first game, between the girls teams, was refereed by former West Hartlepool player Bob Pailor.

The girls, as expected, showed little

knowledge of the game and the ball never travelled far when kicked, but there was no amount of fun and excitement. Some of the girls wore outsize football boots, loaned by men, some wore the latest style of ladies boots and others played in flat shoes. The Expansion team won 1-0, with the goal from Miss Lizzie Kane.

The girls churned the ground up badly, so the condition of the pitch for the other game was poor. The all-male teams played out a scoreless draw.

Girls Teams Take Centre Stage

AS the Pools team were all working and dedicating their time to the war effort, the girls teams seemed to get an appetite for the sport and started playing on a more regular basis, with Expansion playing Browns Sawmills at Expansion's ground and on April 19, 1917 more games took place at the Vic. The first, between Browns and Central Marine girls, ended in a 2-2 draw.

The second was between the 3rd Yorks Regiment and Murton Colliery of the Wearside League, the military side winning 2-0.

On May 28, a Military Tournament offering 'Music, Muscle and Merriment' took place at the Victoria Ground. A broad, somewhat bizarre range of events were on show, such as pillow fights, bayonet training, wrestling on horseback and tug of war.

On June 29, the Club's annual meeting took place at the Commercial Hotel. As there was no football to discuss one of the few topics on the agenda was the state of the ground, after the air raids.

There had been much destruction of the dressing tent and even two of the baths were missing. The Club had no alternative but to report the matter to the police.

The death of one of the Club's most loyal players, Jack Bennett, was discussed. He would be missed by all at the Club and at West Hartlepool Cricket Club, for whom he played during the summer months.

Vic Hosts Summer Sports Day

ON July 7, it was the Military Girls Sports Day at the Vic.

For entertainment there was three and four legged races, hubble skirt races, tug of war and so on. At least it was for good causes with takings split 50/50 and going to The Crippled Childrens Guild and the West Hartlepool Indiginent Sick Society.

BROWN'S GIRLS ATHLETIC CLUB FOOTBALL TEAM, 1917-18.

M. McKENZIE.
M. HODGSON.   E. CAMBRIDGE,   C. KELLEY,   N. HENDERSON,   H. KNIGHT,   M. BOOTH.
M. DORRAIN,   N. MURRAY,   N. STOTT (Capt.),   M. McPHERSON,   E. FERGUSON.

Browns Girls Athletic Club Football Team, 1917-18. Back Row: M McKenzie; Middle Row: M. Hodgson, E. Cambridge, C. Kelley, N. Henderson, H. Knight, M. Booth; Front Row: M. Dorrain, N. Murray, N. Stott (Captain), M. McPherson, E. Ferguson

This feast of fun was followed by another girls match between a mixed team of Hartlepools Girls and a team from the North East Engineering Works in Wallsend. The home team won 3-2, with goals from Norris, Plummer and Murray.

An unusual game took place on August 24 between Browns Girls and a male team representing the 347 Works Company of the DLI. In order to provide good entertainment and even matters out, the men played with their hands tied behind their backs. The game ended in a ten-goal affair with no winner. The scorers for the ladies were Mary Hodgson (2), E Snowball (2) and Alice Allan. Private Williams (2), Lance Corporal Brown, Foster and Grange netted for the men.

On October 3, 1917 another former player passed away, Sergeant Richard Hegarty, one of the players from the first season of the Club. He died from his wounds in hospital on Tyneside, and was later buried in West Hartlepool.

Progress Made By Allies In War

THE town became the subject of a third air raid on March 13, 1918 with an estimated seven fatalities.

More were called to arms as the need to apply pressure on the continent increased. The upper age limit for conscription had been raised and the war – and the country – faced a most uncertain future.

However, with the Americans and other countries finally joining the war, coupled with the efforts of those at home and on the continent, progress was being made.

At 5am on November 11, 1918 an armistice was agreed with fighting scheduled to stop at 11 o'clock. A lot of players from all clubs had died between 1914 and 1918.

Without trying to understate the importance of this ceasefire, the FA met only two days later and announced that football would be reorganised without delay.

How tricky this was going to be for Pools with their ground in such a state of severe disrepair was an issue that needed to be resolved – and quickly.

Games Re-Commence For Pools

EARLY the following month, the Club was invited to join the Northern Victory League of eight clubs – Newcastle United, South Shields, Sunderland, Middlesbrough, Scotswood, Durham City and Darlington Forge Albion.

Councillor Harry Salmon

Steps were taken to pull a team together and an advert was placed in the press by Jack Manners, who was to continue as manager, appealing for players of a first class nature. He was assisted in the role by Bob Pailor.

Due to the kindness of Cllr Harry Salmon home games were to take place at the Expansion Club in the Foggy Furze area of the town. Mr Salmon was a former stalwart of the West Hartlepool Cricket Club and had owned the Expansion Company since 1895. The Vic was not going to be fit for football for some time.

Members of the NVL met in the Grand Hotel, Sunderland on December 19, 1918 announcing the competition would commence on January 11 the following year.

Pools' chances of success were slim, as the team was to be made up of soldiers stationed nearby and a few demobbed players or those who had provided greater service to their country by utilising their skills on the home front.

Several players offered their services – notably Waugh, once of Derby County, W Thompson and Mitchell, both of QPR and R Thompson of Preston.

On Boxing Day the first friendly took place between Pools and a side representing the

Yorkshire Battalion.

Pools won 3-0 in front of a sizeable 8,000 attendance at their temporary new home, and it was announced that steps would be taken to make the Foggy Furze ground more accommodating for the public.

A friendly took place on New Year's Day away to the newly-formed Durham City club – their first game. Peart thought he had levelled for Durham after Jimmy Hibbert opened the scoring for Pools, but he was ruled offside. Gardner equalised but Metcalf netted the winner for Pools.

In time for the first home game against South Shields on the opening day of the league, two additional entrances had been placed in the back street and eight in the front. The pitch had been subject to a lot of attention and ashes had been spread around the ropes encircling the pitch to allow fans to stand in areas devoid of mud.

Although the Victoria Ground was unsuitable for Pools, the Central Marine team played there twice on January 8, 1919 against Westcliffe and a week later against the Cheshire Regiment.

As expected, results in the NVL were inconsistent. Wins of 7-1 against Darlington Forge Albion, when former Preston player Thompson scored six, and a 6-1 victory over Durham City were cancelled out with equally heavy defeats of 6-2 to Sunderland and 8-2 at Middlesbrough.

On March 15, the Club had to fulfil two fixtures in one day playing at South Shields in the NVL and at Darlington in a DSC replayed game.

At a meeting of the NEL in Newcastle on April 11, five new clubs were admitted for the following season – Durham City, Darlington Forge Albion (who rescued the Darlington club), Leadgate Park, Palmer's Jarrow and Scotswood.

Just before the end of the unsuccessful NVL season, the team played three friendlies. Two took place on April 18, one at Middlesbrough and one at home against a good Scottish team of the time, Renton. Pools were victorious in both. The following day they beat Scotswood and also won the final NVL game of the season, beating Newcastle 6-1.

The season's leading scorer was again Reuben Butler, who had top scored in the last full season four years ago. He got 17 goals in 15 games, but later rejoined Middlesbrough and enjoyed a long career playing league football into his late 30s.

The following month it was announced that the military would terminate their occupation of the Victoria Ground and were in negotiation with the board regarding making good all damages.

Ralph Toward, once of Durham City, who played in the NVL and R Topping, formerly of the army, both signed in June 1919 along with J T Dickinson, an 18-year-old forward from Northumbria.

Concern For State Of Victoria Ground

ON June 27, the 11th AGM was held with the first and most important item on the agenda being the damage to the ground by both the Military and the air raids.

The amount of £2055 15s, which was practically all of the Club's assets had been lodged with the foreign claims office, an amount to be claimed from the German government.

Damage caused by the military was assessed by an officer of the Land Survey Office. Following an inspection he stated that the state of the ground was disgraceful and it must be made good. Barricading around the pitch needed replacing along with the turnstiles and their housings and the entrance square. The pitch near the goalmouths had to be re-turfed and the rest of the pitch to be harrowed, with seed thrown in.

It was agreed that the military would continue to pay rent until the ground was in proper order and it had to notify the Club when work would commence. The Club wanted the ground fit for the start of the season, however, the situation was hopeless.

Arrangements had been made to again use the Expansion ground at a cost of £102. Central Marine FC wanted to use the Vic again, but the board refused.

The Club declared a profit of £324 10s. Plenty of difficulties beset the Club, until they were approached by Middlesbrough to join the NVL. The board praised Boro for their interest.

Further assistance was gained from Jack Manners and Bob Pailor who fought to get sides playing in the NVL and during the war. It was also declared that, due to a huge oversight, the damaged grandstand had been uninsured.

The Club still had ample shares available and wanted prominent businessmen and local people to invest as the board felt that they weren't receiving deserved local backing.

In July 1919 Charlie Hewitt, once of Greatham, who starred for his battalion team during the war, and also featured in wartime friendlies and the NVL for Pools, signed along with an army teammate of his, JF Reed, who was once with Brighton & Hove Albion.

No expense or effort was spared to make the Expansion ground a suitable venue. A new stand was in the course of construction which was to be built in sections, so that when the Vic was ready it could be readily transported.

In order to provide somewhere for the players to get changed, huts 24-foot in length were removed from the North Sands (where the military had a base) and transported to the ground.

Owing to the increases in expenditure encountered, such as the ground situation and the elevated costs of running a team, it was impractical to run the Club with the pre-war prices.

Even with an entrance fee of one shilling, the Club believed themselves to be worthy of public support. A quarter of the gate price was due in entertainment tax, so the Club was receiving only 9d, an increase of 50 per cent.

However, the keen sporting spirit of the townsfolk and the eagerness to enjoy themselves after the long war years had been demonstrated in the taking up of some more of the 10s shares.

1919/20

THE first game of the new NEL season, ended in a 1-1 draw at home against Ashington. Pools line up was G Gill, W Scott (captain), T Shields, J Spink, F Knowles, R Topping, R Toward, C Hewitt, W F Reed, G Jobey and G Bryden. The goal came from the penalty spot courtesy of George Jobey.

After the game, the guest player and scorer took up an option to move on to Leicester City. McCarron, who had impressed in the pre-season games, was signed on amateur terms.

In September, Cardiff's George Burton and James Wood from Palmer's (Jarrow) signed. Wood joined Jarrow when he was only 14 and had been a prolific scorer there pre-war. In the two games he played for Jarrow this season prior to signing for Pools, he scored three goals. The decision to change clubs came after he moved to West Hartlepool to work.

Ground Repairs Continue At Vic

WORK on the Victoria Ground was progressing well, with more huts transferred from the North Sands, and the Club hoped the game against Sunderland Reserves on October 25 would see the re-opening of the ground.

A 12-foot gate was erected at the Clarence Road side with a small door for entrance for players and officials, with the same built on the Mill House side. New fencing was installed

George Jobey

along the Clarence Road side, with the work done by Harry Salmon's Expansion Company. Despite the on-going repairs, other concerns wished to use it and both West Rugby and Nursery Villa (a local side) were refused permission.

Pools bad run of luck continued as Woods was injured on his debut against West Stanley on September 27, the last time they played at Expansion's ground. Two weeks later he returned at South Shields reserves and was again badly injured after only ten minutes, with Pools losing only 3-0. He never appeared again as injuries brought his career to a premature end.

In October Charlie Hafekost signed. Born in Sunderland, apparently of Norwegian parentage, he arrived after some fine NVL displays for Darlington the previous season. Despite offers from bigger clubs he chose to stay in the area and was expected to be a force of strength in the forward line. George Gray also agreed to join after his demobbing from the army, refusing offers from Swansea and Sunderland for regular first team football.

The Vic Becomes Home Once Again

AFTER failing to win a league game at Expansion's ground, the Victoria Ground finally reopened on October 25, 1919, the opponents a strong Sunderland Reserve side.

The Military had yet to hand over the first instalment of funds due for restoring the ground, so the board were landed with the responsibility of funding.

But even a return to the home ground didn't help matters as Pools failed to win – although the game was a creditable draw with Walter Scott scoring a penalty for Pools in front of 4,000 fans.

Three days later, after four defeats and five draws, United finally registered their first win – a 4-2 triumph at Houghton Rovers, with Charlie Hewitt grabbing all four goals.

Following the FA Cup defeat at the hands of Bishop Auckland in November, United had cause to complain. At a meeting of the DFA, the Secretary reported receipt of communication from the FA which enclosed a report by Pools.

United alleged that George Atkinson and Thomas Maddison of Bishop Auckland had received monies whilst playing in the DSC the previous season for St Helen's Auckland. The FA sent the letter to the DFA for further investigation.

At a later meeting in December, it was said that the players involved received money following the DSC third round game against Darlington Forge Albion. St Helen's Auckland advised that the players received a bonus and compensation – authorised by the Club committee – for not being able to work. The players never admitted receiving payment and a further meeting was scheduled for a week later.

In between these meetings, Pools played Whitburn, the Wearside League leaders, in the first round of the Sunderland Shipowners Cup on November 29. The game was stopped by the referee with only four minutes remaining due to bad light.

This angered everybody, as they wondered why the referee let the game go on so long, cancelling affairs with only moments left. Nevertheless, Pools won the second encounter the following week 3-0.

As an attempt to continuously cut costs, after he only appeared in four games, winger George Bryden was paid £10 to allow his contract to be paid up.

The final meeting regarding the FA Cup match at Bishop Auckland occurred on December 8, when the books of St Helen's Auckland were investigated. The Treasurer insisted he advised Hartlepools of the situation in order to hurt their bitter rivals Bishop Auckland. The outcome was that three officers of St Helen's – Mr Thompson, the chairman, Mr Brown, the secretary, and Mr Iceton – were suspended.

The DFA committee were sure that monies had been paid, but evidence couldn't determine how much and to whom. No players were charged and the result was to stand.

Spink and Hibbert were injured in the defeat at Scotswood on December 6. Hibbert was advised to give up the game by doctors, due to the damage to the cartilage of his right knee.

Pools Look For Better Fortunes

BY the turn of the new decade United had won only two league games and were struggling at the wrong end of the table. The start of the New Year didn't begin any better with a 2-0 loss to Middlesbrough reserves and a

friendly defeat to a Hartlepool & District XI the following day.

George Burton

Towards the end of January the Club announced the signing of Tom Crilly, a full back from Stockton. He signed amateur terms, but soon put pen to paper on professional forms. The Club had seemed to turn the corner and, with two decent goalkeepers in Gill and Summerfield, it was hoped that performances would improve. By mid-February Pools had gone on a five-game unbeaten run, drawing once, to pull out of the mire.

A large away following, travelling on special trains, saw Pools knocked out of the DSC at Darlington in the third round, losing 2-0. The Club were also knocked out of the SSC at the semi-final stage, to South Shields, 3-1 in a replay.

The players, who normally travelled by train, were moving with the times and getting to the odd game via charabanc, an early form of a coach, traditionally open topped and with a single deck.

Action Taken Against Supporters

THE board were unhappy that people were reportedly attempting to watch matches from positions of advantage for free.

This disgruntled the board, particularly after the struggle they had endured to put things in order.

Regular supporters were also surprised to note members of the Quoits Club at the Gasworks End abusing their position. It was understood that there was a rule in the Quoits Club that anyone taking such an advantage was to be fined 2s and 6d – opinion was that it was high time the fine was levied and paid to the fund for the erection of new grandstands, or that those guilty of this practice should be sportsmen enough to pay for admission.

Despite hardly making any appearances, Crilly was attracting attention and at the end of March, Pools slapped a £300 transfer fee on his head to deter the likes of South Shields and Middlesbrough. A similar approach was adopted with Thoms and Billy Bratt.

Club Set For Reserve Team

ON April 13, 1920, it was again announced Pools hoped to run a reserve team. Admittance to the Hartlepool & District League had been applied for and it was assured a formality as the team would enhance the league.

Although such a venture would be ideal for keeping players fit and for taking a look at trialists, it was intended that the side would mainly be made up of local players.

Changes were afoot and Jack Manners was to retire from his post. Applications were invited.

Just over a week or so later, for the home game on April 24 against Spennymoor, Pools were to be without the services of one of their most consistent performers, Harry Thoms – he was getting married that day.

Change In Management For Pools

THE season ended on a high, as Pools lost only one of the last ten games, ending the campaign with a 2-0 victory over Durham City. After the game, the retiring Manners was awarded with a presentation in praise of his hard work, particularly in the war and the post-war seasons. Charlie Hewitt topped the scoring charts with 21 goals.

Cecil B Potter, 29, was appointed player/manager. He played for Norwich City before the war and later he donned the colours of Hull City, from where he joined Pools.

He had intended to coach Glasgow Academicals in the summer of 1920 but agreed to become manager at Pools, even turning down a healthy offer from Hull to stay. He was selected ahead of former Roker Park hero George Holley.

Potter's job was made easier as a good stock of Pools' professionals had already been re-signed.

Gill, Summerfield, Franks, Crilly, Thoms (who the Club had rejected an approach from Sunderland for), Topping, Short, Maughan, Bratt and Hewitt all put pen to paper. It was the nucleus of the team that had performed so well at the end of the previous season. Prospects seemed good and amateur forward Tommy Yews also signed.

In the middle of May a meeting took place in Sheffield regarding the proposed third division and details were submitted to the Football Association for consideration.

The following week and it was the turn of Manchester to hold a meeting. All 22 Southern League clubs and 30 from the north and midlands, including Pools, were represented.

All agreed to submit their application to the FA for the formation and membership of a new division and the FA would deliberate at their AGM.

The venture was to involve plenty of meetings and Pools even held a public meeting at the Town Hall in early June. It was well attended and Alderman Coates stated that the Club needed to be more financially sound before they joined the Football League.

Funds Not Forthcoming For Repairs

THE Club had endured great difficulties, but before the war they were one of the better NEL sides. Things only started to go sour when the military took possession of the ground. Pools had, at that time, received nothing from either the military or the Germans for the damage both parties had caused. All repair work done at the Vic had been paid for by the directors.

The claim for the bombing damage had been submitted to the Government.

However, there could be no prediction as to when the funds were going to be received from the Germans. The Club owed £450 for external fencing, £120 to A Stephenson for repairs and other minor debts of £65. All in all, they had carried a total cost of £650 for putting the ground into order. They had also paid £214 for

Cecil Potter

Army huts.

There wasn't much of a bank balance and until the Military, and Germany, paid up the situation remained in a near perilous state. A further appeal for public and trade help was issued as there were still plenty of ten shilling shares available. While the sectioned stand, which followed the Club from the Expansion ground, was satisfactory it was seen as temporary and a new grandstand would cost around £2,000.

A new open stand was suggested for the Mill House side. Public spirited businessmen were asked to advance cash on the understanding they would be paid back in cash instalments from the takings of every home game.

Division Three – But Not For The North

REPRESENTING the Middlesbrough Club, Phil Bach, stated that the proposed admittance to the Football League was backed by his team. The towns of Hartlepool and the surrounding district deserved a good standard of football. No Club had fought poverty more than Middlesbrough and he understood the predicament that Pools were in. He concluded with the statement that he believed Pools should be invited to join the new division and that they could rely on his Club for support.

Mr Walker, from the FA, stated that no footballing centre in the country had suffered like Hartlepools United did in the war and that the Club and the townsfolk had come through this adversity with great credibility.

He believed that the Division Three northern section should go ahead and he hoped that Pools would be in it, but they had to do their utmost to guarantee their admittance. It had already been announced that there was to be a Division Three in season 1920-21, but it was to be a southern section.

The news obviously aggrieved the northern teams but the FA claimed they knew a great deal more about the southern sides and teams from the north had to be put on probation as more information was obtained.

Mr Walker was to visit Colonel

Harry Thoms

Kentish, who represented the Army at the FA, to resolve the situation regarding the monies owed to Hartlepools.

The meeting concluded with the hope that Division Three football would be nearer if the Club

Tom Crilly

could achieve some financial backing and continued to play good football. The future looked promising, but plenty of work needed to be done.

More Investment Required In Club (Despite A Cheque From The Military)

FOLLOWING the intervention of Harry Walker, Pools had finally received a cheque from the Military for a sum in excess of £1,200. Most of the funds were absorbed by the cost of putting the ground in order. Despite receiving these monies the claim for the air raid damage was still outstanding and public backing was still needed.

Just 24 hours later the AGM was held and, all things considered, the Club had not fared too badly. However, few people had taken out shares and a disappointing amount were subscribed to. More investors were needed.

An increase in expenditure was expected for the forthcoming season as the weekly wage bill stood at £48, with more players to sign. The figure for the previous season was £40.

On July 7, Club accounts were issued. Gate receipts had risen to £3520 13s 7d, of which £831 14s 1d was paid in tax. Wages stood at £1631 5s 8d and the total loss for the year was £305 12s 9d. The board announced they were not alarmed by the deficit in the accounts.

The proposed open stand would now not be ready but improvements to the covered grandstand were complete. The Club had considered the stand at Hartlepool Rovers rugby ground, The Friarage, and had also travelled to Ripon to view some stands for sale.

On July 24, 1920 Paul Firth was named new trainer. A reputed 120-yard sprinter, an event in which he had won tournaments nationwide, Firth had been training English clubs for 20 years. Starting at Sheffield Wednesday in 1900, he spent nine years there, he then moved to Middlesbrough and, despite the offer of a job on the continent, he decided to stay in the area.

Chapter 4

1920s

1920-21

THE season began with a visit to Durham City and Pools lost 1-0 after gifting City a goal.

In the next match, home to Middlesbrough Reserves, Crilly missed a penalty which was retaken for encroachment. He wasted the second chance too and the game ended 0-0. This run of misfortune continued as in the return fixture a week later, Topping was injured and taken from the field. As there were no substitutes, Pools were down to ten men and Middlesbrough immediately scored the winning goal. As Pools piled on the pressure searching for an equaliser the home crowd started barracking their own players with extreme ferocity, so much so that the referee halted the game for four minutes until the crowd calmed down.

Pools Suffer Poor Start To Season

WITH only one NEL win out of five under their belts by the middle of September, respite came in the form of a Sunderland Shipowner's Cup tie. Drawn at Seaham Harbour, the game was played at the Vic following an inducement of £50.

Pools won 3-0 in front of 3,000 fans and it was followed by a 7-0 win in the FA Cup against South Bank East End, with Bill Short bagging a hat-trick in front of 5,000 fans.

The next round of the cup saw Pools drawn at Haverton Hill but once again a sum was paid and the game took place at the Vic. In front of 4,000 supporters the game ended in a 3-3 draw, with player/manager Cecil Potter missing a penalty.

The replay was hopefully an end to the affair but, with Pools missing another penalty, this time through Short, at full-time the game was goalless and it was agreed to play 30 minutes of extra time.

In this period Short tripped Boswell, the opponent's rugged full back, who in turn retaliated resulting in both men being sent off. Despite Pools' bombardment of the Haverton Hill goal, there was no joy and a further replay was needed.

The draw was no surprise as Potter was suffering from flu and played up front, out of position, former Hull player Stephenson was laid up and keeper Gill was absent with a poisoned foot.

Pools eventually saw off their neighbours in the second replay at Ayresome Park, Middlesbrough when, in front of 3,000 fans, makeshift forward Potter scored the only goal.

In order to boost the forward line Pools signed much-heralded youngster Cecil Hardy from Blackhall Colliery.

A poor start was not aided by the fact that some players were turning up for

Jackie Stephenson

An Invoice from the Hartlepool Gas and Water Company in 1920

training only one night per week. A notice was subsequently posted in the dressing room, advising that three nights per week training was expected.

After nine games Pools stood a disappointing 17th, fourth bottom with just one victory.

Club Moves For Division Three Status And Warns Spectators Not To Throw Stones!

ON October 21, a further board meeting was held where the matter of division three football was fully considered and it was unanimously agreed to press for admission. Plans were established to ensure that immediate steps could be taken to ensure that all requirements regarding the ground, finances and players were met. The board hoped that this announcement would dispel any doubts on the Club's behalf. The board again reiterated the need for greater support, both through the gate and financially.

Once again Pools were drawn away in the FA Cup at Scarborough. Inducements failed on this occasion and the team made the short journey down the coast, running out 4-1 winners.

A meeting of the NEL on November 4 advised Pools that they must post up the Association's notice warning spectators against stone throwing both during and after games. The NEL also gave Hartlepools, Darlington, Durham City and West Stanley permission to proceed with their application to the proposed northern section of Division Three.

In the next round of the FA Cup, Pools entertained Loftus Albion – who had not lost for over a season and a half, and so far this term had not conceded a single goal. Pools won a tight game 2-1 and their reward was a tie against Houghton Rovers.

Meanwhile, the reserve team withdrew from the Hartlepool District League and transferred to the Palatine League which featured stronger opposition.

On November 20 in the game against Houghton Rovers, Pools were leading by one goal when Crilly and Thoms collided with each other. Injuries were enough for both to leave the field of play and Pools played the rest of the game with nine men, scoring two more to win 3-0.

Yet another meeting was held in Manchester to discuss the proposed new third division.

The main topic of discussion was to evaluate if all clubs could afford the increase in travel expenses involved with playing further afield every other week. It was estimated that the cost of 16 persons to travel to all away games would

be around £365 for Hartlepools in the forthcoming season.

A resolution was passed stating that all clubs in the upper two divisions of the Football League would be canvassed for support.

Following the win over Houghton in the FA Cup, United were drawn at home to Bishop Auckland, the game due to played on December 4, but delayed a week due to inclement weather.

It was not called off until 1.45pm after heavy rainfall – and the pitch was full of lakes and mud, resembling a bog. A week later the game ended in a 1-1 draw at the Victoria Ground and United coasted through the replay at Bishop, scoring five goals without reply, with Lister getting a hat-trick. Pools were then handed a tough draw away to third division Swansea Town.

The squad set off for Wales on Friday, December 17 and didn't arrive until 10.30pm.

On the morning of the game they visited the Vetch Field and were very impressed with the facilities and accommodation. Swansea had lost only once in the previous two months and a crowd of 20,000 saw Swansea take a 2-0 lead. Despite Pools tightening up after the break the game ended 3-0 in Swansea's favour. One benefit for Pools was the near £400 received as a share of the gate.

Despite the FA Cup setback the Club recorded victories over Darlington RA and Felling in the DSC. They also played a team from Middleham, comprising jockeys from the stables – this time the match ended in a bizarre 8-8 draw.

Lister, eight goals in his last eight games, injured his collarbone during the Christmas Day victory in Darlington and was likely to be missing for up to four weeks. William Bratt, who had scored four goals in his last three games, had to miss the match on January 8 at Scotswood as he was getting married.

Hard Work In Bid To Reach Football League

IN January 1921 a fact-finding questionnaire was sent to all clubs wanting to enter the proposed new venture.

Details of the Club's status were required – condition of the ground, gate receipts, capacity and so on. United still hadn't received any funds for the air raid damage over four years before and the hopes of getting it looked slimmer and slimmer as the months progressed.

In the end, the Club never received a penny from the German government and the tale has gone down in football folklore.

Even with limited funds, the board went about the costly task of carrying out repairs and improvements to the Vic and many more would be needed for the crowds expected if they managed to secure a Football League spot.

They set up a ground committee and work proceeded on installing baths, hand basins and toilet facilities in the visiting dressing room. New turnstiles were to be provided but the terracing of the banks was held in abeyance for the moment.

Cecil Potter badly injured his left ankle at West Stanley on January 29, at a time when form was improving with the Club moving into 12th place in the NEL. He left the field, unable to return, with his side leading 1-0 and Pools ended up losing 3-1. Second choice keeper Summerfield was also suffering from a knee injury.

Former Bolton and St Mirren player James Lawson showed promise on his month-long trial, although his idea of his own value did not coincide with that of the board and he was on his way at the end of January. In February, Pools made a surprise signing in the form of Leonard Boswell from Haverton Hill. The defender was dismissed against Pools earlier in the season in the FA Cup, but the sturdy half back signed on amateur terms although he played only one game and soon returned to Haverton Hill. In the next round of the DSC, United hammered Spennymoor 6-0 away from home. A special train was laid on and a healthy and vociferous away support saw Pools coast through to the semi-final.

Jack Harris, an occasional reserve team player and captain of Hesleden Celtic, signed on at the age of 19 for a fee of £10.

In the semi-final of the DSC Pools beat South Shields 2-0. A collection was made at half-time for the local unemployed, for despite the war being over for 26 months or so, business and industry were still recovering.

Elected To Division Three (North)

FOLLOWING the success of reaching the final of the DSC came the news Pools had wanted. At a Football League meeting it was decided a Division Three (North) was to proceed in season 1921-22 and Pools were elected to join.

Other teams who made the grade were Accrington Stanley, Barrow, Chesterfield, Crewe Alexandra, Darlington, Durham City, Lincoln City, Nelson, Rochdale, Tranmere Rovers, Walsall and Wrexham. Four more were elected following a further vote – Halifax Town, Southport, Stalybridge Celtic and Wigan Borough. Two more were still to be admitted, to be determined at a later date.

Some reports claim Pools had to finish in the top half of the North Eastern League to qualify for the new venture – but there is no evidence of its requirement and Durham City qualified for the new venture despite finishing in the lower half of the NEL.

This news certainly seemed to lift the team and they won four out of their next five NEL games.

A new centre-half, Valentine Lawrence, signed from the Shildon club and, at a board meeting three days later, manager Cecil Potter was appointed to the post of secretary/manager.

Pools were to play Horden Athletic in the semi-final of the SSC and the match was rearranged to a lunchtime kick-off, so that on the afternoon a second game could take place,

Pools take on Leadgate at Roker Park in 1921

Jack Harris

a friendly against Greenock Morton. They were one of Scotland's biggest clubs and could include at least five Scottish internationals in their starting XI.

The first game ended in a goalless draw watched by 5,000 fans. In the afternoon a Pools XI, including several new faces on trial, led 1-0 before the Scots won 2-1.

Another Cup Final Appearance

ON April 2, Pools were involved in the DSC final against Leadgate Park at Roker Park, Sunderland in front of 12,000.

The Pools squad was decimated. Lawrence and Ashton were cup-tied and injuries to Stephenson, Topping, Potter and Dougherty meant wholesale changes. Hardy scrambled home an equaliser in the dying seconds to force a replay but was injured in the process.

The Pools line up was G Gill, A Franks, T Crilly, W Bratt, H Thoms, W Short, C Hewitt, T Mulholland, J Lister, C Hardy and L Kessler.

At Feethams in Darlington four days later, with youngster Tommy Yews replacing Hardy, Pools were one-up through Lister at the interval but lost 2-1 after extra-time in front of a crowd of 8,380.

Not only did Pools lose, but Franks, Thoms, Short, Lister, Kessler and Mulholland were all on the receiving end of some rough treatment and suffering from injuries.

Looking To The Future In The Third Division (North)

WITH the manager looking to keep his better players on for the forthcoming season and sign new ones to improve the squad, the board were also looking at improving the ground.

Among the ideas were increasing the seating in the grandstand by 250, with a directors room built underneath, together with improvements to the standing areas.

Due to the injuries, an understrength Pools were humbled by Horden Athletic on April 11, 1921 in the replay of the SSC semi-final, losing by an embarrassing 4-0 scoreline.

Pools were then hammered 5-0 at home by Carlisle United. Charlie Hewitt had to leave the game before half-time with a badly wrenched knee, further decimating an already depleted squad. Keeper Harry Summerfield, who was on the army reserve list, was called up for military duties to the Hillsborough barracks in Sheffield.

With some of the injured players returning to the fold, United finished their final season in the North Eastern League in a good run of form.

They lost only one of their final seven games with Lister scoring a staggering three hat-tricks in the last five games. They finished the season in eighth place, some 18 points behind champions Darlington, who were to join them in the Football League. Lister, who only made his debut in October, finished top scorer with 30 goals.

Hope And Optimism – And A Profit!

THE accounts for the season revealed a more than healthy profit figure of £527 4s 7d. The Club was spending a great deal to improve the ground and the player salaries, with their new elevated status, would obviously increase.

With the nucleus of the squad agreeing to sign up for the inaugural first season in the Football League, along with a clever and somewhat frugal board who wouldn't just throw money at players, and a fairly astute manager to lead them, the Club could look forward to the future with great hope and optimism.

Work was beginning in earnest on and off the pitch to ensure that Pools were as ready as they could be to compete in Division Three (North). On May 11, top scorer Jimmy Lister, put pen to paper for another year and Lauchlan Henderson from Paisley Juniors, signed as a professional.

Pools had 16 professional players under contract. Crilly, Thoms and Topping had been offered good terms and the Club were still waiting to hear from them. Pools officials were also confident that keeper

Tom Yews

Summerfield would rejoin when his military duties had ceased.

Just over a week later the NEL held a meeting at the City Hotel in Newcastle. Pools reserve XI applied for membership but Workington, Darlington Reserves, Preston Colliery and Seaton Delaval got the four places up for grabs.

The chairman of Blyth Spartans believed that the reserve sides of Football League teams would reduce the general standard of the NEL, as he thought that teams in his league were of a similar standard to those in Division Three (North). Darlington's reserve side were elected. As a result of the refusal, the Club announced they were to continue in the Palatine League.

Continued progress was being made with ground improvements. The bulk of the work was carried out to the Clarence Road side, with alterations made to both seating and standing accommodation. The board hoped that the capacity would be up to 20, 000.

On June 3 a major new signing was announced. Experienced centre half William 'Pop' Hopkins, 32, joined from South Shields, for whom he was a regular. He had also played for Leeds City and Sunderland. The fee was 'substantial but undisclosed' and he was appointed captain.

It was hoped the greater importance of matches to come would see increased attendances and ultimately higher revenue. Directors gave themselves a note of self congratulation for reaching the Football League. They had every confidence that the team being built would perform credibly and would merit the expected increase in support.

Two more signings followed before the month was out, Fred Ashton and schoolmaster and former Blackpool and Sunderland player Bill Gregson. As amateurs they were expected to feature in the reserve XI.

The arrival of full back Harry Pullen was another promising capture. Born in 1888 he had played for Kettering and Queens Park Rangers and also appeared in the Football League with Newport County.

'Tea And Buns Alone'

ON the final day of June 1921 a meeting took place at the Commercial Hotel, West Hartlepool, with some strange items on the agenda.

One of the first and seemingly important matters raised was in relation to the accounts, in particular refreshments. At one game during the previous season, the team were required to play on 'tea and buns alone'. At another game, the post-game refreshments were not provided,

Pop Hopkins

which was deemed unacceptable. The board had to explain that the first complaint related to a game when they fed substantially and healthily, albeit not on their usual fare.

On the second occasion, it was declared that the end of the match was so close to the train time that there was simply no opportunity to buy a meal. The players did, however, receive the expected value of the meal in cash. The explanations were accepted as satisfactory.

The meeting eventually got down to serious business and the chairman explained that Pools had started the previous campaign under difficult circumstances.

The squad was not up to scratch and again they struggled to settle as they were forced to build the team throughout the season. Progress wasn't helped by having to play in the FA Cup preliminary qualifying rounds, which took a lot out of the team and caused a fixture backlog.

The Club's share capital remained unsubscribed and another appeal was made to existing shareholders to invest further, while asking again for new investment from the public.

The chairman announced he had worked in close harmony with Middlesbrough to secure help and advice about being a Football League Club. He believed there was not a club in the proposed new venture who had suffered as many problems as Pools to recommence proceedings after the Great War. The board were more than grateful for the help that they received from the Expansion club in this matter and also from the 50-plus players who represented the Club during this mini-season. Less than 18 months after the delayed return to the Victoria Ground, Pools were in the Football League and could not have done this without all of this immeasurable help.

Cecil Potter, the manager, was last to speak and he relayed that he was overjoyed to be in the Football League, believing the future of the Club was bright. If Lister, Mulholland and Cec Hardy could carry their goalscoring exploits (61 goals between them) from the previous campaign, there should be no problem scoring goals.

What seemed to be the final signings were made towards the end of July. Durham student

George Gill

and outside left Robert Donald joined, as well as utility man Ben Nicholson and forward Bert Lee. This brought Potter's squad up to a compliment of 29.

Three keepers were at his disposal. The ever dependable George Gill would have competition from William Summerfield and fish merchant Fred Aldridge.

There were five players in contention for the two full back positions. Regulars from last season Tom Crilly and Tony Franks would see Harry Pullen, Rob Hubery and South Hetton amateur Sam Benson vying for a start. Eight half backs were on the books – Joe Dougherty, Pop Hopkins, Harry Thoms, Bill Short, Fred Ashton, John Strickland, Lauchlan Henderson and latest signing Ben Nicholson.

And at Potter's disposal up front were a dozen eager forwards. As well as the form men of last season – Mulholland, Lister and Hardy – there was also the ageing Charlie Hewitt, local prospect Tommy Yews, Jack Harris, Bill Bratt, N Robertson, Young, Laurie Kessler, Tot Parkinson, Gregson and Donald.

All players would be under the watchful eye of new trainer, Ed Wynter who hailed from South Shields.

Work On The Vic Continues

MEANWHILE, improvements at the ground were carrying on at a fair pace. Part of the additional 'garden' ground on the west (Mill House) side had already been taken inside the boundary and banking up was proceeding. A telegraph board had been erected at the North end of the ground which would display certain half-time scores, including the first XI's when the reserves were at home. Efforts were also being made to link the press box with a telephone.

The pitch even received some attention, returfed in certain areas and the whole of the playing surface had been top-dressed and re-sown. Assisting with the works on the ground was half back Lauchlan Henderson and also the cricket clubs of West Hartlepool and Seaton Carew. The former lent the Club a roller and a line marker machine and the Seaton club loaned a grass cutter.

1921-22

Third Division (North)

THE fixtures for the inaugural season were released near the end of July and the first opponents for Hartlepool United in the Football League Division Three (north) on August 27, 1921, was to be the only team from North Wales in the division, Wrexham.

Despite having an abundance of players, Cecil Potter signed more squad members before pre-season training. Arthur and Stanley Butler, from Stillington near Stockton-on-Tees and brothers of former player and twice top scorer Reuben (now with Oldham), agreed amateur terms.

Practice Makes Perfect For Pools…And A Substitute Is Used

TRAINING commenced on August 8 and at the first session the players were hampered to a certain extent by members of the public entering the playing ground and distracting them. They decided almost instantly to adopt the policy of closing the ground to the public when players were training.

Pre-season practice games were played on August 13, 17 and 20. Crowds averaged just over the 2,000 mark, with trialist Peter Robertson impressing with four goals. In the second game Lauchlan Henderson injured his ankle and was substituted by Bill Bratt. Albeit in a practice match, this was the first recorded use of a substitute being used by Pools.

In the third and final match, Cec Hardy and Peter Robertson swapped sides at the interval and after scoring for the Whites in the first half, Robertson went on to score for the Stripes after the restart.

Club Makes Football League Debut

THE first Football League game was approaching and, on the day before the game, recent signing Harry Pullen was rushed to hospital suffering from appendicitis. He was expected to be out for two months.

The team departed West Hartlepool train station on a mid-morning train, arriving in Wales seven hours later.

While the reserve team defeated familiar opposition in the form of West Hartlepool St. Joseph's, the first XI were treading on new ground.

The history-making XI that took to the pitch and triumphed 2-0 were G Gill, T Crilly,

H Thoms, J Dougherty, W Hopkins, W Short, L Kessler, T Mulholland, J Lister, P Robertson, R Donald.

Wrexham began shakily and Pools took an early lead, when Mulholland bagged their first Football League goal. They took control and never looked like losing.

The defence was sound, with Gill outstanding between the sticks. The full backs, Thoms and Crilly, had great games, playing safely and clearing well. The rest of the team also impressed, finding each other with ease with some accurate passing. Lister showed excellent ground work and he scored the second and final goal. Pop Hopkins dominated the midfield and Kessler's touch caught the eye.

It was an impressive victory and showed great promise for the remainder of the season.

In order to attempt to preserve the first XI for league games, the Club asked the Durham FA for permission to play their reserve team in the Durham Senior Cup. However, the DFA advised them of the importance of the DSC and advised that they should play their strongest team available, or be fined up to a rather substantial £150.

On the evening before the return home fixture with Wrexham, both teams were entertained free of charge at The Empire Theatre in Lynn Street, a trait which was continued throughout the season.

However, this hospitality seemed to favour the visitors as they upset the majority of the 10,000 spectators present, winning by a solitary goal, meaning Pools lost their first Football League game at Victoria Park.

After beating Washington in their second Palatine League fixture, Pools played a Hartlepool & District League XI and won 2-0. The opposition contained many players who had featured for Pools reserves over the past few seasons, such as Gilhespy, Redshaw and Bell. Jack Harris scored the first, with the second coming from Tot Parkinson, direct from a corner kick.

Following another defeat, amid an uneven start to the season, changes were made for the home game with Southport.

Tony Franks was brought in at full back with Thoms rested. Starting places were also handed to Cec Hardy and Chuck Hewitt, with Mulholland

Charlie Hewitt

and Kessler dropped. The changes seemed to do the trick as a Lister goal sealed the points. But he suffered an ankle injury and was to be out for a month.

Supporters Form First Association

ON October 14, at a meeting of followers of the Club in the Villiers Hall, Villiers Street in West Hartlepool, a supporters association was established.

The hope was that such an organisation could benefit Hartlepools United financially by taking out shares and by offering friendly criticism. The Club's vice chairman, Mr Stonehouse, fully endorsed the scheme. They later rented premises in the renowned Empire Theatre in Lynn Street, West Hartlepool.

The following day, Lister returned for the game against Grimsby but as well as suffering from a lack of form, the squad was burdened with more injuries with Hopkins, Kessler, Hewitt, Pullen, Peter Robertson and Hardy absent. A much-altered Pools team did well to hold the Mariners to a draw.

Tom Crilly submitted a transfer request which was granted by the board, providing a suitable bid was received. Also placed on the list, but not at their own request, were Tom Mulholland, Laurie Kessler, Fred Aldridge and Charlie Hewitt. Leeds United immediately enquired about the services of Crilly who was valued at £1,500, a fee which caused disagreement in the boardroom as some thought it should be higher.

William Thompson, who played for the Club in the Northern Victory League and had since played for South Shields, Queens Park Rangers and Newport County returned in October.

Good news on the injury front followed as player/manager Cecil Potter reported for training. With no win in five games, it was hoped that his arrival would bring some stability and experience.

The team struggled for form until, on November 12, they beat Halifax at the Vic 4-0, with goals from Peter Robertson, Bert Lee, Tot Parkinson and recent signing John Scorgie. It was only United's fourth win from 12 games and in the 11 matches prior to this they had scored just five times.

After failing to turn up for training, James Dougherty was transfer listed and suspended for a breach of Club discipline. However, he soon settled his differences and was taken off the list.

Scorgie failed to agree terms and left after a month-long trial. The Club wanted him to stay as he showed great promise in his four outings, scoring twice. However, he refused to move to the area and wanted to continue to commute from Birmingham, where he lived and had a business. He wanted travelling expenses on top of his salary, and the Club was not enamoured by his demands.

In the Reserve Sunderland Shipowner's Cup fixture at South Shields on November 20, Cecil Potter made his return, playing his first game for nearly ten months. A week later he was back in the first team, at Stalybridge in the fifth qualifying round of the FA Cup. Pools went into the game with five successive defeats behind them on the road and lost 2-0.

It was to be Potter's final first team game for Pools – in this country at least.

Pools Move In To Transfer Market

TO halt the slide Manager Potter made several new signings. Bill Rumney returned and he also captured forward Tommy Thompson from Seaton Delaval, striker Billy Hick of Consett Celtic and outside left Billy Rowe from Teesside League side Loftus Albion.

These new signings hastened the departure of last season's top scorer Jimmy Lister. He was recalled to the first team for the first time since early November, after being placed on the transfer list and touted to clubs. South Shields were offered him for £500 and later Darlington, who could have had him for just £150.

He demanded his papers believing that he should be playing first team football on a more regular basis and was allowed to leave. With no takers for Mulholland or Aldridge their contracts were paid up for £25 and £5 respectively.

Three days before Christmas the board held a meeting at the Commercial Hotel in West Hartlepool, when the chairman highlighted the fact that more capital needed to be taken up as only £2,256 of a possible £5,000 had been subscribed.

On current revenue this season the Club had done little more than pay their way. Gate receipt money was being spent on ground improvements, when ideally this expenditure would come from share capital and £1000 already was needed to cover the cost of funds spent to date. Several shareholders present again declared to dig deep and purchase more shares.

After failing to score in their last four league games and winning only two of 12, by Boxing Day Pools were in 14th place and crowds had dropped to 6,000.

Pools faced Stalybridge, who had knocked them out of the FA Cup just three weeks before

at home and they ended the rot winning 3-1. They won three in a row, including scoring five against Halifax on New Year's Eve.

With no game on January 7, Pools arranged a friendly against Manchester United's reserve side. Pools romped home 4-0, with Tot Parkinson grabbing a brace, trialist George Crowther netting once and the fourth coming from the penalty spot, scored by keeper George Gill.

To bolster an improving team, more signings were made in the second week of January. Trialist and former Huddersfield and West Ham centre forward George Crowther joined, along with Jimmy Chesser of Stockton.

Crowther was handed an immediate start and scored in his second and third games, both against Nelson, who Pools put ten goals past over two weekends. They had now won six games from seven and climbed to eighth, nine points adrift of leaders Stockport County.

Despite the league form, Pools were knocked out of the DSC at Darlington in a replay on January 23. At 2-1 down, keeper Gill split the palm of his left hand and had to go off, replaced in goal by Harry Thoms. Pools played the remainder of the game with just ten men and conceded one more.

Debate On Gate Prices

MEANWHILE the Mayor of West Hartlepool wrote to the Club asking if they could reduce the price of admission for the unemployed. However, hands were tied as under rule 26 of Football League regulations, clubs had to charge a minimum of 9d plus tax, making a total minimum entrance for adults of one shilling.

Early in February, after playing in the last three games, young winger Tommy Yews was taken to hospital before the 2-1 reverse at Chesterfield suffering from appendicitis .

In the return fixture a week later, Pools gained revenge by thrashing them 7-0, a winning margin that would not be equalled in the Football League for 12 years. Recent signing Crowther scored the Club's first Football League hat-trick.

Rumours were circulating that the northern section of Division Three would be axed at the end of the season, because many of the clubs involved were in a trying economic position after encountering difficult seasons. None were receiving the support through the gates expected.

But, at a meeting in Manchester during the last week of February, the rumours were quickly dispelled. A statement was issued advising that the division would continue and an increase in the number of sides (there were currently 20) would be considered.

Never seemingly satisfied with his lot, Cecil Potter added amateur forward Thomas Towse to his squad early in March. If he could match his performances at Northern League South Bank for Pools, he would be offered professional terms. Rated by his Club as one of the best amateur forwards in the country, Pools got him to sign his contract on the side of a railway truck in Linthorpe in Middlesbrough, where he was employed. He had 17 goals so far that season and was courted by other clubs such as Crystal Palace, Bristol City, Bradford PA and South Shields.

On March 18, Pools played Darlington at the Vic in front of 11,700 fans, the biggest home crowd of the season. Despite a recent upsurge in form – Pools stood in seventh spot – the sides failed to deliver and played out a goalless draw. Top scorer Peter Robertson, who had been suffering from a groin injury for a few weeks, needed time out to recover and missed the next six matches.

George Crowther

Post Season Tour Planned

DESPITE economic difficulties, plans were afoot for Pools to go on their travels at the end of the season. They had been invited to play in Spain, at the request of some recently-formed clubs.

It was intended that Pools play matches in Bilbao, Santander and San Sebastian, with a game in Paris hopefully on their return journey. Provided the hosts could come up with a suitable guarantee to cover the cost of the trip, Pools would leave on May 10, returning two weeks later.

It was also announced that keeper George Gill was to be rewarded for his long service with a benefit match. The game was set for April 19 – and the opposition would be put together by Newcastle United star Wilf Low, a Scottish cap who briefly appeared for Pools during the war. He planned to bring a vastly experienced side, with plenty of international stars on view.

Two days before this game, Pools played a friendly against Greenock Morton, who had just won the Scottish Cup. A hard fought game ended in a 1-1 draw with Cecil Hardy grabbing the equaliser.

For Gill's benefit match, as promised, a line-up packed with talent turned out. A crowd of 6,210 attended to see a Pools XI play the following team: Tim Williamson (Middlesbrough & England), Jock Marshall (Middlesbrough & Scotland & USA), Frank Hudspeth (Newcastle & England), Cecil Potter (Hartlepools), Wilf Low (Newcastle & Scotland), Tom Curry (Newcastle & Football League XI), Stan Seymour (Newcastle & Football League XI), Charlie Hewitt (Hartlepools), George Elliott (Middlesbrough & England), George Holley (Sunderland & England) and Jimmy Low (Newcastle & Scottish League XI).

It was a great coup and a mark of respect for Gill to have such players turn out. It proved a fitting end to the careers of Potter and Hewitt. The game ended 1-1, with England forward Holley scoring first and Marshall equalising when he put the ball through his own net. The gate raised around £300 in benefit for the dependable Gill.

At Ashington four days later, Pools ended up with nine men on the pitch. Chuck Hewitt twisted his knee just five minutes in and Tot Parkinson was injured shortly after. He played as much of the game as he could while suffering from lameness, before giving up ten minutes from the end and leaving the pitch. Pools were hammered 4-1.

Despite struggling financially and suffering from an ever increasing injury list, Pools agreed to travel to Durham on April 25 to play a money-raising friendly. The game, however, seemed to be a fruitless exercise as only 300 turned up to see Jack Harris and Bert Lee score in a 2-1 Pools win.

Even though the season was not over, a further friendly took place on May 3, against Middlesbrough at the Vic. All proceeds were to go to Pools' coffers. A crowd of 1,000 saw Tommy Towse score twice in a 2-2 draw.

The final game of the season saw Towse on the scoresheet again, getting the only goal at Barrow.

Pools ended the season well, losing just one of their last nine. They ended in fourth spot, no mean feat, considering the injury problems and constant changes to the team.

Stockport were promoted as champions, with Darlington and Grimsby the other sides above Pools. Top scorer was Peter Robertson with 12. No players were ever present.

Club's First Manager Passes Away

AS Pools were playing their final game, a sad event happened in West Hartlepool. The Club's first player/manager and former England international, Fred Priest, died at his home after a brief illness.

He resided above the Market Hotel in Lynn Street, where he was the landlord. He was aged only 47 and left behind a widow and family. He was a popular, amiable man who did much to give the Club a solid start in their infancy. The funeral was held on Tuesday, May 9 at the new cemetery and was well attended with fans and officials from the football world and licensing trade in attendance.

Spain Excursion Gets Under Way

THE following day the team were set sail for Spain. Players heading away were Gill, Dougherty, Crilly, Nicholson, Harris, Bratt, Chesser, Thompson, P Robertson, C Hardy, Rowe and Longmore. However, the night before they were due to travel, Cecil Hardy had to withdraw following the death of his father at his home in Blackhall. The word was put out to Thoms to get him on board.

The train carrying the squad left West Hartlepool mid-afternoon and the party was to stay overnight in London. Travelling with the players were vice chairman Stonehouse, Cllr Brown, Cecil Potter and the trainer Mr Wynter. The intention was to travel to Calais by ferry and then by train to Paris, Bordeaux and arriving in Bilbao on the Friday and Santander the following day.

Two games were scheduled there, before moving to Oviedo on Thursday, staying until the Monday. It was then intended to return to Santander for a final game and return to England on May 26, via Paris and Boulogne.

As well as Hardy, Crowther was also left behind due to injury. Thoms, even at 11 o'clock on the day of travel, promised he would make it and would meet his team-mates at the station. However, he failed to show.

Upon arrival at Kings Cross they had a pre-arranged meeting with a West Hartlepool councillor, Mr Candler, who was acquainted with London and would guide them to their hotel. Surprisingly he was accompanied by Mayor Wilson of West Hartlepool who wished the team well and a safe successful journey.

The next morning Cllr Candler saw the team off from Victoria station. Despite being in financial difficulties, the Durham City team were also there, rewarded for their season with a break in the sun. They agreed to travel with Pools to Paris, but they were later bound for Madrid and Barcelona.

Despite the travelling party being a happy little crowd, manager Cecil Potter was not too optimistic. Not only were they undergoing a long journey they were also going to be playing in high temperatures with a lack of playing cover.

The weather on the journey to Bilbao was fine all the way, but too hot for some. Two unnamed players managed to get lost in Paris and had to travel on a later train, intending to meet up with the rest of the squad in Santander. The others spent the night in a rainy Bilbao.

They arrived at their destination in the afternoon and were shown the pitch that they were to play on. While it had a good covering of grass, it was very uneven.

Big Welcome For Pools On Continent – And A Sunday Game

POOLS had the honour of being the first team to visit Santander, who boasted a decent side with an international in their XI.

They were also managed by former England and Middlesbrough player Fred Pentland, who had formerly been in charge of the French national team and took the position in Spain at the same time as Pools entered the Football League.

He was known as El Bombin in Spain, due to his likeness for wearing a bowler hat. He later had great success managing Atletico Madrid, Bilbao and Real Oviedo.

His Santander side recently beat French side Racing Club 4-0. On the Saturday evening the party from the Hartlepools were entertained and were taken to watch a local game known as Boletto, which was similar to a sport indigenous to the North-East known as fives.

The opening game of the tour took place on Sunday, May 14 1922, the first time Pools had played on a Sunday, an option which would never have been entertained in England at the time or for many years to come.

Pools were two-up at half time and the Santander side had a chance to pull one back through a penalty which was put wide. They managed a consolation in the second half, but the goals from Robertson and Bratt, were enough to earn victory for Pools.

The itinerary of the tour changed slightly and two more games were played against the same opposition on May 17 and 19. Pools won 5-1 in the first game, with Harris netting two and Bratt getting a hat-trick. In the final game, manager Potter swapped sides and appeared for Santander with their manager Pentland appearing for Pools. Pools were 2-1 down at half-time, but won 4-2 with goals from Rowe, Chesser and another brace from Harris.

The following day the Club left for Oviedo. The journey was an 11-hour train ride in poor accommodation, made through some scenic countryside. The team looked on as an electric storm took place, with the lightning playing around the hills in the failing light, a sight all would remember. The rain fell heavily, but it was still dreadfully hot. Keeper Gill was likely to miss the first game due to illness.

On arrival at Oviedo a large crowd greeted the Pools party at the railway station and the Hotel Paris. Large streamers advertising the game stretched the length of the main street and photographs of the Pools players were on display in shop windows.

Pentland travelled with the team as he agreed to referee the two games. He reckoned that Pools had never created as much excitement at home as they had in Oviedo. Never before had an English team visited the town and following Pools' successes against Santander, Oviedo declared that they may have to bring in some outsiders to help them out,

Fred Halstead

particularly as they has recently lost 6-1 to Santander.

The first match was another Sunday game and Pools took to the field without a recognised keeper, so Ben Nicholson went between the sticks. The game was played on a pitch devoid of grass in soaring temperatures and Pools were thumped 5-0. George Gill returned for the next match on the following day and, in front of 4,000 fans, Pools won by a single goal. The Oviedo team were described as physical; "they played with their elbows up and fouled frequently".

For the rest of the week the squad were treated to some Spanish hospitality. They visited a bullfighting arena as preparations and training was underway for the weekend event. They also visited the King's Palace.

Pools travelled back to Santander early on the Tuesday morning and were trying to arrange to meet up with Durham City at Santander for an exhibition match.

Santander, who now had more visitors in the form of St Mirren, wanted to play Pools again on Sunday. However, United were due to leave on the Friday morning and were anticipated back in West Hartlepool 72 hours later.

After arriving in Hartlepools, barely a week had passed when a new professional was added to the playing staff. Former Deaf Hill Old Boys and Trimdon Grange player Tommy Mitchell put pen to paper. He was only 17, a speedy inside left forward who promised plenty. A week later Middlesbrough reserve player Francis Dowson signed. Just a few players were expected to be signed this summer due to financial constraints.

Annual Report Shows Good Results On The Field For Pools

THE annual report expressed the board's satisfaction with the results on the field, despite a very difficult position throughout the first half of the season. The reserves had ended the season as runners up to Ferryhill Athletic in a close fought contest. They were to compete in the NEL the next season following their acceptance after a good performance in the Palatine League. Off the pitch the Club lost just under £1,500 putting their total indebtness marginally over £2,500.

Following the destruction of the stand in WW1, the only news received was that once the German nation had been in touch with the British Government, Pools would hear further.

Despite this loss, Pools still captured Charlton Athletic centre half Walker Hampson. The 27-year-old had also played for South Shields and Burnley. Walker's signature was made all the sweeter when it was later reported that he was signed under the noses of Darlington at the last minute.

At the AGM just before the end of June, the board announced they were satisfied with performances, but less than content with the finances.

There was a depression in trade which had once again damaged support. In particular the board referred to the number of men at every home game who stood outside of the ground waiting for free entry when the gates would open 15 minutes before the end. The chairman added that he was devastated to see these men in such a desperate financial position and the gates would be opened an hour into each game for the benefit of the impoverished supporters.

The first team had performed well, but the board believed they could have performed better if they hadn't been robbed of the services of Pullen, who never appeared for the first team following his bout of appendicitis. He later suffered a severe knee injury playing for the reserves and was of little use afterwards.

The board also confirmed that Potter and

Thoms had been offered terms but had not yet signed. Goalkeeper Summerfield had yet to get back to the Club regarding his intentions if he wanted to continue as a professional footballer.

Search For New Manager Begins

POOLS were soon seeking a new manager, as, in the first week of July, Cecil Potter was announced as manager of Derby County, the selection from 90 applicants. He had retired from playing and Pools deemed it necessary to reduce his salary accordingly. Harry Thoms followed him shortly after.

Pre-season trials began on August 12 and a couple of days later the Club announced David Gordon of Leith was the new manager.

Particularly impressive on trial were Hampson and Fred Halstead, another centre half. The towering Halstead had joined from Southend United.

With the pre-season games out of the way, the Club was dealt a blow when Tom Crilly followed Thoms to Derby County.

1922-23

THE team began the season with optimism after their finish to the previous term, but after a draw on the opening day at Walsall what followed was not just a season mediocrity and struggle, but nigh-on 80 years of such form, albeit with a few exceptions. The Club took five games to record their first victory, when they beat Ashington 3-1 on September 23.

		P	HW	HD	HL	HF	HA	AW	AD	AL	AF	AA	POINTS
1	Stockport County	38	13	5	1	36	10	11	3	5	24	11	56
2	Darlington	38	15	2	2	52	7	7	4	8	29	30	50
3	Grimsby Town	38	15	4	0	54	15	6	4	9	18	32	50
4	**HARTLEPOOLS UNITED**	**38**	**10**	**6**	**3**	**33**	**11**	**7**	**2**	**10**	**19**	**28**	**42**
5	Accrington Town	38	15	1	3	50	15	4	2	13	23	42	41
6	Crewe Alexandra	38	13	1	5	39	21	5	4	10	21	35	41
7	Stalybridge Celtic	38	14	3	2	42	15	4	2	13	20	48	41
8	Walsall	38	15	2	2	52	17	3	1	15	14	48	39
9	Southport	38	11	6	2	39	12	3	4	12	16	32	38
10	Ashington	38	13	2	4	42	22	4	2	13	17	44	38
11	Durham City	38	14	0	5	43	20	3	3	13	25	47	37
12	Wrexham	38	12	4	3	40	17	2	5	12	11	39	37
13	Chesterfield	38	12	2	5	33	15	4	1	14	15	52	35
14	Lincoln City	38	11	2	6	32	20	3	4	12	16	39	34
15	Barrow	38	11	2	6	29	18	3	3	13	13	36	33
16	Nelson	38	7	6	6	27	23	6	1	12	21	43	33
17	Wigan Borough	38	9	4	6	32	28	2	5	12	14	44	31
18	Tranmere Rovers	38	7	5	7	41	25	2	6	11	10	36	29
19	Halifax Town	38	9	4	6	37	28	1	5	13	19	48	29
20	Rochdale	38	9	2	8	34	24	2	2	15	18	53	26

Football League Division Three (North 1921-22)

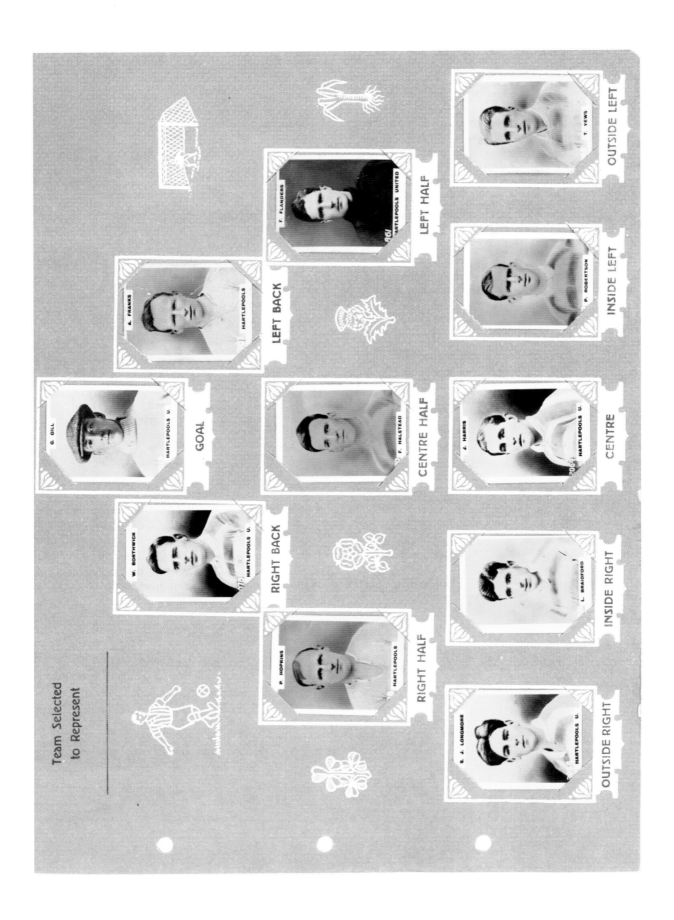

Hartlepools United 1922-1923. Top to Bottom, Left to Right: George Gill, Walter Borthwick, Tony Franks, Tot Hopkins, Fred Halstead, Fred Flanders, Jimmy Longmore, Lowe Braidford, Jack Harris, Peter Robertson, Tom Yews

Fred Priest
Benefit Match

George Keenleyside

ON October 11 a benefit match for the family of the late Fred Priest took place at the Vic. He was to be honoured by three former team-mates of his at Middlesbrough who where now all England Internationals.

The Hartlepools United XI included goalkeeper Tim Williamson as well as their prolific striker George Elliott and fellow forward Tom Urwin. They played a team from Sheffield which had nine players from another of his former teams, Sheffield United, as well as two players from Wednesday, the other team in the city. In a game refereed by another former famous Middlesbrough team-mate Alf Common, just 1,500 fans turned up to see the Sheffield side win 2-0. A sum of £66 was raised for his widow and children.

The Club were suffering from the loss of Crilly and Thoms and were struggling to find a settled line up. With Chesser sidelined because of knee ligament damage, manager Gordon went to Scotland on a scouting mission. He returned with half back David Connell from Greenock Morton, who joined on a month long trial. A month later he also added Boro reserve full back Charlie Dixon to the books.

Pools won their first FA Cup match as a league Club when they beat Durham City in the fifth qualifying round, winning by a solitary goal in the form of a penalty by former Boro player Francis Dowson. They were, however, knocked out by the same score in the next round at Wrexham. The Club progressed in the DSC the next week when two days before Christmas they beat Bishop Auckland 4-0. League form was poor and by the end of 1922 they had won just once in nine attempts.

However, the return of Hampson to the half back line on New Year's Day helped Pools to a 1-0 win over Darlington and they enjoyed a silver streak, dropping just one point in the next four games, pulling them away from the foot of the table. Centre forward Lowe Braidford had scored four goals in seven games and displaced George Crowther from the side. Crowther grew disgruntled and moved on to Tranmere a route which a home sick Fred Halstead followed in March.

Crowd Trouble At Victoria Ground

ON 6 March 1923 Pools were issued with a warning by the Football League and the Football Association.

A section of the home crowd had gained a notorious reputation and this had come to a head on February 24, during the game against Tranmere.

The referee was so annoyed by their abuse and behaviour that he went over to the part of the ground where the words were coming from and demanded that the impoliteness should cease immediately. He complained to the authorities and Pools were warned that the ground could well face closure if there was a repeat incident.

After the good form in January, Pools again went on another shocking run, failing to win in eight. It was halted on the last day of March with a 5-0 win over Chesterfield. Less than two weeks later though, United were beaten in the final of the DSC at Darlington 1-0. The season ended in early May with the Club finishing four points and seven places above bottom club Durham City. The second lowest placed team, Ashington, along with Durham were re-elected, for the following campaign. The division expanded by two sides, with the inclusion of New Brighton and Doncaster bringing the complement of clubs up to 22.

In preparation for the next term, the Club signed experienced forward George Keenleyside from South Shields, for whom he had made more than 100 outings. At 34 years old it was believed he would still give good service. He was seen as a possible replacement for the consistent Tommy Yews who had been monitored by several top flight clubs for some time. Pools also added the signature of Darlington skipper and former Norwich player Percy Sutcliffe to the squad.

The Club lost around the £400 mark over the season which wasn't as bad as many had expected. Considering the harsh employment situation, the board had earlier adopted a prudent money management regime which had been of good use. Following the change of the reserve team to the NEL, their gate receipts were up by over £900. The

Percy Sutcliffe

first team lost in excess of £1,500. Tommy Yews eventually left, which had added the sum of £150 to the coffers, from the purses of West Ham United. He became an early legend for the Hammers, appearing in over 350 games for them.

Just a couple of days after Yews' departure, the top scorer from the previous season, Peter Robertson, joined Doncaster Rovers. After a disappointing season he was allowed to leave on a free transfer. He later moved to Australia where he settled and played his football and found himself appearing for the national side.

Due to the financial crisis, the Club enlisted the help of several local amateurs. Schoolteacher Thomas Hunt from Seaham Harbour signed, Alec Gledden from the St. Oswald's club and Alf Young, from Wingate Athletic, arrived along with another schoolteacher, Thomas Sawdon.

1923-24

IN mid-August the usual round of pre-season games commenced. They were fairly uneventful affairs with nobody standing out, promising very little for the forthcoming season. The forecast after these drab affairs was not wrong either – after winning the first two games, both against Barrow, Pools went six games without a win including an embarrassing 5-0 reverse at Feethams. They were even knocked out of the DSPC by Shildon.

In order to try and halt the slide, the Club signed William Smith, once of Huddersfield. He had been a prolific scorer for their reserve side and had just finished a trial at Southend. He scored in his third game and then didn't score for another five weeks.

However, he did bag seven goals in the next game he scored in. Pools beat Tynesiders St Peter's Albion 10-1 in the fourth qualifying round of the FA Cup on November 17 – the biggest win since April 1910.

He then got a brace in the next round two weeks later when they beat Shildon. Despite the cup results Pools failed to score in five consecutive league games, a spell so bad it would not be repeated for another 15 seasons.

Pools Hit Another Bad Patch

KNOCKED out of the FA Cup at Ashington in mid-December, Pools beat Accrington Stanley 3-0 the week after and then went on to win only one in 15 Division Three games. During this poor run, striker WE Smith was sent off in the home game with Walsall on January 5.

He was suspended for a month due to his poor conduct. Both the player and the fans were once again urged to improve their language and a notice was put up at the Vic stating that a repeat would mean closure of the ground. The Club had also been thrown out of the Durham County Challenge Cup after the reserve XI fielded an ineligible player in the tie against the Wood Skinners club.

Players Agree To Reduce Wages And The Manager Quits

NOT only were the Club in a sorry state on the pitch, affairs were just as poor off it.

Gates were down and concern was raised at the fall in revenue. The Club had been operating in very difficult circumstances since the Great War. The £4,595 spent on ground improvements over the past few years had caught up. They were still owed money from the Government for the bomb damage. The situation had become so drastic that the board were contemplating scrapping the Club.

All the players had, not for the first time in the Club's brief existence, agreed to take a pay cut. Players Rob Carswell, John Birnie and John Duthie were allowed to go in a cost cutting exercise. The Club needed financial assistance and they needed it soon.

On February 16, Pools were hammered 5-1 at Chesterfield and it proved the final straw for manager Davie Gordon who quit, citing the quality of the side and the lack of money. Since the formation, teams had been selected jointly by the directors and the manager at a meeting a few days prior to each game. The squad would continue to be selected in this manner, but by the directors only until such a time as a new manager would be appointed.

Gordon's departure didn't improve results. A 3-2 reverse to Chesterfield in the return match was the first managerless game, followed by conceding five in the ensuing two matches against Rotherham County, leaving the Club rooted to the foot of the table.

A rare collector's card, 1924

William Smith

Joe Osmond

Pools Sign International Player, Win A Cup And Seek Re-Election

A couple of new recruits were drafted in for the second Rotherham game. The much-travelled Jack Bell from Weymouth was a speedy, versatile forward who had previously won a Southern League title with Plymouth Argyle in 1913.

The other signing was, for the time, most unusual – a former Egyptian International who went under the name of Tewfik Abdallah (occasionally Tawfik Abdullah, or any combination of these names). Also known as Toothpick, he had previously played in Egypt and arrived in Britain a couple of years ago, playing for Derby County. Further spells with Cowdenbeath and Bridgend Town followed before he came to the Vic. His papers were not cleared in time for the second Rotherham game, but he made his debut the following week in a 4-0 victory over Wrexham, a game in which he and the other new signing, Jack Bell, scored.

In the remaining 11 games, Pools won only once more and the team finished second bottom, ahead of Barrow thanks to a slightly better goal difference. The Club scored a meagre 33 goals, a poor record. The second string did somewhat better, finishing eighth in their division and winning the regional (Durham) section of the National Orphanage Cup, beating Shotton Albion 4-2 with a hat-trick from Jack Cook and a fourth from Cecil Hardy, in a game played at Wingate. They lined up as follows – W Summerfield, J Storey, J Boulton, A Lonie, W Walsh, R Shaw, T Hunt, C Hardy, W Mills, J Wrightson, J Cook.

They also excelled in winning the Sunderland Shipowner's Cup defeating Darlington on a replayed final with keeper Summerfield getting the only goal from the penalty spot. The teams for the final and the replay were – Summerfield, Storey, Boulton, Walsh, A Young, B C Nicholson, G Keenleyside, Cook, Mills, Wrightson, T Mitchell.

These were the Club's first successes since 1910.

At the end of the season, few players were kept on after a re-election battle (the first of many to come). After only three seasons in the league, Pools could have been kicked out. Abdallah moved to America and Canada, where he had a decent playing and coaching career, later returning to his homeland and managing his country for a few years during the Second World War. Journeyman Jack Bell moved on and Tommy Mitchell was transfer listed for a fee of £1,000. Amateur player Alf Young signed a professional contract and committed himself to the Club for the following season, as did top scorer W Smith.

As well as the usual local league cup finals, the schools held their finals there too, along with a bizarre football match played on motor bikes. It was not the only game of such a nature to take place at the Vic raising money for charities, and it also surely raised the eyebrows of the groundsman. Crowds of around the 2,500 mark turned out for these spectacles.

Due to the threat of re-election the Club were compelled to hold their AGM early.

Once again the board claimed that the first team were unfortunate with injuries. They did, however, praise the efforts of the reserves and congratulated them on their successes. Earlier in the campaign the players had taken pay cuts of between 25 per cent and 33 per cent to aid the financial plight and the Club still recorded a loss of over £750. The board had done well to reduce salaries and other expenses and they had to, as gate receipts were down by in excess of £350. There was still no news on the air raid damage and the board declared that it seemed unlikely that they were to receive any funds in relation to this as the Club had been advised by the Government that there were cases much more deserving.

Pools In Re-Election Drama

JUST a couple of days later in early June came the first re-election meeting.

The Football League Management Committee decided that they wanted both Barrow and Hartlepools to stay in the Football League without the need for a vote, a puzzling decision but a lucky escape.

After four months without a manager, former boss Jack Manners was handed the reigns again. He had previously spent seven years in charge from 1913 to 1920 and wasted no time in recruiting new players.

He re-signed Sydney Hardy, brother of Cecil. He also captured half back Thomas Jobson who had spent two years at Plymouth. Tommy Mitchell moved to Stockport County for a decent fee, but less than the £1,000 that Pools valued him at. The former Trimdon Grange winger was easily Pools finest player last season and had been placed on the transfer list at his own request. Preston North End were also after his signature, while Liverpool and Wolves had been known to have monitored his progress.

More signings followed and by the end of July the Club had signed George Chape from South Shields, Jack Foster from Luton Town, Thomas Potter Smith from Hull City and former Clapton Orient captain Joe Osmond. Manners had also added a good stock of local amateurs who were able for the reserves, including Ord of Bankhead Albion who had scored 37 goals the previous season and had previously had been on trial with West Ham.

1924-25

THE Club started the season in much the same form as the previous one – poorly. Only one win in the first six games, and a DSC cup loss to Darlington, saw a new keeper sign and signal the end of Bill Summerfield's long reign as number one. The new keeper was Billy Cowell, from Huddersfield. The Club also dipped into the market to sign centre half Charles Storer of Bradford City.

Cowell made his debut on September 27 in the game against Rotherham County in a goalless draw. While it slightly stabilised results there was a down side as Tom Lilley broke his collarbone. The Club struggled along and former player Syd Hardy made his first start of the season on October 25 at Tranmere. He scored, but Pools still lost by the odd goal in seven.

However, Hardy's return to the side saw an upturn in results and he scored in the next three games as Pools gathered two draws and a victory. In between this spell of league games, Pools were knocked out of the FA Cup by Ashington for the second season running. However, it was found that Ashington had fielded an ineligible player and Pools were reinstated.

Progress Made In The FA Cup

DESPITE the continuing indifferent league form, Pools beat Bishop Auckland in the

The team that beat St. Albans in the FA Cup qualifying for the first round proper for the first time. Standing: Jack Allen, Ernine Butler, William Cowell, Jack Jobson, Charles Storer, Ed Smith, Cecil Hardy, Alf Young. Seated: Syd Hardy, Jack Cook, Thomas Potter Smith

Tom Lilley

cup and two weeks later on December 13 1924, Pools played St. Albans in the sixth qualifying round. It seemed the perfect chance to proceed, even though they were one of the top amateur sides in the Home Counties and they stood third in the Isthmian League.

Their star player was Wilf Minter holder of two English Amateur caps who, at the start of the season, had scored 132 goals in 135 games. Pools won easily 4-0, meaning they were through to the first round proper for the first time. The reward was a fantastic one, away to Newcastle United on January 10.

The following week Pools signed three amateur players for trial in the reserves. Thomas Reid from Stakeford United, Redyers Tunnell from the Middlesbrough Church League and a 24-year-old striker, William Robinson, from Pegswood United of the Ashington District League. He was to prove an inspired choice.

On New Year's Day, Billy Smith was injured

as he bagged a hat-trick in a 3-0 victory over Walsall. Neighbours Darlington were held to a 1-1 draw two days later without his services.

The following Saturday, Pools played the biggest match in their existence to date when they made the short journey to St James' Park. Pools were not overawed or embarrassed and put up a decent performance, despite losing 4-1 in front of 36,632 fans, with Syd Hardy getting Pools' goal. The gate earned £850, proving the importance of good cup runs to lower league clubs.

The following week at Bradford PA, Tom Lilley broke his collar bone again, just a month after returning to the first team. It was to be ten weeks before he returned to first XI duties. Although it was only January, it seemed to be the end of the season for Pools as it fizzled out almost immediately.

Billy Smith was once again top scorer for the season, weighing in with a meagre 12 goals. They fared slightly better than the season before, finishing third bottom and just avoiding re-election. The reserves finished tenth in the NEL and failed to repeat their cup successes of the previous campaign, with William Robinson, who joined in December, top scoring with 11.

The Club had lost just over £160 during the course of this season but the loss was felt less than it would have been as they reached the FA Cup first round proper.

Although there was an improvement

The team pose before a game early in the 1925-26 season. Back Row: Paul Frith (Trainer), Fred Robson, Jack Jobson, Tom Lilley, Billy Cowell, Jack Foster and Alf Young; Front Row: Ernie Butler, Fred Birtles, Harry Wensley, Cecil Hardy, Syd Hardy

financially, the situation was still unsatisfactory and the prospects did not look rosy.

There was still a grave depression in trade and abnormally high unemployment levels. Once again, due to the financial situation, there would be difficulty in signing any more than a few new players, with the Club compelled to pursue a policy of signing local juniors rather than a procession of experienced, but maybe past their best, players.

The Club signed a few amateurs, but in mid-July they got their hands on 28-year-old Harry Wensley from Shildon, who had been top scorer in the NEL for the past two seasons, netting 52 goals the previous campaign.

He was signed as a replacement for Billy Smith who moved to Rochdale. Centre half Morris moved to Crewe and full back Ed Smith departed.

1925-26

FINANCIAL problems were so dire that pre-season training had to start a couple of weeks later than normal and this clearly showed in the first game of the season when they suffered a crushing 6-0 opening day defeat at Rochdale. However, the Club then went on to win five out of the next six games, with Wensley grabbing eight goals in the process, to move up to fourth in the league.

Towards the end of September they trounced Durham City 5-0 in the first round of the DSPC, with Wensley bagging another two. The team then settled into a consistent run of league form including a 6-1 drubbing of New Brighton.

Fred Birtles who had joined in the summer after playing football in the Cheshire area, netted twice during this game, but suffered cartilage damage to his left knee. He was sent to Newcastle to see a specialist and didn't return for action until he appeared for the reserves almost four months later.

The FA Cup saw Pools play at St James' Park for the second season running, but only in a second replay for the first round (for which Pools automatically qualified) tie against Blyth Spartans. A 1-1 draw saw them lose 2-1 in the third replay, played at Roker Park.

Benefit Match For Cecil Hardy

ON January 23 1926, Pools treated a mere 3,358 fans to a 9-3 victory over Walsall, with the Hardy brothers, Cecil and Syd, getting five of the goals, Cecil claiming a hat-trick.

He was awarded a benefit match in April,

Harry Harrison

when Newcastle legend Stan Seymour brought down a team of local stars including future Scottish star and team-mate Hughie Gallacher and Middlesbrough's Billy Birrell and Maurice Webster. Also playing was former Pools player Charlie Hewitt who was in the crowd and answered a plea for help when Seymour's XI arrived with only ten men.

Just a week after his 40th birthday, Hewitt played the full game, out of position, at right back. Hardy, who was suffering from an injury so was unable to play, saw his Pools side win 5-3, with Harry Wensley getting another hat-trick, in front of 3,000 fans, who raised £134 for the fans' favourite.

Pools went on to stay in the top eight throughout the season and reached the final of the DSPC, playing Darlington and losing 2-0 with the following team – Cowell, Lilley, Kell, Young, Jobson, Richardson, Best, Carr, Wensley, Robinson and Boland. The reserves struggled, placed 13th in the NEL, and were defeated in the semi-final of the SSOC by the Sunderland reserve team.

Wensley top scored with 21 league goals, with Cecil Hardy not too far behind on 15.

Also impressive was William Robinson, top scorer for the reserves last season, who notched seven goals in 13 league games towards the end of the season, including a last day hat-trick in a 5-0 drubbing of Wrexham.

The summer of 1926 saw plenty of comings and goings. Goalkeeper Billy Cowell, who had been an ever-present over the season, moved to top-flight side Derby County. Tom Lilley made a shorter journey when he signed for Sunderland for a handsome £750.

Despite the good league performance and the sixth placed finish, the Club still lost just under £200 during the season. The average attendance was 4,500, up on the 4,123 from the previous season, but still not enough to even start to look at breaking even.

Even though things were bad on the overall financial perspective, buoyed by the funds from the sale of Lilley, Pools strengthened the team that performed so well and added to the ranks former Exeter and QPR forward Colin Myers.

Also joining were ex-Grimsby full back William Arch and Durham City's former

Middlesbrough goalkeeper Harry Harrison, with out of favour forward Ernie Butler, making the trip in the opposite direction. He saw out the rest of his career with Durham, continuing to play for them until he retired in the summer of 1931, three seasons after they lost their league place. This wasn't the end of the dealings with Durham though, as former Pools player Pop Hopkins, left them to take up the position of trainer with Pools.

1926/27

THE transfer dealings that were intended to boost the squad quite simply didn't work out. From the off the season started badly, winning only one game in the first five. Of all of the players, only Harry Wensley stood out, bagging 16 league goals, with Myers his closest contender to the top scorer slot, netting only half that amount. The Club were knocked out of the DSPC to Durham, lost in the first round of the FA Cup in a woeful display at Carlisle, where they were on the receiving end of a 6-2 drubbing. It resulted in complaints in the local press from fans that travelled that day.

Emergency Shareholders Meeting Called

IN February, just five days after being hammered 7-2 at Accrington, the board held an emergency shareholders meeting, where it was revealed that the lending limit with the banks had been reached.

The Club had, for many seasons, survived on funds raised from banks, the directors, local

Ernie Butler

companies and wealthy gentlemen, as on the whole, support had decreased each season. They had even borrowed £500 from Middlesbrough. Already this season the average gate was under 3,200, with a low of 1,278 turning up in early November for the home defeat to Bradford Park Avenue.

From the second the Club left the non-league ranks, the area seemed to have been hit by high unemployment, a financial depression and major industrial action, with this season's strike taking place in the coalfields.

Add to this atrocious weather throughout the winter, with record rainfalls recorded, it was hardly surprising that attendances were dipping drastically.

Pools were also stuck in the position where they had to exist by being a selling Club (a path

Team from 1926/1927 season. Back row: Bertie Hall, Bobby Best, Paul Frith (Trainer), Harry Arch, Robert Little, George Kell, Jack Manners (Manager), Jack Jobson. Front row: Jim McGlen, John Craig, Bob Thompson, Billy Robinson, Harry Wensley, Jack Foster

they would follow until 1997) – agreeing to the departure of any decent players if a suitable bid came in. It went some way to balancing the books, but wrecked chances of advancement.

The End Of The Club Nears?

THE crisis was so bad that the members of the board discussed the winding up of the Club. The only question was whether it was done immediately or at the end of the season. It was estimated that closing straight away would probably save between five or six hundred pounds before the end of the term and already several board members had lost more than they could afford.

However, once again the board decided to plod along and make a go of it but they really needed the support of the townsfolk. West Hartlepool had a population of around 70,000, yet only 280 people had subscribed for shares.

Several members of the Supporters Club were at the meeting and the secretary, Mr Tripp, stated that they would do whatever they could to raise funds, but would need the involvement of the players and directors who should turn up at events they organised and not just ignore it. A fund raising committee was set up.

House Offered As Raffle Prize

THE Supporters Club began a series of meetings to raise money for the Club and came up with ideas such as a whist drive and dance to be held at the Town Hall on March 25, 1927. They were also to raise money at games, including collections and most bizarrely was the raffling of a bungalow in Oakland Avenue, West Hartlepool.

The property was worth £615, would be fully furnished and the deeds would be handed over to the winner. The whist drive was attended by over 60 people with the winners of the ladies dance event winning a chicken and the gents event a box of cigarettes. This and other dances raised nearly fifty valuable pounds.

The bad luck of the team continued right up to the last game of the season when at Wrexham and drawing 0-0, keeper Harrison damaged his arm and had to leave the field of play. He never returned in the second half and Wrexham piled on the misery, scoring four goals without reply.

The reserves qualified for the final of the Orphanage Cup again defeating Ferryhill Athletic and they were also triumphant in the inaugural NEL Challenge Cup Final.

The team of Harrison, Carr, Errington, Hall, Gardner, Nicholson, Best, Robinson, Dobell, Cec Hardy and Boland beat Newcastle's reserve XI 2-1 at the Vic, with Danny Dobell netting both goals in front of 5,120 fans.

At the end of a disappointing season, in which the first team finished 17th, the board acted quickly and in early May they retained only 14 professionals after using 26 all season.

The financial position was well known and they advised that nobody was to be paid any

Bungalow Raffle

summer wages.

Unbelievably, the future of the Club depended on the property raffle, but at that stage only £170 worth of tickets had been purchased. The board decided to make a decision about the future at the end of June. Another effort to raise funds was allowing the Vic to be used for a cricket tournament.

Accounts showed another loss, this time in excess of £1,000 bringing the total indebtness above the £5,000 mark. Average attendances dipped below the 3,000 level for the first time and despite this, pleas were made to the public and businesses to donate whatever they could to keep the Club afloat.

Financial Crisis Forces Coach Out

JACK Manners was let go as the Club simply did not have the cash to afford him or keep him on during the summer. His departure was announced at the AGM in June when only 20 out of 280 shareholders bothered to turn up. The Club now had no manager, no players as there were none contracted, increasing debt and dwindling support. The Club was declared 'as dead as dishwater'.

The following month, the sheer determination and fanaticism of the board were probably the main reasons that the Club is still around today.

Despite the costs they had decided that they wanted the Club to survive. The money raising efforts had so far been only moderately good in raising revenue, but once again board members would provide the cash to keep the Club afloat and applications for players and a manager were invited.

In the last week in July, Bill Norman was installed as manager. He had extensive experience and had been a trainer at Barnsley for eight years, as well as spending three years at Birmingham, had been in charge at Blackpool and was assistant manager at Leeds since June 1923.

Once again pre-season training was to start less than two weeks before the kick-off, due to financial pressures. The Club started signing players including Billy Mordue of Horden, former Leeds player Cuthbert Robson, George Richardson of Hull, a former FA Cup winner in 1922 with Huddersfield, ex-Leeds player William Poyntz and local keeper Joe Hickman.

Just before the season started the winner of the bungalow competition was announced.

In order to win the competition, entrants had to write down an estimate as to how many bus tickets were sold on the local Corporation bus and tram services over the Whit holidays.

Uncannily, Mrs Kate Christelow of Cornwall Street, guessed the exact amount of 188,426 and was presented with the deeds to 'Poolvilla' at the Vic before the first home game of the season against Doncaster. More importantly, after initial sluggish sales of tickets, the Club ended up receiving £189 11s and 2d from the Supporters Association, much needed income. The Club still remained well in debt and the only bill being paid on time was the rent.

1927-28

THE new season started with a win at Wigan Borough. With the plight well publicised, 5,314 fans turned out to see a 1-0 win over Doncaster on September 3, the largest home

A rare photo of Hartlepool Reserves taken in 1927

attendance since January 1926. The Club then followed their now adopted mediocre displays, failing to win for eight games from September 24, until November 12, with a defeat in the DSPC at the hands of Darlington tucked neatly inside these games. In the middle of the run, John Mordue, who was related to Billy Mordue, arrived.

After being dumped out of the FA Cup to Halifax on the last Saturday of November 1927, the Club hit a purple patch the next month, when they won five from seven league games, with forward William Robinson scoring nine goals in the process to move into the dizzy heights of 11th.

Reserve keeper and occasional first team pick Joe Hickman moved to Aston Villa for a fee of £500 – a great deal, for not only was the money much needed but it was a good price for a player with only seven league outings under his belt.

Goalscoring Hero Emerges For Pools

AFTER the New Year, the Club stood ninth, but form dipped once again and they finished the season in 15th.

The only bright spots were the goalscoring exploits of Robinson, who topped the scoring charts with 28 league goals.

Amazingly it took 63 years for the total to be equalled.

He was ably supported by Billy Mordue who chipped in with 16.

During the course of the season, the board re-engaged the services of manager Norman with a new three-year contract which included the clause entitling him to five per cent of the net income from any transfer fees. The Club were also approached to see if they would consider the running of greyhound races on the Vic, which they declined.

The reserves finished 11th in their league and conceded a record 113 goals. They won the Durham section of the National Orphanage Cup, beating Tow Law 2-1 in the final, with Syd Hardy netting a brace. They also were victorious in the final of the NEL challenge cup, beating Middlesbrough reserves 2-1 with goals from J Young and Dobell.

Things On The Up Financially

WITH attendances increasing by an average of 500 a game, good transfer income, monies raised by the Supporters Club and an investment by the local Chamber of Trade, the Club turned in a profit of over £800, bringing

the total indebtness down to under £4,250. Again the Club paid no summer wages but vowed to make improvements to the terracing behind each goal.

In June Cecil Hardy, who was freed in May, was appointed player/coach and

Billy Richardson

put in charge of the reserves. Powerhouse centre half back Alf Young, who had spent five seasons with the Club, moved to Gillingham.

Several other players departed. Top scorer Robinson moved to Bradford City and Dicky Boland ventured further afield when he joined Reading, both after seeking improved terms with the Club during the summer. The Club must have not been impressed with Boland's request as they withdrew their offer of a contract of £3 10/- a week and gave him a free transfer.

The Club signed a few new players, including Jackie Fell of Southend and William Spry of Blackpool, but not enough quality to replace players who had departed.

The playing stock was further decimated when Tommy Robertson and Tom Mackey, who had both joined from local non league sides, were banned for allegedly receiving illegal payments while amateurs. Around 200 North-Eastern non league players were also charged.

The close season saw work commence on the Mill House side of the ground with a covered stand erected and terracing replacing the banking around the ground, at a total cost of £725.

1928-29

Record Transfer Fee Received But Still Poor Accounts

THE season got underway innocuously, sharing four goals at home with Nelson, but on the first day of September the Club were hammered by eight clear goals at Carlisle.

A couple of days later, the Club dug into their pockets and signed former Newcastle United striker Tucker Mordue from Sheffield United for a fee of £100. He was the younger brother of Billy and both were the cousin of the other Mordue who was on the books at the time, Jack. He made an instant impression,

Frank Barson

scoring on his debut, along with Jack, in the 2-0 win over Darlington. Including this game, Pools scored only ten goals in ten games, with Jack and Tucker Mordue monopolising the scoring.

Mackey and Robertson had their appeals against their suspension lifted in September and were two of only a few players, who were fortunate in getting the bans overturned.

Towards the end of October, Sunderland enquired about the services of left back Tommy Robertson. Pools succeeded in putting them off, by stating they wanted £2,500 for his services, but they circulated his details around all top flight clubs as he was considered something of a prospect.

When the Club again fell at the first hurdle of the FA Cup, this time losing to Spennymoor, they had already been knocked out of the DSPC and were firmly rooted at the bottom. The only good bit of news in November was the sale of Tommy Robertson to Bury for £1,000, the highest fee received to date.

The start of December 1928 saw Joe Hickman return only 12 months after joining Aston Villa. A handsome 5-2 win followed over New Brighton, with Tucker Mordue grabbing a brace, to take his total for the season to eight. In the next game, the Club were on the receiving end of a 7-4 drubbing at Rochdale, when former reserve and bus driver Billy Richardson scored his first of the season.

During December, Jack Mordue and Bobby Mason were summoned before the board on a charge of gross misconduct – the exact nature not known.

Mordue was interrogated at length and was warned that if he broke Club discipline he would be instantly dismissed. Mason failed to appear and was given 14 days notice, handed a free transfer and moved to West Stanley to play alongside his brother Thomas. He appealed to the FA but his case was rejected by an appeals commission and was officially dismissed in February 1929.

The Club struggled for form but the reserves were performing well in the NEL and on March 20 they played Murton in a replay of the Sunderland Shipowner's Cup semi-final. With the score at 1-1 in the closing minutes, Pools reserve keeper Smith, who once had a spell at

Arsenal, was beaten by the Murton forward. The referee awarded a free-kick for hand ball but the large crowd thought that he had signalled for a goal and poured on to the pitch.

When they realised that the referee had ruled the goal out, they started barracking the official who rushed to the pavilion for safety. After the game a crowd of around 200 demonstrated outside the ground, before being dispersed. Murton did, however, win the replay three weeks later.

The Club finished second bottom of the league, three points ahead of Ashington, despite the best efforts of Billy Richardson who scored a fantastic 19 goals in 23 games. Tucker Mordue also weighed in with 12 goals.

Ten players were freed at the end of the term, including Tommy Carr, Billy Spry and keeper Joe Hickman, who later moved to Scarborough, but returned to the area and spent many years associated with Horden. New contracts were signed by the remainder of the squad including the three Mordues, Billy Richardson, Tom Mackey and winger Bobby Dixon, but none were going to be paid a summer wage yet again.

Hospital Charity Match At The Vic

AT the end of the season, a grand charity match was held at the Vic on 6th May 1929 to raise funds for the Hartlepools Hospital.

Former West Hartlepool and Newcastle player Bob Pailor and his brother Tom, a future board member and mayor, arranged the game between sides, selected by Jackie Carr of Middlesbrough and Hughie Gallacher of Newcastle. They comprised some of the area's finest players including the two 'managers' with the rest of the teams consisting of Middlesbrough, Newcastle and Sunderland players. The game ended 1-1 with Gallacher netting for his team, and Sunderland hotshot Dave Halliday on target for Jack Carr's side.

In May 1929, Pools signed Spennymoor player William Race and former England International and one of football's original hard men, Frank Barson. Although aged 38, it was expected that the former blacksmith could do a good job for Pools in the role of player coach. Barson, who had previously played for Manchester United and Aston Villa, moved after spending all but one month of the previous season suspended for violent behaviour while playing for Watford. He was to be paid £8 per week when he played and £2 less when not in the first XI – around double what other squad members were earning.

Early in June the plea was heard and they

were re-elected gaining the most votes of the nine clubs in contention. Bottom side Ashington were voted out at the expense of York City.

Just over a week later Pools found themselves following their recent tradition of being a selling Club, when top scorer Billy Richardson was sold to West Brom for a fee of £1,250.

He was to carry on working in West Hartlepool as an inspector on the buses until he had to report to Albion for pre-season training. Pools weren't keen on selling and thought him to be a tad undervalued, but with the situation so bad that the manager had agreed to take a £100 a year pay cut under mounting pressure from the Club's bankers, the move went through.

Richardson went on to become a legend at the Hawthorns. After knocking in over 50 goals for the reserves in his first season, he scored twice in the 1931 FA Cup final, which is still known as the 'Richardson Final'. He won only one England cap, a surprise given his goalscoring record of 451 goals in 550 games. He died while playing in a charity match aged 50.

Players arriving during the summer included Ralph Pedwell, Albert Pape and Jackie Stephenson. Pedwell joined from amateur side Durham West End after scoring 58 goals the previous season, while 31-year-old Pape was a former Manchester United and Fulham forward. Stephenson had previously played almost 150 first games for Durham City and Norwich.

As well as signing these experienced men several local players were recruited including Joe Buller, a miner from Spennymoor United and the sturdy Steve Bowron from Ferryhill Athletic.

End Of Year Report Makes Dismal Reading

THE annual report showed a disturbing loss of over £500.

Contributing to the deficit was the very poor season on the pitch resulting in an average attendance reduction of 200. The Club had also spent a good deal of money on ground repairs.

At the AGM in July it was announced that the manager Bill Norman had good relationships with many first and second division clubs and it was his experience that ensured the likes of a new trainer being signed.

It was revealed to all at the meeting that the manager had an unusual condition in his contract. When Pools sold a player that he had signed, they had to pay him five per cent

commission on any transfer fee received. When the deal was agreed, the board didn't expect to be receiving the high transfer fees that were coming in.

Some shareholders believed they may turn into even more of a selling Club with this clause in mind and many believed that if Richardson had stayed he may have turned into a £2,500 player. Norman was also on a weekly salary of £8 which was £3 and 10 shillings more than the previous post holder.

It seemed that the board thought that some players were not fit, with some of them overweight and a lot of hard work was needed to get them shipshape for the season.

Barson, who was trying to get fit after a season out of the game, along with a few other players 'cajoled' by him, reported for training early to shake off any excess.

The Club believed they had a squad capable of promotion and were also licking the ground into shape, carrying out much-needed repairs to the main stand, patching up the roof to halt water leaks and altering the main entrance. The away team dressing room had a new bath fitted and the home dressing area was repainted.

1929-30

PRE-SEASON promise didn't last long as Pools were hammered 5-2 by Darlington on the opening day, with Pape netting a brace on his debut.

Despite five goals from Pape in his first three games, Pools failed to register a win until the eighth game of the season, when two more goals from the in-form striker proved enough to send Tranmere away from the Vic pointless.

Barson had only played in the first four games and didn't figure again until October 19 when he scored in a 2-1 reverse at home to Nelson. He was admitted to hospital four days later with appendicitis and spent four weeks in hospital.

Pape set a Club record at the time, scoring in each of the next five league games, setting the side up for their FA Cup tie at Midland League Scunthorpe & Lindsay United. However, Pools were dumped out by a solitary goal, ending interest in all first team cups, as they had lost to Darlington earlier in the month in the DSPC.

Wheeling And Dealing Continues

EARLY in December it seemed Pools were to move into the transfer market. After rejecting an offer from Bolton Wanderers for Tom Mackey, Pools offered Ed Bell to

Middlesbrough for £1,000, but they failed to show much interest.

A 5-2 reverse at Crewe four days before Christmas left Pools firmly entrenched in the lower half of the table and it also saw the departure of Mackey and Bell. They both moved to Sheffield Wednesday for a fee of £2,750, with a further £250 if the players stayed at Hillsborough for more than one season – which they did – which bailed the Club out of their financial mess, representing great business.

Mackey had only established himself as a regular halfway through the previous season and Bell had played just five first team games. Bell never played for Wednesday in the 30 months he spent there and played little first team football at his other clubs. Mackey fared little better and after four games at Hillsborough he moved to Luton where he stayed for six seasons.

Pools received some festive cheer, beating South Shields 2-1 on Christmas Day and turning them over 5-3 the following day with Pape notching another brace, taking his total to 15.

With Barson returning to training and a replacement for Mackey signed in the shape of Tow Law captain Percy Thornton, 28, it was hoped there would be a turnaround in fortunes after they lost only once at the end of January, climbing to seventh.

Despite the special clause in Bill Norman's contract, the Club re-engaged him on a new five-year deal, at £400 per annum.

Barson returned for the reserves on February 15, but figured in just four more first team games during the season and announced his intention to leave towards the end of April, when he advertised his services in the Athletic News.

Good Form To End The Season

POOLS hit a consistent run of form, but still left space to lose 7-1 at Tranmere and 8-2 at Rochdale (3-0 down after five minutes) before the season was out.

Eighth place was a decent end after such a poor start and the top scorer was Pape, with 21 to his credit, ably assisted by nippy winger Ralph Pedwell.

The reserves again earned silverware, winning the Orphanage Cup, with Danny Dobell and Billy Mordue scoring twice each in a 4-0 victory over Chilton. They also had their best season to date in the NEL, finishing sixth.

Free transfers were handed to Dobell, Barson, Pape, Stephenson, Billy Mordue and

Jock Miller. Barson later approached the Club in August to see if they would sign him back but the offer was declined and he moved to Wigan Borough.

Albert Pape

Once again the annual summer dip into the transfer market began, to add to players whose services had been retained.

In May, left half Jimmie Dickenson joined from Wearside League champions Hetton United, along with Wolves reserve forward Percy Robson and West Hartlepool-born half back and part-time boxer Billy Thayne, who returned to his hometown after a season in the reserves at Crystal Palace.

Pools also signed Harry Simmons, 21, a prolific scorer with Bankhead Albion and Pallion FC. He had already been on trial with Sunderland and West Ham United. A new assistant trainer was appointed in the guise of Nicholas Evans.

Pools Settling In To Football League Life

AT the Club's AGM it was announced they had recorded a profit in excess of £1,850. A lot was due to a vast rise in gate receipts, with an average attendance of just short of the 4,700 mark, the highest since entry into the league.

After a few years of struggle it was believed Pools were starting to settle in the Football League and the time was right to adopt a policy of signing the best local players in the area. There were 26 players on the books, only one over 25-years-old, Percy Thornton.

Despite the positive outlook it was announced during the pre-season practice games that there would be no season tickets this year due to the fact that only 58 were sold the season before.

Evenwood Town forward Joss Hewitt was added to the books. The teenager had previously had a trial with Everton and made an instant impression at the Vic when he scored twice in the first practice match.

Chapter 5

1930 – 1938

1930-31

A youthful team took to the pitch on August 30 for their opener at Halifax. Thornton bagged the only goal in a 3-1 defeat and he scored twice the following week when Pools beat New Brighton 4-1. Other goals were scored by ex-Whitby forward Jimmy Thompson and Percy Robson.

With one win in five by mid-September, yet another former international joined, Scotsman Billy Cowan, who had played for Newcastle, Manchester City and St Mirren. He was on trial and wanted to move near his parents who lived in Billingham. A former FA Cup winner who had commanded some high transfer fees in the past, a lot was expected of the 34-year-old.

He scored on his debut against Gateshead in a 3-2 home loss on September 20 and again two weeks later in a 3-1 defeat at the Vic to Hull City, which became the last of the three games that he played in for Pools, with the team bottom of the table.

He left to go to Darlington on trial and after a handful of outings there, despite wanting to stay in the area, he moved to Bath City.

Poor Start To The Campaign

DESPITE the sorry form, Pools put five past Darlington in the semis of the DSPC and managed wins over Accrington and Barrow towards the end of October.

Earlier in the month secretary Robert Nicholson passed away. He had been in the role since March 1921 and was replaced by local accountant Frank Perryman.

Billy Cowan

On November 5, the final of the DSPC took place against Gateshead at Roker Park, Sunderland. In front of a meagre 2,000 fans, Jackie Mordue put Pools in the lead, but they conceded two in the second half.

Poor form continued and the defence leaked five goals in consecutive games, despite scoring seven goals in the two matches. Defeats of 4-5 at Tranmere and 3-5 at home to Carlisle preceded an FA Cup exit at the first time of asking once more, losing by the odd goal in five at home to Stockport.

Financial troubles were again lingering and manager Bill Norman took a pay cut to help the Club out, this time of £3 per week, with the Club paying him the shortfall as and when they were able.

New keeper Arnold Swift was signed from South Durham Steel & Ironworks early in December and despite making his debut in a 4-2 win over Rotherham, in which local boy Horace Waller scored a hat-trick, he lost his place the following game to Jimmy Rivers and spent the rest of the season battling for the reserve jersey with Jack Bruce.

Swift returned for a brief two-game spell in February, resulting in a broken collar bone in the second of these two games at Barrow.

Hartlepool v Darlington, 1930

Bruce was an amateur keeper who Pools signed from Station Town and he never played a first team game, but later figured for Clapton Orient.

Brief Upturn In Fortunes At Christmas

SUDDENLY in December the team clicked and went unbeaten for five games, winning four. Two 4-0 wins were recorded and Harry Simmons scored seven goals over the period, including a record five in the 6-1 New Year's Day victory over Wigan Borough at the Vic.

Pools moved up to 11th in the table, but they weren't to stay there for long as they went on a run of eight winless games and found themselves one off bottom.

Finances were increasingly worse and by January 1931 they had already lost over £1,100 that season alone. Stockport County were casting an eye over Simmons and Jack Mordue and Pools, who believed the players were jointly worth £3,000, agreed to accept £1,250. They didn't want to part with either, but money talked. Stockport baulked at the valuation and failed to follow up their initial contact.

Towards the end of January the Club's first signed professional, Fred Mearns, died as a result of an accident, aged 52.

After leaving Pools in the summer of 1909, Mearns joined Barnsley where he won a winners medal in the 1911 FA Cup final. He later played for Leicester Fosse before returning

Hartlepool v Rotherham, 1930

Hartlepool attack through Joss Hewitt

to the area playing for several local clubs as he worked as a joiner.

The dire form continued and if it wasn't for the goals of Simmons and Ralph Pedwell then it would have been much worse. The fans stayed away and the game at home to Crewe on March 7, 1931 attracted a reported crowd of only 853, the lowest at the Vic in a Football League game and a total that was to stay for 42 years.

The reserves knocked nine past Hetton United in the semi-final of the SSOC. The following month though they were hammered 7-0 at Jarrow in a game which ended early after four players collapsed.

The referee ordered the match to be stopped for ten minutes while the players regained their composure, but when the official approached them in the dressing room to resume they refused to come out of the bath and the result was later made to stand, with no charges levied.

Financial Problems Continue To Bite, Especially During The Great Depression

THE chairman was called before the bank manager in the middle of April as the dire financial situation escalated.

After the result of a lengthy interview the manager of the bank decided that the directors' guarantees would not be called in to alleviate the burden as seemed to be requested by his head office. The Club was only

Cliff Ferguson

allowed to continue for the following season as long as they did not pay any summer wages.

The reserves were beaten by Middlesbrough's second string in the final of the SSOC by three clear goals on April 27, but won the final of the

Joe Buller

National Orphanage Cup when they beat Ferryhill 5-1, with former Durham City reserve Cliff Ferguson adding a brace to his tally for the season. Despite having a good season, Ferguson played just the once for the first XI and was one of many players freed at the end of the season. He joined Crook and later had a spell at Tottenham, before joining their Nursery side Northfleet and returning to Crook once more before appearing for Blackhall CW and Horden CW.

The first team's pathetic season ended the day after the final with a 2-0 reverse at Southport. After reaching the heights of 11th after the turn of the New Year, they won just three out of the last 20 games, finishing third bottom.

Top scorer was Harry Simmons who netted 17 goals after signing a quarter of the way through the season. Without his goals and the 11 of Ralph Pedwell, together with the tireless performances of the over-worked full backs Steve Bowron and Joe Buller and centre half Billy Thayne, the Club would have suffered the fate suffered by the bottom team, Nelson, who failed to gain re-election and were replaced by Chester.

Billy Thayne

Departures Ease Financial Struggles

MANAGER Norman had been struggling with illness for some time, so the board drafted the retained list and released keeper Jack Bruce, long-serving defender Albert Errington (who had spent six years with the Club), reserve team players and brothers Tom and 'Tarzan' Harland along with several others including Cliff Ferguson, Tucker Mordue and three other fringe players.

The signings started as soon as the season ended with Cockfield inside right Arthur Robinson joining along with experienced half back and former Army boxing champion, Jimmy Hamilton, who left Crystal Palace after nearly 200 games. He joined them in 1924 following service in the Coldstream Guards, choosing a career in football over that of a boxer. He had bought a business in Thornaby and had chosen Pools over Darlington.

Towards the end of the following month, the Club reported their heaviest loss of almost £1,850.

Again, the main cause was a drop in attendances due to the region's economic situation, with an alarming drop of over a quarter down to an average of 3,438, with another contributing factor being the early dismissal from the FA Cup. The policy of playing youth over experience was openly criticised, but with manager Norman too ill to attend, he was not able to defend himself.

On July 17, Norman's illness was so advanced that he was no longer physically or mentally able to act and the reigns were handed over to chairman Bill Yeats until such a time when a replacement was found, or if Norman recovered.

The end of the month saw the leading scorer from the previous season, Harry Simmons, move to Preston North End for a reduced fee of £1,000. The situation was so bad that they accepted a low fee.

On the day he departed schoolteacher Johnny Wigham, who had scored 30 goals in the Tyneside League for Hebburn Argyle joined Pools ahead of other clubs further afield so that he could continue in his role as a schoolmaster.

A couple of days later Pools made the significant signature of Jackie Carr. One of the famous Carr brothers (his brother Harry played for Pools some 20 years previous) who had featured for Middlesbrough, he joined from Blackpool, after making nearly 450 appearances at Ayresome Park.

The former England international was almost 40 years old and wasn't expected to make a great contribution at that age, which is why he joined in the capacity of player/coach, in the hope his vast experience would instil some quality virtues in the squad.

More players followed. Former Greenock Morton left back Billy Allan joined on trial and West Hartlepool cricketer HE Bailey (later to become a director of the Club) arrived on amateur terms. Bob Shotton, 20, once of West Stanley, who had just been released by Leeds after failing to make the grade, also arrived.

The traditional possibles v probables pre-season game took place and impressive were reserve team player Bobby Dixon and trialist Syd Lumley. He had played midweek football in Sunderland for his employers the Sunderland District Omnibus Company, for whom he scored 50 goals the previous season. A couple of goals from Lumley saw him snapped up.

1931-32

WITH Allen, Carr, Hamilton and Lumley all making their debuts in the opening game of the season, the towns seemed to have renewed their interest as the crowd for the opening game against Carlisle at the Vic was 5,295, the highest home gate since the New Year's Day drubbing of Wigan Borough the previous season.

Despite two goals from Lumley, Carlisle returned home with a point. It turned out to be Billy Allan's one and only game and he returned to Scotland after being replaced by Bob Shotton for the following fixture. Jackie Carr was also sidelined after sustaining an ankle injury and looked after the team in the continued absence of manager Bill Norman.

Trounced by six clear goals at Lincoln two days later, the team was chopped and changed over the next few games and by the time

Jackie Carr

Pools won their first game of the season, five games in, 18 different players had been used, including local forwards Wigham and Joss Hewitt.

Another forward was added to the list of players in the form of 31-year-old County Durham lad Billy Brown. He returned to his native county after playing for West Ham, Chelsea, Fulham and Stockport. The former England cap had also been on the losing side in the very first Wembley FA Cup final in 1923 and had joined initially on trial, signing for the season after this four-week period was up.

Manager Passes Away

A Lumley hat-trick secured the first win at Chester on September 16, the day the death of manager Mr Norman was announced.

The former member of the Border Regiment passed away after a long illness and left behind a widow and three sons. He was buried in the town and his coffin was proudly borne by players Jimmy Thompson, Arthur Mason, Percy Thornton, Steve Bowron, Joe Buller, Billy Thayne and reserve team player Arthur Mason.

Jackie Carr was appointed acting manager, in place of the chairman, as well as player/coach on September 24, 1931.

Struggling for form, a further blow was dealt with an injury to Lumley, who despite the poor start to the season had managed seven goals in nine games. Four different players were tried in the No 9 shirt in his six-game absence with little success. Knocked out of the DSPC during his absence and out of the FA Cup shortly after his return, the Club was robbed of any vital additional finance that a cup run would have yielded.

Pools Go On The Attack

WITH Lumley back in the fold, and Hewitt and Wigham alongside him in the inside positions, Jackie Mordue and Ralph Pedwell were running the wings as the goals flowed at the turn of the year.

One of the front five was guaranteed to score as the team pulled away from the lower reaches of the league. Lumley bagged ten in ten and Wigham eight in six during this purple patch. Then, almost as soon as it started, it was over – five defeats in a row followed, shifting 18 goals in the process, pushing themselves closer to the foot of the table. With Syd Lumley injured, another re-election battle was a possibility.

However in this season of contrasting form, Pools knocked seven past York at the Vic on

April 2, 1932 with Joss Hewitt and Bobby Dixon both getting hat-tricks, in front of a meagre 2,590 fans. Wigham got the seventh and netted two more a week later in a 2-1 win at Southport.

The following match at the Vic saw a 5-0 victory over Doncaster in Joe Buller's final game for the Club, before he signed for Stoke the Monday after the game for £500.

On April 21, Pools announced that caretaker manager Jackie Carr was to be appointed on a permanent basis and he soon made the decision to place Jackie Mordue, Jim Rivers and half back Jack Tither on the transfer list.

The Club won the final two matches of the season with Hewitt getting another hat-trick in the final game, a 4-3 win over Lincoln, with promising amateur Dick Hardy scoring the other. The run of five wins dragged Pools into 13th and the top scorer for the season with 18 goals from only 25 outings was Syd Lumley. Johnny Wigham was close behind with 13, all

Fred Burluraux

Team photo taken prior to game with Halifax in September 1932. Back row: Jackie Carr (Manager), Tommy Harland, Percy Thornton, Jimmy Hamilton, Charlie Owbridge, Steve Bowron, Billy Thayne, Frank Hewitt (Trainer). Front row: Jimmy Dixon, Dick Hardy, Joss Hewitt, Johnny Wigham, Ralph Pedwell

coming in a 12 game spell.

The reserves failed in their quest for minor trophies and finished in ninth place in the NEL for the second season running, having a goal difference of ten for the second season in a row and scoring over 100 goals for the second consecutive season, one more than the previous season with 103.

The Club started dipping their toes into the local transfer market in May, snapping up promising local players.

Former Birmingham City trialist, amateur keeper Joe Murray moved from Shotton Colliery Welfare as well as South Bank's former Middlesbrough reserve full back Fred Burluraux. At the same time Pools were trying to keep their better players and Aston Villa were kept at bay when they tried to pick up Dick Hardy, expressing their interest, but refusing to pay a fee.

They also managed to keep Grimsby away from Ralph Pedwell, as well as Thayne and Wigham, whom Bury and Wrexham were both keen on.

The Club reported only a small loss of over £22 mainly due to the large amount of transfer fees received of more than £1,160. The AGM confirmed the Club was indeed a selling Club,

annually parting with their better players just to ensure survival.

1932-33

14th In The League But Clubs Queue To Take Pools Stars

REGULAR left back Bob Shotton moved to Barnsley, where he stayed for many a year, appearing in around 400 first team games. Tom Harland returned to Pools as his replacement. Also coming back was former reserve trialist Ralph Makepeace who had been playing in Canada and more recently for Sunderland reserves. His brother Rob joined later in the season for a short trial with the reserves. Former Newcastle trialist and Portsmouth amateur forward Harry Proctor replaced the Annfield Plain-bound Billy Brown. Another forward departing was Jimmy Thompson, who, after spending the best part of the previous season in the reserves, moved to Falkirk.

Once again there was no change to the pre-season format and the only player to make an impact was Johnny Wigham, who blasted a hat-trick in the first of the two practice matches.

The season opened at Tranmere with Proctor scoring twice on his debut to help bring Pools home a point as they shared six goals. A 4-0 thumping at Halifax followed a game in which Wigham couldn't play as his travelling was restricted because he had to teach.

Leaky Defence Leads To Lean Spell

Results were predictably unpredictable and the defence was leaking goals, including another four at Walsall. A change was needed

Joss Hewitt Playing Contract from 12 August 1933

between the sticks and former keeper Jimmy Rivers made what was to be his final appearance, as he fared even worse as Stockport put six past him towards the end of September.

Regular No 1 Charlie Owbridge returned, but he didn't last long. After beating Darlington 2-1 on October 1, Pools conceded four at Doncaster and two weeks later at Accrington, seven found their way past the local keeper in his last first team game. He remained a regular for the reserves until he joined Trimdon Grange Colliery at the turn of the year.

Jack O'Donnell made his debut in the Accrington game, a player who Jackie Carr had been after for some time after knowing him from his days at Blackpool.

He played for five years in the top flight with Everton, who paid Darlington £2,700 over seven years ago. He had been placed under an indefinite suspension at Blackpool for failing to honour his contract, once going on a fishing trip to the Icelandic seas in December 1931.

Pools got the suspension lifted and agreed to pay Blackpool around £500 for his services based on an initial payment of £100 and £15 per match played. He was swiftly made captain and his job was to improve the defence.

In his first game they beat New Brighton 3-2.

After being knocked out of the DSPC at Gateshead, the first XI's next spot of cup action was in the FA Cup and they made the journey to Liverpool County Combination side Marine.

Marine qualified for the first round proper for the first time, but the game proved to be a nice break from the pressures of the league and Pools forward line remembered where the net was as they ran out 5-2 winners.

But there was immediate failure to take their form back in to the league and defeats of 6-2 at Crewe and 6-3 at Southport sandwiched the exit in the second round of the FA Cup at Walsall.

Hewitt Deal Falls Through

AGAIN, under mounting pressure from the bank, the Club were forced to sell players at any reasonable price and agreed with Stoke City that they could buy Joss Hewitt for £500. The deal was all but done, only for Stoke to pull out at the last moment.

A week before Christmas the Club had no first team cup interest, sat bottom of the league and it had been reported in the national press that the Club were almost in the process of, not for the first or last time, going under.

The Great Depression and dropping attendances didn't help, but the loyal fans

An Agreement made the _Twelfth_

day of _August_ 19 33 between _Frank Smyth Perryman_ of 6, _Scarboro' Street, West Hartlepool_ in the COUNTY OF _Durham_

the Secretary of and acting pursuant to Resolution and Authority for and on behalf of the HARTLEPOOLS UNITED FOOTBALL CLUB, of _West Hartlepool_ (hereinafter referred to as the Club)

of the one part and _John Joseph Hewitt_

of _12 South View Evenwood_

in the County of _Durham_ Professional Football Player

(hereinafter referred to as the Player) of the other part **Whereby** it is agreed as follows :—

1. The Player hereby agrees to play in an efficient manner and to the best of his ability for the Club.

2. The Player shall attend the Club's ground or any other place decided upon by the Club for the purposes of or in connection with his training as a Player pursuant to the instructions of the Secretary, Manager, or Trainer of the Club, or of such other person, or persons, as the Club may appoint. [This provision shall not apply if the Player is engaged by the Club at a weekly wage of less than One Pound, or at a wage per match.]

3. The Player shall do everything necessary to get and keep himself in the best possible condition so as to render the most efficient service to the Club, and will carry out all the training and other instructions of the Club through its representative officials.

4. The Player shall observe and be subject to all the Rules, Regulations, and Bye-laws of The Football Association. and any other Association, League, or Combination of which the Club shall be a member. And this Agreement shall be subject to any action which shall be taken by The Football Association under their Rules for the suspension or termination of the Football Season, and if any such suspension or termination shall be decided upon, the payment of wages shall likewise be suspended or terminated, as the case may be.

5. The Player shall not engage in any business or live in any place which the Directors (or Committee) of the Club may deem unsuitable.

Joss Hewitt Playing Contract from 12 August 1933

6.   If the Player shall prove palpably inefficient, or shall be guilty of serious misconduct or breach of the disciplinary Rules of the Club, the Club may, on giving 14 days' notice to the said Player, or the Club may on giving 28 days' notice to the said Player, on any reasonable grounds, terminate this Agreement and dispense with the services of the Player (without prejudice to the Club's right for transfer fees) in pursuance of the Rules of all such Associations, Leagues, and Combinations of which the Club may be a member.   Such notice or notices shall be in writing, and shall specify the reason for the same being given, and shall also set forth the rights of appeal to which the Player is entitled under the Rules of The Football Association.

The Rights of Appeal are as follows :—

Any League or other Combination of Clubs may, subject to these Rules, make such regulations between their Clubs and Players as they may deem necessary.   Where Leagues and Combinations are sanctioned direct by this Association an Appeals Committee shall be appointed by this Association. Where Leagues and Combinations are sanctioned by County Associations an Appeals Committee shall be appointed by the sanctioning County Associations.   Where an agreement between a Club and a Player in any League or other Combination provides for the Club terminating by notice to the Player of the Agreement between the Club and Player on any reasonable ground the following practice shall prevail: A Player shall have the right to appeal to the Management Committee of his League or Combination and a further right of appeal to the Appeals Committee of that body.   A Club on giving notice to a Player to terminate his Agreement must state in the notice the name of the League or Combination to which he may appeal, and must also at the same time give notice to the League or Combination of which the Club is a member. A copy of the notice sent to the Player must at the same time be forwarded to the Secretary of this Association. The Player shall have the right of Appeal to the League or Combination, but such appeal must be made within 7 days of the receipt of the Notice from the Club.   The Notice terminating the Agreement must inform the Player the reasons or grounds for such Notice.   If the Player proposes to appeal, he must do so within 7 days of the receipt of the Notice from the Club.   The appeal shall be heard by the Management Committee within 10 days of the receipt of the Notice from the player.   If either party is dissatisfied with the decision, there shall be a right of further appeal to the Appeals Committee of the League or Combination, but such appeal must be made within 7 days of the receipt of the intimation of the decision of the Management Committee, and must be heard by the Appeals Committee within 10 days of the receipt of the Notice of Appeal.   The League or Combination shall report to this Association when the matter is finally determined, and the Agreement and Registration shall be cancelled by this Association where necessary.   Agreements between Clubs and Players shall contain a clause showing the provision made for dealing with such disputes and for the cancelling of the Agreements and Registrations by this Association.   Clubs not belonging to any League or Combination before referred to may, upon obtaining the approval of this Association make similar regulations.   Such Regulations to provide for a right of appeal by either party to the County Association, or to this Association.

7.   This Agreement and the terms and conditions thereof shall be as to its suspension and termination subject to the Rules of The Football Association and to any action which may be taken by the Council of The Football Association or any deputed Committee, and in any proceedings by the Player against the Club it shall be a sufficient and complete defence and answer by and on the part of the Club that such suspension or termination hereof is due to the action of The Football Association, or any Sub-Committee thereof to whom the power may be delegated.

Joss Hewitt Playing Contract from 12 August 1933

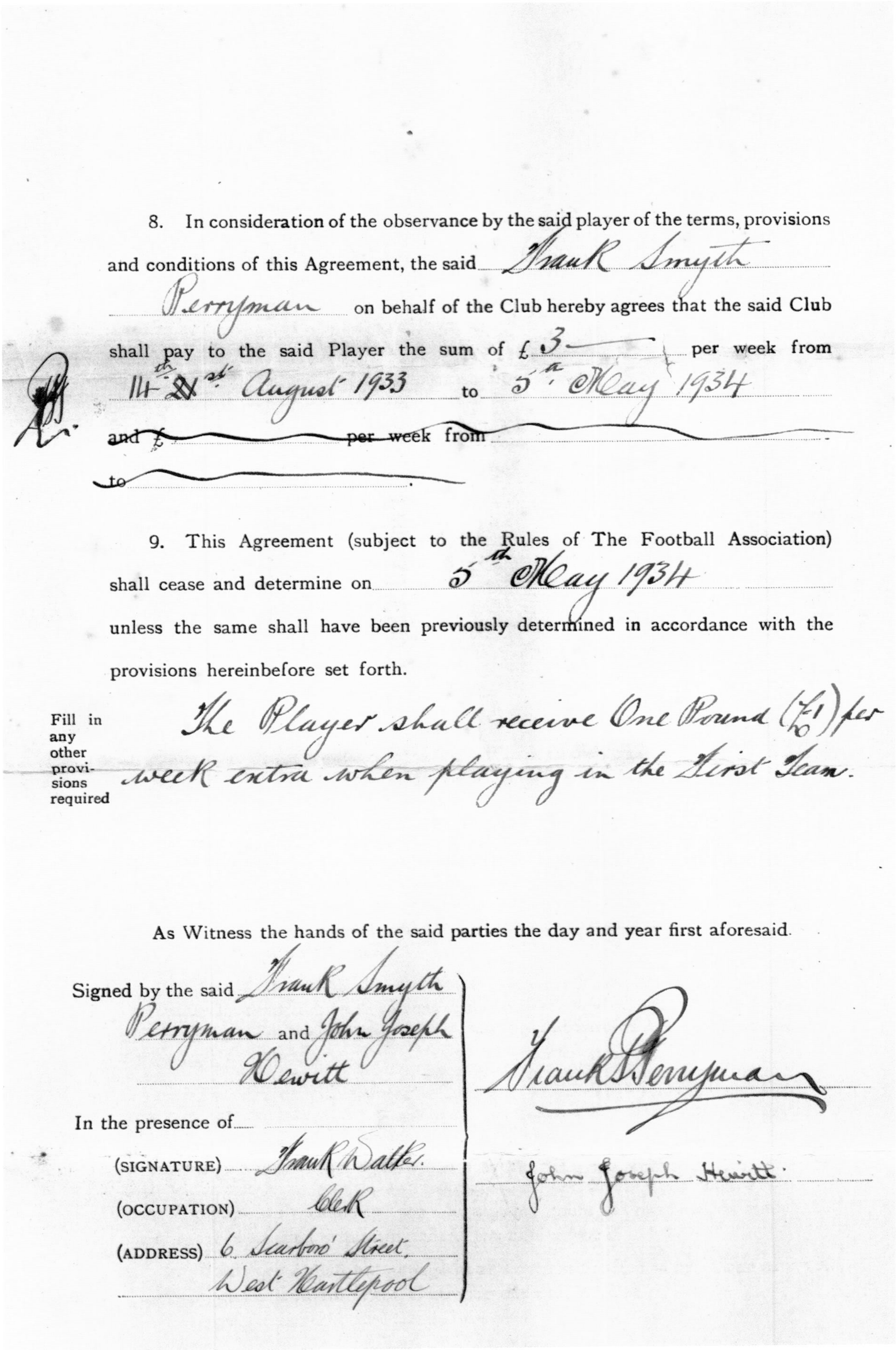

8.   In consideration of the observance by the said player of the terms, provisions and conditions of this Agreement, the said _Frank Smyth_ _Perryman_ on behalf of the Club hereby agrees that the said Club shall pay to the said Player the sum of £ _3_ per week from _14th & 21st August 1933_ to _5th May 1934_ and £ _____ per week from _____ to _____.

9.   This Agreement (subject to the Rules of The Football Association) shall cease and determine on _5th May 1934_ unless the same shall have been previously determined in accordance with the provisions hereinbefore set forth.

Fill in any other provisions required

The Player shall receive One Pound (£1) per week extra when playing in the First Team.

As Witness the hands of the said parties the day and year first aforesaid.

Signed by the said _Frank Smyth Perryman_ and _John Joseph Hewitt_

In the presence of

(SIGNATURE) _Frank Watts._

(OCCUPATION) _Clerk_

(ADDRESS) _6 Scarboro' Street, West Hartlepool_

Frank Perryman

John Joseph Hewitt.

Joss Hewitt Playing Contract from 12 August 1933

rallied round and 3,872 souls, the highest home crowd for more than two months, turned out on Christmas Eve to be delivered the perfect gift, with Pools putting Mansfield to the sword 6-3. Joss Hewitt scored twice to take his total for the season to ten, with the others coming from a brace by Bobby Dixon, Ralph Pedwell and Jonny Wigham.

Defeats Continue For Pools

BEATEN by the odd goal in five at Barnsley on Boxing Day, Pools notched six the following day against the same team at the Vic, with Joss Hewitt netting a hat-trick.

But results took a turn for the worse and Pools found themselves on the end of their heaviest defeat to date when they were humiliated at Wrexham on January 7, losing 8-1.

The game seemed to signal the end of the line for keeper Fred Wilks, but with Owbridge moving to Trimdon, Pools only had young amateur keeper Syd Tremain to fall back on and

Joss Hewitt in 1932

he was still gaining experience in the reserves.

Successive home victories handed Wilks a lifeline, but a 3-1 reverse at Gateshead saw him pull on the first team jersey for the final time, with Tremain thrown into the deep end with the Club just above the re-election zone and by no means out of danger. The youngster, who had previously played for employers Pease & Partners and worked in a nearby mine during the week, seemed to have a stabilising affect.

Results Pick Up For The Club

THE return of Makepeace, injured since early November, brought some composure to the half back line along with the signature of Reg Hill, who joined from Tranmere Rovers, after spending some time in the RAF.

With Tremain in goal and with O'Donnell and the dependable Steve Bowron in front results improved. Better service to the forwards came from Makepeace, Hill and workhorse Billy Thayne and the forward five reaped the rewards. Pedwell ended with 15 goals, as did Jonny Wigham, but top scorer was Joss Hewitt who managed 24, the best return from a Pools player for five seasons.

The Club finished a healthy 14th, although once they knew they were safe they let their foot off the pedal, beaten 6-2 at Rochdale and 7-1 at Mansfield, a game in which the unfortunate Fred Burluraux played his one and only game.

The reserves made the final of the Shipowners Cup when they beat the current holders Sunderland's second string. It was Pools second success in this tournament, the first some nine seasons before. The line up for United on May 3rd,, 1933 was Tremain, Burluraux, T Harland, Thayne, Hill, Hamilton, Hardy, Hewitt, Catton, Proctor, Dixon.

Several first team regulars played in front of 8,000 fans at the Vic with goals from Hewitt and former Eden Colliery player and reserve team forward Ed Catton.

Clubs Circle To Take Pools Stars

DESPITE a mediocre season, clubs from higher divisions were showing interest in some players. Want away Jack O'Donnell was being tracked by Leicester, Southampton and Gateshead, but all were stalling at the £500 transfer fee.

Stoke were also chasing Dick Hardy and it was only when manager Carr decided to stay that Hardy stayed. Hardy, though, could have had the pick of clubs that summer if initial enquiries were later followed up. Arsenal had enquired and Leicester had been in touch about a deal for both him and Ralph Pedwell. They were quoted £750 for the pair, but it later transpired that Leicester were encountering the same form of financial difficulties as Pools and couldn't afford them.

Pedwell was also subject to a bid from Chester City, which at £200 was rejected as somewhat derisory.

Following this, Carr snapped up Matt Johnson, a 21-year-old centre forward who spent the previous season playing reserve team football for Sheffield Wednesday. Promising keeper Syd Tremain soon moved to Preston North End, where he signed a professional contract, leaving behind his 18 brothers and sisters.

In July 1933, the Club reported a loss of in excess of £1,300 with a sizeable overdraft of £3,437 and loan indebtness of £426.

The Club again paid no summer wages and the board were resigned to struggling on despite the huge debt.

The lack of summer wages was one of the factors for Tremain leaving, as Preston offered him such payment. Despite this loss the Club still rejected a bid from Stoke City for Hewitt.

The National Provincial Bank were again putting pressure on and, in an attempt to bail the Club out again, the majority of the directors loaned the Club an additional £25 each – an essential move as the indebtness was at it's height and any further problems could have seen the Club fold.

The bank delayed any action until the New Year, when they would review the situation further and call in their loan and overdraft if needed.

1933-34

Trouble (Again) With The Bank

MORE new signings followed in August, without summer wages of course. Thomas Hird, who had played in a pre-season trial last summer, signed after impressing on the wing for West Stanley. Half back George Brown moved from Cockfield, Northampton full back Billy Fairhurst arrived along with much-travelled forward William Reilly and Darlington keeper Tom Knox.

Finally on his way was O'Donnell, who moved to Cheshire League side Wigan Athletic, after agreeing earlier to play for Tyneside side Pelaw. As he moved to a non-league club, under regulations at the time, Pools were unable to command a fee. O'Donnell continued with his

unusual behaviour and in November 1933, he went missing from Wigan and ended up playing for Irish side Dolphin FC. In May 1934, he was arrested and remanded for 'leaving his wife and children'. He finished his playing days at West Stanley alongside his brother Bill.

After the pre-amble of the warm up matches, the season got under way at Mansfield with the team made up of the bulk of last season's regulars – Bowron, Thayne, Hill, Hardy, Hewitt, Wigham and Pedwell – and four new signings, – Fairhurst, Hird, Reilly and Knox. Pedwell scored in a 1-1 draw. Home wins followed against Rochdale and York, with Jonny Wigham grabbing a goal in each game, helping Pools to their best start since 1923.

New Hard Line In Financial Battles

A sign of the predicament was highlighted in September, when the board advised the Football League that they were against the live broadcasting of any matches on the radio. The board also refused to allow reductions in price for 'crippled spectators'.

In September, despite the same club being unable to afford any money earlier in the season, Leicester were looking at Pools' talented players again and made a bid of £300 for Billy Thayne, which, irrespective of the hardship that the board were facing at the time, was rejected out of hand.

Pools lost their next game but then won four out of the next five, with a loss to Darlington in the DSPC in the middle of these results. Hewitt, Pedwell and Wigham were knocking in goals for fun and elevated the team to third place following the 3-0 home victory over Accrington on October 7.

Pedwell bagged a hat-trick in the 6-2 thrashing of Darlington at the Vic on September 23. The week before, as Pools were winning at Southport, Pedwell's mother passed away and he gave her the best tribute he could on the pitch in the rout of Darlington.

By the time of the first round of the FA Cup on November 25, Pools stood in sixth place after a 5-2 hammering at Stockport, where a Hewitt brace took him to 13

Matt Johnson

A Hartlepool Trio.

Hartlepool United's leader and left wing pair (left to right): Hewitt (centre-forward), Wigham (inside-left) and Pedwell (outside-left).—[S.D.]

Hartlepool Trio Joss Hewitt, Jonny Wigham and Ralph Pedwell

goals in 12 games.

The FA Cup saw them paired away to York City, with goals from Hewitt, Pedwell and Wigham seeing them home in a five-goal thriller. The victory, however, was the only bright point in a terrible run.

By Boxing Day, Halifax had knocked Pools out of the cup and the Stockport defeat was the first of six successive in the league, unfortunately a new record.

Other clubs continued to hover around the Vic and Leeds placed a bid of £550 for Thayne which was accepted although the deal never went through. Also under watch were Hewitt by Sheffield United, Fairhurst by Brentford (who were told to pay £650) and Pedwell by Bradford Park Avenue, who were informed he was available for £500.

A brief return to form saw three successive wins and the Club back in the top ten, but they were followed by a defeat at York by the odd goal in three on January 13, 1934 in the inaugural match in the Third Division (North) Cup. The cup was an attempt to raise

Ralph Pedwell

revenue for clubs in the lower leagues and also a forerunner of the current day Associate Members Cup, which has been known under various titles.

Once more, and under pressure from their bankers, Pools were forced to sell and keeper Tom Knox joined Notts County for a fee of £350, with five per cent of the deal going to manager Jack Carr as per the condition in his contract. Jack Johnson moved from Gateshead-based Davison Villa as a replacement and in February Jim Strong, a shot-stopper from Pegswood United, also joined.

The usual trend of either inconsistent form or poor results followed. Pools had only won two games in nine when they took to the field against Barrow at the Vic on March 17. A hat-trick from Harry Proctor helped Pools on their way to scoring seven without reply, with amateur keeper Johnson's performance doing enough to gain him a professional contract the following week.

A promising start to the season offered hope, but Pools ended the season in 11th. Making a name for themselves were Dick Hardy (12 goals), Joss Hewitt (20), Ralph Pedwell (18) and Jonny Wigham (15) – a healthy total of 65 goals between them.

Thayne, when fit, and Proctor impressed in the half back line and Thomas Hird was an ever present on the right flank.

The red shirted reserve side again qualified for the final of the SSOC but a strong team were hammered 6-1 by Sunderland's second string. Pools line up was G Strong, W Forster, T Harland, W Thayne, J Shield, R Makepeace,

T Hird, J Hewitt, L Hardy, J Moses, and M Johnson. Only two of the players never played a first team game for Pools, Forster and Shield, although the former had been a regular for the reserves, with the latter playing regularly since March. Billy Thayne scored Pools' penalty consolation.

Pools Forced To Sell Their Stars

THE close season was only five days in when Joss Hewitt and Harry Proctor were sold to Division Three (South) champions Norwich City. The bid for the pair of £950 was enough to sell, and was at least enough to beat the bid Brentford made for Hewitt alone.

Proctor had spent a couple of seasons at the Vic and, after a season up front where he was not a regular, he reverted to the half back line and made the left half back slot his own. Hewitt was a County Durham lad and had been with Pools since August 1930. He departed with a great scoring rate, netting 55 in 117 games, putting him just outside the overall top ten.

Also leaving in May was the freed Billy Thayne. The stocky imposing half back had served Pools well in four seasons and notched up over 100 outings. He joined Luton Town ahead of Leeds and Leicester, with the Hatters so keen to sign him that they obtained his signature at 4 o'clock in the morning at King's Cross station. He spent less than a season at Luton and later joined Northampton.

The following month Pools re-signed Gordon Dreyer from Hull City and allowed Steve Bowron to leave for Aldershot. He clocked up over 200 appearances, giving him the accolade of most outings for the Club since they joined the Football League.

In July replacements arrived for the departed long servants. Former Newcastle defender Os Park had spent the previous three seasons as a regular at Northampton, Bournemouth right back Jack Proctor also signed along with former Royal Artillery inside forward William Westmoreland.

The loss for the previous season was reported as just under £500 with the overdraft at the bank £3,277. Gates dropped and were averaging below 3,700 but some prudent housekeeping and transfer fees kept losses down to a minimum. The board still sought to better the ground and were determined to get a new stand to replace the temporary one built in 1919. They knew that they could not afford it, but were keen to do it as soon as possible.

It seemed that the board wanted rid of some of their long servants because of financial reasons, as Ralph Pedwell was lost to Barnsley in August for a moderate fee of only £200.

The flying winger had been at the Club for five seasons and had averaged a goal every two and a half games, a great record for a winger.

The squad line-up at the start of the 1934-35 season. Back row: Frank Hewitt (Trainer), Jackie Carr (Manager), Harrison, Jack Proctor, Jack Johnson, Billy Fairhurst, Frank Perryman, Ryder. Middle row: Tommy Hird, Bill Westmoreland, Duncan Lindsay, Johnny Wigham, Albert Bonass, Ossie Park. Front row: Jack Graham, Ernie Warren

He was renowned as a great header of the ball, so much so he was known as 'Headwell'.

Once again the Club were given a warning by the bank regarding spending and the drawing of cheques as they were already over their overdraft limit.

1934-35

Carr's Four-Season Spell As Manager Over

IN August 1934, two additional forward minded players joined – former York winger Albert Bonass and ex-Newcastle United striker Duncan Lindsay. The latter, aged 28, had been a prolific striker in Scottish football with Cowdenbeath (82 goals in 126 games for the Blue Brazil).

In pre-season, Lindsay netted a hat-trick in the first friendly game, with Bonass netting in both games played. The pair were offered contracts to the end of the season and it came as little surprise when they netted in an opening day victory at Walsall by the odd goal in three. The squad was greatly altered, with only Billy Fairhurst, Tommy Hird and Jonny Wigham in the opening day line from the team that played in the final game of the last season.

Only four games into the season and the squad needed changing due to an injury to left back Bill Fairhurst, with local teenager Jack Howe making his debut.

Howe, 18, born in West Hartlepool, first played for the reserves in February the previous season and signed for Pools as an amateur after previously playing for Expansion in the Hartlepool and District League aged just 15. He was on the books of Wingate United when Pools signed him on amateur terms in December 1933. Dick Hardy returned to the fray, with ex-Shelbourne player Jack Graham confined to the reserves.

Duncan Lindsay

Howe's first three outings were certainly not his finest as he suffered three defeats. He appeared on a winning side in the 2-1 victory over Darlington in the DSPC tie on September 19, but was dropped for the returning Fairhurst. Preston North End were keen on Howe and offered £350 and former Northern Ireland forward Dick Rowley, although no deal took place.

Efforts Made On Victoria Ground

IMPROVEMENTS commenced on the ground in September 1934, with work starting on a covered stand on the Mill House side. On the pitch though, it was once more an uneventful season, and Pools were three off the bottom of the league on the morning of November 10, before they put bottom side Carlisle to the sword, beating them by 5-2 at the Vic in front of less than 1,600 paying spectators.

Two weeks later and Pools drew 1-1 at Halifax in the first round of the FA Cup, winning the replay four days later 2-1 with Lindsay scoring and Bonass adding to the goal he got in the first tie.

December 8 saw them drawn against Coventry in the second round. Boosted by an impressive away support, a total of 13,054 fans turned out to see Pools routed 4-0. It was some comfort that, despite the defeat, the highest recorded attendance to date would greatly aid their financial plight.

Two of Norwich City's new players—(left) Hewitt, centre-forward, and Proctor, half-back—both from Hartlepools United. Their play impressed the crowd at yesterday's trial.

Norwich's new signings: Joss Hewitt and Harry Proctor

The team had a few regulars in the shape of Bonass, Lindsay, Hardy, Hird and Reg Hill. The latter was a former RAF man and carpenter who had been with the Club since January 1933 and was dependable.

Pools Look For Some Stability

BY the end of January 1935, several players had been tried – without success – to bring some stability to the team. County Durham wing man Fred Coulthard, ex Gateshead half back Billy Cleugh, former Northampton half back Ernie Warren and Billy Westmoreland had all been tried with varying success. The only bit part player who should have been playing but wasn't was Howe. He impressed in both the reserves and first XI, so much so that after only 11 first team games, several clubs were watching his progress. Stoke, Aston Villa, Blackburn, Wolves, Arsenal, Middlesbrough, Huddersfield and Derby all had monitored him on more than one occasion.

While Howe was gaining a reputation, Pools couldn't attract players of repute to the Club anymore. Once able to offer decent wages to ageing stars, when the Club tried to tempt 36-year-old ex-Middlesbrough striker and former England International Billy Pease he refused and took up the offer of running a pub in Middlesbrough.

In 17th place at the end of January, Pools were constantly looking over their shoulder and a reprieve came in the form of a 4-2 home victory over Accrington Stanley, when shining light Lindsay again notched taking his tally to 16. Bonass grabbed a brace to take his total to 11, with the fourth from young town lad Jackie Moses, who although only 18 was in his second spell with the Club previously being an amateur and leaving to play for Sunderland's reserves and Trimdon Grange.

A couple of weeks later, Pools reached the third round of the Third Division (North) Cup, with a 4-0 victory over York. Lindsay scored one, with a pair coming from Jonny Wigham.

Although one of the first on the team sheet, when his teaching allowed, he was having a subdued season compared to his previous three. Also on target was Duncan Colquhoun, in his one and only appearance. Colquhoun, a cousin of Duncan Lindsay, was a journeyman both sides of the border, but he was most noted for his work with Wigan Athletic, when he held every post thinkable from manager to physio to scout. He was associated with them for almost 70 years and passed away shortly after they reached the Premiership for the first time.

Triumph over York immediately followed a league victory over the same opposition, the start of five games in a row in which Lindsay scored. The sequence dragged the Club up to 13th, their highest placing since September. A Bonass hat-trick helped them to a 5-2 victory over Barrow on March 16, but they also suffered a 6-2 reverse at Stockport in the third round of the northern section cup and ran out 6-1 winners over Tranmere in early April.

Board Decide To Make A Change

VICTORIES, however, were not enough and just two days later, on April 15, a board meeting was held when it was announced that the board would not be retaining the services of Jack Carr. The decision was purely a financial one and a cheaper replacement was to be sought.

Carr's four season spell with the Club was over and although they never performed any miracles on the pitch, under his tenure they stabilised to become a mid-table team. Carr had a year in charge of Tranmere and four at Darlington, later working for Head Wrightson's foundry, passing away suddenly at his Redcar home in May 1942.

On May 1, Pools lost 5-1 to Sunderland A in the final of the DSPC, played at Roker Park. The team that played were all first teamers and

Jack Howe

		P	HW	HD	HL	HF	HA	AW	AD	AL	AF	AA	POINTS
1	Doncaster Rovers	42	16	0	5	53	21	10	5	6	34	23	57
2	Halifax Town	42	17	2	2	50	24	8	3	10	26	43	55
3	Chester	42	14	4	3	62	27	6	10	5	26	43	55
4	Lincoln City	42	14	3	4	55	21	8	4	9	32	37	51
5	Darlington	42	15	5	1	50	15	6	4	11	30	44	51
6	Tranmere Rovers	42	15	4	2	53	20	5	7	9	21	35	51
7	Stockport County	42	15	2	4	57	22	7	1	13	33	50	47
8	Mansfield Town	42	16	3	2	55	25	3	6	12	20	37	47
9	Rotherham United	42	14	4	3	56	21	5	3	13	30	52	45
10	Chesterfield	42	13	4	4	46	21	4	6	11	25	31	44
11	Wrexham	42	12	5	4	47	25	4	6	11	29	44	43
12	**HARTLEPOOLS UNITED**	**42**	**12**	**4**	**5**	**52**	**34**	**5**	**3**	**13**	**28**	**44**	**41**
13	Crewe Alexandra	42	12	6	3	41	25	2	5	14	25	61	39
14	Walsall	42	11	7	3	51	18	2	3	16	30	54	36
15	York City	42	12	5	4	50	20	3	1	17	26	62	36
16	New Brighton	42	9	6	6	32	25	5	2	14	27	51	36
17	Barrow	42	11	5	5	37	31	2	4	15	21	56	35
18	Accrington Stanley	42	11	5	5	44	36	1	5	15	19	53	34
19	Gateshead	42	12	4	5	36	28	1	4	16	22	68	34
20	Rochdale	42	9	5	7	39	35	2	6	13	14	36	33
21	Southport	42	6	6	9	27	36	4	6	11	28	49	32
22	Carlisle United	42	7	6	8	34	36	1	1	19	17	66	23

Football League Division Three (North) 1934 – 35

wearing Pools colours were J Murray, J Proctor, R Fairhurst, G Dreyer, O Park, R Hill, T Hird, J Wigham, A Huggins, L Hardy and A Bonass, with Albert Huggins netting the goal.

The final game at Rotherham three days later saw a Wigham goal give them the win to elevate them to 13th place.

At the end of the season, with a managerless side, the board released several prominent players. including Duncan Lindsay, Os Park, Billy Fairhurst, Jack Johnson and Ernie Warren. Fringe players Billy Cleugh, Frank Coulthard and Jack Graham were also shown the door.

Lindsay was already rumoured to have a move lined up to Wrexham but he went to Barrow and later played for York City. Keeper Johnson moved to Chesterfield, but failed to appear for them and a year later he returned to the area playing for Blyth and West Stanley. Also on his way was Gordon Dreyer who went to Hull City for £350.

Former York forward Jimmy Hughes arrived, as well as ex-City of Durham winger Frank Pickard and former Darlington and Clapton Orient full back Billy Allison.

Allison was an experienced player who was rejoining the Football League ranks after a couple of seasons with NEL side Eden Colliery. Os Park later rejoined, as well as former player Jimmy Hamilton who was appointed manager.

He had been playing for Durham and Gateshead while running his business in nearby Thornaby since leaving Pools in May 1933. He made his first signing just a couple of days later, former Newcastle United left half Aubrey Heward.

The Club announced a loss of £571 5s 6d with the overall debt rising to in excess of £7,100. Despite the bumper crowd at the Coventry cup game, gate receipts were down by almost £1,000.

More bad news arrived shortly after when speedy winger and ever present for the past two seasons Tommy Hird moved to Portsmouth with £550 changing hands. He was replaced by Stan Thompson, a diminutive winger from County Durham, who had spent the last six seasons with Brighton.

Thompson made a good impression in the pre-season games scoring a couple of goals. Also finding the net, and hopefully some form, was Jonny Wigham who knocked in a hat-trick.

1935/36

15,000 At The Vic And A Good Cup Run

ON the first day of the season – August 31, 1935 – Pools grabbed a 1-0 victory over Halifax Town, with Thompson grabbing the goal in front of 5,615.

Jack Howe was handed a chance after some impressive displays for both the first team and reserves the previous campaign. Also new were former Luton and Birmingham keeper Jack Mittel and 24-year-old Scottish forward Alec Robertson, who had previously been on the books of Kilmarnock and Aberdeen.

Victory was followed with a home defeat to

Pools team during the 1935-36 season. Back row: Jimmy Hamilton (Manager), George Brown, Jack Proctor, Jack Mittel, Billy Allison, Reg Hill, Johnny Wigham; Front row: Stan Thompson, Dick Hardy, Os Park, Alec Robertson, Albert Bonass

Oldham by the same score four days later and they suffered a 4-2 reverse at Feethams on September 7.

Same Old Story For Pools

AGAIN results were unpredictable, with Pools knocked out of the Northern Section Cup at the first hurdle at Carlisle. They didn't find any form until they trounced Walsall by five clear goals on September 28, when a Wigham brace complemented goals from Robertson, Thompson and Hughes.

Form was struggling to bring the fans in and 4,422 watched the Walsall win, which left the Club in 14th place. Home form picked up and by the end of November, after six home wins and a draw from eight games and some good performances from Bonass and Wigham, Pools were up to 11th.

On the last day of the November they won by the odd goal in five at Mansfield in the first round of the FA Cup. Drawn away to Halifax in the next round, a Robertson goal earned a replay and a goalless draw was endured by 7,713 expectant fans.

The long running financial problems were brought to light again when the bank contacted Pools to remind them of their £3,000 overdraft limit, stressing the implications if this service was abused.

Cup Run Lifts Spirits At The Vic

THE second replay was played at a neutral venue, so two days before Christmas 1935, Pools took to the field at St James' Park, where they ran out 4-1 winners, with Wigham getting a hat-trick in a game that went to extra time. Pools' reward was a home tie with Grimsby Town.

Pools were soon up against Halifax Town again and came out 1-0 victors at The Shay, with a goal from former York forward Jimmy Graham, who had joined in October.

Due to the protracted cup run, Pools had a sequence of six out of eight league games at the Vic, staying undefeated, winning four. The last game in this run saw them beat Darlington 2-1, pushing them to fifth. Wigham nabbed a brace, his fifth double strike of the season to go with his cup hat trick, taking him to 14 goals to date.

The game against Grimsby was the biggest ever seen at the Vic. The opposition finished fifth in the First Division in 1934-35 after winning the Division Two title the season before. The players undertook extra training involving weight lifting, running and even boxing. As well as getting the players into shape, the ground also underwent some changes, with the unemployed carrying out improvements to the terracing and installing new barriers.

The work was damaged to some extent on

the Thursday before the game when the two parishes were hit by a terrible storm, which damaged the roofs of the stands resulting in some additional temporary repairs being swiftly made.

Record Crowd Attracted For Grimsby Town Cup Tie

A record crowd of 15,064 turned out for an exciting goalless draw.

Pools suffered in the first half when keeper Mittel was injured and his place in goal had to be taken by Dick Hardy. Pools, roared on by vociferous support, showed no sign of conceding and more than held their own.

In the replay three days later in Cleethorpes, Pools were hammered 4-1, the consolation coming from Bonass. It might have been a disappointing result, but Grimsby included the likes of future England keeper George Tweedy and some of their longest serving players at a time when they played some of the best football in their history.

They also featured former Pools amateur and reserve team player John Hodgson, who spent time in the North-East in the first half of the 1931-32 season. He lasted 16 years at Grimsby. Grimsby progressed to the semi-final, losing to eventual winners Arsenal.

Exhausted by their cup efforts, Pools failed to register a win in the next six games, including a horrendous six-goal defeat at Walsall. They even managed to draw in a meagre 1,820 fans for the first home game after the Grimsby tie, against Tranmere on a Wednesday towards the end of January. After dropping to tenth, they finally regained winning ways at the Vic, with Alec Robertson and Johnny Wigham getting on the scoresheet against Accrington Stanley.

They then lost their first game in 16 at home, when Chester secured a 2-0 victory.

Once again mediocrity emerged and the only results of any note in the remaining 11 games were a 5-1 home defeat of Rotherham and a victory over already-crowned champions Chesterfield on April 18, by the odd goal in three, with Walter Nobbs and Jimmy Graham on the scoresheet.

In the midst of this spell, Pools lost one of their most exciting prospects.

The underplayed Jack Howe left in March

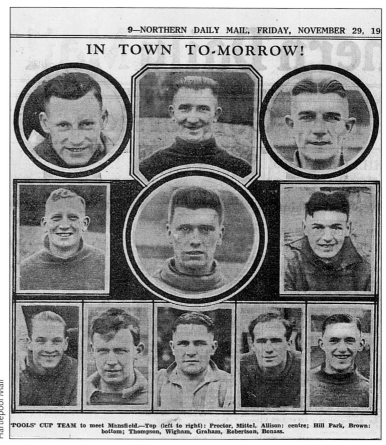

Hartlepool Mail

IN TOWN TO-MORROW!

9—NORTHERN DAILY MAIL, FRIDAY, NOVEMBER 29, 19

'POOLS' CUP TEAM to meet Mansfield.—Top (left to right): Proctor, Mittel, Allison: centre; Hill Park, Brown: bottom; Thompson, Wigham, Graham, Robertson, Bonass.

Pools team to play Mansfield in November 1935

and signed for Derby County. He had played in only eight league games that season and only 16 in season 1934-35. His transfer fee was £750 plus the proceeds of a friendly match to be played at the Vic at the end of the season. If the proceeds were under £250, Derby agreed to make the amount up to a total of £1,000.

Howe went on to become the first and only player born in West Hartlepool to represent England at full level, gaining three caps during 1948 and 1949.

He appeared in around 250 games for the Rams in a career blighted by the war, during which he donned the colours and served many years in India and Burma. He returned to the town as a wartime guest and settled in Hartlepool after his involvement with football was over, passing away in 1987. His grandson, Steve Fletcher, later played for Pools, starting out as a trainee in the late 1980s, before moving to Bournemouth in 1991 where he became a firm favourite in more than a decade of service.

Pools finished in eighth place and, as previously mentioned, performed well in the FA Cup.

They also reached the final of the DSPC again, when they lost at Sunderland 4-1 on April Fool's Day. Pools fielded a team of Mittel,

'Pools Personalities

SAM ENGLISH
(Centre-forward)

Height, 5ft. 8ins.; weight, 11st. 9lbs.

HARTLEPOOLS showed commendable enterprise in signing English during the close season, and if the Irish international justifies his reputation. 'Pools long-standing centre-forward problem should be satisfactorily solved. Besides playing for his country, English has had six years' experience of Scottish and English First League football. He has the reputation of being a first-class footballer as well as an expert marksman.

English by name, Irish by birth, and almost Scottish by adoption, he is an international in more senses than one. A native of Coleraine, English did not reside in the Emerald Isle for long, for at the age of two he moved with his family to Dalmuir, Scotland. As a youth working in the shipyards, he played for junior clubs in Old Kilpatrick and Port Glasgow before joining Yoker Athletic in the Scottish Junior League. After winning a junior cup medal with Yoker, his big chance came in 1930 when he was transferred to Glasgow Rangers. In two and a half seasons with Rangers, English built up a big reputation, won Scottish League and Cup medals and was capped for Ireland against Scotland and Wales, both in 1932-3. In 1933 he was transferred to Liverpool at a fee of £6,000 and for the most part of two seasons at Anfield was a regular member of the League eleven. Injured in a League match at Blackburn towards the end of the 1934-5 season, English was transferred during the following close season to Queen of the South for whom he made 30 Scottish League appearances last term.

Fond of golf and also a keen swimmer. Brother Richard, a full previously with Morton, while another brother, David was formerly well-known as a crack cyclist.

and in the past two seasons he has saved 'Pools almost as many goals as the goalkeepers!

Of the forwards we can say little, except that the new men come with good credentials. The cry all last season was that if 'Pools had a scoring centre-forward Wigham and Robertson would have helped him to goals in every game.

Well, Sam English is an international who has been scoring goals for a number of years. If he continues the good work with 'Pools one of the major problems will be solved.

The new wingers, Scott and Self, are also experienced players, who are expected to fit in with the inside men satisfactorily. By this time next week we will probably be able to say more definitely whether these expectations are likely to be realized.

'Pools Personalities

JOHN SCOTT
(outside right).

Height 5ft. 7ins. Weight 10st. 10lbs.

WHEN Tommy Hird was transferred to Portsmouth, Pools had difficulty in finding a worthy successor. Thompson, Pickard, Moses and Huggins were all tried in the position last season, but none of them gave complete satisfaction. Now, however, Manager Hamilton believes he has found the man for the job in John Scott, a player who has had seven seasons' experience in Second League and Southern Section football.

A native of Sunderland Scott played for Seaham Harbour in the Wearside League before joining Crystal Palace in 1929. After one season in London Combination football he was transferred to Notts Forest, where he was a regular member of the League side for two seasons. Subsequently, he moved to Exeter City and stayed there for four seasons, averaging a dozen League goals each term.

In his first season with the Forest, Scott helped the Second Leaguers to reach the sixth round of the F.A. Cup. The Forest actually went into the hat for the semi-final, but were beaten by Sheffield Wednesday after a replay.

Scott's younger brother, Tom, is an amateur on 'Pools books, and is keen to take up a professional career.

'Pools Personalities

CHARLES MIDDLETON
(Centre-forward).

Height: 5ft. 9in.; weight, 11st. 4lbs.

MANY good judges consider that Middleton will yet make his mark in League football. Only 22 years of age, 'Pools' reserve centre-forward is fast, has bright football ideas, and knows that the goal is there to be shot at. A native of Chester-le-Street, he played as a junior for Ouston Juniors in the Gateshead & District League and then for Ouston Athletic in the Chester-le-Street Alliance. Originally an outside right, he had a trial with Grimsby Town in that position during the 1933-4 season but later decided that centre-forward was his best role.

From August, 1934, until Christmas he played for Walker Celtic in the North-Eastern League and was then transferred to Stoke City, where he was a team-mate of Joe Buller in the Central League side.

Although he scored 12 goals in five Central League games, Stoke released him at the end of the season, and after a spell with Congleton in the Cheshire League he returned to the North-East to play for West Stanley.

Several North-East clubs sought his services this term, but Middleton chose to come to 'Pools in the hope of finding greater scope. To-day he made his first appearance in the league team at Halifax.

Pools Personalities: Sam English, John Scott and Charles Middleton

Hartlepool Mail

"Aim of 'Pools' Board"

SECRETARY'S VIEWS

SPEAKING at a meeting of the local Referees' Association last night, Mr. Frank S. Perryman, secretary of Hartlepools United, referred to the possibility of 'Pools achieving promotion to the Second Division.

"In the present state of the club's finances promotion would be a catastrophe, although I know it is the ambition of the board to achieve this object," he said. "I feel sure that given four or five seasons such as the present one has been up to now we will have gone a long way to achieving promotion, even if it has not already been actually accomplished."

Other interesting points in Mr. Perryman's address were:—

"The first essential in a club manager is tact. By careful handling, a mediocre side can get results because the team spirit is inculcated and encouraged.

"I am one of the few who consider that the standard of refereeing is as good as the human element will allow, and although some referees are rather

MR. F. S. PERRYMAN

lax in their punishment of offences, the fault is rather with the system than with the officials. A referee can have an 'off' day the same as a player with the difference that the latter can probably retrieve his position with the spectators, whereas a referee's mistake is likely to 'dog' him the whole game.

"The system might be improved by a course of training and lectures during the close season when prominent referees could undertake to do this work and educate the younger officials. I would like to see a fair trial of the same referee and linesmen made over a number of matches. You cannot possibly get a perfect understanding between officials when they only meet once or twice in a season."

Football Mail from Saturday 22nd February 1936

Proctor, Allison, Hill, Park, Heward, Thompson, Hardy, Wigham, Scrimshaw and Bonass, with the consolation goal from Dick Hardy. Top scorer was 16-goal Wigham, with Albert Bonass and Stan Thompson tied behind him with 11 league goals each.

The reserves struggled and finished in 14th place out of the 20 clubs. They were knocked out of the SSOC at an early stage but qualified for the final of the Durham Benevolent Bowl, when they lost by two clear goals to Shildon.

The team that turned out on April 11 for the game played at Bishop Auckland was W Norman, J Bradford, G Murray, W Nobbs, G Brown, Pattison, J Moses, J Docherty, W Chatterton, R Owens, J Firman.

As a climax to the season, and as part of the Howe deal, the friendly with Derby County took place on April 30 and 4,500 fans witnessed a 1-1 draw, with Jimmy Graham netting in his final appearance before moving on to Southend United.

At the end of the season, Jimmy Hamilton was issued with a new contract to run for two seasons, paid at the rate of £3 per week in the summer and £5 during the season. The majority of the players offered new terms were paid £4 when in the first team and £3 when not. The Club tended not to pay summer wages and many players continued to work while at the Club, several in jobs found by the directors.

George Brown, Jimmy Graham and, somewhat surprisingly, Stan Thompson had all been granted free transfers along with several fringe members of the squad. Albert Bonass moved to Chesterfield for a satisfactory fee of £250. He later played for QPR and guested for several clubs during the Second World War. He joined the RAF in 1943 as part of the crew of a Wellington bomber as a wireless operator, but later died in a training accident in October 1945 when his Stirling bomber crashed.

1936-37

FEW players arriving were John Scott, a former Nottingham Forest and Exeter City player, soon followed by his brother Tom, who joined from Easington Colliery Welfare. Charlie Middleton was once on the books of Stoke City, but moved from his hometown club West Stanley. Another new arrival was Gordon Dryer, who returned to Pools after an unhappy spell at Hull, where he figured on just five occasions.

Pools had already lost Bonass and Howe and, after having a fairly decent season by their standards, scouts had been attracted to the ground over the course of the previous season. The main target, of course, was Wigham and

Sam English

Huddersfield approached the board towards the end of June to see if they could sign him.

Pools offered him the chance to play in the top flight with the side that had finished third in 1935-36, but he declined seeing himself as more a teacher than a footballer, not wishing to leave his teaching post in Hebburn.

Northampton were also in for Dick Hardy and Chester registered an interest in Reg Hill. Pools agreed to sell Hardy to Northampton, but the Cobblers seemed to baulk at the £350 fee demanded and Hardy stayed.

Club Linked With Move For English From Scotland

POOLS were keen to strengthen their squad and not diminish their prowess, so behind the scenes enquiries were made to see if they could tempt Irishman Sam English away from Scottish side Queen of the South.

English, 26, had previously played for Liverpool and Glasgow Rangers, but endured troubled times and his career seemed on the wane. Pools, however, hoped he would prove a fine buy at this level.

English signed for a reported fee of £1,000, but it was later discovered to be a bargain £275. He received a £10 signing on fee, was paid £5 a week and was one of the few players on the book to receive summer wages.

English ended up at Pools after a troubled time at Rangers, when in an Old Firm derby in September 1931, he collided with the Celtic keeper John Thomson, who as a result of the accidental collision suffered a depressed skull fracture and died that evening in hospital.

English was cleared of any blame but the incident lingered on his mind and he left Rangers after winning the Scottish Cup in 1932, the league title in 1933 and 64 goals in 72 outings. He went to Liverpool in August 1933 for £8,000 and, although not a regular at Anfield, scored 26 goals in 50 matches, before he returned north of the border in July 1935, joining Queen of the South for £1,700.

Pools recorded a profit this season, at last taking a touch of pressure off them from the

bank, although they were still in debt.

The Club announced a healthy profit for trading over the previous year of just under £1,150 due to an influx of transfer fees and a substantial increase in average attendances to 4,289 from 3,114. However, this increase in profit made several creditors press for payment and outstanding bills for rent, gas and water were immediately paid.

The standard amble of pre-season warm up games took place and Charlie Middleton bagged a brace in the first game and Sam English netted four in another, highlighting his obvious talent.

Campaign Begins With Optimism

THE season kicked-off at Southport with long-serving Wigham notching in a draw. English opened his account in the next game, scoring the only goal in the home victory over Accrington on September 2, in front of a healthy 7,342 fans. English was bringing the fans in, as over 8,700 packed into the Vic to see the striker on the scoresheet again in a 2-1 triumph over Tranmere.

Tuesday September 8, saw the manager make a visit to County Durham's Philadelphia Cricket Club and he signed outside left William Barron. He had played for Hetton Juniors and joined Pools after an impressive stint with Annfield Plain. Pools acted swiftly to get him snapped up on amateur terms as it was mooted that Tottenham and Charlton were monitoring his progress.

Charlie Middleton made his debut at Halifax on September 12 in a 2-0 reverse – but he was not registered with the Football League and Pools were fined one pound and ten shillings for fielding an unregistered player.

Improved results continued and, following a 2-1 victory at Accrington on September 26, an amazing 12,220 were at the Vic for the home visit of Chester – the highest attendance for a league game at the Vic. Not for the last time in the Club's history, Pools failed to perform in front of large and expectant home crowd and lost the game by a solitary goal.

After beating Darlington in the semi-final of the DSC, Pools played at Sunderland in the final on October 21 beating their reserve XI 2-0 in front of 2,500 fans.

Pools' goals came from English and former Sunderland reserve Jack Scott. Ex-Southend keeper Billy Moore was kept busy all game, but kept a clean sheet to see Pools home. The team lined up with Moore in goal, J Proctor, W Allison, R Hill, L R Hardy, W Nobbs, J Scott, S Scrimshaw, S English, A Robertson and E Self.

Charlie Middleton (left)

Moore had not even played for the first XI and his performance earned an extension to his month-long trial, signing until the end of the season.

Amateur player William Barron signed professional papers on good terms, as the side was badly in need of a decent outside left to challenge current winger Eddie Self. However, just a fortnight later and after making just a single reserve outing he was signed by Wolverhampton Wanderers for a remarkable fee of £250. He failed to play for Wolves and returned to Annfield Plain, before moving to Charlton and Northampton where he played until season 1950-51. He also continued with his cricket career and played the first class game for Lancashire and Northants.

Jimmy McCambridge

Results stuttered and, including the home defeat against Chester, Pools won only two in seven. Next up was a trip to Feethams on November 21, when an amazing game ensued as the bitter rivals shared the points and shared ten goals in a 5-5 thriller. Joe Scott, Reg Hill, Sam English, Johnny Wigham and Alec Robertson were on the scoresheet for Pools.

Just a week later, Pools shared eight goals with Rotherham in the first round of the FA Cup, winning the replay at the Vic 2-0. Dismissal from the competition at Crewe and three successive league defeats followed and by Boxing Day morning Pools were down to 13th.

Three home games followed in a row and brought victories over Southport, York and Barrow, pushing Pools back into the top ten and into eighth spot.

New Signings And Goals Galore

FOLLOWING a defeat at Tranmere on January 2, 1937 Pools dipped into the transfer market to sign Sheffield Wednesday's Jimmy McCambridge.

The 31-year-old former Irish international previously played for Everton and Cardiff and cost £50. He had a good goalscoring record and was expected to be the perfect foil for English, but with English missing from the line up on his debut against Halifax at the Vic on January 9, McCambridge happily grabbed a hat-trick in a 5-3 victory.

Hat-tricks were in the air and in the following game it was the turn of Jack Scott during the 6-1 drubbing of Gateshead. But just when things seemed to have turned the corner, the next match saw them embarrassed 8-2 at Mansfield on January 23.

McCambridge was rested following the return of English after injury but he was recalled when English missed the game at Oldham on February 20, as he failed to make the train to travel, citing domestic reasons.

Following the dropping of Gibraltar-born Reg Hill in February (he joined Darlington the following month) McCambridge moved to the half back line and results settled, as Pools went on to have one of their better seasons, losing only seven of their remaining 17 games with English, Robertson and Scott to the fore.

Finishing sixth, their best for 12 seasons, the new-look Pools impressed many. Top scorer was English, with 20, supported well by Scott (13) and Robertson (12).

The reserve team finished a disappointing 13th but reached the final of the Durham Benevolent Bowl, facing Shildon for the second successive year and reversing the 2-0 loss of last season with goals from Stan Scrimshaw and Norman West.

The line up was Moore, Bradford, Copeman, Dreyer, Harris, Nobbs, Tom Scott, Scrimshaw, Wigham, West, Owen.

A few reserve team players were released, including Jimmy Bradford, Richard Owens, as well as first teamers Mittell, Dreyer, Os Park and Walter Nobbs.

In June, reserve team forward Harry Harrison headed for Chesterfield for £50, despite never playing a first team game. He never played for the Spireites either, but did enjoy a lengthy spell with Southport.

Also on the move were Dick Hardy and Stan Scrimshaw for a combined fee of £625. Hardy had been the subject of transfer speculation and had made 168 outings in five years. Squad member Scrimshaw had barely been with the Club 18 months. Hardy's spell at Bradford was a short one and he later moved to non-league Shrewsbury, while Scrimshaw stayed with Bradford throughout the war and also guested for Pools.

Some of their transfer monies were spent, albeit just £50, on former Liverpool and Newcastle half back David Davison, an FA Cup winner in 1932, who found first team chances limited on his return to fitness after injury. Also joining were North Shields centre back Tom Reid, Ashington centre forward Norman Thompson and former Spurs keeper Allan Taylor.

Another FA Cup winner arrived in August. Ernie Curtis, a 1927 Cardiff City hero. The former Welsh International was the youngest player to appear in the cup final aged just 19, some ten years ago.

1937/38

A Poor Season But Pools Survive

THE season started with a 2-1 reverse at Lincoln. A victory and a draw against Accrington and Hull respectively saw Pools up in ninth place and they seemed to be following on from where they left off at the end of the last season. However, what followed proved disastrous. They lost their next five games, conceding 18 goals, including six at Wrexham on September 13.

Slight respite came with a home victory over Darlington on October 2 when English and Wigham netted to give Pools a 2-1 victory, but they were still rooted in bottom place and victory was soured by a knee cartilage injury to Curtis, who was not expected to be fit again until the New Year.

Worse was to follow, as following the 5-1 defeat at Port Vale, David Davidson left and moved to join Gateshead as a player/coach for their reserve side, citing personal reasons. He ran a business in Whitley Bay and couldn't commit himself to the Club. Pools then endured their worst run in the league, failing to win in 11 attempts.

Despite re-signing Os Park and blooding a new keeper in the guise of Jock Rutherford they couldn't stop the rot. Several fringe players were tried and the only success came in the FA Cup first round against Southport in November, although they were easily despatched at Tranmere in the next tie.

Bother Brewing For Misbehaving Players

TROUBLE wasn't far away off the pitch either and on Monday, December 6 after failing to score in six outings, Sam English was spotted drinking in the Crown Hotel in Stockton Street, just along from the ground. He was advised to return to his lodgings by the manager but refused and was still in the alehouse some 40 minutes later. The board of directors immediately suspended him for 14 days.

With gates fluctuating and the team firmly rooted in the bottom two, brief respite came on January 1, 1938 when English and Scott found the net in a two-goal victory over Lincoln.

Players, clearly disillusioned with their form, developed problems and another was found drinking on the eve of the game against Port Vale on February 19. Also in bother was former Sunderland reserve Jimmy Rodger who managed somehow to miss the team train to Southport when Pools were knocked out of the Division Three (North) Cup. He made the game, arriving later than his colleagues.

A couple of victories followed in early February, but once again the team went on another terrible run, failing to win in nine following a 4-0 triumph over Rotherham United on March 6, starting with a 2-2 home draw against Rochdale which saw them climb to the dizzy heights of 20th place.

Thrown into

David Davidson

HARTLEPOOLS UNITED (1936-1937)

DATE	HOME or AWAY	OPPONENTS	WIN LOSE or DRAW	GOALS For/Agst	POINTS
Aug. 29	A	Southport	DRAW	1-1	1
Sept. 2	H	Accrington Stanley	WIN	1-0	2
" 5	H	Tranmere Rovers	WIN	2-1	2
" 12	A	Halifax Town	LOSE	0-2	0
" 19	H	Mansfield Town	WIN	3-0	2
" 26	A	Crewe Alexandra	DRAW	1-1	1
" 29	A	Accrington Stanley	WIN	2-1	2
Oct. 3	H	Chester	LOSE	0-1	0
" 10	A	Rochdale	DRAW	1-1	1
" 17	H	Oldham Athletic	WIN	1-0	2
" 24	A	Port Vale	LOSE	0-1	0
" 31	H	Rotherham United	LOSE	0-2	0
Nov. 7	A	Stockport County	DRAW	1-1	1
" 14	H	Wrexham	WIN	2-0	2
" 21	A	Darlington	DRAW	5-5	1
Dec. 5	A	Hull City	LOSE	0-1	0
" 19	A	~~Lincoln City~~ York City	LOSE	0-3	0
" 25	A	York City	LOSE	1-4	0
" 26	H	Southport	WIN	2-0	2
" 28	H	York City	WIN	2-0	2

DATE	HOME or AWAY	OPPONENTS	WIN LOSE or DRAW	GOALS For/Agst	POINTS
Jan. 1	H	Barrow	WIN	3-1	2
" 2	A	Tranmere Rovers	LOSE	0-1	0
" 9	H	Halifax Town	WIN	5-3	2
" 16	H	Gateshead	WIN	6-1	2
" 23	A	Mansfield Town	LOSE	2-8	0
" 30	H	Crewe Alexandra	WIN	4-1	2
Feb. 6	A	Chester	LOSE	0-3	0
" 13	H	Rochdale	WIN	4-1	2
" 20	A	Oldham Athletic	LOSE	0-2	0
" 27	H	Port Vale	WIN	2-0	2
Mar. 6	A	Rotherham United	WIN	4-2	2
" 13	H	Stockport County	LOSE	2-4	0
" 20	A	Wrexham	WIN	1-0	2

Pages from Richard Noble's Scrapbook, 1936-1937

Eddie Embleton

the team to make his debut the following game was Harry Oliver, who at just 17 years and 31 days was Pools youngest player to start a Football League game. He didn't seem out of place as the last four games of the nine were all draws, and he played in the last two games, both goalless draws. The left back, playing alongside a rejuvenated Jack Proctor with former Houghton-le-Spring keeper Tommy Johnson behind them brought steadiness to the rearguard.

Pools Plot The Great Escape

NEVERTHELESS, with three games to go, Pools remained bottom with Barrow and Accrington just above them. With their financial problems mounting, and support dwindling, re-election could see the Club voted out.

Then, in front of just 2,766 fans on April 30, Pools took on Carlisle United, turning in their best performance for weeks, winning 4-1 with goals from English, Jack Scott, Eddie Embleton and Jack Hughes.

Fortunate to have their last three games at home, Pools went into the match against Halifax on May 4 determined.

With a gate of just under 5,000, goals from former Bradford player Embleton and reserve team centre forward Norman West who was called into the squad in place of the injured English proved enough. Victory pulled Pools clear of the bottom two, but they still needed to win on the final day of the season at home to Wrexham three days later.

Adopting the never say die attitude, Pools showed great resolve and West scored again with Embleton getting his third in three games. The goals proved vital as Pools finished third bottom on goal difference, just three better than second bottom Barrow.

It was a great

Harry Oliver

escape, but the campaign was a massive let down.

Dogged by poor form, bad attitudes and injuries, the Club followed one of their better seasons with one of their worst with two woeful spells of inadequacy. English and Wigham topped the scoring charts with a mere nine each, as Pools failed to register an away win for the first time since 1922-23, earning just four points on their travels.

Bids Fly In For Talented Youngster

ONE positive to come out of the season was the discovery of Harry Oliver. The former Durham County and England schoolboy international (when aged 14) had played for Doxford Juniors and Houghton Colliery Welfare before joining Pools in October 1937 as a 16-year-old amateur, turning professional in March the following year.

Even before the end of the season, scouts had noticed his prowess and Pools were open to offers in excess of £1,000 if one came in. It seemed a bidding war was to commence

Bill Allison

Harry Race

as Birmingham, Derby and Newcastle were hovering.

Huddersfield offered £1,000 plus a reserve half back but were outbid by Brentford who laid £1,500 on the table, with a further £500 payable after a dozen outings and an additional £250 if he played international football.

Not surprisingly the reserves limped along and ended up in 15th place in the NEL and failed to reach any cup finals.

At the end of the season, manager Jimmy Hamilton was granted a two-year extension to his deal irrespective of the poor form.

Both he and the board agreed that Ernie Curtis, Jack Scott, Allen Taylor, Billy Allison as well as several others could be freed. Eddie Embleton was offered new terms but when the Club refused to increase their offer he demanded to be freed and was ready to approach the Football League when the board agreed to grant him a free transfer.

English was also offered terms, but as they were at a vastly reduced rate he refused and was transfer listed with a fee of £500 hanging over his head. Jonny Wigham almost departed, as cash-strapped Pools were ready to accept a fee of £100 for his services, but personal terms could not be thrashed out and he stayed for what was to be his eighth season.

Several replacements were signed – Hexham keeper Joe Robinson, Bury reserve and former Pools trialist half back John Chapman, forward Rob Love who had scored 35 goals for Winsford in the Cheshire League the previous season and former Derry keeper Jock Wallace. Arriving on trial were former Liverpool and Manchester City forward Harry Race and Scottish half back Robert Don. A third new keeper arrived in the shape of 18-year-old Eric Garbutt who had been on the books of Middlesbrough as an amateur.

The poor season reflected in a bad financial performance with the Club losing just under £600. Gate receipts were down by almost £1,000. The board again decided they had to look to young players after being let down perennially by experienced, well paid players.

Meanwhile, the landlords of the ground, the local railway company, LNER, were in negotiation with the local authority, the West Hartlepool Corporation over a deal to sell the ground. The Corporation had contacted the Club to get their agreement to a change of landlord, which the chairman gave immediately.

The board of directors was changing and appointed to the board in the week before the season commenced was Tom Pailor, the brother of former assistant manager Bob Pailor. He was yet another member of the board who was a councillor.

On August 15, 1938 Pools lined up against Darlington to raise funds for the League Jubilee Fund. Pools won 2-1, with Wigham and Eddie Self netting. The following week Pools played in a return match at Feethams, when both clubs played their reserve sides, with Pools losing 3-1, Harry Race getting their consolation.

Jock Wallace

1938-39

A Box Of Kippers And War Teams

THE season kicked off on August 27 with the line-up including eight new signings – Wallace, Don, Love, former Newcastle and Port Vale full back Harry Johnson, Shotton-born winger Jackie Price, Joe Musgrave, once of West Ham and Swindon, Paddy Robbins (ex-Oldham) and new captain Jim Wright.

But the batch of new signings failed to impress straight away and Pools returned from Carlisle 2-0 losers. They then lost their next four games without scoring to equal their worst ever run 15 seasons earlier.

Pools brought in former trialist John Douglas from Ferryhill and promoted reserve forward Tommy McGarry, previously a prolific scorer for Newcastle's reserve side, to the first team along with former Blackhall CW winger Fred Lealman.

Desperate Start To New Campaign

ON September 14 Pools won their first game of the season, beating Darlington 3-0 with Johnny Wigham, Lealman and McGarry on the scoresheet, but the result failed to lift Pools off the bottom and the good run at the end of the previous season was long gone. Yet again the Club were struggling.

Next up were Doncaster and Rotherham who beat Pools 3-1 and 5-1 respectively. Joe Musgrave opened his account for Pools in the Doncaster defeat when he scored direct from a corner but despite these losses, Pools were

Joe Musgrave

second bottom as Lincoln City had a slightly worse goal difference.

Victory over Rochdale, 4-2, in the following game was soured when captain Jim Wright left the field with a knee injury expected to keep him out for a couple of months. Making his bow was John Chapman, who replaced the injured Joe Musgrave. His introduction stabilised things and form picked up a touch.

By the end of November, Pools had qualified for the second round of the FA Cup and were off the bottom of the division, in no small way helped by McGarry netting six goals in four games, including a hat-trick on November 5 in the 4-2 home defeat of Stockport County.

During the midst of this bad spell the Club agreed to join a midweek league with the reserve sides of Gateshead, Sunderland and South Shields. Pools' second string met the other teams home and away over the course of the season when other fixtures permitted. The new venture was to be known as the North East Combination.

December saw Pools knocked out of the cup at home to Division Three south outfit Queen's Park Rangers on the second Saturday in December when 11,924 fans packed the Vic to see them lose by two goals. League form stuttered and coincided with the return of Musgrave and the dropping of Chapman. After an embarrassing 5-2 home defeat to Chester on Boxing Day, Pools were hammered 8-2 in the return fixture the following day.

Despite this shocking run of form Pools had no fear of finishing bottom as they were nine points ahead of Accrington Stanley, who had managed only six points.

Dance Drama Hits The Club

THE dropped Chapman saw himself released on a free transfer early in January 1939 when he and squad player Jimmy Mackie were found to have been at a dance between the hours of midnight and 5am on the morning of Boxing Day.

At the dance with them was keeper Joe Robinson, who was deemed more vital to the cause and spared dismissal, instead fined £3. Also leaving was young keeper Eric Garbutt,

who had never played first team football. He refused professional terms offered and declined on occasions to play for the reserves. He was signed by Newcastle United, who paid Pools a transfer fee of £100 and remained on the books of Newcastle until the end of the 1949-50 season.

Winning three league games during February and early March, as well as McGarry having another good spell with five goals in five games, failed to lift Pools from the re-election spots. With the board once more under mounting pressure from the bank, several cost cutting procedures were undertaken. Trainer Frank Hewitt and scout Nichol Evans were released as soon as possible and Fred Lealman was granted a free transfer and allowed to move to Blackhall CW. It was also intended that several others were to be contacted by the manager over the course of the next week or so to consider having their contracts paid up to reduce overheads.

Some respite to the financial burden was received when top scorer McGarry was sold to Bradford Park Avenue in March for £500, enabling the trainer Hewitt and scout Evans to be kept on but on a reduced retainer. Pools also faced increased competition for support for midweek matches when it was announced that the Greyhound Company, who had taken over the premises adjoining the ground, would be running a full race card on Wednesday evenings.

Pools finally progressed in the Third Division north cup and after a 5-1 demolition of Gateshead, when former Swansea player JJ Diamond netted four, Pools were beaten 5-2 in the semi-final by Bradford City.

Threat Of War Emerges Once Again

FOR many months now matters had been brewing on the continent with the threat and the rise of Germany, with their domestic politics and threatening overtures made to other European countries, Poland in particular.

National Service was being considered and in April the Club commenced loudspeaker appeals for supporters who expressed an interest to apply for National Service registration. The threat of war was increasingly evident as preparations were being made across both Boroughs with the recruitment and training of air raid patrols and wardens.

But the season was one of struggle for Pools and they lifted themselves out of the bottom two for just a short spell following their penultimate game of the season, a drawn affair at Barrow. The season ended with a goalless draw at home to Wrexham and they ended second bottom, seeking re-election for the third time in their history, along with Accrington Stanley.

In the Sunderland Shipowners Cup the reserves reached the final but were hammered 6-1 by Sunderland reserves on May 3. The reserves who finished 13th out of 20 teams were represented on the field by John Vaughan, Harry Johnson, John Wilson, Joe Musgrave, John Douglas, John Spencer, J Lynch, Paddy Robbins, John Calder, A Francis and R McInnes, with Pools failing even to score their consolation, as a Sunderland player netted an own goal.

This defeat followed a further cup loss to Sunderland reserves, who only two days earlier had beaten the first XI in the final of the DSPC at the Vic. The team losing 1-0 that day were Joe Robinson, Jim Wright, Charlie Brown, Jack Price, Ron Peart, Richard Woffinden, Jonny Wigham, Rob Love, Cyril Woods, Norman West and Paddy Robbins.

Squad Shuffling Takes Place

A mass clearout of players took place and the Club bid farewell to Johnson, Love, Robbins, Les Rose, Woods, Wallace, Musgrave, Calder, Diamond as well as Barnsley loanee Woffinden. However, Johnson, Woods and Love had the decision overturned and they were to stay.

In early May, Ron Peart was sold to Derby County for £650, which was much needed by Pools and deemed good business for a player who had played just eight games. Pools also stated they were open to offers for any other players.

Re-election took place in early June and Pools won more votes (38) than any other club. Accrington were also re-elected with Shrewsbury, South Liverpool, Scunthorpe, Wigan and Burton missing out.

£10 And A Box Of Kippers

THE Club started signing players, former Sunderland and West Ham player John Foreman among them for a nominal fee

John Foreman

of only £30 from Workington. Foreman had been in dispute with Swansea, his club before Workington, and dropped out of the league to play for Pools. He is assumed to be the player behind the deal who Pools once signed for "£10 and a box of kippers".

Jimmy Deacon

In June 1939 the Club was warned by the War Office that players aged 20-21, and therefore eligible for Military Service, would not be exempt from or allowed to postpone their military training. Thankfully for Pools there was only one player affected – Jackie Price.

Towards the end of the month manager Jimmy Hamilton made a frantic dash around a golf course to finish his game off and travel through to Darlington to sign the former Wolves and Southend left half back Jimmy Deacon. The manager had to act quickly, because as he was driving to his home to sign him, a telegram was on its way from Walsall who were trying to arrange a visit for the following day.

The Club announced a small profit over the previous season of just under £70, mainly due to the transfer fees received which were in excess of £2,000.

Pools then signed two players from London clubs. Stocky centre half Charlie Turner joined from West Ham. The former Southend, Leeds and Republic of Ireland international had only joined West Ham in February 1938 for £2,000 and was seen as a vital signing at a fee of £550, a record for Pools at that time. Another half back joined from Crystal Palace, George Daniels.

Additional funds were needed when it was announced that they had to purchase numbers for the players' jerseys in accordance with the new Football League requirements.

1939-40

TRAINING for the new season began on August 8 with concern constantly growing over what was taking place on the continent. Blackout trial runs had been held in the two towns and a major military operation took place the day before Pools training began with

60,000 personnel involved.

Pools again played two games against Darlington for the League Jubilee Fund. The first game took place between the first XIs on August 19 at the Vic with Pools romping to a 6-1 victory with two goals each for former Hearts forward Joe Mantle and John Foreman and one each for Daniels and ex-York player Sam Earl. Three days later the reserves lost 6-2 at Feethams.

Preparations For War Made In The Town

EVEN though war had not been declared the intent of the German nation was clear and the Hartlepools again prepared further, hopefully in order to prevent the deaths seen in the aerial bombardment of 1914. From August 23 all street lights were to be extinguished during the hours of darkness and all windows in properties were to be covered with dark blinds bringing blackout conditions.

The season kicked off on August 26 with a fairly healthy crowd of 6,380 seeing a new-look Pools perform in an old style manner and share two goals with Barrow, with Mantle netting the first goal of the new campaign. On the Wednesday, the Club were beaten by three clear goals at Gateshead leaving them with just one point from the first two matches.

On Friday September 1, the expected happened and reports were coming through from Poland that the Germans had invaded. The actions invoked the Anglo-Polish treaty and, if it was confirmed, Britain would go to Poland's aid.

Townsfolk continued with a frenzied pace readiness for war. In the borough of Hartlepool, first aid posts had been constructed, trenches were being dug and all available gas masks had been distributed. In West Hartlepool air raid shelters had been built in Raby Road and the Old Cemetery.

Pools were meant to travel to Crewe on September 1 on an afternoon train, but with the railway authorities already faced with a formidable task with the mass evacuation of children, they could not guarantee an easy journey for the players. The Club agreed to leave on the Saturday

Neville Chamberlain

morning without keeper Joe Robinson who had been called up for military duties, replaced by Jock Wallace. The Home Office decreed that the invasion of Poland did not mean all matches should be cancelled, the full programme went ahead and Pools played out a drab scoreless draw.

Charlie Turner

Declaration Of War On Germany

ON the morning of Sunday September 3 1939, at 11.15am Neville Chamberlain, the Prime Minister, declared war on Germany.

Almost instantly Whitehall placed a ban on the gathering of crowds and also closed down places of entertainment including all theatres and cinemas.

Three days later an emergency meeting of the FA in Crewe saw an end called to organised football and the three games played so far this season were to be classed as cup ties.

If permission was granted at a later date for football to continue, teams could be made up of amateurs or guest players.

Several of the Club's professionals had left the area come the middle of September to either gain employment in other towns, or to enlist.

Rob Love and Ernie Thomas had enrolled in the Auxiliary Fire Brigade, Charlie Turner moved to Manchester to work and Foreman returned to Crewe. George Oxley and Jackie Price were due for military service. The Club decreed that if permission was given they were happy to take part in friendlies.

League Football Affected By War

ON September 21 it was announced there was little chance of football restarting for a couple of weeks. The public had expressed a desire to see the sport continue and the Club wanted to. Although the board had already lost a considerable amount of money due to the abandoned season they didn't want to make money from any games in wartime, they just wanted to break even where possible.

The Hartlepool and District League secured permission to resume and, on September 25, it

George Daniels

Raich Carter

was announced that some form of football at Pools was to resume. The Football League were considering imposing a travel limit of around 50 miles and Pools would try to field as full a team possible in any sanctioned regional tournament. After being unable to arrange games with Newcastle and Middlesbrough, a match was lined up at Feethams to take on Darlington.

The team that took to the pitch in this friendly included six players from different league clubs who were playing for Pools as guests. Jack Howe had returned to West Hartlepool from his Derby base to work and to get married as he was intending to sign up. Former Leeds forward Jack Kelly and Wolves winger John Marshall were both living in their home town of Hetton-le-Hole, another Derby player Jimmy Wilson was resident in Seaham Harbour and coming from Houghton-le-Spring was Grimsby wingman Billy Wardle.

Regional Competitions Organised

ON October 2, 82 English Football League clubs agreed to take part in regional competitions. Eleven were named in the Regional League North-East Division. Along with Pools were Newcastle, Middlesbrough, Huddersfield, Leeds, Darlington, Halifax, Hull, York and the two Bradford sides, Park Avenue and City. The competition was to commence on October 21 and run until May 4.

The Club lined up a reverse fixture of the friendly against Darlington at the Vic and even more new guest faces were in the XI. Blackhall-born Manchester City player Dick Neilson, Wheatley Hill lad and Arsenal forward Teddy Carr, Wolves winger Teddy Maguire along with two of Sunderland's longest serving players, and Scottish internationals, Bert Johnston and Alec Hastings.

A final friendly took place at Middlesbrough the following week before the season was to start proper. Again Pools fielded whoever was available – players included Portsmouth keeper James Hall, Billy Smith Stockport's full back, Barnsley's John Logan, Jim Stephens of Leeds and Jimmy Isaac of Huddersfield. In front of

1,500 fans, Pools lost the game by the odd goal in five despite being 2-1 up at the break through Stephens and Wolves player Marshall. Not one Pools player appeared in this game as they were all appearing as guests of other clubs.

The first official wartime league game at the Vic was on October 21 when 4,000 fans turned out to see a Newcastle side run out 2-1 victors. Jimmy Wilson scored for Pools as the team went into the break tied at 1-1 but he was injured early in the second half leaving Pools to see out the game with ten men. Again not one Hartlepools player was in the side, all were guests of other clubs. The following week Pools chalked up their first victory with a 3-2 scoreline at Hull, goals from Jim Stephens and Teddy Maguire.

Famous Players Guest For Pools

RESULTS were almost meaningless, as they merely provided some form of entertainment for the townsfolk and ensured that some of the locally born players from bigger clubs were able to continue playing. The games provided good entertainment and Pools were blessed with having some of football's greats pulling on their colours that season.

Wilf Copping, holder of 20 England caps, a wing half with over 300 league appearances for Leeds and Arsenal figured while he was based nearby in the Army where he was a PT Instructor.

Some other former Pools players such as Stan Scrimshaw and Norman West also pulled on the Club's colours again. Scrimshaw appeared courtesy of Bradford, but West never left the Club and was one of the very few Pools players to play for the Club that season.

Stockton-born former England Schoolboy International and Middlesbrough full-back Norman Fowler figured on a few occasions as did Sheffield Wednesday and England inside forward Jackie Robinson. Leeds forward and former long serving Liverpool record scorer Gordon Hodgson also guested.

Eclipsing all of these though were quite

possibly two players who were among the biggest names in football.

Auxiliary fireman Horatio Stratton Carter, known to all as Raich, and former Scarborough Working Mens' Club wing half Bill Nicholson featured for the Club all too briefly.

Carter was Sunderland's star in their 1937 FA Cup success and was lauded as one of the greatest players of his generation, but was close to giving up the game permanently during the war years due to his love of the Fire Service. He went on to have a long career both as a player and a manager.

Nicholson, who made his bow at the Vic on March 30, 1940 in a 3-1 victory over Darlington, was only at the start of a promising career with Tottenham when war was declared.

After the war he went on to be one of their most famous players and managed the team that did the double in season 1960-61.

Money Lost On Regional Venture

POOLS finished the season 10th out of the 11 teams participating in the regional league. Despite the quality on display, crowds were low and money was being lost at an alarming rate, leaving their future participation in doubt.

Jimmy Hamilton, the manager, had played a massive part in arranging for these players to play, getting them through to West Hartlepool and to the away venues – and all for no salary.

In August 1940 the Club published a loss of just under £1,500. Gate receipts were low which was a surprise considering the good players (who had also been on fair money) that had represented the Club. It seemed certain they would not take part in any official football during 1940-41, but may consider some friendlies if the opportunity arose.

Vic Used By Other Teams During War (And Bombed Again)

OCTOBER saw the Club announce that they were not to participate in any tournaments the Football League had permitted to run that season.

The Vic was used for a variety of matches during the traditional 1940-41 season, normally with proceeds going to local fighting funds and involving the Police and military sides. The Army XI side also played at the ground that season and took part in the local Church League and brought a trophy to the Vic when they won the title that year.

To say nothing much happened during these war months and during 1941 through to the summer of 1943 would not be far from the mark.

A Navy XI played at the Vic during season 1941-42 and Church League team St Nicholas used the ground the following season. Various sections of the military used the ground for drills and training.

Events that did occur were the West Hartlepool Council purchasing the ground from the Railway (albeit agreed back in 1939, but not announced until this period) and Pools becoming their tenants in June 1942, and the bombing of the ground again by German forces the same year.

Pools Rejoin The Action

THE regional tournaments continued without Pools and in the summer of 1943, Darlington applied to rejoin.

One thing standing in their way was the fact that their inclusion would have made the number of northern clubs competing 49, and they would have stood a better chance of rejoining if they could make the numbers even.

They subsequently contacted Pools to see if the Club were keen on recommencing activities. After prolonged discussion and examination of the financial difficulties and other insurmountable barriers to an early recommencement of the game, it was decided by the board that they carry out whatever action was deemed necessary to start again.

The Club needed permission from the new ground owners to get the nod to play there. Pools officials immediately made contact with the local authority and the Admiralty, who occupied the premises and used the ground, to enter into an earlier than expected reoccupation of the Vic.

Once the Club agreed to begin activities again, they wasted no time in appointing a new manager and Fred Westgarth was placed in charge of affairs. He had previously held the reins at Carlisle United, Bradford City and Stockport County. He was gritty and smart enough to take on the task of running the team in such difficult circumstances in time for the start of the Football League North

Jim Barrett

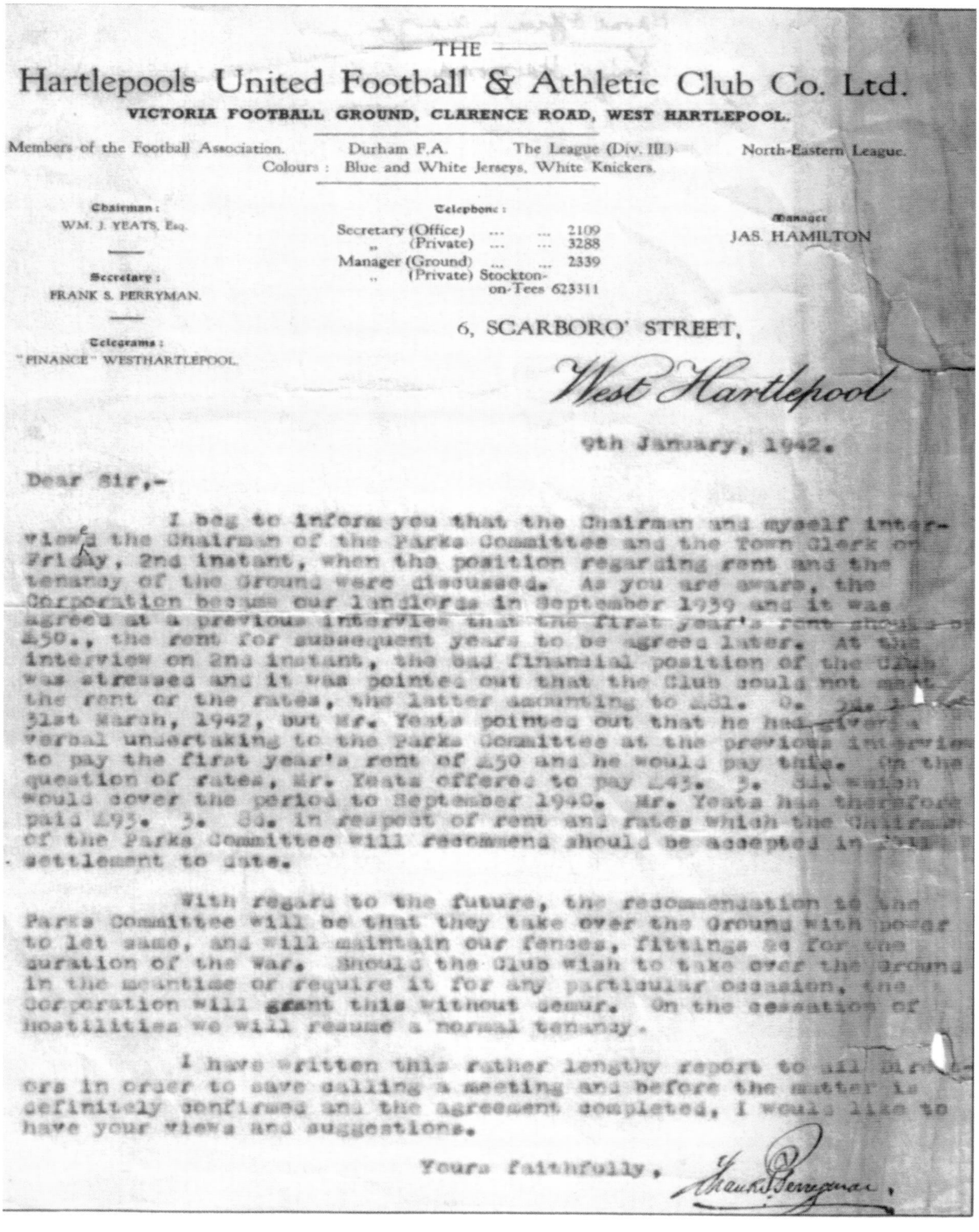

THE
Hartlepools United Football & Athletic Club Co. Ltd.

VICTORIA FOOTBALL GROUND, CLARENCE ROAD, WEST HARTLEPOOL.

Members of the Football Association.   Durham F.A.   The League (Div. III.)   North-Eastern League.

Colours : Blue and White Jerseys, White Knickers.

Chairman :
WM. J. YEATS, Esq.

Secretary :
FRANK S. PERRYMAN.

Telegrams :
"FINANCE" WESTHARTLEPOOL.

Telephone :
Secretary (Office) 2109
" (Private) 3288
Manager (Ground) 2339
" (Private) Stockton-on-Tees 623311

Manager
JAS. HAMILTON

6, SCARBORO' STREET,

West Hartlepool

9th January, 1942.

Dear Sir,-

I beg to inform you that the Chairman and myself interviewed the Chairman of the Parks Committee and the Town Clerk on Friday, 2nd instant, when the position regarding rent and the tenancy of the Ground were discussed. As you are aware, the Corporation became our landlords in September 1939 and it was agreed at a previous interview that the first year's rent should be £50., the rent for subsequent years to be agreed later. At the interview on 2nd instant, the bad financial position of the Club was stressed and it was pointed out that the Club could not meet the rent or the rates, the latter amounting to £81. 0. 0d. to 31st March, 1942, but Mr. Yeats pointed out that he had given a verbal undertaking to the Parks Committee at the previous interview to pay the first year's rent of £50 and he would pay this. On the question of rates, Mr. Yeats offered to pay £43. 3. 3d. which would cover the period to September 1940. Mr. Yeats has therefore paid £93. 3. 3d. in respect of rent and rates which the Chairman of the Parks Committee will recommend should be accepted in final settlement to date.

With regard to the future, the recommendation to the Parks Committee will be that they take over the Ground with power to let same, and will maintain our fences, fittings etc. for the duration of the War. Should the Club wish to take over the Ground in the meantime or require it for any particular occasion, the Corporation will grant this without demur. On the cessation of hostilities we will resume a normal tenancy.

I have written this rather lengthy report to all directors in order to save calling a meeting and before the matter is definitely confirmed and the agreement completed, I would like to have your views and suggestions.

Yours faithfully,

Frank Perryman,

1942 – Letter to ground owners from the Football Club asking for permission to play there

127

championship. The league was to split over two periods, the first from August 28 to Christmas and the second from then until May 1944.

In order to assist Pools with their restart, the West Hartlepool Corporation allowed the Club to have use of the ground without rent or rates for the first year subject to Pools producing a balance sheet for the first 12 months after they were 'back in business'.

More Work Required On The Vic

THE ground was again in a sorry state of disrepair. The Clarence Road stand was in such bad condition that it was considered a danger to the public.

The cost of repairing the stand was estimated to be £380, but the Club could not commence repair until a license was granted by the Ministry of Works. The turnstiles were either damaged or missing, heating to the dressing rooms was not working and the stand needed repairing. With no goal nets the Club borrowed some from Seaton Holy Trinity.

Something 'Fishy' About New Campaign

THE line up for the first game of the new season 1943-44 one again showed a team full of guest players with one exception.

The line up was Albert Heywood (Sunderland), Phil Tabram (Swansea), W Milne (Rochdale), Billy Scott (Brentford), Jim Barrett (West Ham), George Daniels (Pools), George Robinson (Charlton), Tommy Bamford (Swansea), Stan Scrimshaw (Bradford City) and former Pools reserve player Billy Adams (now Spurs). Scrimshaw netted the only goal, giving Pools a winning start in the new competition. Phil Tabram, who was serving in the RAF, broke his right forearm, but completed the full game with the injury.

Future games were also played using mainly guest players who on certain occasions were picked up from Catterick Garrison by the manager and fellow director William Hodgson, a local fish merchant, who brought the soldiers to the games in his fish van!

Manager Westgarth was very persuasive and would telephone all his players on a Thursday to ensure that they were playing at the weekend.

In the first mini season Pools fared well and benefited greatly from having the likes of Scott and Barrett in the half back line, alongside Hearts player W Phillips. With Sunderland keeper Napper Heywood between the sticks protected during most games by two out of

Allenby Chilton

three of either ex-Pools player Ralph Makepeace, Steve Forde of West Ham or Eddie Tunney of Wrexham, Pools were a strong outfit.

The forwards were in the main Robinson, with John Short from Leeds and Spurs pair Billy Adams and George Skinner. Scott, George Robinson and Heywood played in every game and Short topped the charts with 11 goals in the 18 games played.

Pools finished their North-East section in second place, losing out to Sunderland only on goal difference, the winners being better by three.

The Club sought to reach an agreement with the Naval Authority to prevent their team using The Vic. However, no deal was finalised and for the time being, the ground was to be shared by both concerns.

In the first match of the second mini-season the Club drew 1-1 at the Vic with Middlesbrough, in a game which was to be the last for Eddie Tunney and Jim Barrett.

Tunney was relocating, but Barrett suffered a ligament issue and, at the age of 36, he considered retiring, only to return for a spell the following season and then went back to the Hammers where he played a handful of games during the rest of the war and later took charge of the their A side, representing them into his 40s, even playing alongside his son Jim junior.

This part of the competition was not as successful as the first as Pools struggled to get a regular line up with several local players making a handful of outings, such as Skinner of local side Thornville and Slack of Horden. There were also plenty of players who made just the odd appearance here and there who were guests of other clubs such as Arsenal player Louis Delaney, Bob Batey of Preston and former Huddersfield player Sam Malpass.

Relations Strained With Naval Authorities

THE Navy still had not found anywhere suitable to play their games and continued to use the Vic, but relations between the Club and the forces side soured. After a game towards the end of January it was found that three windows in the boardroom had been damaged, subsequently spoiling the blackout blinds. It transpired later that Pools had not

OFFICIAL PROGRAMME – ONE PENNY

DARLINGTON FOOTBALL CLUB

President : Councillor J. Banks.

DIRECTORS :—Chairman : Mr. J. B. Smith ; Messrs. E. Black, R. H. Black, J. B. Haw, D. Jordan, J. Neasham, W. Nevett, T. Rodgers, J.P., J. L. Shepherd.

Team Manager : Mr. J. English.   Acting Hon. Secretary : Mr. J. B. Smith.

FOOTBALL LEAGUE.

SATURDAY, 16th September, 1944.

DARLINGTON v. HARTLEPOOLS U.

Referee : Mr E. W. Arnett, Leeds.

Linesmen : Messrs. J. Gardner, Middlesbrough and J. L. Bolam, Newcastle.

TEAMS :   Kick-off 3-15 p.m.

DARLINGTON

Colours—BLACK & WHITE HOOPS.

1—TAPKEN
(Manchester U.)

2—BURCHELL G. S.   3—STUBBS

4—CASSIDY   5—WHARTON   6—TOWERS, J.
(Gateshead)   (Portsmouth)

7—SHERGOLD, W. R.   8—RUDKIN   9—BROWN   10—WARD   11—SIMPSON
(Wolves)   (Grimsby T.)   (Brentford)   (Sheffield W.)

11—SMALLWOOD   10—NETTLETON   9—HORTON   8—SHORT   7—COPELAND

6—TABRAM   5—MAKEPEACE   4—SCOTT

3—FORDE   2—ATKINSON

1—TOMLINSON

HARTLEPOOLS UNITED

Any change in the teams will be announced.

DARLINGTON'S FIXTURES.

FOOTBALL LEAGUE—(North)			
Aug. 26—Bradford City ....home	6	0	
Sept. 2—Bradford City ....away	2	3	
,, 9—Hartlepools United ....away	2	4	
,, 16—Hartlepools United ....home			
,, 23—Huddersfield ....home			
,, 30—Huddersfield ....away			
Oct. 7—York City...................away			
,, 14—York City...................home			
,, 21—Hull City ....away			
,, 28—Hull City ....home			
Nov. 4—Gateshead...................home			
,, 11—Gateshead ....away			
,, 18—Bradford ....away			
,, 25—Bradford ....home			
Dec. 2—Sunderland ....home			
,, 9—Sunderland ....away			
,, 16—Middlesbrough ....away			
,, 23—Middlesbrough ....home			

CUP QUALIFYING COMPETITION

Dec. 25—Gateshead...................home			
,, 30—Gateshead ....away			
Jan. 6—Sunderland ....away			
,, 13—Sunderland ....home			
,, 20—Hartlepools United...................home			
,, 27—Hartlepools United...................away			
Feb. 3—Middlesbrough ....home			
,, 10—Middlesbrough ....home			
,, 17—Newcastle United ....away			
,, 24—Newcastle United ....home			

NORTH-EASTERN LEAGUE.			
Aug. 26—North Shields...................away	1	5	
Sept. 2—North Shields...................home	1	1	
,, 9—Hartlepools United ....home	8	2	
,, 16—Hartlepools United ....away			
,, 23—Consett ....away			
,, 30—Consett ....home			
Oct. 7—Horden...................home			
,, 14—Horden...................away			
,, 21—Blackhall...................home			
,, 28—Blackhall ....away			
Nov. 4—Gateshead...................away			
,, 11—Gateshead ....home			
,, 18—Eppleton ....home			
,, 25—Eppleton ....away			
Dec. 2—Sunderland ....away			
,, 9—Sunderland ....home			
,, 23—Murton ....away			
,, 25—Xmas Day			
,, 26—Boxing Day			
,, 30—Spennymoor United ....home			
Jan. 1			
,, 6—Spennymoor United ....away			
,, 13—Reyrolles ....away			
,, 27—Reyrolles ....home			

NOTE.—Dec. 16 at Feethams.
Scottish Command v. Northern Command.

The Official Programme from a game against Darlington on Saturday 16th September 1944

Cyril Brown

been informed by the Navy that the game was taking place. For future games, the Club had to be informed and a Naval Officer had to be present and in charge of the team's conduct.

In the final league game of the season at Middlesbrough on April 22, 1944, Pools were so short of players that Fred Westgarth drafted in three soldiers – E Nettleton, Lieutenant John Mitchell and Sergeant G Tootill. Alf Tootill, as he was known, had played for both Plymouth and Sheffield United before the war and Ernie Nettleton had also previously been on the books of the Blades.

John Short netted 11 goals in this closing part of the season, ending with a total of 22.

The summer of 1944 passed and the Club continued to share the lease on a pitch with the Navy so that they could play games there and there was also the subsequent arrangement of a new tenancy agreement between Pools and the local corporation.

The North Eastern League was reactivated, in which Pools were to enter a reserve side, principally to set the foundations for a Football League team as and when hostilities on the continent were brought to a conclusion.

With the league again split into two seasons, the first term of 18 games kicked off on August 26, 1944 at York City, as Pools were on the end of a 3-1 defeat. New players on show were keeper Tomlinson (Norwich), Oldham's Les Horton and former player Teddy Copeland who had returned after a spell with Newcastle.

Enthusiasm For Football Reflected In Profits

JUST over a fortnight later the Club returned a profit of £1,159 from April 1, 1943 to May 6, 1944 showing that the popularity of the game had not waned following

Joe Harvey

the Club's breather.

Appearing during this rather lacklustre first term were Reg Harrison of Derby and centre half Allenby Chilton of Manchester United. With the likes of former guests Wardle, Makepeace and George Robinson only appearing in a few games and with regular showings by only ex-Ashington and Newcastle keeper Tom Rutherford, local lad Atkinson and Steve Forde of West Ham, it was no surprise that the Club struggled.

The chopping and changing of the team, mainly the forward line, continued over the following months. The former Ashington player and now Manchester United forward Bill Bainbridge played a few games, as did Brentford forward Cyril Brown. Several reserve players were used as well when the occasion rose such as Jackie Price and Norman West, stalwarts of the pre-war era.

Also included were the likes of Fred Keeys and Doug Morris. There was a one-off outing from Joe Harvey, a youngster from

Isaac Spelman

Harry Hooper

Cyril Sidlow

William Lloyd

Bradford City, who later went on to become one of the most famous players at Newcastle United.

Before the season was over, on May 8, 1945, victory in Europe for the allied forces was declared.

1945-46

WAR was over and the Football League wasted no time in arranging a series of hurried meetings.

Councillor Tom Pailor, a Club director and brother of former assistant manager Bob, attended several over the course of the early close season when it was decided what was to become of the third divisions.

With the idea of the regional sections split into third and fourth divisions, it was decided the league proper would be delayed and regional leagues would continue.

Pools took on Doncaster on August 25 in the first game of the new season and lined up as follows – Captain Bob Hesford (Huddersfield & The Army), Steve Forde (West Ham), Bill Porter, Isaac Spelman, Fred Keeys, Jackie Price, Eddie Copeland, John Short (Leeds), Norman West, Tommy Barkas (Halifax), James Turney.

The starters contained only four guest players, a great difference from previous seasons. Leeds forward and regular scorer Short netted the only goal in the draw in which Pools ended with ten men as Copeland had to leave the field of play after breaking his nose.

As usual the teams changed regularly with the use of guest players. Harry Hooper, veteran of 300 games for Sheffield United, was based in the area while serving in the forces and on September 22, 1945 played at the Vic in a 3-2 victory over Bradford City.

Also turning out were Boro keeper and former prisoner of war Paddy Nash as well as Wolves keeper Cyril Sidlow, who appeared three times after playing in the area for NEL side Spennymoor.

Other guests were William Lloyd of Swindon, Reg Harrison of Derby and Charlton's George Robinson.

Inclusion Of Guest Players Restricted

TOWARDS the end of October it was announced that, from the third of the following month, clubs were allowed only to field three guest players per match and Pools wasted no time in signing former Sunderland full-back John Foreman.

He had played more than 300 games for

Sunderland and Blackburn and during the war he worked at Hylton Colliery and owned a pub in Sunderland.

They also tried to sign Swindon player William Lloyd who had been a regular guest, but the Robins refused to release him.

Also joining was Sunderland keeper Heywood, an ever-present when he appeared as a guest during season 1943-44.

Matt Johnson, who had previously played 13 years ago, returned. He had a good second spell with the Club and bagged ten goals in five consecutive games at one point.

After four months of discussions they also reached an agreement with the Admiralty that they would no longer use the ground. This did however, lead to a £50 increase in their annual rent.

In February Norman West, Len Robertson and George Daniels were allowed to leave on free transfers, but Jackie Price (who played when his military duties allowed) had been demobbed and signed professional papers.

Also joining the paid ranks were former Sergeant Sam Scott, back from military duties in North Africa, reserve player James Troman and former player Flight Sergeant Jackie Moses.

Pools also failed in their attempt to buy Huddersfield winger Alf Calverley after baulking at the £500 fee. Huddersfield later sold him to Arsenal for £2,500.

Manager's Resignation Shocks Board

WHILE the board were busy making preparations for the forthcoming season, they were dealt a body blow when manager Fred Westgarth tendered his resignation. The reasons behind his decision have never come to light but the board successfully negotiated with him and persuaded him to stay.

At a meeting of the Football League in April 1946, several guidelines were established for the new season, which was to be played in the same format as before WW2.

Ground admission was set at one shilling and sixpence. Players were paid a maximum of £7 10/- in the summer and £10 in the playing season with adjustments for players in essential work or

Leo Harden

in the services. Bonuses for matches won or drawn were to be unchanged.

On May 4, 1946 Pools appeared at the Vic in what was to be the final game of the war era – 4,150 fans turned up to see Pools beat York City 6-2.

The team that graced the pitch was Napper Heywood, Joe Willetts, Bill Porter, Isaac Spelman, Alf Tootill, Jackie Newton, Teddy Copeland, Bill Russell, Jackie Price, Sam Scott and Hughie McMahon. Scorers for Pools were Sam Scott, with Price and McMahon grabbing a brace each.

The sixth was a penalty scored with the last kick of the game by skipper Isaac Spelman. A strangely subdued atmosphere somehow managed to bring about a pitch invasion at the end of the game by local children.

Pools Count The Cost Of War

THE enforced break for the war ended the career of too many players, too quickly and too soon. Those lucky enough to avoid death, injury or imprisonment in the services had to dedicate their time to utilising their other skills or trades for the war effort.

Of particular loss to the Club was schoolmaster Jonny Wigham, who had been the scorer of 95 Football League goals. Aged 28 when the war started he lost another three or four years of playing for the Club he cherished as much as his job.

As soon as the season ended several players were signed on professional terms. Heywood, Leo Harden, Russell, Porter, Willets and reserve team player and former Newcastle United amateur Billy Hughes all agreed terms of £5 per week when in the first team. Jackie Price and Hugh McMahon were offered an extra pound a week.

In view of the fact that so many were in employment, or likely to find employment, it was resolved that in the event of a player signing weekly terms as a full time professional, and who subsequently found employment elsewhere, then agreements would be modified taking into account the salary from the other profession.

The team rebuilding continued apace. Left back Fred Gregory was signed from Doncaster, Eric Lambert from Derby and experienced Middlesbrough right back Billy Brown arrived. He had played in over 250 games before the war, in excess of 60 during the hostilities, as well as almost 100 for Watford. Despite being aged 37, he was made captain.

Keeper Joe Robinson moved to Blackpool, close to his Fleetwood home, with a fee of £150

changing hands. During his time on the west coast he was on the losing side in the 1948 FA Cup final.

It was suggested that several clubs should play friendlies to raise funds for restoration of grounds damaged during the war, but the League, who initially proposed the venture, pulled the plug on the idea.

On the west side (Mill House) work was carried out to ensure the side of the ground was terraced rather than just banked. Repairs were made to the Rink End roof which had been blown off during a summer gale. The roofing sections were replaced with material from Anderson Shelters, which were no longer needed.

1946-47

No More Guest Players

THE season was to start on August 31, at the Vic, against Barrow. There would be no more guest players allowed – no more international players or household names who had been based locally in the services, and it was feared that the decent gates enjoyed towards the end of the conflict would not be repeated.

However, the team for the first post war Division Three (North) game against Barrow was Napper Heywood, Billy Brown, Fred Gregory, Isaac Spelman, Eric Lambert, Harry Jones, Ted Copeland, George Moses, Jackie Price, Hughie McMahon and Leo Harden. Local lad Harden netted Pools goal in a 1-1 draw in front of a healthy 7,259 supporters.

Price had played for the Club before and during the war. Other wartime players, as well as the scorer Harden, included Heywood, Copeland, Spelman, McMahon and youngster Jones who had played once towards the end of the final season.

War Heroes Move To The Vic

INSIDE right George Moses arrived earlier in the month after seeing active service during the war with bomber command. The flight lieutenant had a distinguished war record and was involved in the evacuation of Dunkirk. He represented the RAF at football during the hostilities and before the war he had been on the books of Newcastle United.

With wartime signing Sam Scott released from his military duties in mid-September and with the squad boosted by the signings of Aberdeen's Chris Anderson and John Allison of

Barnsley, a mammoth 12,800 cheered Pools to a 2-1 win over Rotherham, elevating them to fifth place.

Goals were from Moses and Sam Scott, who scored his third goal in his third post war start. Scott had seen service as a Sergeant in the East Yorkshire Regiment 50th Division and was involved in one of the most strategic Allied defeats, but also a turning point, of the North African campaign at Bir Hacheim.

After losing just the once in the first eight games, Pools then went on a horrible run, drawing one and losing seven of the next eight, including 5-1 reversals at Carlisle and Doncaster, plummeting to 17th place.

Football Crowds Begin To Grow

RESPITE came in the first round of the FA Cup when Pools hammered North Shields 6-0, with Sloan netting four goals, making it seven in four starts since his move from Newcastle United earlier in the month, in a part exchange deal for reserve forward Joe Brown.

Results picked up during December with Sloan enjoying a steady flow of goals. However they were hammered 6-1 at home by Rochdale in the second round of the FA Cup – their heaviest home defeat in the competition.

A healthy 8,130 turned out on Christmas Day to see a scoreless draw with Hull City. The following day Sloan netted again at Boothferry Park in front of a staggering Boxing Day attendance of 30,064, the highest Football League crowd Pools had played in front of, proving football was more popular than it was before the commencement of war.

The Flying Dustman Makes His Name

AT the end of February, a significant signing was made when 21-year-old Sunderland left back Ray Thompson arrived following the free transfer of Fred Gregory to Rotherham.

Thompson played for Ferryhill Juniors before moving to Roker Park in November 1945. Although he appeared for them during the war he didn't feature afterwards, despite being regarded as a great prospect. He went straight into the side and that flank had a whole new look about it as local dustman Harden gained a regular slot on the left wing. He was later known as The Flying Dustman.

With a severe winter taking a firm grip, Thompson's third game, his second at the Vic, almost didn't take place with the staff and supporters clearing snow from the pitch enabling the game against Chester to go ahead.

Pools were rewarded with a 5-1 victory on February 8.

Just over a month later and New Brighton fought their way through the snow to reach a Victoria Ground cleared of almost a foot of snow before kick-off.

Ray Thompson

The opponents could only muster nine men so Nichol Evans, 20, son of the Pools trainer and scout of the same name, donned the colours of the opponents for his solitary outing alongside the visiting manager Neil McBain, who, at the age of 51, remains the oldest player ever to play in a Football League game.

Rabbits Out Of The Hat

TRIMDON Station based Evans senior was a Club stalwart, well respected throughout the game with a keen eye for talent. He was responsible for many signings Pools made over the years.

One report, from The Northern Echo, said Evans was: "That unearther of rough diamonds, Nichol Evans, who looks after the Pools reserves and keeps producing young recruits like a conjurer produces rabbits out of hats."

Evans junior's playing experience went as far as appearing at inside-left for Hesleden in the Hartlepools and District League.

Pools won the game 3-0. McBain and his Brighton compatriots were delighted with the gesture. In staying over in West Hartlepool for the night, invitations were extended to the amateur to have dinner with his temporary team-mates, followed up by a dance evening.

Evans senior's finest hour came when spotting the talents of Jack Howe playing for Wingate Albion

Neil McBain

and later sold to Derby for a healthy £1,000.

During the same match George Moses suffered a broken jaw which kept him out for two months.

In normal circumstances, this would have meant the rest of the season but due to the severe winter and a fuel shortage the campaign was extended until the middle of June.

Just two weeks later and Pools entertained leaders Doncaster as 8,310 fans saw the visitors stretch their lead at the top with a 2-0 victory.

Results stuttered and Pools again finished mid-table with Sam Scott's 12 goals enough for him to end up as top scorer.

The board were keen to progress the Club and believed one way to improve was better crowds, resulting in increased funds to buy better players.

Plans Made To Buy The Ground But Corporation Ask Too Much

THE idea was to buy the ground from the Local Authority and overtures were made during April 1947.

The intention was to buy the land already occupied and the allotments on the Mill House side to develop further with the construction of a main covered stand.

The matter had to be placed on hold as meetings continued over the future use of the land, particularly as the borough engineer suggested that Pools extend on the southern side (Town End) and rotate the pitch 90 degrees so that the goals would be on the Clarence Road and Mill House sides.

Pools' idea to build on the west side would not be feasible, as they wanted to erect a large stand to increase capacity to around 27,400.

Perhaps the numbers were optimistic, as although the Club had achieved their best ever-average attendance, it stood well short of the planned capacity at 7,561.

A retained list was released with Pools having only three full-time players on the books – Harry Jones, Jack Price and Billy Brown.

Brown was undertaking coaching with the FA in Leeds and Price almost left in the summer but Grimsby Town failed to come up with the required fee of £600.

The Local Authority came back to Pools advising that the amount needed to buy the ground and land to the west would be a total of £5,931 8/- 10d.

It was a fee out of their means and the idea was once again placed on hold.

Signing during the summer were Peter Baines, Harry Hooper, Jimmy Isaac and Alf Tootill, who had all played for the Club during the war, as well as Newcastle United reserve players, wing half Bobby Donaldson and keeper Cam Theaker.

1947-48

THE season started on a bad note with a crushing 4-2 defeat at Accrington and Pools failed to get a win under their belts – and stood in 20th place – until the 2-0 triumph at Oldham on September 16, which coincided with the delayed debut of Hooper who had been building his fitness up in the reserves.

His full back partnership with Brown added up to a combined age of more than 75 years.

But form remained poor, as Pools won just one in their next nine to sit in bottom spot.

Another Poor Season On The Horizon

DURING this bleak spell, 22-year-old Chelsea centre forward Fred Richardson signed and Bobby Donaldson, who had been injured in pre season training and was deemed fit after just one outing for the reserves, made his debut.

Victory over Darlington in the first round of the FA Cup was followed by defeat after a replay to Brighton and then Pools gifted Gateshead a happy Christmas when they crashed by seven clear goals at Redheugh Park, which proved to be reserve goalkeeper Sid Parkes last first team game. He departed for Blackhall CW.

Pools acted swiftly to sign a replacement keeper in Norman Rimmington from Barnsley.

The second half of the season proved a constant struggle against re-election, although the goals of March signing Laurie Nevins greatly helped.

He was brought in by Fred Westgarth to play on the left wing in place of Harden, netted six goals in six games, and it was considered that his arrival and the return of Hooper at the end of March pulled Pools clear of danger.

Nevins joined a week before Gateshead inside right Harry Hawkins who cost £100.

He was expected to make an impact, but suffered a broken jaw on his debut at home to Bradford City on March 13.

Thankfully the dire form of New Brighton and Halifax ensured Pools were safe from re-election come May 1, when a 5-0 drubbing at Lincoln mattered nothing to Pools, although it sealed the title for the Imps.

Free transfers were granted to Sam Scott, Cam Theaker and Alf Tootill.

It was also arranged with the West Hartlepool Corporation to carry out a programme of repairs to the ground totalling £1,100, with the Supporters' Club offering their services in the form of unpaid labour for menial work.

Watty Moore Joins The Club

POOLS re-engaged the services of the majority of the players, including veteran Billy Brown who was rejecting overtures from York City. Arriving were local youths D Crathorne and Watson Moore, the latter joining from local side Oxford Street Old Boys. He was to prove a record-breaking capture.

In the first week of July, Brown moved to NEL side Stockton to take up the role of player-manager. He went on to be involved at Stockton as a player, manager and chairman and other duties well into his 70s.

1948-49

FOR once the season opened with a clear win, when on August 21, 1948, Pools put Rochdale to the sword, beating them 6-1 at the Vic.

The team of Rimmington, Wilkinson, Thompson, Donaldson, Hughes, Jones, Isaac, Hawkins, Richardson, Price and Nevins netted through a brace each from Fred Richardson and Harry Hawkins, one from a fit-again Jackie Price and an own goal. Price's goal came after only ten seconds – the earliest that Pools have scored in a game.

Despite the poor showing the previous season, football was in boom time and over 10,000 turned out to see the opening game.

A derby loss to Darlington was followed by a draw at New Brighton and a 1-0 home reverse to Darlington on August 30 in front of an impressive 14,585 fans.

Pools Attract Record Crowd To The Vic

SEPTEMBER 18 saw Pools win their third consecutive home game when they beat Crewe 4-1, with Richardson scoring a hat-trick, making it six in four.

It was impressive form and he was closely watched by four or five clubs, in particular Sheffield United who were warned off when Pools slapped a £5,000 fee on his head – however, it did not deter his admirers for long.

On October 9, Pools played host to Hull, who, with former Pools guests Raich Carter and Norman Fowler on their books, were a close second in the division and always attracted

both good home and away support. 17,118 were at the Vic, a record that stands as the highest Football League attendance at the ground, beating the previous best set just a few weeks earlier against Darlington by some margin.

Eric Wildon

But the Tigers headed home with the points after a 2-0 victory in Richardson's last game.

Barnsley met the required £5,000 fee and the move, great from a financial perspective, caused great unrest amongst the fans. President of the recently reformed Supporters' Association, Captain Stathers quit his position.

As much as the board needed the fee, they certainly didn't need this revolt by the fans and most definitely didn't need the one win in the next eight games that followed.

Pools failed to buy a replacement centre forward to start with and tried Eric Wildon in the front line, after signing him from a local factory team. He scored once in three games before being injured, so the Club tried Wattie Moore after he netted a brace for the reserves towards the end of October. He netted on his full debut against Wrexham on November 6, along with Harden, in a 2-2 draw.

Following the recruitment of centre half John Douglas and Grimsby right winger Billy Burnett, a permanent centre forward signing was made in the form of former Arsenal reserve Jimmy Sherratt.

He made an instant impression, netting twice on his debut in a 2-1 victory at Accrington Stanley on December 11. His arrival signalled the departure of long-serving Jackie Price, who moved to York City for £250.

Ground Purchase Is Silver Lining

BESET with injuries, having to sell their best players, blooding local youngsters and playing in front of less than average crowds seemed to

Billy Burnett

135

Les Owens

be the norm for many years before the war.

And now things were returning to this vein.

If ever a season could be labelled as nondescript then this was it. Impressive results were all too rare and form remained patchy, with the Club finishing a poor 16th.

The top scorer was Richardson with nine goals, despite him leaving with 30 games remaining.

However, two matters that season did stand out.

First was the amazing attendances – they played in front of four home crowds in excess of 10,000, with a best average gate so far of 8,796, up from the previous season by more than 1,200.

They also played in front of their highest away crowd when on March 5 they took to the field at Boothferry Park in front of 35,357 followers, when they lost 2-0 to eventual champions Hull.

The other major event was the reduction in price that the Corporation were demanding for the ground and, at the end of January 1949, the Club bought the ground for a total of £3,003 9/- and 2d, with the aid of a mortgage loan of £2,000 from the Football League.

New Optimism For Pools

THE Club now hoped to improve the Victoria Ground, and in particular the west side, with an aim to increasing the overall attendance to 27,000.

Many of the players were retained and the only players given free transfers were squad members and reserve team players and these included Hawkins, Isaac and Nevins.

In July 1949, manager Westgarth was again looking to strengthen and laid out £600 when he signed 29-year-old Southport forward Les Owens. Also joining were former Newcastle United amateur centre half Billy Hughes, Scottish wing half Peter Kerr who signed from Maryhill Harps and one-time Hull reserve full back John Denham.

The Club also negotiated the £750 transfer of Leicester City winger Tom Edwards, but he chose to join Bath City.

Moving south was Jimmy Sherratt, who declined terms and refused to return to the North-East during the summer. He signed for Leyton Orient for a fee of £500. Staying put was Ray Thompson, the subject of interest from Southampton who were put off by the price tag imposed on him by Pools of £7,000.

1949-50

THE league season kicked off on August 20, and United started with a 2-1 victory at Halifax Town.

Two days later Pools beat New Brighton 2-0 at the Vic with goals from Owens and another summer signing, former West Ham inside forward Dick Dunn. It was the first time since 1927-28 that Pools had won the opening two games of the season and they stood in second place, behind Gateshead.

But they fell away and endured a scrappy start, losing the next two, conceding five at home to Gateshead on September 5 and then putting five past Chester at the Vic five days later, with Owens netting four.

Passmore scored all the goals against Gateshead and the game saw the end of the run of 72 consecutive appearances of keeper Rimmington, who was replaced for the Chester game by Wally Briggs.

Poor Start Does Little To Turn Crowd

DESPITE the results, the crowds still piled into the Vic with more than 10,000 present for three consecutive games against Stockport, Lincoln and Carlisle.

The Carlisle game saw Pools net just the once through young forward Moore, but brought their second 5-1 reverse in two games, having lost by the same score at Rotherham.

Rimmington returned after Briggs injured his thumb in the game against Lincoln. Worse was to come the following game when they were thrashed 7-1 at Mansfield.

This abysmal form – they took only one point from the next three games – saw Pools drop to just two points above the drop zone in 18th place.

The FA Cup brought some respite when they won at Accrington thanks to a solitary Owens goal. Pulled out of the hat first for the second round draw they were given a home tie against southern section side Norwich City.

The game on December 10 saw the honours shared in a 1-1 draw, so a replay was needed on a Thursday night at Carrow Road to see who

ROVERS v. HARTLEPOOLS U

Saturday Oct. 1st 1949

Football
League
Third
Division
North

Season
1949-50

No.
8

Official
Programme

THREEPENCE

DONCASTER ROVERS FOOTBALL CLUB

The Official Programme from a game against Doncaster in October 1949

would face Portsmouth in the next round. Over 18,000 were present to see the Canaries put five past Rimmington in the Pools goal, with Harden managing the only effort for the visitors.

Ken Johnson Makes Pools Debut

ON New Year's Eve, following the 3-0 home victory over Bradford City in which Owens, Burnett and debutant 18-year-old amateur Kenny Johnson scored, a leave of absence of a minimum of four weeks was granted to the manager Fred Westgarth, who handed a medical report to the Chairman.

Due to the urgency of the matter, former manager Jimmy Hamilton once more came to the aid of the Club and stepped in as caretaker manager.

He dipped into the market immediately when he arranged the signing of Sunderland full back Barney Ramsden and held off the advances of Newcastle and Carlisle who were tracking Wildon and Thompson respectively.

Fans Unhappy With Off-Field Matters And Allotments Need Protection!

RESULTS suffered away from home, but settled at the Vic under the auspices of the acting manager. With Westgarth not returning within the granted four week period, stand-in boss Hamilton engineered the move of Jackie O'Connor to Spennymoor and the sale of top scorer Les Owens to Norwich City for the fee of £2,000, again representing a healthy profit.

The sale, however, was met with criticism from both supporters and the press. Hamilton also arranged the signature of Joe Willetts after his release from military duties.

Meanwhile, the Club were also receiving complaints from the allotment holders whose land bordered the west side of the ground, principally voicing their concerns over the lack of a fence between their land (what is now the Mill House car park) and the Vic.

The Club had intended to wait until the close season before they started developments

Barney Ramsden

but commenced the necessary procedure to arrange for a ten-foot high boundary wall.

Following the sale of Owens, Pools lost their next game at home to Mansfield Town on March 18 3-1 and found themselves in 19th place, just two points above the three struggling Yorkshire sides – York, Halifax and Bradford City.

Ken Johnson

But Pools went on to win their next three games and pull themselves out of the mire so much so that they enjoyed a seven-point cushion to move to 16th spot.

Driving Drama For Pools Star

THE first game in the run saw major changes to the starting XI and the reintroduction of Rimmington, Harden and Sloan played a part, although Sloan was rather fortunate to make the 2-1 victory at Accrington Stanley.

Based in Tyneside he had to travel to the town to meet the squad. The bus taking him to the train station to get to West Hartlepool was involved in a crash and his father came to his rescue, driving him to Accrington from his home to reach the ground in time to play. Unusually, Sloan's father had never driven anywhere outside the Tyneside boundaries before.

Bobby Donaldson returned, playing alongside Moore, who had converted from centre forward to centre half and was starting to excel in that role.

His form meant the Club was fending off enquires from several teams for the 25-year-old, including Sheffield United.

One player definitely not with the Club the following season was Ramsden, who was moving to America before the campaign ended.

Just as it looked as though the side had turned itself around they went on to lose their final five games of the season, including a 6-0 reverse at Lincoln and a 6-1 final day defeat at the Vic to Crewe.

Finishing in 18th place, just two points off bottom side York, Pools were never in any danger of failing the re-election vote if they had finished in the bottom two, as the division was expanding by two teams.

Shrewsbury Town were elected to the league

John Ollerenshaw

along with Scunthorpe & Lindsay United.

Despite leaving in March, 12-goal Les Owens finished top scorer.

As the season closed, it was announced that manager Fred Westgarth had recovered from his illness and would be returning to first team duty immediately.

With several players released, among them John Douglas, Harry Hooper, Ron Vitty, John Denham and Dicky Dunn, the seasonal dip into the available list took place.

Joining the ranks were Stirling Albion inside right Joe McKeown, former Arsenal man John Ollerenshaw, West Ham United reserve Dick Ballantyne and Scottish forward Billy Bain. The border raids took place after manager Westgarth and chairman Yeats went to Scotland together to meet their scout and returned with the players.

Ground Work Becomes Main Priority

QUOTES had been received for the erection of the west boundary concrete wall and these varied between £2,930 and £3,558.

Further discussions were needed, as a survey of the ground indicated that extensive repairs were necessary.

Stalwart Club secretary and local accountant Frank Perryman, who had recently received a long service medal from the Football League, set about the process of buying up old Anderson Shelter sheets as well as second hand bricks and timber. The materials were to be used by the members of the Supporters Club who were once again offering their services for free. They were tasked to repair the urinals, home and visitors dressing rooms as well as boundary fences and terracing.

The Official History of Hartlepool United Football Club 1908 – 2008

Chapter 7

1950s

1950-51

IN July 1950, Pools made what was to prove a key signing – Tommy McGuigan, an inside left arrived from Ayr United. He spent seven years at the Club and made 350 appearances, becoming a real fans' favourite.

Also arriving was former New Brighton and Preston winger Willie McClure, while ex-player Harry Hooper was appointed assistant trainer and coach.

Pools Youngster Tempted Away

TROUBLE was to follow as former Pools goalkeeper Tommy Knox, in his role as scout for Notts County, induced Pools amateur player Ken McPherson without going through the appropriate channels.

Telephone calls and meetings took place and County were forced to shell out £200 for the services of a player who never even featured for Pools first XI. The Hartlepool-born forward went on to play into his late 30s in a career that saw him play for the likes of Middlesbrough, Coventry and Swindon.

Due to the estimate for building the west wall, the Club redesigned their plans and opted for a wall to be built of concrete and wire mesh, which halved the cost of the project and allowed the project to proceed.

Pre-Season Struggles For Pools

POOLS had just one pre-season game and their lack of preparation showed as they lost the opening game, 2-0 at home to Crewe in front of 10,359.

Another loss two days later at York saw changes to the side with Bain, Ollerenshaw and Sales dropped, with the first two never playing for the first team again. Moore, Donaldson and Willets were restored but a third loss followed, leaving the Club at the foot of the table without scoring.

Respite came with a 4-1 home win over York as McGuigan netted twice with a Willets penalty and a Wildon effort completing the scoring. However, it was another eight games before the Club won again, although it was in some style.

Wildon had been the only bright light of a dour season and a brace against Lincoln in a 2-2 draw on September 30 took his total to five goals in his last seven outings, a run he increased dramatically when he netted all four in a 4-1 victory at the Vic over Wrexham.

The following week, Pools lost by the same scoreline in the DSPC to Sunderland.

Comings And Goings Continue

WITH Bobby Donaldson injured in the Wrexham game, local half back Frank Stamper was called up for the next game at Oldham. Pools returned to their previous poor form, hammered 5-1.

A couple of draws seemed to settle things and, on November 4, Pools put six past Barrow, with Wildon contributing once more, this time with a hat-trick.

A couple of days later and Harry Hooper was on his way again.

Released as a player at the end of the season

and then taken back on the books as coach in July, he was off to bigger and better things when he was appointed as assistant trainer with West Ham United.

He was associated with the London side for many years, overseeing the early years of the career of his son, also Harry, who had a decent career with Wolves, Birmingham and Sunderland.

Just weeks later and Wildon was knocking in the goals for fun again.

A hat-trick in a 6-1 victory over Barrow on November 4 was followed by a further triple haul two weeks later in a 3-1 triumph over Bradford PA, taking him to 16 for the season.

He followed up with another goal seven days later in a tricky FA Cup tie at Worcester when, in front of 10,000, Pools returned home with a place in the second round draw.

Worcester were one of the stronger teams in the Southern League and included in their ranks Hartlepool-born and former Jesmond Road school pupil Alf Newbold who had made his way to Worcester via Huddersfield and Newport.

Jimmy McGuigan netted two goals that day and Billy Burnett the other in a 4-1 win.

The second round of the competition saw Pools lose 2-1 to Oldham in front of the second highest home crowd seen to date – 15,360.

Come the end of 1950 Pools were in 19th place, helped mainly by Wildon's 20 goals.

Illness And Incident Hit The Club

WHILE the two towns and several players suffered from a January flu epidemic, the team had a good run of results and by early February had moved to 15th place.

Off the pitch, however, the Club found themselves in hot water with the FA following reports of a spectator throwing a stone at a Carlisle player during the reserve match at the Vic on January 21.

Details of the offender were known but the Club and the police did not prosecute, although a notice had to be placed in the programme advising customers not to throw stones – a tricky task as the programme was only four pages and consisted of mainly adverts and the line ups.

The next four games were all 1-0 defeats, but an upturn came around on March 17 when McKeown (2), McClure and Wildon got the goals in a 4-2 win.

Good Friday saw an even better result, a 6-1 home victory over Darlington.

The same trio got a goal each and diminutive full back Joe Willetts netted a hat-trick of

---

Shakespeare

DIRECTORS	Let me have men about me that are fat, Sleek-headed men, and such as sleep o'nights. *Julius Caeser.*
MANAGERS	We few, we happy few, we band of brothers. *Henry V.*
SECRETARIES	Into a thousand parts divide one man. *Henry V.*
TREASURERS	O, that we now had here but one ten thousand of those men in England that do no work today. *Henry V.*
PLAYERS	Be swift, like lightning. *Richard II.*
TRAINERS	Oh, that this too, too solid flesh would melt. *Hamlet.*
REFEREES and LINESMEN	Constant in spirit, not swerving with the blood, Garnish'd and deck'd in modest complement, Not working with the eye without the ear, And but in purg'd judgment trusting neither. *Henry V.* —be thou as chaste as ice, as pure as snow, thou shalt not escape calumny. *Hamlet.*

penalties. To date this remains the only post-war hat-trick scored for the Club against Darlington in the Football League.

Pools completed a derby double on Bank Holiday Monday with McClure netting in a one goal victory at Feethams.

Two wins and a draw saw Pools in a respectable 13th place, but once again a poor run followed, with four losses in the last five games.

Sixteenth place was all that the Club could muster with a pathetic nine goals scored away from the Vic.

New Brighton lost their Football League place in the re-election vote, with Workington voted in as their replacements.

THE
HARTLEPOOLS UNITED
FOOTBALL & ATHLETIC CLUB Co. Ltd.

The Chairman, Directors and Officials of the Hartlepools United Football Club send to you their Best Wishes for a Happy Christmas and Prosperity in the New Year.

Victoria Ground,
West Hartlepool

Christmas 1950

Left: 1950 official Club Christmas Card

Below: The official Club Christmas Card from 1950 desinged by Club Secretary Frank Perryman, with quotes from Shakespeare chosen to reflect various football roles

——on *Football*

BANK MANAGERS

He liked not the security.

Henry I V.

PRESS

I must be cruel only to be kind.

Hamlet.

Give every man thine ear, but few thy voice.
Take each man's censure but reserve thy judgment.

Hamlet.

SCOUTS

O, there be players that I have seen play—and heard others praise and that highly—not to speak it profanely.

Hamlet.

SPECTATORS

If all the year were playing holidays,
To sport would be as tedious as work.

Henry I V.

OUR VISITORS

I count myself in nothing else so happy as a soul rememb'ring my good friends.

Richard II.

Bill Robinson

The reserves' efforts mirrored those of the first XI, finishing 15th out of 20 in the NEL.

Pools would have had an even worse season had it not been for Wildon. His total of 27 put him just one goal behind Bill Robinson and J W Smith, who held the combined record for 1927-28 and 1913-14 respectively.

Taking the Durham Senior Cup games into account, Robinson stands with a total of 29 and Smith 32.

Settled Squad Starting To Show Benefits

ONE pleasing thing was that the manager, Fred Westgarth, who now had a clean bill of health, seemed to be building a settled team.

Nine players (Willetts, Newton, Moore, Stamper, Burnett, McKeown, Wildon, McGuigan and McClure) started in three quarters or more of the games. Pools almost lost Westgarth as a prominent First Division club from the south of the country offered him the post of assistant manager, although he declined the offer.

Festival Of Britain Friendly And Joe Harvey Plays For Pools

AT the end of the season, the Club played a friendly against Irish side Limerick as part of the Festival of Britain Celebrations.

Many European teams were playing in Britain as part of the event and Limerick had played in front of very small crowds at Darlington and Gateshead.

In order to counteract this, Pools included two players in their side from Newcastle United – Joe Harvey and Scottish centre half Frank Brennan. Their presence guaranteed a good crowd (7,904) for the game and they even brought down the FA Cup, which they had just won, to the Vic to show off.

Pools played in white shirts and beat the blue shirted Irishmen 4-1 with Brennan, normally Harvey's half back partner but with Harvey wanting to play alongside the precocious talent of Moore, appearing as centre forward.

The role obviously suited him as he put Pools ahead after 30 seconds and ended up scoring the only hat-trick of his career. He only scored three other goals throughout his full career which consisted of more than 300 games.

Only a handful of reserve team players were released when the retained list was announced and added to the squad over the summer were former Sunderland trialist half-back Lionel Richley, Alloa centre forward Sandy Willox, Alex Elder, an inside forward who joined from

Secretary Frank Perryman and wife with Fred Westgarth (back to camera) and wife (on his right) talking to Stan Mortensen at an end of season Football League meeting

Dundee United, and local goalkeeper Robert 'Berry' Brown, who joined from Stockton, but had once played in the top flight for Manchester United.

Chairman Persuaded Not To Step Down

DURING the summer of 1951, the financial matters of the Club were under duress again.

In excess of their £2,000 overdraft with the bank, Chairman Bill Yeats and secretary Frank Perryman loaned the Club £320 and £160 respectively to ensure that summer wages and expenses were met.

Yeats swiftly tendered his resignation to the board after 28 years at the helm.

Seeing the Club through the great depression and rejuvenating them after the war were just two of the major achievements of what is the longest reign as Chairman.

The board met the following day and appointed new directors, auctioneer and valuer Norman Hope, butcher Edward Walker and local businessman Ernest Ord.

A new Chairman – Harold Sergeant – was appointed on July 20, 1951.

Less than two weeks later at the next board meeting, Sergeant and the other members of the board persuaded Yeats to stay in charge, so the decision to install a new man was overturned and Yeats was to turn his 28th season into a 29th.

As well as the new boys, the bulk of the squad from last year had signed once more, although more than half were part-time players and had to seek other jobs, due to the limit on player wages.

1951-52

THE season opened on August 18 with a crushing defeat at Tranmere, McGuigan scoring the only goal for Pools in a 4-1 reverse.

Nevertheless a bumper crowd of 11,394 turned up on Bank Holiday Monday for the game with Crewe.

Keeper Wally Briggs and forward Sandy Willox were dropped and replaced by Berry

Berry Brown

Brown and new signing Alex Elder. The large crowd were treated to a 3-1 victory, and the following week they saw Pools overturn Scunthorpe 3-0.

When The Wind Blows

POOLS soon had another reversal in fortunes, losing consecutive away games at Crewe and Lincoln.

There then followed a pattern of winning at home and losing away until the last weekend in October when Stockport left the Vic with two points, following a 1-0 victory.

In the days before the game, a heavy gale blew half of the roof off of the newly-erected stand on the south side of the ground. It was discovered that the roof securing had not been sufficient and immediate steps were taken to make the rest of the roof safe.

During this period, despite the attempts to build a settled team by Fred Westgarth, the board held discussions with former Hull player/manager Raich Carter who had just resigned from his position to run a confectionery shop in Humberside.

But Pools could not sweet talk him into reconsidering and Westgarth stayed at the helm, with his son Ned remaining as trainer.

Pools Are Up For The Cup In Front Of A Record Crowd

IN the first round of the FA Cup Pools were drawn against a non-league team for the second year running, this time Rhyl, champions of the Cheshire League.

An unbelievably large crowd of 13,037 turned up to see Alex Elder and Leo Harden score the goals to give Pools victory.

In the next round they were paired at Third Division (South) strugglers Watford.

Pools returned from their first visit to Vicarage Road with a win and their name was in the draw for the third round of the cup for the first time since the Grimsby games in 1936 and for only the second time in their history.

The reward was a plum but difficult tie – away to Burnley.

Following a five-game unbeaten run over the festive period, Pools made the trip across the Pennines in good form.

They were watched by 38,608 fans, the biggest crowd that United had ever played in front of (a record which remained for over half a century). Amongst the throng were 3,000 Pools followers.

Burnley included former Pools keeper Jimmy

Strong, who had been a virtual ever present for the past four seasons. Pools lost 1-0, but never looked out of place against their more illustrious opponents, with Moore impressing.

A sloppy goal by Les Shannon just before half-time was enough to seal Pools' fate.

New Nickname Sought For Club

IN the midst of the FA Cup run, town newspaper The Northern Daily Mail ran a regular feature for fans to adopt a catchword or nickname that represented the Club.

The most popular choice was that the Club be called The Monkey Hangers – but the tag was rejected by the board because the history of the story stemmed purely from Hartlepool and not West Hartlepool, where the Club was based, and where the bulk of the Club backers and ultimately board members originated.

Clearly buoyed by their Burnley performance, Pools won their next three games and pushed up to fifth place.

But as quickly as the run started it ended. Away defeats at Southport and Halifax were followed by a home draw with Rochdale and the remainder of the season, with a few minor exceptions, followed the pattern of the start of the season, with home victories followed by away defeats.

The great home form of 17 wins was the best ever achieved, beating the previous record of 16 set in 1936-37, and contributed to the Club finishing in ninth place, their highest position since the pre-war season when they were positioned sixth.

Pools also won their first post-war DSC when they beat Gateshead 3-0 on April 23, 1952, with a Wildon strike and two from the spot from penalty king Joe Willetts.

The team lined up as follows – Brown, Willets, Thompson, Stamper, Moore, Richley, Burnett, Elder, Wildon, McGuigan and McClure.

Wildon again finished top scorer, netting 19 times, ably supported by Alex Elder who scored ten.

Westgarth had a settled team under his wing with ten players or more appearing in 33 out of the 46 games, Watty Moore and Joe Willets ever present.

Billy Linacre

The second string also had a better season, finishing seventh. Pools recorded their best average attendance – 9,247, a rise of 23% on the previous campaign and an average which has never been bettered.

New Chairman Needed As Groundwork Starts

MAY 7 1952 finally saw the end of the reign as Chairman for Bill Yeats.

After his change of heart the previous summer, he refused to stay at the helm but was made Club President. Harry Sergeant finally became Chairman, as was intended 12 months before.

The summer of 1952 saw work commence on the Mill House side of the ground including re-terracing and the building of new turnstile housings. Filling in with hard core was planned and to reduce on the cost, that side of the ground was advertised as a tip, for suitable hard core and ashes.

The local brewery, JW Cameron & Co, had also offered to erect a canopy covering the middle section of the Town End.

The land behind the Mill House side was used as a makeshift car park, but a local rugby concern had approached the local authority for permission to have an enclosed field placed there.

The boundaries would have been within 15 feet of the Vic and Club officials were concerned for the safety of thousands of supporters leaving the ground from that side in such a confined space. The matter took nearly four months to resolve, but Pools got their way and the area was designated as a car park.

A very quiet close season for transfers saw Jackie Sloan move to South Shields and Dick Ballantyne refuse to return north, as he remained at his London base. The only signings were former Preston keeper Brian Powton and ex-Sheffield United forward Brian Weatherspoon.

1952-53

POOLS enjoyed a good 4-1 win over Accrington on August 23, with Weatherspoon scoring on his debut along with McGuigan, Elder and McClure.

It was to prove the highlight of the season.

After such a promising previous campaign, Pools failed to impress this time around.

Weatherspoon departed after just three games and despite the bulk of the squad being retained, little progress was made on the pitch, a flirtation with the top ten during October was the best it got.

November 15 saw a crushing defeat at Grimsby which proved to be the last of the four games that keeper Powton was to play. He conceded seven goals.

Crowd Favourite Returns To The Vic

ELDER and Wildon scored 15 goals between them but the Club sought additional firepower and, after failing to net Newcastle forward Neville Black, they believed they had found their answer during the FA Cup first round victory over Chester.

Among the opposition that day was former favourite Fred Richardson, who had joined Chester via West Brom after leaving Pools some four years earlier. A week later he signed for the Club in a £1,000 deal.

Knocked out of the FA Cup in the next round at Tranmere, it really was a season to forget.

Richardson took ten games to register his first goal and only managed four over the course of the season. Top marksman for the third successive season, despite missing a third of the games, was Wildon with 11.

The poor displays on the pitch saw the attendances dip to just above the 8,000 level, with the team finishing a disappointing 17th.

The reserves had an equally poor season, finishing fourth from bottom in the NEL.

During March the Club agreed to play a friendly at Billingham Synthonia under their newly-installed floodlights. However, set deep in the middle of ICI territory and surrounded by other chemical companies as well, the game was hampered by smog.

Pools sent a full first XI and comfortably ran out 5-0 winners, with McGuigan getting a hat-trick.

Pools did receive a financial bonus when Notts County, who had been negotiating over the fee for Ken McPherson for some months, agreed to pay £100 and send a team up for a friendly to play Pools on April 15, with Pools retaining the entire gate and paying County just travelling expenses.

Pools Gunning For Success

DUE to Fred Westgarth's links and popularity in the footballing fraternity, his side regularly received the shirts of footballing giants Arsenal as an away game option.

But for this game Pools played at home wearing the famous red and white strip and won with goals from Richardson and Burnett.

Once again though, there was a strong consistent line up on the whole to the team.

Keeper Berry Brown played in 42 games, behind full backs Thompson and Willetts, who was ever-present for the second season running, meaning he had now played in 136 consecutive Football League games, way ahead of his nearest contender for this honour, pre-war winger Tommy Hird.

In front of them were Moore and Newton and further forward Burnett, McGuigan and Stamper were always called upon.

The Club believed that they had a good nucleus of a team and surely needed only to fine tune the squad to achieve Fred Westgarth's ambition of having a side capable of fighting for promotion.

During June the Club agreed to a request from the Durham FA for the ground to be used for a match between a County Durham Representative side and the South African touring team to be played towards the end of October.

The Club were also looking into the possibility of having floodlights erected and were receiving tenders for the work, after being impressed by those they had seen at Carlisle United's Brunton Park.

Once more the summer passed with little activity on the transfer market. Dick Ballantyne again refused to re-sign and he offered his services to Millwall for no fee, with the Lions agreeing to pay a sum if he was ever of any service, but he never played for them.

New Signings Arrive At The Vic

POOLS signings included Sunderland reserve wing half Neville Clark, who had spent four years with the Rokerites without breaking into their first team. Alex Elder was allowed to leave the Club on a free transfer and returned north of the border, joining Forfar Athletic.

Also joining during the summer were two former Middlesbrough players. Inside forward Peter Desmond arrived from Stockton, while 29-year-old winger Billy 'Legs' Linacre joined from Goole Town.

He was given that nickname after he had suffered broken legs four times

Peter Desmond

<u>MIDDLESBROUGH FOOTBALL & ATHLETIC CO., LTD.</u>

Ayresome Park,

MIDDLESBROUGH.

Aug. 1953.

The Middlesbrough F. & Ath. Co. Ltd., agree to the transfer of William
Linacre from the aforementioned club to Hartlepools United F.C. on the
following conditions:-

"a"   That in view of us letting you play this transfer listed player
       the Chairman, Directors and Management of the Hartlepools United F.C.
       will fulfil the following.

"b"   That any enquiries by Clubs, or Club Representatives, for his
       transfer from the Hartlepool Club, shall receive every encourage-
       ment.

"c"   That all enquiries shall be immediately submitted to the
       Middlesbrough F.C. for consideration, advise and procedure.

"d"   That any fee received for this player's transfer from the Hartlepools
       Club, shall be paid intact, without reservation, or reservations, to
       the Middlesbrough F. & Ath. Co. Ltd. within seven days of receipt of
       such transfer fee by the Hartlepool United F.C.

       The above conditions are understood and agreed to by the following
       signatories acting for and with the authority of the Chairman,
       Directors and Management of the Hartlepools United F.C.

(Sgd) H J Sargeon   Chairman. Hartlepool F.C.

(Sgd) F Westgarth   Manager. Hartlepool F.C.

Witness:-

Manager, Middlesbrough F.

The conditions relating to Linacre's contract signed by the manager and chairman

throughout his career. Twice it happened in one season with his home-town club Chesterfield, in the top flight with Manchester City and then Middlesbrough.

He had been playing for Goole to regain fitness and his registration was still held by Middlesbrough, who granted him a free transfer, but insisted on a clause stating any transfer fee which Pools may subsequently receive had to be paid direct to them.

Johnson Returns From Hong Kong

THE squad was also bolstered by the return of youngster Kenny Johnson, back from National Service overseas. After scoring on his debut on New Year's Eve in 1949, he played for the reserves as well as Crook Town, before serving with the 34th Royal Artillery Light Attack in Hong Kong.

While still on Pools' books as an amateur he appeared for the British Army as well as the Combined Services and represented the latter in the Hong Kong first division. As well as winning caps for the Army he also played for the Hong Kong national side, technically making him the first player on the books of the Club to win full international honours.

On his return to the country in the spring he was signed as a professional in the Great North Eastern Hotel in King's Cross, London. Pools had moved swiftly to ensure that nobody else got their hands on this blossoming talent.

1953-54

JOHNSON was off and running straight away, netting in a 1-1 draw on the opening day of the season at Chester as Pools lined as follows – Alex Corbett, Joe Willetts, Ray Thompson, Jackie Newton, Frank Stamper, Billy Linacre, Ken Johnson, Fred Richardson, Tommy McGuigan and Jimmy McLaughlin.

Corbett was a former New Brighton and Hull keeper and McLaughlin had also joined in the

Ken Johnson (third from left) returned from Hong Kong in 1953

summer from Alloa Athletic.

With two new wingers, a new keeper, cover in the half back roles provided by Clark and the return of Johnson, manager Westgarth believed he had now got it right and the Club could start a push for a spot in the upper reaches of the table where he believed that a side with such a work-rate and talent deserved to be.

Alex Corbett

But his hopes were futile. Changes were made as Moore and Wildon returned, but after nine games without a win Pools stood second bottom. It was their worst start to a season and, taking into account the two games at the end of the previous season, it was 11 games without a win, equalling their dismal run back in 1937-38.

With Brown restored between the posts and with Desmond making his first (and only) start, Pools finally got a win under their belts with a 3-2 victory over Scunthorpe on September 21, 1953, with Leo Harden, Eric Wildon and Ken Johnson scoring.

New Signing Luke Suffers Bad Luck

FIVE more points from the next four games saw the Club reach 20th and, after spurning an offer of £1,000 from Bradford PA for Wildon, Westgarth popped up the road to Newcastle and signed reserve forward George Luke, hoping he would score the goals to steer them further away from the foot of the table.

But this didn't work either. Luke played two games, missed the next three (including a six-goal rout of Rochdale when Harden bagged four) and played in the two FA Cup games against Mansfield, but during the 3-0 win in a replay at Field Mill he received

George Luke

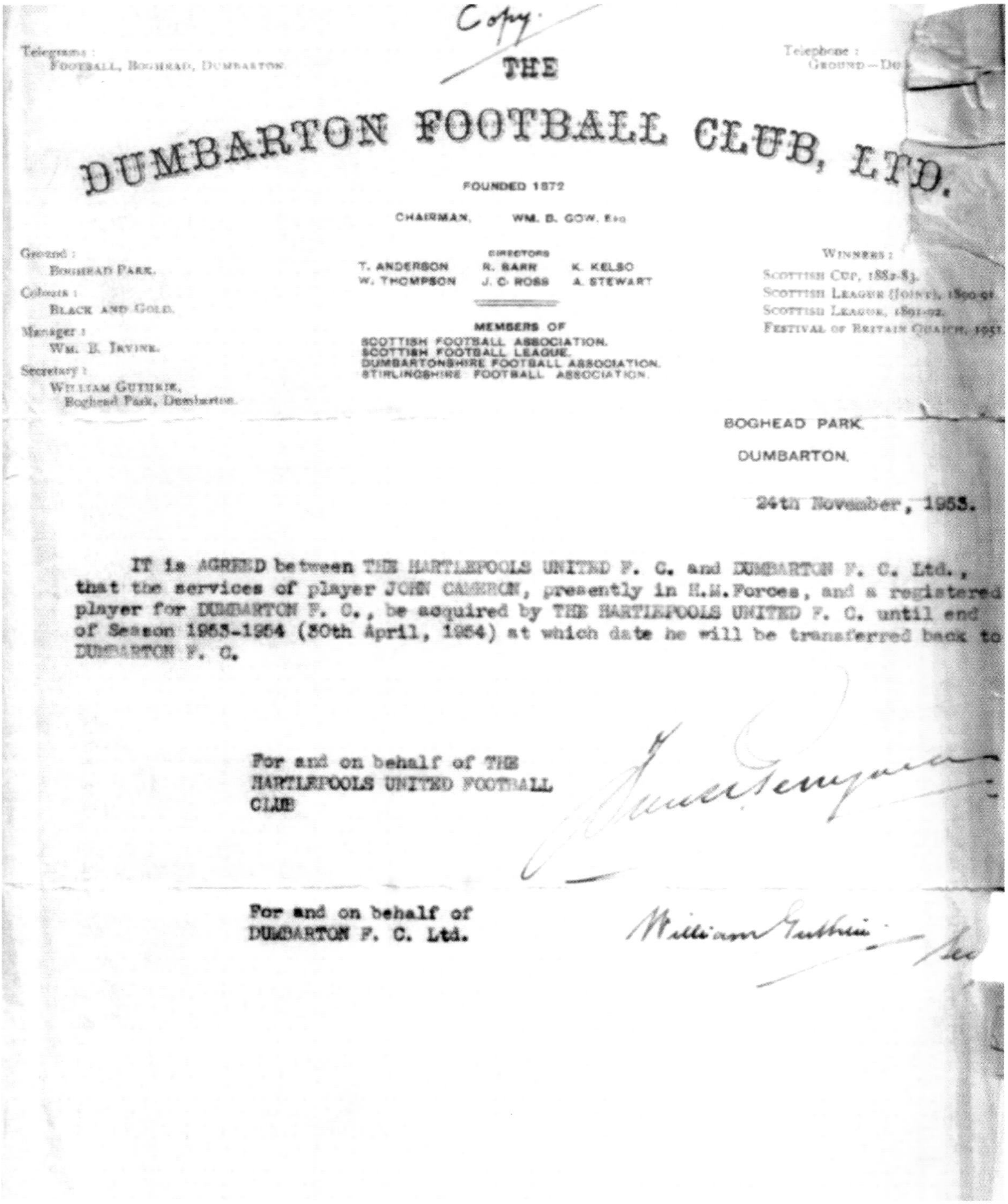

Copy.

THE

DUMBARTON FOOTBALL CLUB, LTD.

FOUNDED 1872

CHAIRMAN, WM. B. GOW, Esq

Telegrams :
Football, Boghead, Dumbarton.

Telephone :
Ground—Du

DIRECTORS
T. ANDERSON   R. BARR   K. KELSO
W. THOMPSON   J. C. ROSS   A. STEWART

MEMBERS OF
SCOTTISH FOOTBALL ASSOCIATION.
SCOTTISH FOOTBALL LEAGUE.
DUMBARTONSHIRE FOOTBALL ASSOCIATION.
STIRLINGSHIRE FOOTBALL ASSOCIATION.

WINNERS :
Scottish Cup, 1882-83.
Scottish League (Joint), 1890-91.
Scottish League, 1891-92.
Festival of Britain Quaich, 1951.

Ground :
Boghead Park.
Colours :
Black and Gold.
Manager :
Wm. B. Irvine.
Secretary :
William Guthrie,
Boghead Park, Dumbarton.

BOGHEAD PARK,
DUMBARTON.

24th November, 1953.

IT is AGREED between THE HARTLEPOOLS UNITED F. C. and DUMBARTON F. C. Ltd., that the services of player JOHN CAMERON, presently in H.M.Forces, and a registered player for DUMBARTON F. C., be acquired by THE HARTLEPOOLS UNITED F. C. until end of Season 1953-1954 (30th April, 1954) at which date he will be transferred back to DUMBARTON F. C.

For and on behalf of THE
HARTLEPOOLS UNITED FOOTBALL
CLUB

For and on behalf of
DUMBARTON F. C. Ltd.

William Guthrie

A letter from Dumbarton relating to the Cameron transfer

George Taylor

knee cartilage damage and wouldn't play again during the season.

The Club were still trying to add to the squad in other areas and signed, on a free transfer, Dumbarton full-back Jack Cameron. He was stationed nearby on military duties and would return to the Scottish side at the end of the season, unless he wished to negotiate terms with Pools.

Attempts to sign Arsenal's Don Rossiter on similar terms were successful, but spoiled when the player was re-stationed from Catterick Garrison to Malaya at short notice. Also arriving, to provide competition for Brown, was former Aldershot keeper George Taylor.

The second round of the FA Cup saw Pools drawn at Northampton and in front of 18,772 fans at the County Ground, a Harden goal earned Pools a replay at the Vic and on 16

December 1953, an extra time winner from Billy Linacre ensured a mouth-watering tie at the other Victoria Ground, home of Stoke City.

The second division side had just been relegated after 20 years in the top flight and would have proved a great scalp for Pools.

However, despite taking the lead through Fred Richardson, Pools were sent packing 6-2 in front of 23,927 fans of which 2,000 were Pools followers.

Boss Turns Down Chance To Leave

MANAGER Westgarth, although happy at the Club, was interviewed for the manager's job at Workington but he failed to agree terms. The job was given to former Grimsby manager William Shankly, who went on to earn legendary status at Liverpool.

The poor form continued after the match at Stoke and a 5-0 drubbing at the hands of Bradford PA on 23 January 1954, saw the pressure on Brown for his goalkeeping jersey tell and for the next game at Carlisle, George Taylor was called up for his debut. His inclusion helped as Pools won 3-2, but he failed to keep a clean sheet in the next four games and his

Hartlepool United – 1954 Durham Senior Cup Winners. Back row: Frank Perryman (Secretary), Ned Westgarth, Billy Linacre, Fred Richardson, Jackie Newton, Watty Moore, Alex Corbett, George Taylor, Berry Brown, Frankie Stamper, Jackie Smith, Ray Thompson, Jimmy McLaughlin, Fred Westgarth. Front row: Ken Johnson, Eric Wildon, Joe Willetts, Tommy McGuigan, Leo Harden

forwards failed to score as the team dropped to 21st in the table.

But, as unpredictable as ever, Pools then beat Stockport County 6-0, with the help of a McGuigan hat-trick.

Away from the first team, the Supporters Association had been running a junior team in local minor leagues and now several of the players were beginning to show promise. As a result, the Association were hoping to get the team entered into the ranks of the Football League's recently-established Intermediate League.

A late run of only one loss in the last seven games saw Pools haul themselves up to 16th place by the end of the season. Wildon finished top scorer for the season with 15 goals from 28 starts. The Club won the DSC once more, beating Sunderland 3-0, with Wildon, Willetts and Harden finding the net.

Extensive Work On Vic Planned

THE board announced that they intended to construct a new stand on the Mill House side, a bold venture but one which signalled the intent of the Club.

The Corporation had a clause set into the sale of the ground back to the Club that they could apply at any time for the widening of Clarence Road, which would result in the possible reconstruction of the east side of the ground.

The authority insisted they had no desire to expand the road within the next ten years, so the Club decided to extend the seating area in the Clarence Road stand at a cost of £1,000. It placed additional financial pressure on the board and a reshuffle of the directors took place to compensate for the signing of additional guarantees with the Club's bankers to accommodate the debt, which was now around £4,000.

Jackie Milburn On Show At The Vic

LONG servants Ray Thompson and Jackie Newton were granted a benefit game towards the end of the season and Newcastle United agreed to send a full-strength XI.

On April 28, a side including Bob Stokoe, Irish International Alf McMichael and the legendary Jackie Milburn were on show as 9,635 fans saw a 1-1 draw. Frankie Stamper put through his own net in the first half and Pools equalised through Kenny Johnson in the final minutes.

It was the first of several benefit games for Pools players that Newcastle had agreed to turn up for over the course of the next few seasons,

Richardson challenging for the ball in the snow during the FA Cup replay at Ayresome Park, with Stamper, Johnson and McGuigan looking on.

Hartlepool Mail

due to more of Westgarth's connections, this time with Stan Seymour.

There was very little transfer activity during the close season with only Jack Cameron joining permanently from Dumbarton.

1954-55

GOALS from Eric Wildon, in his eighth year with the Club, and Tommy McGuigan, his 35th goal for Pools, secured an opening day 2-1 win over Crewe on August 21, 1954.

It instigated a healthy start and, after six games, Pools stood in tenth place after wining their three home games and losing the same number away. A three-game winless run dragged Pools down to 18th place.

After another couple of games they found themselves one place higher and then they turned the corner.

With Berry Brown restored to the side and with Johnson playing inside right to Fred Richardson, Pools won four consecutive games and climbed to ninth.

Draws with Bradford and Barnsley saw them consolidate that position and the game against the Tykes saw the return to the fold of George Luke. He had been out for nearly 12 months but had refused to have another operation on his knee because he wanted to continue playing football for Hartlepools.

The Barnsley game also saw the beginning of the end of the career of Billy Burnett. The right winger had been with the Club for six years but made only 11 starts the previous season, had failed to figure so far this campaign, but was selected as travelling reserve.

He was late to meet the travelling party after missing the train from his home in Gateshead and ended up playing for the reserves at the Vic that day. At a board meeting the following week he was handed a free transfer for his indiscipline. He was also fined £5 and within a month was playing for Consett.

A new winger, George Willis, was quickly recruited. The former Evenwood Town player had been playing for Leeds before starting his National Service with the 7th Battalion Royal Signals based at Catterick.

A 4-2 win over Scunthorpe and a 4-1 win at Wrexham, with McGuigan netting twice in each game, saw Pools climb to the heady heights of fourth, after being unbeaten in eight.

FA Cup Clash With Rivals

IN the first round of the FA Cup on November 20, a second-half goal from Fred Richardson saw Pools progress. Two more victories followed and third-placed Pools entertained Aldershot on December 11 – and sent them packing with plenty to think about on their long journey south, after entertaining the 14,813 home crowd to a dashing 4-0 victory. McGuigan scored twice, a penalty from Joe Willetts and Fred Richardson's fourth goal in four games doing the damage.

Pools made it through to the third round of the FA Cup for the third time in four seasons and were hoping for a plum draw against a top Club.

But there was to be no big fish served before Pools as they were drawn against Darlington. A tie against the local foe was sure to generate interest, with Pools standing an excellent chance of progressing to the fourth round for the first time.

Pools were also due to play their rivals in the Football League on Christmas Day (with an afternoon kick-off so it didn't clash with church services) as well as on December 27.

On both occasions solitary goals from Leo Harden were enough to secure victories, giving Pools a psychological advantage.

Pools were sitting in second place, just a point behind Scunthorpe.

Johnson Forced To Play In Goal

ON New Year's Day, Pools took to the Vic in front of 12,445 fans and a goal by Fred Richardson took them to the top of the table for the first time in their history.

The FA Cup game at the Vic on January 8 saw increased prices applied at the gate of two shillings and sixpence for adults and a crowd of 12,450.

Pools fell behind, but hit back for a 1-1 draw with a second half goal from Harden.

The replay took place midweek at Feethams and in increasingly poor weather, the pitch resembling an ice rink. Pools struggled and were 1-0 down when keeper Berry Brown was injured and had to be carried from the pitch.

With no substitutes the onus fell upon Kenny Johnson to step into the breach (he later went on to appear in every other position for Pools). Darlington were soon awarded a penalty before the half hour mark. But Johnson didn't get a chance to save the kick as Brown was hurriedly restored to service, albeit in vain as Darlington scored from the spot and Pools were two down.

However, the second half was the Fred Richardson show as he netted twice, forcing another replay.

Richardson had been in fine form and his 11 goals had been a pivotal part of the unbeaten run of 18 games. The record run was abruptly halted at Chester on January 15th, when Pools lost by a single goal.

The undefeated stretch equalled that of the Club's second season and was to remain a record for longer than any would have thought possible.

Quakers Win Sets Up Epic Forest Tie

A second replay took place at Ayresome Park on January 17, 1955 when a goal from Richardson and a penalty from Jackie Newton saw Pools through to the next round in front of just under 11,000 fans in a game played on a snowbound pitch.

The reward for Pools was a home tie against second division Nottingham Forest, giving Pools a chance to progress even further. The opposition were having a poor season in comparison to their recent years of challenging for promotion to the top flight.

A record crowd of 17,200 paid the same increased prices for the Forest tie on January 29.

The all-ticket game saw a big demand and long queues were seen at the Vic for days with the game sold out by January 24.

Pools fought for 90 enthralling minutes with Forest and there was nothing more than a cigarette paper between the two sides.

However, after the interval Forest took the

Bobby Lumley

lead and just as it looked as though Pools were on their way out, a moment of individual flair got them level.

With 15 minutes remaining George Luke whipped a ball in from the left and Johnson cheekily back heeled the ball in the direction of the goal. Forest defender Geoff Thomas handled on the line and Jackie Newton converted the penalty, sending the crowd into raptures.

A crowd in excess of 20,000 at the City Ground for the replay saw a hard match and at full time the game was tied at 1-1, Pools netting through Frankie Stamper.

The game seemed destined not to end in Pools' favour as the normally dependable Jackie Newton fired a second half penalty wide.

In extra time Pools could not make their pressure tell and it seemed as though another replay was on the cards when disaster struck with little over five minutes left. Forest scrambled home a winner, denying Pools the chance of a home tie with Newcastle United in the fifth round.

Manager Westgarth kept the pressure on his

		P	HW	HD	HL	HF	HA	AW	AD	AL	AF	AA	POINTS
1	Barnsley	46	18	3	2	51	17	12	2	9	35	29	65
2	Accrington Stanley	46	18	2	3	65	32	7	9	7	31	35	61
3	Scunthorpe & Lindsey United	46	14	6	3	45	18	9	6	8	36	35	58
4	York City	46	13	5	5	43	27	11	5	7	49	36	58
5	**HARTLEPOOLS UNITED**	46	16	3	4	39	20	9	2	12	25	29	55
6	Chesterfield	46	17	1	5	54	33	7	5	11	27	37	54
7	Gateshead	46	11	7	5	38	26	9	5	9	27	43	52
8	Workington	46	11	7	5	39	23	7	7	9	29	32	50
9	Stockport County	46	13	4	6	50	27	5	8	10	34	43	48
10	Oldham Athletic	46	14	5	4	47	22	5	5	13	27	46	48
11	Southport	46	10	9	4	28	18	6	7	10	19	26	48
12	Rochdale	46	10	9	4	28	18	6	7	10	19	26	48
13	Mansfield Town	46	14	4	5	40	28	4	5	14	25	43	45
14	Halifax Town	46	9	9	6	41	27	6	4	13	22	40	43
15	Darlington	46	11	6	6	40	30	6	3	14	23	43	43
16	Bradford Park Avenue	46	11	7	5	29	21	4	4	15	27	49	41
17	Barrow	46	12	4	7	39	34	5	2	16	31	55	40
18	Wrexham	46	9	6	8	40	35	4	6	13	25	42	38
19	Tranmere Rovers	46	9	6	8	37	30	4	5	14	18	40	37
20	Carlisle United	46	12	1	10	53	39	3	5	15	25	50	36
21	Bradford City	46	12	1	10	53	39	3	5	15	25	50	36
22	Crewe Alexandra	46	8	10	5	45	35	2	4	17	23	56	34
23	Grimsby Town	46	10	4	9	28	32	3	4	16	19	46	34
24	Chester	46	10	3	10	23	25	2	6	15	21	52	33

Football League Division Four 1954-55

players after the FA Cup exit when he signed 22-year-old Bobby Lumley from Charlton Athletic. The inside forward was born in the North-East but had been with Charlton since he signed for them as a teenager and cost Pools £1,000. He was thrown straight into action and scored a brace on his debut in a 3-1 win over Rochdale on 12th February.

Pools were still performing well, but the after effects of the cup run saw them drop to fifth in the table.

Club In The Frame For Promotion

WITH a backlog of fixtures, Pools faced two games in as many days. Following a 3-0 defeat at Chesterfield on April 9, Pools went to league leaders Accrington Stanley 24 hours later – but there was no signs of fatigue as Pools ran out 5-2 winners with goals from Stamper (2), Linacre, Johnson and a recalled Wildon.

There was a genuine belief that they could catch the leaders. Although they were five points behind, Pools had a game in hand and also had to play Stanley at the Vic.

Three wins in the next four games saw Pools still in fourth place, but they let themselves down when they were beaten 3-1 at home by Accrington and then failed to win their last two fixtures.

Accrington also slipped up, with Barnsley winning the title. Pools finished in an excellent fifth place, six points adrift of the Yorkshire club.

The cup exploits of the past few seasons had not only benefited the Club financially, but the improvements were there for all to see this season with the team finally meeting the expectations of the fans and finally showing that they were capable of maintaining a challenge for the title under the auspices of Westgarth.

Once again a small squad was used with seven players appearing in more than 40 games.

Jack Cameron, Kenny Johnson, Billy Linacre, Jackie Newton and Frank Stamper were amongst these seven, Watty Moore was an ever present and Tommy McGuigan top scored with 18 goals in his 44 appearances.

Manager Keeps Squad Together

WESTGARTH clearly had faith in his players and, as a result, was again quiet in the summer transfer market.

The main addition to the squad was winger Joe Rayment, a former captain of West

Hartlepool Schoolboys before joining Middlesbrough where he had spent three seasons on the fringes of the first team.

He was the son of Joe Rayment snr who played for Pools in 1927-28. A compact, swift player he was expected to provide great competition for forward places. Also arriving was former Newcastle United reserve Bill Robinson who joined from West Stanley.

Pushing for a start were Jackie Smith, a young local forward, and reserve keeper Jim Dyson. Smith was expected to compete for a place after forward Eric Wildon moved to Billy Brown's Stockton side and a similar role was expected of keeper Dyson who had seen rival George Taylor move to Easington CW. The task of replacing Wildon was a tall one as the 31-year-old had scored 87 league goals in exactly 200 starts.

1955/56

THE opening game of the season brought Darlington as the first opposition at the Vic and a crowd of more than 10,000 saw Pools outclass their neighbours, scoring three without reply, with goals from debutant Rayment, Luke and Jackie Smith.

The full starting XI had a familiar look about it – Jim Dyson, Jack Cameron, Ray Thompson, Jackie Newton, Watty Moore, Frank Stamper, Joe Rayment, Bobby Lumley, Jackie Smith, Tommy McGuigan and George Luke.

It was a side packed with experience and Thompson, Moore, Newton, Stamper and McGuigan had played in well over 1,100 games for Pools. A lot depended on how the rest of the squad would gel with the stalwarts to improve on the excellent performance last year.

Early Optimism Checked By Results

ANY pre-conceptions of an easy season were dealt a double edged blow with two crushing defeats at Workington on August 24 and Stockport three days later. A 5-1 loss and a 4-0 defeat left the Club in 21st place after just three games.

But four wins from the next six games, including a Smith hat trick in a 4-2 win over Mansfield, put Pools in 12th and saw a Monday night fixture at the Vic against Derby County, who had been playing top flight football only three seasons ago.

A hard-fought display in front of 9,170 saw Pools run out worthy winners with goals from Billy Linacre and George Luke, catapulting them to fourth in this tight division.

Newcastle Come To The Vic Again

ON September 21, Newcastle United sent a full strength team to play a testimonial game for Joe Willetts and Watty Moore.

The game was supposed to take place at the end of the previous season, but was delayed due to the Magpies' FA Cup triumph.

A strong Newcastle XI hammered Pools 5-0, with two from Jackie Milburn. A crowd of just under 5,500 were present to pay homage to the players. Willetts had been a great servant and had appeared in over 250 games, including a record 196 consecutive outings. He also figured during WWII.

Moore had been with the Club seven seasons, hardly missing a game over the past four and was considered to be one of the main reasons for the upturn in fortunes.

But Pools then lost four of the next five games, dropping down to 15th, before bouncing back with three straight wins.

Winger Billy Linacre moved to Mansfield Town in October, with his chances for first team starts restricted due to the impressive form of Rayment.

The FA Cup brought a first round tie against Gateshead and a goal from Bobby Lumley and a pair from George Luke gave Pools a 3-0 passage into the second round and a tie at Chesterfield on December 10, 1955.

In between the cup ties, league form was good and wins over Barrow and Chester had left Pools sitting in seventh place.

More Cup Joy As Pools Set Up Chelsea Tie

AT Chesterfield in the FA Cup, it proved to be a closer game than the Gateshead match and the game was 1-1 with just a few minutes to go, when George Luke grabbed his second to put Pools into the hat for the third round.

Pools form building up to the tie was again inconsistent. A 6-1 Boxing Day thrashing of Crewe in which Kenny Johnson netted four was followed by a New Year's Day defeat at Mansfield.

The up and down form was not the best preparation for their FA Cup game at the Vic against last season's first division champions Chelsea, a side that included England caps John Sillett, Roy Bentley and Frank Blunstone.

Try as they might Pools could not break the Londoners down and ended up on the losing side by the single goal, an own goal at that, in front of just under 17,000 supporters.

League form improved and improved and coincided with the return of Rayment. His relentless running and accurate crossing seemed to be the changing point. After his comeback on January 21, 1956 Pools lost only one of eight games to settle in fifth place, with Kenny Johnson on the receiving end of Rayment's crosses, notching eight in eight.

Four defeats in the last ten soured the run-in slightly and Pools finished fourth, equalling their highest placing. Top scorer was Kenny Johnson with 21, supported ably by George

Ken Johnson scores at Blyth

Hartlepool Mail

Luke on 19. In a 20-game stint, Johnson netted a goal a game.

Despite the form of the first XI, the reserves had another disappointing season finishing fourth from bottom of the NEL.

Goals Galore In Season Ending Friendly

ONCE again it was testimonial time and Newcastle United were again the providers of the opposition.

On April 25, it was the turn of long servants McGuigan and Stamper to receive benefits and what a game it was. A crowd of 7,206 saw Pools take a four-goal lead within 20 minutes, with Bobby Lumley netting one and Kenny Johnson smashing a hat-trick.

Billy Robinson made it five just after the half hour mark for a remarkable interval score, with guest keeper Rolando Ugolini keeping a clean sheet. He was born in Italy and spent many seasons at Middlesbrough where he was coming to the end of his career after playing in over 300 games.

Ten minutes after the restart and Newcastle clawed their way back with goals from Bobby Mitchell and Vic Keeble, before a fourth from Johnson put the game beyond doubt.

The exciting end of season finale finished 6-3 to Pools, after Bobby Cummings netted a third for the visitors.

Club Stalwarts Leave The Vic

SOON on their way out were keeper Berry Brown after 126 starts over five seasons. He had lost his jersey to Jim Dyson. Also departing were long servants Willetts, Richardson and Harden.

Joe Willetts was approaching 32, had given the Club great service and moved to Horden Colliery Welfare. Departing for Thornley CW was Fred Richardson, 31, who had been a great asset during his two stints, but he struggled to get a regular start last season. Joining him there was local favourite Leo Harden. Again in his 30s, the Flying Dustman left after notching 52 goals in ten seasons.

After clearing the decks of some older players, Westgarth only made one significant signing during the summer, the capture of West Hartlepool-born keeper Ron Guthrie. The 23-year-old first played as a schoolboy for Elwick Road Juniors. He was on the books of Darlington, but joined Tow Law Town. In May 1953, he made the move to the capital and signed for Arsenal, spending three seasons with The Gunners, appearing in just the two

outings, but he was a member of the side that won the London FA Challenge Cup in 1954 and the Eastern Counties League the following season.

1956/57

THE season started on a high when Chesterfield were thumped 5-1 at the Vic on August 18, with goals from Lumley, Rayment, Johnson, McGuigan and Stamper.

A draw and a win at Wrexham and Chester respectively were followed by a home win over Wrexham and Pools were a point clear at the top.

Exciting Start To The New Campaign

THE players couldn't stop scoring, smashing six past Southport away from home thanks to a brace from Robinson and a four-goal haul from Johnson, and a further five past the same opposition at the Vic six days later.

The result took them back to the top after a minor hiccup and there they stayed for two months until after the first round of the FA Cup in November.

Regularly playing in front of crowds in excess of 10,000, Pools beat most opponents put in front of them. They hit four past Stockport at Edgeley Park and five past Tranmere at the Vic when Johnson again netted four.

They beat Carlisle, Darlington, Crewe and even the much-fancied Derby County. In their first 16 games they had lost only twice – then the wheels came off.

Defeats against Rochdale and Halifax were followed by a draw at Workington, before the chance to refocus came in the FA Cup first round at home to Selby when goals from Luke, Robinson and Stamper saw Pools through against the Yorkshire League outfit.

Defeat at Barrow and a draw at the Vic against Scunthorpe saw Pools lose their grip on the top slot with Accrington Stanley leapfrogging above them.

Pools Handed Giants In The Cup

THE second round of the FA Cup saw them drawn away to Blyth Spartans of the North Eastern League. The game was played in front of over 10,000 fans and Pools scraped through courtesy of a goal by the proflic Johnson, his 16th of the campaign so far.

Some 48 hours later, as the draw was made amid much anticipation, Pools were handed the

The Pools team which took on the Busby Babes in 1957. Back row: Tommy McGuigan, Bobby Lumley, Frank Stamper, Ralph Guthrie, Billy Anderson, Ray Thompson, Ken Johnson; Front row: Billy Robinson, Jack Cameron, Watty Moore, George Luke; Inset: Jackie Newton, Joe Rayment

most glamorous of home ties against a team from the top flight – Manchester United, known proudly as the Busby Babes.

The glee at drawing the most entertaining side in the country did nothing for Pools league form.

The opening day 5-1 victory over Chesterfield was reversed on December 15 and it was another three games before Pools registered a victory, over York at the Vic on Boxing Day.

By this time manager Westgarth was ill once more and bed-bound.

After such a good start to the season Pools managed eight games without a win.

They boasted a new signing in full-back Ken Waugh who joined from Newcastle United where his first team chances were limited. The side was also shuffled due to absence of Rayment who was suffering a knee injury, with Stamper playing in a more forward position.

Excitement Builds For Busby Babes Tie

A home victory over Gateshead and a draw against Hull brought Pools into a promising run of form by the time the third round game arrived.

With the game a sell out, anticipation had been building since the draw was made. Little did they know what they were about to see, a legendary game classed today as one of the greatest ever seen in the town.

Just as the season before when Chelsea were the visiting champions, so were the Red Devils.

But this United team were believed to be a better all round team, the result of years of ground work by the manager Matt Busby.

The Chelsea team were a squad of established older players and hard workers; the Red Devils were a team who played with great flair, brimming with young talent.

They lined up with 25 year old England international Ray Wood in goal. In front of him were Bill Foulkes and the legendary England man Roger Byrne. The half-backs were 20-year-old Edward Colman, 23-year-old Mark Jones and 20-year-old England player Duncan Edwards.

Up front were established England cap Johnny Berry, 20-year-old Irishman William Whelan, English international Tommy Taylor, another England striker in the form of free scoring Denis Violett and finally 21-year-old England international David Pegg.

TEAMS FOR SATURDAY, 5th JANUARY, 1957.   Kick off 2-15 p.m.

F.A. CHALLENGE CUP—THIRD ROUND   No. 2787

HARTLEPOOLS UNITED

Right Wing

1—Guthrie

2—Cameron   3—Thompson

4—Newton   5—Moore   6—Anderson

7—Robinson 8—McGuigan 9—Johnson 10—Stamper 11—Luke

Referee:
Mr. J. V. Sherlock
(Sheffield)

Linesmen:
Mr. P. Rhodes - Red
Mr. N. Haig - Yellow

11—Pegg 10—Viollet 9—Taylor 8—Whelan 7—Berry

6—Edwards 5—Jones 4—Colman

3—Byrne 2—Foulkes

1—Wood

Left Wing   Right Wing

MANCHESTER UNITED

Official Matchday Programme – Hartlepool United v Manchester United

Quite simply, it was a team full of quality and class and the Press were wondering just what Hartlepools' experienced backs could keep the score down to.

Within ten minutes of kick-off Pools had already conceded goals to Whelan and Berry. On the half hour, Taylor made it three.

An embarrassment was on the cards.

The majority of the 17,264 record attendance had their spirits lifted ten minutes before the interval when Stamper netted his fifth goal in the last four games.

When the referee blew for half time, the talk was of how many the visitors would score.

Whatever was said at half-time by the stand-in manager – Fred Westgarth was still bed-bound – seemed to do the trick as Pools came out for the second period full of energy and running and, buoyed by the reinvigorated crowd, they pulled a second back after just eight minutes when Kenny Johnson, suffering from injury, headed home.

Just over ten minutes later and the ground erupted. Pools were level when Jackie Newton hammered in a shot from nothing to bring hope of the biggest upset of all.

Pools pressed and pressed, forgetting about the difference in class and guile they pushed forward at every opportunity, but it was not to be.

After a period of Pools pressure, the Busby Babes settled and broke the hearts of all Pools fans when Whelan grabbed his second with quarter of an hour to go.

Sad News As Manager Passes Away

A month later saw the passing of Fred Westgarth. He had been an inspirational figure, seeing the Club through the war years and the difficult period afterwards. His team of local lads and shrewd signings took on the league champions of the past two seasons and lost by only a goal on each occasion.

They had also topped the league this season for two months and he would never be able to see if his squad could compete for honours.

Shortly before he passed away, his team had risen to the top of the table again following

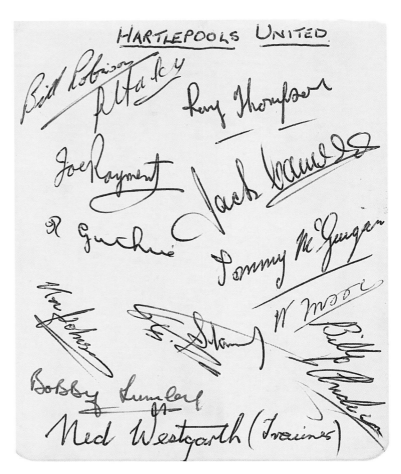

Player autographs from 1956/57 season

successive 4-1 home wins against Stockport and Oldham.

They stayed top until they visited Derby on February 16, where the Rams put Pools to the sword and beat them 2-0 in front of nearly 25,000 fans.

Pools regained top place the following week, but a 3-1 reverse at Feethams knocked them off again, never to return.

Who Would Be Next For Pools Hotseat?

DESPITE a good run of form throughout the rest of the season, they couldn't catch Derby who ended the season four points clear of Pools, making the away defeat at their hands so crucial.

Gone was their figurehead manager and supporters wondered what now for the Club. Who would replace Westgarth? What would happen to the players now their inspirational leader had passed away? These and many other questions were being asked by all.

The failure to get promoted took the shine off a great season.

Pools had a new goalscoring legend of their own in the shape of Kenny Johnson, who netted 24 league goals and he was more than ably assisted again by George Luke who chipped in with 19.

Again there was a great thread of consistency through the team with six players appearing in more than 40 games, three of them ever present – Guthrie, Moore and Thompson. The latter two had now been ever present for the past two seasons.

Attendances at home games had dipped so it was more than pleasing to see an average of 9,225 recorded (the second highest ever), a huge increase from the 7,411 of the previous season. It also brought a much-needed increase to the Club's coffers and a profit of more than £500 was recorded.

Board Surprise Fans With Appointment And A New League Introduced

NOT for the first, nor the last time, a board of Hartlepools directors made a surprise decision when they appointed the new manager in the summer of 1957.

Former Chesterfield and Derby goalkeeper Ray Middleton was handed the role of building on the foundations laid by Fred Westgarth.

Boldon-born Middleton turned professional with Chesterfield in 1937 and went on to appear in around 500 games there, including during WWII when he also worked as a miner. He moved to Derby in June 1951 and spent three years there before joining Boston United as player/manager in the summer of 1954. He came to Pools' attention after leading Boston to FA Cup giant killing heroics.

This was also to be the last season of the northern and southern sections of the third division, as the two leagues were to be split into a new division three and division four with the bottom 12 of the northern and southern sections forming the fourth division and the top twelve from each the third.

The new season was to be Pools' last chance to gain automatic promotion to the second division.

A few new players joined the Club during the summer in an attempt to push for promotion.

The main signings were wing-half Tom Burlison who joined from Lincoln City and former Wrexham forward and English amateur international Peter Thompson, who had scored 18 goals for the Welshmen the previous season.

1957/58

ON the opening day Pools won 2-1 at Accrington with goals from Tommy

Goalkeeper Ray Middleton

McGuigan and Jackie Smith. Interest in the Club was rife and a massive crowd of 15,176 turned up at the Vic on Monday, August 26. Pools didn't let their followers down as they thumped Darlington 5-1, with Jackie Smith scoring again and two goals each coming from George Willis and Bobby Lumley.

Two more wins saw them second in the table behind Bury who also had a 100% record. But a dip in form –one win in five – saw them drop to fourth.

Form continued to be hit and miss but still they flirted with the upper ranks of the division and by the end of October, after 16 games, they stood fourth.

Hit For Seven As Pools Plummet

POOLS were in for a shock as they journeyed to Rochdale on November 2, when Jimmy Dailey scored five of the hosts' seven.

In response, changes were made and dropped were Guthrie, Ray Thompson, Moore and Robinson, in place of Dyson, Cameron, Newton and McGuigan.

The alternations had the desired result – a 5-0 win over Halifax was followed by the same scoreline against Prescott Cables in the first round of the FA Cup, when Peter Thompson netted four.

The following league game saw Moore and Johnson back in the starting XI and Pools scored five again, this time past Hull, with McGuigan's goal adding to a pair each from Johnson and Thompson, who had made it 11 for the season.

A Johnson goal at Bradford the following week was enough for victory and took Pools back into third. Then, overnight, the bubble burst. Pools couldn't maintain their charge. One win in the next seven, including an FA Cup defeat at Stockport, was the start of it all.

Winger Bobby Lumley had agreed to join Chesterfield and the squad changed every game. Although they were only down to fifth in the table, it was a tight league and Pools were finding it difficult to field a regular XI, which had always been a major factor in their ascent to becoming one of the better clubs in the lower leagues.

Hartlepool Mail

1958/59 HUFC Team Photo. Back row: Billy Anderson, Ken Waugh, Jackie Newton, Ralph Guthrie, Frank Stamper, Ray Thompson, Jackie Smith, Frank Perryman (Secretary); Front row: Joe Rayment, Bobby Lumley, Ken Johnson, Watty Moore, George Willis, Tommy McGuigan, George Luke

After the burst of the bubble came freefall, Pools winning just once in the next dozen matches.

Now out of the all-important top 12 and struggling, they were playing in front of crowds of less than 6,000.

Additions such as Workington winger Norman Mitchell failed to help and the final seven games brought just two wins.

Pools had failed to qualify for the third division, ending a season which promised much, but delivered little, in 16th place.

The reserves finished 11th, dropping two places after their performances last year.

Disappointment Inspires Unpopular Changes

A year on and how things had changed. From being within four points of the second division, Pools were now in the new fourth and the Fred Westgarth era was well and truly over.

Average attendances had dropped to 7,852 and the Club reported a loss of just under £2,500. With the bulk of Westgarth's heroes being at the Club for many seasons and advancing in years, the man at the helm decided to axe some of the older wood and replace them with his own younger breed.

Keeper Ralph Guthrie moved to

Winger Norman Mitchell

Horden CW and McGuigan, now 34, went to Spennymoor United after netting 75 goals in his 350 games. Also departing was long serving Jackie Newton after 11 years and 361 starts, Frankie Stamper who joined Blyth after 301 games and Ray Thompson who had clocked up a Club record 423 outings. Joe Rayment made the shock move to Darlington where he was to stay for five seasons.

Drastic changes had been made. The heart of the team for so many seasons was beating no more and now the future direction of the Club would be determined by the quality of players signed.

These decisions weren't popular with supporters, as many believed that the players, crowd favourites among them, had a season or two left in them still.

With players aplenty on the way out, manager Middleton drafted in a player he remembered from his Chesterfield days, a 27-year-old forward called Johnny Langland who had left Saltergate and had been playing and scoring for Blyth Spartans.

Added to the books were local players Harry Herring and Arty Gibbon from Caledonians. A new keeper joined after being released by Doncaster, Stockton-born Norman Oakley chose Pools over Scunthorpe where he had just been on trial.

The major summer signing was forward Harry Clark from Sheffield Wednesday. Although the inside forward had played just once for Wednesday the previous season, he had spent seven seasons at Darlington where he was a constant threat in the 160 plus outings he enjoyed in a black and white shirt. Horden CW inside forward David Nicholson and former Grimsby reserve winger Brian Dunn, 18, also signed on.

"Soccer Star" Vol. 7, No. 30, April 18, 1959

Scoop! Pen Portraits inside

SOCCER STAR

9d.
The only
Soccer
Weekly

Hartlepools

Left to right (back row): K. Johnson, J. Cameron, N. Oakley, K. Waugh, W. Anderson, E. Westgarth (trainer); (front row): G. Luke, S. Nicholson, J. Langland, H. Clark, B. Dunn, W. Moore (captain). (W.1.)

Cover of Soccer Star, April 18, 1959

Clark watches as Smith puts pressure on Palace keeper Vic Rouse at Selhurst Park

1958-59

Biggest League Victory Recorded

DESPITE all the coming and goings, only two new faces were in the squad for the first game of the season – Nicholson and Dunn.

But they brought no luck as Pools lost 2-0 at home to Shrewsbury on August 23, 1958. Two days later and the same XI beat Bradford Park Avenue 3-0, with the goals from Willis, Dunn and a penalty from Billy Anderson. A draw at Southport followed putting them into ninth place, which, sadly, was to be the highest position that season.

Four goals conceded at Bradford PA was followed by giving away nine in their next two home games, 4-2 to Torquay and 5-1 to Port Vale, results which left them in the bottom three. A mini-run of three wins in four offered false hope and the season seemed over from a promotion point of view by November. A run of one win from six in October ensured it was.

Worse was to come when Derby County swooped for Peter Thompson at the start of November after 26 goals in 49 games.

Cup Run Takes Pools To Old Trafford

A neat 4-0 win over Oldham at the Vic on November 8 with goals from Langland (2), Johnson and a penalty by Anderson gave them a welcome boost before the FA Cup first round

game against Rochdale.

George Luke's goal earned a draw in the tie at home, and he scored a pair in a 3-3 draw in the replay with Johnson getting the other.

The second replay was played at a neutral venue and FA Cup officials decided it would be played at a ground closer to Rochdale than Hartlepool – but Pools weren't complaining one bit.

On November 27, Pools took to the pitch in front of 6,126 fans at Old Trafford, the home of Manchester United. And how Pools enjoyed the occasion, goals from Jackie Smith and Kenny Johnson saw them triumph 2-1.

However, that was as good as it got as Pools lost at Barrow in the next round.

The side was going through a period of endless changes to try and find some semblance of form. Middleton used eight players who didn't reach double figures for appearances in the campaign.

Some of his choices – Charlie Denham, Jim Dyson, Harry Herring, Terry MacGregor, Stan Nicholson, Windy Roberts, Bill Welford and George Willis – were squad players given a chance and didn't exactly qualify for the category of Pools' legends.

After the cup exit Pools won only eight out of their 25 remaining games, three of them in March.

A milestone was reached during the poor period when Club captain Watty Moore made his 400th Football League start in the 2-1 home victory over Crewe on January 31, some ten years after his debut.

Pools Record Biggest League Victory

ALL season the Club hovered above the re-election zone and with six games to go, they stood in 19th place.

Pools had a big game coming up, entertaining bottom placed Barrow at home. And the day was a happy one as everything the United forwards touched turned to goals.

A small crowd of just 4,126 saw Pools record what was and still remains their biggest ever Football League win when they beat the visitors 10-1. Clark, Luke and Smith had Pools three to the good with half an hour gone and by half-time it was an astonishing 7-0, after Smith finished his hat-trick off and Joe Scott and Johnny Langland had netted.

The second half saw Barrow score first and it took a full 20 minutes before Luke bagged the eighth.

Harry Clark got his second with ten minutes to go and, seven minutes from time, the tenth came courtesy of an own goal.

A final day victory over promoted Coventry rounded off a miserable season – 19th spot in the table and an average crowd which had dropped by almost 30% to 5,499.

The reserves did marginally better when they

Match Programme from the Rochdale FA Cup game at Old Trafford

finished eighth out of 19 in their first season in the Northern Regional League.

Harry Clark's 12 goals put him top league scorer, with George Luke netting ten league goals with an additional three in the FA Cup.

The goals from Kenny Johnson had dried up after he was moved from the forward line to play a half back role alongside Bill Anderson and 33-year-old Watty Moore.

After the release of a few squad members but no established names, the annual batch of new arrivals commenced.

Joining from Eppleton CW was defensive minded 21-year-old Charlie Atkinson. Carlisle was the source of winger Frank McKenna, who had scored ten goals for the Cumbrians in his second season there. Full-back Eric Oldham joined from non-league Kidderminster, but the 26-year-old had previously seen league action for Gateshead.

1959-60

THE season commenced on a positive note with a 3-0 home win over Aldershot, with local lad Jackie Smith – now in his seventh season with the Club – netting twice and Harry Clark netting the other. Top of the league after the opening game, Pools failed to win in the next six despite the efforts of Smith who had netted six goals and Clark who had netted three.

Defeats Bring About End For Manager

AFTER a crushing 5-2 defeat at Crystal Palace on September 12, Pools were second bottom. Defeat at Palace was followed by victories over Oldham and Bradford PA.

But the wins didn't bring about a drastic change in fortune as Pools lost their next four matches and were in the bottom four again.

Once more they bucked the downward spiral with a brace of wins before disaster struck – on October 13th they were played off the park at Vicarage Road, losing 7-2 to Watford.

It was the last game for George Luke who was sold back to his former employers Newcastle United for £4,000. Further defeats followed to Rochdale and Workington and with a 5-1 rout at Doncaster, Pools were in freefall.

This game also signalled the end of the career in management of Ray Middleton. He had taken on a difficult job following a cult hero at the Club when he replaced Fred Westgarth, but in the eyes of the Club's board he had been given sufficient chance this season to turn things around.

Soccer Star front cover, January 2nd 1960

Tough Start For New Man In Charge

HIS replacement was Bill Robinson, the former Sunderland and West Ham centre forward. He had retired from playing in 1952-53 and had been in charge of the youth team at West Ham before taking up the assistant manager role some years later. His first game was an FA Cup tie at Bury, as Pools were easily despatched 5-0 – proof, if he needed it, that work was to be done.

It took a further eight games before he registered his first win, when goals from Jackie Smith and Harry Clark secured Pools the points at the Vic on January 2, 1960.

Apart from the odd strike from other players, the bulk of the goals were coming from Smith and Clark. Without them Pools would surely have been firmly rooted to the bottom instead of being second bottom.

February 6 saw Pools turned over 6-2 at Bradford PA when Joe Scott and Kenny Johnson scored in a game that saw the debut of former Sunderland player Clive Bircham.

Pools Head For Re-Election Vote

SINCE Johnson swapped roles on the pitch the goals had dried up and it was to be his only effort this season. Further routs followed – 5-0 at Exeter and 6-2 at home to Doncaster. It was an abysmal end to an abysmal season, as Pools won just two of the last 14 to finish bottom and be in grave danger of failing to be re-elected.

They also conceded 109 goals, the worst for nearly 30 seasons. The reserves also had a dire season, finishing third bottom.

The overall average gate had dropped to 3,646, a huge fall, less than half of what it was just two seasons ago.

Finishing bottom meant the Club had to face re-election for the fourth time, but first since 1938-39.

Pools, Gateshead, Southport and Oldham were all to face a vote at the Football League's AGM.

Up against them were former league club New Brighton, reformed South Shields and Wigan, now known as Athletic.

Also in the vote were a further 15 clubs such as Morecambe, Hereford, Scarborough, Romford, Bedford and Peterborough hoping to secure a place in the Football League.

Club Escapes By Skin Of Its Teeth

DESPITE finishing bottom of the league, Pools gained 34 votes, 16 more than Gateshead, but one less than Peterborough United.

The Posh had been winners of the Midland

HUFC line-up 1959-60. Back row: New Westgarth (Trainer), Billy Anderson, Jackie Smith, Norman Oakley, Joe Scott, Ken Johnson, Ray Middleton (Manager); Front row: Ken Waugh, Eric Oldham, Frank McKenna, Watty Moore, Harry Clark, George Luke

League for the past five seasons and also had reached the fourth round proper of the FA Cup the previous season.

There was no doubting that Peterborough were worthy of a place, but the fact that Gateshead were outdone by Pools in the voting caused great consternation to the Tynesiders. They had finished six points above Pools and even five above Oldham.

There were many rumours and attempted explanations to the shock decision, but the fact remained that Pools were very fortunate to maintain their position.

Legend Moore Among Those To Leave As Club Prepares For 'The Swinging Sixties'

LEAVING the Club were Jack Cameron and forward Johnny Langland who returned to Blyth Spartans. Winger Frank McKenna went to play for North Shields and later Gateshead. Local hot-shot Jackie Smith, who had managed 49 goals in 119 starts in seven years, signed for Watford. An ever present this season, he netted 17 times, finishing second to Harry Clark's 21 goals.

And never to pull on the blue and white jersey again would be Watty Moore.

For so long a loyal servant of the Club, refusing offers from bigger clubs in favour of staying with Pools, he had been caught up by Old Father Time and, at the age of 34 after a still-standing record of 447 Football League outings, he made the move to Horden CW.

The scorer of just three goals for Pools, two came in his first four games. His stint at the Club included one run of 162 consecutive appearances and a sequence of 373 games without a goal.

Only Kenny Johnson of the side built by Westgarth in the early 50s remained. Moore deserved his place in folklore and his early death in 1967 was a shock.

Pools had lost a good quality player and the squad desperately needed bolstering after the pitiful season just passed.

Several new signings were made, the most important being the re-signing of top scorer Harry Clark. Former Rotherham forward Doug Cooper arrived with former Newcastle and Gateshead full back George Lackenby. Also joining the ranks were Jimmy Cain from South Shields and Bill Clydesdale, a tough tackling full-back from Aberdeen. Returning to the Club after Gateshead's relegation was Bobby Lumley.

George Lackenby

		P	HW	HD	HL	HF	HA	AW	AD	AL	AF	AA	POINTS
1	Walsall	46	14	5	4	57	33	14	4	5	45	27	65
2	Notts County	46	19	1	3	66	27	7	7	9	41	42	60
3	Torquay United	46	17	3	3	56	27	9	5	9	28	31	60
4	Watford	46	17	2	4	62	28	7	7	9	30	39	57
5	Millwall	46	12	8	3	54	28	6	9	8	30	33	53
6	Northampton Town	46	13	6	4	50	22	9	3	11	35	41	53
7	Gillingham	46	17	4	2	47	21	4	6	13	27	48	52
8	Crystal Palace	46	12	6	5	61	27	7	6	10	23	37	50
9	Exeter City	46	13	7	3	50	30	6	4	13	30	40	49
10	Stockport County	46	15	6	2	35	10	4	5	14	23	44	49
11	Bradford Park Avenue	46	12	10	1	48	25	5	5	13	22	43	49
12	Rochdale	46	15	4	4	46	19	3	6	14	19	41	46
13	Aldershot	46	14	5	4	50	22	4	4	15	27	52	45
14	Crewe Alexandra	46	14	3	6	51	31	4	6	13	28	57	45
15	Darlington	46	11	6	6	40	30	6	3	14	23	43	43
16	Workington	46	10	8	5	41	20	4	6	13	27	40	42
17	Doncaster Rovers	46	13	3	7	40	23	3	7	13	29	53	42
18	Barrow	46	11	8	4	52	29	4	3	16	25	58	41
19	Carlisle United	46	9	6	8	28	28	6	5	12	23	38	41
20	Chester	46	10	8	5	37	26	4	4	15	22	51	40
21	Southport	46	9	7	7	30	32	1	7	15	18	60	34
22	Gateshead	46	12	3	8	37	27	0	6	17	21	59	33
23	Oldham Athletic	46	5	7	11	20	30	3	5	15	21	53	28
24	**HARTLEPOOLS UNITED**	**46**	**9**	**2**	**12**	**40**	**41**	**1**	**5**	**17**	**19**	**68**	**27**

Chapter 8

1960s
Not So Swinging For Pools

1960/61

THE season started badly at Southport on August 20 with a 2-0 reverse. A couple of days later and Pools entertained new boys Peterborough in front of a crowd of 10,784, losing by the same scoreline and the intrigued fans never returned in that number for some four years.

For the next home game against Darlington, less than half that amount turned up to see Pools win 5-0 through goals from Clark, Johnson, Anderson (two penalties) and local lad Bobby Folland.

A close 3-2 defeat in the return game at Peterborough's floodlit London Road where a forward line including the restored Kenny Johnson, who scored twice, was followed by a 2-2 draw at Crystal Palace.

Pools were already struggling and in eighteenth place.

Two home games followed – defeat to Stockport and a 2-1 victory over Doncaster which included a third goal in five starts for Folland. Then a pitiful run of seven games without a win took place and Pools were deep in trouble, second bottom. A Johnson hat-trick secured a 4-1 triumph over Accrington Stanley at the Vic on October 8 and set them up for their first game in the Football League Cup, three days later at Oldham Athletic.

League Cup Introduced

THIS new competition was for clubs from the four Football League divisions only and represented another opportunity for Pools to pit themselves against those from the upper echelons of the Football League. However, it wouldn't be this year as they were beaten by 1-0 by Oldham at Boundary Park.

Four weeks later and they were also out of the FA Cup after conceding five goals for the third game in four, when losing at Halifax. Three wins and a draw restored some hope as they stuttered to 20th place, helped by

Football League Cup

the goals of Doug Cooper who scored four in four.

But what followed can only be described as atrocious, as Pools won once in 15 to leave them rooted firmly to the foot of division four by the middle of March.

A win over Gillingham at the Vic on March 18th came courtesy of a solitary goal from outside left Harry Godbold. At last it seemed some fight was about to be shown – Pools also won their next encounter 3-1 at Bradford Park Avenue, with Kenny Johnson netting a brace and Bob Folland getting on the scoresheet.

Sandwiched between a pair of 4-0 away defeats was a 4-2 home victory over Northampton, with Folland again netting along with a Barry Parkes hat-trick, two of them coming from the spot. Parkes, 20, hailed from Hartlepool and had recently joined from Easington CW.

1960-61 HUFC Team Line Up. Back row: Ken Waugh, Jimmy Cain, Danny Godfrey, Norman Oakley, Joe Wilkinson, Billy Clydesdale, Billy Anderson. Second row: Bill Hesleton (Reserve Manager), Tim Peek, Johnny Dixon, Ken Johnson, George Lackenby, George Patterson, Charlie Atkinson, Wattie Moore, Ned Westgarth. Third row: Clive Bircham, Bobby Lumley, Doug Cooper, Bill Robinson (Manager), Harry Clarke, Ken Butler, Brian Dunn. Front row: Gordon Lithgoe, Barry Parkes, Bobby Folland

Big Win Not Enough – Re-Election Needed

APRIL 15 saw Pools take on Oldham at the Vic and Folland bagged all five in a 5-1 victory, equalling the record for goals scored in the Football League in a game, set some 30 years before by Harry Simmons.

Victory boosted Pools and three more points from the last three games proved enough to pull free of bottom place, but not clear of the re-election zone as they ended up just one off the foot of the table.

By comparison the reserves equalled their best season and finished in fifth place.

Up for re-election along with Pools were Barrow, Exeter and Chester. All were saved from the drop and safely voted in with Pools receiving the fewest number of votes, 32, but streets ahead of Oxford United who came next in the poll with 19, ahead of the likes of Chelmsford, King's Lynn and Bexleyheath & Welling.

Among those playing ending their Pools careers were full back Bill Anderson, forward Harry Clark, Bobby Lumley, Brian Dunn and Doug Cooper. Top scorers for the season were Bobby Folland and a rejuvenated Kenny Johnson who scored a dozen each.

A miserable season had been endured and a big effort was needed to pull the Club out of the doldrums.

The main addition to the squad that summer was York forward Johnny Edgar. He had missed the bulk of the last season but had scored 15 goals in 1959-60 for York and 23 for Gillingham the season before.

1961/62

AT Spotland on August 19, 1961, Rochdale beat Pools 3-1, with United's strike courtesy of an own goal. The team lined up as follows – Joe Wilkinson, Ray Bilcliff, Ken Jones, Kenny Johnson, George Lackenby, Tom Burlison, Clive Bircham, Johnny Edgar, Ken Price, Barry Parkes, and Harry Godbold.

A draw against Oldham was followed by a fine 4-2 home win over Southport with goals from former Tranmere player Ken Price, Johnny Edgar and a pair for Folland. Then, following the course of the last two terms, they failed to win in seven, including a 5-2 reverse at Oldham and a 6-1 embarrassment at Colchester.

There was also a midweek journey to Bristol Rovers in the League Cup when they were beaten by the odd goal in three.

Attendances Drop After Poor Start

A win over Crewe stemmed the flow of poor performances but another five winless games followed. Attendances were dropping and the average crowd was under 4,900, although gates were fluctuating violently between 2,900 and 6,800.

The overdraft was rising and was hovering around the £6,500 mark. Nevertheless two new signings were made. Derek McLean was signed from Middlesbrough for a fee of £5,000, paid in instalments, and Jackie Hinchliffe joined from Workington, with £4,350 changing hands.

October 21 saw a 3-0 win over Doncaster with Folland scoring two to take him to ten for the season. Pools won only two from seven but enjoyed get better luck in the FA Cup, for the first time in many seasons.

An Edgar hat-trick helped them to a 5-1 win over Blyth and in the following round they beat Accrington 2-1.

The third round saw them drawn away to Fulham, a side including George Cohen and Alan Mullery. Thirty Pools fans even chartered a plane for the game.

The Cottagers found Pools easy opposition and sent the team back up the A1 on the end of a 3-1 beating, with Pools at least benefiting from their share of a handsome 18,000+ gate. Pools' only goal was registered by Tom Burlison.

After the Fulham experience several players regained confidence and four unbeaten games followed with Clive Bircham scoring in three successive games.

Clubs Circling To Take Players And Pools Try To Shed Some Light Onto Victoria Park

IN the meantime the board was fending off requests from players to leave and clubs enquiring about some of the squad. Edgar, Norman Oakley and Joe Wilkinson all had transfer requests refused and Darlington asked, with no success, for the services of Oakley and long-servant Kenny Johnson, who was once again playing in a half back role.

Pools also were making renewed enquires into the cost of floodlights as several lower league clubs had them installed. However, it would not be until 1967 that they were installed.

Horrendous Defeat Inflicted On Pools

THE short lived revival led by Bircham's goals was over and between February 10 and April 14 they failed to win in 13 games – a new record.

Within the familiar run of results was simply the worst scoreline in the Club's history.

On March 3, Pools travelled to Wrexham and were despatched by 10-1. Wrexham tore United apart as hat-tricks from Davies, Ambler and Barnes aided the Welshman in their victory, replicating the feat gained by Pools in 1915 when Butler, McGill and Strugnell all netted three in a 10-0 win over Carlisle.

Once again languishing in the nether regions of the table, Pools were saved from a re-election battle by the desperate plight of Accrington Stanley.

Two days after the Wrexham debacle, Accrington had no alternative but to quit the Football League. The team that had mirrored Pools' successful campaigns under Westgarth in the mid-50s were in excess of £50,000 in debt and could not continue trading. Their results were expunged.

For the game at York on March 24, former City player Edgar failed to report and was fined £5 for missing the game that Pools lost 2-0.

Pools' First TV Appearance

EVEN the presence of the television cameras for the match against Gillingham at the Vic on April 7 could not improve matters as Edgar netted the only goal in a 3-1 defeat, in front of a paltry 2,434 fans.

Hartlepool Mail

Ken Johnson in action against Doncaster in October 1961

Pools line-up in the 1961-62 season. Back row: Jimmy Cain, Bobby Folland, Norman Oakley, Ray Bilcliff, Derek Wilkie, Ken Johnson; Front row: Clive Bircham, John Edgar, Barry Hawkes, Ken Waugh, Gordon Lithgo

Part of the game was recorded by Tyne Tees Television and was shown on their channel on that evening.

A reporter from The Northern Daily Mail reported Kenny Johnson for assault after this game. Johnson initially denied such actions, but was later cautioned by the board and the paper was written to and apologised to by the board, with Johnson warned regarding his future conduct.

Re-Election Looms Again

THE run of defeats ended with four games to go as Pools enjoyed a quick double over Darlington. Edgar netted twice in a 2-0 home victory and three days later he did it again at Feethams as Pools brought the points home with a 2-1 triumph.

The season ended with a 5-1 thumping at Barrow when Johnson scored his 94th Football League goal for the Club, leaving him just one behind Johnny Wigham.

Pools again finished second bottom, this time in a division of 23 due to Accrington's absence. Themselves, bottom-placed Chester and Doncaster were voted back in at re-election time, along with Oxford United. Unlucky teams this time around included Gateshead, North Shields Athletic, Sittingbourne and Folkestone.

It was the third season in succession that Pools had been forced to apply for re-election and the third season that they had leaked more than 100 goals. At least Edgar gave a valuable contribution with 20 league goals. The reserves were also disappointing, finishing 11th out of 15 clubs in the NERL.

Three squad members were given free transfers; Hawkes, Cain and Melville.

Transfer listed were Jones at £1,250, Price (£1,000) and Waugh who had a £500 price tag on his head. He later quit the Club and emigrated to Australia.

The rest were offered new terms, several of whom were still part timers.

Manager Sacked By The Board

GIVEN the horrendous recent run it came as no surprise when manager Bill Robinson was shown the door and on June 5, 1962 he was advised by the board that his contract was being terminated.

Two weeks later former player Harry Hooper was interviewed and offered the role of manager with an annual salary of £1,500, almost £500 more than the highest paid player.

But despite the reasonable offer Hooper declined, choosing to stay in the capital with West Ham.

The job was given to another former guest player from WW2, Allenby Chilton, who accepted the role for a salary of only £20 a week and agreed a rolling month to month contract on July 3rd. He enjoyed success as a manager after quitting playing and won the Division Three (north) title with Grimsby in 1956. He had a later spell with Wigan Athletic guiding them to the brink of the Football League.

His first tasks were to ensure that players re-signed their contracts which the likes of Johnson, Folland, Bircham and Bilcliff subsequently did.

1962/63

NEW signings followed. John Brown, a 27-year-old full back moved from Tranmere for £550 and he was joined by Bill Younger of Doncaster Rovers who signed for £1,000. A 2-1 win in a pre-season friendly against Gateshead proved to be handier for the manager in deciding who to play other than the now seemingly pointless blue and whites v red and whites, with both teams consisting of Pools players.

Norman Oakley was restored to the number one spot and new signings Brown and Younger were pitched in for the start of the season.

Also starting were half back Andy Fraser, who had once been on the books of Hearts, and Derrick Wilkie and Derek McLean. There was to be no place for the opening game against Newport for Lackenby, Johnson or Folland.

Despite goals from Bircham and Edgar, Pools lost 3-2 and they took four games to register their first victory when a pair each from Bircham and McLean helped Pools beat Southport 4-0.

Beaten at home 2-0 by Darlington on September 3, Pools were hammered 6-1 by Tranmere in their next game and were perched in 20th place, just above the bottom four.

Swift revenge came at Feethams as United won 2-0 with McLean scoring and Younger getting his first for the Club. But once again things went wrong – Pools failed to win their next six games and were also knocked out of

the League Cup, this time to Barnsley in a replay.

New Boss Dips Into Transfer Market

TO try and improve the situation fresh blood was brought in, in the form of half back Ken Thomson who joined from Middlesbrough for £4,000. He played alongside a recalled Johnson and Jackie Hinchliffe.

Just one defeat in six games followed with McLean netting six times in this spell, although they exited the FA Cup, beaten 3-1 by Carlisle.

By the turn of December Pools stood in a dangerous third from bottom and were beaten 5-1 at the Vic by Crewe.

Pools Embark On A Run Of Defeats To Break Record Set In 1961-62

WHAT followed next was shameful. Pools failed to win in their next 18 outings, surpassing their worst ever run of games set the previous season.

In January 1962, at the start of the run, the board were expressing the view that the manager was not performing as desired and they had received complaints about him from Ned Westgarth the trainer. He claimed Chilton was not assisting with training when Westgarth was attending to injured players.

The board were close to cancelling his

Allenby Chilton and Club Secretary Bill Hillam in 1962

Ken Thomson joined Pools from Middlesbrough

contract and installing a replacement manager, until they settled their differences thanks to the intervention of Ray Bilcliff and Ken Thomson who agreed to assist with training.

During January all the players had to do was train as the winter was so extreme that no games were played from December 22 to February 2 – a gap of six weeks.

Board Take Action To Halt Slump

AFTER seven winless games in March, the board called the manager and the trainer before them.

Not only were results a major concern, but the training of the players had not improved since the previous meetings in January.

On April 1, Allenby Chilton was handed a month's notice for the termination of the contract. It was decreed that if no successor was found in time, the board would take charge of the team. Several directors were keen to appoint Sunderland trainer and record scorer Bobby Gurney, but the matter needed discussing by all before a decision could be made and they still had the option of Club director E Young temporarily taking charge, or even asking a senior player to act as a player/manager.

Gurney got the nod and started on April 12, 1963.

After being 22nd in the table, Pools were soon rock bottom and sat six points adrift after they beat leaders Brentford 2-1 at the Vic on April 22.

They won once more in the remaining seven games and stayed at the foot of the table, seven points behind Bradford City.

Ringing The Changes At Pools And An England Team Plays At The Vic

AT the end of the season trainer and physio Ned Westgarth was released after almost 20 years great service. Also dismissed was former player and scout Tommy McGuigan, who had only been appointed to the role earlier that season. Another casualty of these

lean times was former chairman Harry Sergeant, who handed his resignation after 18 years after becoming a director.

Joining him some weeks later was then chairman Mr Hope. The Club had recently reported a mammoth loss of more than £22,000 and major restructuring was needed.

Re-election time was again worrying as, for the fourth year in a row, they were up for the vote. Yet again they survived mainly because of a lack of any decent non league teams to challenge them.

Pools polled the lowest of the four clubs desperate to maintain their position, but were streets ahead of their nearest challenger Scarborough, who mustered a mere five votes.

Top scorer for the season again was Edgar with a paltry 11 goals, tied for the honour with Derek McLean. Edgar missed the end of the season following cartilage damage. The reserves offered no improvement and finished 13th out of 17 sides.

The Vic played host to an Amateur International on 15 May 1963, when an England team defeated a French XI 3-1 in front of 4,521 spectators.

More Ins And Outs At The Vic As Pools Prepare For A New Season

IT was time for another clearout and time for goodbyes to be said to the likes of Barry Parkes, Bobby Folland, George Lackenby and Terry MacGregor who were all given free transfers. Transfer-listed at various fees were Edgar, Bircham, Godbold, Bill Younger and Joe Wilkinson, although they were all later given frees after their contracts ran out on July 1.

On July 18, Ernest Ord, a local businessman was appointed chairman. He instantly loaned the Club £5,000 to bail them out. Before his appointment the overdraft was more than £18,000 and they owed money to the Inland Revenue and Middlesbrough for the £4000 transfer of Thomson.

Long-serving secretary Frank Perryman was appointed vice chairman.

On the pitch and several new signings arrived, including two from Falkirk – centre forward Ken Cunningham and outside right Hughie Hamilton. Two also came from Ayr, Bert McCubbin and inside left Willie Bradley.

Clearly Gurney had identified talent lay north of the border, as had Fred Westgarth. Whether his signings would prove as fruitful as Westgarth's, time would only tell. Another Scot, Willie Hinselwood, signed, but the forward played in England and joined from Southern League side Tonbridge.

Scandal Hits Pools Player

ON August 11 1963 a story appeared in the Sunday newspapers relating to Ken Thomson regarding the throwing of matches for money, during his time as a player at Middlesbrough.

The FA acted instantly on the allegations and requested a report from the Club and a statement from Thomson. He was later suspended indefinitely by the FA for his role in this alleged bribery case.

After breaching his contract he would no longer receive any monies from Pools, who, due to their financial distress, asked the Football League to pursue any legal avenues on their behalf to recover the £4000 transfer fee, although they later advised against such action.

The Club let the matter lie and accepted the loss of such a large transfer fee for a player who made just 28 outings.

During the court trial it transpired that Thomson had tried to bribe fellow player Andy Fraser to take £20 as a bung to lose the game at Stockport.

Fraser refused and was Pools' best player that day. He recalled Thomson telling Stockport's forwards to take it easy on the keeper as the game was fixed anyway.

Three weeks later Fraser was approached by Thomson with the £20 at half-time during a game. He refused to take it but later found it in his coat pocket after a game and foolishly kept it.

1963/64

INSTEAD of the usual pre-season humdrum of possibles against probables, this season Pools held a challenge match against Leeds United, with 2,887 fans turning out to see Pools win 2-1, goals from new signing from Ayr United, William Bradley. The visitors reply came from Peter Lorimer.

The season started in a familiar and unwanted fashion of a defeat, 4-1 at Aldershot on August 24. A home loss to Torquay by the same score led to a quick response from the manager and former striker Peter Thompson rejoined.

After leaving for Derby in 1958 he later played for Bournemouth whom Pools paid £2,000 for his services – unfortunately he was sent off in his second game back in blue and white. Other players were watched such as Dennis Windross of Doncaster and former England Youth inside forward Keith Havenhand of Derby County. One player who did join was experienced Middlesbrough full back Derek

Stonehouse.

Pools got the first win under their belts at the third attempt when they beat Bradford City, courtesy of a goal from Hinchliffe. Then came the predictable bleak run, this time eight games and a League Cup exit at Notts County.

This sequence included some stinkers against Carlisle. After being disgraced at the Vic by their Cumbrian counterparts on September 16, two weeks later they were pummelled 7-1 at Brunton Park.

Johnson Becomes Club's Leading Scorer

OCTOBER 7 saw not only a crucial two points in the bag, but the creation of a new record as Kenny Johnson's goal in the 3-2 victory at Tranmere was his 96th Football League goal for the Club, overtaking Wigham's pre-war record.

The landmark seemed to perk the team up and they won their next game and drew the following two to drag them up to the dizzy heights of fourth bottom.

Undeterred, the board were prepared to back the manager to the hilt. Rather boldly he was looking at signing Leeds United midfielder John Hawksby, while a more audacious approach for Sunderland's Irish international forward Ambrose Fogarty was on the cards.

And to the shock and delight of all Pools fans they clinched the signature of Fogarty, who made his debut a week after the FA Cup exit at Lincoln. A fine inside forward and aged 30, he had scored 37 goals for Sunderland in around 150 games and was the holder of ten international caps.

His presence didn't help on his debut as Pools went down 1-0 at Stockport. The following week a part-time professional, Terry Francis, joined from Billingham Synthonia. Thrown straight into the melting pot the next week at home to Bradford Park Avenue and in a 4-2 victory he made history as being the first Pools player to score a hat-trick on his Football League debut.

Gurney Pays For Poor Results

THREE defeats out of four in December was followed by a New Year's Day defeat at the Vic to Darlington, which ended the short reign of Manager Bobby Gurney (8 months).

He was dismissed on January 6 and responsible for the team as the post was advertised were 33-year-old former Bradford PA centre half and Club trainer Alvan Williams and secretary Bill Hillan.

SIX   SOCCER STAR, September 14, 1963

Martin Rogers features one of the League's Minnows this week

A Crucial Season for these Stalwarts

HARTLEPOOLS UNITED, traditional cellar-dwellers in the Fourth Division, have been in the Football League since 1921 and as recently as 1957 gained their highest position, second in the Third Division (North).

The last few seasons, however, have been bleak in the extreme and Victoria Road patrons are looking to new manager Bob Gurney, the former Sunderland and England centre-forward, to bring about an overdue revival. The club began as West Hartlepool in 1890, adopting the present name in 1908. All credit to them for managing to continue despite the depression which was rife in the North-East, particularly between the wars. Even at the present time Hartlepools are known to be struggling to survive and the current season may prove to be a crucial one in United's history.

Who's who:

Goalkeeper

Norman Oakley—The only professional custodian on the books, he has been sought after by many prominent clubs and is without doubt one of the most accomplished goalkeepers in the lower divisions of the League. Born at Norton-on-Tees, he was previously with Doncaster Rovers. Last season he did not miss a match in the first team.

Full-Backs

Ray Bilcliff—Solid and experienced defender who hails from Blaydon (of Blaydon Races fame). Joined Middlesbrough from Spen Juniors in 1949 and gave them many years of excellent service before moving along to Hartlepools, for whom he made 32 Fourth Division appearances last season.

Derek Wilkie—Sturdy defender and, like Bilcliff, a former Middlesbrough player. Had 28 senior outings last term and has impressed many Hartlepools followers with his solid performances.

John Brown—Born at Portobello, this former Scotland Under-23 international has recently been experimented with at centre-forward. Gives wholehearted effort wherever he is called upon to

play. Signed from Tranmere Rovers and previously with Hibernian, he was one of two ever-present members of last season's team.

John Milton — Another Scotsman and one of manager Gurney's close-season signings. Promising full-back who made 24 appearances in Ayr United's Second Division team last term and looks a likely acquisition.

Half-Backs

Jackie Hinchliffe — Used to operate on the right-wing and as such had trials with Chelsea, Preston North End and Sheffield United. Signed professional forms

SPOTLIGHT on HARTLEPOOLS UTD.

with Aston Villa in 1956 when 18 and later assisted Workington, who converted him to wing-half. Totalled 28 senior games last season.

Tommy Burlison — Local product who linked up with Lincoln City in 1954 and while there was a colleague of Dick Neal, later of Birmingham City and Middlesbrough. Has been with the Pools for six years now and can also perform on the left-wing. 32 outings last season.

Andy Fraser—One of the Scottish colony at the Victoria Ground. A native of Newtongrange, he was formerly identified with Heart of Midlothian. Made 26 appearances in the Fourth Division side in the last compaign after a spell in Canada.

Charlie Atkinson — From that well-known home of many fine footballers, Washington, Co. Durham. Formerly regarded as a full-back, he moved to centre-half following the suspension of Ken Thomson, former Pools captain who was recently banned for life from the game. Made three appearances in 1962-63.

Willie Hinshelwood — Former Airdrieonians inside-forward who moved to wing-half with success in the latter part of last season when with Tonbridge, the Southern League club. Neat footballer who is readily adaptable.

Derek Turner — Young wing-half signed during the summer from Falkirk, the Scottish First Division club. Found opportunities limited at Brockville and is naturally hopeful of establishing himself in English League football.

Forwards

Derek McLean—Handy inside-forward for Middlesbrough for

several seasons, he has taken advantage of increased chances in the Fourth Division sphere and played 40 times last season, scoring 11 goals.

Ken Johnson — The longest-serving player on the books and a fine clubman who has been on the club's payroll for more than a decade. Can operate at wing-half or inside-forward with equal facility. Signed from local amateur circles. Made 23 appearances last season.

Gordon Lithgo — Gritty utility forward and also a local boy who can be relied upon to give his best when called on for senior duty. Had three outings in the 1962-63 season.

Bobby McCubbin—Signed from Ayr United during the close-season. Last term he had 14 Second Division appearances and impressed as an outside-left who could do well. Began with Pools on the wrong note; a knee injury necessitated a cartilage operation before he had kicked a ball for

Veteran Hartlepools United performer is utility man KEN JOHNSON. He can play in any wing-half, or forward position equally well. (P.N.1.)

them in anger!

Ken Cunningham — Inside-man or wing-forward from Falkirk and another newcomer to the fold. Has the makings of a player who should be a force in Fourth Division football.

Hughie Hamilton — Like Cunningham, he, too, came from Falkirk and made a couple of First Division appearances, scoring in one of them. Inside-forward or winger with the ability to do well south of the Border and likely to thrive on the preponderance of Scottish accents at Hartlepools!

Billy Bradley—Same goes for Bradley, who can play almost anywhere in the front line. Had 10 Second Division games with Ayr United last term and is a handy marksman who possesses the ability to make goals as well.

Soccer Star Article on September 14th 1963

Struggling badly the board approached Middlesbrough and attempted to sign reserve forward Alan Rodgerson and first team regular wing half Ray Yeoman, tabling a bid of £3,000 for the latter.

Boro refused and the incoming manager would have to make do with the squad that he had, particularly after the FA would not allow another potential recruit permission to play.

Former Carlisle wing half Gordon Bradley had been playing in Canada with Toronto Roma and after a spell on trial with Pools he was barred from appearing at the insistence of his former team.

Prospects Remain Bleak For Pools

WITH Williams and Hillan in charge on a temporary basis the Club won one out of five and were now bottom.

Nevertheless, it was enough to appoint Williams permanently.

The decision did little to improve form and Pools won just two out of the next ten, although a couple of draws moved them to second bottom.

Prospects – once again – were nothing but bleak.

Struggling at the foot of the Football League and facing re-election for the fifth successive season, they were also in dire straits financially. Almost £21,000 overdrawn by mid-February, the Club decided that any player who could raise a fee would be allowed to leave, irrespective of who they were.

Less than a month later ever-present keeper Norman Oakley was on his way to Swindon Town after 182 games. He realised a fee of £5,500 which greatly assisted the ailing finances.

Pools acted quickly and signed Wrexham keeper Ken Simpkins. The 20-year-old had played on just four occasions for the Welsh outfit over the past two seasons.

Dressing Room Bust-Up And Pools Play On A Friday Night

THINGS came to a head on March 21 1964 when Pools were beaten 2-1 at home by Workington in front of just 1,805 fans. Long-serving player and record goalscorer Johnson had heated words with the chairman in the dressing room in front of the manager and other players.

Despite his status and standing, his contract was terminated as he was already in hot water with the board for airing his grievances to the local press.

A week or so later and differences were put to bed, as Johnson's contract was reinstated – but the writing was on the wall.

Earlier in the season the Club offered him in a player-exchange with Darlington for former Middlesbrough

Len Ashurst

outside left Ronnie Burbeck. The deal never materialised, but it seemed apparent that with him and Burlison having a joint benefit at the end of the campaign that his time was up.

On the pitch the team lost only one of their final six games, offering a touch of future hope and promise – if they could avoid being kicked out of the Football League.

Amongst the last six matches was a 1-0 win over Chesterfield on April 17, which was the Club's first Friday evening fixture.

Benefit Match Held For Ken Johnson And Tom Burlison At The Vic

THE end of the season saw the joint testimonial game for Johnson and Burlison as a Pools XI took on Sunderland on April 28, 1964.

In order to give Pools a fighting chance and out of respect for the service of the two players, particularly Johnson who had made his debut way back in 1949, Pools were boosted by the services of 39-year-old Gateshead manager Bobby Mitchell and 40-year-old ex-Newcastle stalwart Frank Brennan.

Also turning out were former Leeds and Sunderland player Ken Chisholm, 39, and footballing legend Wilf Mannion, 45.

The former Middlesbrough and England man may have been of an advancing age but had only retired from playing non-league football a year previous.

The oldest player on display was former Pools favourite and England international Jack Howe who played at left back aged 49. A first class crowd of 11,000 saw Pools beaten 6-3 by a full-strength Sunderland side who included Len Ashurst and Charlie Hurley.

The Pools team lined up as follows – Oakley, Williams, Howe (Wilkie), Fogarty, Brennan (Hinchliffe), Burlison, Anderson, Mannion (Hamilton), Johnson, Chisholm and Mitchell.

An Agreement made the .... sixth ....

day of .... May .... 19⁵⁷ .... between .... Frank Smyth Perryman,

National Provincial Bank Chambers, Church Street, West Hartlepool.

of

.... in the COUNTY OF .... Durham ....

the Secretary of and acting pursuant to Resolution and Authority for and on

behalf of the .... HARTLEPOOLS UNITED .... FOOTBALL CLUB

of .... West Hartlepool .... (hereinafter referred to as the Club)

of the one part and .... Kenneth Johnson ....

of .... 16, Romaine Terrace, Hartlepool ....

in the COUNTY OF .... Durham .... Professional Football Player

(hereinafter referred to as the Player) of the other part **Whereby** it is agreed
as follows:—

1. The Player hereby agrees to play in an efficient manner and to the best
of his ability for the Club.

2. The Player shall attend the Club's ground or any other place decided
upon by the Club for the purposes of or in connection with his training as a
Player pursuant to the instructions of the Secretary, Manager, or Trainer of the
Club, or of such other person, or persons, as the Club may appoint. (This
provision shall not apply if the Player is engaged by the Club at a weekly wage
of less than One Pound, or at a wage per match.)

3. The Player shall do everything necessary to get and keep himself in the
best possible condition so as to render the most efficient service to the Club, and
will carry out all the training and other instructions of the Club through its
representative officials.

4. The Player shall observe and be subject to all the Rules, Regulations
and Bye-Laws of The Football Association, and any other Association, League,
or Combination of which the Club shall be a member. And this Agreement shall
be subject to any action which shall be taken by The Football Association under
their Rules for the suspension or termination of the Football Season, and if any
such suspension or termination shall be decided upon the payment of wages shall
likewise be suspended or terminated, as the case may be.

5. The Player shall not engage in any business or live in any place which
the Directors (or Committee) of the Club may deem unsuitable.

6. If the Player shall be guilty of serious misconduct or breach of the
disciplinary Rules of the Club, the Club may, on giving 14 days' notice
to the said Player, or the Club may, on giving 28 days' notice to the said Player,

Ken Johnson's contract with Hartlepool Uniteds Football Club from 1957

on any reasonable grounds, terminate this Agreement and dispense with the services of the Player (without prejudice to the Club's right for transfer fees) in pursuance of the Rules of all such Associations, Leagues, and Combinations of which the Club may be a member. Such notice or notices shall be in writing, and shall specify the reason for the same being given, and shall also set forth the rights of appeal to which the Player is entitled under the Rules of The Football Association.

The Rights of Appeal are as follows:—

Any League or other Combination of Clubs may, subject to these Rules, make such regulations between their Clubs and Players as they may deem necessary. Where Leagues and Combinations are sanctioned direct by this Association an Appeals Committee shall be appointed by this Association. Where Leagues and Combinations are sanctioned by County Associations an Appeals Committee shall be appointed by the sanctioning County Associations. Where an agreement between a Club and a Player in any League or other Combination provides for the Club terminating by notice to the Player of the Agreement between the Club and Player on any reasonable ground the following practice shall prevail: A Player shall have the right to appeal to the Management Committee of his League or Combination and a further right of appeal to the Appeals Committee of that body. A Club on giving notice to a Player to terminate his Agreement must state in the notice the name and address of the Secretary of the League or Combination to which he may appeal, and must also at the same time give notice to the League or Combination of which the Club is a member. A copy of the notice sent to the Player must at the same time be forwarded to the Secretary of this Association. The Player shall have the right of appeal to the League or Combination, but such appeal must be made within 7 days of the receipt of the Notice from the Club. The Notice terminating the Agreement must inform the Player the reasons or grounds for such Notice. The appeal shall be heard by the Management Committee within 10 days of the receipt of the Notice from the Player. If either party is dissatisfied with the decision, there shall be a right of further appeal to the Appeals Committee of the League or Combination, but such appeal must be made within 7 days of the receipt of the intimation of the decision of the Management Committee, and must be heard by the Appeals Committee within 10 days of the receipt of the Notice of Appeal. The League or Combination shall report to this Association when the matter is finally determined, and the Agreement and Registration shall be cancelled by this Association where necessary. Agreements between Clubs and Players shall contain a clause showing the provision made for dealing with such disputes and for the cancelling of the Agreements and Registrations by this Association. Clubs not belonging to any League or Combination before referred to may, upon obtaining the approval of this Association, make similar regulations. Such regulations to provide for a right of appeal by either party to the County Association, or to this Association.

7. This Agreement and the terms and conditions thereof shall be as to its suspension and termination subject to the Rules of The Football Association and to any action which may be taken by the Council of The Football Association or any deputed Committee, and in any proceedings by the Player against the Club it shall be a sufficient and complete defence and answer by and on the part of the Club that such suspension or termination hereof is due to the action of The Football Association, or any Sub-Committee thereof to whom the power may be delegated.

The Player may apply to The Football Association for a personal hearing to answer a charge of misconduct under F.A. Rule 45. He may also be represented at the hearing by the Players' Union provided that such representative is not a member of the legal profession.

8. In the event of the Player being called for Military Service and notwithstanding anything contained in the Rules of The Football Association, the Club may retain the playing services of the Player until the end of the Season in which he is demobilised, provided that the Club make an offer to the Player of a weekly retaining wage of £1 0s. 0d. plus any such match fee that may be mutually agreed by the Club and the Player.

9. In consideration of the observance by the said player of the terms, provisions and conditions of this Agreement, the said Frank Smyth Perryman .... on behalf of the Club hereby agrees that the said Club shall pay to the said Player the sum of £ 8 -------- per week from 1st July, 1957 to 16th August, 1957 3rd May, 1958 to 30th June, 1958. and £ 10 ------------- per week from 10th August, 1957 to 3rd May, 1958.

10. This Agreement (subject to the Rules of The Football Association) shall cease and determine on 30th June, 1958. unless the same shall have been previously determined in accordance with the provisions hereinbefore set forth.

Fill in any other provisions required

The player to receive £4. per week extra when playing in the First Team.

Full-time service.

As Witness the hands of the said parties the day and year first aforesaid

Signed by the said Frank Smyth Perryman .... and ....

Kenneth Johnson

In the presence of

(Signature) ....

(Occupation) Clerk

(Player)

(Secretary)

Three of the old heads were changed at half-time for three young Pools players.

Johnson fittingly notched the first goal from the spot with the other goals coming from Hughie Hamilton and manager Williams.

The retained list saw the Club hold on to Ken Simpkins, Derek Stonehouse, Peter Thompson, Hughie Hamilton, Billy Bradley, Amby Fogarty and part timer Terry Francis.

Goal Hero Johnson Set To Leave

TRANSFER listed for various fees were Hinchliffe, Burlison, Bilcliff, Wilkie, Fraser, Brown and McLean and handed free transfers were Lithgo, Hinshelwood and Kenny Johnson.

It marked the end of an era, the last of Westgarth's boys had gone. After making a scoring debut in 1949, home-town hero Johnson scored 98 Football League goals and eight FA Cup goals.

He stands tied at second place in the all-time scorers list with Wigham (1931-39), just five goals behind the prolific Josh Fletcher (1908-13). But considering he spent a good half of his career as a half back and was never a true out and out centre forward, more of an inside right, it can only be imagined how many goals he would have notched in his 415 starts if he had played them all upfront.

After the game he ran a successful fish and chip shop in the town for many years and, following retirement, was and still is, employed by the Club in a corporate capacity at home games.

Burlison spent a season playing with Darlington before later becoming heavily involved in Trade Union circles becoming Lord Tom Burlison, an Honorary Life President of the Club, before his death in 2008.

1964/65

FROM the previous season Hinchliffe, Simpkins, Thompson and Stonehouse had all signed. Fogarty was expected to sign, but due to the financial plight, Lincoln City were advised that the player could be grabbed for the same fee Pools paid – £10,000.

He hadn't set the world on fire at the Vic but made the 11th and last of his Irish international appearances against Spain during the spring of 1964 and was a current international – the only player to earn full international honours while playing for Pools.

But Lincoln baulked at the fee, Fogarty stayed and was joined by new signings Alan Fox and Cliff Wright. Fox was a central defender with 350 games under his belt for Wrexham and played alongside manager Williams as a player.

Wright was a 20-year-old Middlesbrough reserve who had yet to break into the first XI at Ayresome Park. Making the move from neighbours Darlington was full-back Stan Storton.

Final additions saw former Bolton winger Neville Bannister, Oldham full back Billy Marshall and ex-Halifax central defender Eric Harrison bolster what manager Williams hoped would be a refreshed squad capable of pushing the Club away from re-election worries.

Hartlepool Mail

Ken Johnson runs out ahead of Tom Burlison for their benefit match

Lining up before the Brighton home game on August 29, 1964. Back row: Peter Gordon (Trainer), Stan Storton, Ken Simpkins, Bobby Morrell, Alan Fox, Eric Harrison, Billy Marshall, Alvan Williams (Manager); Front row: Hughie Hamilton, Cliff Wright, Peter Thompson, Terry Francis, Willie Bradley

Re-Election Lives Running Out

POOLS had once again survived the vote at the end of the 1963-64 season, but competition in the ballot had offered no real threat in the shape of clubs such as Guildford and Poole, but that wouldn't always be the case and a move in the right direction was needed.

The opening game, on August 22 1964 at Lincoln City, saw the promise fail to blossom as Pools were beaten by 4-2, Willie Bradley and Eric Harrison netting. The new look XI took to the field as follows – Ken Simpkins, Stan Storton, Billy Marshall, Bobby Morrell, Alan Fox, Eric Harrison, Neville Bannister, Amby Fogarty, Peter Thompson, Cliff Wright, Willie Bradley.

It was practically a full new XI and only Bradley, Thompson, Fogarty and Morrell (a local youth) had appeared the previous season. On paper they looked a solid and experienced unit.

The first home game ended in a 2-2 draw with York, Hughie Hamilton and Terry Francis given a run out with Francis and Bradley scoring in front of 6,473 optimistic fans, a vast improvement on last term's average of 4,169. However, Fogarty broke a bone in his arm and he was to miss the next five games.

After a couple of draws and a defeat at Oxford, the Club were in 19th place and seemed to be heading for familiar territory.

They made their now customary first round exit from the League Cup, this time at Chesterfield.

Moving Up In The Table After 5 Years

PLAYING his preferred line up from the first game of the season, Williams saw his side beat Stockport in an exciting 4-3 home game, with Peter Thompson netting twice and Bradley and Bannister completing the scoring. They followed up with wins over Barrow and at Stockport and for the first time since August 25, 1959, Pools were in the top ten.

Alas, it didn't last long and by the time of the opening round of the FA Cup on November 14, Pools were 21st after a dire run of six defeats from eight October games.

Corby Town In The FA Cup

THE first round of the FA Cup saw Pools face a journey to Southern League side Corby Town, easily seeing them off 3-1, with Fogarty scoring one from the spot. The other two were claimed by Bobby Entwistle who joined until the end of the season following a short trial. The second round pitched Pools with Darlington and over 9,000 turned up at the Vic to see a lifeless 0-0 draw.

Ahead of the replay the draw for the third

round was made and the winners were handed a home tie against Arsenal. Over 14,500 packed into Feethams for the replay and Pools were embarrassed, swept away 4-1 by a rampant Quakers.

Pools managed revenge on their neighbours when they beat them 4-3 at the Vic in front of just 3,166 followers and then secured a double over them, winning 4-3 at Feethams on February 22.

Small bursts of form and a regular line up brought stability and a goalscoring contribution of 16 by Peter Thompson, ably assisted by Bradley and Fogarty who both crept into double figures. Pools managed to climb to 15th place come the end of the season.

It was their highest finish in the fourth division since its establishment.

Eight of the 19 players used that season appeared in 39 or more games – Bannister, Bradley, Fogarty, Fox, Harrison and Marshall with Storton and Simpkins being ever present.

The signature of Southend utility man Barry Ashworth provided extra cover and experience in the last weeks of the campaign. His arrival coincided with the departure of Francis, who agreed to a fortnight's wages to have his contract paid up.

Ground Improvements Back On Agenda

DURING the course of the season, the board were contacted by a concern contemplating converting the greyhound stadium that adjoined the Town End into a ten pin bowling alley and then develop the Victoria Ground at the same time.

The officials had already been discussing the possibility of ground development and at the forefront of their thoughts was the building of a social club at the ground.

The company intended to take over the greyhound stadium and the football ground and construct various entertainments. Part of their thinking was the possibility of the widening of Clarence Road into a dual carriageway, a clause that had always threatened Pools home.

In return for taking over the Vic, the bowling company would provide a new playing area, stands, accommodation and floodlighting.

It would be rent free as long as Pools stayed in the fourth division. The Club were certainly impressed and interested with the suggestion, but they did not own the ground and had to discuss the matter with the borough engineer and town clerk.

Mr Carter, owner of the Ten Pin Bowls (Durham) Limited, had submitted plans showing that they intended to develop the stadium in two stages which was not acceptable to Pools.

A lack of replies and information from Mr Carter left the matter closed for several months. This worked to the benefit of the Club as they planned to repurchase the ground from the council and proceed with their own outlined improvements.

Manager's Exit Shocks The Club

TOWARDS the closing weeks of the season it became apparent that Fogarty was growing unsettled and expressed a wish to be released from his contract in summer of 1965 to go to play in Canada, which was refused. He then later advised that he was to return to Eire for family reasons.

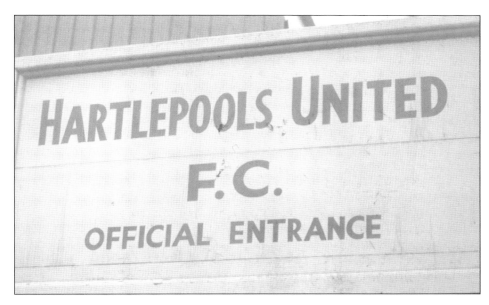

Entrance to the ground in 1964

Leaving, however, was manager Alvan Williams.

Recently awarded a £50 bonus for performances and enhanced terms, he accepted the role of manager at Southend United in early June. He later had a spell in charge at Wrexham.

With two candidates ruling themselves out of the running for the job after they had been offered the post, the board turned to Geoff Twentyman. His playing career had begun at Carlisle, he made nearly 200 league starts for Liverpool, before joining Ballymena as player manager in 1959.

He later had spells at Carlisle and Morecambe before taking over the hot seat at Pools.

Twentyman accepted the role on June 29 1965 and although making enquiries about several players, he only managed to pin a few.

From Brighton arrived Scottish winger Jimmy Cooper, expected to provide good service for fellow new boy Ernie Phythian.

A former English Youth international, he had made his debut for Bolton in the top flight aged 17 and after three seasons on the fringes of first team as understudy to the legendary Nat Lofthouse, he became part of the deal that took Wyn Davies to Bolton, moving to Wrexham where he played and scored regularly.

Pools Pick Up Some Silverware

POOLS won the Durham Senior Cup for the first time in several seasons after beating Darlington 3-2 on aggregate in a two-legged final.

This pre-season Pools played a Newcastle side in a friendly and won 3-2 with Peter Thompson and Ernie Phythian on the scoresheet for Pools, with the third and decisive goal scored by Newcastle's Bob Moncur who put past his own keeper.

They also beat Leeds 2-1 – the third close season in a row that they had played them at home.

1965/66

THE season kicked off with a home win over Southport on August 21 with goals from Ashworth and on their debuts, Mulvaney and Phythian.

24-year-old Jimmy Mulvaney was a former lorry driver and a forward with Whitby Town who played for Pools reserves a couple of seasons back, along with Lincoln player Brian Drysdale.

The following game was a crushing 4-0 defeat at Doncaster. No-one could tell which way the season would go, but they needed a great season from star name Fogarty – and to emphasise the fact he was warned by the manager to concentrate on the skilful side of his play rather than his over physical side.

A draw at Wrexham was followed by a bad home defeat to Bradford PA and a 5-0 reverse at Aldershot, a game in which left back Drysdale became the first substitute to be used by the Club in a Football League game.

Twentyman Under Pressure From Board

ALTHOUGH some respite came with a 2-0 win over Doncaster on September 13 1965, the board were already expressing their disapproval over the results and training methods under the current manager.

It was clear there was unrest in the dressing room and although a Phythian hat-trick helped a 5-2 victory over Newport, successive defeats to Torquay, Chesterfield and Barrow ended the reign of Geoff Twentyman after the board agreed his dismissal on October 5.

He did oversee their first victory in the League Cup at the sixth attempt, the win resulted in a visit to Elland Road. Reminiscent of the FA Cup draws of the mid-50s, Pools had been tied against one the best teams in the country.

Leeds had finished runners up in both the FA Cup and the league, missing out on goal difference to Manchester United and had little problem in beating Pools 4-2

Twentyman managed only ten division four games in which the side gained only seven points.

This run of results certainly was not the worst encountered but behind the scenes, things were amiss. It transpired that the manager could not bring it upon himself to berate players after a defeat and the board found this quiet, friendly approach unacceptable as did some senior players.

Twentyman went on to become chief scout for Liverpool and Rangers, and while at Anfield for 21 years he uncovered many of the greats of that time such as Alan Hansen, Phil Neal and Ian Rush.

Pools Appoint Brian Clough – As Second Choice...

TWO weeks later the board had decided that they wanted Alvan Williams back at the helm. Respected by the board for his training methods and keenness to keep the players fit, he was first choice.

They offered him a deal of £2,000 basic, with £250 extra in finishing in the top half of the table and an additional £250 if promoted. On October 26, they offered him £2,500 basic plus bonuses, but they could not get their man. Reluctantly, the board opted for their second choice for the role.

Little did chairman Ord, vice chairman Perryman and their colleagues realise what impact this decision would have on football in England for years to come.

A 30-year-old ex-forward named Brian Clough, who retired from the game in November 1964 after a suffering a knee injury best described as horrific, had been youth coach at Sunderland before being appointed to the Victoria Ground post on 29 October 1965.

Somewhat confident and free with his opinions, he won only two England caps despite being one of the most prolific scorers of his generation with an amazing 267 goals in 296 first team games for Middlesbrough and Sunderland.

Recommended by Len Shackleton, Clough accepted the role with a struggling Club for a basic salary of £2,000 with an additional payment of £500 to be paid if the Club finished in the top half of the table.

The youngest manager in the Football League appointed former Boro keeper, Burton manager and teammate Peter Taylor as trainer. His arrival brought a quick response from the team and they turned out a 3-1 win at Bradford Park Avenue with a goal from youngster Cliff Wright and a brace from Jimmy Mulvaney.

By now though a sceptical Pools audience refused to turn out in great numbers to see yet another new manager and 4,302 saw a 4-1 home victory over Crewe. More optimistic of progress in the FA Cup, just under 7,500 were present to see Pools beat Workington 3-1.

Tony Parry Arrives At The Vic

CLOUGH made his first signing in November when, under the recommendation of Peter Taylor, Pools signed young wing half Tony Parry from Burton Albion, the club where Taylor was manager before taking up the role at Pools. The initial fee was £300 up front with an additional £250 to be paid following a dozen first team starts. Moving in the same direction earlier in the season was keeper Les Green.

A second round home win over Wrexham saw Pools tied away to second division Huddersfield and they prepared in the worst possible way by winning once only in seven

games, including a 6-1 reverse at Tranmere.

Brian Clough

The game at Leeds Road saw Pools take the lead just after the hour through Peter Thompson, but a couple of controversial goals were allowed for the hosts and Pools went down 3-1. A share of the crowd of over 24,500 was good news for Pools' ailing coffers.

Pools had a record £40,000 overdraft at the bank and disagreement in the boardroom saw the resignation of the chairman Ernie Ord and his son on January 4 1966.

The ex chairman demanded the rest of the board quit to allow him to return with a board of his own. Initially the directors bowed to Ord's directive, but he returned without his own men in place, although a new director, John Curry, joined the following month.

Clough never had a good friendship with the chairman but swiftly made his mark on the players.

February saw transfer requests handed in by Stan Storton, Eric Harrison and Barry Ashworth because of great unrest in the dressing room. Jimmy Cooper and Billy Marshall had their contracts paid up.

Cooper followed the trend of players moving to South Africa for the chance of better money and lifestyle in a wonderful climate. Marshall, on the other hand, stayed local and played for Horden CW.

In order to add more steel to the back line, Clough signed Mansfield hard man John Gill.

The burly defender was a no-nonsense stopper and soon had the Pools fans singing his praises. Form in February and March picked up and while nothing spectacular, the Club hauled themselves precariously above the bottom four.

Clough's Style Ruffles Some Feathers

STILL the personality clashes in the dressing room took place and a clear divide seemed to be there.

Storton, with a transfer request lodged, was suspended for two weeks following the home defeat against Torquay in March after being far from pleased with the forthright way the manager and his assistant aired their opinions.

He had also phoned the chairman direct to

complain at the way he thought he was being treated.

Pools ended the season strongly with wins over Lincoln and Barrow and draws with Rochdale and Bradford.

This run pulled the Club up to eighteenth place and although it was lower than they achieved last season, the emergence of new blood boded well for the future.

John McGovern Makes First Appearance

MAKING his debut in the Pools midfield in the last game of the season against Bradford was John McGovern.

Born in Montrose, but now living on the Central Estate in Hartlepool, he was given his debut 160 days short of his 17th birthday, a record that beat the previous best by 191 days, which was set 28 years before by Harry Oliver. Also making a scoring debut that day was former Middlesbrough centre forward Joe Livingstone.

Top scorer for the season was the hard working Ernie Phythian who netted 17. He was supported by youngster Cliff Wright (11) and Thompson and Mulvaney who scored ten apiece.

Pools had started to entertain and started to score goals again. Although they only scored 63 goals, it was their highest total for five campaigns.

The reserves finished in 13th place in the NERL and during the close season a decision was made to move them to the Wearside League after a failure to re-launch the North Eastern League.

Victoria Park

THE ground was in a bad way and was often the object of derision from visiting supporters and players alike. There were no floodlights as there were at the majority of league clubs now and the stand in Clarence Road was in a dilapidated patched up state. This stand was constructed as a temporary replacement in 1919 and had stood now for almost 47 years. The board, despite all of the financial woes, still intended to buy the ground back from the council. Ownership of the site would leave them in a better position to carry out improvements and contact was yet again made with the corporation regarding this.

Several players were involved in Clough's end of season cull, but leaving of his own accord was Peter Thompson. After three seasons into his second spell with the Club he left to consider taking a college course in youth work and was given a free transfer. He netted 56 goals for Pools in 138 league starts.

Released on free transfers were Barry Ashworth, Willie Bradley, Bobby Brass, Hughie Hamilton, Eric Harrison, Willie McPheat and Stan Storton.

Ashworth and Storton made the move to Tranmere and Hamilton ended up at Scarborough.

Tough-tackling Eric Harrison moved on to Barrow, Southport and Scarborough. He later became a successful coach with Everton and then the youth team coach with Manchester United, where he oversaw the early careers of the bulk of the great Old Trafford outfit of the 1990s.

Clough Works On Ground And Signings

DURING the summer of 1966, maintenance work was carried out at the Victoria Ground. As usual the Supporters Association chipped in as did the manager and assistant manager who assisted with painting.

They were involved in signing players as well and got their hands on some players they assumed would give good service.

John McGovern, fifth in from left, with the Pools Youth Team 1967-1968

The Vic in 1966

From Notts County came experienced wing half John Sheridan and defender Tony Bircumshaw. Torquay United winger Mick Somers put pen to paper, as did another former Burton Albion player, Terry Bell a forward who joined from Nuneaton Borough.

Clough was of the belief that the Club needed to play other teams in pre-season and this summer saw three games against Middlesbrough (2-1), Billingham Synthonia (5-0) and Leeds (1-0). To the fore in these games was Phythian who scored five times.

1966-67

BRIAN Clough's first full season in charge of a football team started shortly after England had been crowned world champions.

On August 20, 1966 at The Recreation Ground, Aldershot, Pools drew 1-1 and lined up as follows – Les Green, Brian Grant, Brian Drysdale, John Sheridan, John Gill, Tony Parry, Cliff Wright, Ambrose Fogarty, Ernie Phythian, Joe Livingstone and Mick Somers.

The team had a gritty feel to it. Players like Grant, Gill and Parry were determined characters. Drysdale and Sheridan provided stability and the speed of Wright and Somers would provide good service to the rest of the forward line.

Livingstone's goal in the opener increased expectations. He scored in the next match alongside Phythian as they beat Wrexham 2-1 in front of 5,664 fans. The pair were on the scoresheet again in the League Cup draw game against Bradford Park Avenue, with Phythian

scoring again when they were knocked out 2-1 in the replay.

The board had to accept that the West Hartlepool Corporation were unwilling to sell the ground, but they arranged to ensure that floodlights were fitted as soon as possible with an increase in the amount paid to cover the cost.

Defeat at Southend followed by a home win over Barrow saw Pools up into tenth, but they lost three consecutive games.

They then put together an impressive run, losing only one in six and climbing to eighth. At the fore was Phythian who had already notched his 11th goal by mid-October.

John Sheridan

Club Pays For Parry With Burton Match

POOLS, in the financial state they were, agreed to play Burton Albion in a friendly at their ground with the hosts taking all of the gate receipts to cover the cost of Pools' payment for Tony Parry.

Pools won 3-2 with Mulvaney, Bircumshaw and a Phythian penalty netting in front of a 716 crowd.

League form stuttered but despite being embarrassed in the FA Cup at Shrewsbury when they were soundly beaten 5-2, four wins out of five in December saw them reach fourth place.

Pools Fight To Hold On To Phythian

WORK on the floodlights finally commenced (they were first discussed in 1961), but all had not been so bright behind the scenes.

With Phythian again performing well he was attracting attention from other clubs such as Colchester and Southend, who were put off

First floodlight tower rises above the ground in December 1966

when they were told that the price needed to prise him away was £10,000.

It was a bold move to stick such a tag on his head considering the financial state. In the past always a selling Club, Pools were determined to hang on to him.

The stubbornness became even more unrealistic when the cheque for the players' wages early in November had been refused by the Club's bankers.

The wages were covered by a personal cheque from the chairman Ord. However, at a board meeting on November 10, 1966 he demanded payment from takings of the next home game, which was approved.

He also stated that he had spoken to all of the directors relating to offers for Phythian and should accept the £6,000 that Southend had bid.

However, John Curry said that he had not been contacted by Ord about the sale. After an argument Ord stormed out of meeting, stating once more that he was quitting.

This put paid to the plans of Clough who had intended to raise several matters before the board at the meeting, but rather diplomatically he refused to address these issues without Ord's presence.

Clough Told To Leave Boardroom Meeting

THE board asked him to leave momentarily and his in absence passed a unanimous vote of confidence in Clough, relayed upon his recall moments later.

They also decided to reluctantly notify Southend to up their bid to £7,000 if they wanted Phythian but would not contact them direct and would wait for them to return.

The Club also launched an appeal for funds and financial assistance – not for the first time and certainly not for the last.

At a meeting five days later, Councillor John Curry was appointed as chairman with stalwart Frank Perryman staying as vice chairman, after Perryman advised that he had spoken to Ernest Ord who declared there was no chance of reconciliation.

Curry wrote to Ord advising that he was still welcome at matches and it was hoped he wouldn't embarrass the board by pressing for his loans and guarantee to be repaid immediately.

Not only was Phythian the subject of admiring eyes but also after just 11 starts was John McGovern. He was attracting the attention of Wolverhampton Wanderers, who were flying high in the second division.

Wolves made an offer, but the board and manager resisted. Once again, despite being in dire straits financially, they were determined to see things through. Offers of assistance and aid were coming in from businesses in West Hartlepool and a handful of investors took out shares.

Rather regrettably, the Ord incident refused to go away as he almost immediately requested settlement of his loan.

The Club declined and an arrangement was later made to pay him back at £20 per week. He was also allowed in the boardroom at home games and if he so desired was permitted to travel on the team coach to away games. The board also declined the request of Clough to forgo his wages while the finances were in a state.

Three straight defeats saw them drop to eighth by mid-January, but it didn't deter Wolves – now joined by Arsenal – from chasing McGovern. Both were informed that offers over £10,000 would be welcomed.

Successive home wins over Bradford and Chester saw Pools in seventh but also saw the fans answering the desire for more support. An average of 8,025 had attended the last four home games bringing in much needed revenue. It also helped that the team were playing better, but it was hoped that these supporters would remain hardcore.

New Lights Cast On The Vic Despite The Club's Financial State

ON January 16, 1967 Pools played a friendly against Sheffield Wednesday to mark the switching on of the new £15,000 floodlights.

After originally trying to get Burnley to appear, Pools lined-up neighbours Sunderland.

However, after the Rokerites suffered eight injuries at the weekend prior to this Monday night fixture, they contacted manager Clough advising that they couldn't send down a full-strength team. In typical Clough terms, he told them not to bother and contacted his former manager at Sunderland, Alan Brown who was now in charge of Wednesday, the current holders of the FA Cup.

With less than 12 hours notice, the opponents arrived and fielded a full-strength

team, exciting the 6,241 crowd as they played out a 3-3 draw.

Pools scorers were Mulvaney and Phythian (2), his second and Pools' third, hitting the bar and bouncing in off the back of a Wednesday defender who was stood on the line.

A good February and March saw Pools in sixth place and just one point outside of the promotion places. Could Clough's team press on and manage what was unthinkable in the middle of September?

Clough Plays In Benefit Match

POOLS then played a testimonial fixture for Amby Fogarty against a Charlie Hurley XI which Pools won 6-3 in front of more than 7,000 fans.

Hurley's XI consisted mainly of Sunderland first teamers and other prominent players of the day; Pools were fortunate to field two special guests. One was 57-year-old director Bert Young who came on as a substitute for manager Clough.

While Clough didn't score, the part he played showed what a loss to the game his talent was – and his appearance showed his respect for the long-serving Fogarty.

Drama In The Boardroom

BEHIND the scenes, the Ord drama dragged on with the former chairman bad mouthing the Club to guests at home matches.

The Club monitored the situation for a while, before withdrawing his privileges. He was informed that if he wished to attend games, he would have to pay and sit or stand with the rest of the fans.

The ex-chairman simply turned nasty, again demanding immediate settlement of his loan and insisting that keeper Les Green vacate the new property that he lived in on the Fens Estate in West Hartlepool that was owned by Ord.

Buoyed by new shareholders, new board members and increased crowds, Clough was able to sign much-travelled midfielder Albert Broadbent, 32. It was hoped his vast experience would be of benefit to Pools. They did lose the services of keeper Les Green to Rochdale though, but managed to hang on to Phythian and McGovern.

Boroughs United As Hartlepool

ON April 3 1967, Pools played leading Scottish side Hearts in a friendly to mark the amalgamation of the boroughs of West

Hartlepool and Hartlepool, which from April 1, 1967 were to be called Hartlepool.

A full-strength Hearts side, including several Scottish internationals such as Jim Cruickshank and David Holt and Norwegian international Roald Jensen, graced the Vic and 3,433 fans saw Joe Livingstone score for Pools in a 1-1 draw.

Through April and May, Pools ran out of legs and could only win three out the last eight games to finish in eighth place.

Few, however, were disappointed as it had been a fantastic season by recent standards and for once future matters seemed bright and not bleak. Average crowds were up by almost one thousand to 5,778.

They ended the campaign on a high when they once again won the Durham Senior Cup, beating Gateshead 10-0 on aggregate, scoring five in each leg, with Mulvaney getting four.

Contract Talks For Impressive Clough – Who Drives The Team Bus – And Leaves

BEFORE the season ended the chairman was also trying to negotiate a new contract for Clough.

Not only had he turned the team around, but off the pitch did as much as he could to promote the Club and did what he could to help them with their financial plight.

Something that he resurrected was regular pre-season friendlies against teams other than possibles and probables. He even got the Press to see him drive the team coach in an attempt to gain exposure for Pools and no doubt for himself as well. But while he had taken lessons in driving the coach, he never took to the wheel in an official capacity.

He was offered an increased salary which, including bonuses, totalled £3,250. Clough declined the offer as he had been approached by Derby County and on May 16, after a discussion with John Curry, he was released, but with an official leaving date of June 3. Pools offered the post to Peter Taylor with a salary the same as that offered to Clough. He also declined and the Clough-Taylor partnership went on to become one of the most successful and controversial in the modern game.

New Manager Required As Duo Depart

ON May 30 after interviewing several candidates, including former trainer Peter Gordon, the board appointed Angus McLean. The former Crewe and Wolves full back had gained experience as coach at Hull. He had a hard act to follow but the nucleus of the team remained in place.

His demeanour was very different to Clough, but it was anticipated he would continue in a similar confident vein.

With just three players released during the summer – Bates, Grant and Livingston – the squad was strengthened.

Wilson Hepplewhite

Keeper George Smith was a veteran of over 300 games for Notts County and he was expected to be first choice, exiling Simpkins to the second XI. Winger Wilson Hepplewhite, 21, was added to the squad and making the long move from Exeter City was young defender Alan Goad.

Pools played four friendlies, beating Queen of the South and losing to Carlisle at the Vic, and winning the final two warm-up games at Whitley Bay and Billingham Synthonia.

1967-68

WHAT turned into one of the Club's finest seasons using the Clough years as a springboard, began with a precise 2-0 win over Brentford, with goals from Mulvaney and Phythian. The team that took the field was Smith, Goad, Drysdale, Sheridan, Gill, Hepplewhite, Wright, Mulvaney, Phythian, Broadbent and Somers. They followed up with a victory at Bradford Park Avenue when a single Cliff Wright goal sealed the two points.

Pools were top and remained so after the next home game against Doncaster, a scoreless affair in front of 7,669 spectators, a leap of almost 2,300 on the previous home game.

It came as no surprise to hardened Pools supporters that this was the start of a six-game run when they failed to win a game, including a six-goal hammering at Wrexham, after which they stood in 17th.

At the end of this run Stan Aston, who had played just once this season because of the form of Parry and Gill, was sold to Nuneaton Borough for £850 after requesting a transfer.

By this time Pools had been knocked out of the League Cup, but at least they made the second round and were drawn away to Clough's Derby County. Pools were easily second best and a crowd touching 18,000 saw them lose by four clear goals.

Off Field Worries Rumble On

OFF the pitch former chairman Ord was still trying to turn up the heat in relation to recovering monies owed and requested that the interest rate that he previously agreed to charge of 4 per cent was to be upped to 7 per cent.

He was firmly told that the arrangement he had made was a verbal one between gentlemen and they expected him to behave as such.

The matter was to continue for another two years until the seemingly constant flow of correspondence from Ord and the firmness of the board ended when the loan was eventually repaid and Ord was released from his guarantee that was held with the bankers.

League form continued to be poor and come the October 21, after a 3-0 defeat at Halifax, United were in trouble in 19th spot.

Goalkeeper Play Up Front For Pools

FOLLOWING the close season signing of Smith, Ken Simpkins had not featured. But a crisis up front bizarrely saw him pull on the No 9 shirt for the game at home to Newport. He went on to make six starts that season as a striker and even managed to notch one goal.

Jimmy Mulvaney signed for Barrow for £2,500 after Notts County pulled out of a deal at the last minute.

Pools were also close to losing Ernie Phythian, with Colchester again showing interest and a bid of £7,000 lodged. The board rejected both that and the £7,500 which Notts County bid for Brian Drysdale. With Albert Broadbent seemingly on his way as well, fresh blood was needed.

In came former Watford forward Tony Smith on trial, along with part-time professional Dennis White and two young apprentice professionals Eric Tunstall and Peter Blowman.

The latter made an immediate impact, scoring twice on his debut in 3-1 win over Notts County on November 10th, a win which saw the start of a run that saw them unbeaten through to the end of 1967.

Although knocked out of the FA Cup to Bury during this spell, Pools stood in seventh place on New Years' Day and had the extra benefit of a festive double over Darlington with a 1-0 home win in front of 9,488 fans and a 3-2 win at Feethams.

Pools Start New Year In Fine Form

JANUARY 1968 saw a dip followed by an average February, but from then on Pools were in top gear.

Bolstered by the £1,500 signature of striker Bobby Cummings from Darlington at the start of February, Pools went on a great run.

The defence was rock solid and after 17

		P	HW	HD	HL	HF	HA	AW	AD	AL	AF	AA	POINTS
1	Luton Town	46	19	3	1	55	16	8	9	6	32	28	66
2	Barnsley	46	17	6	0	43	14	7	7	9	25	32	61
3	**HARTLEPOOLS UNITED**	46	15	7	1	34	12	10	3	10	26	34	60
4	Crewe Alexandra	46	13	10	0	44	18	7	8	8	30	31	58
5	Bradford City	46	14	5	4	41	22	9	6	8	31	29	57
6	Southend United	46	12	8	3	45	21	8	6	9	32	37	54
7	Chesterfield	46	15	4	4	47	20	6	7	10	24	30	53
8	Wrexham	46	17	3	3	47	20	6	7	10	24	30	53
9	Aldershot	46	10	11	2	36	19	8	6	9	34	36	53
10	Doncaster Rovers	46	12	8	3	36	16	6	7	10	30	40	51
11	Halifax Town	46	10	6	7	34	24	5	10	8	18	25	46
12	Newport County	46	11	7	5	32	22	5	6	12	26	41	45
13	Lincoln City	46	11	3	9	41	31	6	6	11	30	37	43
14	Brentford	46	13	4	6	41	24	5	3	15	20	40	43
15	Swansea City	46	11	8	4	38	25	5	2	16	25	52	42
16	Darlington	46	6	11	6	31	27	6	6	11	16	26	41
17	Notts County	46	10	7	6	27	27	5	4	14	26	52	41
18	Port Vale	46	10	5	8	41	31	2	10	11	20	41	39
19	Rochdale	46	9	8	6	35	32	3	6	14	16	40	38
20	Exeter City	46	9	7	7	30	30	2	9	12	15	35	38
21	York City	46	9	6	8	44	30	2	8	13	21	38	36
22	Chester	46	6	6	11	35	38	3	8	12	22	40	32
23	Workington	46	8	8	7	35	29	2	3	18	19	58	31
24	Bradford Park Avenue	46	3	7	13	18	35	1	8	14	12	47	23

Final league table for Division Four in 1967/1968

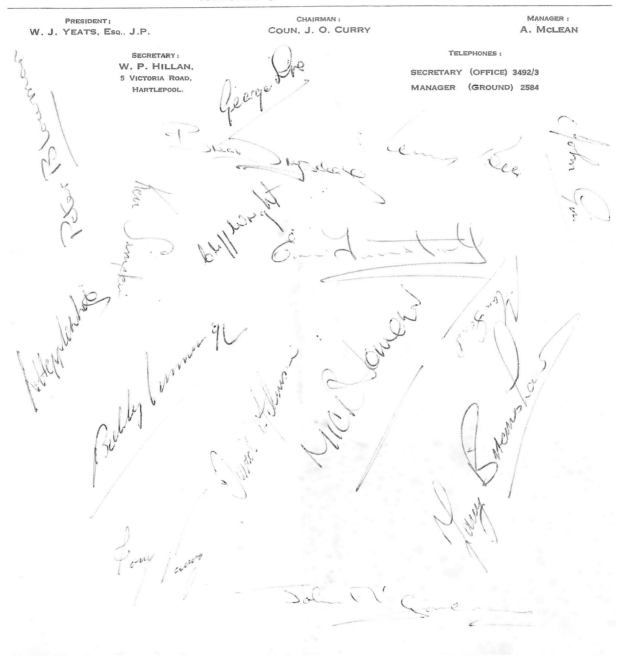

Player autograph sheet from 1967/68 season

Pools players celebrate promotion at Swansea in 1968

Tony Parry, John McGovern, John Gill and director Ben Crosby with fans

home games had conceded only eight goals, the best in the country.

Oddly, in the midst of one of their most important seasons, the Club found it necessary to play Middlesbrough in a friendly on March 4, which they lost 1-0.

The remainder of March saw two wins and three draws and Pools looked to be out of the running for a promotion spot as they stood in eighth place a full seven points behind fourth-placed Barnsley.

Promotion Becomes A Possibility

PLAYERS needed to dig deep for promotion, particularly following the departure of the prolific Phythian, who made the move to South Africa after 51 goals in 124 games.

Pools had seven games to play in April – and they won them all, leaving them in fourth place and in a promotion spot with three games to go.

After a scoreless draw on the long journey to Exeter on May 4, Pools were back in fifth place with two to play.

However, rivals Bradford City and Crewe, who were one and two points ahead respectively, had completed their fixtures. Due to an inferior goal difference Pools needed to win one of their last two games to be sure of promotion.

Both games were against Swansea, who were mid-table with nothing to play for.

In their first game at the Vetch Field since Pools played them in a FA Cup match in their last season as a non-league team, it was hoped that Pools would be playing them in their final year as a fourth division Club.

Step forward Bobby Cummings and Wilson Hepplewhite. Their goals in a 2-0 victory secured promotion for the first time in front of 16 visiting fans.

Almost a month short of 60 years in existence the Club finally managed to achieve promotion. Apart from the local bragging rights gained when winning the Durham Senior Cup, Pools had achieved very little indeed, except for a bad recent record following the death of Westgarth.

Volunteers Christine Flounders and Pamela Beavis, both 15, paint goalposts in 1968

The crowd, though, were enthusiastic and the ground was alive with sound and colour, factors not normally associated with the Victoria Ground.

The team celebrated with a lap of honour and then were guests of honour at a civic reception.

Gus McLean had taken a side that had shown promise, sorted out the defence and built from there.

Many claim he took over Clough's team. But it was he who made them into a promotion-winning team.

The season had been a record-breaking one. Gone went the record for clean sheets as new keeper Smith and his defence marshalled by the imposing Gill gave a return of 20 clean sheets, beating the previous best of 19 in 1954-55.

A Club best of 16 consecutive league games unbeaten was achieved, with seven wins on the trot in April equalling a Club record, set in the runners-up campaign of 1956-57.

Celebrations Begin At The Vic

TO put the icing on the cake, Pools confirmed third place with a record 60 points with another 2-0 win over the same opponents five days later. A somewhat disappointing crowd of 11,011 were present to see Wright and McGovern seal things.

Club Decides To Change Its Name

FOLLOWING the amalgamation of the two towns the previous year, the Club decided on May 11, 1968 to change their name to Hartlepool Football Club Limited.

It wasn't particularly a popular decision at the time as the Club had always been known as

Hartlepool F.C. line-up during the 1968/69 season. Back row: Tony Bircumshaw, John Gill, George Smith, John Sheridan (Captain), Alan Goad, Tony Parry, Eric Tunstall and Brian Drysdale. Front row: David Atkinson, Peter Blowman, Bobby Cummings, Terry Bell, Ron Young, Wilson Hepplewhite

Pools or United and some of the supporters from West Hartlepool took great offence. The board believed that as there was only one Borough of Hartlepool that the name should represent this. However, the name Pools still remains to this day.

Following the promotion and name change, the usual close season affair of fixing up the ground occurred.

There were also meetings with the Council, still the owners of the ground and it was agreed that a new grandstand would be erected on the Mill House side, with a fence erected. It would bring around a huge increase in rent, but at the same time, the Vic would be transformed.

1968/69

PRE-SEASON saw victories over Shildon and Watford. After a trial of 35 youngsters at the Vic, three hopefuls were included in a friendly at Tow Law, which a Pools team mainly consisting of reserves lost 3-2.

They finished the friendlies off by sharing four goals with Dundee United at home on August 6.

But considering the team had just been promoted to a more competitive division, very little activity took place on the transfer front.

Hull City youth player David Atkinson arrived and that was about it. Come the first game of the season played on August 10 against

Bournemouth, there were no new faces in the starting XI – ten of the players appeared in the final game of the previous season.

Terry Bell scored Pools opening goal in a new division in front of 6,791 fans in a 1-1 draw.

Rising Star Leaves The Club

THE following game may have ended in a 3-2 defeat at Bradford in the League Cup, but it was an entertaining affair in which McGovern netted twice. Another six games passed, including a 7-0 reverse at Reading, before they picked up their first win over Watford, when a Cummings penalty and a goal from Ron Young, making his debut after joining from Hull City, were enough to see Pools through by the odd goal in three.

Young was recruited to replace the outgoing McGovern who had been signed by his former manager Brian Clough and moved to Derby County, for a fee of £6,000.

It was truly an awful season. Confidence and belief from promotion was soon erased.

Pools Struggle And Relegation Follows

A club that could not afford to go up and with no new playing staff was always going to struggle. The months went by with no general improvement after October when they won two games.

November, December and January all saw one victory. Draws were frequent, as the defence was solid, but let down by struggling forwards.

February went by winless and a valiant run of just two defeats in the last 13 games saw Hartlepool FC finish third bottom and be relegated.

The squad was hardly added to and there were several players used who had just the briefest of careers with Pools – the likes of Kenny Allen, Derek Oliver, Ken Gate, John Pearson and John Young can be included in this number.

Top scorer was Peter Blowman, whose meagre total of eight was one better than last year's top scorer Terry Bell's total.

Records were set again this season, but the wrong kind. Failing to score in 20 games set back in 1923-24 was equalled, and the players scored a pathetic 40 goals, their lowest total in 45 years. A new record of 19 drawn games was also set.

Clearly hindered by a lack of investment and an inability to score goals and turn those drawn games into winning ones proved costly.

After one year in Division Three and returning to Division Four, the Club had a bit of an overhaul.

Out went Cummings and Hepplewhite, who followed the path laid by Phythian just over 12 months ago and headed to South Africa. Wingate-born Drysdale was signed by Bristol City for £15,000, where he went on to become a legend.

A bunch of local players joined, including Keith Forrest and Tommy Lee. The manager decided to stick with his experienced defence but try to introduce local talent throughout the team.

He signed Bobby Dobbing, 20, a full back from Coventry City where he had spent two years without breaking into the first team.

1969/70

AMID little investment on the playing side, the Club once more had to sell to balance the books. The sale of Drysdale assisted, so did the release of some of the better paid players.

Would the team that still included the bulk of the promotion-winning defence be capable of firing Pools back up a division?

Disappointing Season On The Horizon As The Next Decade Approached

THIS was one of the greatest seasons of disappointment. So many expected the Club to be challenging for honours and not to see them back in the nether regions of the Football League again, following the good work of the past few seasons.

The hard work of Clough and McLean in earning promotion was wasted away.

Friendlies before the start of the season

Hartlepool Mail

1969 – 70 Hartlepool United Team. Back row: Peter Thompson, Tommy Lee, John Gill, John Sheridan, Les Green, Peter Pearce, Tony Bircumshaw, Alan Goad; Front row: Cliff Wright, Tony Parry, Terry Bell, Peter Blowman, Bobby Dobbing, Ron Young, Derek Trail, Andy McCluskey, Robert Longstaff

didn't indicate that they could rekindle success. A single-goal victory over Shildon saw Pools use seven substitutes, one of whom was fifteen-year-old goalkeeper Peter Pearce (the youngest player to appear for the first team).

A draw against St.Mirren was followed up with a 3-0 reverse at home to Barnsley.

However, the campaign didn't start too badly. A new-look Pools took to the Vic on August 9 and played out a scoreless draw against Brentford. The eleven on display were – George Smith, Dennis White, Bobby Dobbing, John Sheridan, Tony Parry, Alan Goad, Ron Young, Tommy Lee, Malcolm Thompson, Cliff Wright and Derek Trail. The substitute Peter Blowman was used.

White was a youngster who debuted in the promotion season playing just once, but had never figured at all last year. There were also debuts for Dobbing, Lee – another local youngster – and Derek Trail who joined from Workington.

Another Encounter With Clough In The League Cup

THE first win came four games in when a couple of goals by Bell and one from Ron Young sent Swansea home pointless. Already through to the second round of the League Cup after victory over Scunthorpe, they were paired with Derby County, who Clough and Taylor had now taken up to the first division.

Up against Pools on September 3, 1969 were John McGovern and former keeper Les Green who had moved to Derby from Rochdale. A healthy 7,700 saw the Rams score three second-half goals with a Pools consolation from Terry Bell as Clough and co had a comfortable 3-1 victory.

An unbeaten September saw Pools in 14th place. The defence seemed to be holding steady, even introducing 18-year-old defender Bill Green for his debut on September 15 at Newport.

However, by the time they were beaten 2-1 at Chester on October 11 they were back in the re-election zone.

Darlington were the source of a player who all hoped may help them out of their predicament. Winger Harry Kirk had

previously been with Dumbarton and Middlesbrough and made an immediate impact when he scored twice on his debut as Pools beat fellow strugglers Bradford Park Avenue 5-2 with Terry Bell helping himself to a hat-trick. This win halted a run of seven games without a victory.

FA Cup success was limited to the second round. A first round victory over North Shields was followed by a defeat at Wrexham.

An unbeaten December brought a rise up the rankings to 16th. With games over New Year cancelled due to weather Pools continued their December league form with a Kirk goal securing a draw on a thawing pitch at Colchester and the following weekend 2,382 fans saw them rout Peterborough 4-2 to put Pools within nine points of a promotion place, but only five above the re-election zone.

And that was as good as it got.

Des McPartland with Gus McLean in 1969

Things Start To Fall Apart –
Re-Election (Again) Needed To Save Pools

A fair start, followed by a small decent run was followed by sheer capitulation. A 6-0 humiliation at Exeter led to another six straight defeats. An attempt to bolster the squad by signing Tony Boylan and Lance Robson from Bishop Auckland and Darlington respectively was followed by the signing of Northampton's former Middlesbrough keeper Des McPartland and full back Jim Walker from Derby on loan.

An upturn in form was achieved with three wins in six, but the Club were still languishing in 21st place with seven games remaining.

Not that they could rely on these last few games to pull themselves out of the mire, as never mind registering a win or even a draw, they didn't even manage a goal.

This abysmal run saw them end in 23rd place, above Bradford Park Avenue by a gap of seven points.

An unwanted record of 22 games without scoring (20 had been the previous record set in 1968-69) wasn't helped by the sale of Bell to Reading at the end of February for £8,000, but he had to go as dwindling attendances affected the dire financial plight.

He ended top of the scoring charts with 15, despite last playing his last game in February.

Pools were again fortunate to be re-elected, but such favour did not smile on Bradford Park Avenue. Out of the Football League they went and in came Cambridge United, champions of the Southern League for the past two seasons.

Cambridge polled 31 votes as Bradford PA managed only 17. They were even beaten by Wigan Athletic who received 18 votes.

Manager Decides Enough Is Enough

THAT was it for Gus McLean and on April 24, two days after the season ended with a 4-0 defeat at Darlington, he quit.

Three seasons, one great and two diabolical, but he will always be remembered as the manager who won promotion for the first time.

Nobody had a bad word to say about him and he was deemed a good manager, but couldn't get the best out of his players. He was eventually replaced by trainer John Simpson, officially appointed to the role on May 6, 1970.

Once again there was a mass clearout. Ageing goalkeeper Smith was freed, along with striker Peter Blowman, Bobby Dobbing, Tommy Lee, Andy McCluskey, Derek Trail and Malcolm Thompson.

Another player not returning was Lance Robson. The former Darlington man only

Bobby Dobbing

played part-time as he was a dentist out of town and refused to train. After a period of suspension his contract was terminated.

To make up for the batch of departures, Simpson was active in the market, very much so for a manager of a struggling Club who had just been loaned £2,000 by their chairman.

Former Scottish cap George Herd joined from Sunderland, along with his former teammate Nick Sharkey who signed from Mansfield, Aldershot's Malcolm Dawes and Malcolm Clarke of Bristol City.

They decided to no longer enter the Durham Senior Cup due to the problems it was causing with fixture congestion at the end of each campaign.

No one – fans, board and players – believed they could have a season as poor as the last.

For the new decade approaching, the board certainly wanted an increase in the gates. When they got promoted the average was 6,189, this fell to 4,200 in 1968/9 and now it was down to a record low of 2,562. The Club was running on empty, the overdraft was at its limit and they were losing money left, right and centre. The new Millhouse Stand was also under construction.

SOCCER DRIVER

MAN and *MANager*

GUS McLEAN (Hartlepool F.C.)

ADD UP THE HOURS a manager crams into his working week, and you will find that a proportion of his life is spent sitting in front of a steering wheel . . . on the way to a game . . . travelling home after a match . . . rushing off to meet a player.

☐ A man who agrees with this is Hartlepool manager Gus McLean. For him, and the other bosses of clubs off soccer's beaten track, the problem of travelling to watch matches and players can become a fair sized headache.

■ So important is this part of a manager's life though that Gus McLean reckons a car is a vital piece of equipment for the modern manager.

☐ "There is always a game on somewhere to take in . . . always a player to check on . . . **without a car, the job would be almost impossible.**"

☐ Not surprisingly Gus clocks up a big mileage during the course of a season . . . most of it on soccer travel. "I would not like to guess what my annual mileage is," he told us, "but I reckon it would certainly make the

average motorist sit up and take notice. In a couple of months I reckon to tot up around 5,000 miles."

☐ *Most of the motorist-managers we know seem ideal candidates for the Advanced Test run by the Ministry of Transport, and McLean admits:* "My driving has improved since I became a manager. It is like football . . . practice makes perfect."

☐ The time spent behind the wheel allows McLean to work out some of the problems that face every manager. "I can ponder over team selection . . . work out schedules," he says.

☐ But like many of the men in his profession, Gus McLean occasionally likes to relax and forget about work for a while. He reckons to have found the perfect answer . . . a hobby that demands the utmost concentration, that wipes everything else out of his mind.

☐ "Tapestry is a pastime that I find soothing and restful," Mr. McLean explains. "You just cannot think about anything else, for me it makes a nice change." **The McLean household is decorated with the end products of his hobby . . . firescreens, rugs, pictures.** "It all began when I broke a leg while playing for Wolves. I was laid up for a lengthy period with nothing to do, and became so bored that my wife went out and bought me a tapestry kit," he explains.

☐ *"I became so interested in the subject that when I was back in action I kept up the hobby and I still like to do a bit when I have an odd moment."*

☐ Gus reckons that tapestry is tailor-made for managers as a pastime. "It is not a hobby that has to be done all at once, you can leave it on one side for months and pick it up to start from where you left off. It's a hobby that is satisfying as well as relaxing. **You make something out of nothing.**"

☐ Could be that the Hartlepool manager has hit on the answer most managers would like to know . . . just how to release the pressures of the game, for once in a while.

■ *AS GUS McLEAN SAYS:* "IF I READ A BOOK OR WORK IN THE GARDEN I SOON GET TO THINKING ABOUT THE GAME . . . BUT THERE IS NO CHANCE WHEN I'M WORKING ON MY TAPESTRY. TIME JUST FLIES PAST."

Vital Statistics

Appointed manager of Hartlepool in June 1967 after a playing career with Wolverhampton Wanderers, Bury and Crewe Alexandra. Took over as trainer at Bury in 1957 and filled a similar post with Hull City.

Above: Gus McLean setting out on yet another long car journey.

Gus McLean in the Football League Review

1970-71

THE mundane run of friendlies prior to the season started with a behind closed doors affair at Catterick Garrison in which they romped to a 10-1 victory.

On August 1, Pools played the first game at home in front of the now-completed £30,000 Mill House Stand, a cantilever build above the terrace.

A crowd of 1,884 saw Pools beat Raith Rovers 2-1, with new signing Nick Sharkey netting both goals.

The friendlies ended with an embarrassing 2-0 defeat at South Shields, a game in which trialist keeper Peter Heaume severely dislocated his shoulder resulting in his return to his home town of Huddersfield to recover.

The new stand stood sparsely populated, as gates were poor from the start and, after losing the opening game at Colchester and being knocked out of the League Cup by York when 3,734 turned out, around 800 less attended the home draw with Workington.

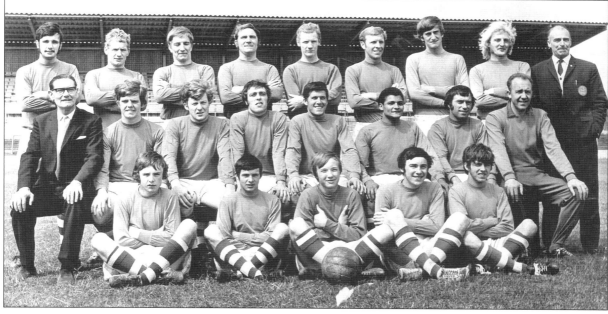

Hartlepool United line-up in 1970. Back row: Les Crook, Malcolm Clarke, Alan Goad, John Gill, Des McPartland, Tony Bircumshaw, Bill Green, Cliff Wright, John Simpson (Manager); Middle row: John Curry (Chairman), Peter Barlow, Harry Kirk, Ron Young, George Herd, Tony Parry, Nick Sharkey, George Henderson (Trainer); Front row: Kevan Thompson, Gordon Winter, Peter Pearce, Dennis White, Keith Forrest

Shaky Start Made Worse By Cup Embarrassment

THE start to the first season in the 1970s was less than average but not desperate, losing only twice in the opening seven games, but four of these were draws. However it soon appeared as though events were mirroring last season as the team seemed to go into freefall and won just once in the next 12, the last seven all defeats. Sharkey was the only scorer in that time with three to his name.

Harry Kirk was sold to Scunthorpe United for £1,550. Earlier in the season he became the first Pools player to score after coming on as a substitute in the 2-1 reverse at Stockport on September 11.

Further shame was to come, when on November 21, Pools were dumped out of the FA Cup at the first hurdle by non-league Rhyl. The Cheshire County League side won by a single goal scored within the first ten minutes of the game. The following week Pools travelled to the same area, facing top of the table Chester. Expectations were not great, but another Sharkey goal saw them come home with the points.

Sharkey scored again on December 19 in a 1-0 win at Workington, but Pools were still down in 22nd place.

He was now the only Pools player to score since Tony Bircumshaw netted in the 1-1 draw at Exeter on October 10. Pools may have had only 15 points but were still way ahead of the two teams below them. Barrow had eight points but Scunthorpe had managed only three and at the halfway point of the season they had failed to register a win.

Poor Form Puts Manager Under Pressure

THE Boxing Day game at home to York may have guaranteed a bumper gate in the past, but only 2,368 turned out. Poor, but still an increase on the last three home games which had all been sub 2,000.

It also was the last encounter in a four game spell that saw Pools draw one and win three games, which persuaded the board not to discuss John Simpson's position, although they were still gravely concerned at the state of affairs.

There was no New Year cheer as all four games in January were lost.

President Bill Yeats passed away after serving the Club for around 50 years, through thick and thin – on several occasions thinner. He was replaced by fellow Club stalwart Frank Perryman.

Falling Crowds Impact On The Club

FEBRUARY saw John Gill given permission to work part-time as a trainee manager in a pub, as long as it did not affect his training or playing.

It also saw another winless month and home games were being watched by less than 1,300 fans.

The Club were seeking money from as many sources as practical and the possible use of the ground for a pop concert on May 29, 1971 was looked at. The Club also approached the Corporation for financial assistance.

They were on their knees and in March were given £10,000 in the form of a grant on the understanding that it was not to be used to reduce the overdraft or to pay off debts to directors or former directors. The payment of rent for February to May inclusive was also waived.

The Corporation also agreed to lend the Club up to an additional £5,000 if they could raise any funds up to the end of May 1971. If the Club were able to raise any figure up to that amount, it would be matched. At the end of this period, the Club had a list of donations totalling £1,735.10.

Boss Stands Down And New Man Is Sought – Len Ashurst Appointed

JOHN Simpson resigned, the 5-0 defeat at Southport on March 5 proving the final straw. After just five wins in 34 games he conceded defeat.

To get the most out of a new manager the Club had already decided that a player/manager was needed and had already been courting Sheffield Wednesday to see if vastly experienced central defender Gerry Young was free.

He was deemed unavailable, so Sunderland player Len Ashurst was interviewed and was appointed the following day. A veteran of over 400 games, he was a few days short of his 32nd birthday when appointed. His former Sunderland team-mate George Herd was appointed player trainer/coach.

The fund raising efforts pressed on. The Northern Daily Mail agreed to donate providing that the new manager assist them with the promotion of their Spot the Ball scheme. Fund raising evenings at various nightclubs were arranged and as well as the pop concert at the Vic, a concert was organised to take place at the Town Hall.

Ashurst was never realistically going to pull Pools out of the mire and in the 14 games he oversaw they lost nine of them. Barrow finished below Pools and when re-election day came, Pools again escaped, tying with Newport on 33 votes. Hereford with 22 votes and Wigan, 14, were the top of the non-leaguers.

Pools needed to sort out their away form, they had won only two and drawn the same number, scoring a paltry six goals all season. They only managed 28 at home all campaign.

Ashurst Swings The Axe In Summer

ANOTHER close season brought another clearout. Man-mountain John Gill moved on after his testimonial. A veteran of well over 200 games, he moved to Nuneaton Borough and later worked in an abattoir. Heading to the same club was Tony Bircumshaw, another permanent fixture in the defence. Keeper Des McPartland, who had never missed a game since he signed, was also released after keeping only nine clean sheets in 56 games.

Forward Peter Barlow signed for Northern Premier League side Stafford Rangers, while winger Ralph Wright made the short move to Darlington. Also released from his playing contract was George Herd, who was to stay on as coach.

To reward Gill for his commitment and service, he was allowed a testimonial match. A Pools XI took on an all-star XI with Pools winning 4-1 in front of 1,198 fans, a poor turnout for such a stalwart.

The opponents included Middlesbrough's Peter Creamer, Alan Foggon and Derrick Downing, Whitby's Billy Veart, twin brother of Pools player Bobby, and Gill. Goals from reserve team players Billy Lewis and Gordon Winter were added to two from Bobby Veart.

1971-72 – Hope

THERE was no talk of promotion ahead of the new season, only survival. Ashurst was still young enough to perform well at this level but wanted to focus on the management side.

Midfielder Malcolm Clarke had been

Len Ashurst was named Player Coach

adequate, but much more was expected of him and the other Malcolm (Dawes) was a different proposition. The utility man had never let the Club down when needed.

Another young player grabbing the headlines was centre half Bill Green. Club captain and aged only 20 he was another in a long line of central defenders nurtured or introduced over the decades. Whether the Club would be able to hold onto him given their financial plight was unlikely.

Winner of the first ever Player of the Year award, in 1968, defender Tony Parry was also part of the scene.

Progressively Hartlepool seemed to be turning into a Club of hope. Hope that their better players would stay, hope that the Club would keep their heads above water financially, hope that they may be able to attract a decent player or two and of course hope that they could keep away from the bottom four.

Shakespeare ——on Football *(Twenty-second Year)*

DIRECTORS

And for my means, I'll husband them so well
They shall go far with little.
(Hamlet)

If the great gods be just, they shall assist,
The deeds of justest men
(Antony and Cleopatra)

MANAGERS

Sir, you have wrestled well, and overthrown
More than your enemies
(As You Like It)

In each thing give him way, cross him
in nothing
(Antony and Cleopatra)

SECRETARIES

...what he hath scanted men in hair
he hath given them in wit
(The Comedy of Errors)

Remuneration! O! that's the Latin word
for three-farthings
(Love's Labour's Lost)

TREASURERS

Money is a good soldier, sir, and will on
(Merry Wives of Windsor)

PLAYERS

Full of strange oaths, and bearded like the pard,
Jealous in honour, sudden and quick in quarrel,
Seeking the bubble reputation
(As You Like It)

Seven hundred pounds, and possibilities, is
goot gifts
(Merry Wives of Windsor)

TRAINERS

Sir, I will use
My utmost skill in his recovery
(Pericles)

REFEREES & LINESMEN

My scars can witness, dumb although they are
That my report is just and full of truth
(Titus Andronicus)

Read not my blemishes in the world's report;
I have not kept the square, but that to come
Shall all be done by the rule
(Antony and Cleopatra)

BANK MANAGERS

We will our Kingdoms give
Our crown, our life, and all that we call ours
To you in satisfaction, but if not,
Be you content to lend your patience to us
(Hamlet)

PRESS

Write till your ink be dry; and with your tears
Moist it again; and frame some feeling line
That may discover such integrity
(Two Gentlemen of Verona)

SCOUTS

Truly, I have him: but would not be
the party that should desire you to touch him
(Antony and Cleopatra)

For by my scouts I was advertised
(King Henry the Sixth)

SPECTATORS

Alas, sir;
In what have I offended you? What cause
Hath my behaviour given to your displeasure
That thus you should proceed to put me off
And take your good grace from me
(King Henry the Eighth)

What shall be our sport, then?
(As You Like It)

OUR VISITORS

... when I was at home I was in
a better place; but travellers must
be content
(As You Like It)

Official Club Christmas Card 1971 – the Shakespeare theme is still being used by Pools

Neil Warnock Wings In To The Vic – Leeds Beaten Pre Season

ASHURST then dipped into the transfer market and signed wide man Neil Warnock from Rotherham. The 22-year-old was classed as a good signing by many. Also joining in June was former York keeper Mick Gadsby. George Potter was an intimidating presence and the former Torquay man was seen as an ideal replacement for Gill. Added to the ranks as well was former Scarborough front man Ken Ellis.

Behind the scenes, Tommy Johnson and Bobby Lumley were put in charge of the reserve and youth teams respectively.

Pools met Middlesbrough in a warm up and drew 2-2. They then played a decent Leeds side who included the likes of Gray, Yorath and Jordan and beat them 3-1. Ellis scored a pair in each match.

The form in these two games looked promising, until contradicted by a 2-1 reverse at North Shields.

Opening Win Offers Pools False Hope And All Players Are For Sale

THE opening day of the season saw Pools beat relegated Reading 3-1 at home, with Ron Young and a pair from Ken Ellis giving a good start to the season. However, once again it was short lived.

Knocked out of the League Cup in the first round by Barnsley, they then failed to win in

Neil Warnock

their next six league games, including a 6-0 thumping at Brentford, and were bottom of the league by the middle of September.

Two home wins over Barrow and Peterborough brought the slightest break, as they once again capitulated and failed to win in the next eight.

At the end of October, six games through this less than illustrious run, the Club were facing deep financial peril once more.

The board wrote to all clubs circulating the fact that all players were available for transfer. Parry and Goad had price tags of £5,000, while £6,000 would have got Ellis or Warnock. Pre-empting some departures the Club brought in Mick Spelman on a short term contract and Bobby Smith, initially on loan from Chester.

Ashurst Already Under Pressure From Above

THE FA Cup brought a home tie with non-league Scarborough, who had reached the first round the season before and performed well in the Northern Premier League finishing in the top four on the last two occasions. 3,374

Pools line up in 1971-72. Back row: George Herd (Trainer), Billy Veart, Dennis White, Malcolm Clarke, Mick Gadsby, Eric Hulme, Alan Goad, Malcolm Dawes, Jimmy Kelly; Front row: George Potter, Neil Warnock, Tony Parry, Ron Young, Bill Green, Nick Sharkey, Ken Ellis, Tommy Cheetham

Bobby Veart, Alan Goad, Ron Young, Barry Watling and George Porter 1972

saw Pools surprisingly breeze through 6-1. Young and Veart nabbed two apiece, assisted by Warnock and former Scarborough man Ellis.

Victory saved Ashurst from the sack as the board had expressed the seriousness of the team's plight to him before the game.

Boosted by this win they beat Crewe in their next home game and the second round of the FA Cup saw them drawn against another non league side, Boston United. The NPL side had been regulars in the top four with Scarborough.

Pools were simply poor and, driven on by their player/manager Jim Smith, it was little surprise when Boston opened the scoring on 50 minutes, through a Smith free-kick.

With a quarter of an hour to go, Ashurst brought on the experienced Sharkey to replace Eric Welsh. The substitute soon brought a great save out of the Boston keeper, but within a couple of minutes, they were 2-0 down, when John Froggat netted after a cleverly worked corner caused confusion in the Pools defence.

		P	HW	HD	HL	HF	HA	AW	AD	AL	AF	AA	POINTS
1	Grimsby Town	46	18	3	2	61	26	10	4	9	27	30	63
2	Southend United	46	18	2	3	56	26	6	10	7	25	29	60
3	Brentford	46	16	2	5	52	21	8	9	6	24	23	59
4	Scunthorpe United	46	13	8	2	34	15	9	5	9	22	22	57
5	Lincoln City	46	17	5	1	46	15	4	9	10	31	44	56
6	Workington	46	12	9	2	34	7	4	10	9	16	27	51
7	Southport	46	15	5	3	48	21	3	9	11	18	25	50
8	Peterborough United	46	14	6	3	51	24	3	10	10	31	40	50
9	Bury	46	16	4	3	55	22	3	8	12	18	37	50
10	Cambridge United	46	11	8	4	38	22	6	6	11	24	38	48
11	Colchester United	46	13	6	4	38	23	6	4	13	32	46	48
12	Doncaster Rovers	46	11	8	4	35	24	5	6	12	21	39	46
13	Gillingham	46	11	5	7	33	24	5	8	10	28	43	45
14	Newport County	46	13	5	5	34	20	5	3	15	26	52	44
15	Exeter City	46	11	5	7	40	30	5	6	12	21	38	43
16	Reading	46	14	3	6	37	26	3	5	15	19	50	42
17	Aldershot	46	5	13	5	27	20	4	9	10	21	34	40
18	**HARTLEPOOL**	**46**	**14**	**2**	**7**	**39**	**25**	**3**	**4**	**16**	**19**	**44**	**40**
19	Darlington	46	9	9	5	37	24	5	2	16	27	58	39
20	Chester	46	10	11	2	34	16	0	7	16	13	40	38
21	Northampton Town	46	8	9	6	43	27	4	4	15	23	52	37
22	Barrow	46	8	8	7	23	26	5	3	15	17	45	37
23	Stockport County	46	7	10	6	33	32	2	4	17	22	55	32
24	Crewe Alexandra	46	9	4	10	27	25	1	5	17	16	44	29

Football League Division Four 1971/72

Never Say Die was recorded in 1972

Although Bobby Veart pulled it back to 2-1, Pools were embarrassed and out of the competition.

As if losing wasn't bad enough, there was fighting on the terraces during which a number of Hartlepool followers were arrested.

Victims of a giant killing act, hooliganism, bottom of the league and nearly bankrupt, it wasn't going to be a happy Christmas.

New Year Offers New Resolve

BUT January 1972 saw an improvement, with two wins from five to drag themselves off the foot of the table. Former Northern Ireland international Welsh, who had been a bit part player since joining in the summer, had his contract terminated at his own request and moved to South Africa.

Arriving on loan was keeper Ron Hillyard from York City, to replace the injured and out of form Gadsby.

Clough's Parry Bid Helps Save Pools

HEADING through the exit door was Tony Parry. Player of more than 200 games for the Club he was on his way to Derby County for a fee of £3,000, reunited with former boss Brian Clough. His place was taken by full back

Bill Green who had been playing as a makeshift centre forward for the past few weeks.

The Club entered February slightly better off, but still in dire straits.

Money Making Schemes Turn Musical

AGAIN ways of making or saving money were being explored and the most bizarre event happened in February – when the team entered the recording studio to press a record – 'Who Put Sugar In My Tea?' and a b-side titled 'Never Say Die'. There was also a celebrity football match, followed by a benefit gig.

On the pitch only Young's goals brightened up a dull February, with him scoring seven since the turn of the year. In March a minor miracle happened as Pools actually won an away game when they beat Newport County 2-0 with old hands Ashurst and Sharkey getting the goals.

After a run of 28 games without a win on the road, it still wasn't a record – that was set at 31 games in the 30s.

Behind the scenes things weren't so rosy and Ashurst dismissed trainer George Herd, leaving himself solely responsible for the management, training and coaching of the squad.

The following game saw the debut, as a substitute, of loan signing Willie Waddell who had joined from Barnsley. The loan signing had

Damaged dressing rooms after fire started by vandals in 1972

watched by 5,537 and the Scunthorpe win was seen by 6,197.

Townsfolk had rallied round, their desire to see the Club pull away from the re-election zone was huge as many assumed that this time there would be no turning back for Pools and they would be cast aside from the Football League family.

The Scunthorpe win had seen Pools escape the bottom four and they stayed outside of the zone even following a defeat at Barrow on April 3.

Dramatic Derby Win Completes Miracle

THEY then won five of the final seven games, including a memorable triumph at Feethams when more than half of the near 9,000 crowd had travelled from Hartlepool.

Darlington took the lead through Colin Sinclair. Ashurst brought himself on for Young and in a desperate measure pushed Dawes into the middle of the park. The change worked with a goal from Green in the 70th minute and another from Waddell with less than five minutes remaining. The win saw Pools safe from the drop.

The 'never say die' attitude was epitomised throughout, but in particular by Neil Warnock. Kicked from pillar to post by Darlington hard man John Peverell and injured early in the game, he persevered and supplied the cross from which Waddell scored.

After the game Warnock was taken to hospital and it was found he had played with a fractured ankle and a ruptured spleen.

Pools ended in 16th place and Ashurst had pulled off the impossible by keeping the Club safe, a feat that was seemingly unbelievable just over a month before.

Waddell was the catalyst for the upturn in the form. Not only did he notch seven goals in 14 games, his dynamic wing play and great delivery was complemented by that of Warnock on the left flank, who had been the most consistent performer throughout and was named Player of the Year, although he had to wait several years for the trophy!

Top scorer was Ron Young with 18.

Barrow, third bottom and eight points above

been on the books of Leeds but after failing to make any impact he returned north of the border to Kilmarnock, before he joined Barnsley. A thick set former Scottish schoolboy winger, he scored a late consolation in a 2-1 defeat.

He replaced Sharkey for the next game and was again on the scoresheet as Pools beat Colchester 3-2. This win saw the Club move off the bottom and heralded the start of one of their greatest ever fightbacks.

Pools Hit Form At The Right Time

APART from a two-week stint in October, Pools had been in the bottom four since the third Saturday of the season, spending most of the time propping up the table. A draw at Workington was followed by three successive home victories over Exeter, Stockport and Scunthorpe.

The crowds had flocked back as the team showed their 'never say die' spirit on the pitch. Gates had been hovering around the 3,000 mark, but the 5-0 win over Stockport was

Hartlepool United in 1972. Back row: Tony Toms (Trainer), Neil Warnock, Malcolm Dawes, Alan Goad, Barry Watling, Bill Green, Bobby Smith, Rob Smith, Len Ashurst (Player-Manager); Front row: George Potter, John Honour, Willie Waddell, Bobby Veart, Billy Ward, John Coyne, Mick Spelman, Jimmy Kelly, Ron Young

bottom club Crewe, failed to gain re-election, with their place taken by Hereford on a second vote.

At the end of the season a new trainer was brought in. Instead of following the normal approach of appointing an ex-player, Ashurst went for Royal Marine Tony Toms.

An outstanding athlete, he was expected to bring the best out of the players with disciplined training aimed at improving fitness and stamina.

Waddell signed permanently after Pools paid Barnsley £1,000. Also putting pen to paper were John Coyne, Barry Watling and Robert Smith.

Coyne, 21, joined from Tranmere, Watling was a keeper who had seen promotion with Notts County in 1971 and considered a fantastic capture replacing Hillyard, whose loan spell had finished, and Gadsby who had been freed along with Ellis and Sharkey.

Robert Smith, a full back from Grimsby Town also moved in, making it a confusing two Robert Smiths on the books, the latest recruit to be known as Rob and the other as Bobby to try and avoid this confusion.

1972/73

THE run in to the new season saw a home friendly against Czech outfit Bohemians Prague, who were touring the country at the time.

In a close game watched by a curious 2,927 fans, Pools lost 1-0.

This was followed up with a 1-0 win at Crook, with friendlies against Middlesbrough and Blyth Spartans cancelled due to a mounting injury crisis at Pools, eight players struggling for fitness.

Positive Signs In The New Campaign

THE new season started with a 2-1 win at Lincoln with goals from Coyne and Bill Green, the first time the Club had started a campaign with an away victory since 1957.

For once they even won a League Cup tie at home to Doncaster and after a second win in the division things looked positive.

Pools were handed a draw at Coventry in the second round of the League Cup and although not one of the more fancied sides it still offered Pools a chance to test themselves against a top-flight team. It proved to be a great game for Pools, who although beaten put on a good show.

Trailing to a controversial Willie Carr penalty, Pools rallied and the impressive Coyne had an equaliser ruled out for offside. They failed to break through the Sky Blues' back line and returned on the end of a 1-0 reverse.

Back in the league, following their second away win at Bradford City on September 23, the side stood in a healthy sixth place and it seemed that the run at the end of the previous

DON HEATH

HARTLEPOOL may be a humble outfit but Don has had his taste of glory en route to the Victoria Ground.

Apart from making 88 League appearances for Swindon Town, it was while with the Wiltshire club that he won for himself a League Cup winners medal, being a member of the side that defeated Arsenal 3-1 at Wembley in that never-to-be-forgotten Final of 1969.

A year later The Robins became the first club to win the Anglo/Italian tournament beating Napoli 3-0, Don earning for himself another treasured medal.

Before playing for Swindon he'd seen service with Middlesbrough and Norwich City, later starring for Oldham Athletic and Peterborough United, before signing for 'Pool in July, 1973.

Born in Stockton, Don is a midfield player and was appointed club-captain at the start of this season.

Don Heath feature in Soccer Star

Hartlepool United in 1973. Back row: Alan Goad, Kev McMahon, Eddie Guy, Barry Watling, Bryan Conlon, George Potter; Middle row: Don Heath, Rob Smith, Billy Ward, Mick Spelman, Malcolm Moore, John Coyne, Willie Waddell; Front row: Brian Gribben, Dave Embleton, Terry Ward, Hartley Maddison

season was not a one-off from Ashurst's men.

But, following suit for so many seasons in the past, a decent start was followed by a poor run of just one win in the next nine.

Off Field Problems Hit The Vic

PROBLEMS were encountered once more away from the pitch, but in a different form.

With the Clarence Road side of the ground overlooking the railway line and dock area, it was an isolated place and had always been easy prey for vandals.

In October a fire was started at the ground damaging the dressing rooms. The playing kit was destroyed and due to their financial plight they made a plea to other clubs asking for replacement kit. They went on to play in the strips of Hereford, Chelsea and Ipswich for a short while.

Towards the end of this sequence the Club lost the services of Warnock who moved to Scunthorpe after Pools accepted a bid of £3,250.

The remainder of his career as a player was spent in the lower leagues but it was for his prowess as a manager that he became better

known and achieved success with Scarborough, Notts County, Huddersfield, Plymouth and hometown team Sheffield United who he guided to the Premiership before standing down in the summer of 2007.

There was a quick reunion with Warnock, as Pools played out two scoreless draws with Scunthorpe in the FA Cup. The second replay took place at Sunderland's Roker Park. In front of a crowd of 7,917, the game was tied 1-1 after 90 minutes, with Pools losing out in extra time.

It signalled the start of another bad run for Pools. Just two wins followed in the next 13 games, a paltry four goals netted in the process.

But in February and March they won four out of six games, climbing to 12th place, but still only scoring five goals in the process. It could have been down to Thoms' intense training methods, but some blamed his style for causing the sluggishness.

A Promising Season Fizzles Out

THE final eight games saw Pools fail to win and again embarrass themselves in front of goal, netting on only six occasions, two being own goals. They dropped to a final position of

20th, five points clear of the re-election places.

The good start had offered hope, but the loss of Warnock and the inability to find a forward line hit the team hard. Watling was ever present and the back four in front of him of Green, Goad, Potter and Smith practically picked themselves.

The defence kept 17 clean sheets, but the rest of the team was the problem and Coyne was top scorer with an embarrassingly low nine goals.

The summer saw the departure of centre half Bill Green. Aged only 22 he had already played in more than 130 first team games for Pools and his sale to Carlisle raised £15,000. He was set to sign for Swindon, but as he was completing a medical Ashurst had negotiated a better deal with the Cumbrians which allowed Green to stay in the north and earned Pools more money. He captained Carlisle in the top flight and later played for West Ham, before a spell as manager with Scunthorpe when he quit playing after a career total of around 500 games.

Also leaving was Bobby Smith who moved to Bury as player/coach. The former Manchester United reserve later became Bury boss in November 1973 when aged just 29.

Bobby Veart and Ron Young both made their way to South Shields. Veart was a dependable player but never a regular, while Young enjoyed five seasons when he notched up around 200 appearances.

1973/74

NEW to the Club were Silksworth-born Tranmere forward Malcolm Moore, former Bury man Dave Embleton and the much-travelled midfielder Don Heath. He hailed from Stockton and had first been on the books of Middlesbrough.

Kev McMahon moved from Barnsley where he had failed to make an impression after previously playing for Consett, Newcastle and York. Also added were former teammates of Ashurst at Sunderland – left back Jimmy Shoulder and forward Allan Gauden. Shoulder had spent several years at Scarborough whereas Gauden joined from Grimsby after a long spell with Darlington.

Friendlies included a behind closed doors game against Newcastle which Pools lost 1-0 and victories over South Bank and Blackburn with a draw against Grimsby. John Coyne was making an impression and scored in each of the last three.

Also new was chairman Tom Aird, who replaced John Curry on August 7.

New Faces Fail To Inspire Team

A home victory over Brentford with a goal from Gauden hailed the start of the campaign, but this was followed by a failure to

Hartlepool Manager Ken Hale in 1974

win in the next six, including the expected departure from the League Cup in the first round losing 5-3 at Rochdale. The run was halted by a 2-1 victory over Gillingham at the Vic when Moore and Dawes notched their first goals of the season.

Over the next eight games Pools again failed to win and scored just four goals in the process. Pools were again flexing their shoulder muscles as they propped up the Football League. The mean defence from the previous season was as non existent as the forwards – they had kept only two clean sheets in the first 15 games and scored 19 goals.

FA Cup Exit Compounds Club Financial Situation/Country In Crisis

FOR the third time in four seasons Pools were drawn away to non-league opposition in the first round of the FA Cup and for the third time in four seasons Pools were knocked out. Altrincham outplayed Pools and sent them home on the end of a 2-0 scoreline.

This defeat seemed to be it for most Pools fans. With average crowds standing at just over 2,000 and with the last six home games pulling in less than this figure, a mere 1,101 turned out for the visit of Barnsley on December 8, as Pools lost again.

A lot of the low attendance issues can be put down to the fact that the country was in crisis.

There were enough problems with rising oil prices without electricity and coal workers

The Vic in 1974

starting an overtime ban back in November 1973. Fuel deliveries were reduced by 10 per cent to conserve stock after the Arab oil producing states reduced their production.

The following month things got worse as a

Barry Watling makes a finger-tip save against Darlington in 1974

1974/75 Hartlepool United Line Up; Back row: Clive Baker (Coach), Malcolm Poskett, Don Heath, Alan Goad, Eddie Guy, David Ambleton, Kevin McMahon, Bobbie Parks, Ken Hale (Manager); Front row: Billy Ward, George Potter, Micky Spelman, Robbie Smith, John Honour, Malcolm Moore, Alan Gauden, Jimmy Shoulder

50 mph speed limit was imposed and restrictions on heating and lighting were placed on businesses. With the town bordered to the north by several collieries, those in that trade or related trades were feeling the pinch.

Then came the announcement of an industrial three-day week as requested by the Government. Factories had to open and work either Monday to Wednesday or Thursday to Saturday. If the factories were open on the traditional match day, how were supporters supposed to get to the game?

Attendances Drop As Country Continues To Struggle

THE great uncertainty, as well as poor form, led to the home game on the December 22 against Scunthorpe being seen by only 844 fans.

The already struggling Club would further suffer if crowds followed this pattern. Yet the players put on their best show of the campaign so far and ran out 3-0 winners thanks to two goals from Malcolm Moore and one from Alan Goad.

A Boxing Day victory at Workington and a respectable draw at Reading at least saw the Club end the year on a decent note.

Pools Set To Play On A Sunday For First Time

JANUARY was a great month for the team. Three wins and two draws saw them push up to 14th place and despite the industrial problems, the crowds had risen to an average of around 2,500.

Politically the Conservative Government lifted some restrictions on events taking place on Sundays and permitted football to be played, to accommodate the tens of thousands who now had to work Saturdays.

Sunday, February 3 1974 was the date that league football was first played on the Sabbath at the Vic. And it proved a popular venture as 5,747 fans streamed through the gates to see Pools make it nine games unbeaten with a comfortable 3-0 home win over Stockport County.

Days later the miners went on strike as expected and Sunday games became the norm.

Although Pools lost to second-placed Gillingham on February 10, the following Sunday they put four past Mansfield.

A Friday defeat at table-topping Colchester was followed by further Sunday victories over Workington and Doncaster, both 3-0.

The miners strike was soon over and usual working practices were adhered to.

With the 'never say die' spirit to the fore, they won three and drew one of the next four and come time for the derby match against the old foe, Pools were in eighth spot, albeit six points off promotion, while Darlington loomed just one spot above the re-election places.

Pools failed to overcome their neighbours, losing 2-1, and then failed to win any of their last five games, although they managed a draw in the return at Feethams to prevent the double being done and save some face.

Alan Goad in action

Decent Finish After More Solid Campaign

AFTER a great second half to the season they ended in 11th place – the highest position in five years. The defence kept 18 clean sheets, average crowds rallied to 2,720 but this was almost 1,000 down on last year.

The season marked the end for several players. Big centre forward Bryan Conlon, after netting just three goals in around 40 games, joined his home town club Shildon. John Coyne moved to America and later Australia where he settled and represented the national side.

Winger Waddell And The Boss Move On

RECIPIENT of cult status in his early days, Waddell – whose transfer fee was contributed to by fans' whip rounds and local schoolchildren holding jumble sales – was idolised on the terraces. He had already been farmed out to Workington on loan and had made just five starts during the 1973-74 season. Waddell moved to Ireland but later went on to spend several years in South Africa.

Joining them through the exit door were manager Len Ashurst and trainer Tony Toms.

Impressed by their resilience and ability to grind results out, Gillingham – who had finished in second place – took them as a pair down to Priestfield almost as soon as the season finished.

Ashurst went on to have a long career in management with several clubs including Sheffield Wednesday, Newport, Cardiff and Sunderland. Toms followed Ashurst to Hillsbrough but left football when Ashurst moved to Wales. He later moved into private coaching and bodyguard work and looked after a wide range of people from female bodybuilder Donna Hartley, senior military figures and singer Madonna.

Pools Appoint Successor To Ashurst

THE Club turned to former Newcastle and Darlington midfielder Ken Hale.

Hale had appeared in well over 400 games and had been in charge of the Quakers for three months on a caretaker basis, two years previous. He didn't make many close season signings, the main signature being midfielder Bobby Park from Northampton.

He inherited what seemed to be the best squad for a few seasons. The bulk of it were regulars and Watling was again ever present. Twelve-goal top scorer Allan Gauden and Alan Goad had both played 44 games last season with the likes of Dawes, McMahon, Honour, Shoulder, Potter and Moore missing just a few games.

1974/75

THE season kicked off with a 2-0 home win over Newport, goals from Moore and Gauden and 2,557 fans, less than last season's average of 2,790, saw Barry Watling make his 100th consecutive appearance. Lining up with him were George Potter, Jimmy Shoulder, Malcolm Dawes, Alan Goad, John Honour, Bobby Park, Allan Gauden, Malcolm Moore, Kevin McMahon and Billy Ward.

They followed up with a 2-1 win in the League Cup

Billy Ward

at Workington. Pools stuttered along, but form was good enough to keep them away from the bottom.

Pools Embark On League Cup Run

THIS season, for once, saw interest in the League Cup, with a four-game marathon in the second round against Bournemouth.

The first game ended 1-1 at Dean Court with Gauden netting for Pools. A week later on September 18 at the Vic, Moore scored twice but so did Bournemouth and another lengthy trip to the south coast was needed for a second replay.

So five days later Moore scored again in another draw before Pools put an end to the long journeys for both sides when a Billy Ward goal put them through to the third round for the first time in the 15 seasons the tournament had been in existence.

Their opponents were Blackburn Rovers, who were flying high at the top of the third division in only their fourth season out of the top two flights since the start of the Football League in 1888.

Unlikely Win Sets Up Clash With Aston Villa And Pools Reach Fourth Season Without Re-Election

DESPITE the attractiveness of the tie, less than 6,000 turned up at the Vic. Moore again scored but the tie needed a replay. Pools went to Ewood Park on October 16 and upset the odds by making it through to the fourth round winning 2-1, the scorers Potter and McMahon.

Their reward was a home tie against another one of the original founders of the League, Aston Villa.

Over 12,000 fans, the highest crowd in almost 18 years, crammed into the Vic and saw Pools fight back to earn yet another draw through another goal from Malcolm Moore.

Pools went into the replay on the back of important wins over Darlington and Brentford, results which had moved them into mid-table.

The replay was a different affair though as Pools first visit to Villa Park ended with United on the end of a 6-1 reverse.

The FA Cup failed to offer as much success following a second round defeat to Lincoln, which won't have been helped by the dismissal of John Honour. Leaving in December was Gauden who followed Ashurst and Toms to Gillingham.

After the Lincoln defeat, the rest of

December saw two wins, followed by a New Year's Day victory over Northampton.

The rest of the season was similar to the first half. Winning on the road was a problem once more, as they lost just once at the Vic in the second half of the campaign. Pools ended in 13th, making it four consecutive seasons where they had avoided re-election.

Hale Turns To The Loan Market For Players

IN February they bolstered the squad by signing tough tackling midfielder Kevin Johnson from Workington. Hale also used the loan facility to it's fullest by borrowing Bob Worthington from Southend. Worthington was the brother of the maverick forward Frank, but was nothing like his sibling on the pitch.

Whereas Frank was full of flair and controversy, Bob had the reputation of being a solid workhorse defender. Also loaned was Bolton forward Mike McBurney. The pair never set the world on fire and were back with their previous employers after the month's loan was up.

Of the playing squad, there was still a regular line up.

Dawes had clocked up over 200 appearances and keeper Watling had played 137 consecutive Football League games.

The first game he missed was the final outing of the season, when he was replaced by Eddie Guy, ironically for what was to be his one and only appearance. Defender Alan Goad was

Malcolm Dawes in 1974

doing his usual and had clocked up almost 300 appearances by the time the season had come to end.

One pleasing thing this term was that it looked as though there were actually two forwards – Malcolm Moore and Kev McMahon – working as a pair and scoring plenty. Moore ended top of the scoring charts with 14 goals.

Don Heath, Hartley Maddison, Bobby Park, Billy Ward and Jimmy Shoulder all departed.

All bar one moved to various northern non-league outfits – Shildon, Gateshead, Eppleton and Gateshead respectively. Shoulder retired because of a knee injury and moved to Australia, where he later became the national coach before returning to the UK several years later and being appointed the Welsh under-21 manager.

Several new players joined during the summer including two new keepers, which was surprising considering the dominance of Watling.

Graham Richardson had previously been on the books of Darlington as an amateur. John Hope was the second keeper who had also been on the books of Darlington earlier in his career, but he had spent the last four and a half years at Sheffield United.

Cult Hero Watling Impresses In The States

WATLING had spent the summer plying his trade in America playing for Seattle Sounders and was to be late home for the start of the English season.

Across the Atlantic he made the NASL all-star team as best goalkeeper. Also in this select XI

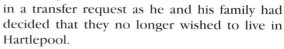

was John Rowlands, a team-mate of Watling's at Seattle, who joined Pools in the summer, along with Middlesbrough reserve midfielder Bobby Scaife.

Rowlands was top scorer for the Stateside outfit in the summer.

Watling handed in a transfer request as he and his family had decided that they no longer wished to live in Hartlepool.

In an American newspaper he stated: "I would love to play football, but I would rather play it somewhere else besides Hartlepool."

Hope and Richardson were preferred to Watling in the first four games of the season. Watling was given a couple of games, and then Hope was given the job on a permanent basis after winning an initial power struggle with Richardson.

Watling was loaned to Chester and then Rotherham before being allowed to move to Sheffield Wednesday. Another long serving player who had found himself playing in America and on his way out was Malcolm Dawes.

He had spent the last two summers playing for New York Cosmos and upon his return he played just one more game before heading for Workington. He enjoyed the next summer playing in Denver.

Hartlepool FC season 1975-76: Back row: Billy Horner (Coach), Mick Spelman, Brian Albeson, Alan Goad, John Hope, Dave Embleton, Kevin Elliot, Steve Griffiths, Ken Hale (Manager); Front row: Kevin Johnson, Steve Crowther, John Honour, Jimmy Shoulder, George Potter, Rob Smith, Malcolm Moore, Keith Skillen, David Smith

1975-76

IT was an unflattering start with three draws – Bournemouth, Brentford and Lincoln – and Pools were knocked out of the League Cup. Now a two-leg format in the first round, Pools lost 4-1 at Halifax and could only manage a 2-1 triumph at the Vic. Just one win in seven followed and, by the middle of October, Pools were in familiar territory in the bottom three.

A great run of five wins in six saw Pools climb to 12th, with the final win in this series at Bradford on November 15, when former Manchester United reserve winger Paul Bielby made his debut. Next up and Pools comfortably beat Stockport in the first round of the FA Cup 3-0.

The second round saw them tied away to Marine, of the Cheshire County League.

Poor results over the past few seasons against non league teams saw Pools approach this game with trepidation – and rightly so, for Marine put up a strong fight and Pools could only draw 1-1.

In the draw for the third round the winners of the replay would meet Manchester City. With a big incentive to progress, Pools beat Marine 6-3, with Malcolm Moore getting a hat-trick.

Pools Visit Manchester City In FA Cup Tie

ALMOST 27,000 fans at Maine Road saw Pools hammered 6-0. Not only that, but George Potter had his cheek bone broken in an altercation with Dennis Tueart. Not only was he injured, but Potter was also sent off.

The City defeat saw Pools lose form and they failed to win in the next 13 games, including a 5-1 hammering at Scunthorpe. The fans who were so vocal and travelled in great numbers to Maine Road were staying away and only the derby defeat against Darlington on February 7 attracted anything resembling a crowd – and this was a poor 3,689.

With the team in 16th and the transfer deadline approaching new signings were made including former Watford and Charlton forward Barry Endean, ex-Halifax full back Paul Luckett and former Hereford defender Dave Rylands.

The last game of this poor run was Endean's debut when a point was gained from the trip to Torquay. The following weekend saw Pools on the road again on another long trek, but at least this time the journey home was a sweet one as Moore netted for the third consecutive game as Pools beat Newport County.

Home wins over Swansea and Rochdale saw Pools pull out of the mire. Two victories in the next three games – as Endean scored in each – virtually secured safety and avoided the need to apply for re-election.

Hale Continues To Make Steady Progress

ALTHOUGH they suffered heavy defeats at Cambridge and at runners-up Northampton, Hale had managed to guide his team to 14th place with 42 points, twice that of bottom placed Workington, who had now finished in the bottom two for the third consecutive season.

Hale had done something that very few Pools managers had ever done and that was to make the team look an average one.

It doesn't seem much of an achievement, but taking into account recent problems it was something of note. Worryingly though, this improvement was seen by fewer fans than before with the season average of only 2,182, the lowest to date.

Vince Barker Begins Involvement At The Club

THERE had also been changes in the boardroom. Tom Aird, who replaced John Curry in 1973, quit and was replaced temporarily by Ernie Ord. It was a highly unpopular decision following his bitter dispute after his previous time in charge. This time, however, his spell was short lived and he was replaced by local farm owner Vince Barker.

Vince Barker

Hartlepool FC season 1976-77. Back row: Ken Hale (Manager), Paul Bielby, Barry Endean, Tony Maggiore, Graham Richardson, Alan Goad, Bobby Scaife, Bob Scott, Jon O'Donnell, Billy Horner (Coach); Front row: Malcolm Moore, Mick Spelman, George Potter, Kevan Elliot, Chris McMasters, Paul Luckett, Kevin Johnson

Top scorer Malcolm Moore left during late summer to Workington, keeper John Hope moved to Whitby and Rob Smith went to Scarborough.

New this summer was keeper Eddie Edgar. The 19-year-old had spent two years with Newcastle but played just once before being released. Giant defender Bob Scott arrived from Wrexham and Cambridge player Jon O'Donnell signed on.

Changes were aplenty and a new coach was appointed, former Middlesbrough full back Billy Horner.

He had spent nine years at Ayresome Park and had been with Darlington for the past six years, chalking up over 400 first team career games. Aged 32, he was deemed young enough but experienced enough to develop the squad under the direction of the manager Ken Hale.

1976-77

THE season kicked off with the usual League Cup dismissal, this time to Huddersfield. This was followed up with a 2-2 draw with one of the promotion favourites Exeter City, with youngster Kevan Elliott – who had broken through to the first team last season – and Barry Endean scoring.

Pools lined up as follows – Richardson, O'Donnell, Goad, Veitch, Scott, Maggiore, Spelman, Elliott, Endean, Scaife and Bielby.

Poor Start Puts Paid To Manager Hale

HOWEVER, by the end of September, Pools had failed to win and were second from bottom with three points. They had also been forced to sell Kevin Johnson to Huddersfield when a £12,000 offer landed on the chairman's desk.

Hale wasn't going to get the chance to spend any of the money though. Chairman Barker was less than impressed with the poor start and dismissed Hale, despite his decent record over the past two seasons. He was replaced by first team coach Billy Horner who appointed Alan Goad as player/coach.

Horner spruced the squad up by signing defender Dave Wiggett from Lincoln City and threw him into the side for the game at Colchester on October 16, playing him at centre half. Pools lost 6-2. The following week at home to Rochdale saw the introduction of another defensive signing, Peter Creamer, who had joined from Doncaster for £5,000.

The former England school-boy and

Eric McMordie

ex-Middlesbrough man lined up at right back in front of Edgar with Goad moved to centre half partnering Scott. Wiggett moved to left back displacing Luckett, who had occupied that slot since joining from Halifax seven months before. Luckett never played for the first XI again and later moved to Australia.

The new look defence held firm against Rochdale and goals from Scaife and a penalty from short term contract forward Hugh Reed were enough for the first win. However, it was another five games before they won again, beating Brentford by the same score.

It was no surprise then the following week that they lost by a single goal at Chester, in the first round of the FA Cup. Pools youngster Kevan Elliott was sent from the field of play making it three successive seasons that a Pools player had seen red in the competition – a record almost as unwanted as their recent form against non leaguers.

Horner Tries To Further Improve The Squad

STILL struggling in early December 1976, the need was seen to bring in more players.

Former Middlesbrough and Northern Ireland midfielder Eric McMordie arrived from York. Chris Simpkin made the move to the North-East. The defender joined from Huddersfield after making his debut for Hull in season 1961-62.

The new look squad took time to settle and it wasn't until January 8 that they registered only their third win of the season when a Malcolm Poskett hat-trick helped them on their way to a 4-0 win over Torquay. Tall and ungainly

Billy Horner

looking, Poskett had been signed by Horner in November from Whitby Town after previously being released by Pools following a short non-playing stint in 1974.

Five home wins on the bounce followed by a 2-2 draw against Colchester saw them stand in 21st place on March 26. Away form was again poor and they could not get out of the re-election places, where they had been nearly all of the season.

Then it was time to lose the plot, as they won only three of their following 11 games, despite a cameo role from Terry Turnbull who joined from Crook. He scored three of the paltry eight goals in that period. Finishing 22nd wasn't what the fans wanted to see – what was left of them anyway. Average attendance was 1,911.

They weren't the only club to experience low crowds at home though, as they played in front of 858 at Rochdale on April 2 and a month later saw 880 turn up at Southport.

Re-Election Time Again At The Vic And Club Changes Its Name Again

SOUTHPORT were one of the three teams up for re-election with Pools, the other two Halifax and Workington.

After periods of consolidation under Ashurst and Hale, new man Horner had taken them to the vote again for the first time in six seasons. It was their 11th application overall and on the surface they looked in trouble.

However, the other three candidates were in equally bad, if not worse, financial trouble and going by the form of recent seasons Pools had done comparatively well.

Halifax had been relegated from division three the previous season and went straight into the bottom four after a woeful year. Second bottom were Southport for a second consecutive season and bottom for the second successive season were Workington.

It was their fourth year in a row in the re-election zone and it was also to be their last. They polled only 21 votes, five fewer than Southern League side Wimbledon.

During the close season the Club's name changed for a second time. The name reverted back to United, but since the amalgamation of the two boroughs the team was renamed Hartlepool United.

In the nine years that the Club had been named Hartlepool they had been relegated once, applied for re-election three times and had finished in the top half of the table only once.

Perhaps a change in name would bring a change in fortunes.

1977-78

SUMMER departures saw Kevan Elliott move on to Willington before later having stints in Belgium, Hong Kong and Australia.

The consistent Jon O'Donnell moved to Scunthorpe and Bob Scott went to Rochdale.

Several local old hands joined, including 32-year-old former Middlesbrough winger Derrick Downing. He had appeared in over 300 league outings for his various clubs and was expected to provide that added extra touch of experience to the flanks. Joining him was another 32-year-old, former Newcastle and Sunderland player Tommy Gibb and 1973 FA Cup winner Dick Malone from Sunderland.

They were followed by two lesser known players, centre half Billy Ayre and forward Bob Newton who joined from Scarborough and Huddersfield respectively. They might have been lesser known, but their impact was far greater.

As usual the team were knocked out of the League Cup, losing 5-1 on aggregate to Grimsby and followed up with two league defeats.

However, four home wins in September saw them sit in 12th place.

The changing of the seasons brought about a change in form and October and November saw just one win as Pools slipped down the table to second bottom in a period of bad luck

Alan Goad was named Player/Coach

and misfortune.

Dick Malone suffered a knee ligament injury when he caught his studs in a Grimsby player's laces in September and was only playing his third game back from injury when he broke his arm at Barnsley at the end of October. In the same game McMordie damaged knee and ankle ligaments and Poskett was struck down with appendicitis.

Poskett was the only player on form, he had scored six in four games, taking his total to nine for the season so far. His goals came from his on the field relationship with Newton and the delivery from Bielby and the graft of Linacre.

Cup Brings Welcome Distraction From The League

THE first round of the FA Cup saw Pools drawn away to third division Tranmere Rovers.

Pools had only gained two points on the road all season and had been thumped at Stockport just two weeks earlier by six clear goals.

With Poskett injured, not much was expected but a goal from reserve player Trevor Smith, who played in place of Simpkin, earned a deserved replay at the Vic three days later.

A crowd of 4,827 – the highest home gate for two seasons – witnessed Pools outclass the visitors with Bielby and Newton both netting their second goals of the season and Billy Ayre netting his fifth of the term in a 3-1 victory.

With league form still poor Pools took on non-league Runcorn in the second round and beat the Merseyside outfit 4-2 with goals from Bielby, Newton (2) and Poskett in front of more than 6,000 followers. A third round tie against Crystal Palace of the second division was Pools' reward.

A Boxing Day defeat at York was followed up with another derby match the following day when Downing and Poskett scored in the win over Darlington in front of 5,299 fans, the highest league gate at the Vic since the Easter derby against the same foe in 1974.

Palace FA Cup Tie Captures The Imagination – Pools Through To Fourth Round

FINALLY there seemed to be some form of renewed interest in the side that Horner was building.

Palace, managed by the former England player Terry Venables, were classed as the most exciting side outside of the top flight and included the likes of Vince Hilaire, Kenny

G. LOWE AUTOMATICS
sponsor
ALAN GOAD'S TESTIMONIAL

HARTLEPOOL UNITED F.C.
VERSUS
NOTTINGHAM FOREST F.C.

KICK OFF 7-15 p.m.   ·   ·   ·   ·   PROGRAMME 10p.

Official Programme from Alan Goad's Testimonial Match

Miss Hartlepool United FC 1979 – Jan Innes, aged 21

Sansom and Terry Fenwick.

From the start Pools tortured Palace and two great goals in the first half from powerhouse Newton sent the majority of the 9,502 fans home happy. Pools were through to the fourth round for just the third time in their history.

But there was to be no attractive home tie as a reward, as they were drawn away to Ipswich Town.

They had finished in the top six in the first division for five seasons. Managed by Bobby Robson, they were established and were a team full of household names and internationals – Cooper, Burley, Mills, Talbot, Hunter, Beattie, Woods, Viljoen, Mariner, Turner and Lambert. Ipswich faced Pools with a full strength XI.

United, roared on by a large vocal away support, were simply outclassed and suffered a 4-1 defeat to the team that went on to win the coveted trophy that year with a Wembley win over Arsenal.

The gate at Portman Road was 24,207 and Pools' share again showed them the added financial benefit of a good cup run.

Cup Run Prompts Interest In Pools Squad

THE only drawback was the attention paid to some of the team and in particular Poskett. After ample speculation he was sold to second division Brighton for £60,000, a record fee.

Newcastle United came in with a bid of £80,000 after the deal had been arranged and Pools lost out on a valuable £20,000 as Poskett missed the chance to stay in the area.

He was replaced by a loan signing from Southend, former Newcastle, Middlesbrough and Sunderland forward Alan Foggon. The 28-year-old had played plenty of top-flight football but his career was on a dramatic slide.

He was considered to be past it by many fans, resentful at the sale of Poskett.

Also signed was a 17-year-old striker who, although born in Middlesbrough, had joined from Chesterfield. Keith Houchen would soon be forced into the first XI under very unfortunate circumstances.

Tragedy As Dave Wiggett Is Killed

ON Thursday March 23, 1978, Bob Newton was driving Dave Wiggett back to his digs on Stockton Road in the town, when, yards from his home, the Ford Capri that Newton was driving left the road and crashed into a wall near the Traveller's Rest pub.

Wiggett, a left back who had joined Pools from Lincoln City in October 1976, had just returned to the side died instantly. Newton, who was on his way to the Catcote Road flat he

Hartlepool FC season 1979-80. Back row: George Smith (Trainer/Coach), Mike Fagan, Mark Lawrence, Billy Ayre, Graham Richardson, Trevor Ramshaw, Steve Brooks, Keith Houchen, Gordon Larkin, Derek Loadwick, Willie Maddren (Coach); Front row: Wayne Goldthorpe, Martin Gorry, Michael O'Moni, John Linacre, Paul Staff, Billy Horner (Manager), David Norton, Tony Duncan, Graham Normanton, Roy Hogan

shared with Eddie Edgar, was taken to hospital for treatment of his injuries, which were not life threatening.

He was to miss the remainder of the season and was later sentenced to prison for nine months for driving offences relating to the accident. A collection of £120 was raised for the left-back's family at the next home game.

Two days after this tragic event, Foggon and Houchen became the front line and they did all they needed to do to make them crowd favourites – score against Darlington.

Both scored at Feethams in a stormy game that saw Downing sent off as Pools completed a double.

Downing had battled all match with Darlington's former Huddersfield winger Lloyd Maitland.

Pools became only the third team in history to win an away game after having a player dismissed – although dismissals were a rare event at the time.

April Fools Result Is No Joke For Pools

THE following game was at Swansea on April Fools' Day and those Pools fans who didn't make the long trek thought a prank was being played on them when they heard the score.

Swansea had put eight past Richardson, who had performed so well at Darlington the week before, without reply. Before the game, Pools coach George Smith had told his players that he fancied his side to turn the Swans over.

They bounced back well with wins at Rochdale and at home to Stockport but a fixture backlog meant in the remaining six games that season, all played in April, they won only once when Billy Ayre netted his 11th and 12th goals, making the centre half the top scorer.

Pools Bid To Survive Re-Election Again

DESPITE the cup exploits, for the second season running Pools were up for re-election. The teams also in the mire this year were York, Southport and Rochdale.

In early June at the league vote, Wigan Athletic and Southport were level with 26 votes split between them, with Pools safe once again. A second vote saw Wigan through with 29 votes compared to Southport's 20. Bottom team Rochdale, who had seven points less than

Southport, stayed up.

The season also saw the end of the career of long servant Alan Goad. He spent eleven seasons with the Club, through more thin than thick and only this season had moved up to third place in all-time appearances for Pools, behind Ray Thompson and Watty Moore.

In 418 games he only netted 11 goals and went from March 2, 1970 to December 22, 1973 without scoring, a run of 157 games. He was awarded a testimonial match when former manager Brian Clough brought his Nottingham Forest team to the Vic – the scoreline was 2-2 with Pools' goals coming from Bob Newton and Billy Ayre. Goad later moved to Canada and played for Vancouver Whitecaps.

Also leaving was winger Paul Bielby. After two and a half consistent years he was snapped up by Huddersfield. Peter Creamer joined Gateshead, a common escape route. Derrick Downing moved on to Scarborough and after several more clubs settled in the Doncaster area where he ran several businesses. Another player who was once on Middlesbrough's books also leaving was 32-year-old Eric McMordie who retired from the game.

He had worked part-time in the building trade throughout his career in this country and was ready to retire from the playing side when his former team-mate Horner persuaded him to come to Pools.

Also retiring was Tommy Gibb, another who turned his back on the game, and he returned to his native Scotland.

1978/79

PUTTING pen to paper was swarthy defender Steve Brooks who arrived from relegated Southport. He was joined by former Barnsley full back Martin Gorry, ex-Newcastle youth player Keith Guy and Ian Crumplin, a 23-year-old forward from Newcastle Blue Star. Wayne Goldthorpe, the Huddersfield forward had already had a spell on loan with Pools back in January 1977 and Horner signed him on a permanent basis.

A few youngsters were expected to make the grade this season after Roy Hogan, Gordon Larkin and Mark Lawrence made their debuts as teenagers towards the closing days of last season.

Hogan was the fourth 17-year-old that Horner had blooded in the first team during his short time in charge.

Once again the annual embarrassment of being dumped out of the League Cup took place with Rotherham being the opponents.

The league programme began with Pools on

the wrong end of a seven-goal thriller, losing by the odd goal to Doncaster, but they gained credible draws at Northampton and at the Vic with promotion favourites Portsmouth.

A rare away win came at Bournemouth courtesy of a Newton penalty, before a 2-1 home win over Hereford when Hogan, 17, scored, making him the sixth youngest in the Club's history with McGovern and Houchen first and second.

Negotiations With The Council To Buy The Ground (Again)

FORM through the early part of the season was inconsistent, but certainly no way as bad as that of the previous two campaigns. Big fees and big salaries were off the agenda and the dilapidated ground and settings they played in wasn't going to pull in those used to greater comforts. Despite the state of the Victoria Ground the board, led by Vince Barker, had started negotiations to buy it back from the local council two seasons before.

Nothing had been heard despite the agreement between the two parties to pay £60,000 for the site. The Club wanted the ground to develop it and make it more attractive to all.

They planned a gym, new dressing rooms, a clubhouse and better facilities for spectators. The space was there underneath the Mill House stand for works to be carried out and, as tenants, when the ground was repaired it was done on the cheap. Every time the wind got up it was expected that parts of the temporary stand on Clarence Road would end up on the near railway lines. However the sale did not progress.

By the end of October Pools stood ninth following a 5-1 victory over Rochdale. Goals from Ayre, Goldthorpe (2) and one each from teenagers Houchen and Lawrence saw Pools score five at the Vic for the first time in nearly four years.

The first three outings of November were winless and Pools faced fifth-placed Grimsby at the Vic in the first round of the FA Cup on November 25.

Pools Paired With Leeds In The FA Cup

JUST over 3,500 fans saw a repeat of the 1-0 away win at Blundell Park when Pools won through a Goldthorpe strike. The second round ended in a 1-0 victory for Pools as well, with a Crumplin goal seeing them through at Crewe.

Pools were handed a plum draw for the third round – a home tie against Leeds United.

The Yorkshire outfit were not the team they used to be two or three years previously, but were still flying high and were in a battle at the top of the first division.

The weather in January 1979 was atrocious and the game against Wigan at the Vic had been postponed. The Leeds game was called off a couple of times before it was eventually played on January 18. Some 16,000 shivering fans crammed into the Vic and saw Pools easily beaten 6-2.

A starting XI of Richardson, George Smith, Gorry, Lawrence, Trevor Smith, Norton, John Linacre, Goldthorpe, Crumplin, Newton and Loadwick took to the field.

United were robbed of their regular centre half pairing of Ayre and Brooks, so Trevor Smith was called up to the ranks for only his sixth start of the season. His partner was David Norton, a 20-year-old who had joined from Whickham and was making his first start against one of the best teams in the country.

Leeds Refuse To Use Vic Changing Rooms

THE Elland Road stars were accustomed to better conditions than the ramshackle Clarence Road stand and refused to get changed at the Vic – instead using the nearby Grand Hotel as a giant changing room!

This didn't detract from the job in hand and despite Newton getting two penalties for Pools, they conceded goals to Frank Gray, Eddie Gray (2), Carl Harris, Paul Hart and Arthur Graham. For the third time in four seasons, Pools had been knocked out of the cup by a top flight team.

The weather still had a hold on the county with only one game played in January 1979 as Pools beat Grimsby 1-0 for the third time that season, two days after the Leeds loss.

February 10 saw Newton grab another two goals, this time in a 3-2 win over Torquay which kept Pools mid-table.

However, these were to be his last two goals for some time as he was jailed for his role in the Wiggett tragedy.

The departure of their talisman badly affected all. Horner couldn't find an organised or settled line up and a fixture backlog took its toll.

A replacement for Newton was not signed until mid-March and by that time Pools had failed to win in six. His replacement was Alan Harding from Lincoln, but he failed to set the scoring charts alight and got just one in 15 outings that season, although the goal was a crucial one giving them their first win in 17 games on May 2, 1979.

Strong Finish Helps The Club

LUCKILY for Pools after such a barren run the players dug deep, winning five of the last six games.

The return to the defence of Steve Brooks, who had missed 11 games due to injury, made a difference.

Also moving into the back four was forward Wayne Goldthorpe who took over the right back spot. He played there in an emergency to allow old hand George Smith to get to grips with the midfield and it worked a treat. Goalkeeper John Watson found renewed confidence behind Ayre and Brooks.

Youngster Mark Lawrence scored six goals in a four-game spell during this revival. He nabbed a crucial winner at Darlington on May 7, when he starred in a 4-2 win at Halifax a week after the Feethams triumph.

He also scored in the final game on May 17 when beating Northampton at home in front of just 1,769 fans – the lowest crowd at the Vic for two years.

Amongst those leaving was keeper Eddie Edgar. He had been playing his summer football in America, missed the start of this season and was replaced by loan signing Jim Platt from Middlesbrough. He failed to regain a regular place and moved on to Gateshead.

In America he played his football for New York Cosmos. Trevor Smith left for Dartford.

1979-80

THE following season saw Chesterfield put Pools out of the League Cup after an opening day defeat at home to Portsmouth.

Three wins out of the next four saw them elevated to ninth. A good run was followed with a bad one and they won just two of the next nine. Keeper Watson was replaced by an October signing from Darlington, Martin Burleigh. The former Newcastle reserve had lost his place at Feethams to Phil Owers after a dispute. Also arriving were Peter Carr, Graham Normanton and Alan Sweeney.

		P	HW	HD	HL	HF	HA	AW	AD	AL	AF	AA	POINTS
1	Huddersfield Town	46	16	5	2	61	18	11	7	5	40	30	66
2	Walsall	46	12	9	2	43	23	11	9	3	32	24	64
3	Newport County	46	16	5	2	47	22	11	2	10	36	28	61
4	Portsmouth	46	15	5	3	62	23	9	7	7	29	26	60
5	Bradford City	46	14	6	3	44	14	10	6	7	33	36	60
6	Wigan Athletic	46	13	5	5	42	26	8	8	7	34	35	55
7	Lincoln City	46	14	8	1	43	12	4	9	10	21	30	53
8	Peterborough United	46	14	3	6	39	22	7	7	9	19	25	52
9	Torquay United	46	13	7	3	47	25	2	10	11	23	44	47
10	Aldershot	46	10	7	6	35	23	6	6	11	27	30	45
11	Bournemouth	46	8	9	6	32	25	5	9	9	20	26	44
12	Doncaster Rovers	46	11	6	6	37	27	4	8	11	25	36	44
13	Northampton Town	46	14	5	4	33	16	2	7	14	18	50	44
14	Scunthorpe United	46	11	9	3	37	27	4	8	11	25	36	44
15	Tranmere Rovers	46	10	4	9	32	24	4	9	10	18	32	41
16	Stockport County	46	9	7	7	30	31	5	5	13	18	41	40
17	York City	46	9	6	8	35	34	5	5	13	30	48	39
18	Halifax Town	46	11	9	3	29	20	2	4	17	17	52	39
19	**HARTLEPOOL UNITED**	46	10	7	6	36	28	4	3	16	23	36	38
20	Port Vale	46	8	6	9	34	24	4	6	13	22	46	36
21	Hereford United	46	8	7	8	22	21	3	7	13	16	31	36
22	Darlington	46	7	11	5	33	26	2	6	15	17	48	35
23	Crewe Alexandra	46	10	6	7	25	27	1	7	15	10	41	35
24	Rochdale	46	6	7	10	20	28	1	6	16	13	51	27

Football League
Division Four 1979/80

Newton Returns As Promotion Is Mentioned

THE team plodded along and by the time it came to FA Cup duty they stood in 17th. There was no FA Cup run this year though as they were turned over 5-2 by Barnsley. Afterwards, however, they lost just the once in December and January with Newton and Houchen netting 17 between them. Newton returned to the team at the start of September and was enjoying his partnership with the young Houchen as their goals had pushed Pools into the top ten. Talk was of promotion.

It proved cheap talk, however, as things deteriorated and, somewhat bizarrely, Pools lost six of the next dozen games by the same scoreline, 2-1.

There was a blank return from the final six games and when the prospect of promotion had been discussed as a possibility, the reality was that Pools were just two points above the re-election zone, finishing 19th. Houchen pipped Newton to the top of the goalscoring charts, beating Bob's 12 by two.

Youngsters Make Their Mark At The Vic

POOLS used 31 players this season including Paul Staff who made his debut two days after his 17th birthday and 18-year-old Ged McNamee who made his debut against top of the table Huddersfield at the end of January.

Utility man Phil Brown, 20, broke through after some time with the reserves.

Several loan signings were used as well as short term deals, including Frank Pimblett, once of Stockport, and Martin Fowler loaned by Blackburn.

Those leaving were Derek Loadwick, who had his contract terminated in March, Wayne Goldthorpe and Martin Gorry. They moved to Whitby, Crewe and Shildon respectively. Peter Carr returned to America to play for New England Teamen, where he had played the previous summer. Steve Brooks headed back to the west coast and joined Barrow.

Pools managed to hang on to John Linacre for whom they had rejected a £60,000 bid from Rotherham earlier in the season.

The struggle relating to the ground purchase dragged on and on.

The Club cleared a large amount of rent arrears at the end of the season and the saga had rumbled behind the scenes for almost three years. The council increased their demand for the ground and both sides seemed to be getting sick of the bickering. Club chairman Vince Barker at one point even threatened to take the Club out of town, much to the anger of supporters. With the new season and decade around the corner the offer remained on the table.

Chapter 10

1980s

1980-81

HORNER plumped for a couple of local old hands to bolster the squad. John Bird, 32, joined from Newcastle after spending five seasons with the Magpies, and Sunderland legend Bobby Kerr arrived. Captain of the Wearsiders' successful 1973 FA Cup final side, Kerr moved back to his adopted North-East after a year and a half at Blackpool. Added to the frontline was Whitby Town striker Geoff Forster.

Pools suffered their usual loss in the League Cup, this time York City being the victors. The League campaign itself began with a great 3-0 win at Wigan who had just missed out on promotion last season, with Forster netting twice on his debut. However it took a while for this season to settle down, with Pools winning more away from home than at the Vic.

Wimbledon put five past them at Plough Lane in the middle of October but in the first weekend of November, Pools cracked six past Crewe in a 6-2 triumph with goals from Kerr, Hampton, Houchen (2) and Newton (2) – but with complaints from Horner that his side didn't score enough after being 5-1 up at the break.

Despite the clear improvements all were not happy and midfielder Linacre put a transfer request in after being played out of position and then being barracked by sections of the crowd. After complaining he wasn't receiving enough of the ball on the right of midfield, manager Horner simply dropped him.

Decent Start Improves Crowd Figures

THE Crewe game was watched by just over 3,000 fans but 1,400 more were present for the next game at home to Scunthorpe. Victory at Halifax and a draw at Bury set them up nicely for the home game with Wigan on November 15 – Pools stood third and Wigan were struggling at the bottom.

Hartlepool Mail

John Linacre in action against Bolton in pre season of 1980

Houchen rounds Crewe keeper Mulhern to score Pools' second in the 6-2 win

Bob Newton celebrates a goal against Lincoln at the Rink End in October 1980 – John Bird added a second as Pools won 2-0

Horner Builds Promising Squad Of Players

ON the pitch the team was a fine blend of youth and experience.

Burleigh in goal was pushing 30, but his nous at this level stood him in good stead.

The regular full backs were Alan Sweeney and Phil Brown. Sweeney had played the bulk of last season and had previously been on the books of Huddersfield. Brown was aged only 21 and had broken through to the first team last season and was playing left back, but could play anywhere.

Wearing the No 4 shirt was home-grown Hogan. The diminutive midfielder was only 20 but was now in his fourth season of first team action and had already clocked up almost 60 appearances. John Linacre, 24 and already a veteran of more than 180 games, Mark Lawrence, a 21-year-old with around 100 games under his belt, and legends Bird and Kerr made up the rest of the defence and midfield.

The bulk of the goals came from Houchen and Newton but also chipping in was 28-year-old Derek Hampton, another in a long list of players who Pools had sourced from Whitby Town.

FA Cup Time Again

IN the first round of the FA Cup at Scunthorpe, Pools took over 1,000 fans with them, but were beaten 3-1 in a match troubled by crowd violence.

Missiles were thrown at both keepers by both sets of fans – and a flask was hurled towards Scunthorpe keeper Joe Neenan, as Police and supporters clashed on the Old Show Ground terracing.

Towards the end of 1980 things tailed off and Pools failed to win in five, including a woeful effort at Darlington when they were played off the park in a 3-0 reverse.

They did, however, still stand in fourth place. A revival – one loss in the next five – saw them retain their grip on one of the promotion spots. The run coincided with the return to the Club of Kevin Johnson, who was on the books of

Pools tore them apart, playing football not seen at the ground for many seasons. The tireless Hogan netted the first goal from the edge of the box after a corner from the recalled Linacre. Houchen tapped in the second after a goalkeeping error following another Linacre corner before knocking in his second.

The highest crowd of the season so far of 5,035 almost couldn't get in. After alleged problems over gate takings some gatemen were dismissed and a number walked out before the match. The chairman, his daughter and the Club secretary were forced to take over the turnstiles.

The remaining gatemen faced large queues with hundreds of angry fans missing the kick-off.

HUFC Team, July 1980. Back row: Willie Maddren (Coach), Jed McNamee, Geoff Forster, Mark Lawrence, Mick Fagan, Eddie Leighton, Trevor Ramshaw, Martin Burleigh, Graham, Richardson, Keith Houchen, Billy Ayre, Graham Normanton, David Howard, George Smith (Coach); Middle row: Bobby Kerr, Alan Harding, John Linacre, Billy Horner, John Bird, Phil Brown, Alan Sweeney, Stephen Vass, Derek Hampton; Front row: Tony Duncan, Barry Stimpson, Roy Hogan, Paul Staff

Halifax, and Pools arranged a swap deal with Billy Ayre going in the opposite direction.

Ayre had been in a contract dispute at the end of last season and by the time it was settled he had lost both his place and the captaincy to John Bird. Johnson didn't get straight back in the team, but Horner was utilising him when a space was free.

Results Falter And Pools Slip Down Table

POOLS faced a tough February. Middle of the table Northampton beat them 3-1 at the County Ground in a match when John Linacre was dismissed after just five minutes.

A week later they took on table toppers Southend at the Vic. Missing Linacre and Newton (suspended following a dismissal) just 3,748 fans saw Pools beaten 3-1. The next week they were turned over at struggling Hereford.

In freefall, they faced Aldershot in what was Pools' 1,000th division four match. The Shots were challenging for promotion and sent Pools packing and on March 14, Wimbledon came to the Vic and took the points.

Five straight defeats in just over a month saw them drop to tenth place and end the best chance of promotion to Division Three in years.

The shocking run ended when a recalled Alan Harding netted the only goal in a surprise win in a Monday night game at fourth-placed Mansfield.

Two days later, Pools took on American side Washington Diplomats, who were touring England looking for talent before their season kicked-off later that month, in a friendly.

Pools beat them by three clear goals – Newton, Houchen and youth team player David Howard netted.

Newton played his last game of the season in the middle of March and returned to America to play for Jacksonville Tea Men after spending the previous summer there (when they were known as New England) when he finished top scorer.

The team was changed around for the game against Stockport and another two youngsters made their bows – left back Barrie Stimpson, 17, and towering centre half Andy Linighan, 18 – in a 1-0 win.

Horner later recalled teenager Paul Staff and also gave another 18-year-old the nod, forward Howard.

Physio Tommy Johnson with missiles thrown at Martin Burleigh in an FA Cup game at Scunthorpe in November 1980

Best Finish Since 1968 Can't Hide Disappointment

THE new blood and the workrate of the rest of the squad saw Pools win four of their last seven in a late surge which saw them end the season in a disappointing ninth place after being in amongst the promotion places for so long. It was their best finish since 1968.

They gained some revenge over Darlington for the costly reverse at Feethams earlier in the season when a team including six teenagers ran out 2-0 winners on April 17, with goals from Howard and Linacre, who was now back in the side.

Pools finished just six points (in these days three wins) adrift of the promoted four – Wimbledon, Doncaster, Lincoln and Southend – showing that the poor run in February and March had cost them dear.

Harold Hornsey Makes First Move To Help Club

THROUGHOUT the last two months of the season the ground purchase saga took a new twist.

Local businessmen Harold Hornsey offered to stump up £100,000 to buy the ground (if the Council would sell) and pay for the proposed gymnasium to be built.

However, his proposal was met with a counter-offer from Chairman Barker which proved the stumbling block. Among Barker's demands were that all of his shares and those of his family were bought by Hornsey and that any loans to the Club he had outstanding were re-paid with interest.

However, Hornsey refused to meet these demands and angered Barker by telling the press that "the letter I received from Pools is not a reply to my offer – it is a way out for the board with financial benefits for them. On these terms, I admit defeat."

Pools Set For Move To Scarborough?

WATCHING from afar with interest were Scarborough, a wealthy non league club at the time.

Around the turn of the year they had tried to buy Halifax Town and it was revealed they had been in contact with Pools for some time about buying Hartlepool United. Discussions had taken place with the Football League and the two clubs.

However, Pools could only leave the Football League if they resigned or failed to be re-elected and Scarborough could only join through election – Pools would not be able to transfer their home games to Scarborough.

Scarborough, who had bid £120,000, believed that they would get their way and that Pools would have to play further down the east coast.

Hornsey put in a complaint and pressed the board – public feeling was bitterly against the move.

Eventually the prospect petered out as the protracted negotiations came to an end. Many assumed the dealings affected the players and had ultimately scuppered the promotion chances that season.

The issue over the ground buy back still hadn't been resolved and now the Club were in dispute with the council over unpaid rent.

Just a couple of noted players departed during the summer, Geoff Forster returned to his non league roots signing for South Bank and Richardson retired from professional football after a knee injury, but he later played for Easington CW and continued to play cricket for Hartlepool. He was replaced by former player John Watson who rejoined after initially deciding to quit football.

Despite the promising batch of youngsters at the Club, there was no summer investment in the playing squad. The now usual financial issues were biting and funds to boost the playing staff were not available.

1981-82

A new competition was introduced – the Football League Group Cup. Pools were in a league of four in the early stages, with Rotherham, Bradford and Hull and the games would be played before the normal season had begun.

But Pools made a mess of it and lost all three games 1-0 and the League Cup also brought the usual result with Northampton dumping them out of the competition.

Injury In Pre Season Hinders The Club

POOLS were not helped by the absence of Mark Lawrence. During pre-season Lawrence, Houchen, Linighan and Linacre all took part in a six-a-side tournament – without the Club's consent. Lawrence suffered a double leg fracture while playing and didn't return until April.

The season started with a 3-1 home reverse to the hands of Colchester and things got even worse when Bob Newton scored for

HUFC Team Photo taken on August 11, 1981. Back row: Barry Stimpson, Roy Hogan, Mick Fagan, Andy Linighan, Keith Houchen, Marin Burleigh, John Linacre, Alan Sweeney, Alan Harding, Kevin Johnson; Front row: Bobby Kerr, Paul Staff, David Howard, Willie Maddren (Coach), Billy Horner (Manager), George Smith (Coach), John Bird, Phil Brown, Derek Hampton

Jacksonville Tea Men to put them through to the league play-offs in America, delaying his return to the North-East.

Defeat at Rochdale followed and Pools finally looked set to lose John Linacre – he went to Doncaster on trial following a pay dispute. However, his time in South Yorkshire was cut short as he wanted to stay with Pools and Doncaster were encountering financial problems.

His return perked the squad up and they recorded their first win, beating Wigan 2-1. It was a first victory under the new three points for a win rule brought in at the start of the season to try to revitalise the game. Many clubs were struggling financially and crowds were down across the land. The country was also in the grip of another financial crisis, high unemployment and riots throughout the summer.

Newton was back in the middle of September and he had an eventful day at York. He scored, earned a penalty, had a goal disallowed and was also booked, all two days after scoring on his return in the League Cup loss at Northampton on September 16.

Wins over Halifax and Hull and a draw with Hereford moved Pools into eighth place, with fans hoping last season's form could be improved upon. Newton was back from America in fine form, with four in five.

A lean spell followed, this time five winless games. A second away win of the season at Aldershot arrived on the last day in October, with goals from Newton and John Linacre, now playing alongside his brother Phil who had

been called into the team.

They then struggled along, but managed to reach the second round of the FA Cup after beating Wigan in a replay. Newton netting with a powerful run and finish at the Vic.

Coach Decides To Leave The Club

THE shoddy form saw the resignation of coach Willie Maddren. Disappointed with the lack of investment during the summer, he believed the side had no future prospects.

Being demoted from first team coach to reserve coach was the final straw. He returned to Middlesbrough and became coach there and later manager. He passed away in 2000 from Motor Neurone Disease aged only 49. Horner remained as Manager.

In December Pools played just once, a 1-1 draw with Bournemouth on the fifth. The rest of the month was written off due to bad weather, which further impacted on the cashflow of the stricken Club.

Financial Problems, Tax Demand, The Big Freeze And Industrial Disputes

JANUARY saw Hull repeat their Group Cup success with a victory over Pools in the second round of the FA Cup. League form was up and down but the Club was facing a new challenge.

It was rumoured the Inland Revenue had demanded £50,000 by the end of January for unpaid PAYE contributions. Pools were skint.

They hadn't played a home game between December 5th and January 30th when, in front of only 2,291, the beat York 3-2. They weren't the only club in a bad way. It was estimated after six weeks of the big freeze that 80 of the 92 clubs were suffering financially.

It signalled the start of a long period of financial woe, far worse than any encountered in the past.

Further bad news followed in February. The Council were chasing late rent and Pools had also been advised it would cost around £14,000 to repair the 64-year-old wooden stand on Clarence Road.

Commercial manager Frankie Baggs was working flat out to raise money locally. The then 47-year-old former engineer had been with the Club for two years and was arranging concerts at local social clubs to raise drastically-needed funds. He acted as a singer, comedian and compere and his endeavours raised several thousand pounds for the coffers.

The Club won only one in six during February but still managed to remain in a decent 12th place, commendable considering the uncertainty.

Striker Houchen notched a hat-trick in a 4-4 draw with Peterborough at the end of February to take his total to 17 for the season.

Keith Houchen in March 1982

He admitted he wanted to be away from the Club, but didn't officially ask for a transfer. As much as the Club wanted to hang on to him, if an offer came in for him, then they would have to let him go.

Fan Violence Mars The Beautiful Game

MARCH saw Pools win just once in seven, but enjoyed a healthy gate of almost 4,500 for the visit of future champions Sheffield United, which was a close 3-2 defeat.

However, the game itself was marred by violence before, during and after the game. Trouble not only spilled onto the pitch from the terraces, but also in to the town centre afterwards.

Hooliganism was once again on the rise across the country and like all clubs Hartlepool had their own problems. Organised violence, or merely just the threat of it, was nationally believed to be one of the reasons for low crowds, along with the grip that the mini-depression, industrial disputes and high unemployment was taking.

Houchen Departs And Injuries Hit Pools

MARCH saw the departure of Houchen. Still aged only 21 he had scored 66 goals in 175 games and was allowed to go to Orient for a bargain £25,000 – Pools had knocked back a bid of £80,000 from Portsmouth the previous season. The funds would bail the Club out short-term, but it was little consolation for losing such a talent so cheaply.

Pools were also hammered by injuries and were blooding more and more youngsters every week. The likes of David Linighan, Paul Dobson, Kenny Lowe and Terry Bainbridge were all youth players introduced to the first team.

April saw just one win, as they were also soundly beaten 5-2 at Bournemouth and by the same score by Darlington the week before.

The 100th Football League meeting between the two sides saw a four-goal haul from Hartlepool-born Alan Walsh help the Quakers cruise to victory.

Victory over Port Vale was a crucial one as Pools were in danger of slipping into the re-election zone, but the return of Newton, who had missed six winless games due to a fractured toe, did the trick and goals from him, Staff and Phil Linacre helped them to a 3-1 win in front of just 1,439 fans.

Pools ended in 14th place, a decent and steady return after such an arduous season.

Cutting Costs And Raising Money Becomes Priority

IN order to cut costs several players were freed. Kerr, 34, was on his way after making only a handful of starts, spending most of his time playing for the reserves in the Wearside League. Derek Hampton's contract expired and half a dozen players still under contract were offered free transfers – Martin Burleigh, Trevor Ramshaw, Kevin Johnson, Alan Harding, Alan Sweeney and Ged McNamee.

Defender Andy Linighan spent a week on trial at Everton but was determined to finish his apprenticeship as a plumber first and stayed at Pools.

Pools played a friendly against Newcastle at the end of the season with the aim of raising money, but only 1,037 fans turned up to see Pools hammered 6-2, with Newton scoring twice. Newcastle's Imre Varadi netted five of their tally. Another money raiser took place later in the summer when a mini–marathon raised £2,000.

No new players arrived during the break due to the financial plight and Pools were in need of an increase in crowds after the average last season of 2,054 was the second lowest on record. Judging by the crowds in the Football League Trophy of 962 against Hull and 655 against Bradford there didn't seem to be much chance.

1982-83

A miserable start to the new season was to come. A dire goalless draw at home to Scunthorpe on August 28 was in front of a mere 1,009 fans. Supporters were at loggerheads with the Club and busy organising meetings when every aspect of the Club was scrutinised and criticised.

Financial Crisis Looms As Fans Begin To Turn

AFTER defeats at Peterborough and Rochdale, the disgruntled group of fans attempted to organise a boycott for the home game against Northampton on September 11. It is difficult to tell if the boycott worked – just 947 turned out, but that was only 62 down on the last gate.

Nevertheless, the die-hards witnessed the first win of the season, 2-1 with goals from Hogan and Bird. Four days later they won through to the second round of the League Cup (known as the Milk Cup after sponsorship) after beating Chesterfield over two legs.

Missing from the second tie was Bob Newton, who had moved to Port Vale the same day for a ridiculous £20,000. The desperation for cash meant he was given away for a fifth of his value from last season when Aldershot tried to buy him. Newton, a real crowd favourite,

HUFC Team Photo, 1982. Back row: John Linacre, Kevin Johnson, Roy Hogan, Paul Staff; Middle row: Barry Stimpson, Mike Fagan, Phil Linacre, Bob Newton, John Watson, Mark Lawrence, Terry Bainbridge, David Linighan; Front row: Kenny Lowe, George Smith (Coach), Billy Horner (Manager), John Bird, Vince Barker (Chairman), Phil Brown, John Fullard (Director), Tommy Johnson (Physio), Trevor Hogg; Mascot: Ryan Whittle

netted 60 goals in 170 games.

Life without Big Bob began with a draw at Hull and wins over Tranmere (4-0) and Crewe (1-0). Despite living on the edge and having little support, Pools were up to ninth.

But the following game at Torquay was nothing less than a shambles.

Pools were 2-1 up and then capitulated, fell down 3-2 and Roy Hogan was sent off. With a minute remaining, Pools embarrassed themselves even more when they had Kevin Johnson and Trevor Smith sent off for arguing with each other. Smith had rejoined on a part-time basis a couple of weeks into the season.

PFA Involved To Settle Pay Disputes And Another Offer To Buy The Club

TROUBLE on the pitch was followed by trouble off it. The Club decided they could no longer afford to pay what they considered to be handsome win bonuses – the £50 a win and £25 a draw was to be reduced to £15 and £5 respectively. Not surprisingly, the players refused to accept this and as the row rumbled on Lawrence and Hogan were put on weekly contracts.

Emergency talks were held with PFA secretary Gordon Taylor. Some players had already waived cost of living increases and loyalty bonuses. But there was no instant result and it was a problem for some time until an agreement was reached.

After losing the first leg of the Milk Cup second round at Derby 2-0, a local consortium put forward a bid to buy the Club.

The takeover was agreed by Barker, but he insisted that if he went the rest of the board would follow suit. The idea was financially and operationally impractical and the deal stalled.

The team slipped to 13th in the table by the time Derby came to town for the second leg of the Milk Cup tie.

After being forced to field promising youngsters Paul Dobson and Kenny Lowe in recent weeks due to suspensions, Horner picked what could only be described as his first choice XI.

Taking to the pitch were Watson, Brown, Stimpson, Hogan, Bird, Andy Linighan, Staff, Trevor Smith, Lawrence, Kevin Johnson and Micky Barker, a former Newcastle and Gillingham player who had joined just a month ago. Despite it being an experienced XI, eight of the players were aged 23 or under.

Derby were struggling in the second division and Pools' young side were in front through Barker within ten minutes and by the break they were 2-1 up after Smith restored the lead.

Almost 3,600 fans – a very good gate considering the circumstances – saw Staff score immediately after the restart and with the aggregate score at 3-3, extra time was played.

Derby went 4-3 up overall, but Pools levelled when Kevin Johnson netted. Despite applying immense pressure, Pools couldn't break through and went out on the away goals rule.

Problems Set To Spiral Out Of Control

IN typical fashion a good result was followed by two shocking ones, a 5-1 reverse at York was coupled with a 4-0 home humiliation against Mansfield, with defender Billy Ayre bossing the lacklustre Pools' forwards.

Horner was critical of his team, calling them novices and accusing them of letting the Club down. He made four changes for the next game and the side got a result with a 1-0 win over Wimbledon, but again followed up with a defeat, this time at Hereford.

Respite came in the form of a win in the FA Cup over Lincoln City but they lost the next round in a replay to York.

Pools then won just two in 11 and dropped to 20th place by the mid-February. More trouble was mounting.

Not only was the players' dispute still ongoing and the Club was living on the breadline, they had to deal with internal disciplinary issues.

Keeper John Watson was sacked in mid-January after he went missing following Christmas. He had already been in trouble earlier in the season when he was late for the Football League Trophy game at Halifax, when he was suspended and fined, and he also missed training regularly. In his place came Eddie Blackburn on loan from York.

They then lost the printer for their programme and had to resort to a shabby four-page affair.

Horner Forced To Step Aside As Manager

A brief sojourn followed with three wins in five as Staff scored in three consecutive games but they remained deep in trouble in 18th place. That was as good as it got.

With the Club under threat of eviction it all seemed to get to Horner as he made some bizarre signings. Easington CW's John Langridge arrived, as did former Mansfield manager Stuart Boam and ex-Northern Ireland forward Dave Stewart, both of whom hadn't played league football for a while. In a more sensible move, he drafted in David Linighan to

Andy Linghan scores in 4-0 win over Tranmere in September 1982

play alongside Andy in the heart of the defence.

That was the only one that worked. David, aged 18, was the perfect foil for his brother. Boam and Langridge were failures. Boam played once and Langridge failed to score in the six games he featured. Stewart did little to impress.

A 1-0 home defeat to Hereford in March 1983 was Boam's first and last game. It was also the end for the manager. Horner was relieved of his position and moved back to the coaching role he previously occupied.

After 343 games in charge over nearly seven seasons he was back where he started.

And his time in charge was a horrendous one for him, as he struggled with no financial support. On the plus side, he developed the youth side and some outstanding players made it to the very top of the game.

He was replaced on April 2 by John Duncan, 34, a Scotsman who had played at the top level for Dundee, Spurs and Derby, but had been dismissed as player/manager at Scunthorpe in February.

With only nine games remaining and the Club sat third from bottom, it wasn't the easiest of tasks.

His first game was a home defeat at the hands of Bury and followed by a 2-1 loss in the derby at Feethams.

New Boss Handed Unenviable Task

POOLS were second bottom with seven games to play and were penniless. Amid constant threats of writs and litigation, it was unlikely a record 13th application for re-election would be successful.

Yet things went from bad to worse.

Mark Lawrence was on loan at Port Vale. Pools wanted him back, but he chose to stay at promotion-challenging Vale. Duncan's hands were tied, there was nothing he could do.

Several clubs were hovering like vultures waiting to pick up the scraps of his team for next to nothing, one of them Newcastle who were sniffing around the consistent Andy Linighan.

Pools On The Brink As Hornsey Returns With Another Offer

THERE was a rare victory, when a goal by 20-year-old Paul Dobson saw Chester off.

Two days later and yet another body blow was landed. It was some punch.

The Inland Revenue filed papers on April 11 to wind the Club up the following Monday. They were believed to be owed £51,949 and the Club was rumoured to owe other creditors a sum in excess of six figures.

The crowd against Chester was a paltry 1,039. There was no way the Club could continue without a new backer.

So back on the scene came Harold Hornsey, who again expressed an interest in buying the Club if the liquidation went through. Barker, however, wasn't going to give up.

Unpopular with the crowd – or what was left of it – he had put countless thousands into the

Club and was a fan himself. He had rescued the Club when he took over and had saved it in the past before.

He adopted the "Never Say Die" attitude which was missing from the stay-away fans and the majority of the playing squad and he was determined to see it through.

Chairman Makes Bizarre Merger Suggestion

AFTER the team lost a Friday night game at Crewe 3-0 judgement day arrived. And Barker won a reprieve, but not before one of the most bizarre comments ever made about the Club, which would have turned the remainder of the fans against him.

At the time Reading and Oxford, like many clubs, were encountering financial difficulties and a proposed merger was discussed at length to create a new team – known as Thames Valley United.

Whether it was the stress of the situation no one knows, but Barker had the temerity to raise the idea of Pools merging with Darlington.

Not only did this astonish fans of both clubs, but it also astonished the Darlington board. The public comments were the first they had

heard of it and they quickly brushed it aside.

Barker, though saviour of the Club in the past, had lost whatever credibility remained.

He and his fellow directors could not raise any money in the town. People wouldn't put money into his Club the way it was. A huge emergency loan was arranged to clear the debt, but it would only increase the interest payments over the coming months.

Players Set To Take Strike Action

THERE were five games to go. The desperate situation was made even worse when the players decided to stop training, stating they hadn't been paid.

The Club's bank account had been frozen after the High Court issue with the Inland Revenue and the players' PFA spokesman Phil Brown claimed that three weeks wages and five weeks bonuses were due and a strike was imminent unless it was swiftly received.

Brown insisted that unless they were paid by 2pm on the afternoon of Friday, April 29 they would not play the game at Halifax that evening.

The threats attracted more unwanted

John Bird leads Alan Hardip and Phil Brown to a PFA meeting in April 1983

attention for the crippled Club, but they paid up in the end, citing cash flow problems due to the legal action.

Come the game at The Shay, Dobson's third goal in four games earned a point, but they remained in the bottom four and would have needed Houdini up front alongside Dobson to get out of this predicament.

Did the fans back the Club after the recent endless sagas? Not a hope of it.

The 804 who turned up to see Colchester play them off the park in a 4-1 hiding confined Pools to the bottom four and re-election.

Anyone who hoped the town would rally round was sadly mistaken. Many stayed away in disgust at the complete hopelessness of the situation – the planned strike, the winding-up order, the proposed merger and the atrocious team.

Duncan made changes for the penultimate game at home to Rochdale, some enforced, some by choice.

He pushed Andy Linighan into midfield and brought Mike Fagan and David Linighan in as centre backs. John Bird was rested after sustaining a cut near his eye in the Colchester game which needed five stitches, meaning he had now notched up around one hundred stitches in similar injuries during his career. Brown was dropped to the bench, replaced by Kenny Lowe.

Six changes brought a 3-0 win, in what many thought would be the last Football League game at the Victoria Ground. Re-election was looming and many forecast the bid would fail.

Despite the possible relevance, the game still only saw a feeble 1,015 trickle through the gates, giving an average of 1,367 that season, another unwanted record low.

Fans Raise Money With Cycling Effort

NOT all Pools fans were giving up though. For the final match of the season at Blackpool a total of 13 fans decided to cycle to the game, stopping halfway at Kirby Stephen on the Friday night.

The 127-mile journey was to end on the Saturday at Blackpool's Bloomfield Road. With the trip sponsored it was anticipated that the money raised would be around the £2,000 mark. It was to be given to the Club with other money they had raised for what the group described as forward thinking projects.

The pedal power fans must have done Pools some good as they won the final game 2-1, with David Linighan and Dobson scoring.

The latter ended the season as top scorer with nine goals, five of them in the last seven games of the season. The Club still ended up third bottom and faced a nervous few weeks.

Graham Spence and Pools Supporters Action Group sponsored bike ride raising money for the Club in May 1983

Business had to go on as usual and Duncan was still preparing for the following season when he released eight players.

Eyebrows were raised when he showed the door to experienced Hogan. The battling midfielder had been an integral part of the team and his release – and that of Phil Linacre – was a shock.

Manager Duncan also freed Terry Bainbridge, Dave Stewart, Alan Harding, Dave Howard, Mike Fagan and Ged McNamee. Dobson also departed.

Tough Re-Election Fight While Ken Bates Makes Football League Proposal

POOLS were up against it at the re-election meeting and were in the vote with Blackpool, Crewe, Hereford and Maidstone United, champions of the Alliance Premier League.

Maidstone had invested £4,000 to attempt to get into the Football League and applied pressure on clubs in the top two leagues, indicating openly that they thought that they should replace Pools. Their campaign included a 20 minute video and they published a glossy magazine extolling the virtues of the club.

It didn't matter how much money they threw into the scheme, there was nothing like understanding a situation.

The past few seasons hadn't just been tough for Pools, most of the 92 clubs had suffered.

At the vote Pools were bottom of the clubs hoping to stave off the big boot with only 36 votes, but it was ten more than the stunned Maidstone outfit.

The meeting also rejected a proposal by Chelsea chairman Ken Bates for automatic relegation of one club from the Football League to the Alliance, described in some quarters as 'horrendous'.

Supporters were happier still when the news came through that John Duncan was quitting to take over as manager of Chesterfield, after less than ten weeks in the role.

Rumoured to be in the running for the Victoria Ground role were former Newcastle and Sunderland forward Bryan 'Pop' Robson, another former Newcastle player John Connelly who was in charge at Blyth and Sunderland youth team coach Mick Docherty.

The son of former Manchester United manager Tommy got the job, following Brian Clough and Len Ashurst who had made the same move from Sunderland's youth team to the hot seat at Pools.

New the 1983/84 season were experienced former Brighton defender Harry Wilson who

joined from Darlington, Mick Whitfield, who followed Docherty from Sunderland, and ex-Liverpool and Leicester striker Alan Waddle. Mick Buckley, who had known Docherty from his days at Sunderland, came on a non-contract basis and also being given a fresh chance under the new boss was Bainbridge, previously released by Duncan.

1983/84

THERE was no Football League Trophy this season after the tournament was cancelled due to lack of interest, so as usual Pools were knocked out of the Milk Cup at the first hurdle, this time by Rotherham.

The Football League had attracted a sponsor and it was now known as the Canon League, with the money from the deal aiding all clubs.

The campaign started with a 3-1 defeat at Peterborough, followed up with a home defeat against Aldershot. Former manager Duncan had an early return to the Vic on September 7 and Pools held his strongly fancied side to a 2-2 draw with Andy Linighan and Waddle making the scoresheet.

Bird Sacked – But Then Quickly Re-Instated

MEANWHILE, Barker sacked John Bird due to his business interests in Whitley Bay where he still lived. It was an oddball decision as 35-year-old Bird would run through a brick wall for the team and was a regular in the side, injuries permitting. He took the Club to the Football League Management Commission and won his case, being reinstated at the end of the month.

A first win of the season arrived when Docherty's side beat top of the table Doncaster in the fifth game, which elevated them to 20th place. After this win it was 15 games before the next triumph and Pools spent the rest of the season in the bottom four.

In early October audacious attempts were made to buy former England player Dave Thomas and ex-Newcastle man Mick Martin. Both had talks but couldn't agree terms as Pools couldn't afford their salaries and even the nominal fee agreed for Thomas was raised by the Supporters Association.

Three draws and a 5-0 hiding at Mansfield followed with only two goals scored in a six-game spell coming from recalled defender Bird. A long season lay ahead.

Forced into action to recruit a forward, Docherty went to Carlisle and signed Kevin Dixon on loan after burly Alan Waddle moved to Peterborough. A different player to Waddle, the slight Dixon netted on his debut in the 3-1 home defeat by Bury on October 23.

Desperate Manager Swings The Axe

DOCHERTY was struggling. While Horner, Clough and Westgarth could throw young players in who could perform, he was hampered by the likes of the easily forgotten Graham Bassett, Paul Campbell and Phil Ray.

After nine games in a row without a win in early November, Docherty had had enough. He sacked Mark Lawrence, operating on a week-to-week contract, stating that his heart wasn't in it after a £15,000 move to Port Vale fell through. Paul Staff was transfer listed and Barry Stimpson was picked up on loan by former manager Duncan at Chesterfield. Sunderland reserve keeper Mark Prudhoe arrived on loan to try and shore up the defence. He kept a clean sheet on his debut and then let six in during his next (and final) two games.

Drawn away to Rotherham in the FA Cup, Pools mirrored the scores from the Milk Cup games, scoreless away and a 1-0 defeat at the Vic. Still 2,635 made their way to the ground that night, the highest crowd since last Christmas.

Docherty also tried two new faces in the FA Cup games. Youth team keeper Jeremy Roberts, 16, and former Boro player Billy Woof.

Pools Unveil Massive Transfer Coup

THE new manager made one more signing, but he was unfit and probably wouldn't be ready for another month. One of the biggest captures the Club had ever made was completed – 32-year-old Ray Kennedy signed a monthly contract. The former Liverpool, Arsenal and England star had, at the time, won more medals than any other player. He had been freed by Swansea three weeks previously and wanted to return to the North-East.

Beaten at home to York and stuffed 6-0 at Colchester, Kennedy had yet to debut, and after being with the Club a month refused to accept any pay as he had been injured and unable to appear.

HUFC Team Photo, 1983. Back row: Micky Barker, Terry Bainbridge, Eddie Blackburn, Andy Linighan, Barrie Stimpson; Middle row: Billy Horner (Coach), Tommy Johnson (Physio), John Bird, Harry Wilson, Phil Brown, Kenny Lowe, Mick Whitfield, Mark Lawrence, George Smith (Coach); Front row: Alan Waddle, Paul Staff, Mick Docherty (Manager), Mark Robinson, Kevin Johnson

But Docherty never got to see Kennedy make his debut as he was dismissed on December 15.

The chairman stated that the Club were rooted to the bottom of the table and a board meeting the previous day had voted unanimously to oust the manager. Docherty had been heralded by Barker as a great prospect when he was appointed but he never breathed the expected life into the Club.

Barker's timing did not benefit Docherty though, for Docherty had just that week moved into a house in Hartlepool. Docherty had also failed to sign the two-year contract offered at the start of the season.

Horner Back In Control And Making Changes

FORMER manager Billy Horner was placed in temporary charge as caretaker manager.

Next up was a trip to fourth-placed Reading. Pools returned on the back of a 5-1 defeat, with their goal coming from debutant Kennedy. Pools were now five points behind second bottom Chester.

Horner had to act and soon. He re-signed Roy Hogan from Crook and brought John Linacre back to the Club, who was recovering from injury after a trial in Malta. He was also keen on signing Paul Dobson from Horden and other former Pools players Derek Hampton and Phil Linacre.

Both were on the books of Whitby but Linacre was at Newcastle on an extended trial and he was hoping to make the move to the big time.

He also had to contend with an outbreak of flu with several players laid low and the ground was closed for two days to prevent the bug spreading.

Boxing Day came and after 14 games without a win, Pools finally notched their second victory of the season – over Darlington. In front of a crowd totalling less than 3,000, two Dobson goals saw Pools home in a 2-1 triumph. Five days later and they won again, beating Northampton.

But January 1984 saw nothing but trouble. Pools played three games and gained one point.

On the plus side Phil Linacre got fed up of waiting for Newcastle to make up their mind. With manager Arthur Cox wanting to take another look at him in another reserve game, in spite of him being there five weeks already, Linacre went back to Whitby and agreed to sign for Pools. His signature was much appreciated by Horner who saw efforts to capture Kevin Dixon on loan for the rest of the season fail.

Dixon appeared in just six games but

managed three goals. At the time he left the Club in the middle of December he was top scorer.

Horden Colliery Welfare were threatening to take Pools to the Football League over the re-signing of Dobson. Horden claimed that they had given United permission to sign him for free, but then changed their minds and demanded payment. The League decided to take no action and agreement was eventually reached between the clubs.

It also emerged that Phil Linacre had been on a pre-season tour of Belgium with a North-East select squad.

He played a couple of matches against Belgian teams and issues were raised over international clearance.

It was suggested that he may have signed a deal for a club while he was over there.

The team which travelled to the continent was made up North-East players from all clubs and managed by former Pools player Ken Ellis who had left in the early 70s to play in Belgium.

Three players were offered terms, Linacre being one of them, but they all believed they were signing work permits and not contracts.

Financial Issues Continue To Cause Concern

THEN the Club also got hit with an outstanding Police bill. Cleveland Police were pressuring both Pools and Middlesbrough for a total just short of £86,000, with Pools' share of this £25,065.

Boro were as desperate as Pools for cash and both were going to struggle to meet this demand.

With the Council owed months of rent, they did their best to pacify the Police and agreed to hold on payment until the end of the season.

Regardless, Barker made an appeal across the North-East for financial assistance. He announced the Inland Revenue were once again on the Club's case, chasing them for £29,000.

Bizarrely he suggested that if the Club could draw 15,000 fans to the next home game against Bristol City then there would be no more problems. His notion fell over 13,000 short as only 1,881 turned up.

To try and help the situation, the players agreed to forgo two weeks wages.

Pools' problems stemmed from being unable to cover their outgoings. Income totalled just £140,500, which was £32,500 short of the wage bill, never mind the rest of the outgoings, which totalled an additional £56,050.

The entrance fee to games was only £1.70, but the town suffered from 24%

unemployment, one of the highest rates in the country.

Oil Company Comes To Pools' Rescue

MOST clubs in the lower leagues were in a predicament, but none as badly hit as Hartlepool. With £80,000 of debt they were on the brink of being the first Club to go out of existence since Accrington during season 1961-62.

As the staff and the players stood firm, help finally arrived.

Local oil marketing company M & M Oils offered much-needed assistance as did former Northern League footballers turned businessmen Peter Mulcaster and John Smart.

The latter, a Tynesider, who was ill in bed at the time, got his company secretary to contact Barker to say he would get involved.

Smart and Mulcaster ended up bailing Hartlepool United out, investing heavily and becoming directors on the board, with Smart's company, New County, becoming the first shirt sponsors of the Club, who had just appointed Ray Kennedy as a player-coach.

Seemingly resurrected by the investment behind the scenes, a Phil Linacre goal earned Pools three points at Tranmere, their first away win of the season after 16 attempts.

The Club received a Council report stating that the Clarence Road stand was unsafe and also discovered that now they had been rescued, the authority was about to chase them for rent arrears.

Officials argued away the stand issue, but couldn't do anything about the arrears. The council needed money as much as the Club.

Back on the pitch though Pools had a decent February, won four of their five games and increased their points total from 15 to 27 – but were still five points from safety.

A Dobson hat-trick at Wrexham secured a 4-1 win and moved the side up to 22nd place and only three points from safety.

Late Collapse Plunges Pools In To Danger Zone

JUST as it looked as though Horner had masterminded a great escape, the side folded and they failed to win in the next ten, finally ending the run with a last day victory at Doncaster. Just like 12 months earlier, the final game of the season was expected to be the last.

A lowest ever league crowd of 790 turned out for the Stockport game on May 5 and a week later 1,214 were present for the final home game against promoted Reading, although around 400 them were visiting fans.

Re-election beckoned again, for a 14th time, and once again the Club pushing for their place was Maidstone. Pools had sold towering central defender Andy Linighan to Leeds United for an undisclosed fee assumed to be anywhere between £20,000 and £60,000 just after the end of the season.

The sale bolstered funds in perfect time for the vote.

United fought fire with fire when they came

Horner and Barker in front of players and staff contemplating the Club's future after another appeal for assistance in January 1984.
Back row: Linda Holmes (Secretary), Syd Lavelle (Commercial Manager), Stan Hillhouse (Commercial Manager), Olive Holland (Lottery Assistant), Michael Harrison (Assistant Groundsman), Sheila Hughs (Clerk), Bill Bushnell (Lottery Assistant), Harry Hughes (Lottery Manager), Kevin Johnson (Player), Tommy Johnson (Physio) and George Smith (Coach).
Players (left to right): John Linacre, Alan Weir, Phil Linacre, Andy Linighan, Kenny Lowe, Paul Dobson, Colin Dixon, Terry Bainbridge, Phil Brown, Roy Hogan, Phil Malley, Paul Staff, Scott McEvett, Alan Barker, Ray Kennedy, Mick Whitfield; Front: Billy Horner (Manager), Vince Barker (Chairman)

Kevin Dixon in action in 1984

Kennedy. Bird was offered a new deal as player-coach and Mike Smithies was expected to go part-time.

Chairman Ousted As New Men Take Over

BARKER was under severe pressure. Board newcomers Mulcaster, Smart and local man Keith Sanderson were keen on seeing the back of Barker and taking the Club over.

He initially laughed it off, but by the end of June his long and troubled reign in charge was over. A fan with the Club's best interests at heart, he was in charge during difficult times but once the rot set in there was nothing he could do.

The new chairman was John Smart and despite the Club's short pockets, Horner was allowed to rebuild.

Kennedy had accepted a substantially better financial offer to play in Cyprus for Pezoporikos. He later returned to the UK and played for Ashington, but was later diagnosed as having Parkinson's Disease.

He played just over 20 games for Pools, but his respect and standing in the game probably

up against Maidstone this time and produced their own glossy brochure and even had player-coach Ray Kennedy fighting their corner, promoting the Club and pleading for their reinstatement. Having a respected figure like Kennedy on board worked as Pools clocked up 32 votes to Maidstone's 22.

Before the vote took place the Club were ruthless with their retained list. George Smith was shown the door after many years as player and coach. The only players retained were Blackburn, Dobson, Hogan, Barker, Brown and

HUFC Team Photo, 1984. Back row: John Brownlie, Graeme Hedley, Harry Wilson, David Robinson, Edie Blackburn, John Bird, Tony Smith, Phil Brown, Roy Hogan; Front row: Bryan Liddle, Les Mutrie, Paul Dobson, Billy Horner, Kevin Dixon, Barrie Wardrobe, Mark Taylor

kept the Club in business during the re-election vote.

Horner brought in the needed mass of new faces.

The experienced former Newcastle and Hibs full-back John Brownlie was to add some resolve to the back four and up front was another old head, the burly Les Mutrie.

The permanent signature of Kevin Dixon was sealed and also joining the fray were Sunderland's Barrie Wardrobe, former Middlesbrough player Graeme Hedley and Halifax centre half Tony Smith.

A money-raising pre-season friendly against Newcastle attracted just over 2,000 fans and saw Eddie Blackburn go off injured after just half an hour with a dislocated shoulder that would keep him out until April.

1984/85

POOLS had to start the season with rookie Mike Finch between the sticks. In his three games he conceded 11 goals, against Stockport (1-4), Swindon (2-2) and, in the Milk Cup, Derby (1-5).

Pools soon signed experienced Burnley stopper Alan Stevenson on loan to provide

cover as Blackburn's dislocated shoulder refused to heal.

It wasn't until the fifth game of the season that Pools won when a stunning Hedley strike gave Pools a win over Chesterfield at the Vic.

Defeat at Peterborough saw them back in the bottom four, but Pools recovered with a 3-0 win over Crewe with goals from Hogan, Mutrie and Wardrobe.

A vital Mutrie goal at Feethams earned victory, followed up with a win at Tranmere when Mutrie scored again. Three wins in the space of a week and Pools were up into the dizzy heights of tenth place.

Power Struggles Continue Behind The Scenes

OFF the pitch, former director Ben Crosby was trying to take control and was launching a bid with other directors which split the boardroom. They claimed that the three in charge weren't true directors due to them not taking out shares within a certain timescale.

The players changed the outlook of the situation when they issued a letter giving their full backing to Mr Smart, declaring that they thought if he were removed then the side would suffer.

Players hold crisis meeting in 1984

Crosby, Barker and another former director, Sam Spaldin, withdrew their bank guarantees leaving Pools up the proverbial creek once more, resulting in the Club needing to find a rumoured £47,500 to pay yet another tax bill.

Barker, curiously, issued a writ for £82,398 which he claimed was owed to him.

It was a plan hatched with the aim of taking over as chairman by forcing Smart to resign. Local businessmen joined the board and backed Smart resulting in Barker, so many times a saviour, becoming a pariah as his writ fell apart. Barker later agreed to an arrangement of £2,000 a week following a £25,000 down payment.

On the pitch only one loss in the next seven kept Pools in the top ten come the first round of the FA Cup, when they played Derby County, who had beaten Pools in the Milk Cup twice in the last three seasons.

Crowds Begin To Return To The Vic

POOLS had been struggling on low crowds for several seasons, but this year they had broken the 4,000 barrier for games against Southend and Mansfield.

It came as no surprise to many when they recorded a thumping gate of 7,431 for the visit of Derby.

Pools even refused a £15,000 offer from Derby to take the game to the Baseball Ground, seeking home advantage – and it worked.

In a game hampered by terrace violence, Pools took the game to their once-illustrious opponents sending them away with a 2-1 defeat. Pools goalscoring heroes were Kevin Dixon and Mark Taylor.

The second round saw Pools tied against last season's runaway division four champions York City, who had settled well in the third division.

Included in the City ranks was former Pools goal machine Keith Houchen, who had joined from Orient in March 1984. York dominated and goals from defender John MacPhail and Houchen saw them through by two clear goals in front of a welcome crowd of 8,554.

York went on to have a great run that year with Houchen at the fore, scoring the penalty that knocked out Arsenal in the fourth round, before losing to Liverpool in the next round, after holding them to a draw at Bootham Crescent.

The revenue from the FA Cup gates was very helpful, and throughout the season they had been on the increase, despite the fear that they would be affected by the mining dispute.

The town had a few pits to the north and while the majority of football fans from these areas tended to follow Sunderland, Pools still had a loyal bunch of supporters. The important East Durham fan base remained strong.

The knock-on effect of the dispute could not be measured against Pools' attendances as they actually increased in the two seasons that the strike covered from March 1984 to March 1985.

Pools continued to perform well and following a Boxing Day victory at Halifax they stood in eighth place.

Mark Taylor scoring in the FA Cup win over Derby

Kevin Dixon was on target twice in the 3-2 win over Halifax

Predictably only one win in the next ten followed and a slide down the table ensued. Darlington were top of the league and five points clear of second spot, 19 points ahead of Pools.

Sponsorship Deal Agreed To Boost The Club

AT least during this fall some good news came off the pitch. Sixty local businesses each weighed in with £300 of sponsorship and even better was the involvement of local brewery Camerons, who had for so long shied away from involvement despite having major deals with Middlesbrough and York.

They chipped in with £5,000 to signal the start of a long and cordial friendship.

Pools only win in March was 3-1 at home over Torquay and saw them dip to 14th by the end of the month.

Defender David Linighan moved to Leeds on loan until the end of the season and as part of that deal winger Mark Gavin, who was educated in Hartlepool, moved the other way.

Pools also signed Peterlee's former Darlington midfielder Brian Honour who slotted straight into the right wing position.

Early April saw the Council threaten to close the old wooden stand in Clarence Road after a report indicated serious wood rot.

They only agreed to keep it open as long as the Club could ensure that the structure had adequate liability insurance should a spectator be injured.

The performances on the pitch were also rotting away. Pools won only two in their final nine, ending up in re-election free 18th place, but only two points above the zone and three defeats in the final three games saw them perilously close.

Club chairman John Smart with a cheque from Jim Mackenzie of Camerons Brewery in 1985

Clarence Road Stand in 1985

Horrendous Fire Disaster Strikes Football

THE 200 or so fans that travelled to Chester on the final day of the season were unsure of the Club's fate until the final whistles blew around the country on May 11.

As Pools succumbed to a Stuart Rimmer penalty at Sealand Road in a 1-0 defeat, a tragedy that would change the shape of the Vic occurred.

Darlington had lost their grip on the top of the table and the champions of the division were Bradford City, who were presented with the trophy before their final home game of the season against Lincoln City, in front of over 11,000 fans.

Just before half time, fire ripped through the old wooden stand at Valley Parade, killing 56 fans. The cause of the blaze was put down to a discarded cigarette setting fire to rubbish underneath the stand.

Anxious Club officials invited the fire brigade to the Victoria Ground to carry out a detailed inspection of the 500 capacity stand.

Urgent work was needed to bring the building up to standard. The Club could not see the point in spending money upgrading a stand that had already been condemned. The stand was sealed off within ten days of the Bradford tragedy and was demolished in the middle of July – but not before manager Billy Horner had contacted the West German national side.

He asked them to play a friendly game to raise money for a new stand as the Club had never received any compensation for the stand destroyed by bombs in the First World War

Needless to say there was no friendly against the Germans. The dressing rooms were replaced by temporary units and Portakabins purchased from the fire brigade.

With the stand demolished the usual plans were announced to utilise the space underneath the Mill House stand. Needless to say, as in the past, these ideas were nothing more than pipe dreams.

The Club was still in massive debt despite additional sponsorship from Camerons' Brewery to the tune of £40,000 and crowds which increased from 1,505 to 2,348 on average, a lift of over 56%.

Comings And Goings During The Summer Months

THE close season saw some major changes in the playing personnel. Experienced defender Bird retired from playing and took up a coaching role. Phil Brown, who had played in almost 250 games, moved on to Halifax on a free transfer.

Never to appear for the Club again were the likes of John Brownlie, Graeme Hedley and

Pools line-up for the annual photograph in August 1986

youngsters Mike Finch and Craig Farnaby. Also playing his last game during the season was experienced striker Les Mutrie who retired after a knee injury. After just a handful of first team outings home-grown defender Mark Venus left.

Released by Horner, he was picked up by Leicester City and went on to make his name with Wolves and Ipswich.

Horner was busy recruiting and signed former Halifax defender Keith Nobbs, ex-Hibs left-back Tom Kelly, Nigel Walker from Chester and diminutive forward Alan Shoulder from Carlisle.

Also putting pen to paper and making a return was last season's top scorer in the division, Bob Newton.

He failed to agree terms at Chesterfield after leading them to promotion and Pools broke their record fee when they forked out £17,500 for his services. Midfield enforcer Alan Little joined, after being a difficult opponent of Pools for many years.

1985/86

THE pre-season included a morale boosting 4-1 victory over Darlington in the Durham Senior Cup, but the season began for real with a trip to Cambridge on August 17

A group of fans flew to the game after first attending a wedding in Hartlepool but despite goals from new strike force Shoulder and Newton, Pools lost 4-2.

They lined up as follows – Eddie Blackburn, Keith Nobbs, Tom Kelly, Alan Little, Tony Smith, David Linighan, Alan Shoulder, Brian Honour, Bob Newton, Nigel Walker and Kevin Dixon.

For the third time in four seasons Pools were drawn against Derby County in the Milk Cup. The first leg saw Pools beaten 3-0 away from home, but United fought tooth and nail at the Vic and won 2-0, with David Linighan and Hogan scoring.

In spite of the excitement and recent history of games between the two, the game was watched by a poor crowd of 1,611, in what again was a thrilling encounter as Pools lost out 3-2 on aggregate.

Sandwiched between these games, Pools opened up their home league programme with a 4-1 win over Crewe, goals from Shoulder, Dixon, an own goal and Newton.

Pools Find Strength In Adversity

NO wins in the next three, including a 2-0 defeat on their first league visit to Burnley saw them in 20th place. Shoulder and Little were missing from injuries sustained in the previous game against Orient – a bad tempered affair.

Little was on the receiving end of a sickening tackle which resulted in a broken leg which would keep him out until mid-March. Newton was sent-off in this game along with two Orient players and he watched the remainder of the game from the touchline on the Clarence Road side.

After being injured, he was replaced by local lad John Borthwick, a prolific scorer for the reserves and on the fringe of the first team action since making his debut as an 18-year-old in January 1983.

Like Little, Newton was out of action for too long and made just three more starts that season.

With the first-choice little and large strike force of Newton and Shoulder out and the strength of Little missing, Pools were expected to struggle. Yet the opposite happened and spurred on by the classy wing play of Walker and Honour, Pools won four out of five and moved up to sixth place.

Following a defeat at Port Vale in the last game of this run, Shoulder returned to the starting XI at Peterborough in place of the unfortunate and now unsettled Dixon.

John Borthwick

The team in high spirits after winning the DSC at Darlington. Back row: Bob Newton, Brian Honour (obscured), Kevin Dixon, Alan Little, John Gollogly, Alan Stevenson, Tom Kelly, David Linighan, Billy Horner; Front row: John Bird, Nigel Walker, Tony Smith, Keith Nobbs, Alan Shoulder, Eddie Blackburn

The 32-year-old Shoulder was considered a bit of a risk when he was signed. The former miner and hero of Blyth Spartans famous FA Cup run of 1977-78 he joined the professional ranks late, just a couple of months shy of his 26th birthday.

How he proved the doubters wrong. After victory at Peterborough he scored in the next two games, to take Pools to third place.

Shoulder bagged a brace in a first round FA Cup win at Macclesfield, but couldn't do anything when Northern Premier League Frickley Athletic knocked Pools out at home in the second round by a single goal in a coma-inducing affair in front of 4,100 appalled fans.

Weather Break Interrupts Pools' Momentum

POOLS remained around the top four promotion places from October to March. Shoulder's goals, helped by the hard work of Hogan, Honour and Walker, and a defence marshalled by skipper Tony Smith meant Pools were sniffing some success.

Pools had lost just once in 11 games when they froze. Momentum was lost when a bad spell of weather and a big freeze brought a three-week enforced break.

When they returned on February 25, it was ten games before they recorded another win. Yet they still hovered in sixth although seven points behind fourth place, with eight games remaining.

Newton's days were over and the £17,500 spent on his capture, for all the joy and hope it brought, was proved to be money wasted.

A character much loved by Pools fans he was struggling to impress in the new-look side after an injury-ravaged season and was loaned to Stockport in March 1986, with another Pools legend coming in the opposite direction, Malcolm Poskett.

Newton was released in February the next season after not figuring at all and even training with Southend and had a short stint with Bristol Rovers before spending time with several non league clubs as well as having spells in Cyprus and Hong Kong.

Poskett was brought in to rekindle some of the form he had shown at Carlisle with Shoulder, but it didn't work and he was soon back at Stockport.

Pools reignited hopes of promotion with three wins in four putting themselves in fifth, just three points behind. However, one point in the last 12 saw Pools finish the season in seventh place.

The season almost mirrored that of five years previous and ended disappointingly. Shoulder ended the season as top scorer with 19 goals and he was supported well by midfielders Honour and Hogan, who netted 11 and nine respectively.

While the promotion assault faltered, there were problems aplenty off the field at the same time.

Season Over And Off Field Problems Take Centre Stage

THE Victoria Ground capacity was forcibly reduced to 3,200 following problems identified with the Town and Rink Ends. The stands, deemed unsafe, had to be demolished. Pools were offered the use of Middlesbrough's Ayresome Park but refused.

Kevin Dixon scores at The Vic in 1985

Club Secretary Malcolm Kirby examines some vandalism of the Victoria Park offices in April 1986

In March 1986 the board also chased former chairman Vince Barker though the court stating that they believed that Barker allegedly breached his duty between 1975 and 1984, in essence claiming that he damaged the position of the Club during his reign. Barker died in April and the High Court ruled in favour of his estate, after Hartlepool United kept pushing the case despite his death.

There were also moves in the boardroom and calls on the terraces for Horner to be replaced after missing out on promotion.

But while they did fall out of the leading group, the season still represented a healthy improvement.

Players who would no longer appear for the Club and on their way out included Paul Dobson, left back Phil Chambers, Tom Kelly and David Linighan.

Kelly was injured in an October home win over Hereford when he was poked in the eye by an opponent and only returned for the final two games.

The Club turned to Tony Chilton for three games before capturing the experienced Chambers. David Linighan moved to Derby County for £20,000, after almost signing for Blackpool. It was another case of the poor financial state being exploited.

As Horner was trying to discover what funds, if any, were available, it was again time for Pools to be put under severe financial pressure, when a director claimed to be owed money.

Ben Crosby announced he was due almost £3,000 and bailiffs were empowered to remove whatever they could. The goal nets and posts, a seed machine and a grass cutter were taken. They were returned within a few weeks, but ill-

Vince Barker

Rob McKinnon

Cup. Fair to say he ended up watching events from afar.

Former Halifax forward Simon Lowe signed, along with experienced defender Tommy Sword from Stockport County and left back Rob McKinnon moved down the A19 from Newcastle after just one appearance in a black and white shirt – a 5-1 thumping at Tottenham.

1986/7

PRE SEASON saw United hammer Darlington 7-1 in the Durham Senior Cup final at the Vic.

Two Games In A Day At The Vic

POOLS season kicked-off with two games at the Victoria Ground on the opening day.

Horner's side hosted Cardiff City, who were playing their first season in the bottom flight after two successive relegations.

But Middlesbrough had suffered a desperate financial plight and were placed into liquidation with the gates at Ayresome Park locked.

Now in the third division, Boro were in danger of getting thrown out of the Football League if they were unable to fulfil their opening game.

Returning the hand of friendship made to

publicity stemming from the matter could have made it increasingly difficult to attract players.

But attract players they did. Burly young striker Dean Gibb joined from Brandon United. Full of promise and confidence, the player infamously boasted of his desire to make the England World Cup squad for the 1990 World

Fans at The Vic in August 1986

Pools last season, Boro were offered use of the Vic and drew with Port Vale after Pools and Cardiff were tied at 1-1, Tony Smith's goal cancelling out a strike from Robbie Turner, who weeks later moved to Pools on loan.

The game is remembered more for the violent nature of the Welsh followers, who gathered in the Mill House stand and started ripping out and throwing seats at the Hartlepool fans. A total of 12 people were arrested.

Crowd Turn On Club, Horner Dismissed And Board Shake-Up

MORE trouble was to follow as Pools were drawn against Middlesbrough in the Milk Cup with rival fans clashing in both legs, a tie which saw Boro win 3-1 on aggregate.

Form was poor and after eight games they had failed to win. The last game of this run was an evening encounter at home to Crewe on October 1.

Pools were played off the park and after David Platt notched Crewe's fifth the Pools fans in the crowd of 1,512 voiced their displeasure.

Police intervention was needed as crowds headed for the Club offices after the game to call for the heads of Smart and Horner.

The manager was subsequently dismissed from his second spell in charge, replaced by his assistant John Bird, albeit on a temporary basis.

As tends to be the case, the team, which showed five changes, played a blinder in the first game under the new manager and returned from Lincoln with a 4-1 victory. John Gollogly got two, there was one from Nigel Walker and the other was courtesy of an own goal by Lincoln defender Gary Strodder.

The result was merely a blip on the radar though as five more games went by without a win and Pools were second bottom, a dangerous position to be in.

Re-election had been scrapped (three years after Ken Bates had suggested the idea), replaced by automatic relegation for the side that finished bottom. For the top end of the table, play-offs were introduced giving automatic promotion for the top three teams with four other clubs competing for a spot in the third division. It was to be some years before the play-offs interested Pools.

Early in November, former keeper and successful commercial manager Alan Stevenson left to take up the same role at Middlesbrough, following long-serving physio Tommy Johnson.

It was rumoured that John Smart wasn't keen to give Bird the manager's job permanently and was looking elsewhere. It

didn't go down well with some members of the board who called for his resignation. Malcolm Lancaster, Mick Brown and John McArdle all left after Smart failed to budge.

He did, however, appoint Bird as boss and youth team coach Alan Little was promoted to work alongside Bird. Gary Henderson was the new physio.

Boosted by Bird's permanent appointment, Pools won three out of four games and moved to 18th place by the end of November.

New Boss Bird Swoops In To Transfer Market As Chairman Resigns

DECEMBER saw Pools slip back into old habits and they failed to score in three games, resulting in Bird getting the green light to bring in some players.

He had already tried Keith Lockhart from Wolves, but he didn't suit and he returned to the midlands after two games. Mike Smithies was brought back after an absence of three seasons, former Middlesbrough midfielder Terry Cochrane made a brief cameo and loan forward John McGinley figured just twice.

Bird did, however, bring in some faces that would last longer. From Billingham Town came former Grimsby right back Tony Barratt and, from Bishop Auckland, ex-Lincoln midfielder Andy Toman.

The turn of the year saw Pools lose just once in five and they pulled nine points clear of bottom placed Rochdale. They struggled until

Wayne Stokes

HUFC Team Photo, 1987. Back row: Paul Haigh, Paul Baker, Kevin Carr, Stuart Dawson, Dean Gibb, Wayne Stokes; Middle row: Andy Toman, Tony Barratt, Paul Butler, Andy Dixon, John Tinkler, John Borthwick, Rob McKinnon, Keith Nobbs; Front row: Alan Little (Coach), Alan Shoulder, John Bird (Manager), Tony Smith, Brian Honour, Gary Henderson (Physio)

mid-March when they were boosted by the return of Shoulder who had missed a fair bit of the season due to an Achilles problem. Shoulder netted six in seven games as Pools dragged themselves up to 17th.

Although they only won one of the final seven games, they ended the season 18th just three points above Lincoln City who were relegated to the Conference, replaced by Scarborough.

Lincoln dramatically fell from a comfortable mid-table position and took a mere nine points from their final 16 games. Torquay, Tranmere and Burnley all climbed above them on the last day.

The campaign was a let down as Pools failed to build on the successes of the previous year.

Smart again offered little confidence in manager Bird when he called a board meeting and cited that the team showed no desire or ambition and, as he could not persuade the board to dismiss Bird, he resigned himself.

Within a month he was back after resolving his issues with Bird.

As usual the close season saw players come and go. On his way was 30-year-old keeper Eddie Blackburn, who after 175 appearances was given a free transfer. He moved to Sweden for a spell but suffered a career ending injury six months into his two-year deal with Halmstad.

Striker Kevin Dixon had refused to budge on a new contract and made the move to

Scunthorpe after spending a stint on loan there in early 1986.

Midfielder John Gollogly was allowed to leave earlier in the season by John Bird and attacking youngster Marty Hewitt also departed.

Bound for Australia was hard-grafting midfielder Hogan. He had spent ten seasons with the Club and was released aged only 27. After over 300 games and several dodgy hairstyles he went on to play semi-pro football with some success for Perth Italia, settling there and later running a ranch. Also on the way out were Nigel Walker and Tommy Sword.

1987/88

Rule Change Allows Two Substitutes

NEW to the ranks were former Southampton and Carlisle central defender turned forward Paul Baker and team-mate Paul Haigh. Former Wolves and Hereford winger Paul Butler was signed as well as former Newcastle stopper Kevin Carr and ex-Stockport defender Wayne Stokes.

Carr entered hospital for treatment for kidney trouble after colliding with a post during training, leaving Pools with no experienced cover in goal.

With Bird not wanting to use untried Stuart Dawson he signed Brandon's 32-year-old Phil

John Tinkler

Toman scoring the other.

The result pleased the decent and vocal away support. In the habit of having low crowds at home, Pools were still attracting a handsome and enthusiastic following at away games. The backing away from home was always vociferous and optimistic; the atmosphere at the dilapidated Vic was subdued and negative.

The following home game Baker scored twice in a 2-1 win over Cambridge and then in a 3-1 victory over Colchester three days later, he scored all three.

Next up was an enthralling encounter at Bolton, where Pools won the first game between the two sides by the odd goal in three with Baker finding the target once more.

A Baker hat-trick in the next home game over Exeter saw Pools climb to sixth and the home crowd had risen to 2,971 in less than four weeks. Baker made it seven consecutive scoring games when he netted his 13th goal in this run in a 1-1 draw at Crewe.

But as abruptly as he started finding the net he then couldn't score at all and he went on a seven game run where he was out of luck.

He broke his lean spell, when he added a second to Gibb's opener at Chorley's Victory Park in the first round of the FA Cup. The second round of the cup saw Pools paired with York.

While Baker had been shy in front of the goal, Toman wasn't and his goals had kept Pools in the top ten.

A crowd of 3,394 were at Bootham Crescent when Baker scored his 17th of the season in the closing stages to earn a replay and send the travelling contingent snaking back up the A19 happy.

Once again Pools took a large away following to this game, but an alarming total of almost 70 Hartlepool fans were arrested for crowd disturbances. In the heavily-policed replay, Toman tore York apart and helped himself to two goals to take him into double figures, with Baker netting the other in a 3-1 win.

The third round saw them drawn at home to Luton and Pools prepared badly by winning just one in six.

A crowd of marginally over 6,000 saw Pools edged out 2-1.

The gate included the directors of Crystal Palace who were in dispute with Newcastle, where they were due to play, and instead decided to attend the Victoria Ground and pay a total of £600 for the privilege.

Luton, with the pacy Stein brothers up front and Danny Wilson bossing the midfield, edged a close encounter with Toman grabbing a late consolation from close range at the Rink End.

Owers who had previously been on the books of Darlington and had last played in the Football League eight seasons ago.

Another new signing unable to play was former Sunderland and Liverpool full back Alan Kennedy. The two-time European Cup winner had agreed to move after playing in pre-season games but manager John Bird agreed to let him go if he received a better financial offer.

Just before the season started Swedish second division outfit Husqvarna made their move.

The season opened with a dreary goalless draw against Newport County at the Vic in front of just 1,848 and followed up with a defeat at Wrexham.

Scunthorpe put paid to any chance of progress in the League Cup (now Littlewoods Cup) and Pools were thumped 5-2 at home by Darlington. The game saw Pools use the now permitted two substitutes for the first time.

After two games Owers was replaced by Mark Prudhoe, who had joined on loan for a second spell. Also missing were Borthwick and Gibb with a broken toe and foot respectively and Shoulder who had damaged ligaments in his neck. Also unavailable were youngsters David Stokle and John Tinkler who had broken into the first team last season.

Baker's Goals The Highlight For Pools

A couple of games after the Darlington loss, Pools drew 2-2 at the Vic with Leyton Orient in front of 1,110 supporters and were second bottom.

Just as another long season of strife looked on the cards, Pools came good at Carlisle in an eventful away trip on September 12. Their first visit to Brunton Park in 24 years saw Pools romp home 3-1, with Baker netting twice and

Pools Drawn At Sunderland In Freight Rover Trophy

FEBRUARY saw Pools beat Carlisle in the first round proper of the Freight Rover Trophy, the newly-sponsored Associate Members Cup, and were handed an away draw at Sunderland.

Backed by a fervent 2,000 fans, Pools beat their neighbours by a single Brian Honour goal, scored direct from a left wing corner in the final stages. It was an awful night for football, with driving rain and a swirling wind taking hold.

This famous win saw the Club progress to the northern area semi-final and they were given a home tie against third division Preston on March 9.

In between these two ties Pools only lost one in five and were just short of the play-off places in tenth. The last of these games was played at Torquay United, just three days after playing at Exeter.

Despite the distance, Plainmoor had always been a favourite destination for Pools fans – but this season only a couple of dozen were present.

Torquay, like Luton before them, had banned away fans from their ground. Some Pools fans gained entrance by gathering the handful of complimentary tickets available from the players, but some also got a few by a chance meeting with a pub owner just before the game who was pulling them a pint and happened to be former Pools keeper John Watson!

After Baker was sent-off early in the game, Pools went behind and fought back through a Tony Barratt goal.

The game against Preston attracted just under 5,000 and, for a midweek game, a following in excess of 1,000 visiting fans.

A confident Preston comfortably beat Pools by two clear goals.

This game came just over a week after Shoulder was announced his retirement due to a neck injury. He had played five games all season and had been out since September. During a friendly arranged to gauge his fitness against Alnwick, the decision to quit arrived after he was injured again.

The Preston defeat seemingly took the wind out of Pools' sails. Two wins in the last 11 saw them end the season in 16th place.

Ace Striker Attracting Positive And Negative Attention

THE campaign offered more but the end result was still promising due to the form of

HUFC Team Photo, 1988. Back row: Paul Haigh, Paul Baker, Kevin Dixon, Simon Grayson, Andy Toman, John Tinkler; Middle row: Tony Barratt, Russell Doig, Paul Norton, David Stokle, Roy Tunks, John Borthwick, Rob McKinnon; Front row: Brian Honour, Alan Little (Coach), Tony Smith, John Bird (Manager), Wayne Stokes, Gary Henderson (Physio), Keith Nobbs

Baker and Toman. That was if Toman was still going to be at the Club, for during the last game of the season, a 2-1 reverse in front of a disinterested 823 fans, he ended the season with a goal and a v-sign directed towards the Mill House stand.

Pools needed his goals, but whether they needed his attitude was a different matter. His form had attracted a great deal of interest and he believed a move was imminent, with WBA interested.

Baker top scored for the season with 25, the best return from a Pools player since the halcyon days of the mid-50s. Perhaps better things were soon to be round the corner.

At least Bird had signed up some existing players for the following season. Young midfielder Tinkler, Barratt, midfield dynamo Honour and skilful left back McKinnon had already signed new deals.

The Club had also signed Leeds midfielder Russell Doig for a fee of £10,000, with £2,000 coming from the supporters' association, as well as former Sheffield United reserve forward Simon Grayson.

Bird had a mini-clear out in the close season. On their way were Carr, Andy Dixon and Gibb.

Carr left the professional game and became a Policeman.

Dixon played for several Northern League clubs before several spells abroad, returning to Pools for a fleeting cameo spell in 1995-96 season. Dean Gibb, released without earning international honours, returned to Brandon

United. Jon McCarthy, a youth team player, made just one substitute appearance in the final game of the season. He turned down a professional deal to go to University and went on to win 18 Northern Ireland caps.

During the summer the Club finally proceeded with work to replace the roofing on the Town End and even incorporate a new stand at the Rink End.

Authorities Target Football Hooliganism

WITH hooliganism an issue across Europe, the problem at Pools had always been there since the mid-seventies.

However, during the summer Pools were quick to distance themselves from a tale which appeared in the local press. Calling cards, supposedly representing a group of followers calling themselves The Moose Men, were discovered and caused uproar.

The supporters' association disassociated themselves from the group and it was hoped that as they were a minority they would not affect the improvements the Club and the association were making to bring more people to the games.

Signings wise the close season was worryingly quiet. Two goalkeepers arrived, but late in pre-season, namely former Sheffield United trainee Paul Norton and experienced former Wigan keeper Roy Tunks.

After a year away, Kevin Dixon returned.

John Tinkler fires past Manchester United keeper Chris Turner in 1988

1988-89

Chris Turner's First Visit To The Vic

THE Club played their usual seemingly run-of-the-mill friendlies, with a Manchester United reserve side coming along to the Vic.

The visitors included several experienced professionals and internationals such as Paul McGrath, Norman Whiteside, Viv Anderson, Mike Duxbury and Chris Turner in goal. Pools tore them apart and ran out 6-0 winners, in the whole mainly due to an inspired performance by the returning Dixon who notched a hat-trick.

This result put the team on a high and they opened the league campaign with an away win at Lincoln courtesy of a Toman goal. The following game saw Pools draw at home to Sheffield United in the first leg of the Littlewoods Cup and next beat rivals Darlington at the Vic 2-1 and a mere 2,477 fans turned up.

The second leg of the Sheffield tie saw Pools lose out and the following Saturday was the long trek to Torquay, who had now lifted their away fan ban. Those who travelled wished it was still in force. On-loan keeper Dave McKellar conceded twice as ten-man Torquay won 2-0.

Indifferent Start As Manager Bird Leaves For York

WINS over Leyton Orient, York and Cambridge saw Pools climb to second place. No prizes for guessing what Pools failed to do in the next eight games – just one point was gained and they dropped to 19th. Only their second ever win at Peterborough stopped the rot when Simon Grayson scored his first goal for the Club in his 14th game.

Three games into this poor run and days after a defeat at Doncaster, John Bird quit to become manager at York City, and following him was coach Alan Little.

Managerless and in freefall, Pools were on the lookout for a new boss. Several names were touted – Billy Bremner, Mick Martin, Frank Gray and Glenn Roeder.

Bobby Moncur Is Named As New Man In Hotseat

BIRD was replaced on October 14 by former Newcastle skipper Bobby Moncur, a friend of John Smart, who had been in charge at Plymouth, Hearts and Carlisle. Pools were calling on his experience to lift the team to better things.

Cecil Yuill with Chairman John Smart during building work at The Vic in August 1988

After four years away from management he joined initially as caretaker boss with his assistant former Newcastle and Sunderland forward Bryan 'Pop' Robson.

Moncur realised that Grayson needed more support up front and signed former Newcastle United player Joe Allon on loan from Swansea City, shortly after dropping Baker into the centre of defence.

His arrival saw the departure of Kevin Dixon who headed down the A19 to join former manager Bird at York. Moncur quickly noticed that there were problems in the goalkeeping department too and that young keeper Paul Norton was not up to scratch. Therefore he entered the loan market once again to bring Leicester stopper Carl Muggleton to the Club.

The AMC had seen Pools lose group games against Burnley and York, but the FA Cup saw Pools play some of their best football of the winter and they beat three division three teams in the opening three rounds.

Wigan were beaten 2-0 thanks to Smith and Borthwick. Next were Notts County who were despatched by Joe Allon's opening goal for the Club, a header from a McKinnon cross. Bristol City followed suit and were seen off by a Baker penalty in front of 4,000 celebrating fans.

In the fourth round for just the third time in their history, Pools were underwhelmed when handed a tie against Bournemouth.

They may not have been a big name team,

Catching the bus to play Bournemouth

Simon Grayson, Paul Dalton and Brian Honour during 1988-89

Simon Grayson after scoring against Lincoln in January 1989

		P	HW	HD	HL	HF	HA	AW	AD	AL	AF	AA	POINTS
1	Rotherham United	46	13	6	4	44	18	9	10	4	32	17	82
2	Tranmere Rovers	46	15	6	2	347	13	6	11	6	28	30	80
3	Crewe Alexandra	46	13	7	3	42	24	8	8	7	25	24	78
4	Scunthorpe United	46	11	9	3	40	22	10	5	8	37	35	77
5	Scarborough	46	12	7	4	33	23	9	7	7	34	29	77
6	Leyton Orient	46	16	2	5	61	19	5	10	8	25	31	75
7	Wrexham	46	12	7	4	44	28	7	7	9	33	35	71
8	Cambridge United	46	13	7	3	45	25	5	7	11	26	37	68
9	Grimsby Town	46	11	9	3	33	18	6	6	11	32	41	66
10	Lincoln City	46	12	6	5	39	26	6	4	13	25	34	64
11	York City	46	10	8	5	43	27	7	5	11	19	36	64
12	Carlisle United	46	9	6	8	26	25	6	9	8	27	27	60
13	Exeter City	46	14	4	5	46	23	4	2	17	19	45	60
14	Torquay United	46	15	2	6	32	23	2	6	15	13	37	59
15	Hereford United	46	11	8	4	40	27	3	8	12	26	45	58
16	Burnley	46	12	6	5	35	20	2	7	14	17	41	55
17	Peterborough United	46	10	3	10	29	32	4	9	10	23	42	54
18	Rochdale	46	10	10	3	32	26	3	4	16	24	56	53
19	**HARTLEPOOL UNITED**	46	10	6	7	33	33	4	4	15	17	45	52
20	Stockport County	46	8	10	5	31	20	2	11	10	23	32	51
21	Halifax Town	46	10	7	6	42	27	3	4	16	27	48	50
22	Colchester United	46	8	7	8	35	30	4	7	12	25	48	50
23	Doncaster Rovers	46	9	6	8	32	32	4	4	15	17	46	49
24	Darlington	46	3	12	8	28	38	5	6	12	25	38	42

1988/89 Barclays League Division Four Table

but they were a good unit and Pools battled for a 1-1 draw at the Vic with a goal from Honour.

The replay, three days later on the last day of January, saw Pools fans head south in their masses only to be beaten 5-2, as they conceded two own goals.

A great deal of interest was held over the replay as the winners were lined up for a home game with Manchester United.

Pools were now in 14th and had started to improve. A new keeper was brought in from Bradford City, Rob Moverley. The chunky 19-year-old had never played first team football for

the Bantams and made his debut in the Notts County cup game as Muggleton was not given clearance by his employers to play.

He acquitted himself well, but less than two weeks after letting in five against Bournemouth he conceded six at Cambridge, in a performance so dire that many Pools fans made their way from the ground at half time.

Moncur Moves To Strengthen The Squad As Team Finish 19th

DESPITE the efforts of Grayson up front, Pools were struggling and, in March, Moncur made permanent the signing of Allon and also recruited Manchester United youth Paul Dalton on loan. The winger was thrown into the first XI immediately and offered some fantastic service from the left wing, but Pools were out of balance with Honour absent due to injury.

Pools played some attractive football going forward but weren't helped by some of the defending and ineffective members of the squad, such as Tony McAndrew who was also signed in March.

Bob Moncur with Chairman John Smart

The full Pools squad line-up ahead of the 1989/1990 season

The experienced former Middlesbrough man played four games in which Pools lost all four and shipped ten goals in the process.

Skipper Tony Smith returned from injury for the last four games of the season and a vital win over Peterborough in the third last game saw Pools climb out of the bottom three and leave the automatic relegation spot for Colchester and Darlington to fight over.

Pools rivals didn't have the heart and lacked the never say die spirit that Pools had embraced so many times in the past and dropped out of the Football League.

Rob Moverley

Pools ended up nineteenth. Not the best of finishes by a long shot but it was now five seasons in a row that they had avoided the drop and had stayed out of the bottom four, the old danger zone.

Top scorer for the season was Grayson who netted on 13 occasions. Baker, last season's top scorer, played most of the season as centre half and Toman netted just seven times.

1989-90

POOLS once again needed to rebuild. Toman, who had expressed his intention to leave for bigger and better things twelve months ago, signed for non league Darlington for a fee of £40,000. Also joining the ex-Football League outfit was Borthwick.

Former manager John Bird approached the Vic to sign Tony Barratt. Skipper Tony Smith hung up his boots, opting for a change of career as he went to work for car manufacturer Nissan.

Goalkeeper Problems, Two Points From 21 And Moncur Goes Sailing!

SUPPORTERS were entering the season with little hope or belief. T-shirts were printed proclaiming this season as the "Farewell Tour".

From the off, the T-shirts weren't far away from the truth.

Just as the season before, Pools were to start without a regular keeper after an injury to Rob Moverley.

In goal for the first game was loan signing Ian Bowling, borrowed from Lincoln City. He conceded four goals as Pools crashed to a

Team celebrate their win over Bristol City in 1989

humiliating opening day defeat at Halifax Town. Afterwards, Chairman John Smart claimed to have been in great fear and danger after he was accosted by disgruntled fans at the lack of investment in the team.

Next in goal was youngster Graham Carr who played in the two Littlewoods Cup games, as Pools lost to York 7-4 on aggregate, and in the opening home league game of the season when he shipped another three goals.

Absent from this game was manager Bob Moncur who was away with prior sea-faring commitments.

It was the final outing for Grayson. He was substituted after just quarter of an hour when an old knee injury flared up and was forced into retirement.

The third keeper filling the void was Tottenham youngster Kevin Dearden. The 19-year-old had a 15-game spell on loan at Cambridge the previous season and made his Pools debut in a 3-0 defeat at Southend.

A first league goal of the season came from

Paul Dalton in a 2-1 home reverse to Gillingham.

The poor run was made worse with a six-goal thrashing at Stockport. A week later and Pools finally got their first points of the season with draws against Peterborough and Rochdale.

Pools had a pitiful two points from a possible 21.

And yet it got worse – a 6-0 hiding at the Vic by Doncaster, who before the game had scored only six goals all season.

More Power Struggles As Garry Gibson Arrives

VOCIFEROUS crowd protests aimed at Smart and Moncur followed and Roland Boyes, a Club director and MP, arrived on the scene to try and pacify the faithful.

The protests were followed by a first win of the season at the ninth attempt when Pools beat Scunthorpe by the odd goal in five, with goals from Baker, Tinkler, and a McEwan penalty.

Once again a behind the scenes power struggle was erupting. When Smart issued a plea for help, Wheatley-Hill born businessman Garry Gibson joined the board.

Another North-East entrepreneur, Sunderland-based Phillip Bennison then offered a package of around £80,000 to see him installed as chairman.

The power struggled would run for sometime.

Moncur had tried several players to get the balance right, although many hardly figured.

Wayne Stokes, David Stokle and Sean Curry all played in the opening match at Halifax but never again. Kenny Davies and Paul Ogden were soon forgotten.

He then introduced the likes of Scottish journeyman Gardner Spiers, Ian Dunbar, Wayne Entwistle and Alan Lamb, signed from Nottingham Forest.

Also thrown into the side by Moncur was scrawny youngster Don Hutchison, who had joined from a famous Tyneside breeding ground, Redheugh Boys Club.

The 18-year-old was an attacking midfielder who had received glowing reports playing for the youth team. Also making his bow in the Club's first win was ageing midfielder John Trewick who had seen a decent career with West Brom, Newcastle and Oxford, but joined Pools from

Paul Baker and Pop Robson in 1989

Bromsgrove Rovers.

Some much-needed defensive steel arrived at the back, with ex-Wimbledon hardman Mick Smith returning to the Football League after playing for Seaham Red Star.

But for all their experience, another five winless games followed, although youngster Hutchison had showed some signs of promise in a badly disorganised team. The return of regular keeper Moverley halfway through this sequence didn't help.

Boardroom Disruption As Chairman Stands Down And Gibson Moves In

SMART resigned in the last week of October 1989, after having enough of the takeover shenanigans and, as a direct result of Bennison being voted on to the board, Boyes stepped up to the role of acting chairman.

A 3-0 home win over Wrexham on November 4 was merely a blip in a dire run – in the following Associate Members Cup game at York, Pools were trounced 7-1, a game which Moncur decreed his 'worst moment in football'.

However, there was an improvement in the following game. Pools went to Aldershot and only lost 6-1.

Things were coming to a head in the boardroom. Gibson paid £200,000 for the privilege of bailing the Club out and being able to sit at the head of the table.

He decided his first job should be to persuade Moncur, on the verge of quitting, to stay. Bennison resigned his role as director and took his £20,000 with him.

Pools were knocked out of the FA Cup in the first round, albeit unluckily to two penalties, by Huddersfield.

With even more bit part players thrown into the mix like Jade Sinclair and Paul Williams, and with Trewick released after a month and McEwan away to Boston, the Club was in a perilous state.

Manager Moncur Finally Steps Aside

LOSING 3-1 Chesterfield was the final straw for Moncur and he finally resigned two days later on Monday, November 27.

Pools were 24th, with nine points from 17 games, had scored only 16 and conceded 46 times.

Despite long-standing calls for his exit, Moncur stated he was committed to the Club which is why he never left earlier. His summer business hardly endeared him to supporters, and, while it is feasible that the boardroom struggle left him in place longer than he should

Garry Gibson chats with Pop Robson and Bobby Moncur in February 1990

have been, his record in charge speaks for itself – the Club had been bottom all season.

In 61 games in charge, Pools won only 14, scoring 65 times and conceding precisely twice as many.

Robson And Craggs Installed As Five Fans Turn Up For Game

POP Robson and John Craggs were installed as joint caretaker managers. They were in charge for a defeat in the Leyland DAF cup at Rotherham – a game in which Pools fans showed so little interest that only five paid through the gate.

Chairman Gibson Makes Crucial Appointment

WITH the likes of Kenny Wharton, Tommy Cassidy, Cyril Knowles and Malcolm Allison in the running for the job, Robson and Craggs lasted just two games.

On December 13, chairman Gibson made an appointment which he could not afford to get wrong. Cyril Knowles was installed as manager.

The former Tottenham defender had already had decent spells at this level in charge of Darlington and Torquay and it was seen as an astute move by Gibson.

Two defeats in December saw Knowles dip into the transfer market and he made three significant signings – Ian Bennyworth and Paul

Olsson from Scarborough and Steve Tupling from Cardiff joined the ranks. The latter had played under Knowles at Torquay.

He quickly decided that Moverley was not up to the job, citing he 'could tell he wasn't a keeper by the way he walked' and brought in Jason Priestley from Carlisle as the fifth custodian of the season.

Knowles Begins To Mould His Squad

COME Christmas, Pools remained at the bottom, had played 19 games and had only nine points on the board. Colchester were only one point above.

Boxing Day saw a clash with struggling Scarborough. The new-look side was Priestley, Nobbs, Smith, Bennyworth, McKinnon, Tinkler, Olsson, Tupling, Dalton, Baker, Allon.

Only Tinkler, Baker and McKinnon remained from the opening match of the season.

The highest crowd for exactly two years – 3,698 – celebrated a 4-1 win with Smith, Baker, an own goal from Chris Kamara and a strike from former Scarborough man Bennyworth bringing much-needed relief.

Four days later they were at it again and, after putting four past Grimsby, the side had finally dragged themselves off the foot of the table, swopping places with Colchester.

After 21 games Pools had 15 points and had won only four games, all at home, scoring just 27 goals with eight of them coming in the last

Pop Robson

Paul Dalton

two. Thirty six players had already been used, the latest of these being former Middlesbrough and Darlington striker Garry McDonald, a substitute in the Grimsby game.

Pools started 1990 with a huge game – a January 1 clash at Colchester. Hutchison, who had dropped to the bench recently, didn't turn up to travel and was sacked for his indiscipline. After much soul-searching the talented teenager was reinstated, given a second chance to succeed.

Colchester won 3-1, Pools were back at the bottom and they won only once in January when goals from Mick Smith and a sharp-looking Joe Allon saw off Halifax.

Pools Battle Against Relegation At Start Of New Decade

BY the end of the month they had risen off the bottom again and Wrexham took their place on 19 points with Pools and Colchester tied on 20.

Knowles terminated the contracts of several players – Carr, Moverley, Stokes and Doig.

The latter had signed under much publicity from Leeds for £10,000, but failed to live up to expectations. He blamed previous manager Bird for stating that he would deliver more than he could. Also going were bit part players Lamb, Williams, Mark Robson and Paddy Atkinson.

Pools climbed all the way to third bottom in February when a 2-0 win in a re-arranged game at London Road shocked play-off hopefuls Peterborough.

They then pulled six points clear of Wrexham with an outstanding 5-0 win over Stockport at the Vic which included four goals from Baker, one of which was a memorable 25-yard overhead kick.

The football was gritty rather than pretty, but when on song they were a finely tuned, well-drilled outfit at home.

Pools would often struggle in the first half, before a half-time blast from Knowles saw them raise their game and come out on fire for the second period. They wouldn't have dared return to the dressing room without an improvement.

Pools suffered 4-1 defeats to Hereford and Lincoln, but a 2-1 win over Rochdale at the Vic saw Pools reinstate their six-point gap over the Welsh outfit.

The following game on March 17 was Pools' first at Scunthorpe United's new home, Glanford Park. The only goal came from winger Paul Dalton and his name became the first to appear as a scorer on the electronic scoreboard

after the Irons' move from the Old Show Ground.

Making his debut for Pools was much-travelled keeper Barry Siddall, who Knowles had persuaded to join and replace the impressive Priestley, who had been recalled by Carlisle.

The Scunthorpe game was in the middle of a seven-game unbeaten run with Allon, Baker and Dalton to the fore.

The next three games were all defeats, including a crucial one to Colchester at the Vic and while safety was in sight, there was some work to be done.

On April 21 the visitors to the Vic were Maidstone – Pools reversed the 4-2 scoreline they were on the receiving end of in December.

This result put Knowles' charges eight points clear of Colchester and it wasn't until a home win over Aldershot in the penultimate game of the campaign that they were safe from the drop. The Essex outfit were confined to the Conference, replaced by Darlington who had won the GM Vauxhall Conference.

Pools ended in 19th , 12 points clear of the drop.

Allon netted 17 league goals, with Baker chipping in with 15 and Dalton 11.

Knowles had certainly made his immediate mark and, if it wasn't for his hardline management, there's every chance Pools would have dropped out of the Football League.

After ringing the changes during the season, summer moves were rare. Tony Barras and Stephen Plaskett left, defender Andy Davies arrived from Torquay and experienced goalkeeper Brian Cox was signed.

Steve Tupling

Chapter 11

1990s

1990-91

FOR the new campaign Knowles needed a new keeper, and another defender. He got experienced Brian Cox in goal and centre half Andy Davies to fill the breach.

Pools were well catered for up front with Allon and Baker, along with promising youth team player Steve Fletcher and the now-forgiven Hutchison who returned to the fold.

Leaving were Tony Barras, Grayson, who retired due to his knee injury, and Plaskett, who had only played in around 20 games over the last two seasons, signed for Gateshead. Jade Sinclair, David Stokle and Phil Wilson also never figured again.

The start of the season saw Pools travel to Chesterfield twice in the opening four days, first in the league and then in the League Cup. Knowles led his side to two victories.

The first encounter was on August 25 and Pools took to the field in glorious sunshine as follows – Brian Cox, Paul Olsson, Rob McKinnon, John Tinkler, Mick Smith, Ian Bennyworth, Joe Allon, Steve Tupling, Paul Baker, Steve Fletcher and Paul Dalton. Brian Honour made a substitute appearance, after putting an end to his knee problems.

Pools started the season on a high note, winning 3-2 in an exhilarating contest with the scorers Tupling, Baker and debutant Fletcher.

Pools were 3-0 up before coming under pressure and only the heroics of Cox, who made a fine finger-tip save at the death, preserved the lead.

Pools followed this up by winning the first leg of the cup tie 2-1 thanks to Allon and Honour.

Brian Cox in September 1990

Gazza On Show At The Vic In League Cup

DEFEATS to Cardiff and Gillingham were followed by a draw in the second leg of the League Cup, a game in which Pools were so desperate for defensive cover that they signed

Andy Harbron, 35, from Billingham Synthonia on a non-contract basis.

The second leg had been postponed because of an injury and illness crisis at Chesterfield and, by the time the game took place, the reward for victory was known – a tie against Tottenham Hotspur, who, in the months after England's 1990 World Cup heroics, included Paul Gascoigne and Gary Lineker.

Pools made it through to the second round for the first time in eight years thanks to goals from Allon and Baker in a 2-2 draw.

Gazza-mania was taking a hold in town and demand for tickets was great.

Pools introduced a voucher system and fans needed to attend the home game with Rochdale to give them priority, even though the Spurs home tie was three weeks away.

Making his debut in the Rochdale game was experienced John MacPhail. The 34-year-old Scotsman moved from Sunderland, after making a start on the opening day of the season in the first division.

However, his debut didn't go to plan as, in front of 5,725 – a bumper gate with one eye on Spurs – he netted an own goal in a 2-2 draw.

With Pools preparing for the trip to White Hart Lane with a defeat at Carlisle, just under 20,000 saw Pools hammered 5-0 by Spurs.

Backed by in excess of 2,000 fans, Pools were without MacPhail, while Honour and Hutchison were on the bench.

The Spurs team included seven internationals including Lineker and Gascoigne. They did the damage at White Hart Lane, with Lineker netting once, and Gascoigne grabbing four goals.

Pools keeper Cox had the satisfaction of saving a Lineker penalty – after the striker had

Don Hutchison

been lethal from the spot in Italia 90.

For the return leg, Pools warmed up with successive 1-0 home wins over Aldershot and Maidstone, moving them up to 15th.

Hutchison and Honour returned and Pools had more impetus about them. The Spurs team for the second leg was not full strength and even included in goal former Pools loanee Kevin Dearden. The rest of the squad were household names though – Sedgley, Howells, Mabbutt, Walsh and Samways to name but few.

A keen crowd of 9,631 turned up to see Pools compete well in a game which former bad boy Hutchison put in a virtuoso performance and stole the show. Pools lost 2-1,

Joe Allon and Don Hutchison pictured alongside Gary Mabbutt and Paul Gascoigne during the game with Tottenham Hotspur in September 1990

Frank Reid/Hartlepool Mail

Hartlepool United Line-Up 1990 – 91. Back row: Steve Fletcher, Paul Baker, Chris Berryman, Rob McKinnon, Ian Bennyworth Middle row: Jon Craggs (coach), Garry MacDonald, Mick Smith, Keith Nobbs, Alan Lamb, Gary Henderson (physio), Ian Dunbar, Andy Davies, Steve Tupling, Kenny Davies, Bryan Robson (coach). Front row: Paul Olsson, John Tinkler, Joe Allon, Cyril Knowles (manager), Paul Dalton, Brian Honour and Don Hutchison

with the goal coming from Dalton, who struck from the edge of the penalty area.

There was no Lineker, and Gascoigne only made a brief appearance from the bench, after spending time warming up with a posse of mesmerised youngsters on the touchline.

A couple of days later Pools lost at York, the final appearance for striker Garry Macdonald, who was forced to quit with a persistent back problem.

Form wasn't great, but eight points from a possible 15 saw them move into tenth place, before a 3-2 defeat at Northampton saw them slip to 14th ahead of a visit to Feethams to face Darlington, who were back in the Football League after a year in the GM Vauxhall Conference.

Pools' rivals had come back in form and were standing in fourth place. But the visitors were made of strong stuff and the difference was MacPhail. He marshalled the defence with calm authority.

With the reliable Nobbs employed at right back and Brian Cox confident with such a unit in front of him, they weren't going to crumble at Feethams. The left back was Rob McKinnon, a crowd hero, fast and hard in the tackle and with great energy up and down the wing, his link up play with Dalton was worth the entrance fee alone. Never mind the rest of the squad. This was some defence.

Darlington's No 9 John Borthwick spent so much time in MacPhail's pocket that he was only found during the washing of the kit after the game! Darlington had a good unit with the

likes of 34-year-old hardman Mick Tait and ex-Pools man Toman in midfield, but they had no answer to Joe Allon whose direct running frustrated skipper Kevan Smith all game.

Allon got the winning goal, cleverly lifting the ball over keeper Mark Prudhoe and tapping in, to send the ranks of jubilant Pools fans in the 5,311 crowd home happy.

The only downside was the loss of Nobbs,

John MacPhail

Keith Nobbs

who suffered a broken jaw when Quakers' midfielder Steve Mardenborough attempted an overhead kick and only managed to connect with Nobbs' face. Legend has it that Nobbs was desperate to carry on and prove his worth in such a game despite having a mouth missing a number of teeth.

The side now sat in 12th after 15 games, only three points off an automatic promotion place.

Gibson Advertises Hutchison's Services

POOLS were drawn at Runcorn in the FA Cup. The Merseyside outfit had finished third in the Conference last season and had qualified for the second round proper of the FA Cup in four of the last five years. Pools brushed them aside, or at least Allon did, as he notched all three goals in the 3-0 win.

The next game saw them creep into the top ten when Baker and Tinkler netted against Scarborough in a 2-0 win, seen by only 2,122 fans.

Despite things looking good on the pitch for once, things off the park were not so good, despite the recent investment by Garry Gibson.

Impressed by the performance of Hutchison against Spurs, Gibson made a video of his talents and sent it to some of the biggest clubs in the country.

The Scarborough game was his last for Pools

and after just 19 starts, he was sold to Liverpool.

It was a good decision indeed by Knowles to retain him on the books after the Colchester debacle the previous campaign as Pools agreed a fee of £300,000, with £175,000 paid up front and the rest to come in instalments.

Victories followed at Torquay (1-0) and at home to Lincoln (2-0) with Allon scoring all of the goals.

Sandwiched between was an exit from the second round of the FA Cup at Wigan. With the north of England gridlocked by snow the game was on and the team and fans fought their way cross country through the conditions to return home by-passing closed motorways on the end of a 2-0 loss.

With the weather putting paid to home games, Pools played three successive away matches between December 22 and January 12 and got three points only from a January 1 win at Halifax, courtesy of two goals from Allon, taking him to 15 for the season.

By February 5 he was up to 20 and home wins over Chesterfield, Stockport and Carlisle saw Pools up to sixth. Not only was Allon scoring goals for fun, Baker and Dalton had contributed 13 between them.

Then, as in countless seasons in the past, results went against them. A sloppy defeat at Scarborough was followed by a goalless draw at the Vic with Darlington, as former Pools keeper

Rob McKinnon, 1991

Manager Alan Murray

Mark Prudhoe played the game of his life. Shot after shot, header after header peppered his goal and he somehow kept it intact.

It was a valuable point for the Quakers as after the game they stood at the top of the division, eight points clear of Pools in seventh place.

Defeat at Scunthorpe was followed by a 0-0 draw at home to Torquay and, after a 3-1 reverse at Lincoln, Pools were down in eleventh and a staggering 16 points behind Darlington.

Unlike the seasons of 1980-81 and 1985-86 when Pools endured a poor spell and trailed off, there was justifiable cause why Pools had stuttered so badly on this occasion.

Inspirational manager Cyril Knowles had to step down in January due to serious health issues and Gibson made the somewhat unusual decision of appointing commercial manager Alan Murray as caretaker manager.

On the outside it seemed an odd appointment for a team doing so well but Murray had coached before at Middlesbrough and had enjoyed a playing career between 1970 and 1978, the bulk of it spent with Doncaster.

The team clearly took time to react to the shock news regarding Knowles and also adapt to having a new man in charge, but they seemed to pick up on March 12 when they hammered Aldershot at the Recreation Ground 5-1, thanks to a Dalton hat-trick.

It was followed by a crucial home defeat to Blackpool, who before the game were only one point ahead of Pools and in a play-off place. Rob McKinnon netted Pools goal amid talk of interest from Leeds and Aston Villa.

All Eyes On Promotion

THERE were 14 games to go and if Pools could gain some momentum they were in with a chance of a play-off spot, as they sat just two points away from the zone.

After just one win in seven games, the squad dug deep, drank from the bottle marked never say die and washed it down with a chaser of momentum.

On March 23 Pools won 4-1 at Maidstone when an inspired performance from Brian Honour tore the Kent team apart, with his two individual efforts straight from the book of great goals.

It was followed three days later with two Allon goals seeing Walsall off, before Pools enjoyed a very Good Friday.

Another pair from the blonde Geordie and one from Baker saw Pools take three points home from fourth placed Stockport, where a new loan signing from Middlesbrough, keeper Kevin Poole, made an inspirational debut.

Three games within a week, nine goals and nine points, Pools were sixth, in the play offs and a point off an automatic promotion place.

A hard fought 0-0 draw against fifth-placed Burnley saw no change, and a controversial last minute Allon winner at Walsall on April 6 still saw Pools in sixth.

With nine games to go, Pools were level on points with Stockport, but with a far inferior goal difference. In fourth spot lay Blackpool on 62 points, one ahead of Pools and above them were Northampton and Peterborough both on 65 points and 38 games, all behind runaway leaders Darlington on 72 points.

Talk was now of automatic promotion and, between April 9 and 20, Pools had four successive home games crammed in. April 9 – Scunthorpe, 2-0 (Dalton and Baker), now up to fifth; April 13 – Halifax, 2-1 (Baker and Allon), up to fourth; April 16 – Doncaster, 1-1 (MacPhail), still fourth; April 20 – Wrexham, 2-1 (Allon and Baker), still fourth and two points clear of fifth-placed Blackpool.

Despite promotion being a real possibility for only the second time, the Wrexham game was watched by barely over 3,000 fans.

Away draws at Rochdale – when over half the 1,686 gate were from Hartlepool – and Peterborough saw them maintain fourth place.

A midweek win over Gillingham on the last day of April saw Pools up to third and with two

Joe Allon receives his North East Footballer of the Year Award from Graham Taylor in 1990/91

games remaining they were with a chance of winning the title, now just four points behind Darlington.

Just as back in 1968 when they first got promoted, Pools last away game was a lengthy one.

Not Swansea this time, but Hereford United. Edgar Street was never the happiest of hunting grounds for Pools and in 13 visits since Hereford joined the Football League in 1972, they had never won.

Hundreds made early morning starts and were treated to a fine display. Pools oozed style and goals from Baker and a pair from the classy Dalton put them on the edge of promotion.

They entered the final game of the season at home to Northampton on May 11, 1991 in third place, with a multitude of different outcomes on the cards.

Pools were one point behind Darlington and tied on 79 points with Stockport. Blackpool, Peterborough and Burnley were all on 76 points, all with a chance of promotion and all with a similar or better goal difference to Pools. Victory was essential.

Northampton, who had been in the promotion battle all season and had spent several weeks on top, had faded in the past month and were now only in with an outside chance of a play-off spot.

Pools, roared on by an expectant 6,957 recorded crowd scored three divine goals through the terrific trio of Allon, Baker and Dalton.

Dalton scored first, another individual effort to add to his collection and calm the nerves.

But Trevor Quow gave the Bovril a bitter taste at half-time, squaring the scoreline. There was no need to worry, however, as Baker's volley from 20 yards looped into the Town End net and Allon put the seal on victory, stooping to head home.

At the end of the game euphoric fans streamed on to the pitch and held the players aloft as the news came through that Darlington had won, as had Stockport, putting Pools up in third place. Peterborough snatched fourth place off the unfortunate Blackpool.

Top scorer for the season was Allon who tied Billy Robinson's tally of 28 league goals, but he ended up with a record 35 in all competitions and was crowned the North-East Footballer of the Year for his efforts.

Despite Allon's goals, the force of Baker, the skills of McKinnon and Dalton, and the grit and hard work from the likes of Nobbs, the player of the year award went to the mercurial Honour.

The local hero had recovered from a career threatening injury to play a substantial role in one of the greatest seasons in the Club's history.

"We expected to be in the play-offs, so going up automatically is a bonus," admitted caretaker boss Murray. "And you can't take it away from us – it's down in history."

It was hoped that promotion would put a smile on the face and offer some hope for the now gravely ill and absent Cyril Knowles.

Murray had done a great job in taking the team to fourth spot, but this was the team that Cyril built.

Paul Dalton opens the scoring against Northampton as Pools head for promotion

1991-92

Division 3

POOLS had been a thoroughly entertaining side during the latter half of the previous season, with their 14-game unbeaten charge leading them into a new division.

Scoring 35 goals was no mean feat and it came as no surprise when Allon followed Hutchison onto bigger things. After a mooted move to Middlesbrough fell through, he signed for Chelsea for a Club record £300,000.

Goalkeeper Brian Cox had been ousted by Poole, and he left to join Buxton of the Northern Premier League, replaced by the vastly experienced Martin Hodge who arrived from Leicester.

Other players leaving included bit-part players Kenny Davies and Ian Dunbar.

In addition to Hodge, Murray brought in Darlington youth player Nicky Southall and the experienced former Manchester United and Northern Ireland international David McCreery, who signed from Scottish side Hearts.

Murray had been unable to invest any of Allon's fee in a new forward and for the start of the season he had to rely on the loan services of Sunderland's highly-rated David Rush.

The first game of Pools second season out of the bottom flight, saw them face the long trek to Torquay United on August 17. In the middle

Fans invade the pitch to celebrate promotion to Division 3

McCreery, pictured with Eddie Kyle, physio Gary Henderson and manager Alan Murray after signing

of a glorious summer around 500 Pools fans made the journey in party mood – but it was a wasted one as Pools returned on the back of a 3-1 loss.

The first home game of the campaign was a single goal victory over Bury in the League Cup followed by a league game against Reading.

The Royals were expected to prove a stern test, but just 2,858 fans saw Pools win 2-0 courtesy of goals from Baker and Olsson. A 2-2 draw at Bury in the second leg of the League Cup presented a second round tie against Crystal Palace.

Sad News Hits The Vic

TRAUMATIC news arrived as Pools prepared for a game at Bradford City on the last day of August. Cyril Knowles had passed away, aged just 47.

Cyril was idolised for the hard work he had put in until he was forced away from the game he loved in February. The entire Valley Parade crowd of 5,872 paid tribute to Knowles with an exemplary minute long silence and the away support of around 700 paid tribute, with a constant chant of "Cyril Knowles' Blue and White Army''.

The seemingly irrelevant result saw Pools draw 1-1.

In the run up to the Palace tie, Pools form was not too bad and they played a close game at Stoke, losing 3-2, before embarrassing fallen giants Birmingham City, when Paul Baker's sixth goal of the season was enough to earn three points and move them into the top half of the table.

As Palace visited, 6,697 saw a Brian Honour volley earn a 1-1 draw against a mainly second string side.

But there was to be no upset as Palace put out their first XI in the return leg – fielding the team who had finished third in the first division last season. They also included new £1.6m recruit Marco Gabbiadini, the older and somewhat more talented brother of Pools striker Ricardo.

There was to be no surprise as Pools lost 6-1.

No win in five games in the league followed. The low point was a 4-0 Saturday lunchtime reverse at Feethams, after which manager Murray questioned his side's "moral courage". It was a turning point for Murray, who never played Bennyworth again. Pools dropped to 19th place and were seemingly set for a season of struggle.

November 9th saw an end to this run with

A minute's silence is held for Cyril Knowles prior to the game at Valley Parade

victory over Fulham at the Vic, followed by a 3-2 win over Shrewsbury in the first round of the FA Cup.

The next Saturday saw Pools head to the Welsh border again and play the Shrews. Sporting a rarely seen silver away strip, some accurate shooting from Olsson saw Pools win 4-1.

Local Derby In The FA Cup

MURRAY'S men were soon to face Darlington in the second round of the FA Cup at Feethams, but the game was postponed. Back in action at Deepdale on December 14, they repeated their impressive performance at Shrewsbury, recording a first win at Preston and on a plastic pitch.

When the FA Cup tie was played, Pools gained swift revenge for their league humiliation, seeing off Darlington 2-1.

Although the Quakers scored through Toman, United won comfortably with spectacular strikes by Honour and Dalton to earn a third round tie at Ipswich Town.

Pools remained unbeaten in another three December games taking the run to nine and elevating them to eighth place.

The New Year started with defeat at Brentford and three days later 1,500 Pools fans headed for Portman Road. A Baker volley secured a deserved 1-1 draw, but the replay comfortably went the way of Ipswich through goals from Jason Dozzell and Simon Milton.

February brought a bad run – Pools were knocked out of the Associate Members Cup by Stockport and won just two out of seven league games.

Cyril Knowles

Pools were struggling without Rob McKinnon, veteran of almost 300 appearances, who had moved to Motherwell after the first Ipswich game for £150,000.

McKinnon's powerful play had brought him to the attention of many clubs. He had refused a move to Reading in the past and also had a fruitless trial at Manchester United in the summer of 1991.

Murray signed Paul Cross, a steady left back who had spent eight years at Barnsley. At the end of February, after two goals in five games

Andy Saville on his debut v Darlington

Murray made a permanent signing – striker Lennie Johnrose for £50,000 from Blackburn Rovers.

After four games without a goal, Baker netted in a 1-0 win at Stockport on March 6, a game which was to be his last for the Club as he followed McKinnon to Motherwell.

His replacement soon arrived, as Murray went back to Barnsley to sign Andy Saville for £60,000.

He couldn't have made a better debut. Playing against a Darlington team struggling at the foot of the table, Saville scored on his debut making him an instant hit.

But while celebrating his success that night he broke an arm, forcing him out for the season.

Pools ended the campaign in a more than respectable 11th place with 65 points, some 28 ahead of bottom placed Darlington and 17 behind champions Brentford.

Following the loss of top scorer Allon and the death of Knowles, it could have been a season of struggle. Instead, Murray ensured it was quite the opposite, as his new-look side more than held their own.

Bennyworth returned to Scarborough and stylish midfielder Dalton, who had finished joint top scorer with Baker, made the move to Plymouth Argyle for a fee of £275,000. Defender Ryan Cross arrived as a makeweight in the deal.

Also heading to the south coast was youngster Steve Fletcher, who made a surprise move to Bournemouth for £30,000. Midfielders Tinkler and Tupling went to Walsall and Darlington respectively. Defender Mick Smith

hung up his boots and moved onto the coaching staff.

Honour, MacPhail, Nobbs and Olsson were now the only four players left from the promotion season.

Murray pulled off something of a coup when he signed Coventry midfielder Dean Emerson, who had spent five seasons with the Sky Blues in the top flight. The experienced Mick Tait arrived from Darlington, and much was expected of winger John Gallacher from Newcastle.

1992/93

Pools In Division Two – Without Promotion!

POOLS had consolidated at a higher level, but overnight they changed divisions, now being part of the newly-named second division. In a controversial move the old first division was rebranded the Premiership.

Football was seemingly past the dark days of the hooligans and the tragedies of the 1980s, with Bradford, Heysel and Hillsborough still fresh. The powers that be were attempting to rise from the ashes with a hyped-up new sport – all-seater, all glamour and family orientated, with no drinking in view of the pitch.

Dean Emmerson in action

Honour In Spat With Palmer And Murray Replaced

A decent start to the season, League Cup wins over Halifax and no defeats in the first six league games, saw Pools in third by mid-September.

A first leg 3-0 reverse in the second round of the League Cup at Sheffield Wednesday didn't slow Pools down and wins at Preston and over Blackpool saw them rise to second place behind West Brom – the highest position ever achieved.

The second leg of the League Cup saw Pools draw 2-2 with Wednesday at the Vic and lose out on aggregate. The game was best remembered for the childish baiting of Honour by the ungamely England cap, Carlton Palmer. He is alleged to have ridiculed Honour and Pools, while asking what Honour was doing in the summer while Palmer was playing (and failing miserably) for England in the European Championships in Sweden.

Victory at Bolton on October 10 saw Pools in second place on goal difference. They won just one more in five, but by the time the first round of the FA Cup came round they stood in eighth place. Pools won 2-1 at Doncaster, and in the second round triumphed over Southport courtesy of a Saville hat-trick, giving Pools a home draw against Crystal Palace.

United warmed up for the tie with wins over Hull and at Fulham and took on Palace on January 2, 1993.

Pools fielded Steve Jones in goal as first choice Hodge refused to train over rumours that he hadn't been paid his signing on fee. The youngster played the finest game of his short career.

After chances were missed and saved at both ends, with minutes remaining Richard Shaw upended Southall in the box and Saville smashed home the spot kick.

Palace and manager Steve Coppell were utterly furious with the penalty award, as Pools made it through to the fourth round for the second time in four years.

That, however, was as good as it got.

Pools Wound Up In The High Court

P OOLS season was to collapse as their future was again thrown into serious doubt.

Just three days before the trip to Bramall Lane to take on Sheffield United, Hartlepool United Football Club was wound up in the High Court in London.

The Club chairman, Garry Gibson, was caught out by the news and a frantic period

Mick Tait pictured in August 1992

ensued to ensure the Club could continue operating.

With the attendance and gate receipts taking on more importance than the game, almost 4,000 Pools fans embarked on Bramall Lane. "You'll never wind us up" was the defiant chant of the day.

An Alan Cork goal proved the difference, but Pools, without classy midfielder Emerson who fractured a cheekbone the previous week, couldn't find a goal to secure a financially welcome replay.

Before the Palace game and the subsequent troubles, Pools were comfortably in fourth spot. Clearly affected by events, Pools went an appalling run of 13 games without scoring a goal, dropping to 16th and seeing the crowds at the Vic drop to under 2,000.

A new record of 20 winless games was established and it took until April 5 to end the rot when a Honour goal sealed victory over Plymouth, their first win since 28th December.

The players celebrate after beating Crystal Palace

Viv Busby Named Manager

NINE games into the run, Murray was replaced by former Sunderland coach Viv Busby. He had experience as youth team coach at York.

United had to wait five games under his tutelage before they notched a goal, by Saville at Bloomfield Road, Blackpool ending the embarrassing run of 1,227 minutes without a strike.

Saville was soon sold to Birmingham in a cut price deal.

With four games of the season to go, Pools were one place and one point off the relegation zone. Form under Busby was appalling, the last four games were crucial and the prospects were bleak – away to table toppers Stoke, away to Swansea, home to Brighton and away to Bradford, all the latter three fighting for a play-off place.

The game at Stoke was in front of 17,331 fans all ready for the home banker. After Johnrose netted for Pools in the seventh minute, the leaders piled on the pressure but Pools stood firm to record the most unlikely of victories.

One game gone and Pools were up to 18th, A week later they travelled to Swansea, lost 3-0 and were fifth bottom, with three of the teams below having a game in hand.

The crucial game was at home to Brighton and a 2-0 victory, thanks to second half goals in a seven minute spell from Southall and Nicky Peverell, saw Pools safe from relegation.

Keeper Hodge had been through enough and moved to Rochdale. Surprisingly he was the only major departure. The squad was added to with the signings of former Sunderland keeper Tim Carter and ex-Dundee forward Colin West.

There was a reportedly promising crop of youngsters on the books and it was expected that the likes of Scott Garrett, Stephen Halliday, Denny Ingram, Chris Lynch and Antony Skedd would all have roles to play in the forthcoming campaign.

1993-94

IN front of just over 2,500 fans, the season commenced with a home defeat to Fulham and followed with 1-1 draws at Brighton and at the Vic against Bournemouth.

John Gallagher scored at Brighton, but he made his final appearance the following week and was on his way back to Scotland after an injury ravaged spell.

Andy Saville brings to an end 1227 minutes without a goal for Pools with his strike at Blackpool

Saville celebrates his goal against Blackpool

Nicky Southall takes on Sheffield United's Brian Gayle

Houchen Returns To Pools

AFTER beating Stockport over two legs in the League Cup, Pools got a little run going winning three in four with Nicky Southall grabbing a couple of goals.

The second round of the League Cup saw no glamour tie this time – Pools were drawn against Grimsby and they lost both legs. Busby's Boys also lost five in a row in the league, dropping them to 20th place.

Denny Ingram at training in 1993

The season never improved. Busby's managerial prowess was questioned by all and his record stood fairly low in the rankings.

He had managed to persuade Keith Houchen to return at the age of 33. The striker had enjoyed a great time during his spell away from the Vic and had played at the top level. He arrived from Port Vale.

Busby's Managerial Reign Comes To An End

BY the first round of the FA Cup on November 13, Pools had won just one in ten, had been knocked out of the group section of the AMC and were in no form to face a trip to non-league Macclesfield Town. The Conference outfit easily beat an out of sorts Pools team 2-0, the result not helped by the dismissal of Paul Olsson.

Pools were in crisis. Midfield general Dean Emerson returned to Stockport after failing to ignite the side as he had the previous season. Paul Cross left, making the shortest of moves to Darlington. After a defeat by Wrexham at the Vic the following Saturday, common sense prevailed and chairman Gibson finally dismissed Busby. His 42 games at the helm had produced only nine wins.

New Man At The Helm For Pools And Relegation

THE board appointed the vastly experienced John MacPhail as manager, but he had to do the best he could with the bedraggled players already at his disposal. Several had already left to ease the wage bill and both Lennie Johnrose and Ryan Cross moved to Bury before the month was out, with keeper Tim Carter heading to Millwall.

Pools were in the bottom four and stayed

John MacPhail was
appointed Manager

there. It was a terrible campaign. MacPhail's team did not have the financial backing that his predecessors had, but from his appointment until March 19, Pools won just once in 16. Home crowds were once again back to sub-2,000.

With ten games remaining they stood 15 points from safety. MacPhail dropped himself and placed young Ian McGuckin into the centre of defence alongside Gilchrist, who was one of the few players to impress.

There was a sign of life in March, when a three game run at the Vic saw Cardiff, Burnley and Swansea all beaten.

Houchen scored in each game and helped bridge the gap to ten points. However, the revival was over as soon as it started. A must win game at Huddersfield was drawn and followed by a home defeat to Hull. The next game confirmed their relegation as Pools seemingly gave up and shipped seven goals at Rotherham.

Hammering For Pools At The Vic

JUST 1,409 turned up to see Pools beat Bristol Rovers in their next match at the Vic and the season ended on a particularly embarrassing note when MacPhail's side recorded their highest ever home defeat.

Promotion-chasing Plymouth hammered Pools 8-1, with the last goal in a sorry season netted by Nicky Peverell. Southall's nine made him top scorer and the average attendance had dropped from 3,201 in 1991-92 to a mere 2,071.

The financial problems dug deep, players were not always paid and there was no investment in the playing squad. Amid the troubles, Pools dropped from being second top to relegation in 18 months. The fans, those that had not turned their back in disgust, clamoured for Gibson to go.

And boardroom changes were afoot.

Gibson Era Comes To A Welcome End

HARTLEPOOL businessman Harold Hornsey, who had tried to buy the Club at least twice in the past, this time got his wish after a somewhat drawn out process of removing Gibson.

He finally managed it in June 1994. Gibson may have been in the big seat (and it had to be big as he stood at six foot six inches) during promotion, but his appointment of Busby, the subsequent decline and his failure to ensure that the bills were paid had seen his departure.

Hornsey was a self-made man on the back of several hardware and electrical retail outlets and knew the job at Pools was never going to be resolved overnight. He was prepared to work at it and turn around the fortunes.

But new blood was needed, particularly in midfield after a servant of nearly 200 games, Olsson, made the move to Darlington.

1994-1997 – The Hornsey Years

1994-95

MACPHAIL remained in charge for the new season and Hornsey dug deep to allow the manager scope to introduce several new players.

He had done well to get hold of former Portsmouth and Millwall stopper Brian Horne, a move which would allow Jones to be taken out of the firing line.

Added to the midfield was Jason Ainsley, a 24-year-old rated as one of the best midfielders outside the professional game, who joined from Spennymoor. One-time Newcastle prospect Scott Sloan also moved in.

The opening game of the campaign saw a drab scoreless draw at Gillingham, who included one-time Pools hero Paul Baker.

Beaten 2-0 at Bury in the first round of the League Cup, Pools had to contend with Darlington as the opening home encounter and 3,000 saw a Chris Lynch drive seal the points.

Buoyed by victory, Pools put five past Bury in the second leg of the League Cup match to earn a fantasy football tie against Arsenal.

Honour Retires And MacPhail Is Fired

MISSING from the Darlington game and second Bury test was Brian Honour. His knee had taken one knock too many and he was forced to call it a day, after just under 400

Garry Gibson (right) smiles in spite of a chorus of boos as he takes his seat

Lenny Johnrose and John MacPhail show off the new home and away kits with manager Viv Busby and Derek Andrew, MD of Camerons

Harold Hornsey at Victoria Park

first team appearances. He was the last remaining player from Murray's promotion side.

League defeats at Bury and at home to Barnet and Chesterfield saw Pools looking rocky again and Hornsey made the bold decision to fire MacPhail and his assistant Alan Hay just five league games into the season.

Familiar Face Returns To Pools

HORNSEY brought David McCreery back to the Club. He had left in September 1992 to take over as Carlisle boss, but lasted only a season. The new player-manager knew a lot of

the younger players at the Vic and his experience was being called upon.

MacPhail admitted: "I was devastated when I was sacked. Although they retained me as a player, for some reason David McCreery refused to play me. Having to turn out for the reserves was demoralising.

"Because of the circumstances of my sacking, I sued the Club for unfair dismissal. I never had my day in court because, acting on solicitors' advice, I settled.

"Why did my one attempt at management fail to work out? Basically because the players were not always being paid by the then chairman (Gibson). How can the players be totally committed if they are not sure of their wages?

Hartlepool United Line-Up 1994 – 95. Back row: Nicky Southall, Phil Gilchrist, Keith Houchen, Steve Jones, Ian McGuckin, Brian Horne, Matty Hysenm Jason Ainsley, Paul Thompson, Gary Henderson (Physio); Front row: Scott Garrett, Chris Lynch, Denny Ingram, John MacPhail (Manager), Brian Honour, Alan Hay (Assistant Manager), Antony Skedd, Stephen Halliday, Keith Oliver.

New Manager David McCreery with skipper Phil Gilchrist

I can recall countless occasions when the lads met to decide if they were going to play on the Saturday.

"I would have to ask the chairman if they were going to receive their money. Sometimes the answer was yes, other times the money just was not there.

"We never found where the money was going. All I do know is this situation made my job virtually impossible.

"There was no way of bringing in new players and some of them were earning as little as £70 a week. I tried to bring in David Moyes from Preston as my number two – we played together at Bristol City – but that fell through because we could only pay him £400 a week, half of what he was on at Preston.''

MacPhail left as a player in March 1995.

It took three games for McCreery's new side to get a win, doing so in the home game over Gillingham on September 17 when Houchen, 34, and Alan Walsh, 37, scored in a 2-0 victory.

Hartlepool-born Walsh was a record breaking scorer at Darlington in the early 80s, at one point putting four past Pools in April 1982. He had found his way to the Vic from Taunton Town after a distinguished spell with Bristol City and several other clubs, including a stint in Turkey.

Not long after turning up for a Sunday League game on the Rift House Recreation Ground, Walsh was up against Arsenal, holders of the European Cup Winners Cup.

Arsenal At The Vic In The League Cup

THE Gunners paid Pools the utmost respect and put out a full first XI, including many internationals and returning to the Vic in the heart of the Arsenal defence was Andy Linighan. Only 4,421 fans saw goals from Tony Adams, Alan Smith, Paul Merson and a pair from Ian Wright secure a 5-0 win. The return leg saw Pools put in a much better performance against an equally strong Arsenal side, losing just 2-0 in front of more than 20,000 at Highbury.

Just one win in October saw the side drop to 19th and another season of struggle beckoned.

In the FA Cup, Pools equalled their worst-ever defeat when they were stunned 6-0 at Port Vale.

McCreery let Walsh go, and signed another ex-Quaker and another left back, Mitch Cook, 33.

The following month was a touch better with a 2-1 win at Feethams through goals from Southall and Houchen, followed with a Houchen hat-trick in a 3-1 victory over Bury, a game in which he was also sent-off.

Reaching as high as 16th was a nice Christmas present for Hornsey, who was trying to balance the books on sub-2,000 crowds.

A fair gate of 3,854 turned out for the Boxing Day game with Carlisle. That was as good as it got – Pools lost 5-1.

It heralded the start of another slide and a 12-game winless run, ended when Southall netted a hat-trick against Colchester on March 11.

Jason Ainsley in October 1994

Stephen Halliday in action against Arsenal's Paul Davis and Ian Wright

The squad was strengthened with the signing of striker Damien Henderson and the loan arrival of defender Steve Holmes. Form picked up slightly but after defeat against Fulham on April 8, Pools were deep in trouble and in danger of the drop. Despite victory over Carlisle on April 17, a new manager was in charge in the shape of Houchen come April 20 – Pools' fifth boss in four years.

A senior player and coach under McCreery, he had endured an uneasy relationship with his boss.

Honour, Tait and Horner Join Coaching Team

IT came to something of a head when, on returning from a coaching course, Houchen discovered McCreery had invited former Hearts coach Sandy Clark to the Club for a few days in an advisory role.

Houchen felt something was amiss when one of the players approached Clark to discover what the plans were for that day's training session.

Once it was over, Clark addressed the players: "You lot are the lowest of the low. You can't get any further down than this poxy little Club."

Houchen, proud of the Club where he made his name, was furious. He told McCreery what he thought of Clark's cameo and then told the Scot he was no longer welcome. Clark was not seen again.

Houchen's coaching staff had a more familiar feel – Brian Honour, Mick Tait and Billy Horner.

His first game in charge was a 4-0 win over Hereford and enough to see Pools safe. A final day hat-trick from Halliday in a 3-0 win over Mansfield saw Pools finish 18th, nine points clear of bottom side Exeter City who were not relegated as the ground of the Conference champions, Macclesfield, was not classed as being up to league standards.

1995-96

OUT of the signings made 12 months previous, only Horne had made any impression. He made himself a favourite with the fans with his whole-hearted displays, slightly marring his copy-book though with a sending off at Scarborough when a goalkeeper was used as a substitute for the first time with Jones entering the fray.

Ainsley didn't make the impression expected and moved overseas playing in Australia and Singapore. Sloan only scored twice, but was retained.

Winger Paul Daughtry went to Sweden after being involved in just 15 games. Youngster Scott Garrett had been involved for three seasons but had made just one sub outing last campaign and was off, alongside Paul Thompson, Archie Gourlay, Matty Hyson, Tony Skedd and Mark Sunley.

Ingram had been a regular and Halliday offered promise on occasion but was far from the finished article. His seven goals in 19 starts would put him in good stead.

Pools also lost the services of two of their better players. Defender Gilchrist moved on to Oxford for a much-needed £100,000 in February and the versatile Southall went to Grimsby for £70,000.

Added to the squad during the break were Port Vale's centre half Peter Billing, Tony Canham, a 35-year-old veteran of more than 400 midfield appearances for York, and Steve Howard, 19, who signed from Tow Law Town, on the recommendation of Middlesbrough coach Gordon McQueen.

The seemingly trouble spot of left back was filled with the signing of Sean McAuley from St Johnstone.

Houchen was far from impressed with Horne and even plumped for Jones for the first two games of the season, both ending in defeats.

Bruce Rioch's Arsenal Team At The Vic

HORNE returned for a draw at home to Exeter in the League and was between the sticks for the second leg of the League Cup tie against Scarborough, a game in which Ian McGuckin levelled the tie forcing extra time, and for the first time, Pools entered a penalty shoot out.

After four kicks each (Henderson, McAuley, Houchen and Halliday scored for Pools) the scores were tied at 4-4. Keeper Horne then buried his spot kick.

With the Seadogs pulling level, Keith Oliver saw his kick saved. Horne kept Pools in it by saving the ensuing kick, but Kelly matched him and saved Canham's effort.

However misses from Richard Lucas and Lee Thew, and conversions from Billing and Tait saw Pools through – and for the second year running they were rewarded with a tie against Arsenal.

By the time they played the Gunners at the Vic in the first leg, Pools had won just one of their eight opening games.

An Arsenal side again crammed with quality boasted new multi-million pound signing Dennis Bergkamp. The Dutchman had so far failed to score in England and was expected to break his duck against Pools – but it didn't happen.

Arsenal beat Pools 3-0, goals scored by Ian Wright and Tony Adams (2) and Pools' cause wasn't helped when keeper Horne was sent-off for handling outside the penalty area.

The game is remembered by many for Gunners' boss Bruce Rioch storming away from a pitchside interview after the game when the prowess of Bergkamp was called into question.

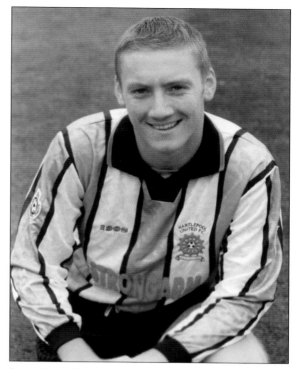
Steve Howard

There was no need to question it two weeks later. After breaking his duck in a Premier League game, Bergkamp netted two and Ian Wright grabbed a Highbury hat-trick, when young stopper Jones was on end of a 5-0 drubbing.

The second leg took place in the middle of an upturn in fortunes as Pools went on a run of three wins in four, propelling them to 14th, helped mainly by the goals of Howard and the form of Kenny Lowe, who left in summer 1985 and returned on loan from Birmingham via, Scarborough and Stoke, as well as a spell in Australia.

Allon Gets Back Into The Swing Of Things

HOWEVER the form was just temporary in another bad season and no win in four was hardly preparation for the FA Cup tie against Darlington at the Vic, a game the Quakers won 4-2. It came just weeks after an 8-0 drubbing at Crewe in the AMC – United's second heaviest defeat.

The return of former Pools hero Joe Allon had failed to reignite any spark in the squad. He had failed to become a permanent feature at Chelsea and signed for Brentford and spells followed at Southend, Port Vale and Lincoln before he returned to Pools in the middle of October for £50,000.

His goal in a 2-1 home reverse to Cambridge saw Pools stretch their winless run to eight,

Brian Horne in action against Darlington

placing them third bottom, six points ahead of Torquay.

Houchen and Halliday then came to life and started scoring, as did Allon. A run of just one loss in eight was promising, but too many draws pegged them back. By the middle of February they were still struggling, sitting fourth bottom but with a ten-point gap over Torquay.

The remainder of February and March can best be described as average, but the introduction of youth team forward Paul Conlon did breathe some life into things. By the end of March, Pools were up to 16th, safe with eight games remaining. Pools then won just one in the last eight and were back to playing in front of only the die-hard fans, with the lowest attendance that season being below 1,200.

The second game in the last eight was away to Gillingham. A struggling side witnessed a public falling out between keeper Horne and Houchen. The goalkeeper was substituted by Houchen on the spot during an on-field spat and the much-maligned Steve Jones was called off the bench to replace him.

It was the final straw for Houchen and the final game for Horne. "What is he doing in my dressing room?" asked Houchen. "When he took his kit off, it was revolting. He was an absolute slob."

Pools had used several loan keepers – Andy De Bont, Lance Key, Ben Roberts and Paul O'Connor – during the season as they tried to find an answer to their keeper problems. Jones was also released at the end of the season.

A final placing of 20th again offered no hope of achieving promotion. Chairman Hornsey was working hard behind the scenes to set the Club up as a business and ground improvements had transformed the Vic, but he wasn't being rewarded on the pitch nor backed through the turnstiles. It was unsure how long he could continue to bankroll the Club.

It looked like some money was on its way, as Halliday caught the eye of Sunderland. After training with the Wearside club, they were keen to sign him.

With the clubs unable to agree terms – Sunderland offered £50,000 – a Football League tribunal was called into action to set the fee.

They decided a deal worth £375, 000, including instalments and bonuses. It would be welcome money for Pools and Hornsey – but Sunderland boss Peter Reid refused to go ahead with the deal.

On leaving the hearing at the Football League HQ, he pulled out on the grounds that he didn't feel Halliday was worth that much.

1996-97

New Faces Arrive For Pools

FROM his office at the renamed Victoria Park, Houchen was busy during the close season and signed several players as he attractively reshaped his squad.

Liverpool reserve goalkeeper, Stephen Pears, formerly of Middlesbrough, joined – surely an end to the long-running number one problems.

Glen Davies, 20, moved after being released by Burnley and Houchen made three signings in midfield.

Mark Cooper, son of former England player Terry Cooper (who had almost joined Pools 18 years earlier), made the trek from Exeter City. Chris Beech, 21, joined from Blackpool and completing the threesome was David Clegg who had been released by Liverpool, with Anfield boss Kenny Dalglish labelling him the free transfer signing of the summer.

The new-look side made a good start and after three games stood top on goal difference.

Paul Conlon in April 1996

Micky Barron Joins Pools On Loan

AFTER being knocked out of the League Cup to Lincoln over two legs, Houchen wanted defensive reinforcements and brought in on loan Middlesbrough reserve team skipper Michael Barron.

He had caught the eye while playing for Boro's second string during their games which were played at the Vic.

Two weeks later and winger Kona Hislop, brother of Newcastle United's Trinidad and Tobago international keeper Shaka, signed.

Barron was part of a 1-0 win at Hereford on

Paul O'Connor was one of the loan keepers used by Pools in 1995/96

his debut, and a 2-0 win over Chester at the Vic thanks to Allon and Cooper's fifth of the season saw Pool rise to seventh spot by the end of September.

No win in October saw more tinkering. In came Adie Mike from Stockport for a fruitless loan spell and also a brief cameo from Madagascar-born trialist Alain Horace.

Pears also left and in his place Pools signed Paul O'Connor who had made one outing during a previous goalkeeping emergency. He joined on part-time terms as he continued to work for Black & Decker.

He made his second debut in a 3-2 home defeat to Brighton, a result which extended the winless run to eight, as Pools dropped to 23rd from 7th in just over a month.

Houchen's playing days had recently been ended by injury – and his days in the hot seat were over as well.

When the manager's dug-out was surrounded by demanding fans in the closing minutes of the Brighton game, Houchen walked away.

New Manager Named

IT was announced on November 4 that he had left by mutual consent, replaced by Mick Tait.

Tait opened his spell in charge with victory at Scarborough, with Pools showing four changes to the starting line up in a 4-2 triumph.

Under Tait, Pools were knocked out of the FA Cup by York City after a replay, and made a slight improvement, ending 1996 in 17th place.

January was a winless month, but a Cooper

Glen Davies, Mark Cooper, David Clegg, Chris Beech, Stephen Pears, Chris McDonald and Steve Tierney with Keith Houchen, July 1996

goal saw them do the double over Scarborough on February 1.

However, the following weekend they were thumped 5-0 at Brighton. Tait acted quickly and snapped up Russell Bradley on loan from Scunthorpe, who made his debut against Torquay.

His introduction did not help initially as their poor run continued and by March 22, Pools were bottom after losing at Fulham and had won just once in the last 14 games. Ageing former Middlesbrough midfielder Mark Proctor made his debut.

Transfer deadline day was a desperate scramble for Tait – he needed new signings who could breath some much-needed life into the squad, who were facing a relegation battle.

He had to sacrifice Sean McAuley, who had missed just one game in two consistent seasons, in a swap deal with Scunthorpe for 1991 promotion hero Paul Baker.

Scarborough full backs Richard Lucas and Darren Knowles were landed and Tait went to Morpeth Town to sign attacking midfielder Jon Cullen.

The biggest coup came when Manchester City manager Frank Clark allowed midfielder Michael Brown to move on loan. The 20-year-old had made 20 Premiership appearances and was about to help out his home-town Club in their hour of need.

All five made their debut in a 1-0 home win over Colchester on March 29. A defeat two days later at Mansfield was followed by a 3-1 win over Leyton Orient, courtesy of goals from Bradley, Baker and the unpredictable Halliday.

Pools stood second bottom, tied with Hereford and five points ahead of Brighton who had been docked two points for failing to control spectators.

They had four games left to play but a poor home defeat to play-off chasing Cambridge left them just two points above Brighton with the trickiest of fixtures next on the agenda – Darlington away.

The long standing foe were not having the best of seasons but were five points better off than Pools.

In another crucial derby Pools had to change their line-up after just six minutes when the increasingly influential Bradley was replaced by Denny Ingram.

Just two minutes later and Pools were in front. Brown struck home a gem of a free-kick from 20 yards to send the travelling fans into raptures. However, just when it looked as though Pools would be going into the break one up, Quakers equalised.

With time ticking by, Tait swapped Brown for Cullen and then played his joker, replacing Howard with Allon.

Deep into injury time, Allon increased his status from hero to legend. A corner by Proctor landed deep at the far post, Glen Davies headed it across goal and Allon's attempt to divert it in was blocked.

As he fell to the floor, an outstretched leg returned the ball towards goal and, from a prostrate position, Allon scored.

Cue wild celebrations. For the second time, Allon had scored the winning goal for Pools in front of Darlington's Tin Shed end.

Mick Tait was named Manager

Dedication

HE dedicated the goal and the win to chairman Hornsey, reward for his efforts in saving the Club and finding the funding for Tait to make some vital new signings in the closing weeks of the season.

Although the win didn't guarantee safety it was almost enough. Pools then pummelled Barnet at the Vic the following week with Allon grabbing a pair in a 4-0 win.

Pools ended 20th. Brighton escaped the drop on goal difference with Hereford United falling into the Conference to be replaced by Macclesfield Town, whose ground was now up to League standards.

1997-98

New Owners Arrive – IOR Era Begins

TAIT released the usual crop of youngsters but also a few first teamers moved on. Chairman Hornsey had taken the Club a long way without additional investment and, while he wished to be involved, he needed extra financial help.

Tait helped by trimming the wage bill.

David Clegg and Kona Hislop were freed. Ian McGuckin headed to Fulham for £50,000 and keeper Paul O'Connor decided to move to Bedlington Terriers and seek more secure employment away from the professional game.

Mark Proctor returned to the local leagues.

The only major signing was Middlesbrough defender Barron. After returning to the Teessiders after his loan spell, he was allowed to leave on a free transfer.

Once again Pools found themselves starting the season without a regular keeper and loan signings were the order of the day with Luton reserve Kelvin Davis starting the season at Exeter. He was soon recalled and replaced by Warren Dobson.

Steve Harper Joins On Loan

POOLS were knocked out of the League Cup by Tranmere, after which Tait contacted Newcastle United and obtained the services of reserve team keeper, Steve Harper. It was an impressive signing.

He made his debut in the home draw against Macclesfield on August 30, a game which marked the final outing for Allon. Last season's hero of Feethams was suffering from a long-standing knee problem.

His 35 goals in the promotion season earned a place in the record books and in folklore. His last – numbers 78 and 79 – goals came in the 3-2 win over Colchester in August.

League form in August and September offered optimism, as Pools lost just once.

But, while hard to beat, Pools couldn't turn draws into wins. Aided by the goals of the strong running Cullen, they had risen to seventh place.

Darren Knowles

INCREASED OIL RECOVERY Ltd

SEPTEMBER saw a big, surprising and welcome change as Hornsey's plea for financial assistance bore fruit, when Aberdeen-based company Increased Oil Recovery Ltd (IOR) became the new owners.

The company were little heard of, but were experts in their field of oil exportation and oil production, and Ken Hodcroft was appointed chairman with Hornsey remaining as a paid consultant and still being involved with the running of the Club.

Hornsey had spent much time steadying the Club after the Gibson debacle and the new owners weren't going to destroy his good work. They were to build on a steady platform.

October also saw just one defeat and some impressive performances from Harper and a rejuvenated Steve Howard, who was revelling in his new up front role.

IOR exploited their Norwegian contacts and pulled off a great coup for Pools when they persuaded Norwegian international midfielder Jan Ove Pederson to join.

The 28-year-old Brann Bergen player had been capped 17 times for his country. With the Norwegian season finished, he arrived in the North-East with the intention of getting some much-needed games under his belt to try and force his way into the Norwegian 1998 World Cup squad.

He settled instantly and his utter class shone in this league. He created so much space for other players, which Cullen exploited in particular.

More New Faces Brought To Club

DESPITE getting knocked out the FA Cup at home to Macclesfield in a game in which Pools were always under the cosh after Ingram was sent off after 20 minutes, they fared well in the league and stayed in the top ten.

November saw Harper return to Newcastle after a great contribution. Pools had agreed a deal to make his signing a permanent one but a new manager at St James Park saw that move thwarted and Harper was replaced at Pools by another Norwegian and another former Brann player – Martin Hollund.

Also joining was Ian Clark, a utility player from Doncaster, but midfielder Cooper soon departed.

With Pedersen pulling the strings, the good form continued and by January 3, Pools were sixth and in a play-off place on goal difference.

Two weeks later Cullen played his last game for Pools and was sold to Sheffield United for £250,000.

His departure affected performances, his goals from midfield were missed, and, after eight games without a win, Pools were out of the play-off picture, down in 14th place.

Pedersen had also left, in mid-February after the most impressive of cameos. His 21 appearances, and professionalism in moving across the North Sea, made a huge impression on everyone.

Without him, Pools were never the same and for all the effort of Tait and the team, the season didn't have the impact once promised.

The manager introduced new signings Craig Midgley and Argentinian Gus Di Lella. Midgley was signed from Bradford to replace Halliday, who had moved to Scottish outfit Motherwell.

Steve Harper in action for Pools

Martin Hollund in December 1997

Youngster Tommy Miller was brought into the side in the place of Pedersen and former Newcastle and Millwall winger Paul Stephenson arrived towards the end of the campaign.

Pools won just twice in the last 11 games and ended in a disappointing 17th position, 11 points short of the play-offs, but a huge 39 points above bottom placed Doncaster Rovers, who were heading to the Conference.

They drew a record-equalling 23 Football League games, the same number as Cardiff City that season.

The final game at Peterborough was overshadowed by the temporary departure of Tait, who refused to travel to the game amid rumours of a disagreement with the owners, which was incorrect. Coach Honour picked the side for the 0-0 draw, but Tait soon returned.

1998-99

AFTER a season of consolidation, could matters improve? A solid base offered a decent platform, but Tait needed to move things on a stage.

Glen Davies, Richard Lucas, Warren Dobson, Andy Elliott, Marc Nash and Paul Walton all departed.

Defender and captain Bradley was offered a new contract but chose to return to the Midlands and join non-league side Hednesford Town.

Tait added very few players to the squad

believing that those brought in towards the end of the previous season would be up to the job.

Focus Turns To League After Cup Exit

KNOCKED out of the League Cup by Bolton, the season started fairly well with midfielder Chris Beech to the fore, scoring five times in the first eight games and seeing Pools in the top ten.

The sixth game of this spell was a Friday night match at Halifax, a game broadcast live on Sky TV – Pools first live TV appearance.

If Tait's side won the game by enough goals they would be top of the table.

Hundreds of Pools fans were squashed into the Shay in a spot with poor visibility, despite improvements having been made to the most uncomfortable of surroundings.

And the game was marred by clashes with Police – for which the Club and fans later received some apologies.

The game saw Chris McDonald go off injured after only 13 minutes, replaced by Nicky Evans in what was to be his only game, meaning his full career was broadcast live on TV. He was the son of former trainer Nichol Evans, who for many years worked for the Club.

As usual a slide down the table followed a good start and just one win in the next eight saw them in more accustomed territory.

The final game of this run was the last that Beech was to play. He made the move to Huddersfield with a tribunal deciding on a seriously unjust fee of £65,000 for a player who has been with the Club for over two seasons and had already netted nine goals this season.

Beech had fallen out with the Club over the terms offered to him during the summer and was placed on a weekly contract when a move to Sheffield United fell through.

Peter Beardsley Comes To Town

NOVEMBER brought stability and a first round FA Cup win over Carlisle. In the second round, Pools were drawn away to Fulham, but despite goals from Howard and Midgley, they were beaten 4-2.

They lost all four December league games and by the turn of the year were standing fourth from bottom, but ten points clear of Hull.

Pools needed an injection of form and fast.

The owners, IOR, reacted quickly and met with Peter Beardsley who had also been contacted by Carlisle United. IOR convinced him that he could help Hartlepool and also be

Hartlepool United Line-Up 1998-89. Back row: Stuart Elliott, Jeff Smith, Micky Dunwell, Tommy Miller, Glen Downey, Denny Ingram, Chris McDonald, Paul Walton, Craig Lake; Middle row: Gary Hinchley (Physio), Chris Beech, Nicky Evans, Graham Stokoe, Graeme Lee, Steve Howard, Martin Hollund (GK), Stephen Hutt, Gareth Downey, Martin Pemberton, Paul Stephenson, Paul Baker, Tommy Miller (Snr Scout); Front row: Stuart Brightwell, Stuart Irvine, Gustavo Di Lella, Mick Tait (Manager). Micky Barron (Capt.) Brian Honour (Asst Manager), Darren Knowles, Ian Clark, Craig Midgley

Peter Beardsley fires home on his Pools' debut

Chris Turner Is named Manager of Pools

closer to home. IOR succeeded and making his debut in the home game against Cambridge was the 37-year-old ex-England great Peter Beardsley. His career was always in the limelight and he was simply one of the best players of his generation.

His debut attracted an extra 1,500 on the gate and he didn't let the fans down with a stunning strike in the 2-2 draw, with the other a first strike for Micky Barron.

However with no victories after the next two games, and Tait asking the owners if he had to play Beardsley, he had picked his last XI and left Victoria Park.

Promotion heroes from 1991 Baker and Honour took over as joint caretaker managers. Baker was still registered as a player but was suffering from a recurring back problem and had made just two substitute outings in the last 14 months. Honour had been involved with the youth team and reserves.

They were in charge for just five league games, won only one, and suffered a humiliating 4-0 drubbing at bottom-placed Hull City.

By the time their brief flirtation with management was finished Pools were in a worrying situation, just six points above bottom team Scarborough and once again fighting a battle for their survival.

After a 2-1 loss at Exeter on February 20, a game in which the hosts scored two injury-time goals, Howard was sold for £120,000 to Northampton Town.

Chris Turner Appointed Manager

JUST like with the arrival of Cyril Knowles in 1989, the installation of the next boss was a vital appointment.

IOR implemented their expertise in making the decision and candidates went through a tough interview process.

The list of applicants included Newcastle coach Derek Fazackerley, their chief scout Chris McMenemy, Burnley's Jimmy Mullen, former Sunderland stopper Chris Turner, and others such as Russell Slade and Chris Waddle.

It was widely assumed that Beardsley may have got the job.

But on February 24, Chris Turner was appointed. The ex-Manchester United keeper was in charge of the successful Wolves youth team, twice winners of their league under his eye.

His new task was simple – keep Pools in the Football League with 14 games remaining.

Tait and Honour/Baker had made some emergency, almost panicky, loan signings in the shape of Newcastle's Stuart Elliott, and ex-players Ian McGuckin and Rob McKinnon.

Turner's first signing was Gary Strodder from Notts County for £25,000, who was to prove a rock at the back.

Pools were still short of goals and on March 13 Turner gave a debut to new signing and proven scorer, Gary Jones who had won the Third Division Golden Boot the previous season.

Pools continued to fire blanks and on deadline day the new manager signed his former Wolves youth team defender Chris Westwood, midfielder Danny Hughes and also snapped up another scorer in the form of Northampton Town's Chris Freestone.

Despite the improvements to the playing squad, Pools failed to win in Turner's first six games in charge. The positive point was that four of these games had been drawn.

With eight games to go, Pools were propping up the table, one point behind Scarborough who had a game in hand. It seemed a two horse race as Carlisle were five points ahead of Pools.

The game at Shrewsbury on Tuesday, April 6 was a turning point.

With only one goal to their name in Turner's six games – a run which included a 3-0 humbling at Torquay – Pools were running out of time.

Relegation Fight

IT was a poor game and with 12 minutes to go, Jones was replaced by old hand Baker.

With three minutes remaining, Pools were awarded a penalty when Strodder's header was handled on the line.

Pools had a lifeline – and one they couldn't pass up.

But Ingram's weak penalty was saved and Pools hopes were hit. However, Baker came to the fore, racing in to slot in from a tight angle.

Their first victory under the new regime was on the board, but Pools remained bottom as Scarborough also won. Carlisle were sucked into the battle and there was only two points between the bottom three.

Freestone and Jones broke their duck in the next game, as Pools saw off Chester 2-0 – their first back to back wins since August.

A midweek defeat at Swansea led Pools into their next match – Scarborough at home.

Some 5,098 supporters dug out the roadmaps and located the ground on Clarence Road, the biggest gate for a league game at the Vic since Boxing Day 1991, when Baker scored the only goal in a win over Bradford City.

Scarborough were bottom on 41 points after 40 games and Pools on 43 points after 41.

It didn't take a genius to work out that Pools had to win. With Tommy Miller back in the starting XI and learning more by the minute by playing alongside Beardsley, Pools pushed from the off.

Beardsley came to the fore, he split the Vic apart with the pass for Freestone to open the scoring. Then his quick thinking saw a hurried free-kick put Scarborough under pressure and

the keeper brought Miller down when he was through on goal.

Pools were 2-0 up at the break, held on easily and Baker, playing with the enthusiasm of a man half his age, brought a cross down on his chest and sent home as crisp a volley as he ever scored.

A 3-0 win and the pressure was off for now, United were now five points clear of the Seadogs and two ahead of Carlisle.

Almost 1,000 Pools fans turned up at Mansfield for the next game, but they witnessed a flat 2-0 defeat.

Fifth-placed Orient were next up and an early strike from Beardsley calmed nerves, eased the pressure and Pools were safe.

As Stephenson scored only his second goal of the season on the last day at Southend, high drama was afoot for Scarborough and Carlisle.

It was full time at Scarborough's McCain Stadium and as results stood they were safe. Carlisle were drawing 1-1 at Brunton Park with Plymouth Argyle and the game was into injury time. Scarborough were on the pitch celebrating their safety.

Carlisle's keeper, a loan signing made after the deadline, Jimmy Glass went up for a 95th minute corner and drilled in the winner.

Cue dramatic celebrations in Cumbria and shellshock on the east coast, Scarborough were down and out.

1999-2000

Turner Builds His Squad

AFTER the escape from relegation, Turner started to make his mark on the squad. Graham Stokoe, David Rush, Stuart Brightwell, Stuart Irvine and Paul Baker were released along with Beardsley, who departed the Club with special thanks from IOR.

Turner's main signings were Burnley striker Kevin Henderson and Chesterfield left-back Chris Perkins.

A bundle of pre-season games took place, with victories over Billingham Town, a Sheffield Wednesday XI, Telford and Oswestry Town, with Falkirk and Middlesbrough beating them at the Vic, which was now free of West Hartlepool Rugby Club's tenancy.

New Manager Builds Good Platform For Pools

POOLS were knocked out of the League Cup in the first round by Crewe, winning just one in the first seven in the league and sitting second bottom.

Anther Norwegian joined, Thomas Tennebo from Fana and he made an impressive bow in a 3-0 win at Carlisle.

Turner also signed Burnley defender Rune Vindheim, former Coventry player Sam Shilton and had taken Blackburn midfielder Lee Fitzpatrick on loan.

September 18 saw Pools win their first home game at the fourth attempt, goals from Freestone, Graeme Lee and Henderson seeing off Plymouth 3-0. Defeat against Orient the following week saw Chris Perkins play his last game just nine games in. Claiming he was homesick, Turner agreed to let him go. Orient were chasing Ian Clark.

October 2 saw Turner's first derby match, when Darlington breezed into town. Riding high in third place and bankrolled by George Reynolds, Darlington were expected to beat third bottom Pools with a reported win bonus of £2,000 per man on offer.

Turner started Fitzpatrick and Shilton for the first time. Miller had matured after his stint alongside Beardsley and Turner was finally getting the best out of Paul Stephenson. The 31-year-old had been out of sorts, but a move into the middle of the park revamped his career.

After Shilton opened the scoring, Fitzpatrick joined him with a strike from 25 yards.

Three wins out of the next four games saw Pools sitting in 16th place before they got involved in the FA Cup. Millwall made the journey north on Sunday, October 31, for an all-ticket game.

A tedious affair was best remembered for the debut of new Club mascot H'Angus the Monkey, before Jones scored in the last minute.

November saw Miller make his name, he netted a hat-trick against Barnet and scored the only goal in a victory over Chester.

The second round of the FA Cup saw Pools play at non-league Hereford in a live televised game. But there was no success as Pools lost 1-0 amid a rather embarrassing performance.

Pools regrouped and surged up the table and by the end of the year, after winning four in five, and playing some exciting football they were in fifth place, only four points behind fourth-placed Darlington.

New Millennium, Boyd And The Play-Offs

THE Millennium arrived and Pools stuttered in the first month, but remained in fifth place.

On February 5, Pools took on Shrewsbury at the Vic and sneaked victory in the last minute.

Making just his fifth substitute appearance was a slight youth team player, Adam Boyd. He chased a lost cause as the Shrews' keeper was trying to allow the ball to go out of play, dispossessed him and hit the ball into the net from the narrowest of angles.

Next came just two wins in nine, as Pools dropped out of the play-off places with seven games remaining.

Pools had bolstered their squad with two loan signings as Jamie Coppinger and Paul Arnison joined from Newcastle. Pools knocked back a bid of £400,000 from Wigan for top scorer Miller.

Defeat at Rochdale was sandwiched between home wins over Exeter, Lincoln and Mansfield. Turner's charges were back in the play-off spots, but it was tight – very tight. Cheltenham, Plymouth and Rochdale were all hot on Pools' tail.

The problem for Pools was their remaining three games. Away to third-placed Darlington, home to second-placed Rotherham and a tricky trip to Hull on the last day of the season.

The game at Feethams was a tense 1-1 draw. Miller put Pools ahead, but former Pools loanee Paul Heckingbottom equalised. Darlington had the upper hand and jaded Pools hung on for a point.

The Rotherham game was a

H'Angus made his debut at the Vic in 1999

Adam Boyd hits his first goal for Pools

disappointment and Pools lost 2-1 in a game which saw the Millers promoted.

Pools were eighth and had to go to Boothferry Park in need of a win and hope that Cheltenham slipped up.

Pools tore into Hull from the off and makeshift forward Graeme Lee scored in the second minute. Six minutes later, Coppinger made it two.

Around 1,200 away fans made the trip and saw Pools dominate, despite having Gary Strodder sent-off.

News filtered through that Cheltenham were one-up, it all seemed over. Kevin Henderson scored after 37 minutes to put Pools three up and then news came through that Cheltenham had been pegged back to 1-1.

The second half was a nervy affair, but Southend beat Cheltenham to put Pools in seventh spot and the play-offs for the first time. Their opponents? Darlington.

Darlington Derby In The Play-Offs

WITHOUT Strodder, Knowles and Henderson, Arnison, Paul Beavers and Midgley were in the starting line up.

Ten minutes before half time, Darlington were in the lead through Craig Liddle.

After Midgley missed the most gilt-edged of chances, Quakers soon doubled their lead.

Glen Naylor was brought down by keeper Hollund and the Norwegian was dismissed.

Turner sent on reserve keeper Andy Dibble in place of Arnison and despite a valiant effort he couldn't keep Gabbiadini's spot kick out.

With tempers frayed and visiting manager David Hodgson and scorer Gabbiadini on the end of the fury, there was an appeal for calm ahead of the second leg.

But the returning Strodder put through his own goal after eight minutes to make the aggregate score 3-0 and that was how it stayed.

Darlington went to Wembley, where they lost to Peterborough.

Despite the disappointment in the play-offs, the season had far exceeded expectations

In Turner, Pools had an astute and promising young manager. He knew he had a good platform to build on for next season.

Chapter 12

2000 – 2008

2000/01

The Early Years

AMID Turner's post play-off clearout, Beavers, Freestone and Jones left, leaving Pools short on the striker front. The only major signing was goalkeeper Anthony Williams from Blackburn Rovers.

Turner also recruited Tony Lormor and Norwegian Tim Sperrevik, who impressed Turner playing for Fana during the pre-season tour of Norway.

The day before the season started, James Sharp, a stocky defender, signed from Andover Town and he made an instant debut in the opening day win at Lincoln – but it was their only victory in the first five outings.

Tommy Miller got the season going with a spectacular winner at Blackpool and Pools were 14th at the end of September.

The Darlington derby approached and Pools won 2-1 with strikes from Henderson and Miller – both in fine form with 11 goals between them. The game was watched by just 3,265 fans.

The end of October saw Pools make the significant signing of former Leeds and York midfielder Mark Tinkler, who joined from Southend for £40,000.

Pools had developed a habit of winning home games and losing away, a sequence which ran throughout October and November, including a first round FA Cup reverse at Scunthorpe.

This run ended when Pools won at Halifax on December 16. A 6-1 thrashing was handed to Barnet in the next game, when Midgley – the

Tommy Miller

smallest player on the pitch – grabbed a hat-trick of headers.

Pools were in top gear and went on a run of 21 league games without defeat, from a 3-1 home win over Kidderminster in November to a loss at Southend on March 21, by which time they were fourth behind Cardiff, Brighton and Chesterfield.

Pools lost the next three, but recovered to win the last three and end the season fourth in the league and earned a Play Off place.

Saltergate – Gate

EARLIER in the season Chesterfield had been taken to task for being late with payments for striker Luke Beckett, signed from Chester City. Chesterfield had also broken several other rules and the activities of a former chairman were under investigation. The Football League brought charges, among the possible punishments was being kicked out of the league or a penalty of up to 50 points.

On April 11, a Football League disciplinary panel found them guilty of financial irregularities. They had also not declared true salaries and attendance figures. They were docked a rather convenient nine points – enough to keep them in the top three and clear of Pools. They were fined a paltry £20,000 after they had broken eight league regulations. Pools, privately furious at the decision, were

badly hit by Saltergategate.

Play Off Time Again

FOR the second season in a row, Turner's Pools were in the play-offs, this time against Blackpool.

Pools had done the double over the Tangerines in the league, but didn't perform in the knock-out.

The first leg saw Blackpool coast it 2-0 and the return at the Vic was a disappointing one. By the time Jermaine Easter was dismissed ten

Darren Knowles in action at Blackpool

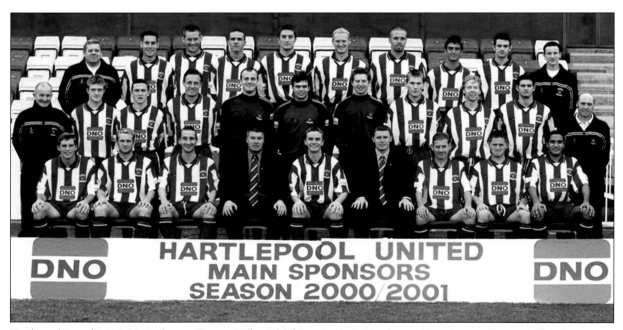

Hartlepool Squad 2000-01. Back row: Tommy Miller (Chief Scout), Kevin Henderson, Tony Lormor, Tommy Miller, Graeme Lee, James Sharp, Tim Sperrevik, Paul Stephenson, Adam Boyd, Martin Scott (Youth Team Coach); Middle row: John Murray (Head Physio), Lee Fitzpatrick, Paul Arnison, Gary Strodder, Anthony Williams, Martin Hollund, Chris Porter, Thomas Tennebo, Ian Clark, Rory Barker, Cedric Forster (Kit Manager); Front row: Sam Shilton, Andy McAvoy, Mark Robinson, Chris Turner (Manager), Micky Barron, Colin West (Reserve Team Manager), Darren Knowles, Craig Midgley, Chris Westwood

		P	HW	HD	HL	HF	HA	AW	AD	AL	AF	AA	POINTS
1	Brighton & Hove Albion	46	19	2	2	52	14	9	6	8	21	21	92
2	Cardiff City	46	16	7	0	56	20	7	6	10	39	38	82
3	Chesterfield	46	16	5	2	46	14	9	9	5	33	28	80
4	**HARTLEPOOL UNITED**	46	12	8	3	40	23	9	6	8	31	31	77
5	Leyton Orient	46	13	7	3	31	18	7	8	8	28	33	75
6	Hull City	46	12	7	4	27	18	7	10	6	20	21	74
7	Blackpool	46	14	4	5	50	26	8	2	13	24	32	72
8	Rochdale	46	11	8	4	36	25	7	9	7	23	23	71
9	Cheltenham Town	46	12	5	6	37	27	6	9	8	22	25	68
10	Scunthorpe United	46	13	7	3	42	16	5	4	14	20	36	65
11	Southend United	46	10	8	5	29	23	5	10	8	26	30	63
12	Plymouth Argyle	46	13	5	5	33	17	2	8	13	21	44	58
13	Mansfield Town	46	12	7	4	40	26	3	6	14	24	46	58
14	Macclesfield Town	46	10	5	8	23	21	4	9	10	28	41	56
15	Shrewsbury Town	46	12	5	6	30	26	3	5	15	19	39	55
16	Kidderminster Harriers	46	10	6	7	29	27	3	8	12	18	34	53
17	York City	46	9	6	8	23	26	4	7	12	19	37	52
18	Lincoln City	46	9	9	5	36	28	3	6	14	22	38	51
19	Exeter City	46	8	9	6	22	20	4	5	14	18	38	50
20	Darlington	46	10	6	7	28	23	2	7	14	16	33	49
21	Torquay United	46	8	9	6	30	29	4	4	15	22	48	49
22	Carlisle United	46	8	8	7	26	26	3	7	13	16	39	48
23	Halifax Town	46	7	6	10	33	32	5	5	13	21	36	47
24	Barnet	46	9	8	6	44	29	3	1	19	23	52	45

Nationwide Football League Division Three Table 2000/01

minutes after half-time, Pools were 4-1 down on aggregate and in the end, Blackpool added another.

Pools had been much more consistent this season, but they met a Blackpool side who had peaked at the right time.

2001/02

Watson, Widdrington, Williams and Humphreys

AFTER back to back play-offs, Pools needed something extra to go one step further. Turner had the makings of a very good side, but he was brutal at the end of the season.

It was a summer of change. Released were Strodder, Aspin, Fitzpatrick, Shilton, McAvoy, Brownrigg, Sperrevik, Midgley and Knowles,

Turner went for quality over quantity. In came former Birmingham defender/midfielder Jon Bass and Darrell Clarke from Mansfield who could play out on the right wing or in the middle of the park and cost £80,000.

Former Sheffield Wednesday youth prodigy Ritchie Humphreys also joined after a spell at Cambridge.

Possibly the most significant signing at the time was that of holding midfielder Tommy Widdrington. He had been released by Port Vale, was vastly experienced and had spent four years in the top flight with Southampton.

Tommy Miller moved to Premiership side

Chris Turner following the defeat to Blackpool

Frank Reid/Hartlepool Mail

Gordon Watson was to prove a big hit at The Vic

The Official History of Hartlepool United Football Club 1908 – 2008

New signings Jon Bass, Darrell Clarke and Tommy Widdrington

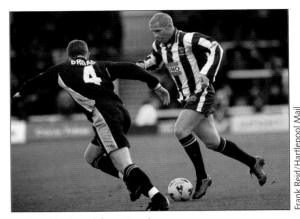

Paul Smith signed from Burnley

Ipswich Town for a fee of £750,000, after briefly heading to Norway to train with Champions League hopefuls Brann Bergen.

Graeme Lee was fit after an injury blighted season and was likely to be joined in the squad by left back Mark Robinson and Adam Boyd who had made just three starts in 2000-01.

An opening day draw with Mansfield and a win at Shrewsbury seemed OK, but a poor display in an ITV Digital Sport televised game against Nottingham Forest in the League Cup was followed by an equally lacklustre performance at home against Darlington, with Pools losing 2-1.

Keeper Martin Hollund was dropped and replaced by Williams. Hollund would once again spend the bulk of the season on the bench.

Pools failed to score in the next four games and in total contrast to their form of last year they were in 23rd place.

Turner then took a big risk, one, however, which was to pay a rich dividend. He signed Gordon Watson, a flamboyant centre forward who had already been on the end of a career threatening injury.

In February 1997, Bradford striker Watson suffered a double leg fracture following a challenge by Huddersfield defender Kevin Gray. He had a metal plate and screws inserted into his leg following immediate surgery, needed five more operations and a court case ruled in his favour, as he was awarded £950,000 in damages related to loss of earnings.

Watson was thrown straight into the first team and scored the goal that earned Pools a point against Kidderminster.

Ian Clark was soon on his way to Darlington for £15,000, but Pools didn't miss him as they beat Carlisle 3-1 with Watson scoring again, along with Tinkler and Boyd.

Turner signed Paul Smith, a left winger from Easington who had spent eight seasons with Burnley.

But Pools were still 23rd and a couple of good performances were followed with some horrific displays, and Pools scored just once in the next four games. After defeat to Plymouth on November 3 they were propping up the Football League once more. It was a long journey back from the south coast, especially with high-flying Hull City next up.

Ritchie Humphreys signs on the dotted line as Chris Turner looks on

Chris Turner signs James Coppinger on loan

The scorers celebrate after a demolition of Swansea City

On November 6, the Victoria Park fireworks arrived 24 hours late, as the season was turned around.

Watson put Pools in front, and he made it two with an unstoppable shot from distance. Skipper Micky Barron scored a rare goal, before Watson completed his hat-trick.

Two home wins sandwiched an FA Cup defeat at Swindon then a win at Swansea courtesy of Graeme Lee, as Pools dramatically climbed to eighth.

In need of a further lift, Turner again signed James Coppinger on loan from Newcastle and his debut against Rushden saw Pools destroy them 5-1.

Four games and three wins later, Pools were back in the top ten, desperate to get in the play-off places, just four points ahead.

Without Widdrington, victim to a long-term hamstring problem, there was little consistency. A 5-1 thrashing of Southend was followed by just one win in seven.

Torquay striker Eifion Williams was a long-time Turner target. The former Wolves apprentice had played in the Welsh League with Caernarfon Town and then Barry Town where he had smashed all scoring records.

A fee of £30,000 was enough to tempt the Welshman to the North-East.

After a couple of substitute outings he was handed a chance in the starting line up at Oxford on March 30. He scored twice on his debut and two days later Pools took on table toppers Plymouth, a team 33 points ahead of Pools and already promoted. Clarke netted the all-important winner with just minutes of the Easter Monday game remaining.

Three games to go and Pools needed three wins, an improved goal difference and a lot of luck to make the play-offs.

A visit to Halifax was next on the calendar and 1,100 Pools fans in a total of 1,838 spectators saw Pools win 2-0.

Once again so much depended on the outcome of the final two games.

On the penultimate weekend of the season,

Gordon Watson celebrates his hat-trick against Hull City

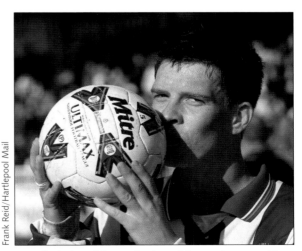

Darrell Clarke celebrates his hat-trick over Swansea City

303

The Pools' fans turn out in force for the Cheltenham play off game

Ritchie Humphreys missed his penalty against Cheltenham in the Play Off Semi Final

Pools were ninth and looked out of the picture, relying on other results to have any chance.

Without worrying what the others were up to, Pools just had to play their own game and try to overcome Swansea. It wasn't a problem as goals from Williams, Clarke (hat-trick), Boyd, Watson and Henderson saw them run out 7-1 winners.

It all boiled down to the final 90 minutes of the season and Pools were at Exeter. Around 1,200 fans made the trek south and how they were rewarded.

Watson blasted home his 18th goal of the season and Williams made it two.

With results going happily in their favour, Pools were in the end of season shake-up for an unprecedented third year in a row, this time against Cheltenham.

Agonising End To The Season For Pools

THE first leg at the Vic saw Williams put Pools in the lead on the stroke of half time – the first time Pools had been ahead in a play-off game – but the crowd of 7,135 were stunned when Grayson got an equaliser with a minute to go.

With 1,500 Pools fans crammed into the compact away end at Cheltenham, the second leg was a thriller.

Arnison put Pools ahead with a brilliant

		P	HW	HD	HL	HF	HA	AW	AD	AL	AF	AA	POINTS
1	Plymouth Argyle	46	19	2	2	41	11	12	7	4	30	17	102
2	Luton Town	46	15	5	3	50	18	15	2	6	46	30	97
3	Mansfield Town	46	17	3	3	49	24	7	4	12	23	36	79
4	Cheltenham Town	46	11	11	1	40	20	10	4	9	26	29	78
5	Rochdale	46	13	8	2	41	22	8	7	8	24	30	78
6	Rushden & Diamonds	46	14	5	4	40	20	6	8	9	29	33	73
7	**HARTLEPOOL UNITED**	**46**	**12**	**6**	**5**	**53**	**23**	**8**	**5**	**10**	**21**	**25**	**71**
8	Scunthorpe United	46	14	5	4	43	22	5	9	9	31	34	71
9	Shrewsbury Town	46	13	4	6	36	19	7	6	10	28	34	70
10	Kidderminster Harriers	46	13	6	4	35	17	6	3	14	21	30	66
11	Hull City	46	12	6	5	38	18	4	7	12	19	33	61
12	Southend United	46	12	5	6	36	22	3	8	12	15	32	58
13	Macclesfield Town	46	7	7	9	23	25	8	6	9	18	27	58
14	York City	46	11	5	7	26	20	5	4	14	28	47	57
15	Darlington	46	11	6	6	37	25	4	5	14	23	46	56
16	Exeter City	46	7	9	7	25	32	7	4	12	23	41	55
17	Carlisle United	46	11	5	7	31	21	1	11	11	18	35	52
18	Leyton Orient	46	10	7	6	37	25	3	6	14	18	46	52
19	Torquay United	46	8	6	9	27	31	4	9	10	19	32	51
20	Swansea City	46	7	8	8	26	26	6	4	13	27	51	51
21	Oxford United	46	8	7	8	34	28	3	7	13	19	34	47
22	Lincoln City	46	8	4	11	25	27	2	12	9	19	35	46
23	Bristol Rovers	46	8	7	8	28	28	3	5	15	12	32	45
24	Halifax Town	46	5	9	9	24	28	3	3	17	15	56	36

Nationwide Football League Division Three Table 2001/02

strike from distance, only to see it cancelled out ten minutes later. Pools dominated for long periods, but couldn't find the net and the season was decided by a penalty shoot-out.

Paul Smith scored his then Stephenson missed his strike, but after Arnison scored Duff missed for the Robins. Henderson and Watson converted and Alsop netted for the hosts to put them 5-4 in front.

Humphreys stepped up and hit his strike towards the top of the net. It hit the underside of the bar and dropped down towards goal, but hit the keeper on the way out.

Agonisingly, it didn't cross the line and Pools season was over in the most cruel and dramatic of circumstances.

Turner remained defiant: "Next season starts here," he vowed.

H'Angus appeals for votes at The Vic

2002/03

The Mayor, H'Angus, Newell and Promotion

BEFORE Turner announced his retained list, Pools were in need of another staff member after H'Angus, the Club's mascot, had stood for Mayor in the local council elections.

Stuart Drummond, 28, beat off his opponents landing a £53,000-a-year job as the town's first elected Mayor. The Club paid his deposit (£500) but did not get involved in any other way in the campaign.

The mascot, who had first appeared on October 31, 1999, was controversial under Drummond's guise and certainly got the Club exposure and column inches, but not always for good reasons.

His Mayoral campaign was built on the promise of free bananas for schoolchildren.

Drummond, initially available to back at odds of 100/1, was no fool though and he beat the Labour candidate and expected winner by over 600 votes.

A couple of squad members were also entering a new chapter of their careers. Lormor moved to Telford, as the likeable Hollund returned to Norway.

Turner was confident his squad was capable of promotion and added only released Newcastle youth player Steven Istead to the books.

There was no pre-season Norwegian venture this year, but Pools were still off to Europe, heading for Holland to stay at the training camp of the Dutch national side.

Stuart Drummond – the man behind the monkey

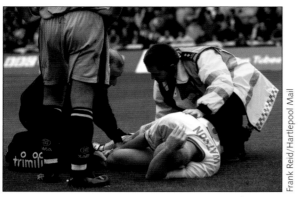

Gordon Watson broke his leg in the game with Darlington

Frank Reid/Hartlepool Mail

They played two games in two days and won them both 12-0. Against Theole, Watson got five, with the rest scored by Henderson (3), Boyd (2), Humphreys and Clarke.

Turner changed his team to face SV Nootdorp, when Easter grabbed six, Boyd scored his second pair and Simms, Arnison, Bass and Stephenson got on the scoresheet.

There was a genuine belief that Pools were going to go one better this time around and they started the season with an impressive 3-1 win at Carlisle, followed up with a 2-0 home win over Boston.

The season was going well, a Watson goal at Oxford saw Pools top and next up were Darlington, no longer the side heading for big things.

It took just three minutes for Williams to drill in the first after Watson cleverly back heeled the ball to him.

Against the run of play former Pools player Ian Clark enjoyed his moment of glory when he made the most of a mix-up to score.

Parity didn't last long, as Watson set Williams up again for his second, Humphreys angled home the third from outside the box and Tinkler turned in a fourth.

However, the game wasn't all roses, for, with ten minutes to go, Watson suffered a broken leg during a challenge with Matt Clarke.

It was to be the last Pools saw of the real Gordon Watson.

Pools were brimming with self-belief and continued their form, even without Watson.

October 19 saw Wrexham visit, and Pools won 4-3 with a Tinkler hat-trick and a goal from new boy Marcus Richardson.

The youth policy was one of the key developments under IOR and in the home game against Bristol Rovers ten days later, winger Istead was introduced for his debut with four minutes remaining.

At 16 years and 189 days he became the youngest player to appear for Pools, beating John McGovern's record, but he wouldn't hold the accolade for long.

Then it was all-change. After drawing with York City on a rain-soaked Friday night at Victoria Park, Pools were in need of a new manager.

Turner Leaves For Pastures New

CHRIS Turner had gone back to his roots to take over at Sheffield Wednesday who were struggling in the Championship.

Colin West was named caretaker manager, but after two games in charge – a win at Exeter and an FA Cup draw at Southend – he followed Turner to the Owls, despite being offered the job at Victoria Park and several efforts made by Ken Hodcroft to convince him to stay.

He may have been out injured, but Watson wasn't one to keep quiet and, as Pools looked for a permanent replacement, the striker announced that "this bus drives itself".

New Manager In Place At The Vic

POOLS, though, needed a new bus driver and the task of steering Pools to promotion was given to a surprise candidate – Mike Newell, the former Everton and Blackburn forward, who had experience of running Tranmere's reserve side.

He vowed though, to keep things as they were, without making unnecessary changes. Perhaps the bus was capable of steering itself.

His first game in charge saw a 2-1 win at Leyton Orient but they were then knocked out of the FA Cup by Southend, as the visitors scored two late goals in the replay.

December wasn't so hot for Pools and they won only once, losing one game in front of 22,000 fans at Hull's new KC Stadium in the first game there.

Mike Newell was the new man in charge at Pools

Pools went to Rushden needing a win to take the League title

However, the first two months of 2003 saw Pools unbeaten in eight and concede just four goals in the process. With 13 games remaining Pools stood a massive 14 points clear of Rushden. Surely silverware was finally on the way.

The Run-In To Promotion

MARCH 1 saw Pools visit Feethams and in a game much more closely contested than the derby at the Vic, Darlington were on top in the first half. Barry Conlon opened the scoring, but three minutes into the second half Matt Clarke needlessly bundled over Williams in the box and Boyd stepped up to the mark.

Five minutes later and it was 2-1, when Darrell Clarke headed home, before Darlington snatched a leveller through Liddle in the last derby game at Feethams before it was demolished.

Pools got the jitters and lost badly at Lincoln and drew at home to Bury. Pools had ten games left to play and still had a ten point lead, but Rushden had two games in hand. Just one win in five saw the gap narrow to a point with both teams having five games remaining.

Pools bounced back to form with a 4-1 win over Orient. One point ahead, four games to play.

Promotion was clinched early, but in the most surreal of circumstances. April 19 saw Pools travel to Scunthorpe, where they were beaten 4-0.

What should have been a day of celebration ended in muted farce and Rushden's win took them ahead of Pools into top spot.

Three games to go, two points behind.

A draw against Rochdale on Easter Monday in the next game at the Vic wasn't enough as Rushden won again. Two games to go, four points behind.

Hope came in the penultimate game. As Pools were condemning Shrewsbury to the Conference, Rushden drew.

Pools were one point behind, with one game to play – at Rushden.

The tiny town of Irthlingborough was invaded by hoards of travelling fans and the locals had not seen anything like it. Pools away support was reaching unprecedented levels and, again, well in excess of 1,000 made the haul down the M1.

The leaders controlled the first half and were one-up at the break. Pools, who now had Watson back, lost him through a hamstring injury, were better in the second half and thought they had levelled when Graham Lee scored, only to be denied as it was harshly ruled out for a foul on goalkeeper Billy Turley.

The equaliser through Westwood came two minutes from the end, but despite the crazy finish, Mark Tinkler going close with a last-gasp header, the scoreline remained. Pools ended in second place.

So near, yet so far and while the season was a complete success, it was tinged with a feeling of what might have been.

Pools went up as runners-up after Rushden just edged it in the league

Pools celebrate promotion to Division Two with the fans at The Vic

		P	HW	HD	HL	HF	HA	AW	AD	AL	AF	AA	POINTS
1	Rushden & Diamonds	46	16	5	2	48	19	8	10	5	25	28	87
2	HARTLEPOOL UNITED	46	16	5	2	49	21	8	8	7	22	30	85
3	Wrexham	46	12	7	4	48	26	11	8	4	36	24	84
4	Bournemouth	46	14	7	2	38	18	6	7	10	22	30	74
5	Scunthorpe United	46	11	8	4	40	20	8	7	8	28	29	72
6	Lincoln City	46	10	9	4	29	18	8	7	8	17	19	70
7	Bury	46	8	8	7	25	26	10	8	5	32	30	70
8	Oxford United	46	9	7	7	26	20	10	5	8	31	27	69
9	Torquay United	46	9	11	3	41	31	7	7	9	30	40	66
10	York City	46	11	9	3	34	24	6	6	11	18	29	66
11	Kidderminster Harriers	46	8	8	7	30	33	8	7	8	32	30	63
12	Cambridge United	46	10	7	6	38	25	6	6	11	29	45	61
13	Hull City	46	9	10	4	34	19	5	7	11	24	34	59
14	Darlington	46	8	10	5	36	27	4	8	11	22	32	54
15	Boston United	46	11	6	6	34	22	4	7	12	21	34	54
16	Macclesfield Town	46	8	6	9	29	28	6	6	11	28	35	54
17	Southend United	46	12	1	10	29	23	5	2	16	18	36	54
18	Leyton Orient	46	9	6	8	28	24	5	5	13	23	37	53
19	Rochdale	46	7	6	10	30	30	5	10	8	33	40	52
20	Bristol Rovers	46	7	7	9	25	27	5	8	10	25	30	51
21	Swansea City	46	9	6	8	28	25	3	7	13	20	40	49
22	Carlisle United	46	5	5	13	26	40	8	5	10	26	38	49
23	Exeter City	46	7	7	9	24	31	4	8	11	26	33	48
24	Shrewsbury Town	46	5	6	12	34	39	4	8	11	28	53	41

Nationwide Football League Division Three Table 2002/03

2003/04

Neale Cooper's Reign In Charge

FOLLOWING the Rushden game, there was a civic reception and an open top bus tour for which thousands of fans turned out.

Leaving Pools was Lee – out of contract and

Marco Gabbiadini joined Pools in a shock move

teaming up with Turner at Hillsborough – Widdrington, Smith, Sharp and Simms. Watson retired and soon following out of the exit door was Newell.

Well-liked within the dressing room, Newell was never taken to by supporters and Pools were seeking their third manager in nine months.

Another surprising choice was made by owners IOR. Neale Cooper, who had managerial experience at Ross County in the Scottish leagues, was the new chief.

At the same time, Pools announced the £70,000 signing of Michael Nelson from Bury.

Cooper pulled off a shock in the transfer market when he signed former Darlington striker Marco Gabbiadini. He had been training with his former Club and was set to put pen to paper, but Pools quickly moved in.

Also joining was former Darlington and Newcastle forward Paul Robinson, who was once famously selected ahead of Alan Shearer against Sunderland in the Ruud Gullit days at Newcastle United, Andy Jordan, the son of Scottish international Joe, and on the eve of the new season Gavin Strachan, son of Gordon.

Debutant History

AUGUST 9 saw Pools begin their new season at Peterborough following their third promotion.

Neale Cooper was the man to replace Newell at The Vic

Frank Reid/Hartlepool Mail

The team included new signings Nelson, Jordan, Strachan, Robinson and Matty Robson was making his first league start.

In excess of 1,200 fans made the journey and in scorching sunshine Pools were two down within 23 minutes and looking as if they were going to be taught a harsh lesson of life in the new division.

Debutant Strachan curled in a free-kick to give Pools hope. Yet just five minutes into the second half they were 3-1 down. Robinson tapped in a debut goal to make it 3-2, before Robson scored to make it 3-3. With time running out, Nelson picked up possession 40 yards out, brushed team-mate Robinson aside and unleashed the most spectacular of debut goals.

It was the first time in the Football League that four debutants had all scored in the same game. The feelgood factor was back at Victoria Park.

League Cup Action For Pools

FOUR days later Pools travelled to Sheffield Wednesday in the League Cup. They fell behind to a Graeme Lee goal – on his home debut – before Paul Robinson levelled from the spot. The game went into extra time and Istead put Pools ahead, but with five minutes remaining Wednesday equalised to take the game to penalties.

Jim Provett, who was a shock replacement for Williams in goal, saved the Owls' second penalty and Pools converted all five to knock former boss Turner out of the competition.

Turner was to later say that he was shocked to see Provett on the teamsheet and had to re-

plan his team talk ahead of the game.

Draws against Tranmere and Bristol City were followed by a home victory over Port Vale on August 23 when David Foley came off the bench with eight minutes to go. He was aged only 16 years and 44 days and broke Istead's recently-set record.

A solid start – Pools were 12th – turned into a spectacular one when Grimsby visited. Pools ran riot, running out 8-1 winners, with Robinson helping himself to a hat-trick in Pools' second biggest win in the Football league.

It was followed by a goal from Eifion Williams and an absolutely sublime strike from Gabbiadini to give Pools a 2-1 win at Stockport and put them in second place.

John Brackstone's Only Pools Goal Comes In The FA Cup

IN the FA Cup in November, Pools were handed a home tie against Whitby and a comfortable 4-0 win was secured thanks to a pair by Gabbiadini one from Humphreys and a stunning free kick from youth team player John Brackstone.

It was to be Gabbiadini's last goals, as he was soon forced to retire with knee trouble.

Boyd was loaned to Boston United in an effort to get him back in shape, goalkeeper Williams moved to Swansea on loan and Easter and Richardson were told they could leave.

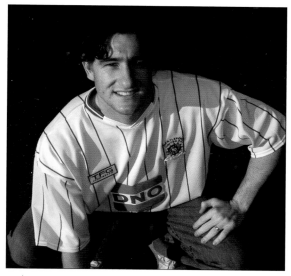

Joel Porter scored his first Pools goal in the televised FA Cup game at Burton Albion

Mark Tinkler challenges Sunderland's Ben Clark at the Stadium of Light

Cooper then received clearance to allow Joel Porter to play. The Australian international had made his way to Pools via trials in Spain and Sunderland and made his debut in the 2-0 home win over Swindon.

The second round of the FA Cup saw Pools win 1-0 in a televised game at Burton Albion , the game settled by a Porter strike after 70 minutes.

Pools Drawn To Face Sunderland In The FA Cup

POOLS were handed a plum draw in the third round at Sunderland.

A massive 9,200 tickets were sold to visiting fans.

Sunderland, relegated from the top flight the season before, included four players who were later to join Pools – Michael Proctor, Darren Williams, Ben Clark and Tommy Butler.

Julio Arca scored the only goal, eight minutes after the break when he fired home a low shot. The closest Pools came to scoring was when Eifion Williams sent a header in with just two minutes to go that Phil Babb hacked off the line. The 40,816 crowd was the biggest that Pools had played in front of.

Out of the cup, Pools enjoyed a 5-2 win at Port Vale in the snow, which saw them back up to eighth

and seriously contending for a play-off place.

Hammer Time At The Vic

COOPER went to Scotland to sign Alloa defender Scott Walker and Hugh Robertson, a left back from his former club Ross County.

With Mark Robinson, Matty Robson and John Brackstone all tried in that position by Cooper he gave Robertson a go and soon displayed an extra dimension to his game – the free-kick.

Against Blackpool he fired in a 25-yarder which was disallowed as the referee had ruled that it had been taken too quickly. So he stepped up and did precisely the same again with consummate accuracy. Hugh the Hammer had arrived.

Pools won their next three but were given a lesson by QPR, who completed a 4-1 double over Pools.

Adam Boyd returned to the bench for the game against Stockport on March 16. He had spent three months on loan at Boston and scored four goals in 14 games but had put on weight during this spell.

His talent was there to see but it wasn't always applied and now it was down to the player to perform. He was sitting in the last chance saloon. He was also given a talking to by owners IOR and told to get his life in order.

Frank Reid/Hartlepool Mail

Hugh Robertson was to become a cult hero at The Vic

Boyd was restored to the starting line up at Grimsby and responded by scoring both goals in a 2-0 victory. Going on loan to Boston and his meeting with IOR had proved the kick-start he needed and Pools were to reap the benefits.

Sad Losses At The Club

THE Club was then hit by the loss of two Club stalwarts in the space of a week, Frankie Baggs and Harold Hornsey.

Baggs was a well-known character in the town, who worked tirelessly for the Club in the Commercial Department, raising funds, arranging events and always carrying a smile and a joke.

His funeral took place on Thursday, March 25 and as mourners were celebrating his life in his old haunt, Hartlepool Cricket Club, news filtered through that former chairman and saviour of the Club Hornsey had passed away.

Some 5,206 fans observed perfect silences for both men before the Brentford game two days later.

Boyd, now a reshaped and rejuvenated player, scored again but Brentford won by the odd goal in three. The next game saw Pools lose 2-0 at Brighton and put them in ninth place. They had to play Luton (8th place) and Bournemouth (6th) next, games which would decide if their season was going to hold further interest.

Antony Sweeney had been given his first start of the season in the Luton game and the midfielder opened his account on the quarter-hour mark when he equalised Steve Howard's opener.

Boyd levelled to make it 2-2 against Mike Newell's new side, but then came one of the most fiercely-struck goals Victoria Park has ever seen.

Robertson picked up a free ball 20-yards out and leathered home his goal of the season. Luton made it 3-3, before a late Boyd penalty won it.

Two more Boyd goals saw off Bournemouth, making it seven in five starts as Pools went into overdrive.

A 2-1 win at Wrexham was followed by a classy 4-0 win over Notts County.

The next game showed how much improvement Pools had made this season under Cooper. On April 24, 1,100 Pools fans again plodded down to Rushden as they stood in sixth place, five points above their nearest contenders Port Vale.

Rushden were in the relegation zone. Goals from Williams and Boyd, following a schoolboy error from Rushden keeper Turley, gave Pools

Dimi Konstantopoulous

the points.

The result put Pools fifth and with two games remaining only Port Vale could stop them in their hunt for the play-offs.

But Pools lost at home to champions Plymouth and again it all hinged on the last day.

Pools had to travel to Swindon, both teams on 72 points and both needing just a point to secure a play-off berth over Port Vale who were two points behind, but with an inferior goal difference.

The game at Swindon was played in a windy downpour, with 1,500 Pools fans massed on an open terrace.

Swindon went in front, but Pools levelled and, of course, it was Boyd who scored. He met

It was Danny Wilson against Neale Cooper at Ashton Gate

Pools players had to be escorted from the pitch at full time in the game at Ashton Gate as City fans celebrated

Frank Reid/Hartlepool Mail

a Robertson cross to plant a header home and clinch Pools a play-off spot.

Port Vale had managed a victory and missed out due to goal difference.

Bristol City Prove Tough Play Off Opponents

POOLS were to take on Bristol City, who had finished nine points clear of Pools.

The first play-off game took place at a raucous Victoria Park.

City, managed by Danny Wilson, took an early lead. Pools got into their stride and were denied a penalty on the hour when City keeper

Steve Phillips took Williams out.

But with just over 15 minutes remaining, Porter nipped in between defender and goalkeeper to roll the ball into the net and send Victoria Park wild.

It was all down to 90 minutes at Ashton Gate four days later.

The tension was clear to see in the first 45 minutes and there was little between the sides, although a piece of Boyd trickery saw him shoot against a post.

Pools took the lead when Williams, out on the right flank, fired over an inch perfect cross which Sweeney guided into the net. Pools were 2-1 up on aggregate.

		P	HW	HD	HL	HF	HA	AW	AD	AL	AF	AA	POINTS
1	Plymouth Argyle	46	17	5	1	52	13	9	7	7	33	28	90
2	Queens Park Rangers	46	16	7	0	47	12	6	10	7	33	33	83
3	Bristol City	46	15	6	2	34	12	8	7	8	24	25	82
4	Brighton and Hove Albion	46	17	4	2	39	11	5	7	11	25	32	77
5	Swindon Town	46	12	7	4	41	23	8	6	9	35	35	73
6	**HARTLEPOOL UNITED**	46	10	8	5	39	24	10	5	8	37	37	73
7	Port Vale	46	15	6	2	45	28	6	4	13	28	35	73
8	Tranmere Rovers	46	13	7	3	36	18	4	9	10	23	38	67
9	Bournemouth	46	11	8	4	35	25	6	7	10	21	26	66
10	Luton Town	46	14	6	3	44	27	3	9	11	25	39	66
11	Colchester United	46	11	8	4	33	23	6	5	12	19	33	64
12	Barnsley	46	7	12	4	25	19	8	5	10	29	39	62
13	Wrexham	46	9	6	8	27	21	8	3	12	23	39	60
14	Blackpool	46	9	5	9	31	28	7	6	10	27	37	59
15	Oldham Athletic	46	9	8	6	37	25	3	13	7	29	35	57
16	Sheffield Wednesday	46	7	9	7	25	26	6	5	12	23	38	53
17	Brentford	46	9	5	9	34	38	5	6	12	18	31	53
18	Peterborough United	46	5	8	10	36	33	7	8	8	22	25	52
19	Stockport County	46	6	8	9	31	36	5	11	7	31	34	52
20	Chesterfield	46	9	7	7	34	31	3	8	12	15	40	51
21	Grimsby Town	46	10	5	8	36	26	3	6	14	19	55	50
22	Rushden & Diamonds	46	9	5	9	37	34	4	4	15	23	40	48
23	Notts County	46	6	9	8	32	27	4	3	16	18	51	42
24	Wycombe Wanderers	46	5	7	11	31	39	1	12	10	19	36	37

Nationwide Football League Division Two Table 2003/04

Ritchie Humphreys can't hide his disappointment as Pools are defeated at Bristol City

Pools held firm and were on the verge of glory until, on 88 minutes, substitute Marc Goodfellow headed beyond Provett. Extra time beckoned – or so Pools thought.

In six minutes of additional time, Christian Roberts went on a run, beat makeshift defenders Tinkler and Williams, before shooting under Provett.

Once again, Pools fell at the final hurdle. This, however, was the most agonising of their play-off campaigns.

2004/05

Cardiff Here We Come…

COOPER'S summer task was a fairly simple one. He had a confident and successful side which didn't need much changing.

Paul Robinson, Anthony Williams, Scott Walker and Mark Robinson departed and in came Jack Ross, a right sided midfielder/full back and captain from Clyde.

The season started at home to Bradford and a rounded display from Pools saw them win 2-1, with Boyd carrying on where he left off, netting a free-kick, Robertson scoring the other.

After losing at Tranmere, Pools travelled to Huddersfield for a game live on Sky Sports. It was the first time Pools managed to win a televised game, loan signing Kevin Betsy

Cooper had to change things around as Chris Westwood, the most reliable of defenders, had to leave the field due to injury and was replaced by Neil Danns.

Tinkler dropped into the heart of the defence, which again had to be reorganised as Barron went down injured and had to be stretchered from the field.

With no defender on the bench he was replaced by Darrell Clarke, as Williams dropped deep to play right back.

Pools had around 20 minutes to see the game out and City manager Wilson, sensing uneasiness in the Pools defence, brought on two subs either side of Barron's departure.

2004/5 Squad. Back row: Matty Robson, Joel Porter, Darren Craddock, Eifion Williams, Chris Westwood, Ryan McCann, Hugh Robertson; Middle row: John Brackstone, Jack Ross, Michael Nelson, Jim Provett, Dimitrios Konstantopoulos, Mark TInkler, Adam Boyd, Antony Sweeney; Front row: Gavin Strachan, Steven Istead, Neale Cooper (Manager), Micky Barron, Martin Scott (Reserve Team Manager), Ritchie Humphreys, Darrell Clarke

Andy Appleby turns home his amazing winner against Bournemouth

Frank Reid/Hartlepool Mail

scoring the opener, with the second coming from Tinkler.

The second round of the League Cup saw them lose at Crystal Palace 2-1 in extra time.

Worryingly, Pools were starting to ship goals but Cooper was able to make a significant signature in the form of Ben Clark from Sunderland.

After back-to-back away defeats at Brentford and Peterborough, Provett was replaced between the sticks by giant former Greek under-21 cap Dimitrios Konstantopoulos.

Just in the top ten by the time of the second round of the FA Cup on December 4, Pools were starting to gel.

Cooper had added to his squad and was trying to get the right mix. Due to a long term injury to Darrell Clarke, loan players like Betsy, Alan Pouton, Lewis Gobern and Martin Woods had all been and gone.

Good FA Cup Run For Pools

POOLS beat Aldershot 5-1 in the second round of the competition and were handed a third round tie with Boston.

League form picked up, with Porter and Boyd becoming a lethal pairing. Pools went on a run of one defeat in eight league games, including a 5-1 win at Wrexham and an overdue home treat when they cruised to a 5-0 victory over MK Dons, a game in which youngster Andy Appleby popped in his second of the season.

He had scored in the game which had started the upturn in form – an amazing 3-2 win over Bournemouth, a thriller where Pools were 2-1 down with two minutes to go. Nelson equalised and then Appleby netted to make it 3-2, but the referee controversially disallowed it for a foul on the youngster and awarded a penalty which Boyd saw saved. In the dying seconds Strachan took a free kick from the edge of the area which was steered home by Appleby.

The Boston FA Cup tie was a drab affair made worse by a last minute spot kick miss by Boyd, who made amends by scoring the only goal in the replay.

The fourth round saw Pools tied against Brentford. Some 1,500 fans travelled to London for a 0-0 draw. After a replay, in which Jack Ross

Adam Boyd chips home his third goal against Sheffield Wednesday

Frank Reid/Hartlepool Mail

was sent off early in the game, Pools were disappointingly knocked out and the chance to reach the fifth round for the first time in their history had gone.

Pools lost four in a row, including an amazing 6-4 reverse at home to Wrexham. Cooper had already added to the squad in February when he signed striker Jon Daly from Stockport and Republic of Ireland winger Tommy Butler.

Friday, April 15 saw Pools take on Sheffield Wednesday at the Vic in a game played in horrendous conditions.

Wednesday were one point ahead of Pools and in fourth place. Within two minutes Boyd had put Pools into the lead from close range, then made it two before going on to net one of Victoria Park's greatest goals.

The conditions were atrocious, the goal sublime.

He dashed onto a pass from Williams on the right edge of the box. A defender powered in and Boyd sold him a dummy, sending him sliding towards the Town End, before doing the same to a defender coming from the opposite direction. All this while the rain lashed down.

He looked up and lifted the ball with the outside of his boot over the keeper into the net. It was a stunning way to seal his first professional hat-trick and Pools jumped above their opponents into fourth with three games to come.

Pools lost 2-0 at Doncaster and stayed fourth, before losing badly at home to Walsall.

Manager Cooper described the performance as 'woeful'. Pools stood fifth on 70 points going into the final game. Bournemouth, their next

Martin Scott replaced Neale Cooper at the helm

opponents, were sixth on 69 with Brentford, Bristol City and Huddersfield all capable of catching Pools.

Once again, everything boiled down to the final day of the season.

Shock Change At The Top

ON the Wednesday before the Bournemouth game Cooper was released from his contract for personal reasons. The news came

Frank Reid/Hartlepool Mail

Dimitrios Konstantopoulos and Ritchie Humphreys celebrate as Pools go through to the Play Off Final

out of the blue and Martin Scott was put in temporary charge for the final game in which a draw was enough get Pools to the play-offs. Defeat and Bournemouth were secured of a place – with Pools missing out.

Pools went one down on 12 minutes, but levelled when Daly headed in his first for the Club. Bournemouth regained the lead, before Butler crossed for Sweeney to head a dramatic leveller and earn a fifth play-off place in six seasons.

Play Off Time Again For Pools

POOLS entertained Tranmere on Friday, May 13 and won 2-0 with Boyd getting both the goals, the second another spectacular effort.

It was the first time in nine play-off games that Pools had gone into a second leg with a lead. It was a lead they would have to defend at Prenton Park.

After Konstantopoulos made a number of saves, and after Pools had created very few chances of their own, Tranmere took the lead midway through the second half.

Pools looked like they were going to hang on, before conceding with three minutes of time remaining.

There was only going to be one way that this was settled – penalties.

Tranmere took the first penalty and Konstantopoulos saved, but Tinkler missed

Pools' second effort. Porter, Robson and Westwood netted and after the compulsory penalties it was 4-4. Beresford made it 5-4 but Sweeney buried his. Konstantopoulos saved Ian Sharps' kick, to give Pools the upper hand.

The next penalty was to be taken by Humphreys. The player who had missed the penalty at Cheltenham three years earlier had now clocked up almost 200 consecutive league games and used all of his experience to plant the ball home to the keeper's left and put Pools through to the play off final.

Humphreys had buried his demons from the Cheltenham game and the 2,300-plus Pools fans had something to celebrate in the play-offs at last.

Into The Millennium... And A Mystery Letter

FOR the showpiece final at Cardiff's Millennium Stadium, their opponents were Sheffield Wednesday.

The town rallied behind the Club for the biggest day of all and in excess of 16,000 tickets were sold.

Not only did Cardiff open their arms to Hartlepool fans but places such as Gloucester, Bristol, Taunton and Newport all saw Poolies spend the weekend there. There were around 40,000 Sheffield fans in an attendance of 59,808 – the highest crowd for a Hartlepool United game.

Over 16,000 Pools fans travelled to Cardiff for the Final

Eifion Williams celebrates after scoring at The Millennium Stadium

Line-Up For The Final

POOLS lined up with Dimi Konstantopoulos, Micky Barron, Chris Westwood, Micky Nelson, Matty Robson, Gavin Strachan, Tony Sweeney, Ritchie Humphreys, Thomas Butler, Joel Porter and Adam Boyd. On the bench were Darren Craddock, Mark Tinkler, Eifion Williams, Jon Daly and Jim Provett.

Scott had taken the decision to drop Daly for Porter and Williams for Butler.

Pools didn't settle and, after 30 minutes, Scott's gamble to play Butler backfired when, in his first start in five, the winger took a heavy knock. On came Eifion Williams, playing on the biggest stage in his homeland.

Pools found their feet and grew in confidence, but fell behind in first half added time when Jon-Paul McGovern tapped home.

It was a fair reflection of how the first half had gone. Boyd, who had rattled in a hat-trick against the Owls just weeks earlier, was man-marked and well shackled even when he dropped deep for the ball.

Pools were on level terms within a couple of minutes of the restart. A long throw by Humphreys on the left was headed into the path of Williams who whacked the ball in to the back of the net, and wheeled away with his traditional goal celebration of his arms extended as if they were wings. Pools were indeed flying.

Strachan and Sweeney took the game by the scruff of the neck and started to dominate.

Pools then lost skipper Barron who turned his knee and was taken off to be replaced by Craddock on the hour. Less than ten minutes later Pools were forced into another substitution when Porter was injured once again. Three injuries – three substitutions.

The final change paid an immediate reward. Daly entered the pitch and rose to meet a Strachan free-kick and power home the perfect header.

Hartlepool United 2, Sheffield Wednesday 1.

If the noise was deafening before the goal it was ear-splitting after.

The Owls poured forward but struggled to get past a now slick and confident Pools. With 13 minutes left the Owls brought on three pairs of fresh legs to try and break Pools down.

Costly Penalty Decision

WITH less than ten minutes left one of the substitutes, Drew Talbot, went down under very little pressure from Westwood. Penalty. Referee Phil Crossley, who was not well-placed to make the decision, had awarded a dubious spot kick for the most innocuous of challenges, the striker making the most of Westwood's positioning.

Westwood, one of the calmest men on and off the pitch, furiously questioned the decision as he was instantly dismissed. With eight minutes of normal time remaining, another substitute, Steve MacLean, held his nerve and rattled in the equaliser from the spot.

Shortly into extra time the game as a contest was over. Pools conceded after just four minutes, when Whelan capitalised on a rare Nelson slip. Pools pressed, pushed and harried but with a man to the good, the players tiring and no more substitutes allowed, the Owls just soaked up the pressure and in the dying minutes of the game, with Nelson pushed up front, Wednesday scored an underserved fourth.

Pools were eight minutes away from glory for the second season in a row.

No consolation could be given to any of the players, who lay crestfallen and in tears on the Millennium Stadium turf, watching the victors celebrate victory and promotion.

Pools weren't beaten by the Sheffield team that day, they just lost.

Jon Daly hit Pools' second to make it 2-1

The Mystery Letter

WHAT really did happen on that fateful day in Cardiff?

Perhaps we will never know but some things were of interest. There were rumours that the match officials had been seen up 'late' the night before.

Player selection was restricted for Martin Scott due to injuries – did that affect the outcome? Injuries to key players caused all substitutes to be used early in the game. There was nobody left to come on in extra time.

The penalty decision? How could the referee have seen the exact circumstances from behind and a long way from the run of play? Was the linesman consulted? Why didn't Sky Sports ever re-show that penalty decision during the match or in the post-match analysis? Usually they analyse such instances in great detail.

Finally, why did HUFC receive an anonymous letter – posted on Friday 27 May 2005 – 48 hours before the game warning of a penalty decision?

The hand-writing is that of an older person and the address on the envelope shows an old Pools address. The envelope was post-marked "Tyneside, 27th May 2005", but not opened by the Club until Tuesday 31 May due to the Bank Holiday Monday.

Who wrote it? The Club were unable to find out despite detailed investigations by all concerned (including the Police).

Did Pools deserve to go into the Championship? Was it allowed? Were Pools big enough?

We will never know – a real Sherlock Holmes mystery – but perhaps the Club needed to hire Life On Mars star detective Gene Hunt to 'establish' the truth…?

So if anyone knows who wrote the letter then please contact the Club.

Jon Daly consoles Gavin Strachan at the final whistle

The fans were in fine voice throughout the game

		P	HW	HD	HL	HF	HA	AW	AD	AL	AF	AA	POINTS
1	Luton Town	46	17	4	2	46	16	12	7	4	41	32	98
2	Hull City	46	16	5	2	42	17	10	3	10	38	36	86
3	Tranmere Rovers	46	14	5	4	43	23	8	8	7	30	32	79
4	Brentford	46	15	4	4	34	22	7	5	11	23	38	75
5	Sheffield Wednesday	46	10	6	7	34	28	9	9	5	43	31	72
6	**HARTLEPOOL UNITED**	**46**	**15**	**3**	**5**	**51**	**30**	**6**	**5**	**12**	**25**	**36**	**71**
7	Bristol City	46	9	8	6	42	25	9	8	6	32	32	70
8	Bournemouth	46	9	7	7	40	30	11	3	9	37	34	70
9	Huddersfield Town	46	12	6	5	42	28	8	4	11	32	37	70
10	Doncaster Rovers	46	10	11	2	35	20	6	7	10	30	40	66
11	Bradford City	46	9	6	8	40	35	8	8	7	24	27	65
12	Swindon Town	46	12	5	6	40	30	5	7	11	26	38	63
13	Barnsley	46	7	11	5	38	31	7	8	8	31	33	61
14	Walsall	46	11	7	5	40	28	5	5	13	25	41	60
15	Colchester United	46	8	6	9	27	23	6	11	6	33	27	59
16	Blackpool	46	8	7	8	28	30	7	5	11	26	29	57
17	Chesterfield	46	9	8	6	32	28	5	7	11	23	34	57
18	Port Vale	46	13	2	8	33	23	4	3	16	16	36	56
19	Oldham Athletic	46	10	5	8	42	34	4	5	14	18	39	52
20	Milton Keynes Dons	46	8	10	5	33	28	4	5	14	21	40	51
21	Torquay United	46	8	5	10	27	36	4	10	9	28	43	51
22	Wrexham	46	6	8	9	26	37	7	6	10	36	43	43
23	Peterborough United	46	5	6	12	27	35	4	6	13	22	38	39
24	Stockport County	46	3	4	16	26	46	3	4	16	23	52	26

Coca Cola Football League One Table 2004/05

2005/06

Scott, Ross, Stephenson And Relegation

ONCE the aftermath of defeat subsided, Pools appointed Martin Scott as permanent manager. He had progressed through the managerial ranks within the Club, first making his mark as youth coach. He knew the IOR way of working so confidence was high.

On the way out were Jack Ross and Westwood. Ross had looked very promising before he suffered from injury and then homesickness. His contract was cancelled after a Football League enquiry. Ross claimed stress to get out of his contract and owners IOR were not pleased that a player could so easily break his contract with full PFA backing.

Westwood had been a great servant, a consistent performer, and had clocked up just short of 300 appearances. Despite the best efforts of both Scott and IOR to keep the classy defender, he was returning to the midlands for family reasons after five seasons in the North-East.

Also no longer to play for the Club were youngsters Andy Appleby and Jack Wilkinson and former England International Steve Howey who made a single cameo appearance towards the end of the season.

Scott was keen to stamp his mark on the playing squad and made a number of new additions.

From Cardiff came central midfielder Lee Bullock, also arriving from Wales was Wrexham midfielder Chris Llewellyn. Exciting former Sunderland forward Michael Proctor put pen to paper as well as right back Darren Williams, another ex-Wearsider.

Scott's former Sunderland team-mate Steve Agnew was appointed as reserve team coach.

Pre Season Tour

HOLLAND was on the menu again for Pools and youth team player James Brown scored on his first run out for the first XI in a 1-0 win over TOP Oss. Pools lost the second game by the same scoreline to Den Bosch. On returning home a 3-0 win over a youthful Middlesbrough outfit followed and then they bettered this with a 4-0 win at York, with the talented Brown netting once more. Big things were expected of him this season.

But as Pools lost 1-0 to Hibs in Scotland, they were dealt a blow when Brown was carried off with knee ligament damage. His promising career was put on hold.

For the second season in a row Pools started off with a home game against Bradford City, but this time they gave a disjointed display in losing 2-0.

Scott dropped Boyd after an uneasy opening game and replaced him with Daly. After a draw

Paul Stephenson, Martin Scott and Steve Agnew

in the following game at Bournemouth, Scott decided to dip into the transfer market again.

With no replacement signed for Westwood, Scott went to Sunderland and landed Neill Collins on loan.

His debut saw a win for Pools at Doncaster thanks to Daly, followed by a 1-1 home draw with Walsall, who scored through Westwood, making a quick return to Pools with his new employers.

Midweek saw Pools win through to the second round of the League Cup after a 3-1 victory over Darlington. Pools were in need of a

home win and Scott recalled Boyd.

Proctor started the next game, taking the place of Daly, and was again on the mark alongside Eifion Williams and Boyd as they shared six goals with Scunthorpe.

In 17th place and struggling, Pools had the ideal chance to get some points on the board, a home game with bottom of the league Yeovil.

With Collins on international duty for the Scotland under-21 side, it was expected that Ben Clark would start in defence. Instead, Scott opted to give a debut to Carl Jones on his 19th birthday.

Michael Proctor scored two goals in Pools' 3-1 win over Darlington

Martin Scott signed defender Gerard Nash on loan from Ipswich Town

Pools lost 1-0 in a dire game and there was worse news to follow – Boyd suffered knee ligament damage in the early stages. He was to miss the majority of the season.

With Porter also sidelined long-term, Pools were without the two forwards who pushed them to the play-offs.

Pools were knocked out of the second round of the League Cup after a gutsy display at Charlton, losing 3-1 on the night. At the end of September, Pools were third bottom after 11 games with the same number of points.

October promised to be a tricky month, but Pools came through it with wins at Bristol City and Port Vale and a vital home win over fellow strugglers MK Dons. A November 3-1 victory over Gillingham – managed by Neale Cooper – had left them in 15th place before they beat Dagenham and Redbridge in the first round of the FA Cup.

Embarrassment In The FA Cup

THE second round of the cup brought a home tie with Tamworth, managed by former Pools midfielder Mark Cooper. Pools were embarrassing and were embarrassed, losing 2-1.

December saw the start of a dire run of form and, by the time Pools took to the field to face Blackpool on January 28, they hadn't won in the last eight games and were in a battle to stay out of the bottom four.

Pools started with two inexperienced loan players, Gerard Nash and Jon-Paul Pittman, in the side.

Both sides were reduced to ten men, Pools losing Micky Barron as he conceded a penalty in the process.

Scott changed the team around, introducing a far from fit Boyd for Clark.

With around 20 minutes left, Pools were awarded a penalty. Boyd's kick was saved, Blackpool cleared and ran into the home half where Nelson upended the influential Keigan Parker. Peter Clarke netted his second penalty. Parker himself added a third and Pools were easily beaten.

The result was met with a crescendo of disapproval and demands for the manager to go.

Amid a post-match dressing-room bust-up, Scott was suspended and later replaced following a thorough internal investigation.

Pools had gone from being eight minutes away from playing in the Championship last season to being thrust into turmoil and a relegation battle.

Paul Stephenson was put in temporary charge of the First Team

		P	HW	HD	HL	HF	HA	AW	AD	AL	AF	AA	POINTS
1	Southend United	46	13	6	4	37	16	10	7	6	35	27	82
2	Colchester United	46	15	4	4	39	21	7	9	7	19	19	79
3	Brentford	46	10	8	5	35	23	10	8	5	37	29	76
4	Huddersfield Town	46	13	6	4	40	25	6	10	7	32	34	73
5	Barnsley	46	11	11	1	37	19	7	7	9	25	25	72
6	Swansea City	46	11	9	3	42	23	7	8	8	36	32	71
7	Nottingham Forest	46	14	5	4	40	15	5	7	11	27	37	69
8	Doncaster Rovers	46	11	6	6	30	19	9	3	11	25	32	69
9	Bristol City	46	11	7	5	38	22	7	4	12	28	40	65
10	Oldham Athletic	46	12	4	7	32	24	6	7	10	26	36	65
11	Bradford City	46	8	9	6	28	25	6	10	7	23	24	61
12	Scunthorpe United	46	8	8	7	36	33	7	7	9	32	40	60
13	Port Vale	46	10	5	8	30	26	6	7	10	19	28	60
14	Gillingham	46	13	4	6	31	21	3	8	12	19	43	60
15	Yeovil Town	46	8	8	7	27	24	7	3	13	27	38	56
16	Chesterfield	46	6	7	10	31	37	8	7	8	32	36	56
17	Bournemouth	46	7	11	5	25	20	5	8	10	24	33	55
18	Tranmere Rovers	46	7	8	8	32	30	6	7	10	18	22	54
19	Blackpool	46	9	8	6	33	27	3	9	11	23	37	53
20	Rotherham United	46	7	9	7	31	26	5	7	11	21	36	52
21	**HARTLEPOOL UNITED**	**46**	**6**	**10**	**7**	**28**	**30**	**5**	**7**	**11**	**16**	**29**	**50**
22	Milton Keynes Dons	46	8	8	7	28	25	4	6	13	17	41	50
23	Swindon Town	46	9	5	9	31	31	2	10	11	15	34	48
24	Walsall	46	7	7	9	27	34	4	7	12	20	36	47

Coca Cola Football
League One Table
2005/06

Stephenson Replaces Scott

YOUTH team manager Paul Stephenson was placed in temporary charge.

For the next game at Rotherham, he made five changes to the starting line up. Back in the fold were Darren Williams, Mark Tinkler, Matty Robson and two youngsters that Stephenson knew well – Stephen Turnbull, 18, and Michael Maidens, 17.

For the next game, at home to Chesterfield, Pools won thanks to a great individual strike from Robson.

Chris Turner Returns To Pools

FORMER manager Chris Turner returned to the Club in a consultancy capacity with the title of Director of Sport on February 20. The popular Stephenson was to continue as caretaker manager until the end of the season.

After a scoreless draw at Tranmere, Pools had kept three consecutive clean sheets, but were hit by a strike from distance in the last minute of the home game with Doncaster which meant a 1-1 draw. The two dropped points would be costly.

Pools were 19th, three points above second bottom Rotherham and five above MK Dons. With 12 games to play the run in was going to be tight.

The next encounter saw Pools play another

Friday night match with second-placed Huddersfield at the Vic. On the bench for the first time this season was Joel Porter. Boyd converted to put Pools one-up, before the visitors levelled.

Nelson and Boyd both went close, before the latter pushed the ball wide to youngster Maidens.

He took a few steps forward and hit a gorgeous strike with the outside of his boot from around 30 yards. The goal of the season award followed.

Michael Maidens hit Goal of the Season against Huddersfield Town

Adam Boyd sinks to the
ground at the final whistle

Porter's return was crowned with a 15-yard volley. Now seven places off bottom and four points above the relegation zone, it was hoped that this win would give Pools the impetus to progress.

Eight Defeats In A Row

HOWEVER, in the following eight games, Pools failed to win and with three games remaining they were second bottom and four points away from safety.

Nottingham Forest came to the Vic in with a shout of promotion.

After a see-saw game, Pools won 3-2 and moved to third bottom on 48 points, behind Rotherham who held the safe spot with 51 points.

Third-placed Brentford provided stern opposition in Stephenson's final away game. Defeat would relegate Pools.

The visitors defended stoutly, but with just six minutes remaining they fell behind. At that point Pools were down and looking at League Two – cue Nelson.

He nabbed an equaliser in the last minute to give Pools an outside chance of survival in the final game.

Pools needed to win the last game with Port Vale and hope Rotherham lost.

Almost 7,000 fans were present, but there was no breakthrough. With 13 minutes to go, Port Vale took the lead. Stephenson brought on James Brown for his fourth substitute appearance in the last few weeks. He netted his first league goal of the season with four minutes to go, but it wasn't enough, the game was drawn and Pools were down. The crowd applauded the players from the pitch.

After the crowd and players had departed and the tears subsided, tied to the terrace in the Town End was a home made banner.

On it were sprayed just three words – Never Say Die.

Ritchie Humphreys distraught as Pools are relegated

A lone banner left in the Town End

Danny Wilson was charged with getting Pools back into League One after relegation in season 2005/06

2006/07

Wilson, Darlington and Promotion

FOLLOWING the trauma and disappointment of relegation, Hartlepool United FC entered the new season with one aim – promotion.

After such hard-work in trying to establish the Club as a League One side, the efforts weren't going to be ruined by a single season.

Entrusted with getting things back on track was new manager Danny Wilson, appointed on June 13. For the first time since Cyril Knowles became manager in 1989, Pools had appointed a new manager with experience of steering teams to success in the English Football League.

Each appointment since then – all ten permanent choices – had experience of youth football, reserve football, Scottish football or was a former senior player.

"This is a long-term job," said Wilson. "I'm here for the distance, just as the Chairman and IOR are, which is fantastic for the stability of the Club and for taking it forward."

Stephenson returned to his post of youth team coach and Wilson appointed Ian Butterworth as his right-hand man.

Winger Thomas Butler who submitted a transfer request, stayed behind when the team went to Holland for their pre-season training stint, and soon joined Swansea City. Chris Llewellyn also moved to Wales, returning to Wrexham almost a year after swapping North Wales for the North-East.

Micky Barron's well-deserved testimonial game brought a 2-1 win over Leeds United, with James Brown scoring twice.

And, as Pools drew with Carlisle, Adam Boyd was on his way to Luton for a reported £500,000.

The real campaign started with a home defeat to Swindon, as Pools missed two penalties and were unable to beat an inspired visiting goalkeeper.

A goalless draw at Macclesfield, home loss to Walsall, draw with Torquay and loss at Hereford proved an unflattering start.

Liddle Debut Comes In The Cup

WILSON moved to sign promising Middlesbrough midfielder Gary Liddle and he

Micky Barron leads his children out for his testimonial game with Leeds United in 2006

made an impressive bow in a Carling Cup win at Burnley, Joel Porter netting the winner from the spot. Willie Boland (Cardiff) and Ali Gibb (Bristol Rovers) also arrived as Wilson added to his squad.

In defeat at Hereford, Wilson put an end to the record run of Ritchie Humphreys. The left-back had made 234 consecutive starts for Pools – from his debut in August 2001 through to August 2006.

Soon after Humphreys went on loan to Port Vale, he missed the next eight Pools games, but returned to play a vital role.

A 3-0 home loss to Shrewsbury then brought about a fine run.

Pools won 5-3 at Peterborough, 4-1 at Grimsby and beat Wrexham 3-0 at Victoria Park to move from 18th to seventh.

At the heart of the run was striker Jon Daly, he scored seven times in a week, including a hat-trick against Wrexham.

But a disappointing loss at Lincoln pegged the progress back and, after losing 1-0 at home to Barnet on November 4, Pools were an unflattering 16th after 17 games.

Wilson signed Darryl Duffy on loan from Hull City to add firepower to his side. His five goals in ten starts helped bring Pools season to life.

The turning point came at Accrington Stanley on November 18. A goal down at the break, Pools were staring at a season of uncertainty.

But Eifion Williams drilled in an equaliser and, with time fast running out, Humphreys surged forward from left-back and bent an exquisite shot into the corner of the net.

Both players and manager revealed a few home truths were said at half-time within the confines of the dressing room. And it proved the key to turning the situation around.

Records galore were broken as Pools hit top form.

They chalked up nine successive wins – eight of them without conceding a goal – went 23 games without defeat, taking 61 points from a possible 69, and moved from 16th to top spot.

Andy Monkhouse's first goal for Pools after moving from Swindon proved enough to beat Notts County on December 5, Ben Clark's first goal for Pools since moving from Sunderland in 2003 helped secure a 2-0 at Bristol Rovers the next week.

Jon Daly's last goal for the Club before moving to Dundee United helped see off Grimsby on Boxing Day.

When Pools won at Mansfield on January 1, another clean sheet was kept as Clark and

Gary Liddle in his first training session with Pools

Jon Daly proudly shows off the match ball after his hat-trick against Wrexham

Richard Barker signs for Pools in January 2007

Micky Nelson kept Richard Barker in check.

The next day a cheque was on its way to Field Mill for the services of the free-scoring striker. Duffy had gone back to Hull and Barker took on the mantle of leading the line.

After a key 1-0 win over promotion rivals MK Dons, Barker's first goal came in a draw at Wrexham, his goal later cancelled out by a Chris Llewellyn leveller.

A big victory came on February 10 over Walsall, as second top entertained top.

When Martin Butler put the leaders ahead, it was the first time Pools had been behind in a game since the victory at Accrington, some 13 games previous.

But Nelson put Pools level before a dramatic ending. A free-kick was rolled to Humphreys and he cracked his shot around the wall and into the side of the net to give Pools an 88th minute lead.

And there was still time for Barker to nab a third to help manager Wilson to his second manager of the month award of the season.

Pools had the momentum – and luck – as proved in wins over Macclesfield and Boston.

Against Macc, Pools were two-up, pegged back to 2-2 before a Humphreys' free-kick in the 88th minute cracked off the woodwork and into the net via a visiting defender.

Next up at York Street, Humphreys had the confidence and audacity to ping a free-kick at goal from nigh-on 40 yards. After hitting the bar it ended up in the net via the back of the goalkeeper.

Danny Wilson picked up the Manager of the Month award three times in the 06/07 season

Derby Delight For Pools At Darlington

A stunning comeback at Stockport, Pools drawing 3-3 after being 3-0 down, set the side up for a trip to Darlington.

Backed by 4,000 fans, it was men against boys as Pools toyed with their rivals, themselves in with a shout of the play-offs.

After Dimi Konstantopoulos saved a deflected free-kick, Eifion Williams tore into the home penalty area and drove his shot home.

The Welshman then scored one of the greatest – and most memorable – goals. Micky Barron played the ball forward, Williams controlled the high pass with his outstretched foot before volleying in from 20 yards in front of the delirious travelling contingent.

As Monkhouse headed in a third, following up a James Brown shot which came back off the post to make it 3-0, Pools were in dreamland.

"We are unbeatable" was the cry – it was hard to argue with the statement as Pools were .

After a 3-0 win over Chester, Wilson's side were nine points clear, although Walsall won their game in hand the next day.

But the run was about to come to an end. Backed by almost 1,000 fans at Barnet, Pools

Eifion Williams celebrates his wonder goal at Darlington

never got going and, while Williams scored what was to prove his final goal in a Pools shirt to make the score 1-1, Barnet soon scored a second.

The undefeated run was over. Pools were top of the table and still had the title in sight.

A win over Accrington led Pools into a game at Wycombe – victory would mean promotion.

Monkhouse crossed from the left, Barker ghosted in from the right and planted home an 81st minute header to get Pools back into

Pools fans celebrate in front of the scoreboard after the win at Darlington

Frank Reid/Hartlepool Mail

Andy Monkhouse was shown the red card for a clash at Rochdale on April 28, 2007

League One.

Promotion assured, Pools had three games to get their hands on a first piece of silverware.

And, with Walsall losing at home to Bury, Pools point with Notts County looked a good one – three points ahead with six points to play for.

But they pressed the self-destruct button at Rochdale. With in excess of 3,500 travelling fans hoping for the win which could clinch it, all they saw was a 2-0 loss, Barker and Monkhouse red-carded, a missed penalty and Nelson injured.

It all boiled down to the final day, Pools at home to Bristol Rovers, needing Walsall, at Swindon, to lose.

Porter chipped Pools in front and all looked good. But a 54th minute penalty equaliser handed the initiative back to Walsall. Recent signing from Consett, Michael Mackay superbly finished from distance, but it wasn't to be as the effort was chalked off for offside.

And when Pools conceded a second goal on 86 minutes, the dream was over. Walsall's winner a minute later meant that Pools missed out once again.

Amid muted celebrations, Pools were presented – again – with the League Two runners-up shield.

The first priority had been achieved, but there was disappointment again at missing out on the title and silverware.

Pools are presented with the runners-up shield in League Two

		P	HW	HD	HL	HF	HA	AW	AD	AL	AF	AA	POINTS
1	Walsall	46	16	4	3	39	13	9	10	4	27	21	89
2	HARTLEPOOL UNITED	46	14	5	4	34	17	12	5	6	31	23	88
3	Swindon Town	46	15	4	4	34	17	10	6	7	24	21	85
4	Milton Keynes Dons	46	14	4	5	41	26	11	5	7	35	32	84
5	Lincoln City	46	12	4	7	36	28	9	7	7	34	31	74
6	Bristol Rovers	46	13	5	5	27	14	7	7	9	22	28	72
7	Shrewsbury Town	46	11	7	5	38	23	7	10	6	30	23	71
8	Stockport County	46	14	4	5	41	25	7	4	12	24	29	71
9	Rochdale	46	9	6	8	33	20	9	6	8	37	30	66
10	Peterborough United	46	10	6	7	48	36	8	5	10	22	25	65
11	Darlington	46	10	6	7	28	30	7	8	8	24	26	65
12	Wycombe Wanderers	46	8	11	4	23	14	8	3	12	29	33	62
13	Notts County	46	8	6	9	29	25	8	8	7	26	28	62
14	Barnet	46	12	5	6	35	30	4	6	13	20	40	59
15	Grimsby Town	46	11	4	8	33	32	6	4	13	24	41	59
16	Hereford United	46	9	7	7	23	17	5	6	12	22	36	55
17	Mansfield Town	46	10	4	9	38	31	4	8	11	20	32	54
18	Chester City	46	7	9	7	23	23	6	5	12	17	25	53
19	Wrexham	46	8	8	7	23	21	5	4	14	20	44	51
20	Accrington Stanley	46	10	6	7	42	33	3	5	15	28	48	50
21	Bury	46	4	7	12	22	35	9	4	10	24	26	50
22	Macclesfield Town	46	8	7	8	36	34	4	5	14	19	43	48
23	Boston United	46	9	5	9	29	32	3	5	15	22	48	46
24	Torquay United	46	5	8	10	19	22	2	6	15	17	41	35

Coca Cola Football League Two Table 2006/07

2007/08

Consolidation, Elland Road And Michael Maidens

NO sooner had he won the goal of the season award for his stylish effort at Darlington, and Eifion Williams was one of ten players released as Wilson prepared for life in League One.

Darren Williams was granted a free, 12 months after he requested a move, along with stalwarts Mark Tinkler and Darrell Clarke, two players who played their part in the Chris Turner revolution, but had been dogged by injury in recent seasons.

Also on their way were John Brackstone, Michael Proctor, Craig Hignett, Phil Turnbull, Tony Davison and Carl Jones.

Dimi Konstantopoulos, after a record breaking 25 clean sheets, moved to the Championship and Coventry City, but Micky Barron signed a contract for his 11th season at Victoria Park.

Arriving were two new goalkeepers – Arran Lee-Barrett and Jan Budtz – Robbie Elliott and Ian Moore from Leeds, Jamie McCunnie from Dunfermline and Godwin Antwi was signed on a season-long loan from Liverpool.

Wilson hailed the summer tour of Holland as a success, as Pools beat RKC Waaljik and lost to Hapoel Shoma of Israel.

On the opening day of the season, it was a repeat of the performance 12 months previous, as Pools dominated but ended up losing.

After Swindon in 2006, it was Luton in 2007, as Pools controversially went down 2-1 at Kenilworth Road.

But Pools enjoyed an encouraging start – and were up to third after a swift 4-2 win at Orient on September 22.

The win at Port Vale, on August 25, however proved a rare event – an away victory as three-point hauls on the road were too scarce throughout the campaign.

Pools lost 2-0 at Elland Road, the home of Leeds United on September 8, in front of 26,877 – the third highest Football League attendance Pools had appeared in front of. Wilson's men played some fantastic football and did not deserve defeat.

In October Wilson signed defender Danny Coles on loan from Hull City to try and put an end to the side's defensive problems away from home and he debuted in a loss at Nottingham Forest.

Tragedy Strikes Football Club

BUT on the morning of their game at Swansea City on October 21, everyone associated with Hartlepool United was left stunned.

Promising midfielder Michael Maidens died following a car crash on Teesside.

Jamie McCunnie, Arran Lee-Barrett, Robbie Elliott, Jan Budtz and Godwin Antwi arrived at The Vic

The game was postponed and a shell-shocked squad made the journey back to the North-East.

The gates at Victoria Park were soon adorned with tributes to the 20-year-old and boss Wilson said: "We as a Club are shattered at what has happened, but it is nothing compared to the pain his family are feeling.

"Michael was an outstanding young lad. Everyone says after tragedies like this what a lovely person he was, but he genuinely was an outstanding boy."

The next game for the Club was against Brighton on October 27 and, following an immaculate pre-game silence in memory of Michael Maidens, Pools set about the task of getting back to playing football.

Richard Barker's late penalty looked like brining late relief as he levelled, but there was still time for the visitors to score an unsavoury winner.

A minute's silence is held before the Brighton game in memory of Michael Maidens in 2007

The gates at Victoria Park were adorned with tributes to Michael Maidens

Gainsborough Hit For Six

POOLS won 6-0 at Gainsborough Trinity in the FA Cup, but were knocked out in the second round at Hereford.

Antony Sweeney's spectacular goal at Millwall, Pools first league game against the Lions since 1965, produced a welcome win, but from then on away form faltered terribly.

Pools lost their next six on the road, including a January 1, 4-2 loss at Carlisle when the visitors twice led.

But it wasn't until Ben Clark's effort at Northampton on January 12 that the rot was stopped. It was, however, temporary as they lost three of their next four.

In the meantime, struggling Championship side Norwich City had made an approach to add Pools Youth Team Coach Paul Stephenson to their backroom staff. Discussions between the two clubs were ongoing when Stephenson walked out on Pools to join the Canaries in early December.

Home form was keeping things together, as Pools were scoring for fun at Victoria Park, with wins over Southend (4-3), Luton (4-0) and Port Vale (3-2).

Alan Thompson, capped once by England, moved on loan from Leeds to offer experience and a cultured left foot in midfield. Wilson also signed commanding defender Sam Collins from Hull City, while striker Moore left to team up with his dad Ian, the manager of Tranmere Rovers.

Disappointing losses at home to Northampton and at Bournemouth raised fears of being dragged into a relegation scrap, but the players were having none of it.

The long haul back from Bournemouth offered time to reflect and, with the senior professionals coming to the fore, the message was clear – Hartlepool United were desperate not to get involved in a scrap to stay out of the bottom four.

And so it proved, as, in their next game, at Oldham a change in personnel was needed. Michael Mackay had scored over 40 goals that season before coming to Victoria Park and had continued scoring the Reserves. His time had come at Oldham and a cheeky lobbed finish by Mackay secured a rare and very welcome win.

On the downside, leading scorer Barker damaged knee ligaments which was to put paid to his season.

But a 4-0 win over Gillingham – a game which brought Joel Porter the goal of the season award – and a 2-1 triumph over Huddersfield pulled the side away from danger.

Pools won only one of their remaining nine games, an Easter Monday win over Yeovil at Victoria Park, a game which saw the return of James Brown after he was injured in the thumping win over Luton on February 2.

Champions-elect Swansea won 3-1 at Victoria

Michael Mackay joined Pools in February 2007

Park, Millwall triumphed 1-0 at the Vic and Nottingham Forest did the same as Pools ended the season with a trio of home losses.

With almost the final kick of the campaign, Brown secured a 2-2 draw at Walsall to bring the curtain down on an unfulfilled season.

Pools never really troubled the play-off spots, while they flirted on occasions with the bottom four – but 15th place was still the fourth best finishing position in 99 years of football but lacked the exciting end to the season that had become the Club's and IOR's trademark.

The Centenary celebrations got underway with a special Player of the Year Night at the Borough Hall on the Headland.

Not only did the fans get the chance to vote for the normal annual awards, but the Club also sought winners for Players of the Decade through from the 1950s to the 2000s.

As well as that, the prestigious title of Player of the Century was also up for grabs on a glitzy evening for the Club, with former players invited along to join the celebrations.

Ritchie Humphreys was the night's biggest winner, scooping the Player of the 2000s accolade as well as being named Player of the Century.

He also won the Supporters' Player of the Year award, while James Brown took the Players' Award.

Coca Cola Football League One Table 2007/08

		P	HW	HD	HL	HF	HA	AW	AD	AL	AF	AA	POINTS
1	Swansea City	46	13	5	5	38	21	14	6	3	44	21	92
2	Nottingham Forest	46	13	8	2	37	13	9	8	6	27	19	82
3	Doncaster Rovers	46	14	4	5	34	18	9	7	7	31	23	80
4	Carlisle United	46	17	3	3	39	16	6	8	9	25	30	80
5	Leeds United	46	15	4	4	41	18	12	6	5	31	20	76
6	Southend United	46	12	6	5	35	20	10	4	9	35	35	76
7	Brighton and Hove Albion	46	12	6	5	37	25	7	6	10	21	25	69
8	Oldham Athletic	46	10	7	6	32	21	8	6	9	26	25	67
9	Northampton Town	46	12	6	5	38	21	5	9	9	22	34	66
10	Huddersfield Town	46	12	4	7	29	22	8	2	13	21	40	66
11	Tranmere Rovers	46	13	4	6	32	18	5	7	11	20	29	65
12	Walsall	46	7	9	7	27	26	9	7	7	25	20	64
13	Swindon Town	46	12	5	6	41	24	4	8	11	22	32	61
14	Leyton Orient	46	9	6	8	27	29	7	6	10	22	34	60
15	**HARTLEPOOL UNITED**	**46**	**11**	**5**	**7**	**40**	**26**	**4**	**4**	**15**	**23**	**40**	**54**
16	Bristol Rovers	46	5	10	8	25	30	7	7	9	20	23	53
17	Millwall	46	9	4	10	30	26	5	6	12	15	34	52
18	Yeovil Town	46	9	4	10	19	27	5	6	12	19	32	52
19	Cheltenham Town	46	10	8	5	23	21	3	4	16	19	43	51
20	Crewe Alexandra	46	8	6	9	27	33	4	8	11	20	32	50
21	Bournemouth	46	10	4	9	31	35	7	3	13	31	37	48
22	Gillingham	46	9	9	5	26	22	2	4	17	18	51	46
23	Port Vale	46	5	8	10	26	35	4	3	16	21	46	38
24	Luton Town	46	10	5	8	29	25	1	5	17	14	38	33

Ritchie Humphreys with his Player of the Century, Player of the Decade and Player of the Year awards

The Centenary Season

THERE was good news for the Club at the start of the Centenary Season with the confirmation that the ever-popular Joel Porter would remain on the books after Pools opted to take up the option year on his contract.

There had been talk that Aussie front man Porter would make a summer move closer to home but the fans were delighted that he was to be staying at Victoria Park

Willie Boland, James Brown, David Foley, Gary Liddle, Michael Mackay, Andy Monkhouse, Michael Nelson, Matty Robson and Martin Young were also all kept on by the Club.

Making way were Scott Allison, Robbie Elliott, Ali Gibb, Tom Haigh, Michael Rae and Stephen Turnbull while Godwin Antwi returned to Liverpool at the end of his season-long loan deal.

Danny Wilson also made moves in to the transfer market to bring young midfielder Ritchie Jones to the Club following his release by Manchester United.

Also signed was Alan Power, who had impressed in the engine room of Nottingham Forest's Reserves against Pools the previous season.

Hartlepool United 2008/2009. Back row: Jonny Rowell, Martin Young, Matty Tymon, Joe Tait, Richard Barker, Alan Power, Willie Boland; Middle row: Gary Liddle, Andy Monkhouse, Ben Clark, Arran Lee-Barrett, Jan Budtz, Mark Cook, Michael Nelson, Michael Mackay, James Brown; Front row: Ritchie Jones, Joel Porter, Antony Sweeney, Danny Wilson (Manager), Sam Collins, Ritchie Humphreys, Ian Butterworth (Reserve Team Manager), Matty Robson, Jamie McCunnie, David Foley

Hamilton Academical won the Centenary Tournament at The Vic

A change of pre-season routine began the campaign as the Club headed north to Scotland rather than to their usual base at the KNVB in Holland.

Based in impressive surroundings in Largs, Pools played two competitive fixtures and defeated Greenock Morton 2-1 before drawing 0-0 with Falkirk in driving rain.

Arriving home, Pools then played host to a special Centenary Tournament at Victoria Park. Huddersfield Town, Sunderland and Hamilton Academical were the invited guests and it was the Accies who came out on top, beating Sunderland in the Final.

The fixture computer had handed the Club what looked a tricky start to the new campaign as they were due to play newly-relegated Colchester on the opening day who had moved in to a plush new stadium and had designs on an instant return to the Championship.

However, a James Brown-inspired Pools were quickly in the driving seat as the young starlet scored twice in the opening 14 minutes to stun the U's and send The Vic in to raptures.

Second half stunners from Willie Boland and debutant Ritchie Jones extended the lead to 4-0 and even two late consolation goals failed to take the gloss of a fantastic start to the season.

League Defeats But Carling Cup Glory

NEXT up a Carling Cup fixture with Scunthorpe United, another side down from the Championship in to League One and they too took a Victoria Park roasting. Goals from Porter, Foley and Brown did the trick as Pools eased in to Round Two.

Things stalled in the League with defeat at Tranmere and an unfortunate home loss to Stockport County, which also saw Willie Boland

stretchered off with a knee injury that would see him sidelined for the remainder of the campaign.

However, things continued to fizz in the Carling Cup and Pools took their first Premier League scalp of the season when they pushed their way past West Brom. Porter had put Pools ahead midway through the second half but Robert Koren's late leveller took the tie to extra time.

Ritchie Jones joined from Manchester United

The majority of the crowd perhaps expected the Baggies to show their top flight fitness, but they wilted under the lights at The Vic and goals from Foley and Richard Barker had Pools in the headlines – even if one local paper (The Northern Echo) chose to cover it with a cartoon due to an ongoing dispute between the Club and the Hartlepool Mail.

Former Pools man Steve Howard scored his regulation goal against the Club as Leicester brushed past Pools in the Johnstone's Paint Trophy, while in the League it was away form that was once again proving troublesome.

An unlikely 2-1 success at promotion favourites Peterborough at the end of January was the only cause for celebration as Pools went on to lose the next four on their travels.

At The Vic the crowd were getting value for their money as the goals flew in left, right and centre. A 4-1 hammering of Cheltenham was as routine as it got with Pools seemingly inclined to go behind by a couple before mounting a fightback.

The first of the incredible sequence of comebacks was against Oldham who led 2-0 at the break after a lacklustre first half which

James Brown celebrates his second goal against Colchester

Joel Porter scored a hat-trick against Swindon

offered no clues as to what was to happen next.

Pools exploded out of the traps in the second half and the visitors had no answer as Danny Wilson's men stormed in to a 3-2 lead within eight minutes of the restart, though the Latics did recover to make it 3-3 and escape with a share of the spoils.

The very next home game also finished 3-3 and this time Pools gave themselves an even bigger mountain to climb having been 3-0 down to Swindon on 52 minutes with all three goals scored by Robins prolific front man Simon Cox.

However, Porter seemed to take particular offence to Swindon's onslaught and the in-form striker helped himself to his own hat-trick, completed with the deftest of lobs in the very last minute. Typical of Porter, he let Cox take the match ball!

The Carling Cup run had come to an end against Leeds despite a spirited performance at Elland Road, while an early goal from Matt Oakley was enough to defeat Pools on their first ever trip to face Leicester City.

And trailing 2-0 at half time against Walsall at the Banks's Stadium in mid-October it looked likely that Pools would extend their winless away run to five games.

However, once again they showed their character with Antony Sweeney scoring the first, substitute Matty Robson smashing home a stunning equaliser before James Brown secured the win with a late header.

Pools seemed to be in the habit of falling behind and did so three times against Huddersfield Town, but goals from loan signing Kevin Kyle (2), Porter (2) and Brown clinched an amazing 5-3 win at The Vic.

Any regular neutrals turning up at Victoria Park may well have been enjoying themselves

Joel Porter and Matty Robson celebrate the fifth goal against Huddersfield

as between the start of the season and the end of November there had been an incredible 51 goals scored in just 13 games!

And the goals kept coming as Pools needed a home replay to see off Brighton after drawing 3-3 at the Withdean Stadium.

Injury Blow Hits Pools Where It Hurts

DISASTER struck at the end of November when with an hour gone in the home game with Bristol Rovers, young starlet James Brown turned awkwardly on his right knee as he looked to jink in to some space.

Having ruptured the cruciate ligament in his other knee in the pre season of 2006, Brown seemed to immediately sense he had sustained a similar injury and slammed his fist in to the ground in agony and frustration.

A trip to the specialist confirmed the striker's worst fears and a he underwent re-constructive surgery to his knee, ruling him out for the remainder of the campaign.

Not only was it a sickening blow for Brown, who had earlier in the season signed a new deal, but also for the Club. Brown had scored eight goals before the injury and his creativity would be sorely missed.

FA Cup Exploits For Pools

AND it was in to Round Two after Pools saw off the challenge of non-league Fleetwood Town thanks to a double from Michael Mackay. The game was featured on ITV's highlights show that night and an incident involving Arran Lee-Barrett was spotted which resulted in the Pools keeper being handed a retrospective three-game ban.

Away form continued to be the Club's Achilles heel. During 2007/2008, Pools had managed just four away league wins, and by December 2008 the new season had offered just two league wins on the road. With the Club sitting in 13th position, the decision was taken to end Danny Wilson's time at the helm in December 2008. The former Sheffield Wednesday manager had stabilised the Club following relegation and presided over a record-breaking promotion season. However, the team's inability to string results together on the road meant he was replaced, and Chris Turner, the Director of Sport, was announced as temporary manager.

Turner's first game back in charge was the Friday night clash with Southend United and Matty Robson's sizzling strike from distance was sandwiched between a Kyle double and secured an impressive 3-0 win.

James Brown lies injured after rupturing his cruciate ligament

Pools extra time heroes

There's no stopping Joel is there?

Oh no. Help

I'd better get out of the way or Sweeney might knock me over with this shot

It's the talk of Victoria Park

Have you heard the Echo are banned?

Pools held firm in defence

James Brown has his admirers

Celtic are here watching Browny

Paul Fraser
CHIEF FOOTBALL WRITER
paul.fraser@nne.co.uk

Hartlepool United 3
West Bromwich Albion 1
after extra time, score at 90 minutes, 1-1

READERS may be wondering why the match report from last night's Carling Cup match between Hartlepool United and West Brom is accompanied by a Roy Of The Rovers-style comic strip.

It is because The Northern Echo was prevented from publishing live photographs from the game due to a growing dispute between the club and local newspapers.

The Northern Echo, along with the Hartlepool Mail, is banned from sending photographers to home matches, and our reporters are denied press access at Victoria Park.

The Mail was originally banned because it refused to sign a commercial agreement which it considers to be unfair. And The Northern Echo was then banned for supporting the Mail by supplying pictures of recent matches and refusing to give a commitment not to do so in future.

Peter Barron, Editor of The Northern Echo, said: "I don't think it is right to give that commitment without being given an explanation of the

WITH Gordon Strachan inside Victoria Park to cast an admiring eye over James Brown, the young prospect's Hartlepool United teammates combined to produce the biggest Carling Cup shock around last night.

While the Celtic manager monitored Brown's every move, it was another promising talent brought on as manager Danny Wilson's cup card that turned out to be the match-winner.

After Joel Porter's opener on the hour was cancelled out by the exquisite thinking from West Brom's Robert Koren three minutes from time, David Foley finished off a quick move in the 11th minute of extra-time to edge Pools in front again.

And, after Richard Barker nodded in Matty Robson's delivery four minutes later,

Arran Lee-Barrett's goal.

Lee-Barrett had been pretty quiet considering the opposition, hovering outside the area, struck a wonderful volley that looked destined for

created the better chances in the opening half.

Sweeney, hovering outside the area, struck a wonderful volley that looked destined for

DRAWING ON INSPIRATION: Pools went ahead through Joel Porter, but the Baggies levelled late on, sending the game into extra time before Pools scored two more thanks to David Foley and Matty Robson to secure victory

MATCHFACTS
Goals: Porter (60mins, 1-0); Koren (86, 1-1); Foley (101, 2-1); Barker (105, 3-1)
Booking: Bednar (54, foul)

With Willie Boland out with the knee injury sustained in the defeat to Stockport on Saturday, the Pools boss had to tinker slightly

The cartoon produced by the Northern Echo following Pools cup win over West Brom. The newspaper had got into a dispute with the Club over the Hartlepool Mail and their photographers were banned from the ground.

Back in the FA Cup and Pools were handed a Third Round tie with Stoke City to be played at Victoria Park on 3 January 2009. Tony Pulis' side had impressed in their debut season in the Premier League and although they arrived at The Vic inside the top flight drop zone, they'd already done enough to suggest they could fight off relegation.

A great atmosphere inside the ground, with a crowd of 5367, witnessed a strong performance from Pools and, after a goalless first half, Pools turned the screw early in the second period when Michael Nelson powered home a header at the back post to send the crowd in to bedlam.

The Potters rarely threatened a comeback and the giant-killing was complete when David Foley rammed home an unstoppable effort from 30 yards as Pools secured a place in Round Four.

With the nation's media fixed on Hartlepool for their Third Round heroics, Chris Turner's men were handed a home tie with three-time

Joel Porter celebrates with H'Angus after scoring against West Brom

FA Cup winners West Ham United, a game that was to be screened live on ITV on Sunday 24 January.

Pools began the game strongly enough, but were dealt a blow on the stroke of half time when Hammers summer recruit Valon Behrami slammed home an opening goal. It got even worse before the break when Michael Nelson was adjudged to have handled inside the area, even though replays showed the decision to be wrong. Mark Noble fired home the resultant penalty and from that moment an upset by Pools never looked on the cards as West Ham kept possession.

The return to league action proved a tough transition and no wins in the next seven games saw Pools slip to 16th in the table and just five points clear of the League One drop zone.

As well as losing ground in the league, Pools also had to cope with the loss of Reserve Team boss Ian Butterworth. The Coach had joined Pools under Danny Wilson in 2006 but walked out to team up with Bryan Gunn at Norwich in February 2008.

Turner responded by adding some fire-power to his squad with some loan signings in the shape of Daniel Nardiello from Blackpool and Lewis Guy from Doncaster. Norwegian import Rune Lange joined on a short-term deal but after scoring on his full debut at MK Dons he dislocated his shoulder in the following home game against Leicester and was ruled out for the remainder of the campaign. It was the type of luck that was to haunt Pools as they

Daniel Nardiello joined on loan from Blackpool

battled against the drop.

Following the departure of Ian Butterworth, Chris Turner was looking for somebody to help him with the workload at Victoria Park. In February, he was able to secure the services of Colin West who left a post at Southend United to be re-united with Turner at The Vic.

Danny Wilson had got back in to football quickly as boss at Swindon Town. Pools' game at Swindon was re-arranged to Tuesday 24 February due to the FA Cup fixture in January. And Wilson was left furious after Pools were awarded a debatable penalty in the last minute of their showdown at the County Ground. Ben Clark stroked the penalty home to secure a priceless three points for Pools.

A creditable 1-1 draw at Colchester the following Saturday and a home win over play-off pushing Tranmere Rovers seemed to herald the turning of a corner, but five straight defeats in the rest of March plunged Pools towards the bottom four.

Relegation Looms Once Again

TURNER raided Huddersfield Town in March for another loan signing in the shape of Keigan Parker, while his Terriers team-mate Joe Skarz joined later the same month to add competition in the left-back area.

A home game against fellow strugglers Hereford at the beginning of April was as must-win as they come and thankfully Pools did produce the goods – eventually. With twelve

Frank Reid/Hartlepool Mail

Chris Turner returned as temporary manager

minutes left the sides were locked at 2-2 with a draw not ideal for either side, but goals from Sam Collins and Antony Sweeney meant a crucial win for Turner's men.

A point at Crewe was seen as a good return, but a home defeat to play-off bound Scunthorpe United hurt as despite goals from Nardiello and Nelson, Pools were beaten 3-2.

Next up was the crunch clash at Yeovil Town and Pools knew they must at the very least avoid defeat to keep their battle for survival in the black. Joel Porter's 22nd and 23rd goals of the season were added to by a priceless header from Nardiello as Pools came away from Huish Park with a 3-2 win.

Defeat to Leeds in the final home game of the season and with Hereford United and Cheltenham Town already relegated, Pools still mathematically needed a point from their last day trip to Bristol Rovers. There were four teams who could take that final relegation spot and many combinations would doom or save Pools.

However, the game did not go according to plan and Pools found themselves two down inside five minutes on a day when they needed to protect their +5 goal difference to ensure they stayed above Carlisle.

Nardiello grabbed one back for Pools before the break, but another horrendous start to the second half saw Pools 4-1 down and staring

Antony Sweeney celebrates his crucial goal against Hereford

down the barrel of relegation if other results conspired against them.

Saved By Leeds United

IN the end it was Northampton's defeat at Leeds which proved pivotal and sent the Cobblers in to the final relegation place and Pools had secured their League One status.

Joel Porter's 23 goals ensured he was named as both Supporters' and Players' Player of the Centenary Season; a nice send-off for the striker who announced he was to sign for Australian outfit Gold Coast United.

On the back of the most sustained period of success, Hartlepool United Football Club, its owners Increased Oil Recovery Ltd, the staff and fans can look back on the last Century of football with pride and a roller-coaster of emotions; equally they can look forward to the next Century of football with optimism but, as the book has shown, there'll be more emotions to follow.

Joel Porter was named Fans and Players' Player of the Year

		P	HW	HD	HL	HF	HA	AW	AD	AL	AF	AA	POINTS
1	Leicester City	46	13	9	1	41	16	14	6	3	43	23	96
2	Peterborough United	46	14	6	3	41	22	12	5	6	37	32	89
3	Milton Keynes Dons	46	12	4	7	42	25	14	5	4	41	22	87
4	Leeds United	46	17	2	4	49	20	9	4	10	28	29	84
5	Millwall	46	13	4	6	30	21	12	3	8	33	32	82
6	Scunthorpe United	46	13	5	5	44	24	9	5	9	38	39	76
7	Tranmere Rovers	46	15	5	3	41	20	6	6	11	21	29	74
8	Southend United	46	13	2	8	29	20	8	6	9	29	41	71
9	Huddersfield Town	46	9	8	6	32	28	9	6	8	30	37	68
10	Oldham Athletic	46	9	9	5	35	24	7	8	8	31	41	65
11	Bristol Rovers	46	11	4	8	44	29	6	8	9	35	32	63
12	Colchester United	46	7	4	12	21	24	11	5	7	37	34	63
13	Walsall	46	10	3	10	34	36	7	7	9	27	30	61
14	Stockport County	46	9	7	7	34	28	7	5	11	25	29	60
15	Leyton Orient	46	6	6	11	32	40	7	7	9	23	30	52
16	Swindon Town	46	8	7	8	37	34	4	10	9	31	37	53
17	Brighton & Hove Albion	46	6	6	11	32	40	7	7	9	23	30	52
18	Yeovil Town	46	6	10	7	26	29	6	5	12	15	37	51
19	**HARTLEPOOL UNITED**	**46**	**8**	**7**	**8**	**45**	**40**	**5**	**4**	**14**	**21**	**39**	**50**
20	Carlisle United	46	8	7	8	36	32	4	7	12	20	37	50
21	Northampton Town	46	8	8	7	38	29	4	5	14	23	36	49
22	Crewe Alexandra	46	8	4	11	30	38	4	6	13	29	44	46
23	Cheltenham Town	46	7	6	10	30	38	2	6	15	21	53	39
24	Hereford United	46	6	4	13	23	28	3	3	17	19	51	34

League One Table
2008/09

Saturday 25th April 2009 | Kick-off 3.00pm
Hartlepool United v Leeds United
Coca-Cola League One

2.50

During the Centenary Season, Pools modelled the front cover of each matchday programme on a different design from a past season at The Vic. This cover was taken from the final home game of the 2008/09 campaign against Leeds United (25/04/09) and it shows a selection of the covers used throughout the season.

Chapter 14
Micky Barron

Micky Barron is in a select group of three at Hartlepool United. In 100 years, only Tony Bircumshaw, Paul Baker and Barron have led the Club to promotion. But add in the five play-off campaigns he has been part of and Barron has no peers.

Micky Barron remains a popular figure with fans at The Vic

Micky Barron in action against Swansea

Frank Reid/Hartlepool Mail

MICKY Barron joined the Club, initially on loan, from Middlesbrough in 1996. He celebrated his testimonial season ten years later and has become one of most respected players ever to wear the shirt.

In sixth place in the Club's all-time appearance chart, with 374 outings, Barron has been part of the IOR revolution at Victoria Park, the Club steadily improving year on year since 1997.

And since retiring from playing after leading the Club to promotion in 2007, Barron has continued his affinity with Pools by taking the role of Youth Team Coach.

His history and his connection with the Club during the period of success, it puts him in a prime position to review the IOR years.

"When I first came here from Middlesbrough we were playing in front of about 1,000 people," he recalled. "But all our success is down to hard work, from people who have been here along the way and everyone at the Club now. A lot of people can take a lot of credit for what we have achieved."

The play-off and promotion successes seemed a long way away when Barron first arrived.

His first few seasons were spent at the foot of the Football League, the 1998-99 season proving a particularly traumatic – and defining one.

Chris Turner took over a Club fighting relegation, with 14 games remaining to secure Football League status.

And for all the big occasions and glory

Barron has experienced, a day at Victoria Park in April 1999 proved utterly pivotal.

Scarborough were the visitors and while it wasn't quite winner takes all that day, the losers were staring relegation in the face.

"We knew we had to win," said Barron. "If we lost we would more or less have been out of the Football League. We won 3-0 and never looked back.

"Chris Freestone scored two and Peter Beardsley made a big difference. It was a day to remember and, thankfully, we have had a few more since.

"Looking back at the Scarborough game now, I don't think we realised the pressure of the day. I was a younger player then and wanted to go out and enjoy it without worrying.

"If we lost that day, we were as good as down. They had a great chance to go one-up but missed and we won 3-0 to secure League status. We had Peter Beardsley in the team and it was an honour to play with him. He is a smashing fella and it was unreal to see him at Hartlepool.

"I grew up watching him for Newcastle and England, so I appreciated having him as a team-mate."

Moving To Victoria Park

"Sometimes it seems donkeys years ago when I came here, you wonder where the time goes.

"People who have been here and watching us since then can see how far we have moved on as a Club. Back then we didn't even have training kit – it was bring along a pair of shorts and a T-shirt to run around in, it really was.

"The ground has improved no end and the facilities we have for training are the best in the lower divisions.

"Hartlepool United is now a great place to work and a great place to play your football.

"I made my debut at Hereford in 1996. We stayed in a hotel the night before and we were in the bar having a drink.

"I'd come on loan from Middlesbrough and was gobsmacked! I was told it was something they did every week, but it's fair to say things have changed a bit since then.

"I played OK that day for my first game and went back to Boro after three months on loan. Bryan Robson called me back and said I had done well on loan, but now I had to go and do well for him as well.

"My last game for Pools was followed by being on the bench at Liverpool for Boro – Robbo was laughing about that, saying what a difference it was for me, but I think I knew I was never going to have a big run in the team there.

"I was always looking to get away at the end of the season because Boro had experienced players who had cost money who he could play and they were played out of position to fit in as well. I was big enough to realise I was going to have to move on.

"I played at Victoria Park a few times for Boro reserves before I came on loan and, being honest, a lot of the lads there didn't like coming over to play here. But I had been to watch the team a few times as well because I knew a few of the lads and that helped me decide to come here.

"I was big mates with Steve Howard before I came on loan and I also knew Joe Allon and Stephen Halliday, so I felt it was easier going somewhere comfortable."

Best Team-Mate

"Jan Ove Pedersen – he was fantastic, a nice bloke and a class act. He came on loan from Brann Bergen in Norway and we all wanted him to stay, but he was always going to go back and play at a higher level than ours.

"It's a shame he was here when he was because at the time we weren't up to scratch, up to his level if you like, and you could see that. If we had him a few years later he would

Best Team Mate - Jan Ove Pedersen

have played in a much better team and he would have been even better.

"Some players weren't on his wavelength or level and that used to frustrate him at times, but you would never know and he never let it be known at the time. He came over and fitted in well, the best I've ever played with."

The Big Turn Around In Fortunes

"Chris Turner came in and brought along a professionalism that wasn't there before. He let us know straight away what his standards were and it was plain that if you didn't meet them you were out the door.

"Looking back, his arrival and that of IOR turned the Club around and we've gone from strength to strength.

"Getting into the play-offs first time in 1999 was a novelty. We went to Hull needing to win and relying on other results to go for us. When they came through for us I've never seen as many happy – and surprised – faces in a dressing room.

"We all know we should have won the League in 2003. I remember going home after a game and watching Rushden get beaten on Sky and really thought we would go up as champions.

"Not winning the league is the one real blackspot on the year. Getting promotion was a great feeling and something to be proud of, but it would have been fantastic to have a trophy to show off on the victory parade.

"At the time you don't think of it so much, it's when you look back and know we should have had a winners medal, not a runners-up."

Micky Barron in action

Promotion, Life In A New Division

"After promotion in 2003 we surprised a lot of people with the way we took to the division. But we got off to a great start and give ourselves a chance of being up there and believing what we were capable of. After the start we had we realised there wasn't such a big gap between the divisions.

"The first game of the season set the tone. I was injured and sat at home listening to it. At 3-1 down I left the house and wasn't going to listen to any more of that.

"By the time I got back, we had won 4-3. Everyone at the Club was on such a high and it went from there.

"We knew if we could fight and scrap we could go a long way. There were a few new players in that year and they all got off to great starts. We had the fans on board and everyone was together.

"Marco Gabbiadini came in and was similar to Flash (Gordon Watson), they were the same type of player. I don't think Gabbers will ever be the best trainer – a bit like Flash – but give either the ball and they will cause problems.

"You always knew when Flash was around. I

Micky Barron in action for Pools

Frank Reid/Hartlepool Mail

don't think you were ever going to agree with him and what he said all the time, but what's wrong with having an opinion in a dressing room?"

Sir Bobby Robson spoke at Micky's testimonial dinner in 2005

The Play Off Years

After leading Pools into every play-off campaign, Micky Barron is a prime candidate to review them all.

v Darlington, May 2000
First leg 0-2; Second leg 0-1;
Aggregate score 0-3

THIS was the first time we made the play-offs and maybe people got a bit carried away. Darlington were a better team than us at the time. We had a good chance in the first leg with Craig Midgley that could have gone in, but everything seemed to run for them at our place.

Then we had to go there for the second leg and we were soon behind. Strods (Gary Strodder) scored an own goal early on and they might as well have called it off then! It was an experience to be in there, but maybe as a team and a Club we weren't prepared to go up at that time. Of course, you take the chance when it comes, but, being honest, we weren't as good as the other teams in the play-offs.

I suppose it was more disappointing because it was Darlington and the chance to play at Wembley. With my mate Craig Liddle scoring as well, it was a bad time all round!

v Blackpool, May 2001
First leg 0-2; Second leg 1-3:
Aggregate score 1-5

WE went into these games feeling a little bit disappointed because we hadn't gone up automatically. Blackpool made the play-offs on the back of a good run and we had been chasing an automatic slot.

It was a red hot day at Bloomfield Road and the atmosphere was a bit flat. We didn't perform and were two down.

We had done the double over them in the league campaign and really thought we still had a good chance of getting back into it at our place, but they were strong and passed the ball well, very difficult to break down.

The games were a bit of a turning point for the Club. Chris (Turner) had given the lads who were here a chance and they did well, but he wanted to bring experienced players in and the team really improved.

v Cheltenham, May 2002
First leg; 1-1; Second leg 1-1;
Aggregate score 2-2;
Pools lost 5-4 on penalties.

THIS was the one which hurt the most for me. We played so well away from home in the second leg. In extra time we had chances to win it, one with Darrell Clarke where he was stretching, but it went down to penalties and it wasn't to be.

It really hurt us losing that because we played so well away from home.

It was our best performance in the play-offs in the game down there, but we were disappointing at home and perhaps that was the difference.

The second the season was over, the gaffer came out and said the next season started there and then. We didn't want to make the play-offs again, we just wanted to go up automatically, and that's what we did.

H'Angus consoles Micky Barron after the loss to Blackpool

v Bristol City, May 2004
First leg 1-1; Second leg 1-2;
Aggregate score 2-3

WE conceded in the first few minutes of the first leg, but from then on we took the game to them. Boydy was on fire that season and their keeper had a blinder.

Eifion Williams was through one on one, but was brought down and we should have had a penalty – it was on Sky and when you saw the replays it was clear. But Joel equalised after their keeper went missing and we were level.

It was always going to be hard in the second leg, but we got in front when Sweens scored. I played the ball wide to Eifion and he crossed for Sweens to score. Even before the goal we had chances and Boydy hit the inside of the post.

I was knocked out in the second leg and carried off with an oxygen mask on. It gave a few people a scare, but I think it looked a lot worse than it was. Five minutes later I was sat up with a cup of tea!

My family were a bit worried. Some of the lads thought I was time wasting because we were in front at the time, but I went off and we later lost Chris Westwood as well, which proved the big difference.

When you look back at the goals, you know we could have kept them out with a full team."

v Tranmere, May 2005
First leg 2-0; Second leg 0-2;
Aggregate score 2-2,
Pools won 7-6 on penalties

BOYDY scored twice to give us an advantage and we were in a strange position be actually winning a play-off game and having a lead to defend.

We knew it was going to be tough in the second leg, it was up to Tranmere to have a go at us and try and break us down. It went all the way to penalties in the end, but it was a tremendous feeling at Tranmere to be able to celebrate reaching the final. We had to look at other teams doing it to us on plenty of occasions.

This time, it was our turn and I can't describe the feeling we had. Fantastic is one word I could use, but it was probably better than that.

I went off injured and we conceded two goals so I started blaming myself for it. In extra

Frank Reid/Hartlepool Mail

Ritchie Humphreys slams home the winning penalty at Tranmere

time we had our best period of the game, but I thought that Micky Nelson and Chris Westwood were fantastic.

If anything we got stronger as the game went on, especially in the last 30 minutes. I was delighted for Ritchie Humphreys at Prenton Park. If there was one person who I wanted to score the decisive penalty it was Humps.

Three years on, he was still getting some stick from the lads about what happened at Cheltenham. No-one can say anything to him

now after that. It shows some character to step up in that situation.

It would have been hard for him if that one had been missed, but he made no mistake. It was a fantastic night for him and a fantastic night for the Club.

At the time, beating Tranmere was something else, it was the relief of finally coming through a play-off and getting to the final instead of being knocked out.

I remember the likes of Tommy Miller and Russ Green coming down on to the pitch and just hugging everyone and realising what we had done. We were going to Cardiff and the emotions just took over.

Frank Reid/Hartlepool Mail

Micky Barron after the first leg play-off win over Tranmere in 2005

V Sheffield Wednesday, May 2005
The Millennium Stadium, Cardiff
2-4 after extra time.

TO go to such a stadium in front of so many fans was something else. It's a day never to be forgotten by anyone associated with the Club.

I've got a DVD of it with some footage I took behind the scenes and when I watch it again, I get the same feeling I did that day. It's something to treasure for the rest of my life and it was a proud time to be captain that day.

Being captain was something I took a lot of pride in.

£5.00 Official Matchday Programme

Coca-Cola LEAGUE 1

PLAY-OFF FINAL

HARTLEPOOL UNITED *v* SHEFFIELD WEDNESDAY

Sunday 29th May 2005
Millennium Stadium, Cardiff
Kick Off 3.00pm

MILLENNIUM STADIUM
CARDIFF ARMS PARK

THE FOOTBALL LEAGUE

League 1 Play-Off Final
Squads

 Hartlepool United

 Sheffield Wednesday

Manager **Martin Scott**	Manager **Paul Sturrock**

Jim Provett	1	☐	☐	1	David Lucas
Mickey Barron	2	☐	☐	2	Lee Bullen
Hugh Robertson	3	☐	☐	3	Paul Heckingbottom
Mark Tinkler	4	☐	☐	4	Graeme Lee
Michael Nelson	5	☐	☐	5	Steve Adams
Chris Westwood	6	☐	☐	6	Glenn Whelan
Darrell Clarke	7	☐	☐	7	Jon-Paul McGovern
Ritchie Humphreys	8	☐	☐	8	Matthew Hamshaw
Eifion Williams	9	☐	☐	9	Steven MacLean
Adam Boyd	10	☐	☐	10	Lee Peacock
Gavin Strachan	11	☐	☐	11	Chris Brunt
Joel Porter	14	☐	☐	12	Patrick Collins
Antony Sweeney	15	☐	☐	14	Rory McArdle
Jon Daly	16	☐	☐	16	Richard Wood
Ben Clark	17	☐	☐	17	Richard Evans
Matty Robson	18	☐	☐	18	Alex Bruce
Jon Brackstone	19	☐	☐	19	Paul Smith
Steven Istead	20	☐	☐	20	Lewis McMahon
Dimitrios Konstantopoulos	21	☐	☐	21	Chris Adamson
Darren Craddock	22	☐	☐	22	James Quinn
Graham Low	24	☐	☐	23	Craig Rocastle
Andrew Appleby	25	☐	☐	24	Zigor Aranalde
David Foley	26	☐	☐	25	Drew Talbot
James Brown	28	☐	☐	26	Danny Reet
Michael Maidens	29	☐	☐	27	Graham Barrett
Stephen Turnbull	30	☐	☐	28	Ross Greenwood
Thomas Butler	32	☐	☐	30	Liam Needham
Steve Howey	42	☐	☐	31	Adam Proudlock
			☐	33	Robert Poulter
			☐	34	Luke Foster
			☐	39	Tommy Spurr

Officials
Referee: **Phil Crossley** (Kent)
Assistant Referees: **Darren Cann** (Norfolk), **Andrew Halliday** (North Yorkshire)
Fourth Official: **Andre Marriner** (West Midlands)

Millennium Stadium, Cardiff

Frank Reid/Hartlepool Mail

Millennium Stadium, Sunday 29 May 2005. Phil Crossley (Refereee), Micky Barron, Hodcroft, Ritchie Humphreys, Chris Westwood, Dimitrios Konstantopoulos, Michael Nelson, Gavin Strachan, Thomas Butler, Joel Porter, Antony Sweeney, Adam Boyd, Matty Robson, Jim Provett, Mark Tinkler, Jon Daly, Darren Craddock, Eifion Williams, Martin Scott

Chapter 15

Chris Turner

As far as Hartlepool United managers go, few can have had as much impact on the Club as Chris Turner.

WHILE the likes of Brian Clough, Cyril Knowles and Gus McLean are much revered by all after their illustrious and respected stints in charge, Chris Turner's influence cannot be under-estimated.

On his appointment at Victoria Park on January 24, 1999, Pools were in a precarious position. He described the Club at the time as being "possibly at its lowest ebb". He wasn't far wrong.

When he left the Club for Sheffield Wednesday in November 2003, his four years in charge had not only heralded success on the pitch, but also a massive transformation off it.

Standards were raised, amid a more professional outlook as the Club changed from top to bottom. The Hartlepool United pre-IOR and pre-Chris Turner is unrecognisable from the one today.

The rewards are still being reaped. If it wasn't for the Turner revolution, Hartlepool United may not be in the position it is today.

"When I came here I said the Club could be in the division we are now or the next one playing in front of 5,000 crowds. People laughed at me," he recalled.

"My first game was against Rotherham. I walked out on a pitch with no grass on it and there were a couple of hundred people on the Mill House terrace. One voice came out and shouted 'Turner, what you doing here, what have you come here for?'.

"People didn't think we could get 5,000 in

Chris Turner

every week, but we have done it and we know it is possible to keep that amount coming through the gates if we play well and entertain.

"I would like to think I had played some part in, not just the revival, but the best years of the Club.

Frank Reid/Hartlepool Mail

Chris Turner celebrates

"There had been a couple of promotions but never sustained success. In my time as manager we had three successive play-offs and, when I left, it was a team clear at the top and destined for promotion which was then taken on by other managers since."

On his appointment, Pools had 14 games to stave off relegation. A few late dramas and a huge effort later, Pools finished in 22nd spot, three points clear of relegated Scarborough, who incidentally had a certain Russ Green working for them.

Turner took the challenge head on and succeeded. Moving to Pools was something of a gamble, but a chance to progress his career.

In charge of the youth team at Wolves in a comfortable position, he was more than willing to take the step up and move to the foot of the old Division Three.

"I had a very good job at Wolves and wanted to make the next progression in my career," he recalled. "Three jobs were up for grabs – Colchester, Hartlepool and another southern club.

"I applied here, had an interview in Newcastle, another interview in Peterlee and then it all went quiet.

"I was in a good job with a good working relationship with everyone at Wolves, so I rang Ken one Thursday night. I asked what was going on and told him I had no youth team game at Wolves that weekend.

"Hartlepool were playing at Exeter that weekend – a long way from Hartlepool, but a few hours from Wolverhampton and I said I could go and watch them.

"I had seen the team at Rochdale, they won 1-0 and I did a report on the players for IOR from that game. Then I watched them at Exeter and said that I wasn't trying to put them under pressure, but I couldn't mess people about at Wolves waiting for a call to find out what was going to happen.

"Ken told me to go to the Exeter game, stay on the Friday night, take my wife down for the weekend and see what happens. Debbie and I stood on the Kop there because I didn't want to be seen in the main stand.

"Denny Ingram scored a penalty to put Hartlepool one-up and Exeter never looked like scoring. Ten minutes to go and we had parked in a car park which went round and round and would take an age to get out of.

"So we left before the end to make sure we got away quickly. It was 1-0 and I thought that there would be no appointment for another week – if they had won away from home there was some breathing space."

Turner was left wondering whether his future would be at Hartlepool United, for with three points on the board a quick appointment of a new boss seemed unlikely.

"We got out of Exeter and put the radio on," he added. "Exeter had missed a chance in about

Chris Turner is named Manager of Pools in 1998

the 94th minute, so that was that as far as I was concerned.

"About half an hour later my son, Jamie, rang. He said 'what a result that was'. I agreed and said it was a good away win.

"He told me Exeter got two goals in injury time – I couldn't believe it, but I knew a decision would come.

"On the training ground on the Monday morning I got a phone call from Ian McRae saying IOR would like to approach Wolves for permission to speak to me to be the new manager of Hartlepool United."

Being appointed manager was only the start. The job ahead was immense, possibly bigger than he realised at the time. Taking over a squad low on confidence, short on fitness and devoid of ability, the battle was on to stay in the Football League.

IOR couldn't afford to get the appointment wrong. They didn't.

"I moved to Hartlepool, brought the family, bought a house, the lot – I was committed."

With goals and inspiration in short supply, Turner needed to make changes to his team for the final run-in and signing two strikers proved decisive.

There was, however, one front man who departed days before his arrival who he would have loved to have worked with.

Steve Howard was a big striker who was more often than not the target of terrace fire. Since leaving Pools he has progressed and reached the Premiership with Derby County and continued scoring goals with Leicester City.

He might not have looked like a top-flight target man at the time, but the new Pools boss spotted something in his game.

"When I came up for one of the interviews, Harold Hornsey talked to me about Stevie Howard," said Turner. "I'd noticed him when I saw the game at Rochdale and he was about a stone overweight and lethargic. But at that level he was just what you require.

"Harold had an offer in from Northampton for about £90,000 but I told him that I wouldn't sell him.

"The day before I got the job, Harold had advised the owners to sell him, so they did. In my first home game with Rotherham I had Stuart Irvine and Craig Midgley as my two strikers – both five foot something against two big defenders."

As Turner coped without Howard, Pools former striker was busy making his mark for his new club – at Pools expense.

"We sold Howard to Northampton – I had Mark McGhee coming up to help me out and we were playing Northampton," Turner recalled.

"Mark was out of work after Wolves and was an extra help. I didn't have an assistant at the time.

"As soon as he saw Howard, who had been through a big pre-season programme and must have lost about two stone, looked the bees knees physically and scored twice that day, Mark said to me in the dressing room 'I don't know what you are going to do, but you are not going to turn this Club around'.

"Look what has happened since then – what a change and that comment came from an experienced manager! I will never forget it."

But Turner had to work without Howard. Goals were at a premium – Pools scored just once in Turner's first six games – but were a necessity. Something needed to be done.

"It was a desperate situation and we needed new strikers," he said. "We got about £90,000 for Howard, but spent more on two replacements.

"And even though Gary Jones and Chris Freestone weren't prolific, they gave other players the belief. Jones had just got the Golden Boot for scoring 28 goals for Notts County and Freestone was an ex-Middlesbrough player who had done well for Northampton when they were televised live.

"People knew of them both and the rest of the team had confidence in the two strikers. We had nine games left to stay in the Football League."

Nine Games Left

APRIL 17, 1999 was a key date, arguably the most important day of them all. With Pools, Scarborough and Carlisle in the relegation mix, the Seadogs were visiting Victoria Park. The stakes couldn't have been higher.

"The biggest game of the lot was Scarborough – Freestone scored twice and kept us up," said Turner.

"There was pressure on. It was all or nothing. But I know IOR would have remained in control and still run the Club the right way like they still do today.

"Winning away at Shrewsbury (April 6) was vital. Denny Ingram missed a penalty and Paul Baker squeezed in the rebound from the narrowest of angles to win.

"We followed up with a home win over Chester and that gave us the momentum to stay up."

The game with Leyton Orient on April 27 was very important. Just two more games remained after that and, with Carlisle and Scarborough meeting on the last day, that 1-0 victory all but secured safety.

The winning goal came from Peter Beardsley, the first big IOR signing. Turner, however, admits it wasn't glory all the way for the former England forward.

"Peter's contribution was experience and he had the ability to create goals, like he did against Scarborough that day," said Turner. "We were at Mansfield with just a few games remaining. It was a big game and we had great support, but were poor. We had a game coming up on the Tuesday night at home. Peter wasn't playing well and I took him off with Orient in mind.

"He wasn't happy about it. Players are like that, but as a manager you have to handle superstars and first year pros.

"Peter got over his disappointment and came to see me on the Monday, apologised and scored the winner on the Tuesday.

"Good management? Who knows, but regardless Peter had done his job."

Keen to play down his role on that occasion, there were plenty more examples of good management to come.

The transformation from relegation battlers to play-off and promotion contenders was spectacular.

Just 12 months after celebrating beating the drop, the celebrations were of a different kind as a place in the play-offs was earned for the first time.

Before then the play-offs were something supporters and officials looked at from afar.

After making the top seven for the first time, the end of season knock-out became the norm as Team Turner, with Colin West in place, made its mark.

Much of Pools success wasn't just down to Turner. All good managers need a good right-hand man, a confidante to lean on, who can be trusted. Turner had West.

"Colin came to the Club because I needed a No 2 and a manager needs more eyes and ears," said Turner. "We spent six years together as a management team, they were great times. He had the same quandary as me in the end – do I stay at Hartlepool or go to Sheffield Wednesday?

"Colin won his one game in caretaker charge of Pools and IOR did all they could to keep him and it was a tough call for him.

"I drove up to meet Ken in his village pub and told him I wasn't going to persuade Colin to leave Hartlepool – it was going to be Colin's call and I would let him decide.

"We had a good strong partnership. It wasn't good cop – bad cop, with one of us having a go at players and the other putting an arm around

Colin West was the man chosen by Turner as his number 2

Frank Reid/Hartlepool Mail

them like some managerial partnerships, we were very similar and Colin had that physical nature about him.

"People who played under us respected us as a pair and I don't think we were a nasty pair or aggressive.

"But one day at Mansfield I kicked a tray of sandwiches across the room. We had been 3-1 up and lost 4-3. I lost it and it was probably a fair reaction to that result.

"I was sat in the stands after the game by myself and Billy Dearden, their manager, came up and said he couldn't believe it. I'd asked the linesman how long was to go when we were 3-1 up – 14 minutes he said. Those 14 minutes were a disaster."

The big successes and achievements came in reaching the play-offs, making it three seasons in a row sowed the seeds of success and, ultimately, promotion.

"Making the play-offs the first time was a big achievement," he admitted. "But on each season the play-offs were a hurdle too far.

"Twice we made it on the last day – one at Hull (2000), one at Exeter (2002). The other time came in 2001 when Chesterfield should have been deducted enough points to stop them going up automatically – we were in fourth place by a mile.

"That year we beat Cardiff at home 3-1 on the last day of the season and they had been promoted – we had a good side. But we couldn't turn winning games into winning play-off games.

"The Blackpool game in the 2001 play-offs was a watershed. It was a red hot day, too hot and I remember Ian Clark, he had enjoyed a good season and was playing well, but he had a stinker.

"He said he couldn't handle playing in that heat – but in a game when we needed a draw or maximum one goal defeat we couldn't do it.

"Cheltenham came the next year and we outplayed them home and away. We conceded a last-minute goal at home to draw 1-1, then they smacked one into the top corner from distance to make it 1-1 away. They hung on, hung on and hung on – then we lost on penalties. That was how it went for us.

"The next season started that night at Cheltenham because I knew I had a squad of players capable of getting in the top three and staying in it."

After reaching the top seven three seasons in succession, Turner was desperate to go one further.

From the moment Ritchie Humphreys' penalty somehow stayed out at Cheltenham, the next season began immediately.

It was a plan which worked.

Watson, Widdrington And Tinkler

WE had a great start at Carlisle on the opening day and followed it up with two home wins. Players like Watson and Widdrington had the nous and they were invaluable," he said.

"You felt confident every week, every game we went out full of belief feeling we could win.

"Maybe the fans didn't understand Tommy when he first came – he was an organiser, a manger on the field. In a positional sense he knew where to play, sitting in front of the centre halves and he contributed immensely.

"He gave Mark Tinkler his best season; he had Tommy looking after him and was allowed to wander, get on the end of things and spray the ball around."

And while Widdrington's expertise dictated the pace of games, one of Turner's signings – the man rated the best capture of the lot – dictated just about everything.

Step forward Gordon Watson. A Hartlepool United talisman if ever there was one.

His swagger, arrogance and outlook was just what was needed. Flash by name, Flash by nature - that was Gordon Watson.

And how everyone knew it.

Frank Reid/Hartlepool Mail

Flash by name, Flash by nature – Gordon Watson

"I always remember a situation at a game at Oxford," said Turner. "Gordon Watson scored two goals to put us in front, but they scored one back right before half-time.

"I got back in the dressing room and, as everyone says, it's a nightmare time to concede a goal just before the break. You know they are back in it and will come back at you from the restart.

"As a manager you have to get the players in, get their heads right, get them focused on the job and what is going to come if there's an onslaught.

"I was in the dressing room first and I saw all the players coming back in. There was only one player not in and that was Gordon Watson.

"He came in last, a little bit late. He opened the dressing room door and had a right go at the lads saying 'I've got you two goals and got you in front and now you have chucked it away' and the like. All the lads went off it and laid into him. There was hell on. Micky Barron stood up and had a right go at him and others joined in.

"My job was done; I moved to the back of the room, made myself a cup of tea and let them get on with it.

"We didn't need a manager that day! We went out and still won the game and maybe Flash had spurred everyone one. But that was Gordon Watson – that was him all over and what he was all about. He was my best signing, without a doubt."

He might not have played for four years after a horrific leg break, he might have only trained with the Club for part of the week, but when he was around, he was around.

He bagged 23 goals in 43 starts. The faithful had a new idol.

"We signed him and he would fly up on a Wednesday afternoon, train Thursday, train Friday, play Saturday, fly home Sunday," revealed Turner.

"And some of the lads – as would be the case – would naturally feel they were putting in the work all week and someone comes up for a few days and plays.

"His first game was at home to Kidderminster and he had four or five chances which all went fractionally wide. I knew we needed someone to come in and put the icing on the cake -he was it. Yes, he was a pain in the backside at times but look what he added.

"The huddle in the middle of the pitch before the game is something we have used a lot now and that was started by Gordon Watson. He was good for supporters, good for Club profile and good for team spirit – the players recognised he won games for them.

"He scored all types of goals and did something players don't do enough of these days - shoot at goal.

"He had one thing on his mind, scoring goals. Look at the goals he scored against Hull City that night he got a hat-trick, each one of them was memorable.

"And he helped other players on the pitch as well. He took Adam Boyd under his wing and helped shape and mould him and he would tell Eifion Williams to do all the running because he was busy scoring goals!"

Gordon Watson was responsible for introducing the 'huddle' at Victoria Park

Frank Reid/Hartlepool Mail

IOR Remain Positive

WHILE Turner's charges took on – and more often than not beat – all comers, the Club's current Director of Sport admits he owes a debt of gratitude to the Club's owners.

There was times when it wasn't easy. It wasn't all top of the table stuff. On November 3, 2001 Pools lost at Plymouth Argyle.

The trek up the motorways of England wasn't easy. Pools were on the football equivalent of the hard shoulder and they had the title favourites next up at Victoria Park.

Cue Watson.

"I think the interest in Hartlepool United grew in those years from IOR. They never put anyone under pressure or made ridiculous demands and it allowed me to grow and develop as a manager," said Turner.

"I could make mistakes without feeling under pressure from it – and that applies to all managers at Hartlepool, but not perhaps elsewhere. These days, managers make a mistake and they are sacked.

"IOR allowed me to come through some difficult spells and be better for it. Their confidence in me was born out of their desire to succeed.

"We lost at Plymouth and went bottom of the table in 2002. In the second half we took the game to them and we came off after the game with a defeat.

"Paul Smith had just signed for us and Smudger came in the dressing room and said if we are at the bottom, are they really at the top? He was spot on.

"On the Tuesday we were playing Hull who were flying, we were bottom and there was

only one result to come. We tortured them and I've always said the real rise of Hartlepool United started that night. From then on we never looked back.

"Paul Smith was a great signing. I asked Mick Docherty about him, I knew Mick from Sunderland and he used to manage here. He said you won't find a better crosser of the ball.

"To be fair, Gordon Watson would have many a go at Paul because all Smudger needed was half a yard to swing a ball over – Flash wanted that extra yard to get up there in the box and finish it off.

"We put a lot of balls into the area which went across goal.

"We racked up some big wins – five, six and seven. Only one team scored more goals than us that season – Manchester City managed by Kevin Keegan, so that shows the sort of attacking football we were playing."

He added: "Colin West and I installed a spirit here and it's gone on – the will to win and the never say die spirit which everyone has today.

"A number of players had played together for a while. After the Cheltenham game we turned our attentions to promotion the next season and Watson was the icing on the cake.

"He wrote on the training ground door in 2002 'Third division champions' – he wanted winners around him.

"And that fixed the mindset – we wanted to the win the league and his cockiness filtered down.

"I wasn't at the Club at the end of the season, but it was a disappointment for me when the team didn't win the league. I left a team at the top and Mike Newell picked up the team and took it over the promotion line."

Turner added Paul Smith to his ranks

Frank Reid/Hartlepool Mail

Sheffield Wednesday – Homeward Bound

TURNER'S last game in charge was a goalless draw at home to York City on November 1, 2002.

The pull of Sheffield Wednesday was too much. Victoria Park was saturated that night, driving rain left the surface flooded.

Turner's thoughts, however, weren't waterlogged.

"Leaving was the hardest and the easiest decision to make for me," said Turner. "I didn't want to leave, but the only club I would have left for – or even thought about leaving for – was Sheffield Wednesday.

"My dad took me in the 60s and 70s, I played for them in the 80s and 90s and being a Sheffield person it was a chance I couldn't turn down.

"Ken Hodcroft tried to convince me to stay and Sheffield Wednesday wouldn't pay enough compensation for me. However, in the end he allowed me to leave and still believes Wednesday owe IOR more money!

"Looking at my playing career I was ever-present at Sunderland for two seasons and won player of the year awards. Manchester United came in for me, I was out of contract, and could have played week in, week out at Sunderland – or do I go to Old Trafford and be No 2 to the England No 2 keeper?

"It was a challenge and I played over 90 times for United, made a lot of friends and gained so much experience. It was the same scenario going to Wednesday – and what an experience.

"Terry Yorath was manager and under pressure, the press started speculating and my name was in the frame as an ex-player.

"It was a disappointment to leave, but it was something I had to do. As a manager you don't want to see your best players leave, but they have to. We didn't want Tommy Miller to go, but knew he had to, to develop and further his career.

"Tommy really flourished at Pools. When I got the job he was on the bench, but I knew he was a good size, with good legs and was what we needed – especially playing 3-5-2. Playing that way extended Paul Stephenson's career because he sat in as a ball player and Tommy pushed on.

"I take great pride in seeing Tommy leave for that money – £800,000 which was unheard of at the Club. Since then we've had Adam Boyd sold for half a million pounds and those sort of transfers had never happened before.

"But that's the IOR philosophy, people are allowed to leave if they are bettering themselves, but they don't just do it for the money."

And Turner offered an insight to the workings of the Club.

"There is no pressure at the Club," he insisted. "IOR create a good working atmosphere – and that's as a player, manager, secretary, any position.

"It's nice to come to work for the company – when you understand how the company works it's not a problem. It is a problem when someone comes and doesn't understand how the company works. That's when problems have arisen in the past.

"The reason why this Club has been successful is because of IOR, it's not Chris Turner, Danny Wilson, Mike Newell, Neale Cooper or whoever.

"It's IOR stabilising the Club, building on what is already here.

"We have built a good name and good reputation within football – but some people still can't understand it and wonder why in recent years this Club is playing the likes of Sheffield Wednesday, Leeds United, Leicester City and Nottingham Forest – and holding their own."

From Sheffield Wednesday, Turner went to Stockport. But, unable to turn the club's fortunes around and with a Supporters' Trust in place, he left in early 2007.

At the same time, IOR were looking for a new manager. Turner was available. An easy choice for all parties? Not quite – Turner had had enough of being an old-school football manager.

He wanted something else, something different. But so did IOR.

Director of Sport

WHEN I left Stockport County I had a couple of ideas of what I wanted to do in the game," he admitted. "It would be easy to sit at home for a couple of months and wait for a manager to get the sack and get a job that way.

"I'm not saying I would never go back into management on a permanent basis, but since I was appointed as the Director of Sport there's a lot of other people appointed in a similar position at other clubs.

"It's a role that people ask 'what do you do?' But it's solely to help. Management today is a different story to what it was in the past.

"It's got harder and harder with media, internet, pressure, and off-field jobs. When I was at Hillsborough I could certainly have done with someone doing this side of the job for me.

"What we are doing here means any manager can concentrate on the team and his players.

The Manager picks them, selects who he wants to sign and trains them. He doesn't have to worry about filling in forms, checking the dressing rooms, making sure arrangements are made for away games – he worries about the team and nothing else. Also, once a new player is identified, I will carry out the negotiations on behalf of IOR.

"People think a manager's job is turning up at three o'clock on a Saturday and you have all week long to do what you want."

He added: "I got a phone call from Ken after I left Stockport and after Martin Scott had left the Club. We met up one Sunday night and Ken said we were looking at a different role – manager but not being manager.

"I was looking for something different rather than being a football manager, you go somewhere for 18 months and move on again. I'd had that before.

"I was looking to develop a niche role and they offered me this position, a position which continues to evolve. I've been involved heavily in the project at Billingham and redeveloping the youth set-up and worked closely with Danny Wilson when he was here."

And Turner played a key role in attracting Danny Wilson to the Club in the summer of 2006.

After leading the Club back into League One at the first attempt in record-breaking style, Danny's appointment certainly rang true.

Like every other manager IOR have employed Danny was given every opportunity to do well with no pressure.

Like all managers at the Club, he was under a normal contract of employment, with no fixed terms, no re-negotiations, just the security and support of a normal employee of the Club.

However, after 30 months in charge and many new faces coming into the team, either on loan or as permanent signings, it was decided that a change was needed and Danny left the Club in December 2008.

Chris Turner, remaining in his role as Director of Sport, and with the help of Colin West is back at the helm and narrowly avoided relegation in season 2008/2009. The role is temporary in the management hot seat but they will remain there for the season 2009/2010 to help the Club through one of the worst economic downturns the world, including football, has ever known. However, the future may be bright with twelve new players brought in for the new season.

2009 saw Turner reunited once again with Colin West on the touchline

Eifion Williams proved a big signing for Pools, he's seen here scoring his second goal in a 3-0 win over Darlington on March 25, 2007.

Looking Back

SOME of Chris Turner's signings at Hartlepool United lasted the distance and played key, key roles in the big turnaround in fortunes.

While plenty of players came and went, some stayed around and became terrace favourites.

Turner built a successful team with good characters. Bad eggs at Victoria Park were few and far between.

Instead, it was players who gave their all for the cause who earned the plaudits.

One of his key signings had previously gone some way to damaging his prospects in his early days in charge.

In just his fifth game as a manager, Turner's side travelled to Torquay. They lost 3-0 as a striker called Eifion Williams netted a hat-trick on his Football League debut.

The Torquay new boy, however, could easily have been wearing a Pools shirt that day.

"I always like to see players before I sign them," confessed Turner. "I was recommended Eifion Williams a week before deadline day. I spoke to someone at Wolves who said 'just sign him'. Barry Town wanted £70,000 and I asked someone else who said he was a bit frail.

"I didn't think I could spend £70,000 in the situation we were in when a doubt had been placed in my head. He was warming up before the game and Brian Honour pointed him out to me – as soon as I saw him I knew he looked like a striker and he went and got three against us."

But Turner eventually got his man. It cost a

few quid, but pound for pound few have given such service to the Club as Eifion Williams.

He departed in summer 2007 with 56 goals in 239 games. Some of his goals will never be forgotten – his leveller in the play-off final at the Millennium Stadium in 2005 or the second goal of his double haul in the 3-0 thumping of Darlington at the home of the old enemy in the 2007 promotion season.

"Further down the line we were looking for a new striker – he wasn't prolific but I was aware of him," recalled Turner. "He cost £50,000 on a three-year deal. Roy McFarland said we wouldn't get goals out of Eifion Williams, but I thought he was an excellent striker.

"Eifion is the sort of player who needed confidence and he lost it a bit. There is a weaker side to him, he's an arm round the shoulder player.

"You have to keep telling him all the time he will score goals – Gordon Watson did it to him every game.

"But other managers came in and he lost confidence playing on the right wing. I'm pleased that late on here he had a little resurgence and got two fantastic goals at Darlington.

"But like all players you come to the end of your days and they move on."

That day when Williams netted three against Pools he was being marked by Chris Westwood – a raw teenager pitched into a relegation battle under his former youth team boss.

In six seasons at Victoria Park, few defenders have been as popular as the central defender.

"Chrissy Westwood was the biggest joke signing Hartlepool had made for years according to some," said Turner.

"He'd been injured and out with shin splints and had missed a lot of football.

"He played left sided centre back which is always a difficult job for anyone, but I think he was very consistent – an eight out of ten every week."

Alongside Westwood was Graeme Lee, another to be polished into a diamond.

"Graeme Lee was sluggish, being booked every week, overweight, no discipline, couldn't stay on his feet," he said. "We worked on him and slowly turned him around."

Perhaps the key behind the transformations of players was Turner's introduction of a new regime.

When Pools utilised the services of former Royal Marine Tony Toms in the early 70s, it was revolutionary.

Yet it was around 40 years later that Pools realised the benefits of a full-time fitness coach. After introducing Nick Ward to his charges, the biggest battle was winning them over.

"I had discussions with Nick and battles with players about Nick's workings," he admitted. "They had to be convinced.

"One of the biggest transformations I ever saw in a player was Paul Stephenson. I had him in my office and he had one year left on his contract. I told him to buck his ideas up and get himself fit or he would be out the door.

"I used Gordon Strachan as an example, look how he extended his career as a player. I told Paul to go away in the summer, work hard and come back fit, ready for the season or he would be a free transfer the next year.

"In all fairness to Paul he came back and did everything I asked. Look at him today he is as fit as ever."

And while Stephenson was the prime example of what a change in outlook could achieve, Turner was a firm believer in the message he was trying to get across – even if others weren't so sure.

DU On Fitness – Three Rules of IOR

IT was hard for everyone introducing Nick Ward as a Fitness Coach from Durham University. There were a lot of factors thrown into the equation – warmups, warmdowns, diet, food, nutrition, rest, drinking the right things everything.

"It was changing the whole philosophy of football. I said to IOR that he would change the Club and make it more professional. I later took him to Sheffield Wednesday with me and I got the same complaints from players, staff and directors about the way things were changing and being introduced.

"With the old Hartlepool United before IOR took over, the aim was to finish second or third bottom, see the season off and get to Magaluf in Spain for a holiday with the lads at the end of it. That was it, that was the outlook.

"It took me two to three seasons to change that because we started at such a low mark. However, IOR were fully supportive and they then introduced a player Code of Conduct which all players and football staff must sign each season.

"It is updated annually and such new ideas changed and shaped the Club inside out."

However, the three requirements of IOR still remain the same:

Enjoy what you are doing

Don't embarrass yourself, the Club or the owners

Don't get relegated

The rest, as they say, is history.

Frank Reid/Hartlepool Mail

Turner saw a big change in Paul Stephenson

The Official History of Hartlepool United Football Club 1908 – 2008

Chapter 16

Kits Throughout The Century

Everyone's got their favourite haven't they? Throughout the ages, Hartlepool United have worn many a fine design in kits – some are easy on the eye, some are a little less conventional!

However, they all have a part in our magnificent history and here we celebrate every stitch worn by the various teams since 1908.

So take a look back in time with us as we remember the good, the bad and the sometimes ugly in Pools kits from the past.

Club strips courtesy of www.historicalkits.co.uk

1908-1911

1912-1920

1925-1930

1931-1932

1932-1935

1935-1936

1936-1937

1937-1939

1946-1947

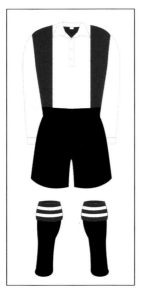

1947-1952

1952-1953

1955-1956

1956-1957

1957-1958

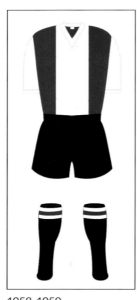

1958-1959

1959-1960

1960-1961

1961-1963

1964-1967

1967-1969

1970-1971

1971-1972

1972-1973

1974-1975

1975-1976

1976-1977

1977-1978

1978-1979

1979-1982

1981-1982

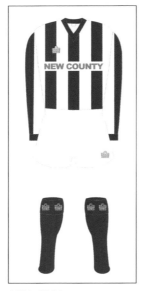

1983-1984

1984-1985

1985-1986

1986-1987

1987-1988

1988-1990

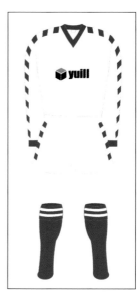

1990-1991

1991-1992

1992-1993

1993-1995

1995-1997

1997-1998

1999-2000

2000-2002

2002-2003

2003-2004

2004-2006

2006-2007

2007-2008 Away

2007-2008 Third

2008-2009

2008-2009 Away

2008-2009 Third

Chapter 17

Club Logos
Through The Years

GENERALLY speaking, the majority of English clubs played without badges regularly appearing on their shirts until the 1960s and 70s. Prior to that, clubs would occasionally adopt their town or city's coat of arms for major occasions. In 1914, for example, Burnley adopted the town's crests for the first FA Cup Final to be witnessed by a member of the Royal family. The primary motivation was to demonstrate the great civic pride felt by supporters, players and board members alike, as the local club were representing their parent town or city at prestigious national events, such as cup finals and semi-finals.

The appearance of town crests at key matches continued until, in the 1960s and 70s, a wave of English clubs adopted permanent badges on their shirts. Many had club-specific logos devised already, but their use was reserved for official correspondence and other important documents. However, as a consequence of the increasing commercialisation of the sport, the majority of English clubs began to adopt the club's logo or badge as a mark of authenticity on an increasing range of shirts, scarves, hats and other products.

It was at this time that a great number of badges were modernised, invented or re-invented, as English clubs sought ownership and copyright over the images for commercial use. As local councils owned the rights to their respective town's coat of arms, many clubs were forced to run competitions in local papers or seek outside expertise in the planning and design of their own distinct crest. Nottingham Forest, for example, abandoned the city's coat of arms in 1972 and adopted a modern logo depicting Sherwood Forest and the River Trent, key features of local identity which are still evident in the club's present badge. Forest are typical in retaining crucial elements of the town's history and identity, yet repackaging and copyrighting those elements in a badge they could call their own.

Although English clubs continue to update or replace the crests they use on shirts and other products, a cursory glance at the badges of league clubs shows that local identity, history and civic pride are still of central importance.

On the following pages you can take a look through the logos that have been used by the Club during their history.

HARTLEPOOL F.C.

Above right: The club's metal lapel badge price 4/6, and the Supporters' Association badge, price 3/-. The address to write to for both badges and information about other items on sale at the Club Shop, is: The Victoria Souvenir Shop, 82 Stockton Road, Hartlepool, Co. Durham. All enquiries and orders should include a stamped addressed envelope.

Right: The club's official crest, not available to the public.

BEHIND THE BADGE

The figures illustrated on the official club crest help to make up the name of the town, i.e. a hart at bay standing in a pool of water. A hound is featured on the back of the hart. The club's badge is adopted from the town's Coat of Arms.

Club logos from 1969/70

Chapter 18

Managers of HUFC

Name	From	To	P	W	D	L	F	A	%W	%Pts
Chris TURNER†	15-Dec-2008	May-2009	28	7	6	15	38	50	25	32.1
Danny WILSON	13-Jun-2006	15-Dec-2008	133	58	29	46	199	166	43.6	50.9
Paul STEPHENSON†	01-Feb-2006	13-Jun-2006	16	3	8	5	15	20	18.8	35.4
Martin SCOTT	04-May-2005	01-Feb-2006	39	11	10	18	42	55	28.2	36.8
Neale COOPER	26-Jun-2003	04-May-2005	110	48	26	36	180	147	43.6	51.5
Mike NEWELL	21-Nov-2002	30-May-2003	29	13	9	7	42	36	44.8	55.2
Colin WEST†	07-Nov-2002	21-Nov-2002	2	1	1	0	3	2	50	66.7
Chris TURNER	24-Feb-1999	07-Nov-2002	193	82	47	64	266	220	42.5	50.6
Brian HONOUR#†	18-Jan-1999	24-Feb-1999	7	2	1	4	8	14	28.6	33.3
Paul BAKER#†	18-Jan-1999	24-Feb-1999	7	2	1	4	8	14	28.6	33.3
Mick TAIT	04-Nov-1996	18-Jan-1999	115	33	36	46	149	169	28.7	39.1
Keith HOUCHEN	20-Apr-1995	04-Nov-1996	75	20	17	38	80	123	26.7	34.2
David MCCREERY	01-Aug-1994	20-Apr-1995	46	10	10	26	41	84	21.7	29
John MACPHAIL	24-Nov-1993	09-Sep-1994	36	7	6	23	32	74	19.4	25
Viv BUSBY	15-Feb-1993	24-Nov-1993	42	9	10	23	32	61	21.4	29.4
Alan MURRAY	17-Jun-1991	15-Feb-1993	97	39	24	34	122	125	40.2	48.5
Cyril KNOWLES	01-Nov-1989	17-Jun-1991	90	41	18	31	138	132	45.6	52.2
Bobby MONCUR	02-Nov-1988	27-Nov-1989	61	14	14	33	65	130	23	30.6

Name	From	To	P	W	D	L	F	A	%W	%Pts
John BIRD	01-Nov-1986	01-Oct-1988	102	35	29	38	110	130	34.3	43.8
Billy HORNER*	01-Dec-1984	01-Nov-1986	100	32	22	46	125	157	32	39.3
Mike DOCHERTY	01-Jun-1983	15-Dec-1983	22	1	7	14	13	40	4.5	15.2
John DUNCAN	01-Apr-1983	14-Jun-1983	9	3	1	5	10	14	33.3	37
Billy HORNER*	01-Oct-1976	31-Mar-1983	343	106	82	155	423	554	30.9	38.9
Ken HALE	01-Jun-1974	01-Oct-1976	119	39	31	49	146	187	32.8	41.5
Len ASHURST	01-Mar-1971	01-Jun-1974	164	50	41	73	162	208	30.5	38.8
John SIMPSON	01-May-1970	01-Mar-1971	33	5	9	19	26	49	15.2	24.2
Gus MCLEAN	01-May-1967	30-Apr-1970	149	48	41	60	155	216	32.2	41.4
Brian CLOUGH	29-Oct-1965	01-May-1967	84	37	13	34	125	126	44	49.2
Geoff TWENTYMAN	01-Jun-1965	19-Oct-1965	14	4	2	8	17	28	28.6	33.3
Alvan WILLIAMS	01-Feb-1964	31-May-1965	68	21	18	29	90	128	30.9	39.7
Bob GURNEY	01-Apr-1963	31-Jan-1964	45	9	11	25	48	94	20	28.1
Allenby CHILTON	01-Jul-1962	01-Apr-1963	35	5	7	23	43	78	14.3	21
Bill ROBINSON	01-Nov-1959	30-Jun-1962	125	27	24	74	162	285	21.6	28
Ray MIDDLETON	01-May-1957	01-Nov-1959	116	38	26	52	190	220	32.8	40.2
Fred WESTGARTH	01-Aug-1943	01-Feb-1957	510	207	99	204	739	746	40.6	47.1
Jimmy HAMILTON	01-Jul-1935	30-Sep-1943	195	65	47	83	283	353	33.3	41.4
Jackie CARR	01-Apr-1932	01-Apr-1935	135	55	22	58	284	303	40.7	46.2
Bill NORMAN	01-Aug-1927	01-Apr-1931	164	53	27	84	270	348	32.3	37.8
Jack MANNERS*	01-Jun-1924	31-Jul-1927	136	46	29	61	207	235	33.8	40.9
Davy GORDON	01-Jul-1922	31-May-1924	85	20	23	42	96	129	23.5	32.5
Cecil POTTER	01-May-1920	01-Jul-1922	88	42	17	29	144	100	47.7	54.2
Jack MANNERS*	01-Aug-1913	01-May-1920	133	55	33	45	244	172	41.4	49.6
Percy HUMPHREYS	25-Jun-1912	31-May-1913	43	19	6	18	79	73	44.2	48.8
Fred PRIEST	01-Aug-1908	31-May-1912	145	68	37	40	311	179	46.9	55.4

* Jack Manners and Billy Horner both had two spells in charge of the club
# Brian Honour and Paul Baker were jointly in charge
† Caretaker

Statistics courtesy of www.inthemadcrowd.co.uk

Chapter 19

Club Statistics

**Most Appearances
(Top 100)**

472 - Watty Moore
423 - Ray Thompson
418 - Alan Goad
413 - Ken Johnson
411 - Ritchie Humphreys
384 - Brian Honour
374 - Micky Barron
361 - Jackie Newton
350 - Tommy McGuigan
326 - Frank Stamper
325 - Keith Nobbs
319 - Roy Hogan
310 - Keith Houchen
306 - Michael Nelson
298 - Rob McKinnon
293 - Chris Westwood
291 - Johnny Wigham
279 - Paul Baker
258 - Joe Willetts
255 - Graeme Lee
249 - Phil Brown
249 - Antony Sweeney
245 - Mark Tinkler
242 - George Potter
239 - Eifion Williams
233 - Tony Smith
231 - John Linacre
228 - Denny Ingram
219 - George Gill
217 - John Gill
215 - Eric Wildon
213 - Malcolm Dawes
209 - Joel Porter
205 - George Luke
205 - Paul Olsson

205 - Ken Waugh
204 - Billy Burnett
203 - Steve Bowron
203 - Tony Parry
203 - John Tinkler
201 - Cliff Wright
199 - Ron Young
196 - John MacPhail
194 - Joe Allon
194 - Tony Bircumshaw
194 - Jack Cameron
193 - Norman Oakley
191 - Darren Knowles
187 - Billy Anderson
187 - Mark Lawrence
186 - Ian McGuckin
185 - Joshie Fletcher
184 - Bob Newton
182 - Brian Drysdale
180 - Leo Harden
177 - Paul Dalton
176 - Rob Smith
175 - Eddie Blackburn
174 - Ben Clark
172 - Kevin Johnson
171 - Jack Proctor
170 - Matty Robson
170 - Paul Stephenson
169 - Adam Boyd
168 - Dick Hardy
165 - Fred Richardson
164 - Ralph Pedwell
162 - Stephen Halliday
162 - Steve Howard
161 - Tommy Miller
161 - Nicky Southall
159 - Ian Clark
158 - Barry Watling

157 - Tommy Burlison
157 - Reg Hill
155 - Billy Ayre
155 - John Bird
155 - Mick Tait
154 - Cecil Hardy
153 - Bobby Lumley
149 - Malcolm Moore
148 - Kevin Henderson
146 - Gary Liddle
146 - Anthony Williams
145 - Peter Thompson
142 - Kevin Dixon
141 - Mick Spelman
139 - Berry Brown
139 - Dimi Konstantopoulos
138 - Bobby Donaldson
138 - Amby Fogarty
137 - Bill Green
136 - Darrell Clarke
135 - John Borthwick
135 - Tommy Carr
135 - Jack Mordue
135 - Ernie Phythian
134 - Ken Simpkins
133 - Martin Hollund
133 - Jimmy Rivers

**Most Football League
Appearances (Top 100)**

447 - Watty Moore
396 - Ray Thompson
384 - Ken Johnson
375 - Alan Goad
358 - Ritchie Humphreys
332 - Jackie Newton

325 - Micky Barron
325 - Tommy McGuigan
319 - Brian Honour
301 - Frank Stamper
284 - Roy Hogan
280 - Keith Nobbs
279 - Keith Houchen
264 - Johnny Wigham
259 - Michael Nelson
254 - Rob McKinnon
251 - Chris Westwood
239 - Joe Willetts
232 - Paul Baker
222 - Graeme Lee
217 - Phil Brown
213 - George Potter
211 - John Linacre
211 - Antony Sweeney
211 - Mark Tinkler
208 - Eifion Williams
204 - John Gill
200 - Tony Smith
200 - Eric Wildon
198 - Denny Ingram
195 - Malcolm Dawes
195 - Ken Waugh
194 - Steve Bowron
194 - Billy Burnett
188 - Tony Parry
186 - George Luke
186 - Ron Young
185 - Tony Bircumshaw
184 - Cliff Wright
182 - Norman Oakley
179 - Billy Anderson
175 - Jack Cameron
173 - Joel Porter
171 - Paul Olsson
170 - Brian Drysdale
170 - John Tinkler
169 - Leo Harden
168 - Joe Allon
168 - Darren Knowles
168 - Mark Lawrence
163 - John MacPhail
161 - Eddie Blackburn
161 - Bob Newton
159 - Ian McGuckin
156 - Ralph Pedwell
152 - Rob Smith
151 - Ben Clark
151 - Paul Dalton
150 - Dick Hardy
149 - Jack Proctor
149 - Fred Richardson
148 - Tommy Burlison
148 - Kevin Johnson
145 - Bobby Lumley
145 - Paul Stephenson
144 - Adam Boyd

142 - Steve Howard
141 - Billy Ayre
141 - John Bird
140 - Stephen Halliday
139 - Reg Hill
139 - Mick Tait
139 - Barry Watling
138 - Tommy Miller
138 - Nicky Southall
138 - Peter Thompson
137 - Ian Clark
135 - Matty Robson
131 - Tommy Carr
131 - Bobby Donaldson
131 - Bill Green
131 - Kevin Henderson
131 - Jack Mordue
131 - Anthony Williams
129 - Malcolm Moore
129 - Jimmy Rivers
127 - Kevin Dixon
127 - Amby Fogarty
126 - Berry Brown
126 - Gary Liddle
124 - Cecil Hardy
124 - Billy Hughes
124 - Ernie Phythian
124 - Norman Rimmington
123 - Darrell Clarke
123 - Alf Young
121 - Ken Simpkins
121 - Mick Spelman
120 - John Sheridan
119 - Jackie Smith

Most Goals (Top 50)

111 - Joshie Fletcher
106 - Johnny Wigham
106 - Ken Johnson
94 - Keith Houchen
92 - Paul Baker
89 - Eric Wildon

79 - Joe Allon
79 - Tommy McGuigan
68 - George Luke
68 - Ralph Pedwell
65 - Joel Porter
62 - Bob Newton
61 - Peter Thompson
60 - Adam Boyd
56 - Eifion Williams
56 - Cecil Hardy
55 - Joss Hewitt
55 - Ernie Phythian
52 - Leo Harden
50 - Jackie Smith
46 - Ron Young
44 - Tommy Miller
43 - Harry Clark
43 - Paul Dalton
43 - Fred Richardson
42 - Malcolm Moore
39 - Billy Robinson
38 - Harry Wensley
38 - Terry Bell
36 - Albert Bonass
36 - Roy Hogan
36 - Brian Honour
36 - Mark Tinkler
35 - Antony Sweeney
35 - Kevin Dixon
34 - Paul Dobson
34 - Kevin McMahon
34 - Cliff Wright
34 - Reuben Butler
33 - Jimmy Mulvaney
32 - Steve Howard
32 - Ritchie Humphreys
32 - Kevin Henderson
32 - Andy Toman
32 - Jimmy Sloan
31 - Jack Mordue
31 - Johnny Edgar
31 - Sam English
30 - Billy Smith
30 - Frank Stamper

Oldest Players on Debut

39 years 276 days, Jackie Carr, 29-Aug-1931
38 years 184 days, Jack Brown, 18-Sep-1937
38 years 143 days, Frank Barson, 31-Aug-1929
37 years 349 days, Peter Beardsley, 02-Jan-1999
37 years 282 days, Alan Walsh, 17-Sep-1994
37 years 247 days, Roy Tunks, 24-Sep-1988
37 years 173 days, Billy Brown, 31-Aug-1946
37 years 77 days, Craig Hignett, 30-Mar-2007
37 years 8 days, Colin West, 21-Nov-1999
36 years 274 days, Harry Hooper, 16-Sep-1947

Most Football League Goals (Top 50)

98 - Ken Johnson
95 - Johnny Wigham
92 - Keith Houchen
87 - Eric Wildon
76 - Paul Baker
75 - Tommy McGuigan
67 - Joe Allon
66 - Ralph Pedwell
60 - George Luke
56 - Peter Thompson
53 - Adam Boyd
53 - Joss Hewitt
51 - Joel Porter
51 - Ernie Phythian
50 - Eifion Williams
50 - Bob Newton
49 - Jackie Smith
47 - Leo Harden
45 - Cecil Hardy
43 - Harry Clark
40 - Ron Young
38 - Billy Robinson
37 - Harry Wensley
37 - Paul Dalton
35 - Tommy Miller
35 - Fred Richardson
34 - Mark Tinkler
34 - Malcolm Moore
34 - Terry Bell
33 - Kevin Dixon
32 - Paul Dobson
32 - Roy Hogan
31 - Jack Mordue
31 - Jimmy Mulvaney
31 - Johnny Edgar
31 - Albert Bonass
31 - Antony Sweeney
31 - Cliff Wright
30 - Ritchie Humphreys
29 - Kevin Henderson
29 - Kevin McMahon
28 - Andy Toman
28 - Jimmy Sloan
27 - Billy Ayre
27 - Bobby Dixon
27 - Sam English
26 - Tucker Mordue
26 - Steve Howard
26 - Dick Hardy
26 - Frank Stamper

Football League Hat-Tricks

Joel Porter, 3-3 v Swindon Town (H), 2008/09
Jon Daly, 3-0 v Wrexham (H), 2006/07
Adam Boyd, 3-0 v Sheffield Wednesday (H), 2004/05
Antony Sweeney, 3-2 v Chesterfield (H), 2004/05
Paul Robinson, 8-1 v Grimsby Town (H), 2003/04
Ritchie Humphreys, 4-0 v Swansea City (H), 2002/03
Mark Tinkler, 4-3 v Wrexham (H), 2002/03
Darrell Clarke, 7-1 v Swansea City (H), 2001/02
Gordon Watson, 4-0 v Hull City (H), 2001/02
Craig Midgley, 6-1 v Barnet (H), 2000/01
Tommy Miller, 3-0 v Barnet (H), 1999/00
Stephen Halliday, 3-2 v Mansfield Town (H), 1994/95
Nicky Southall, 3-1 v Colchester United (H), 1994/95
Keith Houchen, 3-1 v Bury (H), 1994/95
Paul Dalton, 5-1 v Aldershot (A), 1990/91
Paul Baker, 3-1 v Exeter City (H), 1987/88
Paul Baker, 3-1 v Colchester United (H), 1987/88
Paul Dobson, 4-1 v Wrexham (A), 1983/84
Keith Houchen, 4-4 v Peterborough United (A), 1981/82
Malcolm Poskett, 4-0 v Torquay United (H), 1976/77
Terry Bell, 5-2 v Bradford Park Avenue (H), 1969/70
Jimmy Mulvaney, 4-2 v York City (H), 1966/67
Ernie Phythian, 5-2 v Newport County (H), 1965/66
Terry Francis, 4-2 v Bradford Park Avenue (H), 1963/64
Johnny Edgar, 4-4 v Chester (A), 1961/62
Barry Parkes, 4-2 v Northampton Town (H), 1960/61
Ken Johnson, 4-1 v Accrington Stanley (H), 1960/61
Jackie Smith, 10-1 v Barrow (H), 1958/59
Johnny Langland, 4-2 v Aldershot (A), 1958/59
Ken Johnson, 4-1 v Barrow (H), 1957/58
Jackie Smith, 4-2 v Mansfield Town (H), 1955/56
Tommy McGuigan, 6-0 v Stockport County (H), 1953/54
Tommy McGuigan, 6-1 v Halifax Town (H), 1951/52
Joe Willetts, 6-1 v Darlington (H), 1950/51
Willie McClure, 5-2 v Halifax Town (H), 1950/51
Eric Wildon, 3-1 v Bradford Park Avenue (H), 1950/51
Eric Wildon, 6-1 v Barrow (H), 1950/51
Fred Richardson, 4-1 v Crewe Alexandra (H), 1948/49
Tommy McGarry, 4-2 v Stockport County (H), 1938/39
Jack Scott, 4-2 v Rotherham United (A), 1936/37
Jack Scott, 6-1 v Gateshead (H), 1936/37
Jim McCambridge, 5-3 v Halifax Town (H), 1936/37
Albert Bonass, 5-2 v Barrow (H), 1934/35
Harry Proctor, 7-0 v Barrow (H), 1933/34
Ralph Pedwell, 6-2 v Darlington (H), 1933/34
Joss Hewitt, 6-4 v Barnsley (H), 1932/33
Joss Hewitt, 4-3 v Lincoln City (H), 1931/32
Joss Hewitt, 7-2 v York City (H), 1931/32
Bobby Dixon, 7-2 v York City (H), 1931/32
Sydney Lumley, 4-1 v Halifax Town (H), 1931/32
Sydney Lumley, 3-2 v Chester (A), 1931/32
Horace Waller, 4-2 v Rotherham United (H), 1930/31
Jimmy Thompson, 3-1 v Wigan Borough (A), 1929/30
Billy Robinson, 4-5 v Nelson (H), 1927/28
Billy Robinson, 5-1 v Lincoln City (A), 1927/28
Billy Robinson, 5-0 v Wrexham (H), 1925/26
Cecil Hardy, 9-3 v Walsall (H), 1925/26
Harry Wensley, 5-1 v Accrington Stanley (H), 1925/26

Billy Smith, 3-1 v Walsall (H), 1924/25
George Crowther, 7-0 v Chesterfield (H), 1921/22

Ten Highest Attendances (Away)

40816, FA Cup, 0-1 v Sunderland (A), 2003/04
38608, FA Cup, 0-1 v Burnley (A), 1951/52
36632, FA Cup, 1-4 v Newcastle (A), 1924/25
35357, League, 0-2 v Hull (A), 1948/49
30064, League, 1-1 v Hull (A), 1946/47
27194, League Cup, 0-5 v Arsenal (A), 1995/96
26877, League, 0-2 v Leeds (A), 2007/08
26863, FA Cup, 0-6 v Man City (A), 1975/76
25414, League, 0-5 v Hull (A), 1947/48
24644, League, 0-2 v Derby (A), 1956/57

Ten Highest Football League Attendances (Away)

35357, League, 0-2 v Hull (A), 1948/49
30064, League, 1-1 v Hull (A), 1946/47
26877, League, 0-2 v Leeds (A), 2007/08
25414, League, 0-5 v Hull (A), 1947/48
24644, League, 0-2 v Derby (A), 1956/57
24630, League, 1-4 v Bradford (A), 1928/29
22319, League, 0-2 v Hull (A), 2002/03
22126, League, 1-1 v Bradford (A), 1956/57
21182, League, 1-4 v Leeds (A), 2008/09
20873, League, 0-1 v Stockport (A), 1949/50

Ten Lowest Attendances (Away)

290, Div Three(N) Cup, 0-0 v Gateshead (A), 1938/39
300, Div Three(N) Cup, 1-2 v York (A), 1933/34
800, Non-League, 1-3 v Newcastle Utd A (A), 1908/09
800, Non-League, 3-0 v Shildon (A), 1909/10
858, League, 1-0 v Rochdale (A), 1976/77
859, FL Trophy, 0-2 v Carlisle (A), 1992/93
876, League, 1-3 v Halifax (A), 1987/88
880, League, 2-1 v Southport (A), 1976/77
910, League, 3-4 v Rochdale (A), 1984/85
936, FL Trophy, 5-2 v Lincoln (A), 2007/08

Biggest Winning Margin (Away)

7-1 v Darlington Forge Albion, Non-League, 1918/19
6-0 v Gainsborough Trinity, FA Cup, 2007/08
6-1 v Southport, League, 1956/57
5-0 v Durham, Non-League, 1918/19
5-0 v Bishop Auckland, FA Cup, 1920/21
5-1 v Lincoln, League, 1927/28
5-1 v Aldershot, League, 1990/91
5-1 v Wrexham, League, 2004/05
4-0 v Shildon, Non-League, 1912/13
4-0 v Rotherham, League, 1929/30
4-0 v Accrington, League, 1934/35
4-0 v Nelson, League, 1921/22

Statistics courtesy of www.inthemadcrowd.co.uk

Chapter 20

Club Organisation Chart
End of Season 2007-8

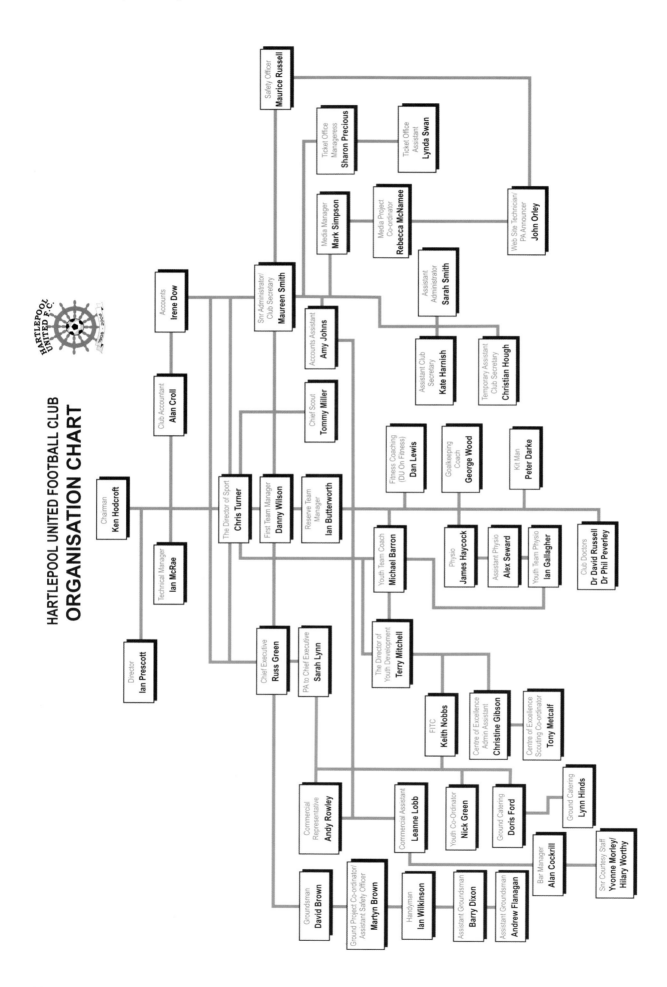

HARTLEPOOL UNITED FOOTBALL CLUB
ORGANISATION CHART

Safety Officer **Maurice Russell**

Ticket Office Manageress **Sharon Precious**

Ticket Office Assistant **Lynda Swan**

Media Manager **Mark Simpson**

Media Project Co-ordinator **Rebecca McNamee**

Web Site Technician/ PA Announcer **John Orley**

Assistant Administrator **Sarah Smith**

Assistant Club Secretary **Kate Harnish**

Temporary Assistant Club Secretary **Christian Hough**

Accounts **Irene Dow**

Snr Administrator/ Club Secretary **Maureen Smith**

Accounts Assistant **Amy Johns**

Club Accountant **Alan Croll**

Chief Scout **Tommy Miller**

Fitness Coaching (DU On Fitness) **Dan Lewis**

Goalkeeping Coach **George Wood**

Kit Man **Peter Darke**

Chairman **Ken Hodcroft**

Technical Manager **Ian McRae**

The Director of Sport **Chris Turner**

First Team Manager **Danny Wilson**

Reserve Team Manager **Ian Butterworth**

Youth Team Coach **Michael Barron**

Physio **James Haycock**

Assistant Physio **Alex Seward**

Youth Team Physio **Ian Gallagher**

Club Doctors **Dr David Russell Dr Phil Peverley**

Director **Ian Prescott**

Chief Executive **Russ Green**

PA to Chief Executive **Sarah Lynn**

The Director of Youth Development **Terry Mitchell**

FITC **Keith Nobbs**

Centre of Excellence Admin Assistant **Christine Gibson**

Centre of Excellence Scouting Co-ordinator **Tony Metcalf**

Commercial Representative **Andy Rowley**

Commercial Assistant **Leanne Lobb**

Youth Co-Ordinator **Nick Green**

Ground Catering **Doris Ford**

Ground Catering **Lynn Hinds**

Bar Manager **Alan Cockrill**

Snr Courtesy Staff **Yvonne Morley/ Hilary Worthy**

Groundsman **David Brown**

Ground Project Co-ordinator/ Assistant Safety Officer **Martyn Brown**

Handyman **Ian Wilkinson**

Assistant Groundsman **Barry Dixon**

Assistant Groundsman **Andrew Flanagan**

Chapter 21

Victoria Park

is a 7,787 capacity football ground, located on Clarence Road, Hartlepool

Cyril Knowles Stand - Home Supporters

The Cyril Knowles Stand is a modern all-seated and houses the Family Enclosure within Victoria Park. It is also the stand in which the players tunnel is situated. The Director's Box is also in the CK Stand, with the Executive Boxes situated at the top of the stand. Official Capacity 1, 599.

Town End - Home Supporters

The Town End Terrace is a standing area behind the south goal, it is usually the most vocal area of the ground. Official Capacity 1,775.

Camerons Brewery Stand - Home Supporters

Formerly the Millhouse Stand. This two-tier stand holds an all-seated upper tier and terraced lower. The Press Box is situated within the upper tier and it is located at the west side of the ground. Official Capacity 1, 617 (seats), 1, 832 (terrace).

Rink End - Away Supporters

This is an all-seated stand in which away supporters are seated. However this is the only stand containing some areas with an obscured view of the pitch, due to a number of supporting pillars. Official Capacity 964.

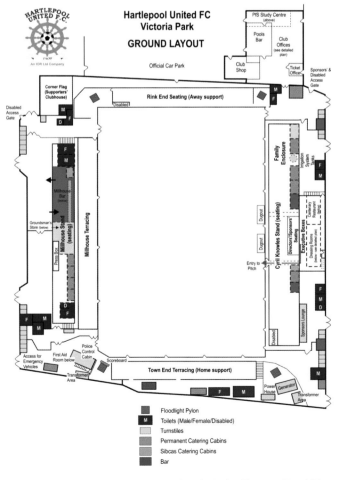

Victoria Park, Clarence Road Plan

Outside of Victoria Park

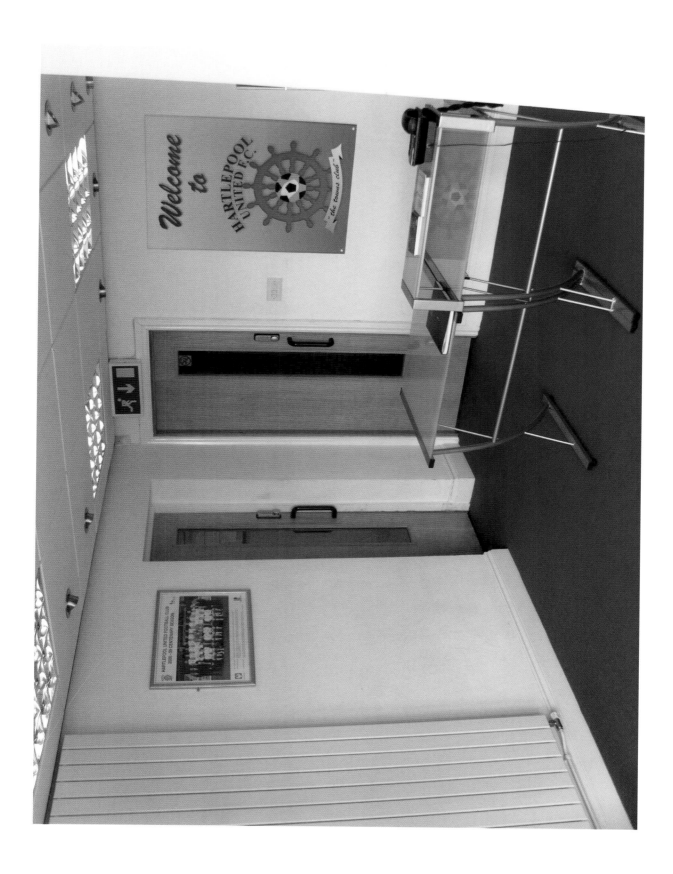

The reception at Victoria Park

The Centenary Wall

Hartlepool United Club Shop

The Cyril Knowles Stand

The Mill House Stand

The Town End

The Rink End

The Club's new Centenary Suite has been available for matchday hospitality, conferences and, most recently, weddings

Player of the Century Ritchie Humphreys alongside his portrait in the Centenary Suite

The Victoria Lounge

The Victoria Lounge

Maidens Suite

Maidens Suite

Executive Boxes at Victoria Park

Executive Boxes at Victoria Park

Pools Study Support Centre

Chapter 22

Centenary Subscribers

Hartlepool United Football Club would like to take this opportunity to say "thank you" to all the supporters of this project and hope you enjoy reading about the history of this great Club.

With best wishes,

Ken Hodcroft, Chairman of Hartlepool United

Gary Welch	Ernie Welch, The Greatest Pools Fan.
Fred Bage	Thanks for the memories, Fred Bage
Mark Wallace	A Fitting Tribute. Mark Wallace
David Garthwaite	Happy 100 to my Club. Forever Pools
Frank Carr	Well done Pools. Here's to another 100…
Peter Jackson	Alan, Peter & Ian Jackson - Coxhoe, Durham
Mr N Wilkinson	Norman Wilkinson - a Yorkshire Poolie
Peter Britcliffe	Peter, Tom & Frances Britcliffe
Christine Gibson	Ryan - HUFC through & through. Mum & Dad
Paul Keay	Paul Keay, blue & white for life
Paul Stoddart	Paul, Andrew, Matthew. Poolies Forever.
Mr R Smith	The best rollercoaster ride! Robert Smith.
Mark Hargreaves	Tom - Once a Poolie, Always a Poolie
	Kate Hargreaves - Poolie Forever!
	The Sea Gull and Chihuahua were Poolies!
	Pools and Lynn: A lifetime's romance
	Mark Hargreaves - Never Say Die!
	CJ - Only 20 years younger than Pools!

Richard Somerville	Madeleine Somerville - 'Poolie Till I Die'
Roy Golding	To Mary, who also has a big birthday in 2008!
John Beetham	John Beetham. Supporter since 1966
John Marsden	Billy, John & Dean - Poolies forever!
Chris Nutt	Chris Nutt & Helen Humber Peter, Maria, Chris & Andrew Nutt
Scott Llewellyn	Living a Cheeky Monkey's Life
Graeme Stonehouse	For my Grandad, Wilf who did so much for Pools
Jayne Gardner	Jayne Gardner David Hodgson
Michael Robson	Always been there, always will be
Errol Bristow	Great Club - Errol & Brenda Bristow
David Wright	David & Linda Wright. Always Poolies!
Libby Suwinski	Keith Thompson
Derrick Jackson	To our 1st Grandson, Alfie. Nana & Grandad.
Martin Randall	HUFC, it's what Saturday's are for!
Geoff Newton	Geoff Newton a Poolie in Darlington
Mrs Leslie	Keith, Paul & Lynne Leslie
Mick Hutchinson	N. Hutchinson - Thanks for the memories. C&M.
Amy Johns	In loving memory of Fred Weegram. Amy Johns
Gail Gould	Keep going to the games & 'Bloody Enjoy It!'
M Thompson	Richard Thompson
Mrs Hunt	John Lonsdale Hunt - 13th June 2008
Brian Mason	Trevor Mason, Pools No 1 USA Fan 2008
Mr Paine	Michael Paul Mitchell - 26th April 2008 William Paine - 26th April 2008
Terje Flataukan	Ski, Norway Hartlepool United Social Club
Tony McManus	George & Tony McManus. Forever Blue & White
David Gray	HUFC heartache and passion. David Gray.
John Allen	Tony Allen - Norwich Poolie For Life

Ian Pringle	In memory of Mike Bulmer. Ian Pringle.
Kevin Bruce	To my Dad, Richard Terence Bruce
Clive Parkes	Simplex Munditiis
Graham Whitehead	William & Graham Whitehead from Jarrow
Mrs Grylls	Sally Harris, life long Poolie fan
Mr R Templeman	Richard Templeman - Supporter since 1963
Eric Burton	Eric, Janet and Ruth Burton
Jill Richards	Once a Poolie, Always a Poolie. Lee Hocking
John Potter	To George Readman. A lifetime Poolie.
Tony Grainger	Poolie Till I Die - Jonny Grainger
Gordon Small	Gordon Small - From 1965-66
Ron Harnish	Never Say Die in next 100 - Ronaldo
Mr Hudson	Andrew M Hudson. A Poolie since 1982.
David Gardiner	In memory of John Gardiner, loyal Pools fan
John Collins	John, Pete & Rick Collins - Forever Pools
Steve Sharp	Glory will come, Poolymads can wait
Miles Harwood	The Harwoods will be Poolies till we die
John Cooper	Those were the days my Friend! John Cooper
Tom Smith	Memories of following Pools. Tom Smith
Iain Kilgour	Iain and Christopher Kilgour
John Raftery	John Raftery - Life sentence began 11-4-68 Jonathan Raftery - Humphreys for England
Steven Bell	Thanks for the memories - Steven Bell
Ray Reed	Ray Reed - Here's to the next 100 years.
Mrs Sewell	Cardiff! Poolie Till I Die. Lucy Sewell
Jill Harker	Jill Harker - Proud to be a Poolie
Dave Sutheran	In memory of Kenneth Sutheran 1940-2005
Glenn Corbett	To Glenn Derek Corbett… Enjoy To Darren Corbett. Love Mum and Dad

Edwin Jeffries	JPR Jeffries, Poolie 'til he died.
Steve Blackwood	Congratulations Alex & Rebecca Blackwood
Wendy Cranney	Jordan, Kirby & Victoria Cranney
Lynne Taylor	Iain Taylor - Granddaughters Rachel & Paige
Nick Gray	Nick, Victoria & Nicholas Gray
Monkey Business	Paul Mullen - much loved Poolie ambassador
James Barker	Dr Jim Barker, Forever a Pools fan
Mrs Johnson	To Martin. From Mum & Dad.
Lynsey Bell	To my Dad, Alan Bell. Love Lynsey
Mrs Addison	Daniel Campbell, Happy 21st Love Nanna
Thomas Hocking	Thomas Hocking, Poolie since 1950
Julie Stanford	Les Stanford. Happy 50th - Rach & Matt.
George Readman	John Potter, The Swindon Poolie Since 1994
Steve Wiles	
Sue Levinson	
David Roake	
Mrs Plant	
Ann Bolton	
Mr Meadley	
Gary Lupton	
Mr Lightower	
Mr Walker	
Mrs A T Daly	
Mr Kyriakides	
Darren Hewitt